1st edition

5.19

Forged in Fire

Forged in Fire

Strategy and Decisions in the Air War over Europe 1940–45

By DeWitt S. Copp

The Air Force Historical Foundation

DOUBLEDAY & COMPANY, INC.
GARDEN CITY, NEW YORK
1982

Library of Congress Cataloging in Publication Data

Copp, DeWitt S.
  Forged in fire.

  Continues: A few great captains.
  Bibliography: p. 505.
  Includes index.
  1. World War, 1939–1945—Aerial operations, American.
2. World War, 1939–1945—Campaigns—Europe. 3. United
States. Army. Air Corps—History. 4. Aeronautics,
Military—United States—History. I. Title.
D790.C66   940.54′4973
ISBN 0-385-15911-0   AACR2
Library of Congress Catalog Card Number 81–43265

This book is dedicated to:

Lieutenant General Ira C. Eaker
United States Air Force, Retired

One of the first and one of the few.
In war and peace he helped to forge
the greatness of American air power.

Foreword

The first book of this history, *A Few Great Captains,* recounted the lives and careers of a handful of unique U. S. Army airmen, principally Generals Frank M. Andrews, Henry H. Arnold, Ira C. Eaker, and Carl A. Spaatz. More than pioneering aviators, they were in the forefront of a twenty-year battle (1919–39) to gain military acceptance for the doctrine of strategic air power and at the same time to win aerial independence from War Department control. Book One concluded with simultaneous and far-separated acts whose linkage was to be of profound importance to these airmen in the years of war that followed.

All could recognize the enormity of Hitler's invasion of Poland, on September 1, 1939. Hardly anyone at that time would equate it with the announcement on the same day that Major General George C. Marshall had been officially named the new U. S. Army Chief of Staff. Hindsight strongly indicates that had any general officer but Marshall been named to the post, this book would tell a different story, for aside from his military genius, Marshall, better than any other ground soldier—including Douglas MacArthur—had a real understanding of air power as a crucial weapon and appreciated the value of the airmen who sought to give it operational credence.

Forged in Fire, the second book of this history, goes forward into combat, political as well as military, with the major characters of Book One and others called on to make command decisions that determined the course of bitter aerial conflict in the skies over Europe. They fought for superiority in the air in order to destroy the industrial heart of Hitler's Third Reich. And from the outset, George Marshall was the quiet, firm presence who stood behind them and with them through the grim years of challenge and response.

On the very day Hitler brought war to Europe, Marshall was airborne. The pilot of the plane, Captain Eugene Beebe, passed word to him of the official announcement of his appointment as well as that of Admiral Harold R. Stark, who had been named the new Chief of Naval Operations. Marshall, wishing to congratulate Stark, asked Beebe to have the radio operator send a message he had jotted down. Since they were near El Paso, Texas, where the Army had a radio station, Beebe sent the message by voice. Two days later he was summoned to the General's office on the double by Colonel Walter Bedell Smith, then Marshall's chief of staff.

"Who handles telegrams to Beebe from Admiral Byrd at the South Pole?" Marshall asked the Captain while studying a cablegram.

"I didn't send Admiral Byrd a cable, sir," came the puzzled reply.

"You know, it's a funny thing," mused Marshall, "but I never heard on the one I had you send Admiral Stark. So you find out what happened."

Since Beebe was also Air Corps Chief General Hap Arnold's aide and pilot, it didn't take him long to uncover the answer. An Army radio operator somewhere between El Paso and Washington, D.C., had changed the name *Stark* to *Stork*. The Navy radio operator who picked up the relayed message figured someone was kidding and sent it off to Byrd in Antarctica.

When Beebe reported his findings to the Chief of Staff, Marshall shook his head and said, "Now, what are we going to do to correct a thing like that? We can't have communications messed up."

"Well, sir," Beebe answered, "if the Air Corps had its own wireless net, that never would have happened. We did our part correctly. That happened on the Army net."

"Don't you have your own communications?"

"No, sir. No airwaves communications."

"Well, you get them," Marshall said.

Captain Beebe reported his instructions to Arnold, who responded blithely, "If he told you to get them, you'd better get them."

And that was how the Army Air Corps, after twenty years of trying, finally came to have its own airwaves net, which enabled pilots and radio operators to communicate directly with their own ground operators and vice versa. Though this was a relatively small matter, it was of considerable importance to the Air Corps, and Marshall's swift action and commonsense approach was indicative of his style. And although it has been correctly stated that, for the good of the nation, he was the right man, chosen at the right time for the right job, the axiom became specifically true for the airmen of this book.

As related in *A Few Great Captains,* Marshall gained his first real understanding of what air power was all about in August 1938 while head of the War Plans Division, just a year before becoming Chief of Staff. In the early days, he had known Billy Mitchell well and had served with and become a friend of Hap Arnold's during Philippine duty in 1913. But it wasn't until he was taken on a nine-day inspection tour by Major General Frank M. Andrews, the Commander of the Army's aerial combat arm, GHQ Air Force, that he came to appreciate the potential of air power. The transcontinental journey in Andrews' plane, with visits to air bases, depots, and aircraft manufacturing companies, made a deep and lasting impression on Marshall, as did the personality of his guide.

Marshall realized that his host was a special person, a leader with a rare combination of abilities. Andrews not only had been a principal architect of the plan to create a combat air arm, but despite continuing shortages of everything, he had in three short years molded it into a cohesive and highly mobile strike force. More, Andrews' clarity of thought and forward-looking approach toward aerial needs aided Marshall in his own evaluation. He saw that "Andy" Andrews was a broad-gauged thinker and a strategic planner who would be of great value in a time of crisis. Directly following their nine-day association, Marshall wrote Andrews thanking him for the indoctrination and saying that he had been given an invaluable education.

Marshall's estimation of Andrews was boldly evidenced when Marshall became Acting Chief of Staff, in July 1939. In March of that year, Andrews, because of his determination to build a modern air force in the face of War Department resistance, lost his job as GHQ Air Force Commander, was reduced in rank to colonel, and was assigned to an innocuous post in Texas. One of Marshall's first acts in office was to take on Secretary of War Harry H. Woodring, Assistant Secretary of War Louis A. Johnson, and retiring Army Chief of Staff Major General Malin Craig in a behind-the-scenes confrontation to rescue Andrews from military exile and command oblivion. Marshall was to remark that their stand against him was probably the only time the three had ever been in joint agreement on anything. But he backed them down and retrieved Andrews, bringing him to Washington as G-3, the Assistant Chief of Staff for Operations and Training for the entire U. S. Army. Theretofore, no Army airman had held such a high General Staff position, and in assuming the position Andrews was only the second Air Corps officer to be promoted to permanent brigadier general of the line.*

The mutual personal regard and professional appreciation that grew between Marshall and Andrews was not only to have its impact on the entire relationship between air and ground forces, it was to bring changes that were long needed.

To add support and stimulate innovation, there was General Hap Arnold, for whom Marshall had a long and abiding esteem. The feeling was returned, almost reverentially. Years before, while serving with Marshall

* Brig. Gen. H. Conger Pratt was the first, promoted to the rank in 1938.

in the Philippines, Arnold had predicted to his wife that one day his hunting partner would become chief of staff. When that day came, Arnold had been Chief of the Air Corps for nearly a year, and again, it was good fortune that placed the two in their respective positions of command. As Marshall had raised Andrews in stature, so in time would he raise Arnold, through a plan that made Arnold a deputy chief of staff and one of the four most powerful men in the Army. Significantly, the essence of the plan had been suggested by Andrews to the General Staff several years earlier, only to be summarily rejected.

In that last summer of European peace, when Marshall had brought Frank Andrews to Washington as one of his principal staff officers, he also had rattled the hidebound traditionalists in the War Department by placing a number of bright young air officers in planning positions on the General Staff. He believed their talents could best be utilized at the center of expanding operations.

A number of these officers had been instructors at the Air Corps Tactical School at Maxwell Field, Alabama. Previously their heretical teachings on the strategic uses of air power as opposed to the accepted support of ground troops had been brought to Marshall's attention by Major General Lesley J. McNair, who then headed G-3. McNair had been sent to Maxwell to investigate reports that an "intolerable deviation" from War Department directives was being taught at the school. He arrived with Colonel William Gruber, who headed the training section of G-3 and was responsible for instruction in all Army schools. The word was that the Air Corps instructors were not teaching the doctrine, tactics, or strategy being given at either the Command and General Staff School, at Fort Leavenworth, Kansas, or the Army War College, in Washington, D.C. The former was considered to be on a higher level than the Tactical School, and the War College was the Army's *sanctum sanctorum*.

Hearing that McNair, Gruber, and a staff of critics were about to descend on them, the instructors decided not to back off. For several days, the visitors were shown how a Japanese sneak attack on Pearl Harbor could be exposed by air reconnaissance and defeated by fast-flying, long-range bombers. McNair agreed that what was being taught by the airmen was at odds with established War Department doctrine, going far beyond the scope of what was intended, but he was impressed. He not only did nothing to stop the instruction; he wanted to have it used in the other schools. McNair's report impressed Marshall, but after evaluation, the plan to block a theoretical Japanese attack on Pearl Harbor was filed away to gather dust with other plans like it dating back to Billy Mitchell.

There were some who saw Marshall's move to place Andrews and bright Young Air Corps-independence Turks in War Department staff and planning jobs as a sagacious method to defuse a resurgence of the drive to create a separate air force. Proponents in the press, the Congress, and the Air Corps were maintaining that since air power was the Administration's accepted key to hemispheric defense, those who must assume responsibility for that defense should command it. Marshall had discussed the idea with Andrews, Arnold, and others. His recognition of its potential volatility could be perceived in his subsequent reorganization of the air arm that will be described in later chapters, but at the time his thinking embodied a larger context.

Two months before war began in Europe, Marshall, then Acting Chief of Staff, gathered ten of the aforementioned junior officers for an introductory briefing. His subject was "Yours Is a Wartime Assignment." This look into a future they all had considered as a growing possibility was somewhat of a shocker to his listeners. Not one of them expected the new chief of staff to expound on it as though its reality was not far down the road. Marshall was not forecasting that the United States would be involved in a war even before one had begun in Europe. He entertained firm hopes that the United States could stay out of the impending conflict. But since the risk of war was so obvious and the United States so unprepared, it was best to assume the worst and work accordingly.

That Arnold and his staff saw in George Marshall the chief of staff for whom they had long been looking, there can be no doubt. That he gave them all they wanted just short of an independent air force, there can be no doubt either. And for most of them, that was good enough. For those, like Andrews, who sought the whole loaf, once the United States went to war, duty, honor, and country came before all else, and the ultimate goal would have to wait the return of peace.

In the beginning, soon after Marshall became the Army's leading general, Hap Arnold found himself caught in a political conflict that could have cost him his post. President Franklin Roosevelt, who in January 1939 had called for a vast air expansion, was determined to supply the French and the British with all the aircraft they wanted to buy. Arnold's job was to organize and oversee the long-sought buildup of his own forces. Secretary of War Harry H. Woodring, a political isolationist, hewing to the overtly avowed Administration policy of strict neutrality and hemispheric defense, was not anxious to cooperate with the President's covert policy of making the Rhine the first line of American defense through the sale of U.S.-produced aircraft. His reasons were political, but he also supported Arnold's assessment of the limited facilities of U.S. aircraft manufacturers, few in number and unprepared to produce the flood of aircraft needed to build up U.S. air power and at the same time supply the British and the French. Roosevelt could call for ten thousand planes one month and fifty thousand the next, and the press could make it seem that such figures were obtainable overnight. But for an industry whose annual capacity until 1939 was about two thousand planes of all types, it would take time and money and organization to produce anything like the numbers called for.

To complicate matters further, Roosevelt had turned over to his Secretary of the Treasury, Henry Morgenthau, Jr., the somewhat *sub rosa* job of handling the negotiations for foreign aircraft sales, short-circuiting Secretary of War Woodring. The President had worked this political sleight of hand for two reasons: Morgenthau, an internationalist, was, along with Harry Hopkins, one of FDR's most trusted confidants. It didn't matter that the Secretary knew absolutely nothing about airplanes. Secondly, Woodring and Assistant Secretary of War Louis A. Johnson, whose bailiwick was procurement, had made a shambles of the War Department in a two-year internecine feud over who was really boss, a situation Roosevelt had also permitted to continue. Although Johnson was anxious to support FDR in all his actions, the artful President felt far more secure using Morgenthau in an area that was extremely sensitive (due to neutrality laws that prevented the sale of armaments abroad).

Once war began, Roosevelt went before Congress and asked for a change in the laws so that arms could be sold to the Allied nations. The Congress gave him what he wanted on a cash-and-carry basis and with the proviso that no U.S. ships could be used to transport the purchases. Then, following the defeat of Poland, its partition between Germany and the Soviet Union, and the latter's costly attack on Finland, which Roosevelt described as "this dreadful rape," the fighting all but ceased and the war settled into a stalemate. The RAF dropped more leaflets than bombs. The Luftwaffe did not send its fighters into French airspace. The poilus sat snug in their Maginot Line. The Wehrmacht rested on its laurels, awaiting Hitler's next command, while he was said to be awaiting overtures for a negotiated peace. The period—the fall of 1939 and the winter of 1940—was called the "Phony War."

It was during this interval that Arnold became engaged in his own war between the demands of the Air Corps and those of the Allies. There was nothing phony about it. Andrews, who was not directly involved, could not help him. Marshall, whose responsibilities encompassed the whole Army, could and did give some support. Harry Hopkins, Arnold's friend and White House protector in previous clashes, was too ill to be of real assistance. Arnold's troops were some of the handful who had served with him since the early days, the few who had been there from the beginning and would remain to the end, no matter what the end was. Colonel Carl "Tooey" Spaatz, Chief of Plans and for twenty years Arnold's closest confidant in or out of the office, was there to advise and shape strategy. Lieutenant Colonel Ira C. Eaker, Arnold's Executive Officer and trusted wing man, was there to backstop his Chief in any encounter. For all of them, there was nothing new or unusual in finding themselves in a one-sided political conflict; it was the story of their military lives.

But now, in the winter of 1940, working to carry out directives approved by Roosevelt and the Congress, it was apparent that Hap Arnold was locked in a confrontation with the President himself.

Contents

Forged in Fire

Part I

One

The Phony War

In the nation's capital, March that year of 1940 came in like a wet blanket. It had been raining intermittently for the first five days of the month when Air Corps Chief Major General H. H. Arnold went up to Capitol Hill to testify before the House Military Affairs Committee. The only change in the weather on Tuesday morning, compared with the four previous days, was that the rain was mixed with snow, and an ice storm was reported blanketing areas to the north. The chill, the wetness, the dark-bellied clouds, the opaque light conspired to fit the general mood reflected in the muddled news from Europe and the uncertainty of its meaning in Washington.

This uncertainty was in part the reason for Arnold's being summoned to testify. A few days earlier, on February 29, President Roosevelt had sent to Congress a letter on the Army's aircraft procurement program for 1941. The Army had already increased its estimated cost for contracted planes by ten million dollars, and the President was asking for legislation to raise that figure by another twenty million. A number of congressmen on the Military Affairs Committee were disturbed by the request. Some believed they saw an attempt by aircraft manufacturers to boost their profit margin; others felt the increases were stimulated by previously placed French and British orders which were forcing airplane prices upward. Whatever their suspicions, their underlying motivation was largely political, dictated by the position of each on the abiding question of U.S. policy toward the war in Europe. On the surface, at least, the Roosevelt administration preached nonintervention, but that policy was viewed by the President's opponents as something quite different.

All of these factors weighed on Hap Arnold in some measure as he left his office in the Munitions Building that gray morning accompanied by three of his trusted subordinates.

Of the three, Brigadier General Barton K. Yount, wearing glasses and looking more professorial than military in his civilian clothes, had known Arnold the longest. They had been classmates at West Point. Now serving as an Assistant Chief, Bart Yount was in command of the Corps's burgeoning training program. Lieutenant Colonel Robert Olds was the antithesis of Yount. Lean and intense, with little time for comedy, Olds was a combat veteran of World War I and the Air Corps's premier heavy-bomber commander. Currently, he was Assistant Director of Plans. The third officer, Major Elmer E. Adler, had first served under Arnold at Wright Field more than a decade earlier. A logistics and engineering specialist, he was there to backstop his chief on any technical points that might come up.

Although they knew the queries would center on the reasons why it was now going to cost thirty million dollars more to produce the planes already contracted for, Arnold could be sure the questioning would also center around a new, very large procurement proposal just made by the Joint Anglo-French Purchasing Mission. The order would undoubtedly be jumped on by isolationist-minded congressmen, not only as the cause of Roosevelt's request but also as a deterrent to the Air Corps's authorized buildup.

Arnold had foreseen early on, and declared often enough, that he was all in favor of French and British money being used to expand U.S. aircraft facilities. During World War I, he had helped direct Army airplane production and had been caught in the middle of the debacle that ensued. Primarily because the small, undernourished U.S. aviation industry lacked the plant capacity and trained labor force necessary to fill the sudden massive demands, it had been unable to deliver as anticipated. Arnold had never forgotten the lesson, and now, twenty years later, he did not want to see the mistake repeated. He was extremely anxious that the industry be expanded, against the possibility of U.S. involvement in the war —an expansion that he foresaw would far exceed the present authorization to build Air Corps strength to a total of fifty-five hundred planes.

Arnold had been in favor of foreign sales, providing three fundamental provisos were observed: No secret equipment was to be sold. Sales must never result in the Air Corps's ending up with second best. And sales must never be at the expense of the Air Corps expansion program.

As the four rode up to the Hill, they knew all three conditions were in jeopardy at the White House. Since January, Arnold had been seeking a solution to a French request that if approved—as both the President and Secretary of the Treasury Morgenthau expected—would compromise the first two conditions. On top of that, the new Allied purchase order just handed to Secretary of War Harry Woodring was a shocker. The French and the British wanted to buy an estimated ten thousand planes and twenty thousand aircraft engines—all to be delivered by July of the next year. Arnold was reluctant to testify on the matter without additional clarification, for he knew the size of the order would indeed have a very serious effect on production for the Air Corps.

When the airmen arrived at the House Military Affairs hearing room, Congressman Andrew J. May, Chairman of the Committee, was waiting to greet them. May, a sixty-five-year-old Kentuckian who had served in the House of Representatives for nearly nine years, was a quiet-spoken, independent-minded legislator. He knew Arnold well and liked him.

After war had begun in Europe, Secretary of War Woodring had arranged to have monthly meetings with key congressional leaders in order to maintain close contacts. Arnold had attended many of the meetings, which had given him ample occasion to discuss with the Military Affairs Chairman what was needed and what was being accomplished.

Now May informed him that the hearings about to begin were going to be held behind closed doors in executive session. No stenographic notes, he said, would be made of the Air Corps Chief's testimony, and Arnold was to feel free to speak out without fear of his words being made public. The Chairman's announcement was good news, but the Air Corps Chief had been given such assurance in the past, with less than reassuring results. Little more than a year previously, the Senate Military Affairs Committee had questioned him in supposedly secret session on foreign sales and the next day the New York *Herald Tribune* and the Washington *Post* had quoted his testimony, in large measure inaccurately.

Hap Arnold was an adroit political pro. As Chief of the Air Corps he had to be, for unlike a *bona fide* politician, he operated within a restrictive framework that was supposed to be nonpolitical and yet was beset by political pressures on every side. When Congressman May said the hearings would be closed, Arnold had to accept that they would be, knowing full well that there were members of the Committee who would be anxious to misuse his words. Still, he had to take his chances, and there was no reason to doubt the integrity of Chairman May. However, in testifying, Arnold would be inclined to follow Colonel Tooey Spaatz's, well-advised congressional axiom: "Tell the truth, but don't blurt it out."

During the session, one of the most determined interrogators was Representative Paul W. Shafer, a Republican from Michigan. Shafer's previous background had been divided between the law and the news. He had been a judge and a newspaper editor and publisher and was a strict isolationist. He also knew how to get himself into print.

The next day, a six-column headline in the Washington *Daily News* read: REP. SHAFER CHARGES U.S. PLANE MAKERS PROFITEERING. The covering story, on page 3, ran a vintage photo of Hap Arnold in helmet and goggles and misquoted him as having told the Committee that the cost of twenty-one hundred planes approved in the Air Corps expansion had exceeded original estimates by about ten thousand dollars a plane because aircraft manufacturers were reluctant to delay on foreign orders for fear the war would end and they would lose business. Consequently, they were charging the Air Corps more than originally agreed on to get the job done.

Arnold had given no such blanket reason for the increases, but the newspaper quoted Shafer as saying, "The trouble is that they [U.S. manufacturers] can sell all the planes they want to Europe, and they are jacking up the price to the U.S. They are taking the taxpayer for a sleigh ride."

More accurately and to the point, the story cited Commerce Department figures on foreign aircraft sales for January 1940 as being 421 percent over the previous January, which gave an indication of the growing pains besetting the aviation industry. France had placed orders in excess of twelve million dollars and Great Britain of more than four million. An additional nine million dollars in orders had come in from eight other countries—one of them Japan.

The damaging thing about the story was that while it did not quote Arnold directly, its inaccuracies attributable to him were the platform from which Congressman Shafer launched his strident attack.[1]

Arnold knew he could expect reaction from within the War Department —maybe from the White House. He called in Bart Yount and Bob Olds to discuss the strategy of response. The result was that Olds, who had taken notes during the testimony, wrote a report on what Arnold had actually said to the congressmen: "Inaccurate account of General Arnold's statement before the Military Affairs Committee."

On the matter of Allied procurement affecting the Air Corps expansion program adversely, he quoted Arnold as having said in substance: "We have no evidence of any delay from such causes to date. In fact, the Army and the Navy are on first priority for the delivery of all aircraft produced in the United States." *To date* was, of course, the key phrase in his statement.

Concerning the question of profiteering on the manufacturers' part, Olds quoted Arnold as saying: "We have absolutely no evidence of any collusion, nor do we suspect any."

And as for the reasons behind the requested increase by the President, Arnold stated that "since Air Corps estimates were drawn up, manufacturers have been faced with increased labor costs, profit limitations, application of the Walsh-Healy Act,"[2] and finally, but of basic importance, "a certain fear factor which has introduced a reluctance to expand facilities at great expense to meet increased demands which may prove of very temporary duration. . . ."

On this last, Arnold had tried to be careful before the Committee, not wishing to rock the boat until he had more details on the newest Allied order. He did know that the aircraft industry was not yet tooled up to accommodate such large increases and that it was not in the mood to invest the capital required to fill these orders with the war's course hanging in the balance. He could have given some prime examples to illustrate the "fear factor."

On a previous French order for seven hundred fifty light bombers, DB-7's, the Douglas Aircraft Company was not willing to expand its plant to produce more than two hundred. It recommended the other five hundred fifty be farmed out to Boeing and Consolidated. In a similar case, the Pratt & Whitney Company, one of the three U.S. aircraft engine manufacturers, informed British and French purchasing agents that it was not prepared to go ahead on a joint order because of a lack of supervisory personnel and the failure of the Treasury Department to give assurances of a tax arrangement that would protect the company against possible financial loss by expanding. As for cooperative relationships, Bart Yount told Arnold that Pratt & Whitney representatives had informed him they were "not going to be pushed around by the Allies." Neither was Henry Ford, but for different reasons. The British wanted the Ford Company to produce its Rolls-Royce Marlin 1650-hp liquid-cooled engine, the best of its kind at the time. Ford said no. He would produce for neither side in a war in which his country was not a combatant.

Bob Olds's corrective report was put on an official Routing and Record sheet, confirmed in writing by Yount, and made the rounds outward and upward.

In view of the *Daily News* article and the response it was bound to bring, Arnold felt he should talk it over with Woodring and Assistant Secretary of War Johnson. Both were scheduled to testify in the near future on the new Anglo-French request, and for the moment at least Johnson appeared to have the President's ear.

In the past, Woodring had made many decisions with which Hap Arnold thoroughly disagreed, but over the issue of who was to receive first pick of military planes coming off U.S. production lines they were in complete accord. In his testimony, Arnold had not blurted out the truth on a long-standing confidential White House demand that both he and Woodring opposed. It concerned the previously mentioned French order placed in January, which they believed, if carried out, would put the Air Corps program in a nasty spiral.

The action on it began some weeks earlier with a telephone call from Lieutenant Colonel Ira C. Eaker, Arnold's Executive.

"General," Eaker said, "I just had a call from Joe Burns, who heard from Pa Watson that the first twenty-five P-40's coming off the line allotted to us are going to go to the French instead."

Colonel Joe Burns was Executive Officer to Assistant Secretary of War

Johnson, and Brigadier General Edwin "Pa" Watson was Roosevelt's valued military aide. Eaker's news was highly disturbing, for the planes were the Air Corps's newest model of the Curtiss fighter, and to hand them over to the French would not only abrogate the joint release policy worked out by Woodring and Secretary of the Navy Charles Edison, but would also compromise the Air Corps buildup and put it in second place on the production line.

Arnold immediately contacted Burns, and the Colonel said yes, that was the word passed from the White House. Arnold asked him if he would come to a meeting at eight-thirty next morning. He then got in touch with Tooey Spaatz, his Chief of Plans, and Bart Yount, and asked them also to be on hand.

The four sat down the next morning to see what strategy they could devise to block a move that Arnold was sure had been instigated by Secretary of the Treasury Henry Morgenthau. He wanted Burns present to supply information on what part Louis Johnson had played in the sudden switch.[3] They could pose the question of how such a transfer to the French could be legal, since the original purchase order had been made by the Air Corps. The real issue was that if the agreement was upheld, a dangerous precedent would be set.

Spaatz felt they had several good arguments to reverse the White House position, not the least of which was support in Congress for the Air Corps's stand. After all, both Arnold and General Marshall had testified before the Senate and House Military Affairs committees on the terms of the release policy. So had Woodring, and a lot of hell could be raised if it was learned that the policy had been reversed.

Arnold asked Spaatz to draw up an outline on the whys and wherefores of the issue. He in turn would give it to Woodring to use as ammunition. Spaatz drafted a typical no-nonsense, one-page, point-by-point statement with an implicit warning of congressional reaction to any change in the procurement policy. He cited as a principal objection the delay that would be incurred in the completion of the Air Corps's expansion. The change, he wrote, would be "providing foreign nations with planes superior in performance to those of our own air force, which is in conflict with testimony given to Congressional Committees by the Chief of Staff and the Chief of the Air Corps."

He recommended that the joint release policy be strictly adhered to, that manufacturers be held to their existing schedules, and "that foreign sale of aircraft and the deliveries of such aircraft be for the primary purpose of building of our aeronautical industry for our own National Defense."

Before Arnold personally carried the memo to the Secretary of War's office, he added two qualifying paragraphs. One spoke again of the desirability of foreign orders that increased productive capacity and made the

United States better prepared for an emergency. The other added protective coloration, portraying him as a reasonable man, always loyal to the Commander-in-Chief, thus leaving a well-defined avenue of retreat.

> There is no need of the statement being made as it is a matter of course, but should a decision be made by those in authority that such diversion should be made the Chief of the Air Corps will carry out his instructions to the letter and cooperate to the fullest extent.

In spite of his disclaimers, it was a dicey situation for Arnold, made more so by a President who was given to making statements in private that he contradicted in public, shifting his course as the situation dictated.

Bart Yount had defined the problem by quoting Roosevelt's statement at a White House meeting to discuss ways of speeding aircraft engine production in order "to meet possible foreign requirements." The President believed the Air Corps, even during its expansion program, could help foreign buyers and that every effort should be made to do so. "There was no definite statement of policy as to what extent this help should go," reported Yount, "but a little help here and there would be beneficial. Each and every problem would have to be handled as a separate item and there would be no general policy on the subject."

To Hap Arnold, a little help here and there did not encompass giving up to the French twenty-five of the Air Corps's newest P-40's.

In the January and February meetings that followed between Air Corps representatives, members of the French purchasing mission, and Burdette Wright, of Curtiss-Wright, the maker of the P-40, nothing was resolved. Each side rejected the proposals of the others. Arnold was not going to approve an idea that would shift the engineering force working on Air Corps P-40's to the French production line. Colonel Paul Jacquin, head of the French group, was not willing to accept the second twenty-five P-40's extracted from the Air Corps's total order of eighty-one. The French planes were to have modifications not incorporated in the U.S. model, and making the changes after the planes were produced would only add to the delay. From January until March the issue went around and around, with Secretary Morgenthau growing increasingly impatient over what he correctly considered was a War Department delaying action fostered by Woodring and strongly supported by Arnold.

On Friday, March 8, Hap Arnold returned to Capitol Hill, this time to testify before the House Military Affairs Subcommittee on Appropriations. Here, too, he would be misquoted several weeks later in a page-one story in the Washington *Times-Herald*.

What he had done was give production figures whose significance was lost in the newspaper's effort to sell isolationist copy. He had said that, at present, aircraft production capacity amounted to three hundred fifty planes a month, or forty-two hundred annually, and that he expected that figure to rise to nearly six hundred a month by September. However, Assistant Secretary of War Johnson had misinformed the dual Committee, saying that production would reach between thirty and forty thousand aircraft by year's end—a 400 percent discrepancy with Arnold's accurate estimates. The reason given for Johnson's hugely inflated projection was "an attempt to justify the sale of planes to Allies."

By the weekend, it appeared to Arnold that his earlier misquoted testimony would bring no reaction, for so far there had been none. Woodring had Olds's memo on what had been said, should anyone raise the matter, and evidently no one had. So all was quiet. But not for long.

Monday came, and with it the Washington *Post*. The newspaper carried a front-page story on the unconsummated sale of the P-40's to the French. It reported that the delay was due to War Department opposition, principally by the Secretary of War and the Chief of the Air Corps. Other newspapers carried the same information, and since the French request of January had been of a confidential nature, the news was an exposé. It became a very busy day.

Ohio Congressman Dow H. Harter, Chairman of the Aviation Subcommittee of the House Military Affairs Committee, called for an immediate inquiry into the government's policy of releasing planes for foreign sale. Harter wanted to know if what Arnold had told the Military Affairs Committee in private could be substantiated in public, or whether in fact the sale of planes to the Allies was curtailing Air Corps deliveries. Andrew May decided that the hearings should be held before his full Committee, and he wanted Harry Woodring as the lead-off witness, the action to begin on Thursday, the fourteenth. Senator Robert M. La Follette, Jr., of Wisconsin, a strong isolationist, moved that the Senate conduct similar hearings.

Treasury Secretary Henry Morgenthau was convinced that his efforts to speed production on Allied orders were being foiled by a War Department twosome: Woodring and Arnold. The emphasis, he felt, should be on the latter, for he believed the Secretary took his cue essentially from the Air Corps Chief. Thoroughly upset by delays and newspaper reports, he went to the White House on March 12 to pour out his woes to the President. Later he gleefully informed his staff, "Oh, boy, did Arnold get it!"

According to Morgenthau, between what he and Press Secretary Steve Early had to say, the General had been dragged over the coals in long-overdue fashion. Early had gone so far as to remind Roosevelt of an episode back in 1926 when Arnold, through the concurrence of Secretary of War John Weeks and by order of Air Service Chief Major General Mason M. Patrick, had been removed from his job as Air Service Director of Information and thrown out of Washington. Early claimed that Arnold had been running a mimeograph machine on government time and government stationery to send out propaganda supporting a separate air force. Early said he himself had been employed in the War Department then, but the details of his story, at least as reported by Morgenthau, were badly twisted.[4] The President had remarked, "Well, if Arnold won't conform, maybe we'll have to move him out of town again."

In the course of their discussion, which included Pa Watson, it was decided Early would tell Arnold that from now on there would be no further publicity from the Air Corps, and that he was to keep his mouth shut. He wasn't to see the press any more. The War Department was going to announce that the twenty-five P-40's had been released, and Early was going to give out the latest aircraft production figures. "These foreign orders," Roosevelt said to them, "mean prosperity in this country, and we can't elect a Democratic Party unless we get prosperity, and these foreign orders are of great importance. Let's be perfectly frank."

The President was saving some of his frankness for the next day, when he summoned to the White House all those most closely involved in the proposed sales. Along with Secretaries Morgenthau, Woodring, and Edison, they included the Assistant Secretaries of the War and Navy departments, Arnold's old buddy Admiral John Towers, Chief of the Bureau of Naval Aeronautics, several aides, and Arnold himself.

The President's voice was sharp and testy, and there was something about the scene, the gathering, the angry Commander-in-Chief, that was coldly familiar to Arnold. This, in fact, was practically a replay of a White House gathering at which he had been present almost exactly a year before. It, too, had been the result of congressional testimony he had given concerning French desires and presidential orders. Europe was not at war; U.S. neutrality laws remained strict and unamended.

His testimony then had centered around a reluctant admission to isolationist Senator Bennett Champ Clark, of Missouri, that Secretary Morgenthau in handling the negotiations on foreign aircraft purchases had overruled War Department opposition to the French mission's access to a new Douglas bomber. The bomber had crashed on a test flight with a member of the French purchasing team on board. Woodring had revealed the secret details of Morgenthau's actions to Clark. With the story of the crash in the press, Clark was free to use Arnold to show how U.S. neutrality laws were being secretly violated to aid the French. Accordingly, Woodring and Morgenthau had been called to testify on the matter before the Senate Military Affairs Committee. Morgenthau had been infuriated and Roosevelt annoyed and embarrassed by the incident.

Arnold was to recount that at the White House meeting that followed, he realized his career was hanging in the balance. He was threatened, he said, by Roosevelt with a one-way ticket to Guam if he didn't learn to play ball.

Now here he was again with the President sounding off on the same subject, his stinging sarcasm double-barreled, aimed at both Harry Woodring and Arnold. In no uncertain terms, Roosevelt went over the necessity for cooperation and coordination in the sale of aircraft and accessories to the French and the British. He wanted absolutely no more trouble on this from the War Department. The direction of his gaze and the sonorous emphasis of his words supplied their own punctuation marks. Everybody, he said, must be on guard in answering questions before congressional committees. He had not liked one bit the manner in which questions had been answered by witnesses—particularly War Department witnesses—and now his eyes were fixed on Arnold. And then the implied threat of a year ago was recited almost word for word. There were places, warned Roosevelt, where officers who could not learn to play ball might be sent . . . "such as Guam."[5] Further, if bureau chiefs were not capable of taking care of themselves on the Hill, it might be necessary to send the second- or third-in-command to appear before the various committees.

No one present was prepared to inform the Commander-in-Chief that much of the problem was of his own making, aggravated by a vague policy that was neither fixed nor clear, influenced on one side by hostile congressional forces and on the other by the reports that he was receiving from the war capitals. The meeting only proved the point, for as Arnold recounted: "Upon a direct question as to whether or not it was advisable to release our latest gadgets and articles to foreign governments before we had something better, the President stated positively that he was *not* in favor of such a release." (Italics added.) Yet he was on record as in favor of releasing the twenty-five P-40's to the French. They were certainly "the latest," and at the moment there was nothing better to replace them.

The question and Roosevelt's answer put an end for the moment to his testy criticism and opened the conference to a discussion attempting to clarify his policy. Morgenthau, who had been enjoying the dressing down of the military, brought up the availability of a new fighter in which there was Allied interest. The President repeated that he would not release any airplane until the United States had a better one, an apparent endorsement of the original War and Navy departments position. What it finally came down to was a decision to work out a new plan on the same theme, in which both sides would get what they wanted even though the problems remained the same. Woodring had already gone through this exercise, with the guidance of Marshall and Arnold, twice before. Presidential spleen demanded that he try again.

When Roosevelt dismissed them, Arnold was to note wryly: "It was a party at which apparently the Secretary of War and the Chief of the Air Corps were to be spanked and were spanked." His attempt to add a light touch was belied by the issue that remained unresolved. A new release policy must be drafted quickly. It must be approved by Roosevelt and be acceptable to the appropriate congressional committees.

In the week that followed, most of Arnold's time was taken up in conferences with Spaatz and the planning staff, General Marshall, and the Secretary of War. Woodring had gotten a delay until March 20 on his appearance before Chairman May and the Military Affairs Committee. Arnold, in order to show exactly what was involved in the release problem, worked out with Spaatz and his people a chart that included every type of plane in the Air Corps production program, showing which aircraft the Air Corps wanted to keep and which they were willing to sell. The differences among them in equipment, physical characteristics, and performance were defined. Arnold wanted the breakdown to show that no matter what was approved for sale, the Air Corps would always keep the best model. Using this basis, a plan was drafted.

On Monday afternoon, March 18, with Spaatz and others in tow, Arnold took his charts and plan to Woodring. The Secretary said he would approve it in principle subject to acceptance by higher authority—meaning the President, which should have brought a chuckle from all present.

The plan was taken to the Treasury Department for Morgenthau's concurrence. The response that came back the next day was a qualified one. The Secretary agreed to the plan's practicability but wished to discuss the details further.

Woodring was already doing that with Arnold at an early-morning get-together, giving the go-ahead to launch some trial balloons on Capitol Hill.

Following the meeting, Arnold briefed the Chief of Staff on the new proposal. Marshall offered a suggestion: Wouldn't the Air Corps have much more to gain than to lose, he asked, if the planes being produced as a reserve were released to the Allies? In place of the reserve planes, the Air Corps would receive later models whose performance had already been proved. Arnold immediately saw it as a workable solution. It was decided that the Air Corps would receive its operational quota plus 15 percent reserve on schedule, the balance temporarily withheld and available for Allied purchase.

At a larger gathering in Marshall's office, with Woodring presiding, this revised plan was gone over, and the Secretary of War announced ten guiding conditions he would present to the President before seeking direct congressional approval.

Of them, the most important to Arnold and the Air Corps were the basic ones: ". . . that no military secret or secret development should be divulged or released . . . no American military plane would be released for foreign sale unless and until a superior plane was actually in the process of manufacture for the War Department. That no delays will be tolerated in our operating requirement needs or in the 15% maintenance reserve. . . ."

After spending much of the day thrashing about on the wording of the new plan—which, except for General Marshall's input, was not new—Woodring, with his ten points inscribed, was still not all that sure of himself. Part of his doubt lay in the unpredictability of the President, to whom he must now sell the proposal; part lay in the gamesmanship of Assistant Secretary of War Louis Johnson. Woodring believed with good reason that Johnson would do almost anything to cut his political throat over this or any other issue. As Arnold and Marshall knew only too well, the Secretary of War seldom made a move or reached a decision without figuring Johnson's reaction into the equation.

Marshall, like Malin Craig before him, handled the problem of the feud by giving his loyalty to the Secretary of War, but, unlike Craig's, Marshall's was a hands-off policy, respected by both men. Arnold stayed clear of their divisive rivalry. Woodring, because of his uncertainty and the fact that he must present the plan to Roosevelt prior to his scheduled appearance before the House Military Affairs Committee, the next day, called for still another meeting in his office. This one was to be at 7 P.M., and he made a special point of informing Johnson that his presence was expected too.

That evening, driving down to the Munitions Building from his home in Bethesda, Maryland, in his sporty Chevy coupe, Arnold turned on the news and received an unpleasant shock. Newscaster Fulton Lewis, Jr., reported that the President, at his afternoon press conference, had announced that all types of U.S. military planes would be available to Allied buyers. Once a plane had come off the production line, it could no longer be considered secret. To a somber Hap Arnold, it appeared that Roosevelt had gutted the new proposal even before it had been presented.

When Arnold arrived at Woodring's office, he found that General Marshall and the other nine conferees knew about the Lewis broadcast. The consensus was *Before we do anything, let's see what Roosevelt really said. Get the story off the ticker tape. Better yet, get the stenographic notes of his press conference.* The wire story was brought in first. Fulton Lewis, it seemed, had been only half right. FDR had stated positively that each sale must be decided on its own merits, but he had declared that once a plane was in production, he could no longer see that it was secret.

To Arnold this had to be a pretty fair example of just how little Roosevelt understood, or for that matter cared, about the technical details of aircraft design and development. The conflict was basic. No army trying to build its own strength and not engaged in a war would be willing to supply other nations, allies or not, with its best equipment.

Roosevelt, of course, had no such qualms. Better to defeat Hitler with American arms than with American blood.

No point of view over the issue could be objective. Woodring's political philosophy was fixed on hemispheric defense and nonintervention. Marshall's energies were directed toward building an army; the politics, he left to the politicians. He hoped America could stay out of a European war, and at the time he believed that it could. Arnold's priorities were fixed as well, but he had an eye to the future. He knew that combat experience was going to bring the sort of rapid changes in aircraft development that would far outpace anything now in the laboratory. He had written a memo on the subject to Woodring, citing the "possibility of having some 1,500 planes now under contract, approaching obsolescence at the time of delivery." It was easy for him to see that if Roosevelt's thinking was followed and the Allies were permitted to pick up the best coming off the production line, the Air Corps would always be in the position of getting second best. That was why Marshall's suggestion on the reserve planes had made such good sense.

While they were all digesting the President's public statement as carried on the wire, the stenographic notes of the press conference requested from the White House arrived. At the same time there came a telephone call for Woodring. The caller, he was informed, was the President.

As Arnold put it, the President was "apparently quite disturbed." Indeed he was. He had been told of Woodring's move to obtain the notes, and being as suspicious as he was thin-skinned, he had misinterpreted the reason for the move. When Woodring sought to explain, Roosevelt told him that what had been said at the press conference was clear enough. It outlined White House policy, and that was going to be followed. Further, if there was any officer there who didn't agree with his position he would take "drastic action" against him! (Arnold could be sure the threat was aimed right at him.) As for those officers scheduled to testify tomorrow before May's Committee, or any other congressional committee, they had better consider themselves on trial! And that went for any statement they might make! Woodring was unable to get in a word of explanation. When he continued to try, the President hung up.

A former governor of Kansas and a politician of many years' standing, the Secretary of War knew how to roll with the punch, but this was the second time in a week Roosevelt had heatedly rebuked him in front of War Department subordinates. Woodring gave those assembled the benefit of Roosevelt's unequivocal warning and orders. The ruffled Cabinet officer made it clear he was absolutely opposed to this latest so-called policy, whether quoted by a newscaster, taken from stenographic notes, or given by the President himself! Obviously, he needed time to settle down, and while he was finding it, Arnold spoke up.

Disappointed as he was, he knew they were in a no-win situation—at least for the moment—and once again he voiced the bottom-line position he had added to the Spaatz memo on the same subject two weeks before. The President as the Commander-in-Chief had made a decision, he said, and "the best anybody could do would be to go ahead and follow the policies of the Commander-in-Chief as well as they could."

Why did he feel it necessary to make the statement? Every military officer present knew you had no choice—you either went along or you got out. Obviously, Arnold wanted it clear for the record that he was going along. It was certain that Louie Johnson would take everything said at the table to Morgenthau, who would repeat it to Roosevelt. Arnold had even less liking for Morgenthau than did Woodring, and he knew that the feelings were reciprocated, so he wanted the word carried that he was going to play ball.

Later Arnold wrote of his statement at the meeting, "All arguments should stop as soon as the policy of the Commander-in-Chief was definitely known." But the arguments did not stop that night. It became a four-man debate—Woodring, Johnson, Marshall, and Arnold—and by the time they adjourned, early the next morning, only one thing was certain: Woodring had called Congressman May and gotten another week's postponement of his appearance before the House Military Affairs Committee.

The next day, it was Marshall, not the Secretary of War, who took the outline they had drafted to the White House. When he returned, he told Arnold that Roosevelt had accepted the conditions in principle—exactly what Morgenthau had said about the earlier effort. Now, once again, all that was needed was a final version.

Five days later the President got what he wanted. The single page bore the title "Government Policy on Aircraft Foreign Sales." Compared with the one drawn up for Woodring, principally by Arnold and Marshall, the difference in outlook and intent was patently clear. The Woodring proposal had been declarative and prescribed. In its place an ambiguous flexibility marked the policy paper approved by Roosevelt on March 25 and defended several days later by Woodring before the House and then the Senate Military Affairs committees. Its preamble stated that with so many planes due to be delivered, productive capacity was increasing and there was no longer such a rush by the Air Corps for early delivery. Therefore when it was "to the advantage of the national defense, the War Department will negotiate for deferred deliveries." Of course, ". . . any authorized delays must not interfere with the delivery of equipment for units immediately necessary for our defense needs." But ". . . the release policy for foreign sales of our most modern design will be liberalized to accomplish the foregoing—each case to be decided on its own merits. . . ."

In his testimony, Woodring stressed Arnold's points. There were, he said, two major advantages in the switch. Changes brought by war threatened Army planes with obsolescence by the time they were ready to fly. By accepting a delay in orders, the changes could be worked into the later models and the Air Corps would benefit. The other was the oft-repeated claim that foreign orders would increase production facilities and thereby benefit the Air Corps, which was now suddenly confronted by a large cut in appropriations.

While there was a certain amount of truth in what the Secretary of War said, there was none in his denial of press reports that he had been vigorously opposed to the changes. The new policy would put the Air Corps in *second* place to the demands of foreign buyers. They could talk about lessons learned in combat, keeping a 15 percent maintenance reserve of aircraft, not divulging military secrets, etc., but the nub of it was . . . from now on the Air Corps would not be first in line.

As John C. O'Laughlin, publisher of the *Army and Navy Journal,* wrote to General Pershing, with whom he corresponded regularly, Woodring had "surrendered and did so in order to hold his job."

Surrender was not exactly the correct word. Woodring had instead carried out a military maneuver that, in the way of the German *Blitzkrieg,* soon to follow, was to become publicly familiar. He had "retreated to prepared positions," very possibly with Hap Arnold as his adviser and guide. And although the Secretary of War's motivation had him marching to a different drummer from that of his Air Corps Chief, their strategy for counterattack was joint. In the Roosevelt-approved policy there was a loophole: a last ditch they could fall back into. It stated: "Each case must be decided on its merits." And the War Department would do the deciding, over the signature of Harry H. Woodring.

In the interim between the unexpected telephone call from Roosevelt on the nineteenth and Woodring's meeting with him on March 25, the Secretary of War had refused to sign a release for the sale of a supercharger General Electric was manufacturing for the Air Corps. The supercharger was considered "one of the Army's most carefully guarded secrets." After the meeting with Roosevelt and the Secretary's later appearance before the House and Senate committees, he continued to balk at requests forwarded by Morgenthau to Johnson. One was for the release of the twenty-five P-40's to the French before the Air Corps had received any of them. At a conference in Marshall's office, Johnson tried to prevail on Woodring to change his mind, but the Secretary of War refused. The planes were slated for Air Corps operational units. They were not in a reserve category.

Practically all of what Woodring knew about military aircraft, the technical details involved in their production, and their end use, he had learned from his Air Corps Chief. Arnold's influence in the struggle, regardless of his written and verbal statements on bowing to the will of the Commander-in-Chief, had to be paramount. It was he who briefed Woodring with the facts gathered by Spaatz, Yount, and others on his staff. It was he who advised the Secretary on the effect of a particular sale. In short, he supplied the ammunition that helped Woodring make up his mind to go on resisting.

Like a whiff of garlic on the breeze, there was the smell of irony wafting about the Secretary of War's bald head. Arnold undoubtedly had little time to reflect on it, but here was a stubborn Harry Woodring, tenaciously battling the President and his foreign-sales czar, Henry Morgenthau, and in so doing working to build a large, modern U.S. air force. Yet, but a short time earlier, in the minds of airmen at least, he had been battling just as hard to accomplish the opposite. His thinking then had been geared to keeping U.S. air power within the niggardly boundaries dictated by congressional appropriations. His outlook had been predicated essentially on the axiom that two small planes could be bought for the price of one large one, without regard to the strategic purpose of either. As Arnold well knew, during the years of meager military budgets, Woodring had consistently demonstrated that like most of his subordinates on the War Department General Staff, he was blind to the strategic uses of military aircraft. In 1938 he had canceled *all* future production of four-engine bombers. Just a year past, if he did not personally perpetuate the Billy Mitchell-type exile of Major General Frank M. Andrews, he had fully concurred in it because of Andrews' unceasing fight to make the long-range bomber the backbone of his air force. Now, as a result, war in Europe and in China, plus Roosevelt's dramatic call to rearm, Woodring was in the forefront of the ranks dedicated to U.S. air power first!

Less than two weeks later, the climax came. The Anglo-French purchasing mission informed Morgenthau they were anxious to proceed with their already announced desire to buy a great many U.S. fighters and bombers. They were being blocked because the War Department had failed to sign the necessary releases. Morgenthau got on the phone to Johnson, who was all in favor of the purchases and asked him to see what he could do about expediting the release. It wasn't a matter of paper work, said Johnson. Woodring wouldn't sign a blessed thing. Worse, Johnson feared the Secretary of War was going to approach Andrew May and ask to be heard by the House Military Affairs Committee again so he could repudiate his previous acceptance of the release policy. One reason influencing Woodring may have been that the Senate Military Affairs Committee had voted by a very narrow, five-to-four margin not to investigate the entire foreign-sale policy. Woodring, in talking to some of his congressional friends, believed that appearing before the House Committee again would persuade it to go ahead with an investigation.

Morgenthau was not inclined to wait on that sort of possibility. He said he was going to call on the President, and he suggested that Johnson do the same. The Assistant Secretary of War needed no urging. He could see this shaping up as his golden moment. The result was that both men informed Roosevelt of Woodring's adamant stand. Roosevelt contacted his Secretary of War at once.

Harry Woodring had been one of FDR's earliest and staunchest supporters. A former National Commander of the American Legion, Woodring knew how to rally the faithful and bring in the votes. Whenever Roosevelt asked him to hit the campaign trail, the results had been positive. This was the early spring of an important election year, and although the President had been quoted in the press as saying he was not inclined to seek an unprecedented third term, he was considering doing just that. If he did, there was bound to be a backlash. He would need all the support he could get, including that which Woodring could deliver. Otherwise, although Roosevelt didn't like to fire anyone, it's fair to assume that the recalcitrant Secretary of War would have lost his job right then and there.

Instead, Roosevelt gave him the option of releasing the requested planes immediately or refusing to do so with the obvious result. The Secretary of War was not willing to give up his Cabinet position over the sale, undoubtedly convinced that he could serve his country better in the post than out of it. Directly after the meeting, Britain and France placed a joint order approved by the War Department for forty-six hundred fighters and bombers, and several weeks later aircraft previously slated for the Air Corps began going to the Allies.

For Arnold, it had to seem that at month's end the long battle with the White House was just about where it had started. Once again he was in the newspapers. This time the Washington *Times-Herald* featured him with a smashing front-page headline: ARNOLD BLASTS ALLIES PLANE SALE BY U.S.

Arnold immediately wrote a letter to Senator Morris Sheppard, the powerful Chairman of the Senate Military Affairs Committee. To the Senator from Texas, Arnold declared:

> In order to correct any erroneous impression or opinion gained from this article, I wish to inform you that I am in full accord with the release policy for the foreign sale of aircraft as was presented to your committee by the Secretary of War, Mr. Woodring, in his recent appearance.
>
> Prior to my concurrence in this policy, my technical and tactical staff and myself made a very careful study of its effect on the Air Corps Expansion Program. I am confident that the new policy will operate to the advantage of the Army Air Corps and thereby the National Defense.

In spite of his denials, the problem was not about to go away. Four months later, and after a great many changes for the worse, Arnold was to record a statement made by Assistant Chief of Staff Major General Richard C. Moore at a private meeting in the Secretary of War's office. He quoted Moore as saying "that we would have to come out and tell the truth some of these days and the sooner the better. That we had continuously told Congress that British production was not interfering with American [aircraft] production when it was. General Moore also stated that apparently we had to wait until England was licked until we could build our own air force."

The remark was an indication of the touchiness of the entire production issue, which could not be separated from personality clashes affecting Air Corps planning on a continuing basis. As an example, Arnold informed

Morgenthau, Woodring, and Johnson that he wanted to confer with representatives of the aircraft industry to find ways of speeding up production on three types of trainers as well as heavy bombers. Johnson called Arnold the following afternoon to say that the conference had been scotched by Woodring with the concurrence of the President. Apparently Woodring was miffed, possibly because Arnold had made the original arrangements through the Assistant Secretary. However, the next morning Johnson was back on the phone to inform Arnold that the conference was on again. The cancellation had been a misunderstanding, which Johnson had managed to correct, and although Arnold did not make note of the way in which the correction was made, it was Johnson's habit to run to the White House to get what he wanted. Johnson now suggested it would be advisable for Arnold to notify Morgenthau that the conference was on again. Morgenthau's reaction to Arnold's call was irate.

"Now, see here, I thought this matter was already settled," he snapped. "The conference is to be held in my office by order of the President!"

"Mr. Secretary," Arnold responded, "that's not the point. All I'm after is information. As Chief of the Air Corps I'm responsible for Air Corps contracts by law, and the—"

"And the conference will be held in my office as scheduled," Morgenthau reiterated archly.

Fed up with this intramural nonsense, Arnold said flatly, "Look, I'm the one who called this conference in the first place. You don't even know why it was called or what's to be discussed!"[6]

His bluntness did nothing to calm the Secretary of the Treasury, who implied that Arnold was refusing to obey the President's orders, which had nothing to do with the matter at hand and was a thinly veiled threat.

Morgenthau, upset by Arnold's frankness and with a penchant for complaining, did so to General Marshall, who in turn asked his Air Corps Chief what it was all about. Arnold informed the Chief of Staff he would do nothing further on setting up the conference until next week. It was a niggling illustration of how personality clashes delayed progress on important matters.

There were at the time, however, other threats that were real and compelling. One concerned the future of the Boeing B-17. This wasn't a matter of who was going to get how many but of whether the Air Corps was going to get any at all. In this case, the battle was not over Harry Woodring's reluctance to approve production of the big Boeing, but Boeing's refusal to accept a reduction in cost. The figure of $205,000 per plane had been accepted in the original contract with the Air Corps, but because the Air Corps was placing large orders for the Flying Fortress, the price, the Materiel Division felt, should be reduced to $198,000. Major General George H. Brett, Chief of the Division, had said, "Not a dime more!"

During the thin years of production, relations between the Air Corps and leading aircraft manufacturers had been good, for the most part. Ruben Fleet, of Consolidated, was a former Army pilot of note, and so, too, was Burdette Wright, of Curtiss-Wright. Glenn Martin, Larry Bell, Donald Douglas, Guy Vaughan, Alexander de Seversky, of Republic, and Dutch Kindelberger, of North American—all were friends or acquaintances of long standing, some more friendly than others. Hap Arnold hunted with Glenn Martin and Don Douglas. Andy Andrews played golf with Larry Bell and Guy Vaughan. As for Boeing, Claire Egtvedt was well known and highly regarded by both Arnold and Andrews as well as many of their colleagues who dealt with the quiet-spoken aircraft design engineer. It was Egtvedt, more than anyone else, who was the creator of the B-17. Through his dedicated persuasion and belief in the plane's concept, the company had been willing to risk its financial neck at the outset to produce the first test model. Now, five years later, Boeing was not about to turn out the plane for a penny less than had originally been agreed on.

James P. Murray, Boeing's Washington representative, was not the sort to knuckle under. After unproductive meetings with Woodring, Brett, Arnold, and Johnson, Murray, a bit dented but not cowed, reported the impasse to Boeing headquarters in Seattle. It was decided that a month's cooling-off period might be in order. The option for the Air Corps to buy was extended, but the word from the West was that the Boeing management was burned up and ready to drop production on any new B-17 orders from the Air Corps.

It was Arnold's problem to solve. With time of pressing importance, he called a meeting which he planned to chair. Present would be members of his staff and representatives from the Boeing Company as well as General Brett and some of his people from the Materiel Command. Shortly before the meeting was to convene, in the Air Corps Trophy Room at the Munitions Building, Arnold was alerted by General Marshall that they were wanted at the White House. It was not an appointment that could be deferred. Arnold immediately notified his Chief of Plans, Colonel Tooey Spaatz, that he was to chair the meeting. He had no qualms about leaving the conference in Spaatz's hands. He simply told the unflappable redhead there had to be some solution or they were facing an almighty disruption in the heavy-bomber program just as it was getting started.

The conferees in the Trophy Room listened with minds already set as Wellwood Beall, of Boeing, outlined the problem from the company's point of view. Boeing could not reduce the charge and make it worthwhile to continue production. It was as simple as that. Spaatz digested it all, and when Beall had finished he asked an equally simple question: "What can you take off the plane to lower the price?"

The idea had never occurred to anyone before. They jointly decided that the electrically controlled cowl flap mechanism could be removed, and the external bomb racks and other odds and ends could be shed. The $7,000 difference was narrowed appreciably. By the time they adjourned, Arnold had returned and Spaatz reported the results. He felt they could get Woodring's approval to go ahead now, possibly finding other expendable items.[7]

Spaatz, a 1914 graduate of West Point, had been coming up with solutions to tough problems for years. Laconic—he was known to say that he had never learned anything by talking—he was a low-key officer with a gift of seeing to the heart of the matter and quickly reaching decisions that usually saved everyone a great deal of time and energy. As a staff officer and planner, his leanness of thought was appreciated by commanders who wanted to act. As a tactical commander, he knew how and where to lead the troops. Directness was his forte and loyalty up and down an ingrained trait.

To those who had never sat at the poker table or quaffed a drink of scotch with him, Tooey Spaatz may have seemed remote and enigmatic. He recognized the trait in himself, for after reading an article by Arnold Bennett on conversation, he observed, "He deplores silent or taciturn people, advised one to talk even if they talk trivia or seem silly—that by this talk life becomes more enjoyable—doldrums at meals, etc. can be made into pleasant moments. Believe he is right and that I am a serious offender." Nevertheless, on the ground or above it, he was known throughout the Air Corps as a reliable professional.

His interest in the Boeing B-17 was as technically deep as it was strategically broad. In 1936 he had been Executive Officer to Bob Olds's 2nd Wing of GHQ Air Force, Langley Field, Virginia. The 2nd became the only wing with a squadron of B-17's, and with them Spaatz saw long-held theories take solid form. In October 1917, he had flown night bombing missions with the French over German lines. He had gained enough experience to know that bombsights were poor, and accuracy was hit or miss and not improved by trying to destroy a target at night.

Ever a realist, he absorbed the strategic ideas of Billy Mitchell, Douhet, and other bomber theorists, but was not ready to accept the practicality of their theories until aeronautical development brought into being bombers that had range, speed, armament, and a bombsight that made it possible to hit a target from four miles up. In the units he commanded during the twenties and thirties he developed tactics, as did other operational officers, on the basis of what experience taught and theory preached at the Air Corps Tactical School. It was a case in which theory was the tail wagging the dog of aeronautical development—at least until the B-17 came along. Spaatz saw the plane as the means of implementing a practical and feasible aerial strategy.

Frank Andrews, as GHQ Air Force Commander, had been the leader in a three-year losing battle with Secretary of War Harry Woodring and the War Department to sell this strategy and to build air strength around the Flying Fortress. Andrews had pointed out publicly in January 1939 that U.S. air power was fifth-rate in a world preparing for war. Roosevelt's almost simultaneous call for a force of ten thousand combat planes was a dramatic reversal of previous policy, the change stimulated by events in Europe.

During the same month that Andrews had spoken out on the lack of U.S. air power and the President had announced a plan to build it, Spaatz joined Arnold's staff. Almost immediately, he became one of five members on a board whose job it was to revise and expand the research and development capabilities of the Air Corps. The situation was one of paramount importance in Arnold's mind, and in discussing it with Spaatz and Assistant Air Corps Chief Brigadier General Walter G. "Mike" Kilner, they decided to come up with a program covering aircraft requirements, including weapons and equipment, spanning the next five years. Arnold asked Kilner, a member of the National Advisory Committee for Aeronautics, to head the board and Spaatz to serve along with Lieutenant Colonel Earl L. Naiden and Major Alfred J. Lyon, both highly regarded Air Corps engineering officers.

In a shrewd move, Arnold added one more member, Charles Lindbergh, to what became known as the Kilner Board. The revered pilot, a reserve officer in the Air Corps, was also a highly regarded member of NACA—he had been offered the presidency of the body—and above all an astute and gifted aviation planner. Beyond that, he was a celebrity who shunned the limelight and despised the press, with good reason. Captain Eugene Beebe, Arnold's aide, smuggled him in and out of the Munitions Building by a little-used side entrance.

Arnold called the findings of the Kilner Board of "inestimable" value. They included much-needed plans for improving the characteristics of all types of military aircraft then under consideration. One recommendation was tied directly to foreign purchases: The French and the British were to be asked to turn over to the Air Corps combat data on flight performance so that aircraft weakness could be corrected and improvements made. The result of this sound policy was that, in February 1940, U.S. aircraft manufacturers began turning out for the first time self-sealing gas tanks, armor protection for the pilot, tail guns for bombers, heavier armament, and a number of other important refinements.

* * *

In January 1940, the War Plans Division passed a study to Assistant Chief of Staff for Operation and Training Brigadier General Frank Andrews stating that 915 long-range bombers would be needed to provide adequate hemispheric defense. The Air Corps at that moment had fifty-two B-17's. Six months earlier there had been only thirteen of the Boeings, a number to which the Air Corps had been blindly limited since 1935. Further, until December 1939, the War Plans Division had never established a requirement for aviation based on the Air Corps's mission in hemispheric defense. Yet, a month later, it was referring to the B-17 and its anticipated but still unproduced counterpart, the Consolidated B-24, as *medium*-range bombers (italics added).

Andrews, like Hap Arnold, thought the figures cited were adequate. But the study's provision for 181 *heavy* bombers was actually the result of a secret project begun more than four years before, in October 1935.

The project was to produce a single bomber, the XB-19, built by the Douglas Aircraft Company. It would not be ready for testing until 1941. Still, it was being cranked into the potential air strength as an aircraft capable of carrying over ten thousand pounds of bombs three thousand miles, or a twenty-five-hundred pound load eight thousand miles. There would be nothing like it in the air, providing it could live up to its expectations. A similar bomber had not made the grade. In 1937, Boeing had delivered to Andrews and GHQ Air Force the results of another secret project, the XB-15. Dubbed "Grandpappy," the XB-15 was a most impressive sight on the ground or above it, whether flying across the country or on a mercy mission to Chile carrying three thousand pounds of medical supplies to earthquake victims. But in speed, altitude, and fuel consumption the underpowered XB-15 could not measure up to the B-17. It remained to be seen whether the even larger XB-19 would make the grade, but in the meantime, in the winter of 1940, the War Plans Division was busy turning out studies that foresaw nearly two hundred B-17's as the key segment of the total 2,726 authorized tactical aircraft required to protect the hemisphere from attack.

Most of what Andrews was dealing with at the time, whether on the ground or in the air, was theoretical, since appropriations lagged far behind projection. He had had to deal with unfulfilled theory for so long there was no difficulty in dealing with it now, particularly when he knew the tangible appeared to lie ahead. For years they had played make-believe in numbers and types of planes, in pretending that three pilots represented a squadron of eighteen, that three hundred fifty aircraft—half of them obsolete—represented a modern strike force of one thousand, always knowing that what was authorized was largely a will-o'-the-wisp. Now, in the air at least, there was change.

When Andrews had taken over as G-3, the entire U. S. Army was in a wretched state. Lack of manpower was only surpassed by lack of equipment, and very little of that could be classified as modern. Enlisted strength for all branches was less than 130,000 men. There were three organized and six partially organized divisions in the entire Army, none of them up to combat strength. There was not a single armored division, and the few scattered tank units boasted fewer than fifteen hundred men.

By January of 1940, Congress had authorized an increase of an additional one hundred thousand men. Small as the number was compared with the military strength of friend and potential foe alike—the German Army mustered eighty divisions of all types—the increase was a slight movement forward, and the psychological impact was far greater than the figures might indicate. Andrews' Plans Division, of approximately one hundred officers and civilians, was at work formulating training and operational plans to encompass what was projected. One such projection was airborne training—an idea espoused by Billy Mitchell in 1918 and demonstrated on a small scale by First Lieutenant Claire Chennault in 1929 maneuvers attended by the visiting Chief of the Soviet Military Mission. Shortly thereafter, the Soviet Union offered Chennault a colonelcy and a thousand dollars a month to train airborne forces in the U.S.S.R. Chennault rejected the offer as summarily as the War Department rejected the idea of paratroops.[8]

It was another eleven years until Andrews proposed airborne training to the Chief of Infantry, Major General George A. Lynch, who thought they should give it a try, and still two more years before airborne elements were ready to be tested in maneuvers. But the airmen—Andrews and Arnold—had supplied the impetus and direction to get the infantry off the ground.

Although, to the Air Corps, Andrews' mandate as G-3 marked a reversal of War Department policy, it did not mean that hard-held attitudes within the General Staff had suddenly vanished. Hostility to the Air Corps was still very much at home in certain offices, particularly in the War Plans Division and in G-1, Personnel.

Andrews' calm adroitness outflanked the opposition, or simply faced it down with a quiet authority that could not be denied. As long as he was G-3, his presence eliminated the long-standing friction between the Air Corps's G-3 section and that of the General Staff. The former was responsible for drawing up training and operational plans and the Planning Section for recommending implementation. But only G-3 of the Army had the authority to approve or reject the Air Corps proposals. Frequently in drawing up its own, parallel programs, G-3 had rejected or modified or delayed Air Corps plans. It had made for some bitter infighting, and was one of the causes behind the airmen's desire to be rid of War Department control. However, with Andrews as G-3, for the first time anyone could remember there was real cooperation, overall understanding of what was involved, and a resultant smoothness of internal operations.

Several of the division's officers were among those whom General Marshall had brought up from the Air Corps Tactical School. One of the sharpest was Captain Laurence S. Kuter. Kuter had first served under Andrews briefly in 1932, when Andrews commanded a squadron of three bombers and a pair of amphibians on a "mass flight" from San Antonio,

Texas, to France Field, Panama. At that time, Andrews was trying to sell
the idea of regular ferry flights to the Canal Zone aimed at improving the
Canal's defenses. He was one of those who believed its security would
depend not on naval forces but on air power.

Kuter, who was in full agreement, had tried to prove the point at some
risk while serving as an instructor at the Tactical School. He had given a
lecture describing what would happen to a naval task force sallying forth
from a harbor when met by an attacking force of B-17's. An attending
naval observer, Commander Miles Browning, was infuriated by the
suggested heavy loss of shipping and registered a complaint that reached
the desk of the Secretary of the Navy. As a result, Kuter was reprimanded
before the students and faculty of the school by its commandant, Brigadier
General H. Conger Pratt, for having dared to advance such a heretical scenario. Pratt then quietly gave Kuter a perfect efficiency rating.
Previously, Pratt had suggested to the War Department that the school's
texts on air matters be made the guiding doctrine followed by Air Corps
tactical units. He was quickly informed by the Adjutant General that
official tactical doctrine was set down in the various service, training, and
field manuals.

But now, in 1940, Larry Kuter, as a project officer in the Training Section of G-3, was at work drafting the Air Corps's first official field manual
—titled *FM 1-5 Employment of Aviation of the Army*. To airmen, the
manual was a step in the right direction, but a breakthrough only insofar
as it was the first of its kind. Even though air operations were still to be
planned in line with and under the direction of surface operations, strategic bombardment was given recognition. It would be used, said the manual, "to nullify the enemy's war effort or to defeat important elements of
the hostile military forces."

Serving in G-3, Kuter also got to fly with Andrews again, only this time
as his copilot. There was one flight he would never forget: They had
taken off in Andrews' DC-2 to fly to Barksdale Air Force Base, in
Shreveport, Louisiana. They ran smack into an ice storm, and Andrews,
who was absolutely indifferent to weather, bored on through. When the
ice-coated radio antenna snapped off and they could no longer bracket the
radio beam into Barksdale, Andrews dropped down and picked up the
railroad track that went to Shreveport and began bracketing the so-called
"iron beam" instead. By now the windshield was a solid sheet of ice, and
he told Kuter to open his side window and keep his eye on the track while
he calmly eased the overburdened plane through the storm. Kuter didn't
know what was keeping them in the air, and directly after Andrews
plunked the Douglas down on the fog-shrouded field, he thought they had
lost a wing, for a great mass of ice dropped off it.

Later, Kuter taxied the plane to a heated hangar and the real melting
began. Soon thereafter, Andrews arrived back on the scene and said,

"Let's go." The landing gear was still heavily ice-coated and his copilot wondered if they shouldn't wait. More, the whole area was still under the influence of the foul weather. "Nothing to it," said Andrews. "Once we pull the gear up the ice will break off."

Engineering Officer Milo McCune, who had been talking with Kuter and admiring the glistening aircraft, wondering with him how it had ever managed to remain airborne, said, "No, sir, that ice won't come off. You'll break the gear when you try to lift it."

Andrews took a closer look, rubbed his chin, and said, "You're right," and then added to his relieved copilot, "Okay, we won't go today."

Kuter also was working with Lieutenant Colonel Harold M. McClelland on a series of programs aimed at developing a balanced air force of trained combat groups. In 1939, Congress had approved Air Corps procurement of more than thirty-two hundred aircraft, doubling officer strength from sixteen hundred to thirty-two hundred and nearly tripling enlisted strength. Programming was, of course, a major Air Corps consideration, but as Andrews was in overall charge of all Army operations and training, G-3 was very much involved in the organization of an authorized twenty-one-group program. It was a program whose figures would grow like Topsy as events overwhelmed it.

To ease the burden of rapid expansion, Andrews organized what became known as the "Miscellaneous Branch" of G-3, in violation of accepted principles of staff organization. He considered the move a justifiable violation to head off any delaying action on the part of the road blockers, in order, he said, "to accomplish things that had to be accomplished." He knew only too well that problems connected with the development of air power were too technical to be handled efficiently and quickly by people not otherwise qualified. Chief of the new branch was Colonel Clinton W. "Jan" Howard.

If Andrews had a blind spot, it was his tendency to overlook personality shortcomings of some of his people. By most old-guard Air Corps regulars, Jan Howard was well known and generally disliked. No one would deny that he had one of the best engineering minds in the Corps, that he had been a driving force in the B-17 from dream to reality, and that in the early days he had helped to bull through ongoing research and development on more advanced equipment. Beyond that, there were few who appreciated his abrasiveness and his treatment of subordinates. Hap Arnold and Howard, formerly brothers-in-law, had little regard for one another on the reservation or off. Aircraft engineering was Howard's strong suit, not commanding troops, and he was quite unaware of how his behavior affected those with whom he dealt. Larry Kuter was an exception, whom he openly disliked. At a future time, when Howard commanded a base in Charlotte, North Carolina, and Kuter flew in on his way to somewhere, Kuter found his picture hanging in the latrine.

Andrews had brought Jan Howard into G-3 because he knew of his technical knowledge, Howard having served both as his G-4 in GHQ Air Force and briefly as his Chief of Staff. Andrews was not unaware of how Jan ruffled the feathers of ranking officers in other branches. Complaints from outside of G-3 had come to him. But he was inclined to discount them, because Howard got results, and if the War Department was over-supplied with anything, it was complaints.

In that regard, the Air Corps had a complaint that was constant. It was a problem more pervasive than all the rest and harbored within it the long-rooted seeds of catastrophe. In the mind of an Andrews or an Arnold it was fundamental and was fixed on the relationship between the Army and the Navy, particularly the role of aviation. Billy Mitchell had brought the conflict to the public eye when he began preaching the obsolescence of the dreadnought. He demonstrated its vulnerability when his bombers sank an "unsinkable" battleship in 1921 and then repeated the performance on a pair of Navy battlewagons two years later. Even before that, however, the lines had been drawn in the minds of Army airmen, who saw themselves in an undeclared war of wits where they were outnumbered and often outmaneuvered politically. As a result, over a twenty-year span certain beliefs became fixed in their thinking, their views on air power shaped around them. Those views added up to this:

1. The Navy wanted to dominate and control the air defenses of the United States and its possessions. 2. The Navy was out to deprive the Army air arm of its mission of coastal defense, even usurping its bases when it could. 3. The Navy wished to limit Army aviation solely to the protection of ground forces. 4. The Navy's influence in the War Department and with successive political administrations worked to retard Air Corps technological and strategic development. 5. The Navy could not be trusted in any joint maneuver, seeking always to make itself appear superior, using any subterfuge available. 6. The purpose of the Joint Army-Navy Board was to work for tactical and strategic harmony. Since each service operated primarily in its own element—land or sea—the only area where there might be disagreement was in the air. Until 1940, the Air Corps had no representative on the Board, whose generals and admirals had, in the airmen's belief, little if any understanding of air power. 7. The Navy, fearing that an independent air force posed a threat to control of its own air arm, would bring all political guns to bear any time the noxious idea appeared on the horizon. Conversely, many Army airmen who believed in a separate air force were sure the Navy would end up running it.

There was a considerable record of tangible evidence to support these unwritten Air Corps tenets, and it seemed the more years one had been involved in the interservice air struggle, the more entrenched was the belief that the real enemy was the Navy Department. It wasn't that the airmen of both services were hostile to each other—quite the contrary. In 1940, Chief of the Naval Bureau of Aeronautics was Admiral John Towers, a friend of Hap Arnold's since 1911, when they had both learned to fly. Andrews, too, had friends of long standing who were naval aviators, but personal relationships didn't change the overall feeling.

More than twenty years after the fact, Andrews' air force commander at Hamilton Field, Colonel John F. Curry, put in writing the story of how in early 1917 he had established the 6th Aero Squadron, at Ford Island, Pearl Harbor. The squadron's mission was "Aviation Seacoast Defense." There was no Navy aviation there until nearly three years later. Curry's point was that coastal defense had originally been an Army mission, but it had been temporarily usurped by the Navy, and was still contested while Ford Island had become a permanent Navy air installation.

It didn't matter that the latter change had been instituted for the good and sound reason that Pearl Harbor was the fleet's major base in the Pacific and it made sense for the Navy's air support to have a field close by. Curry believed the story must be told to show how military aviation had been established at Pearl Harbor not by the Navy but by the Army. And although the Air Corps subsequently established three major bases on Oahu and a number of smaller fields, Army airmen believed Ford Island had been lost to the Navy through some dirty poker played by the members of the Joint Board. To this loss could be added others, principally North Island, San Diego, California, also first occupied by Army airmen and for years their principal training base.

The important but unrecognized point in this tale was not what was lost or gained or even why, but that over the years suspicion and recrimination between the two services lay like strewn wreckage, and one day would contribute to wreckage of a far greater magnitude at the very point of Curry's contention.

* * *

It was to Lieutenant Colonel Ira C. Eaker that John Curry sent his Ford Island saga. As Hap Arnold's Executive Officer, Eaker was privy to all the problems that beset his boss. Curry recognized that if anyone would know how to handle the information to good advantage, it would be the keen-minded Texan who had previously served as Air Corps Chief of Information.

Of the principal tasks facing the Air Corps, Eaker equated negotiations with the Navy over who got what and who was responsible for the defense of what on a par with foreign sales. Bringing the Air Corps to top efficiency while increasing production and training bases was the primary goal, but it was closely interrelated with the two knotty problems of naval and foreign demands.

Eaker was only too well aware of what the Air Corps considered the

Navy's unflagging attempt to stifle and block Army air development, particularly in the realm of tactical operations beyond sight of land. Through the War Plans Division, Arnold and thus Eaker knew that the Navy was preparing to ask that its patrol strength be increased by 500 percent. Andrews, also apprised of this confidential information, had made two points: The numbers were far more than the fleet could legitimately employ for reconnaissance work, and if the Navy was thinking of using the slow-flying PBY's as a strike force, the plan, to put it in its most charitable light, would not be economical. In fact, to pit lumbering, poorly armed amphibians—no matter how long-ranged—against carrier-based fighters could be catastrophic.

These were not considerations that Arnold could address before congressional committees, but when he went to testify on appropriations, or the progress of expansion and the tricky and dangerous issue of foreign sales, it was Eaker who prepared and organized his statements and supporting material. When Arnold wanted to write an article, it was Eaker who was his collaborator. They had written one book together; they would write others. With a degree in journalism, honed by years in the ever-sensitive realm of Air Corps publicity, Eaker had a shrewd sense of public relations backed by more than twenty years in the aerial arena as a premier pilot, staff officer, and tactical commander. He knew how to play cards in the public-relations game as well as he played his cards at the poker table. He was acutely sensitive to the way the isolationist press was twisting Arnold's statements to serve its own ends. His only recourse was to make sure his news contacts had the real story and that whatever he supplied Arnold was accurate.

In those increasingly hectic days, Eaker and his wife, Ruth, lived in a small house just off the end of Key Bridge, on the Virginia side of the Potomac, a good takeoff point for reaching the office by seven-thirty. There, he would go over the work that had not been completed the previous evening so that when Arnold came in, about eight, they could go through it and discuss what lay ahead for the day.

Arnold's secretary of long standing, Edna A. Adkins, was the real majordomo of the office. Everyone who knew her well called her Suzie. Everyone else had better call her Miss Adkins. It was said there was nothing that went on or stirred in the War Department that got past Suzie. Behind those horn-rimmed glasses and that broad forehead lay a perceptive mind that was there to serve and protect a boss to whom she was completely devoted. It was her desk that faced the entry door of the outer office, and although it was Eaker's job to know who was coming to see Arnold, it was Suzie who summed up their qualifications and mentally filed them away for any future reference that might be of benefit to her boss.

As a close observer of Arnold's personality, there was probably no better-informed officer than Eaker. This was so for two reasons, one of which could be detected in his still brown eyes. He was by nature a watchful person who missed little and retained what he saw. Secondly, he had hooked his star to Arnold's a long time ago. Some of those close to the scene, who recognized that Tooey Spaatz was Arnold's right-hand man, may have seen Ira Eaker in the light of a protégé. This was not altogether so, for Arnold was not the type to attempt to mold an alter ego in his own image. He was quick to respect anyone who worked hard and did a good job, but he was not inclined to show favoritism; it was bad policy in any case. Nonetheless, in a shadowy way perhaps unrecognized by both—Eaker never addressed Arnold by his first name—the relationship was there. And it was only natural for a military leader to have around him those on whom he knew he could depend.

Not a West Pointer, ten years Arnold's junior, Eaker, as a twenty-two-year-old lieutenant, had briefly served with both Arnold and Spaatz at Rockwell Field, California, in December 1918. Later, during the Billy Mitchell days, in the mid-twenties, they had come to know each other better. Eaker was Assistant Executive Officer to Army Air Service Chief Major General Mason M. Patrick, and with his office between that of the General and Mitchell he was literally in the middle of the fireworks.

Unlike many pilots of the time, Eaker combined intellectual curiosity with a love of flying. He would break aviation records not for fame and glory but to prove what could be done in the air and, in proving it, point the way ahead.

After long duty in the Washington area, Eaker served once again with Arnold and Spaatz at March Field—first as a pursuit squadron Commanding Officer, then as a group commander. It was during this time that Andy Andrews, who prided himself on being an instrument pilot without peer, heard that Eaker was so good he could perform aerobatics while under the hood. At one of his periodic visits to March Field to discuss the state of GHQ Air Force with Wing Commander Hap Arnold, Andrews looked up Captain Eaker and said, "Ira, I'd like to see you do your stuff."

Eaker invited Andrews to ride as observer and check pilot in the front cockpit while he did the flying from the rear under the hood.

When they had leveled off, Andrews instructed by intercom, "All right, do a loop."

Eaker, concealed by the hood, did as requested, and then leveled off again.

"Try an Immelmann to the right," said the General. Eaker gave him an Immelmann to the right and then one to the left. Thoroughly impressed, Andrews said, "Okay, how about a spin to the right?"

After the Captain had spun the plane, recovered, and resumed normal flight, Andrews cracked, "Ira, I think you can see out of that thing."

"Why don't you give it a try, sir?" suggested Eaker.

They landed and swapped places. Once they had gained altitude, Eaker ordered a loop and Andrews ended up in a spin. Eaker made the recovery, and Andrews, laughing ruefully, said, "You win, Ira. Show me how it's done."

Eaker was only too happy to do so, and Andrews, proficient as he was, caught on quickly.

Ira Eaker's expertise as an instrument pilot offered an insight into his nature. His proficiency had come about through a process of analytical thought and calm daring that began in a nearly fatal spin over Manila Bay in 1922.

During the rainy season, Army pilots in the Philippines had to pick and choose the best time to fly. Someone had said if you got caught in the air in a downpour you could drown. On a flight from Manila, Eaker learned you could do worse than that. Running into a deluge in his DH-4, he ran out of visibility and very shortly thereafter he was coming down in an uncontrollable spin. Plunging earthward through the cloud muck, struggling to gain control, he saw a yellow discoloration out of the corner of his eye and realized it was the muddy water of the Bay coming up at him sideways. At literally the last instant, he hauled the plane out of its descent, the DH-4's wheels smacking the water as he pulled back on the stick. By staying very low he made it to the field, waterlogged and shaken. When he had dried out, he observed to his friend Lieutenant Newton Longfellow, "Newt, you know you can't fly if you can't see the horizon; you can't keep a plane under control."

The question they asked themselves was, What could be done about it besides staying on the ground when the weather was bad? The next morning when Eaker took off he carried two additional pieces of equipment. He had suspended a plumb bob on a string from the instrument panel, and on the top longeron of the fuselage he had secured a carpenter's level. He thought that the bob would indicate a turn left or right and the level would indicate when he was flying in a nose-high or -low attitude.

He began experimenting, first in clear sky. Next, he rigged a canopy over his cockpit and brought Longfellow along to make sure he didn't run into anything. When he was able to fly his DH-4 up through five thousand feet of cloud and back down again, he invited others to join him. With Longfellow on one wing and Captain Charlie Phillips on the other, he guided the formation through long reaches of cumulus. This was real pioneering!

The success of the experiment led him to write to McCook Field, in Dayton, Ohio, where Air Service Research and Development was then situated. When the response arrived he was a bit let down. They sent him a turn-and-bank indicator, explaining that development at McCook was a bit more advanced than plumb bob and carpenter's level.

Nevertheless, Eaker had run into a problem in the air, and on his own initiative he had solved it and used what he had learned to benefit others. This was his style in all things, on the ground or above it. He was a quiet man, like Spaatz, but far more articulate, and what attracted Arnold to him early on was his facility for seeing what was needed even before it was asked, then preparing for it. He had that inbred quality of the sharp pilot who always has a field picked out to set down in should the engine quit.

It was at March Field that a closer connection grew between Eaker and Arnold. They began collaborating as aviation writers, first on magazine articles stemming from the Army Air Corps Mail Operation and then on a book. Although Arnold went to Washington duty in 1936 and Eaker was assigned first to the Air Corps Tactical School and then to the Command and General Staff School, they continued to collaborate. Often the "collaboration" consisted of Eaker writing the article and Arnold making some minor changes, with publication under both their names. Their first book, *This Flying Game,* was published in 1936 by Funk & Wagnalls, and in the winter of 1940 it was still earning them royalties.

Reports on aerial combat in Europe and the Far East inspired them to write another book, *Winged Warfare,* which would be dedicated to the courageous flyers of the RAF when it was published, in 1941. What the authors had to say about a separate air force and the use of strategic air power illustrated a measured and cautious approach to both issues. They were out to rock no boats, naval or otherwise. On the issue of a separate air force, which was once again gaining momentum, they cited the two long-held schools of thought but championed neither one. "Unity of Command" was the battle cry for those who wanted to keep the air under Army control. "Flying leaders for flying fighters" was the way they described the attitude of those seeking separation from the Army.

While the book was being written, Arnold was doing a considerable amount of testifying on the Air Corps expansion program, and on one such occasion he was asked his opinion of a separate air force. Spaatz, who was present, took down his words: "Eventually it may come since the majority of leading actions toward it have been adopted. However, I personally believe that an attempt to institute a separate air force now would confuse the issue and delay this program. I think the most immediate concern is to provide the combat units called for in these supplemental estimates."

Winged Warfare offered a third position, a variation on a theme previously pushed by Andrews and others: Between 1926 and 1933, the Air Corps had had its own Assistant Secretary of War for Air. The post had been dropped by Roosevelt supposedly for economy reasons but primarily because Major General Douglas MacArthur, Army Chief of Staff at the time, felt that it gave the air arm too much clout in the halls of Congress. This was not so, for the controlling factor was still the War Department and the General Staff. Now it was suggested that the Assistant Secretary's position be restored, that the Air Corps have its own staff, and that both be responsible to the Secretary of War. This would eliminate the War Department General Staff as the dictating body. It was a plan that Andrews had discussed at length with Marshall when the two had met in August 1938, and later Andrews had sent the text of the plan to him.

On strategic bombardment, the authors stated a proposition that later they would have been happy to delete. After describing the manner in which a bombing mission would be carried out, they wrote: "Successful bombing is done largely at night."

Those words must have raised the hackles of all who had preached the theory of precision *daylight* bombardment for so long. The statement doubtless was strongly influenced by reports from Europe. The RAF had made one daylight raid that left a powerful impression.

During this period most RAF Bomber Command attacks were against German shipping in the North Sea area, made with little success by twin-engine Wellingtons, Blenheims, and Hampdens. Over land targets, propaganda leaflets instead of bombs were dropped. Conversely, British losses to German U-boats and a successful raid by the Luftwaffe on the naval base at Scapa Flow had brought an angry demand by the First Lord of the Admiralty, Winston Churchill, for the RAF to get off its duff. Why did it not go after targets like the German port of Wilhelmshaven? he asked.

On December 18, 1939, Bomber Command did so. Twenty-two Wellingtons, flying in tight formation at eight thousand feet through a clear blue sky in what was termed by the British Air Ministry an "armed reconnaissance," were jumped by a strong force of German fighters over Heligoland Bight. This was the largest air encounter of the war so far, and it received a large play in London and Berlin, both sides claiming victory. The RAF admitted the loss of seven of its bombers and proclaimed their fighters had knocked down thirty-four of the enemy.[9]

Arnold and Eaker received word of the actual but concealed British losses—twelve shot down and three forced to crash-land—through the U. S. Military Attaché in London, Colonel Raymond E. Lee. It was a fiercely high figure, an unacceptable loss ratio. Admittedly, the Wellington was "very inflammable and burns readily," as one German pilot reported. The need for self-sealing fuel tanks was recognized immediately, but the huge losses convinced the RAF that it must move more and more to night bombing. This switch was obviously accepted by Arnold and Eaker at the time. Eaker was predominantly a fighter commander, his thinking on tactics so oriented, and Arnold was privately keeping his options open. Operations, not classroom theory, was proof of whether daylight bombardment was feasible. Into the strategic question must be fed the quality of the equipment and the training and tactics of those who commanded it.

* * *

On March 23, 1940, *Army and Navy Times* publisher John O'Laughlin wrote General Pershing that the suspicion "has been justified" that FDR had called for building fifty-five hundred planes so he could give two thousand of them to Allies. Whether Arnold would have agreed or not, on April 4 the Washington *Times-Herald* ran the aforementioned headline story on his blasting Allied plane sales. The account said that in recent testimony he had attacked the Roosevelt administration's excuse for permitting huge sales to foreign buyers. The move had been defended by both Woodring and Johnson before the full House Military Affairs Committee on the basis of vastly increased aircraft production. It was here that Johnson had so wildly exaggerated the figures, but there was little doubt that the battle was still going on. A complaint was passed from Morgenthau to Marshall concerning Arnold's failure to cooperate. Arnold's response was that he had the task and responsibility of building an air force as authorized. That's what he was trying to do, and he didn't know any other way to do it. Would Marshall rather he simply acquiesced to Morgenthau's demands? Marshall would not, but they must find a way to work things out.

Then suddenly, on April 9, the whole world changed, and although the problem of aircraft production would become more acute as a result, all attention was focused on Europe. Hitler had struck at Norway and Denmark.

A month later, the stunning swiftness and apparent ease with which German Panzers swept through the Low Countries and into France shook the War Department as nothing ever had. On the thirteenth of May, Secretary Morgenthau, who had come to view General Marshall with respect and with growing understanding of the herculean problems facing the Army, arranged a White House meeting at which the Chief of Staff could tell the Commander-in-Chief just how bad things really were. Present with them were Woodring, Johnson, and Harold Smith, the Director of the Budget. Marshall said he must build a fully equipped army of 750,000 men within a year. He needed $657 million to do the job. Somehow, Roosevelt wasn't getting the message, and Marshall, in his quiet, crisp manner, told him flatly, "If you don't do something, Mr. President, and do it right away, I don't know what is going to happen to this country."

Two days later, Winston Churchill became Prime Minister of England. He informed U. S. Ambassador Joseph P. Kennedy that he believed Hitler would attack the British Isles within a month, and in a private appeal to Roosevelt, he asked for all aid short of war. Prime Minister Paul Reynaud, of France, was even more impassioned in his plea for help.

Ambassador Kennedy's attitude was "that if we had to fight to protect our lives, we would do better fighting in our own backyard."

On the sixteenth, the President called on Congress for the funds that Marshall needed and for the production of fifty thousand planes a year. Included was the request for an additional two hundred B-17's, but it was all a long way down the track.

At a meeting in Morgenthau's office the next day, Marshall asked Arnold how badly his training program would suffer if they sent only 100 planes to the Allies. Arnold said it would mean a six-month delay. He had only 150 pursuit planes for 260 pilots, and only 52 B-17's of the 136 contracted for. Marshall concluded: "If I do this, that accentuates the ineffectiveness of the Air Corps. It is a drop in the bucket on the other side, and it is a very vital necessity on this side, and that is that. Tragic as it is, that is that."[10]

Not altogether. While a frantic effort went forward, first to secure weapons for the British and French and then to find a legal method by which the meager results could be turned over to them, Arnold moved to try to get some essential answers. Could the Allies halt the German drive, and if France was defeated, could the British survive?

These were the paramount questions facing the Administration and the War, Navy, and State departments. All future action was centered on the answers, and the applicable U.S. embassies, among others, were called on to give them.

In every embassy, one of the military attachés was an airman whose reports went to Hap Arnold as well as to G-2. Prior to George Marshall's appointment as Chief of Staff, assistant military attachés were assigned from the Air Corps but their reports were not passed on to the Chief of the Air Corps. Arnold changed that by pointing out to Marshall the stupidity of a military intelligence system that for twenty years had failed to keep its air arm apprised of foreign aeronautical developments. When war began in Europe, he suggested that his office be permitted to send observers to the various capitals and war fronts to learn all they could about the technical and tactical aspects of the air war. Marshall agreed, and Arnold turned the administration of the plan over to Bart Yount, who had his staff draw up a series of questions for each observer, military or civilian. These were to be memorized, with a final briefing being given by Lieutenant Colonel Robert Candee, of G-2.

A few days before the Germans launched their thrust into Holland and Belgium, Yount suggested to Marshall and Arnold that from now on a rotating system be used, with the observer remaining on the scene for three months, his replacement arriving in plenty of time to be filled in. That made good sense. Not only would it expose more airmen to what was going on in the war, but it would also ensure a steady flow of fresh information, along with a widening circle of contacts.

Yount now recommended that Lieutenant Colonel Frank O'D. "Monk" Hunter, senior pursuit specialist, be sent to Paris, Captain Benjamin S. Kelsey to London, and Captain Willard R. Wolfinbarger to Berlin.

Arnold approved, but he wanted a name added to the list, someone who could study RAF fighter and bomber tactics and bring home the answers. If Arnold could not go himself, then Tooey Spaatz was his man, and Tooey, in his usual, no-fuss manner, agreed to go and be—as he put it—"a high-class spy."

Two

The High-class Spy

At high noon on Friday, May 17, 1940 Tooey Spaatz bade farewell to his wife, Ruth, and three admiring daughters and boarded the train at Washington's Union Station, bound for New York City. Joining him were Ben Kelsey, Monk Hunter, and Willard R. Wolfinbarger. With headlines black and the air waves filled with the dramatic news of German victories in Europe, the four wondered if they would get to their assigned stations before it was all over.

Their ship, the U.S. liner *Manhattan,* bound for Genoa, Italy, reflected the severity of the news. There were only a hundred twenty passengers making the crossing in a vessel built to accommodate more than two thousand, but the ship's skipper knew he would be returning with every nook and cranny filled. Aboard ship, the four officers met Ward Davison, of General Motors, who, with a party of engineering colleagues, was on his way to France to see what armament G.M. could produce for the French Army at this late hour. An ebullient public relations vice-president, Davison seemed confident that his efforts would not be wasted. The French had stopped the Germans at the Marne in the First World War. They'd stop them at the Somme in this one. Arthur Nutt, an aircraft-engine specialist with Curtiss-Wright and the *Manhattan*'s Chief Engineer, Pat Brennan, weren't all that sanguine.

At Gibraltar the ship was stopped briefly by the British, but it was not until the *Manhattan* had anchored in the sweeping Bay of Naples, on Monday, May 27, that they saw any real sign of warlike activity. Spaatz noted eight Italian submarines, fifteen destroyers, five cruisers, some transports, and a hospital ship—a formidable array. But when they went ashore with Davison and his party, they found the Italians friendly enough. A taxi driver told them, "We don't like the English, but we don't want to fight them. We don't like the Germans, and we don't want to fight them, either, but we would rather fight the Germans than the British. But—" with a hands-off-the-wheel gesture "—Mussolini knows best."

Aside from wild rumors, no one really knew what was happening in France. The airmen did not know that the British Expeditionary Force had commenced its desperate evacuation from Dunkirk, only that the German attack appeared to have veered away from its southerly thrust toward Paris and had swung northwesterly. Nor could they foresee that Italy was less than two weeks away from entering the war.

For the moment, Spaatz observed no warlike preparations, no unusual troop movements. Later, the four talked with Captain Walter J. Rayne, who had joined the ship at Naples and was returning to the United States. Rayne, the skipper of the freighter *Flying Fish* and a Naval Reserve officer, had been caught with his ship in the harbor of Bergen, Norway, on April 10, when, out of the dusk, RAF bombers and Navy torpedo planes attacked.

He described how the German heavy cruiser *Königsberg,* docked along a cement pier, was hit and moved out into the harbor, where she sank. Rayne also saw a transport ship, an oil storage tanker, an ammunition depot, and bridges destroyed by the bombs. German antiaircraft batteries set up in the nearby hills were notably inaccurate, although they did bring down one British plane. There were no German fighters aloft to repel the raid.

The next day, the *Manhattan* arrived in Genoa. Anchored in the midst of an Italian naval task force was the Italian liner *Rex.* Just two years earlier, General Andy Andrews had given the *Rex* a lead role in a grand illustration of what long-range bombing was all about, proving what B-17's and their well-trained crews could accomplish under the worst of weather conditions.

It was during the East Coast air maneuvers of May 1938 that Lieutenant Colonel Ira Eaker had given Andrews the idea of using the *Rex* as an imaginary attacking fleet. Three of Bob Olds' Fortresses had been assigned the task of finding the ship. The lead navigator, Lieutenant Curtis E. LeMay, whom Olds considered "the best damn' navigator in the Air Corps," had plotted his course through impossible weather to locate the liner some seven hundred miles off the East Coast at a previously announced time. While the significance of the feat made worldwide headlines, Andrews was summarily informed by the War Department that his planes were thenceforth to be restricted to within one hundred miles of the shoreline.

In Genoa, Spaatz picked up his first reports on German *Blitzkrieg* tactics and the Wehrmacht's use of paratroops to capture airdromes. The Germans first dropped two thousand paratroops at Rotterdam Airport, followed by four thousand more the next day. Once the field was secured, transports flew in with more troops and supplies. The Germans took advantage of any opening. "Motorcycles dart at 50 mph across the bridge on Meuse past guards, then cut wires controlling explosive charges—then Panzers come and keep going. When stopped by resistance, call in planes," Spaatz reported.

German fighters, it was said, had orders to avoid combat if outnumbered but were poured into the attack wherever a weak spot was found. The fighters carried their bombs not in racks but in tubes or hoppers beneath the wings. The German Air Force, it seemed, was being employed on a strictly tactical basis, coordinated with the advance of the Army and, with the exception of the bombing at Rotterdam, not used strategically.

Spaatz gained all this information from Captain Bentley, a military attaché who helped him, Kelsey, and Hunter to reach Paris. There was a good deal of doubt about how they were going to make the journey; it was rumored that the border was already closed. Wolfinbarger bade them farewell, his trip to Berlin presenting no problem. The overcrowded train they finally boarded was actually the last one to travel to Paris, and even that was in doubt, with a six-hour halt at the Italian-French border, where they saw many passengers forced off by French and Italian border guards.

After Spaatz had talked to Bentley, he recommended lateral liaison between the attachés serving in the various capitals. That there was not, was an example of how little thought had been given by Army Intelligence to the obvious benefits of the exchange.

On the journey to Paris, the only signs of war they observed were scenes at important rail stops—such as Tours—where young men, suitcases in hand, boarded the train or left it, obviously on their way to report to their Army units. Otherwise, until they checked in at the American embassy on the Avenue Gabriel, in Paris, the war continued to remain in the rumor stage. But in Paris the quiet was not a sign of tranquillity. They could feel the tension, see the sense of despair and shock in the faces of the people. The city's famous blue haze had become a fog of fear, and the sky was full of black smoke from burning oil dumps.

They arrived in Paris on the morning of the twenty-ninth to find that embassy records were going up in smoke. Spaatz and Kelsey spent most of the day being filled in by a pair of Air Corps engineering officers, Captains Frank Carroll and John Gardner, who had recently arrived from England. Kelsey was to be Carroll's replacement as an observer. They discussed Great Britain's aircraft production, but Spaatz took time to relate Captain Rayne's description of the RN's April bombing of Bergen. Arrangements were immediately made to pass the account on to the British Naval attaché, who was most appreciative, for information coming in from occupied Norway was thin and spotty.

Far away, at West Point, on that same day, Norway was very much on the minds of Hap Arnold and Ira Eaker. Sadly, they were acting as honorary pallbearers at the military funeral of Air Corps Captain Robert M. Losey. Losey had been killed in Norway on April 21 during a German air attack, which made him the first American military officer to be killed in the war.

A West Point graduate, class of 1929, the young Iowan was both a pilot and a meteorologist and, prior to overseas duty, he had headed the Air Corps Weather Service. When Russia invaded Finland, in late 1939, Losey went to Arnold and sold him on the idea of his going to Finland to observe aerial combat in the Arctic, an area of major meteorological interest. Arnold pushed Losey's travel orders through in two days and, in January 1940, the Captain was on his way to Helsinki. Four months later, when the Germans invaded Norway, he was in Stockholm on his way home. Because there was no U.S. military observer in Norway and the minister there was a woman, Mrs. Florence J. Harriman, Losey was ordered to join her as she tried to maintain contact with the disassembled Norwegian Government. They met at a country inn, and several days later, after making certain Mrs. Harriman was out of harm's way, he moved up to the front lines, such as they were, to observe the fighting. Standing at the mouth of a tunnel during a Luftwaffe air raid on the town of Dombas, he was killed instantly by shrapnel from a German bomb.[1]

Both Arnold and Eaker had admired the dedicated Captain and recognized the importance of his work in the small but vital Air Corps Weather Service. This was all geographically far away from Spaatz and Hunter and their endeavors, yet they were linked by a common bond, similar pursuits, and a shared danger.

Later that same day, Spaatz met with Ward Davison again. The G.M. official told him the French wanted to buy big, seventy-ton tanks, that they had plenty of pilots but needed planes badly. They were disappointed in the Martin bomber, for although the pilots liked its flying characteristics, lack of self-sealing fuel tanks made it a flaming coffin when hit. The Curtiss P-36 was still being used in combat.

Embassy miltary attachés described the power-driving tactics of the German Army and Air Force. Nothing, apparently, could stop the combination, and the British were continuing to pull out at Dunkirk. As many as eighty planes were said to be operating in support of a single Panzer column, close communication maintained via two-way radio. French and British guns could not stop the thirty-ton Skoda-made tanks. The famous French 75 was unable to traverse fast enough over a large enough field of fire to halt them. The American Ambassador, William C. Bullitt, was sending frantic cables to Roosevelt asking for immediate aid that did not exist, or could not have been made available in time if it did.

With the fall of Paris apparently imminent, how would Spaatz and Kelsey reach London? On Friday the thirty-first, they learned that Prime Minister Churchill was coming to Paris for an emergency meeting with

French Premier Paul Reynaud and Marshal Pétain. There might be room for the two Yanks on the return flight, although that meant leaving behind most of their clothes, including dress attire. As it turned out, Churchill's flight was delayed, but Spaatz and Kelsey did get aboard a small twin-engine Jersey Airways plane that had brought supplies to Paris. The circuitous three-hour flight through hostile skies ended after dark at Hendon Airport, near London.

Spaatz and Kelsey carried no written instructions. Officially, they were classed simply as observers on temporary duty, not attached to but in direct contact with the American Embassy and particularly its Military Section. But, unlike regular air attachés, Spaatz and Kelsey were Arnold's men, his representatives, and therefore, to the British in their hour of great need, they were special.

That night they were joined for dinner at the Cumberland Hotel by an old and savvy comrade of Tooey's, Major George C. McDonald, who had been in England since April 1939, first as an assistant military attaché and then, at Hap Arnold's request, as an assistant military attaché for air, also. He and Spaatz had served together for two years at Langley Field, Virginia, in the 2nd Wing of Andrew's GHQ Air Force, Tooey as Wing Executive and Mac as Operations and Intelligence Officer. Intelligence—such as it was—had been McDonald's specialty for twenty years, first in photo reconnaissance, then in plans and operations.

Spaatz was interested in getting the picture as seen from the U. S. Embassy at Grosvenor Square. McDonald told them that with all the confusion of the incredible cross-Channel retreat from Dunkirk, a lot of friendly planes were being shot down by their own side. Proper recognition signals had not been worked out.

The following morning, Spaatz and Kelsey were presented to Joseph P. Kennedy, who had been the U. S. Ambassador to the Court of St. James's since 1938. Kennedy was not well regarded by the senior officers in the Embassy's military section, particularly those who were strongly pro-British. He was considered a shrewd, abrasive, blunt, and politically devious operator whose appointment to the ambassadorial post was a payoff for campaign services rendered Franklin Roosevelt. His thinking had been in tune with that of Prime Minister Neville Chamberlain, and during the Munich crisis his influence had carried considerable weight in bringing about the original conference among Chamberlain, Daladier, and Hitler. At the time, he had asked Charles Lindbergh to come over from France to draw up a letter appraising German air strength. Lindbergh had done so, declaring the only nation with the potential to equal Hitler's air power was the United States. Kennedy had not only sent the letter to the White House but had also used it to influence Chamberlain and his advisers. Popular with the British at that point for his decisive action in the cause of a negotiated peace with Hitler, his attitude now was considered "defeatist" by the Churchill government and pro-English segments in the Roosevelt administration. British public opinion toward him was turning to enmity. At the time of his meeting with Spaatz on that bright June morning, he was declaring by cable and telephone to the President and Secretary of State Cordell Hull that Hitler could not be beaten and that he would crush England as he was crushing France.

Tooey Spaatz would reach his own conclusions through personal observations and inquiries. They might not carry the same impact on the policy makers at home as would Kennedy's, but they would be of importance to his boss, Hap Arnold, who in turn would bring his own weight to bear.

Spaatz saw immediately that the mood in the streets of London was far from the tremulous quiet of Paris. There was a feeling of stubbornness, a sense of defiance and determination. An eye cocked to the sky, an ear listening for the siren's wail, Londoners went about their business, gas mask and helmet on hip. Sandbags were piled in orderly rows against what everyone was sure was on the way. The newspapers reflected that spirit, proclaiming "the miracle of Dunkirk"—the successful evacuation, in nine days of fierce attack, of nearly 340,000 British and French troops. *BLOODY MARVELLOUS*, clarioned full-page headlines in the London *Daily Mirror*.

The air officers at the Embassy knew that an overriding factor in achieving the miracle had been control of the air. In spite of the loss of Army men and equipment, the RAF was still a formidable force, and Spaatz was eager to find out just how formidable.

He began to do so at once with the assistance of another old friend and seasoned campaigner, Colonel Martin F. "Mike" Scanlon, the principal Embassy Attaché for Air. Scanlon was a vintage airman who had earned his wings shortly after Spaatz, in 1916. Even before that, in April 1912, shortly after he was commissioned a second lieutenant in the Infantry, Scanlon had had his first taste of flying in a flimsy Wright B aircraft with Hap Arnold at the controls.

During World War I, Scanlon had come to know and like the British. He was in England for six months commanding ten U.S. squadrons taking Royal Flying Corps training before going off to France for combat duty. After the war, he had spent eight years on two separate tours as a military attaché with the Embassy in London. Independently wealthy, Scanlon and his wife, Gladys, circulated in the upper levels of British society. Friends of Edward, Duke of Windsor, and Mrs. Simpson, and the Astors and their Cliveden set, Scanlon was an admitted Anglophile. He had entry almost everywhere and had the confidence of key RAF personnel whom Spaatz was looking forward to meeting.

In the next week, the newcomers were introduced to a great many RAF officers, including Air Marshal Sir Cyril Newell, Chief of the Air Staff. Air Commodore Jack Slessor, Director of the Plans Branch in the Air

Ministry, particularly impressed Spaatz. Slessor had learned to fly in spite of the ravages of polio, which had left him with leg braces. Accepted into the Royal Flying Corps, he had become a World War I ace.

Over a lengthy lunch with Spaatz, Scanlon, McDonald, and Kelsey, Slessor played down the effectiveness of the Luftwaffe's dive-bombing tactics at Dunkirk. He said that had the Germans used horizontal bombing instead of depending so much on Stukas, the outcome would have been far more costly to the British Expeditionary Force. He also said that the greatest handicap of the RAF over Dunkirk had been the restricted range of the Hurricanes and Spitfires that were designed for defending England. Their record would have been much better with tanks that held forty-five minutes to an hour more fuel. Slessor admitted that RAF fighter losses had been greater than anticipated and the bomber losses less, but "the neck of the bottle," as Spaatz put it, was trained pilots and combat crews.

What Slessor didn't say on that last day of the incredible retreat from Dunkirk was that in the past three weeks the RAF had lost 250 Hurricanes alone. At that crucial moment in history, Fighter Command had exactly 413 serviceable aircraft to protect the British Isles from an estimated fifteen hundred German fighters and three thousand bombers. Of the RAF total, only 325 planes were Spitfires and Hurricanes. Air Chief Marshal Hugh "Stuffy" Dowding, Chief of Fighter Command, warned Churchill and the War Cabinet that same Monday that if the Luftwaffe struck now he "could not guarantee air superiority for more than forty-eight hours."[2]

When Spaatz asked Slessor why the RAF had failed to launch strategic bombing raids from bases they had held in France, Slessor said the plan for a department of strategic operations had been interrupted by the German breakthrough. Beyond that, French air power was tied to the battle and not to strategic bombing. Spaatz later wrote, "RAF apparently thinks as we do but has been hindered by the higher-ups." At least during the Phony War it had been—when Bomber Command was limited, except in a very few instances, to dropping leaflets proclaiming to the Germans that if British bombers could drop paper on them they could also drop bombs. This had the combined effect of wasting precious fuel and freezing poorly protected air crews.

By "thinking as we do," Spaatz was referring to Slessor's agreement that daylight bombing operations were feasible when the weather was good but only if there was fighter escort to the target. There were also differences in tactics, and they would remain—the differences between day and night.

Slessor pointed out that German pilots appeared to be a mixed bag: some very good, some with less than one hundred hours of combat training. Their losses were estimated at around 20 percent, and if this was true, they all agreed that when the German Air Force moved against England it would stay away from RAF bases.

The circumstances changed abruptly on June 9. The Wehrmacht, 143 divisions strong, began its massive drive against the French Army along a four-hundred-mile front, reaching from Abbeville, on the Somme, to the upper Rhine. In two days of fighting, l'Armée de l'Air was put out of action by the Luftwaffe in its OPERATION PAULA which included successful bombing attacks on aviation installations. No one doubted that when Hitler finished with France he would launch an invasion across the Strait of Dover. The only question was, How soon?

The perilous springtime was full of incongruities. Continuing fair weather stimulated optimism, and siren-like, it helped to create illusions. While the crowds on Westminster Bridge cheered the ragtag fleet of Dunkirk-battered little vessels that chugged up the Thames, the 52nd Scottish Lowland Division embarked for France. It and what remained of the 51st Division, pinned down at Le Havre, were doomed to defeat and capture. While Air Marshal Dowding was warning of the urgent need to keep RAF units at home, four more squadrons were assigned to operations over the Continent, operating from bases in southern England.

At night German aircraft prowled the British skies with little interference, causing no appreciable damage. During the daylight hours, RAF pilots fumed over orders not to attack the marauders. But back in mid-May, Fighter Command's defensive strength had been reduced by a precious ten squadrons of Hurricanes sent to fight in France at Churchill's insistence and over Dowding's objections. He had told the Prime Minister, Air Minister Sir Archibald Sinclair, and Air Chief Marshal Newell that he must have a minimum of fifty-two squadrons to maintain control of the air over England and its sea approaches or the Luftwaffe would gain supremacy. Now he had fewer than half that number: twenty-five squadrons. These figures were known only to a few, even though the public was fully informed on the general gravity of the situation.

Despite all that, traffic moved through the streets, sunbathers at Trafalgar Square sat around the base of Lord Nelson's pedestal feeding the pigeons, the parks were full of strollers and soapbox orators, flowers bloomed in bright profusion. A newly arrived French brigadier general named Charles de Gaulle noted it all "belonged to another world than the one at war."

Ambassador Kennedy didn't think so. When the German attack had been launched, in May, the U. S. Embassy had urged the estimated four thousand Americans living in England to return home while they could. On June 7, a repeat notice was circulated with a warning: "This may be the last opportunity for Americans to get home until after the war."

The response of about seventy of those who had been so informed was to join the 1st American Squadron of the Home Guard, commanded by retired U. S. General Wade H. Hayes. This action prompted Ambassador Kennedy, who was hostile to the whole idea, to inform an officer in the group that the formation of such a unit "might lead to all United States citizens being shot as *francs-tireurs* when the Germans occupied London." That gave a fair appraisal of Kennedy's expectations. The members of the Squadron, however, who sported a distinctive red eagle patch on their jackets, had no sympathy with the Ambassador's assessment or conclusion. They joined in the preparations for the battle with a will.

All road signs lost their heads, villages their names, and milestones their numbers. Roadblocks were thrown up with such vigor that in some places Army equipment could not pass, and everyone who owned a shotgun was joining the Home Guard with the hope of getting a Hun on the wing. Reality was somewhere else for the moment, still across the Channel, and a sense of high adventure seemed to possess almost everyone.

Spaatz was beginning to get the feel of the British. Their long lunches, cocktail gatherings, supper parties, and late dinners were in keeping with the atmosphere of the moment. It was going to take more than this fellow Hitler to interfere with military social custom. That Spaatz, a colonel, and Kelsey, a captain, were meeting socially with air marshals and senior officers from the Air Ministry was more a reflection of underlying British need of U.S. support than any sudden break with military tradition.

On June 10, 1940, Benito Mussolini, the Italian dictator, decided he could risk an attack on the all but defeated French—or, as Roosevelt aptly put it in an address before the graduating class at the University of Virginia, "The hand that held the dagger has stuck it into the back of his neighbor."

The Italian Embassy in London was separated by a single dwelling from the red brick American Embassy. Late in the afternoon, Spaatz watched the sad-faced "evacuation" of the Italian staff.

In the days and weeks that followed, Spaatz found British cooperation "splendid." He also found England changing from somewhat blasé optimism to an armed camp.

Spaatz now began a series of visits to training bases and operational commands. At a gunnery school he was told that German dive bombers like the Ju-87 and -88 were tough on the inexperienced but could not inflict heavy losses, and their effectiveness diminished as antiaircraft defenses increased. That fitted into a general Air Corps disinterest in dive bombing, a U. S. Navy specialty.

At Bomber Command Headquarters, Spaatz met Air Marshal Charles "Peter" Portal, who then headed the command and later was to become a close associate and friend. Then he had a chance to talk with some squadron leaders at a bomb wing equipped with Blenheims. At a fighter base near Paddington, he met several pilots who had flown Hurricanes from fields in France. They claimed to have shot down eighty German planes confirmed in the first five days of action over the Low Countries, and probably an equal number unconfirmed, against a loss of two killed and three missing. Spaatz was not told that in those first five days, RAF Bomber Command on the Continent had lost half of its two hundred planes and that RAF fighter losses were calculated by the Germans to be fiercely high. Despite British and German claims and counterclaims, Spaatz needed no one to tell him that the shattering series of German victories could not have been won without control of the air.

After visiting Fighter Command, where Spaatz and Kelsey saw for the first time film of aerial combat taken by synchronized gun cameras, they witnessed the launching of a Coastal Command strike against six German ships off the Dutch coast. Nine twin-engine Lockheed Hudsons and six Navy Gloucester biplanes went off to make the attack. Spaatz asked Group Captain Primrose if the command always sent out fighters with the bombers. "When we send them out without fighters, they don't come back," he was told. Kelsey, who knew Spaatz's attitude on unescorted long-range bombardment, hid a grin, guessing that the Group Captain's response had disgruntled Tooey.

Kelsey had developed his own views of Britain's situation. He felt that official communiqués failed to give the real picture of what was going on. You had to get out of London and talk to the people, he believed. This he did, and his perceptive conclusion was that in this moment of crisis a great social change was beginning to take place. The British would fight, but things would never be the same again—not in the structure of their class system, not in anything.[3]

But now it was back to London to take part in a welcome-home party given by the Scanlons for Military Attaché Colonel Raymond E. Lee. Lee had been in Washington for six months, and when he had been recalled to the United States, in December 1939, he had not anticipated returning to take up the post he had held since 1935. But because the Army, the State Department, and the White House needed an officer in England who knew the British intimately, yet was perceptive and balanced enough not to be carried away by sentiment, he was being returned to Grosvenor Square.

Before leaving Washington, Lee had lengthy meetings with two State Department officials: James Dunn, an adviser on political relations, and Herbert Feis, an expert on international economic affairs. Both indicated a growing bitterness toward Ambassador Kennedy's position, which Feis called "Defeatist . . . as always."

Lee, attempting to get clarification of U.S. policy toward the Allies, said it appeared to be one of helping as much as the American public would permit. Dunn agreed that that was it in a nutshell.

Upon his return to England, Lee found that a great change had taken place. To him "London seemed as dark as a pocket . . . shops, houses largely deserted with familiar streets barricaded and barbwired."[4] The surface euphoria observed by Spaatz two weeks before had vanished.

Following their welcome-home reception, Lee and Scanlon talked into the small hours. According to Scanlon, one ray of light in all the darkness was "the RAF who have proved themselves better fighters every time they have encountered the Germans."5 The Ambassador, Scanlon reported, expected the British to be beaten.

The next morning, Lee heard it all from Kennedy himself, who declared emphatically that he was opposed to the United States becoming involved or intervening in any way.

* * *

It had been a busy month since Spaatz and Kelsey bade farewell to Monk Hunter in Paris. Although there hadn't been much time to wonder how he was faring, news of the German approach to Paris had stimulated Spaatz to talk with Ambassador Kennedy and Colonel Lee about having Hunter transferred to London. Lee cabled Washington, requesting the move.

In Paris, Ambassador William Bullitt, learning that the French Government was moving its crumbling seat of power to Bordeaux, elected to remain in the capital. Not Hunter. When he received word that his presence was desired in England, he contacted his opposite number in the British Embassy. "I don't want to stay and welcome Germans," he told him. "Can you get me orders to fly out in one of your planes?"

His friend suggested they call on the British Consul. Word was that the last ship would be sailing from somewhere shortly. They made a quick trip to see the Consul, who was only too happy to oblige. Now all Hunter needed was transportation, which he adroitly managed through the U. S. Deputy Ambassador, Anthony J. Drexel Biddle, Jr. Biddle, who had been Ambassador to Poland before the war, was planning to head for Bordeaux to represent the United States there. Hunter asked if he could squeeze on board. Indeed he could, and they were off with a chauffeur whom they agreed was the best driver in all of France, possessed of an uncanny ability to avoid the jammed highways crowded with refugees fleeing southward by every means of conveyance.

In Bordeaux, Hunter found thousands of desperate people of all nationalities trying to get passage to England. His diplomatic papers were quickly stamped, and he was told to get to the port of St.-Jean-de-Luz, where there was a ship waiting. The port was over one hundred miles to the south, near the Spanish border. Biddle again came to his aid, loaning his car and chauffeur to get there. Off they went, this time in style, Hunter insisting they stop to dine at the best hotel en route, figuring they might as well live for the moment. He knew he would not be using French francs for some time to come.

The scene at St.-Jean-de-Luz was a smaller replica of the square in Bordeaux: people of all nationalities, many of them elderly and frail, women and children far outnumbering the men. The ship they were to board was lying three miles offshore, and the passengers were taken out in small boats, the able-bodied climbing rope ladders to the ship's deck, the less able being hauled up in rope baskets.

The little steamer, crammed to the gunwales with escapees ranging from King Zog, the deposed ruler of Albania, and his sisters, to a recent Princeton graduate, headed out into the Bay of Biscay. It was a four-day voyage through rough seas and frequent rain squalls and the constant worry of being torpedoed by a German U-boat. Hunter and some of his newfound companions used canvas awnings to build a room of sorts on the deck. There wasn't much food, but nobody was all that hungry.

On the morning of June 30, they made it safely into Plymouth Harbor, the last British ship from France, its overloaded cargo weary, seasick, but greatly relieved to have escaped the Nazis. Hunter got on the phone to the Embassy and talked to Colonel Lee, who told him how to reach London and that evening picked him up at Paddington Station.[6] He described the traveler as "looking rather wild-eyed." The cause probably had more to do with Monk's discovery that the British refused to honor his American Express travelers checks than his sea venture.

Two days later, a cable from Washington ordered Spaatz and Kelsey home. As far as Tooey was concerned, it didn't make sense. He fired back a request that he be permitted to stay. It was obvious, even in Washington, that the main event was about to begin. An invasion appeared imminent. It had to begin in the air. Whatever was to happen would be decided there. He quickly received permission to remain. No doubt, Arnold saw to that.

Captain Ben Kelsey, who also had wanted to stay, bade Tooey good hunting and departed for Ireland to help shepherd several thousand foreign refugees on their way to the United States. He returned home with views that ran contrary to the generally accepted belief that England could not hold out alone. He told Arnold and others that the German defeat of France had not won Hitler the war but probably had lost it. His argument was that the British, no longer encumbered by having to divide their strength to support the French, could now devote all their energies to their own defense. Kelsey sensed the willingness of the British public at all levels—from the working man to the privileged—to support the war effort, whatever came. He also believed that since the Germans could not invade by surprise, they could not now invade at all.

Hap Arnold found Kelsey's assessment worth circulating. So did General Marshall and others in the War Department. Kelsey and two Army officers who had been on the beaches with the British at Dunkirk were sent off to brief selected audiences within the Army. Their theme was that Britain would not go down as France had, and that their fight was America's, too.

Back in England, on the day of Kelsey's departure Spaatz had written a tally of what he considered RAF Fighter Command's strength to be. The total was 736, based on estimates made at the beginning of the war. He guessed that losses since then would equal new planes produced in the interim. Actually, he was off by a wide margin, for at the time RAF fighter strength was 602 aircraft of all types, including about five hundred Spitfires and Hurricanes. At the same time, he had been told that the Germans were training for the invasion in Baltic Sea ports, using forty ships of five hundred tons or more and other types of landing craft. He thought it both a pity and a point to stress that RAF Bomber Command lacked aircraft with the necessary range to hit these "excellent targets."

After a lengthy visit, with Air Secretary Archibald Sinclair and Air Chief Marshal Newell, which included Lee, Scanlon, McDonald, and Hunter, he came away with some pertinent statistics. According to the official daily reports from the War Cabinet room, RAF fighter losses amounted to 5.5 percent per mission. Day bombers were losing nearly 7 percent and night bombers less than 2 percent. The Air Ministry claimed twenty-nine hundred German planes shot down since the beginning of the war. Admittedly the tally could not be verified, but it was an accepted estimate.

At this moment of relative calm before the storm, there were many unanswered questions on both sides of the Channel concerning the other side's strength and intentions. The British anticipated invasion and were grateful for every day that it did not come, allowing them to build their defenses and husband their air strength, which Dowding knew to be too little to defend all. Hitler's generals and their troops were eager to finish the war, but in the flush of their amazing victory in Europe, plans had not been developed to invade England. The Fuehrer appeared in no hurry and seemed reluctant to launch the climactic battle.

On June 30, under a directive signed by Goering, the Luftwaffe was given a general outline of what was expected of it: "As long as the enemy air force is not defeated the prime requirement is to attack by day and by night in the air and on the ground without consideration of other tasks." The plans for the attack were to be worked out by Goering's Chief of Staff, General Hans Jeschonnek.

Two days later, on July 2, Hitler, while vacationing in the Black Forest and working on a victory speech to the Reichstag, approved the release of a top secret directive to his senior officers. It stated: "The Fuehrer and Supreme Commander has decided: that a landing in England is possible providing that air superiority can be attained and certain other necessary conditions fulfilled. The date of commencement is still undecided, all preparations to be begun immediately."

In retrospect, July 10 was the day when the battle for air superiority began. On that morning of rain and mist and swirling cloud the Battle of

Britain started, with heavy attacks on convoys in the Channel by closely escorted German bombers. The British ships were reluctantly protected by thin patrols of RAF fighters, for Dowding was against the piecemeal commitment of his strength.

At a meeting a few days later with Sinclair and other RAF officers, it was decided that Spaatz and McDonald would settle in with an operational bombing group while Hunter and Scanlon were assigned to Fighter Command. Through much of the remainder of the month Spaatz observed the tactics and growing effort of Bomber Command in its plan to carry the war to Germany by bombing the invasion ports and industrial targets. As the tempo of the air battle over the Channel and the southern part of England increased, his inquiry became fixed on respective bombing results. In a letter to Hap Arnold he said that as far as he could gather, German bombing had been "particularly lousy."

Juicy targets are available all over the island and planes regularly make their appearance usually at night but the damage done scarcely warrants the effort. Whether they are holding back their mass of well-trained crews for an aerial blitzkrieg or whether they have no well-trained crews is not definitely apparent. However, I am beginning to believe that the German Air Force was too hastily constructed and is beginning to be mastered by the smaller but much better trained (apparently at least) RAF. The flights over the English Channel during the past few weeks indicate that smaller numbers of British fighters inflict serious losses on German bombers protected by Me 109's and Me 110's, the latter in most instances outnumbering the British fighters brought into the action. Losses in the aerial fighting recently have been in the neighborhood of 4 or 5 German planes for one RAF fighter. On the other hand, the RAF have been doing some excellent bombing and have a fairly low loss rate particularly in their night raids.

What Spaatz did not know was that by mid-July RAF losses were rising so fast that if the rate continued, Fighter Command would be out of business in six weeks. Unintentional but highly exaggerated claims of German losses by RAF pilots was one crucial factor that led the Air Ministry to believe it could repel the daily attacks.

Spaatz spent nine days at a heavy-bomber station housing twin-engine Wellingtons. He saw one raid of seven planes launched at night. At the mission's debriefing he learned that six of the planes had dropped their bombs, two of them on alternate targets, and one plane could not locate the target and returned with its bomb load. Except for antiaircraft fire, no enemy opposition had been encountered. The moon was bright and the air hazy over Germany. From what Spaatz saw and heard, he drew certain conclusions. "Apparently night bombers are not being used under doubtful weather conditions, and by excessive centralization of control there is not sufficient flexibility in shifting targets in case of weather."

He felt that RAF bombing could be termed "harassment over a large area rather than bombing for destruction," or strategic bombing. However, he believed that the British effort was better than the German, and he gave some reasons why in his letter to Arnold: "Bombs are not dropped wildly and are brought back if the target is not definitely located. This makes weather an important factor. . . . Some of the raids were called off because of anticipated bad weather at the objective, which was deep in Germany." The centralization of control that he had criticized limited the RAF's ability to shift its attack to targets closer at hand where the weather was good.

During his stay with the bomber group only one raid was made with a full squadron of sixteen planes, and after talking with the crews he decided that "effective bombing has been accomplished. Intelligence reports from abroad, received by the military here, confirm this."

He listed the principal targets as gas and oil supplies but added that aircraft factories, munitions factories, and airdromes were given high priority. The RAF's most serious limitation was its lack of a bomber with enough range to reach all parts of Germany and Italy. He reached two additional conclusions: first, that adequate photoreconnaissance of a target both before and after the attack could not be done "due to the lack of an airplane of sufficient speed and firepower to carry out such missions during daylight." The British were using unarmed Spitfires operating at high altitudes, but there were camera problems. Secondly, ". . . whatever means are used it is evident that the most efficient long-range bombing results cannot be accomplished without continuous reconnaissance of the target."

He reported that no effort was made to use weather recon before committing a whole squadron, yet if the weather looked threatening the entire mission was called off. Because of this, he estimated, the Wellingtons flew fewer than fifteen missions a month. The answer to successful bombardment was altitude and speed and daylight attack, preceded by weather reconnaissance when the outlook was uncertain. Only the last was something new in Spaatz's thinking; the rest dated back to Douhet and Billy Mitchell. Firepower with the speed and altitude was programmed into his thinking as it was into the thinking of every daylight bomber advocate. From all that he was seeing and hearing, nothing had happened to change the fundamental approach. Spaatz was simply finding ways to improve on it. The growing British adherence to night operations did not dissuade him.

At the time, Spaatz had not met Vice Marshal Arthur Harris, who then commanded No. 5 Bomb Group. Two years later, Harris would become Commander-in-Chief of Bomber Command, but in July of 1940, while Spaatz was validating conclusions already well entrenched in his own thinking, Harris had decided, and felt everyone around him should agree, that bombing must be done at night. As he put it, ". . . any idea of using [bombers] by daylight is now a busted flush even amongst those who were not seized of this childishly obvious fact before the war started."

Aside from the question of accuracy over the target, there were two related points that influenced these diametrically opposite approaches to bombing. One had to do with humanitarian considerations; the American concept was to kill as few civilians as possible, while the British were fighting for their very existence, with their backs to the wall. The other had to do with aeronautical design and engineering. The British then had no bomber with enough defensive firepower to make it viable in daylight against concentrated fighter attacks. Further, it had no fighter that could fly escort for any great distance.

Spaatz believed the B-17 could defend itself against fighters by daylight, providing it flew in numbers. New bombers would do even better. Also, the B-17 carried a bombsight that made precision bombing possible. On the matter of needing fighter escort, Spaatz appeared ambivalent, his mind not made up. It was apparent that he didn't like the idea. When Spaatz cited the keys to bombing success as speed, altitude, and range, he was citing an engineering requirement, not an intellectual one. On the other hand, when engineering skill was about equal, as in the case of Spitfires and Hurricanes on one side and Me 109's on the other, different requisites came into play, indefinable qualities marked by the etching of contrails high in the merciless sky.

Spaatz offered Arnold an interim appraisal of what he foresaw of the German effort, written six weeks before the climax of the battle. "Unless their attempt to take England is launched in August I am inclined to believe it will have been indefinitely postponed. Unless the Germans have more up their sleeve than they have shown so far their chance of destroying the RAF is not particularly good. I am more inclined to believe that the German effort will be more in the nature of an air and submarine blockade of the British Isles rather than a risk of a defeat in an attempted invasion of the Islands."

On a Sunday evening late in July, Spaatz was invited to have supper with Joseph Kennedy at the Ambassador's estate at Great Park, Windsor. On the first of July, Kennedy had told Winston Churchill that everyone in the United States believed England would be beaten by the end of the month. He did not add that his own view had helped foster the sentiment. At least one official in the British Foreign Office considered the Ambassador to be "the biggest Fifth Columnist in the country."[7] Kennedy was motivated by an inflexible belief that his own country should not become involved in what he considered an attempt to save the British Empire. He was also fiercely against the thought of his sons having to fight in a foreign war. No doubt Kennedy questioned Spaatz on his observations, and Tooey must have responded frankly, for, the next week, Colonel Raymond Lee polled his attachés on how they rated British chances. In the two-hour session, Lee said it came down to whether the Germans could get control of the air. All agreed there was an even chance that Britain would remain free at the end of September. Noted Lee, "I was surprised that my enthusiastic air assistants readily admitted that the country could not be conquered by air alone."[8]

Lee gave as his reason for the meeting his desire to "accurately portray the exact situation" to the War Department. This, he said, had been stimulated by Hitler's long-awaited speech at the Kroll Opera House, in Berlin, on July 19. In it Hitler had attacked Churchill, threatened England with annihilation if she continued, and made an undefined offer of peace, which the British promptly scoffed at.

No doubt Lee's decision to poll his assistants was for the reason given, but there probably were other, contiguous reasons. On that Monday, Spaatz, Hunter, and McDonald had gone down to Feltwell, a bomber base, and were not at Lee's meeting. It would have been natural for Kennedy to have discussed Spaatz's appraisal with Lee and for him to have requested that Lee check out Spaatz's opinion with his other attachés and give him a report. Kennedy was planning a press conference at the end of the week with neutral journalists—most of them American. It was believed he expected to inform them that in his opinion Hitler would be in London by August 15. The conference was not held, but the British, who were reading Kennedy's cables to Washington and listening to his telephone conversations, thought that it would be.

There was still another stimulus to Lee's action, and it was brought about by an unexpected visitor, Colonel William J. "Wild Bill" Donovan. Donovan, famous commander of "the fighting 69th" in World War I and Medal of Honor winner, had become a well-known lawyer and investigator. Although he was a Republican, FDR liked and trusted him, their friendship dating back to Columbia Law School days. Now Donovan had been given a special mission by the President. Greatly concerned over the continuing pessimism of Kennedy and others, Roosevelt decided to send his own agent to England to give him a first-hand personal report on the situation there. Politically a great deal was riding on the U.S. policy of aid for the British.

Although Donovan's mission was to be kept secret, it was nevertheless approved by Churchill's personal agent in the United States, William Stephenson. Stephenson had written that the man chosen to measure morale and scrutinize the new, aggressive leadership must "combine integrity and discretion, compassion and resolve."[9]

The fifty-seven-year-old Donovan left Washington on July 14, flying to Lisbon by Clipper. With him was Chicago *Daily News* correspondent Edgar Ansel Mowrer. Donovan's cover was that of a businessman. Mowrer was along supposedly to gather material for a series of articles. The U. S. Embassy was not informed of Donovan's arrival or the purpose of his journey. When Donovan dropped in to see Lee it was late of a Saturday afternoon, and he knew full well that Kennedy was not in town. Lee was pleased to see him, for, as he said, "I like him. My theory is that I welcome anyone who gets the intelligence and sends it home."[10] As it was, on the following Monday he sent home some intelligence of his own on England's chances and later was extremely pleased to find that it paralleled Donovan's evaluation.

The visitor confided to Lee that the real purpose behind his visit was to gain first-hand knowledge on how the Conscription Law was working and what kind of legislation would be required to set up a counterespionage agency at home. That was only a small part of it, for in a top secret message to King George VI, Stephenson informed the King that Donovan's main purpose was to determine whether the United States should keep England in the war by providing supplies, or give it up for lost.

Although Ambassador Kennedy had been informed that Donovan was coming to London, he was not told why, nor that Donovan would be bypassing the Embassy, using British contacts. Kennedy had protested to Under Secretary Sumner Welles that Donovan could obtain valuable information only through the Embassy military and naval attachés and that his coming would cause confusion and misunderstanding among the British.

None of these political maneuverings directly affected Spaatz until August 2, when he met with Donovan at a very important breakfast gathering at Claridge's. With his ten-day investigation all but completed, Donovan was planning to leave the next morning on a plane the British were putting into service between London and New York via Ireland and Newfoundland. Lee had prepared his own list of requests, which he wanted the special agent to pass on to the President. Since their previous meeting, they had not checked with one another on the way the battle was going, and Lee felt a get-together with all the attachés and Spaatz would be helpful to Donovan. It was a breakfast that went on for more than two hours, and at it everyone was encouraged to speak out. All did. Afterward, Lee wrote: "What greatly pleased me was that (a) our feeling in the office is pretty uniform about things and (b) what D. has found by talking to an extraordinary list of well-posted people, from the King and Churchill down, agrees with our conclusions and is not at all defeatist. He gives odds of 60–40 that the British will beat off the German attack. I will say a little better, say 2 to 1, barring some magical secret weapon."[11]

What Lee did not know and Donovan did was that the British had a magic weapon of their own. Entrusted with the innermost secrets of the Empire, Donovan had been informed that British cryptologists had broken the "unbreakable" German Enigma code and were able to read some of Hitler's instructions to his generals. DAY OF THE EAGLE was to be August 5 or thereabouts, aiming toward air victory on or before September

15. On that date SEA LION, the invasion of England, was to be launched.[12] That the British code breakers, working under the code name ULTRA, were also able to read Goering's orders to his Luftwaffe leaders on where and when to attack, gave Donovan a special kind of insight into the battle. If the RAF knew German intentions before they were carried out, the advantage was obviously theirs. In ULTRA, combined with radar, the gallant "few" that Churchill praised had two weapons on their side that helped offset the numerical odds.

What Spaatz wrote of the breakfast was typically succinct. "Donovan's analysis of chance of attack on England same as mine. He believes movement will be toward East and South, closing Mediterranean with continuous threats against England by air and submarine against shipping and ports." Spaatz also was quoted as saying that he and his fellow observers were convinced the British would pull through, because the Germans could not beat the RAF.

Although his prediction turned out to be correct, neither he nor any American and not very many British knew how costly the fighting had really been so far. In July, Dowding had lost 145 aircraft and eighty experienced pilots. At the beginning of the month, Fighter Command had a total of 675 aircraft, most of its pilots were exhausted, and replacements were only half trained. The Germans had not yet given the signal for launching ADLERANGRIFF, DAY OF THE EAGLE. Mike Scanlon picked up some inflated figures on RAF fighter strength which were nearly double what Dowding had on hand.

Even as Bill Donovan was preparing to return to Washington, the word was circulating around the cocktail circuit that a high-level U.S. military group was coming over for talks on joint strategy. Only the first half of the rumor was correct. The mission was coming, but it, too, was to be secret. Ambassador Kennedy was to maintain not only that he was kept in the dark about it but also that the envoys had been instructed not to deal with or through him. This last was untrue, but there were two reasons for the secrecy, one political and the other a matter of security.

The delegation was made up of Rear Admiral Robert Ghormley, Assistant Chief of Naval Operations; Brigadier General George V. Strong, Chief of the Army War Plans Division; and Major General Delos Emmons, the Commander of GHQ Air Force. The British hoped that the Americans were coming to hold important bilateral talks with their Chiefs of Staff. But like Spaatz and Kelsey and Hunter and others, the trio had been designated as observers, their assignment to "look and learn." They carried no directive, no instructions for policy talks at all. They represented at the time the highest-ranking flow of increasing U.S. military traffic, and in this the British could take heart, although they were annoyed at the vagueness of the mission and its undefined purpose.

The political reason for the visit's being kept secret—Ghormley was to remain in London—was that Roosevelt was running for an unprecedented third term. He knew isolationist forces would claim a high-ranking military delegation in London showed that FDR was bent on dragging the United States into the conflict.

The security matter dealt with a leak discovered by the British in Ambassador Kennedy's Embassy. In June, Tyler G. Kent, a twenty-eight-year-old U.S. cipher clerk who believed the President was leading the United States into war, was caught passing secret cables between Roosevelt and Churchill to a pro-German Russian refuge (who had become a British citizen) suspected to be in league with the Nazis. British counterintelligence, M.I. 5, had apprehended Kent and his accomplice. Kent had stolen fifteen hundred documents from the Embassy, among them exchanges between Roosevelt and Churchill while the latter was still First Lord of the Admiralty. Roosevelt knew that news of his secret correspondence with Churchill would finish his chances to be reelected and used the security breach as an excuse and a reason not to keep Kennedy informed on the details of missions such as Donovan's and the military delegation's.[13]

The answer to predictions of visiting investigators and military observers was being determined not only in the sky above but also in the thinking of the air commanders on both sides of the Channel. Through the entire month of July, Luftwaffe strategy had centered on attacking British coastal convoys. KANALKAMPF, it was called. Its purpose was twofold: to sink ships and, more important, to draw the RAF into combat over the Channel and wear it down by attrition. Dowding fought against committing his slim forces to protect shipping when he felt that he should husband his squadrons against what he knew would be the main onslaught. The Admiralty prevailed, and by the end of the month nearly half of Dowding's pilots were untried replacements. The only bright spot was fighter repair and production.

In May, Churchill had turned the production and repair job over to Lord Beaverbrook, a crusty Canadian-born newspaper magnate. Beaverbrook was a tough, hard-driving businessman who knew how to slash his way through Air Ministry red tape and get the job done. Over his desk was the slogan: "Organization is the enemy of improvisation." Known as "the Beaver," he worked like one. Fortunately for England, "Stuffy" Dowding and the Beaver took to each other. Both had sons who were fighter pilots, and each evening the Beaver's son, Squadron Leader Max Aitken, would telephone to report that he was all right. Also daily, the Beaver would phone Air Vice Marshal Keith Park, the commander of 11 Group, responsible for the air defense of southeastern England, and ask him how many planes he needed to replace losses. Park would receive what he needed the next day. This was possible not only because Beaverbrook had nearly doubled Hurricane and Spitfire production at the expense of bomber production but also because of his system for rapidly repairing damaged fighters.

Most Air Ministry officers did not like the Beaver's manner or his manners, and this feeling was reflected by Colonel Lee, who considered him to be "a violent, passionate, malicious and dangerous little goblin." Dowding wouldn't have agreed, and later was to say, "This country owes as much to Beaverbrook for the Battle of Britain as it does to me."

At the moment, however, the battle had not really been joined, although Fighter Command was flying as many as six hundred sorties a day.

On August 2, the day that Donovan listened to the opinions of the U.S. military contingent at breakfast, Reichsmarshal Goering handed down his final orders for DAY OF THE EAGLE. Two air forces, Luftflotten 2 and 3, were to strike RAF fields, radar stations, and ground defenses in southern England. The following day the attacks were to hit RAF installations farther inland, and on the third day they would repeat the treatment. Goering felt that his forces needed only three days of good weather to break the back of the RAF and win air supremacy. To do the job he had three air forces, which included nearly a thousand medium bombers and approximately three hundred fifty dive bombers. For their protection, Luftwaffe fighter strength stood at just over one thousand aircraft, dominated by the short-range single-engine Me 109's. The twin-engine longer-range Me 110's numbered less than three hundred.

A week was allotted to prepare for the day of reckoning, and then the weather turned sour. During this period, Spaatz spent much of his time with Fighter Command, and particularly at 12 Group headquarters, which was under Air Vice Marshal Trafford Leigh-Mallory. At the flight control center, Spaatz stayed up most of one night, watching the board as WAAF operators vectored night fighters toward lone marauders. Leigh-Mallory explained the difficulties involved: lack of training for searchlight troops, and night fighters having to fly in a given sector marked by kerosene flares on the ground, which attracted bombers and brought the complaints of farmers. Leigh-Mallory did not divulge that RAF night fighters were radar-equipped and could home in on their quarry without the aid of searchlights or the help of antiaircraft guns, whose shells could not reach the attackers anyway.

On August 10, Spaatz visited a Defiant squadron. Squadron Leader was Philip Hunter, a dark, soft-spoken pilot who talked to Spaatz about 264 Squadron's record over Dunkirk—thirty-eight victories in one day—but said nothing about the later decimation of 141 Defiant Squadron, helpless before the speed and firepower of Me 109's. Some of the Defiant pilots wondered why their slow planes with machine guns in turrets were based on forward fields, where they would meet the enemy first, and Hunter had replied quietly, "We are in the place of honor and we must accept it." He had just two weeks left to live before the Me's shot half of 264 Squadron out of the sky.

In his inspection, Spaatz saw two developments that he felt should be installed in U.S. equipment: gun cameras and pip squeak. The latter was the British identification of friend or foe through the use of radar, and he described it as an "ultra high frequency signal which enabled British radar . . . to pick up and enable ground stations to know exact location of all their planes. This is used for recognition signal and also to bring back lost pilots. This should be employed by us."

Two days after his stay with 264 Squadron, in the prelude to all-out attack, sixteen Me 110's armed with bombs took off from Calais. Their targets were four principal radar stations. The attackers succeeded in knocking out three of them and tearing a one hundred-mile gap in the radar screen. Other strikes, by Dorniers, Heinkels, Stukas, and Ju-88's were made on RAF fields and Portsmouth Harbor, but the only factory manufacturing Spitfires in the area was ignored. Even so, it appeared to be an impressive opening by the German Air Force. Yet, that night, when Dorniers approached the Kentish coast again, they found to their amazement that the knocked-out radar stations appeared to be back in operation. This was true of all but the largest and most important of the four. Another station was sending out its signal, which hoodwinked the attackers. Several days and many raids later, Goering was to commit the costliest error of many he made in the following month. He decided there was no point in continuing the attack on radar stations, because none had been put out of commission so far.

In the fighting that followed, when all hung in the balance and the few rose to do battle with the many, Spaatz was on the move, gauging the conflict, measuring the effect of the daily offensive. With Monk Hunter and several U.S. newsmen, he spent three days at Dover, standing on Shakespeare Cliff, watching the action above during the day and the fireworks from RAF bombing of Calais at night. He just missed being in a heavy bombing attack on the airfield at Eastchurch, where the Short plant had been hit. Spaatz took in the considerable damage and made further notes. "Detling airdrome badly hit day before. CO and two squadron commanders and a number of others killed when bomb hit headquarters building. All messes hit, also WAAF's quarters. Six Blenheims prepared for a mission were destroyed. Total casualties about 35 killed, 70 wounded. Dive bombers used. No warning received. Apparently planes came out of clouds."

He did not know that on the day he was examining the bomb damage at Eastchurch, Flight Officer Billy Fiske, fellow American pilot with whom he had had drinks a few weeks before, had flown his last mission. Fiske, attempting to land at Tangmere air base while it was still under attack by a Stuka and a Ju-88 *Gruppe,* managed to set his damaged Spitfire down amid the bomb craters wheels up and was slithering to a stop when the plane exploded.*

On Sunday the eighteenth from Shakespeare, Cliff Spaatz saw an attack on a formation of German bombers. "Too high to see anything but streaks of condensation in the sky. Saw one falling." In the afternoon he watched British antiaircraft fire trying to bring down three German bombers without success. He also watched the same units mistakenly whang away at twenty-six Blenheims with the same results. "AA guns all very inaccurate," he observed. That night several bombers attempted to hit Dover. British searchlights, he saw, were unable to pick the intruders up "in spite of almost ideal conditions of cloud banks at 9,000 feet." And once again, he and Hunter and their newspaper companions saw the RAF attacking targets across the Channel.

News from Dover was that Spaatz and Hunter had been thrown in jail for having tangled with a British Navy Commander, Evan Thomas, at the Grand Hotel. As Tooey could attest, he had not been in jail.

The fury of the air battle over Britain mounted during the last week of August and on into the first two weeks of September. The Luftwaffe's three air fleets pounded Fighter Command's principal air bases: Manston, Tangmere, Biggin Hill, Debden, Hornchurch. . . . Around-the-clock bombing seemed to be Goering's order of the day and night. Spaatz was told that the Stukas and the Ju-88's were being withdrawn from the battle, their losses too high to sustain. On the British side, the venerable Defiants were switched to serve as night fighters. In daylight, German bombers were now coming over protected in some cases by four times their numbers of fighters. And Spaatz wrote: "General opinion is that German fighters will not attack a well-closed-in day bombing formation." What was going on overhead was proof that the RAF certainly would, and that poor as German strategic tactics turned out to be, the Luftwaffe high command, not to mention its bomber pilots, recognized that without escort the chances of daylight survival were very slim indeed.

On the night of August 23, German raiders were over southern England *en masse,* their targets more civilian than military. Hitler had theretofore ordered that London was not to be bombed. Spaatz, returning to the city, was caught in an air raid, and then at midnight a second attack occurred. He had moved from the Cumberland Hotel to an apartment, and in this second raid the planes were overhead. He went up on the roof and saw "fire of some intensity started east along the Thames." There were lots of searchlights fingering the night sky, but they picked up none of the marauders.

* Fiske, who had lived a long time in England and had an English wife, was one of the first American pilots to be killed in combat.

The next day, RAF Bomber Command retaliated. It was not Churchill's decision but the Air Ministry's, to send a mixed force of eighty-one aircraft to hit Berlin. Because the distance there and back was a thousand miles, the planes could not carry a full bomb load. Supposedly, Goering had once said that if Berlin was ever bombed, the citizens of the city could call him Meier. Although the only casualties of the attack were some cows, Berliners were stunned by the RAF's being overhead and were ready to call the Reichsmarshal something a bit stronger. To compound the shock, the RAF was overhead again three nights later, and this time there were human casualties, though few in number. Twice more before the end of the month, RAF bombers struck at the German capital.

Hitler was enraged. He maintained the bombing of London had been an accident, that the targets had been aircraft factories and oil-storage tanks on London's outskirts. An error in navigation had caused the bombs to be dropped on the city, he said. On Wednesday, September 4, he spoke before an audience of women, social workers, and nurses at the Sportspalast. To their enthusiastic cheers, he declared: "When the British air force drops two or three or four thousand kilograms of bombs, then we will in one night drop 150, 230, or 400,000 kilograms. When they declare they will increase the attacks on our cities, then we will raze their cities to the ground. We will stop the handiwork of these air pirates, so help us God! The hour will come when one of us will break, and it will not be National Socialist Germany!"

"Never! Never!" shouted his foot-stamping audience.[14]

No one knew at the time that Hitler's determination to swing the thrust of air attack away from military to civilian targets was to be a deciding factor in the outcome of the battle. Further, daylight raids had cost the Luftwaffe dearly. Its bombers began flying higher, more and more of its attacks coming at night, its bombs no longer as accurately aimed.

In discussing German tactics with the British, Spaatz, Hunter, and McDonald learned that experience had eliminated a few theories. The old concept that you could destroy an air force on the ground had been thoroughly disproved. A well-dispersed air force was almost impossible to knock out, they were told. Bombers used on such efforts were better employed against oil tanks, factories, and other strategic targets. In its raids the RAF was using a few bombers to cover a small area as a nuisance while concentrating the mass over the target, with complete destruction in view. It was called area bombing, and it did not meet with either Army Air Corps belief in strategic, pinpoint bombing or U.S. humanitarian considerations.

After the raid of August 28, Spaatz noted that the antiaircraft fire "has now developed to the point where it delivers a much greater volume of fire much quicker but with the same inaccuracy as the last war." Sardonically, he observed, "It takes close coordination with the Army to obtain the maximum misuse of air power."

At Farnborough, Spaatz got to look over a number of downed German aircraft. He was surprised that the Me 109 did not have either an artificial horizon or a gyro compass. He was not at all impressed with the bomb-sights on the Ju-87, -88, or Heinkel 111. He wrote a detailed description of each plane's salient points, its weaponry, its armor, and its flight characteristics and aerodynamic quality.

Sunday, September 15, would be designated by historians as the day the Battle of Britain was won. It was a day in which the RAF gained a decisive air victory over the Luftwaffe, but more significantly, it was the day beyond which Hitler's naval and army commanders were not willing to commit themselves to attempt Operation SEA LION. Only by daylight could the Luftwaffe expect to win over the RAF, and whatever death toll it could claim by its blitz on London and other English cities, air supremacy could not be gained, and so no invasion could be attempted.

British bombing of the invasion ports had taken a heavy toll as well. During the summer months, Bomber Command had flown eight thousand sorties and lost only 163 aircraft. Even so, on the night of the fifteenth, Londoners and defending forces along Britain's southern coast were fully anticipating invasion under the code name CROMWELL. So was the Churchill government. Then, on Tuesday, Hitler sent out word that he was postponing SEA LION "until further notice." British Intelligence got the news first through decoding a German General Staff order to airfield commanders in Holland to dismantle air loading equipment. ULTRA interpreters recognized the significance of the order, for the equipment was a necessary invasion tool.

The victory was such a near thing that no one in Fighter Command could immediately recognize it as such. In spite of the claims of German losses, they could not know how the severity of those losses affected German air crews. Inconsistent tactics combined with Goering's accusations of cowardice were also a bitter psychological blow to the worn-out airmen of the Luftwaffe. RAF fighter pilots, though stretched to the thin edge of endurance, did not suffer a loss of morale, and while replacement pilots were badly undertrained, the Beaver had kept the planes coming. On September 16, 659 aircraft; four days later, 711; and daily the German pilots and crews were being told, by Goering and Kesselring and Milch, the RAF is finished.

Two weeks prior to the climax, Tooey Spaatz had reached his own conclusion on the outcome of the Battle of Britain. He told Raymond Lee he thought the invasion was off for this year and that he and Hunter should go home and get to work. Some insight into his prediction at a point when most English military men would have given heavy odds that he was wrong was in a letter he had written to Hap Arnold several days before.

The Blitzkrieg seemed to start off with a bang two weeks ago and then pe-
tered out. After a lapse of several days renewed activities are in being but
with slightly different tactics. Apparently the first effort was to determine
the effect of large masses of bombers escorted by fighters on daylight missions, starting with action primarily against airdromes. . . . The net result
of these operations seemed to be excessive losses compared to the damage
done. Airdromes attacked were able to keep right on operating in spite of
damage done to permanent buildings. . . . Whether the strategy of the
Germans was to prepare the way for invasion or to close the English
Channel is a moot question. However it would appear that the basic plan
must be to close the Channel and North Sea thus allowing a concentration
of submarines and airplanes against the western approaches.

He then reiterated several observations: "A well-dispersed air force is a
most difficult target to destroy on the ground. . . . The action of fighters
against hostile daylight raids has been very effective. . . . Since the combat crew eventually becomes the neck of the bottle this makes destruction
in combat doubly effective."

As for German daylight bombing: "Large formations of bombers escorted by fighters are very unwieldy. The fighters do not insure immunity
from attack by hostile fighters on the bombers. A comparatively fewer
number of hostile fighters can by determined effort break up the large formation. . . ."

But then looking at it from the RAF's point of view and his own apparently fixed belief: "A well-trained formation of bombers with adequate
firepower built up of two sections of three planes each is able to cope with
any type of attack so far delivered by German fighters." He then informed
Arnold that the Blenheims, which had suffered excessive losses on their
daylight raids, were now being equipped with much greater firepower and
armor protection for the rear gunner and the pilot. "Pilots of the squadron we visited were confident of their ability to operate on daylight raids
with this armament."

Spaatz again went into the hazards of dive bombing. It was the consensus that the zone between fifty feet and five thousand feet was somewhat of a suicide area due to the heavy concentration of machine-gun and
small-cannon antiaircraft fire. He felt that the concept of a light bomber
like the Douglas A-20 was absolutely sound providing it had adequate armament. On the subject of firepower he said its importance could not be
overemphasized. "In the case of the bomber they cannot hope to outrun
the fighter and nothing less than 4 gun turrets should be considered for
our heavy bombers."

And finally, "The Blitzkrieg for this season will probably have spent itself by the middle of September, and I shall be satisfied to cease being a
high-class spy."

On August 31 Spaatz received orders to return home, but it was another nine days before he would depart on a Dutch KLM plane for Lisbon, during an air raid. In the interim he experienced a steady round of air raids on London. On September 8 he wrote, "Apparently indiscriminate bombing of London has started. Present strength of RAF heavy bombers inadequate to bring same firepower on Berlin." He believed that this kind of indiscriminate bombing would win no wars and launch no invasions.

At six o'clock on September 9, Hunter and McDonald accompanied Spaatz to Imperial Airways House, where they bade him farewell. It had been a long four months since he had left Washington. The KLM DC-3 flew at German sufferance with Dutch pilots at the controls, the windows painted over. He could catch up on his sleep, for it was a long flight, of nearly seven hours, to Lisbon.

In the quiet of the peaceful Portugese capital, Tooey Spaatz had time for reflection. Like all but a few of his Army aviation contemporaries, he had long been a believer in the Douhet philosophy of aerial attack. Billy Mitchell had preached and written his own variation on that theme, as had Air Marshal Trenchard and other air strategists around the globe. There could be no doubt Goering had been attempting to prove Douhet's theory that an adversary could be bombed into submission. That German air fleets were fighting to attain air supremacy there could be no doubt either. But so far the RAF, using superior tactics and aided by radar and code breaking, had stood in the way. Still it did not appear that they could stop the bombing, and into this also came Douhet's unproven belief that sustained aerial bombardment would break the will of the recipients to resist. This belief was one of the two legs on which the Italian General Douhet had built his concept, the second being that destruction by air of an enemy's industrial capacity could win a war without the need of armies or navies.

In bombing shipping and ports and oil-storage depots, aircraft and armament factories—all strategic targets—Goering had sought to carry through the theory, but the effort was helter-skelter and poorly mounted, with no real organizational plan. Excellent targets were ignored; others, of little value, were hit; and losses in planes and crews had been staggering, nearing 50 percent since the battle had begun. Now, because of Hitler's change of mind and his preoccupation with attacking the Soviet Union, British cities were faced with a literal rain of terror. What would happen to the public will? For included in the target area was the entire structure of British society, everything from its factories to London Bridge.

Spaatz believed from what he had observed that there had to be a differentiation made between "morale or will to resist and efficiency of effort due to interruption on account of air raids." He had seen nothing that indicated the British had lost their will. Comparing British character with that of the Germans as it applied to the opposing air forces, he believed the British concentrated on building individual initiative, while the Germans emphasized "masses of automatons led by individuals. Great Britain has developed real air power, whereas Germany so far appears to have developed a mass geared to the Army and lost when confronted with properly applied air effort." Spaatz believed that while Goering could order his commanders to attack strategic targets, the German air crews were not properly trained, nor were their aircraft aeronautically designed to succeed.[15] Above all, they lacked a long-range bomber.

Of the RAF officers Spaatz had come to know, Jack Slessor was the one he liked and appreciated most. Both were engaged in the broad spectrum of plans. Their conversations ranged over a wide area of mutually important subjects. One was training. Spaatz felt that England's rotten winter weather would only pose a drawback in turning out badly needed pilots and air crews. What about using the United States? Slessor felt they would have to borrow U.S. instructors and use Air Corps schools. Spaatz said he figured Air Corps schools would be needed for U.S. expansion. RAF schools could be moved gradually to good-weather areas in the United States. Having to operate in a war zone could be eliminated. The drain on shipping would be reduced, because planes and fuel would be produced in the United States. Further, the men when trained could be transferred to bombers being built there, and they could assist in flying them back over. Slessor could see great merit in the idea.

One evening, driving back to London after tea and dinner at Slessor's home in Alderson, Spaatz raised the question of lessons learned from the war so far. He felt ". . . one distinct lesson from the French collapse should be that an army on the defensive is liable to lose its morale. If England remains continuously on the defensive," he said, "awaiting an attack which never materializes, there may be collapse from within. It would be erroneous to assume that Germany will collapse from within. If Germany should ever learn to use air power as some air enthusiasts think it can be used, then England might starve before Germany." He added this would be particularly so if Germany should move to grab control of the Mediterranean and the trade routes to the Far East and North Africa.

In the privacy of Slessor's car, Spaatz spoke with candor, and what he had to say was an illustration of his perception of things to come. The only way England's policy of starving out Germany could succeed, he said, was by England's becoming a strong operational center to maintain a sea blockade in the Atlantic and continuing air operations against the Reich. But: This must be combined with a strong movement of U.S. air, naval, and ground forces into Africa via Natal, Brazil. The move he proposed must be made to obtain control of the Mediterranean, followed by an offensive against Italy, which was the best approach to defeating Germany.

Slessor was only too happy to agree to any plan that foresaw the United

States actively engaged. Earlier he had described the method by which the British Government—its civilian and military components—arrived at policy decisions. Spaatz saw that there was more coordination in the British method than that used in the United States but still did not feel it was the answer to coordination for a national foreign policy, particularly a policy that might involve the use of force to carry it out. "It must be evident," he later wrote, "that any policy such as the British adopted in guaranteeing Poland should not be undertaken unless the Army, Navy and Air Force are fairly certain that they have the means to enforce it." He thought that in the United States a superior staff with full representation from the appropriate departments "should be the agency which prepares the recommendation for any policy which may involve the U.S. in a war." But certainly, at the moment he was advancing his own ideas of how to defeat Germany by including the United States in the war, there was no one in authority, from the White House down, who would advocate it, even privately.

On September 19, after having been put off several flights, Spaatz, along with twenty other passengers, flew home in style. Two of his fellow travelers were Generals Strong and Emmons, who had arrived from England the night before. Emmons was carrying papers which Colonel Raymond Lee, back in London, had figured the Germans would easily pay a million dollars to obtain.

There would be no measuring the value of what Spaatz carried in his head. All of it was preparation and background for the command assignments that lay beyond.

Three

The Long Summer

The four climactic months Spaatz was out of the country brought sudden changes in Administration personnel, encouraging a shift to a more direct policy of aid, which in its implementation compounded the problems facing U.S. military leaders. The French collapse and the British retreat from the Continent brought a desperate personal plea for assistance from Winston Churchill to President Roosevelt. The British Prime Minister wanted guns, ammunition, planes, and fifty or more decommissioned destroyers "right now."

On the day Spaatz and his fellow observers left Washington to go abroad, Secretary Morgenthau met with General Marshall and asked for a survey that would offer an update on weaponry in U.S. arsenals that could be classed as surplus. If the question hadn't been so serious, it would have been laughable. As Marshall said after the survey had been made, the real question was whether "we pour our slender means into a situation over which we have no control and reduce ourselves to the point where we can't protect our own interests." Yes, there were half a million pre-World War I Enfield rifles, with ammunition, some 75-mm cannon, three-inch mortars, and thirty-five thousand machine guns and automatic rifles. Yes, there were fifty World War I mothballed destroyers, but there were legal barriers to be surmounted in providing what was wanted, and they could not be overcome all that swiftly, particularly with a Congress and a public that had been shocked out of its somnolence by the debacle in France.

Of very direct interest to the Air Corps, aside from surplus weaponry, the British request for planes now included the B-17. With the French surrender, the British Purchasing Mission, under the direction of the Canadian industrialist, Arthur Purvis, moved to absorb all French aircraft orders. This, however, dealt with what was to come off the production line.

The request for B-17's was for what had already come off it, and Henry Morgenthau was anxious to comply.

On June 17, the day the Reynaud government fell, Morgenthau told the President the British were in great need of some B-17's. He had not bothered to check with Woodring, Marshall, or Arnold, but he said he felt ten of the planes could be spared. FDR thought this was fine, not aware that total B-17 strength was only fifty-two aircraft. By the time the Treasury Secretary had discussed his decision and Roosevelt's approval of it with Pa Watson, the President's chief military aide, Morgenthau had upped the number to twelve B-17's. Watson asked what the War Department's reaction had been, and Morgenthau admitted he hadn't bothered to ask. After all, he said, he had the authority to act as he saw fit on the matter. Watson strongly suggested that both Secretary of War Woodring and General Marshall be informed, and in fact, after Morgenthau's departure, he notified Marshall of what was intended.

The meager force of B-17's, many of them nonoperational for one reason or another, was the backbone of U.S. hemispheric defenses, which both Marshall and Arnold believed to be gravely threatened. The Fleet was in the Pacific, and in view of the dangerous world situation, to suddenly strip away one fifth of U.S. heavy bomber strength was a move neither Marshall nor Arnold was willing to accept. Neither was Harry Woodring. The next day, under a memorandum drawn up by Marshall, he sent to the White House a strong protest against Morgenthau's generous decision to seriously weaken the air element of the country's defenses. He was not clairvoyant enough to realize that his position on the issue would cost him his job.

For a number of months Roosevelt had been anxious to replace both Woodring and Navy Secretary Charles Edison. Personalities and politics were involved in the desire. Edison, the son of inventor Thomas A. Edison, was considered ineffective and not all that well-tuned to White House thinking. On the very day France surrendered, he was discussing with Harry Hopkins the possible resumption of German dirigible service for trade purposes with South America. Withal, he was generally liked at the White House, and the Navy's rebuilding program was in far better shape than the Army's.

Conversely, Woodring, as an isolationist and philosophical America Firster, had been fighting Morgenthau and the White House over aid to the Allies even before the war had begun. His running three-year "holy show" feud with Louis Johnson had done nothing to help either his image or his performance. The press had long been filled with rumors that Roosevelt was going to drop him. Possibly he'd gotten so used to reading them that he no longer gave them credence, and so the Dear Harry letter he received from Roosevelt the next morning, June 18, must have come as a thunderous surprise. As a palliative, FDR offered him the governorship of Puerto Rico, and further attempted to blunt the ax by declaring, "This note goes to you with the warmest feeling of friendship on my part—and let me repeat, Harry, that I shall always be thankful to you for your help to me during all these seven years. . . . Affectionately yours."

In his prompt letter of compliance, written in longhand and not made public, Woodring stressed America's unpreparedness: "I trust you will advise those who would provoke belligerency—a state of war for our nation —that they do so with the knowledge that we are not prepared for a major conflict. Billions appropriated today cannot be converted into preparedness tomorrow."[1]

When the President wrote to Woodring, he already knew who the Secretary's successor was going to be. He had been reluctant to fire the stubborn Kansan, not only because he disliked the idea of firing anyone but also because he could be sure the move was going to bring anguished cries from the powerful isolationist bloc in Congress, whose support he would need in building U.S. defenses. His plan had been afoot since late in May, when Navy Secretary Edison announced he would be stepping down to run for Governor of New Jersey. That Edison had been selected as the Democratic choice was due more to the political expertise of Jim Farley, acting on Roosevelt's wishes, than to overwhelming popularity of the candidate.

Talk, long circulating in Washington, was that FDR wanted to form a coalition Cabinet for the time of crisis; it would also help third-term prospects should he decide to run. Privately, back in December, he had approached Colonel Frank Knox, publisher of the Chicago *Daily News,* on becoming Secretary of the Navy. Knox, who had been Alf Landon's running mate in 1936, said he would only consider the office if Roosevelt was willing to bring in another Republican. Even before Edison announced his resignation, Roosevelt was considering Woodring's replacement. He took the advice of Supreme Court Justice Felix Frankfurter, who recommended Henry L. Stimson.

Stimson, at seventy-two, had served every President since McKinley. He had been Secretary of War under Taft and Secretary of State for Hoover. Despite his age, he was a vigorous, extremely active lawyer. A conservative Republican, he was nevertheless an internationalist who saw America's role in the world as a bastion of democratic concepts. Most important to Roosevelt, he was strongly in favor of supporting England in its hour of need.

When Stimson met with Roosevelt, on the evening of June 19, the President told him that Knox had already accepted the position of Secretary of the Navy. Wrote Stimson of their meeting: "The President said he was very anxious to have me accept because everybody was running around at loose ends in Washington and he thought I would be a stabilizing factor in whom both the Army and the public would have confidence."[2]

Stimson stated one condition: He wanted to be able to name his own Assistant Secretary. His choice was Robert P. Patterson, a distinguished and highly respected judge of the New York Circuit Court of Appeals. Roosevelt approved, but he was not all that ready to act on the matter. To do so would mean dropping Louis Johnson, who had been promised the job of Secretary of War once Woodring was out of the way. He happened to be in Roosevelt's office with unofficial presidential adviser Bernard Baruch when he first learned of Stimson's appointment. Wrote Baruch, he "sat in flushed and indignant silence while FDR tried to explain the 'reasons of state' which made it necessary for him to break his promise. After a while Johnson could no longer contain himself. 'But Mr. President, you promised me not once but many times . . . ,' he began to protest, his face flushed and his voice unsteady." Baruch, sensing danger signals across the desk, gave his friend a gentle kick, and Johnson subsided, but he was not going to go quietly.[3] It took another five weeks to ease out the weightier half of the "holy show," who lost thirty-five pounds in the tussle.

During the course of it, Johnson informed Stimson that Judge Patterson could be named a special assistant, but he planned to remain as Assistant Secretary of War. Stimson discussed the seeming stalemate with Morgenthau, who told him, "You have just got to get rid of Johnson." The new Secretary did so by making out the nomination form on Judge Patterson himself and sending it over to the White House. According to Pa Watson, the President instructed him not to put the nomination up to the Senate for confirmation. Bernie Baruch and some of Johnson's friends on the Hill were threatening to raise a hue and cry. Stimson quietly but firmly let FDR know that if he was to remain as Secretary of War, it would have to be on the terms already agreed. And that, before the end of a very hot and muggy July, was that.

The appointments of Henry Stimson and Frank Knox to head the country's key defense posts were far more than a masterful political stroke on Roosevelt's shrewd course to an unprecedented third term. It gave him the united support he needed within his Cabinet to pursue his publicly unclarified policy to aid England and his announced goal to build America's defenses. At their meeting of June 19, Stimson had assured the President he was very much in favor of and anxious to work for a draft law. This at least was good news to the military.

At the War Department—from Marshall, Andrews, Arnold—there was unanimous approval of the change. Although Arnold's battle to build an air force would become even more frustrating, as would his dislike for Secretary Morgenthau, there had been an even earlier change, which he had welcomed with great enthusiasm.

On May 29, Roosevelt had named William S. Knudsen to oversee the country's military production. In this appointment, Knudsen was asked to serve as one of six civilian leaders of a National Defense Advisory Commission, whose members were chosen by Harry Hopkins.[4]

Knudsen, the president of General Motors, was a bluff, good-natured production wizard who spoke with a Danish accent. In what he saw as his country's coming hour of need, he wanted nothing to do with Washington politics. He was, in fact, like Stimson and Knox, a lifelong Republican. Now he was willing to devote his great energy and talent to what he considered a national cause.

Hap Arnold had first met Bill Knudsen in 1917, when both were entangled in the aircraft production problems. Knudsen was working for Henry Ford at his River Rouge plant. While Ford was turning out Liberty Engine cylinders like stacks of cordwood, Knudsen was managing the construction of eagle boats, which were earmarked to quell the German submarine menace. Arnold admired Knudsen's know-how and Ford's production methods. But then, as now, it was a matter of having a cohesive, workable program. Much of Arnold's frustration was over Morgenthau's abysmal lack of understanding of what aircraft production was all about. This lack was tied to the fact that there was no real Administration program or policy covering the problem. As Arnold put it, ". . . there was no schedule that took into account the steady maintenance of our Air Force at a programmed strength—that is a production schedule insuring not only a given number of aircraft at a certain date but thereafter the unfaltering replacement of those planes."[5] Without such a program, the aircraft manufacturers were not willing to extend themselves.

It was said that Knudsen was the first to call America the "Arsenal of Democracy"—a slogan that Roosevelt was quick to borrow. To Arnold, Knudsen knew all the production techniques that would make the slogan meaningful, and he saw the appointment of the automotive genius as a bright ray in the gloom of his most taxing problems. Not that Knudsen's arrival on the scene changed for a moment British needs or the determination of Roosevelt and his closest advisers to fill them. Just a month after Woodring's departure and Stimson's acceptance of Morgenthau's resolve to do all within his power to aid the British at any cost, Knudsen agreed to split U.S. aircraft production equally between the United States and Great Britain.

As necessary as the planes were to the RAF after Dunkirk, Britain's need for naval ships was equally great. Their losses in destroyers, plus the removal of the French fleet and the worry that it would fall into German hands, made the threat of blockade and invasion paramount. In mid-May, directly after taking the reins of power, Churchill had told Ambassador Kennedy that among other things he intended to ask Roosevelt "for the loan of 30 or 40 . . . old destroyers." As the odds of England's survival against Germany rose, the need for the destroyers—now quoted as fifty or one hundred—rose too.

At the beginning of August the British Ambassador to the United States, Lord Lothian, had called Secretary Knox from his dinner and asked if he would please come to the Embassy. Knox complied, and Lothian informed him that the shipping situation in the British Isles was so serious that unless they got the fifty destroyers he didn't know what would happen. Since Churchill's earlier request, which he had also put into a private telegram direct to the President, the matter of the destroyers had been discussed at great length within the Administration. It was not so much a matter of pro and con as it was to find a method that was legal, publicly acceptable, and at the same time beneficial to the United States. Admiral Harold Stark, Chief of Naval Operations, was willing to declare the ships surplus in the same manner that General Marshall was reluctantly willing to supply the British with Enfield rifles and French 75's.

On August 16, at his regular press conference, Roosevelt announced that negotiations were being conducted regarding U.S. acquisition of British bases in the western hemisphere. The President blandly denied that the negotiations involved the fifty destroyers. It wasn't until two weeks later, when all the legal ramifications of the deal had been worked out, that it was admitted publicly the bases and the destroyers were a part of the same package. Churchill later wrote: "The transfer to Great Britain of fifty American warships was a decidedly unneutral act by the United States. It would, according to all the standards of history, have justified the German Government in declaring war upon them."[6] There were many Americans—congressmen and individuals in positions of power—who agreed.

From the War Department's point of view, a great deal of extremely valuable real estate had been obtained in the exchange. Through a ninety-nine-year-lease arrangement, the United States was free to build air and naval bases at eight strategic points in the Atlantic and the Caribbean. They were Newfoundland, Bermuda, the Bahamas, Jamaica, Antigua, St. Lucia, British Guiana, and Trinidad.

This development was naturally of immediate and direct interest to Arnold and his staff. The parameters of hemispheric defense, particularly in the Caribbean, had been greatly expanded, and Arnold quickly appointed a board headed by Ira Eaker to make a survey of likely locations for air installations on the islands.

Eaker and his two fellow board members, Major Harold Clark, a site specialist, and Major Austin W. Martinstein, a finance expert, set out on an aerial and ground inspection of the Caribbean locations. For his flight crew, Eaker had old friends Majors Newton Longfellow and Sam Connell. They departed from Florida in a lumbering four-engine Boeing flying boat, looked the Bahamas over first, and then continued on down through the Leeward and the Windward islands.

There was actually a twofold purpose in Eaker's mission—just as there had been to Spaatz's tour in England. Arnold wanted his Executive to drop in at a potential hot spot: the island of Martinique, lying between Antigua and Trinidad. It was a possession of the Vichy French Government and therefore considered a latent danger in the western hemisphere. Aside from a military force of approximately six thousand soldiers, elements of the French Fleet were known to be anchored in the harbor of Fort-de-France. Most threatening was the aircraft carrier *Béarn,* with a complement of one hundred twenty U.S.-made P-36's. There were two light cruisers as well, and one of them, the *Émile Bertin,* was rumored to have brought French gold reserves amounting to billions of dollars to be secretly stored on the island.

In early July, fearful that the entire French Fleet might surrender to Hitler, the British Navy clumsily attacked elements of it in North African ports. Frenchmen everywhere were enraged by the act, and as a result, the War Department wanted to know: How much of a threat to the area and the Canal Zone did the French flotilla at Martinique now pose? How difficult would it be to take the island? Was it being used by German U-boats as a refueling depot?

The State Department warned that the Vichy government had announced that any American planes flying near or over the island would be fired on, but getting the answers for Arnold was the sort of assignment Ira Eaker relished. Ignoring the State Department warning, Eaker had Longfellow and Connell fly their amphibian over Martinique one bright afternoon. There they circled the harbor of Fort-de-France, closely observing the French warships below, particularly the carrier. They were pleased to see no Curtiss fighters on her flight deck. Eaker signaled Longfellow to chop the power, and they came in to land through the harbor's narrow entrance.

As they taxied in to the refueling dock, they could see sailors standing along the ships' rails watching them, and on the shore there was a military patrol waiting. Eaker climbed out on the dock and explained that he would like to pay his respects to the island's governor, Admiral Georges Robert. Shortly he saw a staff car, flying a large French flag, coming down from the heights. Eaker had noted that the naval ships appeared ready for action. Crossing the port's broad central square, however, he was quick to size up the general air of listlessness: soldiers lazing about, their uniforms untidy, their equipment appearing shabby and poorly maintained.

He found Admiral Robert hospitable enough but obviously under pressure, nervous and preoccupied.[7] Yes, they could purchase fuel, but the Colonel must depart as soon as possible.

Eaker had seen enough to indicate that although the French forces on Martinique might pose a threat at some point in time, they did not at the moment. If, indeed, gold was stored in old Fort Desaix, up on the hill, a resolute invasion force could probably capture it. As for German submarines using the island as a refueling stop, Eaker sensed that the Admiral's jumpiness was caused by something more than meeting a U.S. pilot in need of fuel. He thought he might have a way of finding out.

Once they had the amphibian airborne again and out of sight of the harbor, he had Longfellow bring the plane down to a thousand feet and make a wide circle, approaching the island from the opposite side of Fort-de-France. There was enough daylight remaining for an hour of patrolling. At a thousand feet, they could not be seen from the harbor, although with binoculars they could keep its entrance under surveillance. Near the end of the hour, their reconnaissance was rewarded. In the fading light they saw a U-boat surface and make its way into the docking area. Eaker watched the car in which he had ridden drive out onto the pier, saw Admiral Robert get out and shake hands with the German submarine commander. Then, together, they were driven back up the hill. The watchers turned away, heading north for St. John's, Antigua, and a report for the General.[8]

Arnold's desire to get Eaker's swift evaluation of the potential threat Martinique might pose for the United States was more than another illustration of his direct way of operating, or even his keen sense of intelligence gathering, a rarity even among those who served in the Military Intelligence Division, G-2. It was also symptomatic of a growing sense of alarm at a critical time dating from June 17—a day of divergent but interrelated actions that reflected the undercurrent of tension. Admiral Stark voiced the underlying cause that morning when the Congress, shaken by events in Europe, approved a four-billion-dollar appropriation to build a two-ocean Navy. "Dollars," said Stark, "cannot buy yesterday."

On that same Monday, on which Secretary Morgenthau told FDR the British must have B-17's and Admiral Stark was seeking presidential permission to move the Fleet back to the West Coast, General Marshall held a staff meeting on critical defense problems. Present were Generals Frank Andrews, George Strong, and Richard Moore. They discussed a snowballing array of global danger signals: the French collapse; the fear that Hitler would get the French fleet; indications of German and Japanese sabotage attempts on the Panama Canal, and of Nazi subversion in Uruguay and Brazil; peace agreements between Japan and Russia, and the former's plans to move against the Dutch East Indies; the Soviet annexation of Latvia, Estonia, and Lithuania; and most serious of all, an evaluation on the part of General Strong's War Plans Division that the Japanese were prepared to launch a diversionary raid against Pearl Harbor.

"Thinking out loud," said Marshall to his three advisers, "should not Hawaii have some big bombers? We have fifty-six. It is possible that opponents in the Pacific would be four fifths of the way to Hawaii before we knew they had moved. Would five or ten Flying Fortresses alter this picture?"

"They'd be overwhelmed by hostile pursuit," said Andrews. "We are weak in pursuit and any small force would be destroyed. We shouldn't split our forces. We should send all or none."

Both Andrews and Strong recommended that the National Guard be called up, and Strong felt there would be "a desperate need within sixty days for troops in South America." The belief had been stimulated by a British report that there were six thousand German infiltrators on ships headed for Brazil, where they would join with other Nazis in seizing the government there. From Uruguay, Ambassador Edwin C. Wilson had cabled at the end of May that only swift action by the Uruguayan Government had prevented a take-over by Nazi elements. He asked for a U.S. naval task force of forty to fifty ships to cruise off the coast of South America, and for a flotilla to station itself at Montevideo. Roosevelt's response was to dispatch two cruisers to the scene. Finally, three days before the June 17 meeting, the U. S. Naval Attaché in London, Captain Allan G. Kirk, had cabled: IN MY VIEW SAFETY OF THE UNITED STATES WOULD BE DEFINITELY IN JEOPARDY SHOULD BRITISH EMPIRE FALL, AND WOULD EXPECT ITALO-GERMAN COMBINATION TO MOVE SWIFTLY IN SOUTH AMERICA AND CARIBBEAN AREAS . . . SAFETY OF CANAL SEEMS PARAMOUNT.[9]

When Marshall met with his planners, it was under the not entirely correct assumption that Admiral Stark was about to order the Fleet to leave Pearl Harbor and head for the Panama Canal Zone. This would mean that air and naval installations in Hawaii would be vulnerable to a hit-and-run raid by planes from Japanese carriers. If that happened, the Fleet would have to return to the area, which in turn would leave the Canal Zone and South America open to a German-Italian threat. Admiral Stark, however, was working on an entirely different strategy. With Roosevelt's approval, on June 17 he ordered Admiral Richardson to take the Fleet out of Pearl Harbor and to steam for two days toward Panama, maintaining radio silence but letting leak his position and supposed destination. This would be done to scare off any intended hostile move toward the southern part of the hemisphere, and Richardson would then bring his ships back to Pearl Harbor.

The result of these mixed postulations and uncoordinated plans was that Marshall instructed Strong to send a war alert not just to Major General Daniel Van Voorhis, the Panama Canal Department Army commander, but also to the Hawaiian Department Army commander, Lieutenant General Charles D. Herron. The message to Herron read:

IMMEDIATELY ALERT COMPLETE DEFENSIVE ORGANIZATION TO DEAL WITH POSSIBLE TRANS-PACIFIC RAID, TO GREATEST EXTENT POSSIBLE WITHOUT CREATING PUBLIC HYSTERIA OR PROVOKING UNDUE CURIOSITY OF NEWSPAPERS OR ALIEN AGENTS. SUGGEST MANEUVER BASIS. MAINTAIN ALERT UNTIL FURTHER ORDERS. INSTRUCTIONS FOR SECRET COMMU-

NICATION DIRECT WITH CHIEF OF STAFF WILL BE FURNISHED YOU SHORTLY.
ACKNOWLEDGE.

Herron immediately signaled a full alert, the only type he had. But the
cross-purposes of high command raised a large cloud of doubt in his
mind. He quickly learned the Navy had not sent a similar message to its
principal Hawaiian commander, Admiral Claude C. Bloch, Commandant
of the 14th Naval District.

To view the action and reaction in its most charitable light: Herron,
Bloch, and Fleet Admirals Richardson and Adolphus Andrews wondered
within the next few days just what the hell was going on and why!

In Washington the communications between Marshall's office and
Stark's had not been clear. Stark did not concur with the need to put
naval forces in Hawaii on an alert. His concern was focused on the
Panama Canal Zone and his wish to get the Fleet into the Atlantic, a
move opposed by Roosevelt and Secretary of State Hull. Marshall, for his
part, was working to quickly plug gaps in defenses that he knew were piti-
fully weak, while at the same time trying to do what he could to help the
British without emasculating a yet unclarified defense program. Neither
department communicated properly with the other, and so they failed to
act in concert.

* * *

The survey made by Ira Eaker and his fellow investigators to locate
sites for air bases included not only the Caribbean area but also Canada.
The yet undecided outcome of the Battle of Britain had greatly stimulated
Roosevelt's interest in that country.

As a result, on Saturday, August 17, Roosevelt and Stimson met with
Canadian Prime Minister William Mackenzie King near Ogdensburg, New
York. Roosevelt had more on his mind than good-neighborly chitchat. He
proposed that in the interest of mutual defense they form a permanent
joint U.S.-Canadian board which would include army, navy, and air representatives of both countries. The board's purpose at the outset would be
to formulate plans for the defense of the northern half of the hemisphere.

King was delighted with Roosevelt's defense proposal and was all for
establishing both a U.S. naval base and an air base in the region. To Stimson, the meeting and proposal marked a turning point in Roosevelt's determination to stand with Great Britain. The following Tuesday, Stimson
received word that the Canadian Government wished to convene a meeting in Ottawa on Thursday to establish the permanent joint board.

The air officer appointed to the board was a planner and organizer
General Marshall had come to view as one of the most astute in the War
Department. Colonel Joseph T. McNarney was a vintage airman, noted
for his blunt analytical approach, his ability to cut through to the heart of
the problem. He believed that if the British Isles fell, the whole task of

opposing the Germans would devolve on the American people. There was a certain irony in the appointment of Major General Stanley D. Embick as the principal U.S. delegate. Two years earlier, at the time of Munich, Deputy Chief of Staff Embick had informed a congressional committee that there was no need for the Air Corps to procure long-range bombardment aircraft such as the B-17. The Navy could handle any aggressor approaching U.S. shores. He added that to his way of thinking—like Woodring's—two or three smaller planes for the price of one large one certainly made sound economic sense. Now he had been chosen to grapple with the quickest and best method to build air defenses where none existed so that yet unproduced long-range aircraft could guard the northern approaches and if need be, go on the offensive and strike overseas. It wasn't that Embick was a fool; he was, in fact, a brilliant *ground* officer. But, like so many of his military generation, he had a blind spot when he looked at the sky, and that was one reason why it was so empty of planes in the hour of peril.

That summer, the sky looked discouragingly empty to Hap Arnold, confronted by the twin bottlenecks of aircraft and engine production and pilot training. Encouraged by Arnold, Roosevelt called for fifty thousand planes, but the planes would be useless without trained air and ground crews. Yet, at the moment, the Air Corps had more pilots than it had planes.

Only one hundred fifty members of the 1940 West Point graduating class, of four hundred forty cadets, had selected the Air Corps as their service. That Arnold's eldest son, Hank, could not apply for pilot training due to physical disability was disappointment enough, but Hap wanted to know why so many others had opted for different branches. He chose newly commissioned Second Lieutenant Theodore R. "Ross" Milton to tell him why.

Ross Milton had been a favorite of the Arnold family since 1926 and the days at Fort Riley, Kansas. The son of a cavalry officer, he'd had his first airplane ride thanks to the impulsiveness of Major H. H. Arnold.[10] Since then, his goal had been to become an Army pilot, and following West Point graduation, he had joined the Air Corps. Now, of a Sunday, he received orders to report to Arnold's house. Ross and Hank had gone through the Point together, Lois Arnold had been his first girl friend, and he looked upon Bee Arnold almost as a second mother, so the order did not strike him as anything too serious. But when he arrived at the Arnold home in Bethesda, the look on the General's face was not too reassuring. *What the hell have I done wrong?* he wondered as Hap led the way to his study.

Behind the closed door Arnold got right to the point: "Will you please tell me why the hell more of your class don't go into the Air Corps?"

Milton felt a sense of reprieve and was only too willing to explain. "We were given a rotten time at Mitchel Field," he said.

"What do you mean, 'a rotten time'?"

"We had no fun. It was a dull week. We attended some deadly ground-school courses, one about how to use an oxygen system. They were tough on partying and rough on bed checks, like we were back at the Point."

He didn't have to add that, at the moment, every branch of the Army was extremely anxious to acquire as many of the new graduates as it could. The result was not unlike fraternity rushing, in which the prospective members are wined and dined and made to feel this is the place to be. Even though the Cavalry didn't have much to offer in the way of hardware, its briefing officers had been sharp and friendly, impressing the young men with their manner and projection of things to come. The visitors spent a relaxed and enjoyable week in their midst; many of them had chosen to join up.

"What about flying?" asked Arnold.

"Oh, we got a ride around the field in a B-18." Lieutenant Milton didn't add that the Commanding Officer at Mitchel Field was thoroughly detested by everyone on the base. He didn't have to. The look in Arnold's eyes indicated the matter would be taken care of at once, and it was.

Then came a far brighter development on the manpower front: During the summer months, Congress had been battling over a selective-service bill whose sponsors foresaw a draft and the federalizing of the National Guard for at least a year. In July, after his nomination, Roosevelt came out publicly for the draft, and his presidential opponent Wendell Willkie supported the move in his acceptance speech. Differences were finally ironed out between the House and the Senate, and the Burke-Wadsworth bill was signed into law by the President on September 16. The bill made all American males between the ages of twenty-one and thirty-six eligible for military service, providing an estimated pool of 16.5 million from which to draw, though only eight hundred thousand could be drafted in the first year. No longer would Arnold have to worry about having enough men to build the air force he foresaw, although the Congress had written into the law that continuance would have to be re-voted in a year's time.

In rapid-fire order, following the signing of the draft law, came three moves and countermoves that marked the acceleration of events.

On September 22, Japanese forces began to slip down into French Indochina, the Vichy government consenting to Japanese occupation of three major air bases in Vietnam. For months Roosevelt had been pressed to embargo the sale of potential war materials to Japan. At a Cabinet meeting on September 19 the question of embargoing oil was raised. Stimson and Morgenthau were in favor, as was the President, but Secretary of War Cordell Hull feared the action would provoke the Japanese into attacking the Dutch East Indies. Nevertheless, a week later, on September 26, Roosevelt announced that the United States would no longer sell scrap iron or steel to any nations other than Great Britain and those in the western hemisphere.

Stimson felt the move was three years too late and would not have the effect it would have had earlier. The Secretary of War believed his experience in foreign affairs gave him an insight into the behavior of other peoples—particularly the Japanese—that was unquestionably accurate. The way to handle the Japanese, he lectured Frank Knox and others, was by showing the fist. "When the U.S. indicates by clear language and bold action that she intends to carry out a clear policy in the Far East, Japan will yield to that policy, even if it conflicts with her own Asiatic policy," he concluded in a memo titled "Morale."

On the day following FDR's embargo announcement, the Axis powers —Germany, Italy, and Japan—signed a ten-year mutual-aid pact. Stimson's reaction was that the pact would be "useful in waking up our people."

On most issues the elderly but energetic Secretary of War and Henry Morgenthau were compatible and respected each other's thinking. Stimson quickly developed a far broader and more realistic understanding of U.S. military shortages and demands through briefings by General Marshall. Nevertheless, Morgenthau's influence and actions did not slacken on behalf of the British, and the Churchill government would be eternally grateful for his unflagging endeavors. From Stimson's point of view, the "chaotic condition" between the War Department and the White House had been a result of the previous relationship, but he also believed a part of the continuing confusion was due to the President's unpredictable moves. Morgenthau admitted to Stimson that the situation had been mixed up for so long because Roosevelt had been using him to try out "his haphazard decisions."

Haphazard was perhaps too mild a description of the way in which the desperate British plea for ships, arms, and planes was finally handled after three months of internal struggle. The State Department documents releasing the fifty destroyers failed to include the aforementioned armament and the B-17's. Stimson was to say that the cause for the incredible oversight was "inadvertence." It had to be wondered whose! The glaring question was quickly shoved aside in an effort to correct the error without having to go back to the Congress, which would have been highly embarrassing to the Administration and particularly to Roosevelt in his campaign bid.

The error meant that turning over the bombers was still at issue, and although Lord Lothian and Arthur Purvis were shocked by the "inadvertence," they recovered quickly enough to add additional Army aircraft and Navy PBY's and torpedo boats to their most-wanted list.

Stimson had been somewhat shocked himself to learn from Hap Arnold that although the Navy was fully equipped with enough planes for the present size of the Fleet, the Army was three thousand short of the number necessary to fulfill the Protective Mobilization Plan. He was to learn more than that, for on a miserably hot and humid Wednesday, Arnold gave him some additional hot and humid specifics at a meeting which included the new Assistant Secretary of War, Judge Robert Patterson, and General Richard C. Moore, Assistant Chief of Staff for G-4, whose concern was supply. Arnold began by citing two dates: April 1, 1941, and April 1, 1942. By the first date, the Air Corps was to have a force of 138 combat squadrons, he said, and by the second, 288. Neither could be met as long as the present policy of giving the British priority in delivering continued. He raised Morgenthau's statement of the day before that every other Allison engine would go to the British.

"This will interfere with deliveries of P-40's and delay our pursuit organization," he said. "In my opinion, Mr. Secretary, airplanes going to the British six months from now will be too late. What they're getting right now is all they're going to receive that will help them. The whole crisis will probably be over in a month. What we have to do now is build up the Air Corps, and what's left goes to the British."

Stimson said he recognized the necessity, realized what was at stake, but did not commit himself further. Patterson then advanced the belief that it was a matter of assurance for the United States to give these things to the British. By doing so, he said, we probably wouldn't need them ourselves.

Arnold's reply was, "If we give them to the British and don't have them in our Air Corps, then they can be used against us if the Germans lick the British the way they did the French." Again he pointed out the growing imbalance: The British had ordered so many aircraft engines they would be receiving fifteen hundred a month against five hundred for the Army and the Navy combined—engines that couldn't be used in British planes built in the United States anyway!

Again Stimson indicated he would see what he could do to change the arrangement. He also said he would call Knudsen and outline the urgency of producing aircraft for the Army—something Knudsen appreciated only too well. He suggested Arnold speed up the training of pilots and crews so they would be ready to take over English planes in case the British "went by the board." Arnold said such a plan was already being prepared.

It was crusty General Moore who called the Secretary's attention to the fact "that one of these days we're going to have to come out and tell the truth and the sooner the better. We've continually told the Congress that British production is not interfering with our own, and it is."

Later that day, Arnold and Moore went to Patterson's office and strongly urged that 271 P-36's and Vultee pursuit planes be diverted from a previous sale to Sweden and turned over to the Air Corps to fill gaps in tactical units where there were pilots but no planes. The planes in question, they argued, would not reach England in time to be of benefit any way. Patterson said he would take up the idea with Morgenthau, again indicating the power the Secretary of the Treasury wielded in the entire matter.

Following the meeting with Arnold and Moore, Stimson called Morgenthau. "You know," he said, "I have fully sympathized with the effort to protect the British; in fact I was one of the first shouting for that, long before I came here. We have, however, been so long delayed about it that the situation of the British has become more desperate and we have got to constantly think of the possibility of their defeat. . . . I don't like to do it at all, but when I'm making contracts for airplanes I have to." He continued, choosing his words carefully, "While we should continue to make immediate deliveries in all amounts that we can, in contracts for future deliveries we must be sure that the contracts contain provisions in them which will save us against such a situation as we've seen in France where the Germans have taken over a lot of our American airplanes and they are using them against Great Britain, and eventually against us."

He believed that everything pointed to a drive by Germany to finish the British. It would have to take place within the next six weeks or two months, and that was what must be borne in mind in regard to contracts coming after that time.

"Yes," Morgenthau said, "but what I'm pushing for, and it's about all I can do is to push, up to a certain point, is to get the materiel to fight during the next sixty days. . . . And I've got to take chances," Morgenthau stressed. "That's all I'm trying to do for the moment."[11]

Ten days later, General Marshall, in Arnold's absence, called Assistant Air Corps Chief Bart Yount to his office. He told Yount that what he had to say would be kept as secret as possible. The Army was to be prepared to turn over to Great Britain five B-17's completely equipped except for the [Norden] bombsight. The Navy would probably be handing over five PBY's with the fifty destroyers.

Marshall was in a great hurry. It was a Saturday and he was on his way to Wisconsin to observe maneuvers with Frank Andrews. What he wanted Yount to do was to come up with a recommendation on the method by which the planes could be relinquished should the State Department call for one.

As Yount later recounted for Arnold, Marshall said that the arrangement would not involve any transaction with the Boeing factory. The Attorney General had ruled that both the destroyers and the planes could be released on a certificate of the Chief of Staff and the Chief of Naval Operations to the effect that they were being transferred in the interest of national defense.

Yount recognized that the rationale of national defense was pretty thin ice, saying that "this was extremely political and would involve a headache for someone."

Marshall, perfectly aware of the skating conditions, peremptorily cut him off and said, "If anyone is to get a headache, I'm the one, and you needn't concern yourself. These orders are from the highest possible authority. Be prepared to recommend where the B-17's are to be turned over and also what can be done about training British crews. I understand they're on their way here."

Yount returned to his office and got hold of Captain Marc A. Mitscher who was Acting Chief of the Naval Bureau of Aeronautics in Admiral John Towers' absence. Mitscher, like Towers, had been an early naval pilot. Soft-voiced and circumspect, he told Yount that he had already been directed to release five PBY's to the British. He believed that, like the destroyers that were to be assigned to British crews at Halifax, the planes would be flown to Canada for acceptance as well. What Mitscher did not know at the time was that U. S. Navy pilots would end up flying coastal patrol missions in PBY's from bases in Northern Ireland many months before Pearl Harbor.[12] Roosevelt even then was discussing with Stimson and Knox ways in which American pilots could volunteer to fly with the RAF and not lose either their military rank or their citizenship.

After talking with Mitscher, Yount learned there were exactly thirteen Flying Fortresses operational in the United States. All but two had been equipped with the latest Norden bombsight, which was considered secret even to the British for fear that if a plane carrying the sight was shot down, its secrets would fall into German hands.[13] Yount was informed that although it would take only a few days to remove the bombsights, it would take approximately six weeks to reinstall the automatic pilots. He decided that if he was called into a high-level conference on the situation before Arnold returned, he would describe the difficulties and recommend that the five planes be taken from the total of seven belonging to the 2nd Wing of GHQ Air Force, at Langley Field. After the aircraft had been modified they could be flown to some designated place in Canada by U.S. crews, who should be prepared to check out RAF crews.

Yount was not called by Marshall, and after Arnold returned, there was no further directive on the matter for several weeks, since Roosevelt began to weather-vane on his agreement to turn over the B-17's. He was worried about the political awkwardness of having to admit the gross oversight in the original approval. Further, as Stimson wrote: "Timid members of the Cabinet" persuaded FDR to undo his decision of last night to make delivery of the Forts. The President's ambivalence had his Secretary of War very concerned. Along with the bombing of London, it "weighs on my nerves as much as anything," he wrote.[14] The so-called timid members he referred to were Secretary of State Hull, Attorney General Robert H. Jackson, and Assistant Secretary of the Navy James Forrestal, who argued that to renegotiate the agreement would raise a public howl in the middle of a presidential campaign.

The President's sudden shift might have had his Secretary of War very concerned, but not Morgenthau, who knew that FDR's rejection was one of form and not of substance. A few days later he informed the President, "The English have got to have more planes."

"They can have anything they want," responded Roosevelt, but then added the proviso, "You had better work this out with the Army, Navy, and Knudsen."

"I'm going to work it out," Morgenthau said, "and I will go to it, but you are going to hear plenty about this. . . . I may have to bring them to see Papa."[15]

Indeed he did. Admiral Towers was no more anxious to release five of the PBY's than Arnold was to release five of his B-17's. Morgenthau was informed that while the Navy was willing to revise its production so that the British received every other PBY produced in 1941, it did not want to give up the five right now, particularly with the world situation as it was.

At the same time, Arnold prepared a memo for Marshall on the subject of "Existing Shortage of Airplanes." In it he said: "The acute shortage of planes suitable for advanced training seriously jeopardizes our ability to carry out our pilot training objective. Our combat groups are woefully short of planes. Pursuit groups, which should have 80 planes, average about 40. Bombardment groups, which are authorized 44, average about 20." The Combat Air Force numbered a total of 656 aircraft, he said, with an additional 338 assigned to overseas departments. Figures were the only ammunition he had, to fight what he considered was a fleecing of the country's air strength.

Since aircraft production was running behind schedule, Morgenthau suggested that it might be better if the Air Corps concentrated on producing *only* the P-40 instead of its other new fighters—such as the Lockheed P-38, the Bell P-39, and the Republic P-43. Except for Knudsen, the idea was generally liked by the members of the National Defense Advisory Commission. The Treasury Secretary then proposed that from now on the British would receive half the P-40's and PBY's produced.

With Arnold's and Marshall's prompt objection, Judge Patterson informed the Commission that it simply wouldn't do. The Air Corps needed more of everything, including P-40's. Morgenthau refused to back off. His position was that for the next nine months the British had to have as much as was necessary to continue. Knudsen said the RAF was already getting more than a half of what was being produced, which was certainly more than fair. Morgenthau's reply was that he wasn't trying to be fair, all he wanted was an extra thousand planes for the British. Knudsen refused to go along and suggested sarcastically that maybe the British should

award Henry the Order of the Garter. To which the Secretary shot back
he would prefer something above the belt.[16]

Stimson came away from the meeting troubled in his mind, knowing
that it was Marshall who was caught between the rock of Roosevelt's aim
and the hard place of U.S. defense needs. In an effort to explore what options there were to the division of war production, Stimson invited
Marshall for lunch at Woodley, his home in suburban Washington which
overlooked Rock Creek Park. They dined and then sat on the porch, taking in the bucolic scene and discussing the difficult problem.

Marshall suggested a survey of all the requirements of the Army, the
Navy, and the British, including a projection of what would be needed in
an emergency. Charts of the survey would be kept current so that when
decisions were made on what to give, the giving would not be done
"haphazardly," as was Roosevelt's way, or through emotion, as was Morgenthau's. There had to be an orderly plan.

That there wasn't one was clear on Friday, September 27. At a meeting
in Assistant Secretary of War Patterson's office, Arnold, with George
Brett and Major Al Lyon in tow, got the latest determination passed on
from Morgenthau. The Air Corps had on order sixty-eight B-17C's, of
which the Treasury Secretary wanted thirty-two allotted to the British. In
a second, follow-on order of 291 planes, he wanted another thirty-two.
The Consolidated B-24 was just going into production. The Air Corps
had placed an order for fifty-three and the British for forty-one. Morgenthau wanted that changed to a fifty-fifty split of forty-seven each, the
deliveries to be made alternately. He was also asking for the second-best,
Sperry bombsight, which Arnold assumed would require all the necessary
equipment to go with it such as the automatic pilot.

Morgenthau asked for the plans and specifications of the Martin B-26
medium-range bomber and the Lockheed P-38 interceptor, as well as the
engine specifications for both planes. Arnold believed that the blueprints
were requested so production facilities could be set up in Canada. He already knew that such facilities would have to start from scratch, since
Canada had none of the production components.

Arnold went directly to Marshall, whom he knew was attending a
twelve-thirty White House gathering on the subject. He asked the Chief of
Staff "to object strenuously to turning over any of our heavy bombardment."

Present for the meeting, aside from the President, Stimson, Knox, and
Morgenthau, were Knudsen, Stark, Forrestal, and Patterson. Morgenthau
arrived with the news that he had been informed by the British that they
were turning out pilots in Canada and England at a rate compatible with
the production quotas he was bent on filling. When the key question of
the B-17's was raised, Stimson suggested that the Chief of Staff address
the issue. Stimson reported in his diary that when Marshall stated the Air

Corps now had exactly forty-nine B-17's fit for duty, not counting Hawaii, where there were seven, "the President's head went back as if someone had hit him in the chest. I think the President and Morgenthau at last got it into their heads in what a difficult position we were, and I hope that will end the situation," observed the Secretary.

It didn't, but out of the meeting came a small victory for Arnold and an agreed-upon compromise. As he wrote after talking to Marshall, "It was decided that no B-17's would be given to the British until Army units were equipped," but instead the first six B-24's off the production line would be handed over to them, and twenty more within the next six months. In exchange, the British would give to the Air Corps from their production quotas one hundred twenty engines that were usable in B-17's. As for the Navy, it agreed to relinquish every other PBY.

For the moment, Morgenthau and the President accepted the compromise, but the cross-purposes—Marshall and Arnold on one side, the President and Morgenthau on the other, Stimson, Knox, and Knudsen in the middle—remained. So did doubt about Great Britain's survival and Hitler's plans, not to mention those of Japan.

It would neither have cheered nor surprised Arnold to know how thorough a picture of U.S. military aircraft development the Germans had. Hitler's Military and Air Attaché in Washington since 1933 had been Major General Friedrich von Boetticher, whom Stimson viewed as "a large fat German general" showing arrogance in every step. Airmen who knew Von Boetticher well had a less harsh appraisal. They saw him as a genial officer who since the end of World War I had gone out of his way —in Germany and in America—to build friendly relations with all those whom he wished to cultivate. Because of his virulent anti-Semitism and his close association with Washington isolationist circles, he misjudged and misinformed Hitler on the U.S. political climate during the summer of 1940. But technical information Von Boetticher's office sent home was right on the mark. The amount of accurate information on new and experimental aircraft in his August 1940 report "Recent Types of U. S. Military Aircraft" indicated the laxness of U.S. security.

The conclusion of the report indicated that Von Boetticher was offering his own evaluation of what he had picked up from some of his Air Corps contacts:

> The recognition of the overwhelming importance of air power evidently proven by this war, has come as a stunning surprise not only to the general public but also to military men who have not closely followed aeronautical developments. Quickly-changing world conditions have necessitated revision of armaments. Even the United States in their "splendid isolation" must recognize the tremendous change air armaments have brought to bear on international relations.

By autumn, in spite of a chorus of powerful voices, such as Ambassador Joseph P. Kennedy's, saying that Britain could not survive, it had. The few who had foreseen that there would be no invasion, such as Spaatz, Donovan, Emmons, Strong, and Lee, were not so sanguine as to believe that England could weather the next twelve months without huge amounts of U.S. aid. Supplying that aid was emerging as a principal plank in the Administration's foreign policy. How it would be done remained the central point of the internal struggle.

Following his talk with Stimson at Woodley, Marshall had put his staff to work preparing a secret strategic analysis to determine the country's military needs on the basis of probable Axis moves. Stimson was anxious that Morgenthau be shown the projection, and Marshall put the assessment into his hands on October 2.

The War Department premise was that although U.S. aid to Great Britain might bring some form of retaliation by Germany and Italy, the two could not launch a major strike against the United States until they had defeated Great Britain and were sure of Russia's continued neutrality and support. The planners' fear of a move toward Latin America by the Germans had decreased since midsummer. Conversely, the threat of Japanese action had mounted, due to U.S. economic restrictions and diplomatic opposition to Japanese aggression in China and their threatened military advances into Indochina. The possibility of an attack against the Dutch East Indies and the Philippines was foreseen. It was hoped that diplomacy would prevail in the Far East, at least until the United States had become militarily strong. Priority was put on defending the western hemisphere. Since Germany's nightly bombing raids had failed to subdue the English and with invasion no longer possible until the next summer, some time had been bought. But it had to be used properly, to build defenses against a possible attack within a year or even less.

At the moment, the country did not have the means of production to fill both U.S. and British requirements. Marshall suggested how production could be greatly increased: more shifts, more working hours, rigid priorities, a halt to the exportation of machine tools, and finally, an end to the roughshod acquisition of Air Corps equipment. He proposed that a committee made up of Stimson, Knox, Knudsen, and Morgenthau be formed to oversee these improvements and changes, and schedule priorities.

Morgenthau was in favor of Marshall's suggestions, and participated in forming the committee. However, between the time he was apprised of the Chief of Staff's endeavor to outline a workable plan and the end of the month, when Roosevelt made a memorable campaign speech in Boston, he was busy processing and encouraging larger British orders.

On October 25, Stimson complained that Arthur Purvis, chief of the British Purchasing Mission, was proposing aircraft increases above the twelve-hundred-fifty-a-month figure Knudsen had previously set. "The camel having gotten his nose into the tent," said Stimson, "he's beginning to get his neck in."

Morgenthau's explanation was that the British needed nine thousand more planes. Then he combined politics and opportunity in Britannia's cause: First he convinced Roosevelt that in the President's upcoming campaign speech, on the thirtieth, it would be politically smart to announce Great Britain's production needs. This would show that while the nation was the Arsenal of Democracy, it was not headed for war, and to Morgenthau's way of thinking the announcement would also make the orders a *fait accompli*. After FDR approved the idea, Morgenthau called on Arthur Purvis to give him the glad tidings. "I want a cable from Mr. Churchill on Monday in Churchill's own language that the President can announce . . . what the British want." The cable was to cover *everything* England wished to buy.

He got it, and then some, for as Purvis had signaled the Prime Minister, "The critical moment has arrived." Churchill's response was to explain the British position in terms of the loss of the French Fleet, the U-boat threat, and the British plan for putting a large army in the Middle East within the year.

"So far as aircraft are concerned," wrote Churchill, "would it be possible to speed up deliveries of existing orders so that the numbers coming to our support next year will be considerably increased? Furthermore, can new orders for expanded progress also be placed promptly so that deliveries may come out into the middle of 1941?"

On Tuesday, October 29, at twelve noon in the packed interdepartmental auditorium of the Labor Department, Secretary of War Stimson, with blindfold in place, drew the first number of the draft—the first of eight hundred thousand men of the new Army. The President spoke briefly and solemnly over nationwide radio, referring to the historic occasion as a "muster." There was tension and a feeling of high drama, with strong public and political division over the issue.

The following night, Roosevelt addressed an enthusiastic audience in Boston. Incorporating into his speech Churchill's statement and Purvis' preamble citing previous U.S. aid, he said:

> Building on the foundation provided by orders placed last winter and in the spring, the British are now receiving a steady stream of airplanes. The strength of the Royal Air Force, after three months of blitzkrieg of the air, is actually greater now than when the blitzkrieg began. And this increase in strength despite battle losses is due in part to the contribution made by American airplane industries, and the American contribution will be of ever-increasing importance.

> The British have now asked for permission to negotiate again with American manufacturers for 12,000 additional planes. I have requested the request be given most sympathetic consideration. It will bring Britain's

present orders for military planes from the United States to more than 26,000 and require extra plant facilities so that the present program of building planes for military purposes both for the United States and Great Britain will not be interrupted. Also, large additional orders are being negotiated for artillery, machine guns, rifles and tanks with equipment and ammunition. The plant capacity necessary to produce all this military equipment will be available to serve the needs of the United States in any emergency. . . .

While Marshall and his aides were faced with realities far harsher than those described by the President, the public paid little attention to the recital of production figures and the implicit meaning of more jobs. It focused instead on Roosevelt's unforgettable statement: "And while I'm talking to you mothers and fathers, I give you one more assurance. I have said this before, but I shall say it again and again and again. Your boys are not going to be sent to any foreign wars. . . ."

* * *

As autumn moved on toward winter there could be no doubt that in a year of European war, aircraft had played a decisive role. Until the draft law was passed, in September, the emphasis on building U.S. defenses had been on naval and air power, and the President's call in May for fifty thousand planes was strong enough proof of the latter. Riding on this wave, many Army airmen, as well as civilian organizations supporting them, saw a growing imbalance between the recognized need and subsequent growth of an air force, and the continuing lack of acknowledgment in the councils of the mighty to include those who commanded it.

Although a major general and Chief of the Air Corps, Hap Arnold was not privileged to sit on the Joint Army-Navy Board, where matters of military policy were worked out, all of them to a greater or lesser degree related to the use of air power. Aside from his difficult relations with Secretary Morgenthau and Roosevelt's coolness toward him, during the critical summer months neither he nor any of his ranking staff members were called on to attend White House conferences on the production and disposition of aircraft. Even though, with Marshall's approval, he had set up his own intelligence system by assigning air officers to U.S. embassies around the globe who reported to him privately, he was not made privy to information coming into the Army's intelligence branch, G-2. This was particularly true of information in secret Japanese wireless exchanges obtained by Signal Corps code breakers.

Further, the twenty-year relationship between the Air Corps and the General Staff was built on the demand that everything the former did had to be cleared and approved by the latter. Now there were forces at work that demanded a change in structure. Marshall was aware that the enlargement of Army air power had to mean a concurrent upgrading of command or he was going to be faced by a concentrated resurgence to bring about a separate air force.

Equally aware of both the pressure and the need for change was Secretary of War Stimson. Far more perceptive than many of the senior officers of the War Department, Stimson recognized that air power involved an entirely new element, "not merely a new auxiliary weapon for ground troops [but] independent action quite divorced from both land and sea." He knew that the difficulty was going to be in finding just how far the War Department could go in "freeing them [the Air Corps]" without complete separation. Stimson was of the opinion "that Marshall and his deputies are very much wedded to the theory that it [the Air Corps] is merely an auxiliary force."[17]

This was certainly not true of Marshall. As for his deputies—his ground commanders—they had seen how the German use of air power had been closely tied to the *Blitzkrieg* in Poland and France, the spearhead of the advance. The success of the strategy strengthened their twenty-year-old belief that an air force must be linked to ground forces as a tactical auxiliary.

In London, U. S. Military Attaché Colonel Raymond Lee was living through the nightly aerial blitz and being kept closely informed on the RAF's retaliatory strategic bombing of industrial targets in the Ruhr and elsewhere. As a career ground officer, he clung to the same viewpoint. The thought never seemed to register with him that the success of strategic bombing depended on *how* it was done. Lee took considerable pride in believing that his reports to Marshall on what he saw as the failure of RAF bombing policy influenced the Chief of Staff against strategic bombing. Marshall did become skeptical of the RAF plan, but not of strategic bombing *per se*. This was true particularly at the time in question because he had been so completely sold—in fact oversold—on the potential power of the B-17.

However, in the waning months of 1940, disagreement over the best use of air power was but one of a number of divisions, most of which were matters of structure and not of tactics.

When Frank Andrews, on March 1, 1939, had handed over command of GHQ Air Force to Major General Delos L. "Lucky" Emmons, it was announced that the GHQ Air Force thenceforth would be under the jurisdiction of the Air Corps. Apparently, this supposed joining was authorized as a sop to the feeling of outrage rippling through the air arm at the dumping and exiling of Andrews. Andrews had never been all that much in favor of such a linkage, for he was only too well aware of the internal conflict produced by two staffs competing for manpower and authority. He would have been willing to accept such an amalgamation only if tables of organization underwent major revisions. No such revisions were planned by the General Staff or by Chief of Staff Malin Craig, who was looking yearningly down the road toward retirement.

For the next twenty months, GHQ Air Force was under Air Corps jurisdiction in name only. Arnold did not run the combat air arm; Emmons continued to take his orders from the Chief of Staff's office. The only real change in the scheme of things was geographic. Andrews had long tried to have his headquarters shifted from Langley Field, Virginia, to Bolling Field, near Washington, to save time and money and to afford better communications. The War Department apparently felt he was too close as it was, but with the demands of the expansion program, the change was made.

In August, Emmons had gone to England, returning in late September. He had been amazed at the calmness and unhurried approach of the British commanders and their seeming willingness to listen to ideas other than their own. He was also impressed with Ambassador Joseph Kennedy, calling him a "damn' smart man, a clever man." When Colonel Lee sought to point out that what was needed in a diplomat was wisdom and sagaciousness, Emmons replied, "That's just it. That's what he is. A damned smart fellow."[18] Lee dropped the subject, but it was obvious to him that Emmons was impressed by surface appearances. This must have been apparent to Marshall as well, for when Strong and Emmons gave their report to him on the effectiveness of British defenses, he told them not to "jump to conclusions" on what was going on in England at the moment. It was not defenses that would win a war. Exposure to Marshall's skepticism apparently toned down the two officers' final report.

But as Emmons returned to pick up command of the GHQ Air Force, plans were being finalized to inject a more equitable balance within the War Department for the Air Corps. The change would have a direct effect on the career of Lucky Emmons, proving if nothing else that his nickname was well chosen—that and just how fouled up was the War Department's promotion system.

It was through promotions and not an attempt to reorganize the divided air wings that Marshall, encouraged and strongly supported by Stimson, attempted a greater equalization of command. Late in October, he arrived at Stimson's office with the names of twenty-six officers, whom he was recommending for promotion as general officers, including the first black brigadier, General Benjamin O. Davis.

Stimson went over the list carefully. He found several of the recommendations "quite epochal," particularly the promotion of Delos Emmons to lieutenant general. He commented that this put Emmons deservedly on a par with the commanders of the four continental Army Field Forces, who had received their long-awaited promotions to lieutenant general a month previously.

"Furthermore," he wrote in his diary, "it serves the useful purpose of showing that we are attempting to give real independence to the Air Corps and to keep it free from the domination of other branches of the Army."[19] No doubt some friends would express surprise at the announcement of Emmons' ascension to the rank of temporary lieutenant general. Not because they wouldn't approve, but because he now outranked Hap Arnold, who was senior to him on the permanent list established in 1920, senior to him in length of service, and obviously senior to him in every other way!

As Stimson saw it, this strange convolution was ameliorated by making Arnold a Deputy Chief of Staff while keeping his hat as Chief of the Air Corps. All well and good for the moment, but the question had to be raised as to why Arnold hadn't been promoted to lieutenant general as well. As a Deputy Chief of Staff, he would supposedly be in a position to coordinate the activities of the Air Corps and the GHQ Air Force, but that didn't get around Emmons' having three stars to his two. However, in examining the promotion list, Stimson did not realize that in seeking greater balance, the War Department had come up with a new type of imbalance. Instead, he made an appointment to see Roosevelt, hand-carried the names over to the White House, and found the President very willing to accept everything as recommended.

The promotions were not made public until November 12. The following week it was announced the GHQ Air Force, now to be called the Air Force Combat Command, would no longer be under control of the Air Corps but under the commander of the Army field forces. The original three wings of GHQ were to become four air forces, one for each sector of the country. Two other air forces were also designated: The 18th Composite Wing, in Hawaii, became the Hawaiian Air Force, and the 19th Composite Wing, in Panama, became the Panama Air Force.

Arnold knew that under the circumstances he could not expect to perform efficiently as a Deputy Chief of Staff and Chief of the Air Corps at one and the same time, so George Brett became Acting Chief of the Air Corps, and Major General Oliver Echols became the new chief of the Materiel Division. All of these changes were a reflection of the need for rapid growth and the organizational, industrial, and political turmoil the need produced.

Into this caldron there came a new presence, whom Hap Arnold would term a man of "towering importance." His name was Robert A. Lovett. During World War I, Lovett had been a U. S. Navy aviator, the squadron commander of a night bombing unit. He had learned to fly in 1916 while still an undergraduate at Yale. F. Trubee Davison, friend and classmate, had talked his father, Harry Davison, into permitting the family summer home on Long Island to be turned into a flying school, where eager

members of the Yale Aviation Unit earned their wings. The graduates
went on to become officers in the Naval Aviation Service. All but Trubee,
who had the misfortune of being seriously injured in a crash.[20]

Following the war, Lovett had combined a career of railroading and
banking, but he had also kept an active interest in aviation. During the
spring of 1940 he was in Europe on business. Extremely concerned over
the future, and believing the United States would be drawn into the war,
Lovett realized how important air power would be. He wondered just
what the United States was doing to develop its own potential, and he decided to find out. During the summer, as a director of Union Pacific, he
traveled by train across the country, making a private inspection of the
aircraft industry.

What he learned disturbed him greatly, for it appeared that even with
foreign orders there did not seem to be half enough production going on.
He wrote a report of his observations which his friend and neighbor and
former Yale colleague in Naval Aviation, James Forrestal, the Assistant
Secretary of the Navy, heard about. Forrestal asked if he could read the
critique, and the next thing Lovett knew, he had a telephone call from the
Assistant Secretary of War, Judge Patterson, asking if he would care to
come to Washington for a talk with Stimson.

At their November 28 meeting, Stimson asked the forty-five-year-old
Lovett if he would give up his position as a member of the investment
banking firm of Brown Brothers-Harriman to join his staff, initially as a
special assistant, eventually to become the Assistant Secretary of War for
Air. Lovett didn't take long to say yes.

In his acceptance there lay a line of political coincidence reaching back
into the past. Although Trubee Davison had not been able to earn his
pilot's wings, he had in 1926 become the first—and until 1941 the only—
Assistant Secretary of War for Air. A Republican, he had held the post to
the advantage of the Air Corps until 1933, when the Roosevelt administration came into power. Through the urging of Chief of Staff General
Douglas MacArthur, the office had been left vacant, supposedly as an
economy move but actually so the General Staff of the War Department
could maintain tighter control over the Air Corps.

It was not until September 1939, shortly after war began in Europe,
that the post was very briefly taken out and dusted off as a bribe to shut
up Charles Lindbergh. On September 15 the Lone Eagle was scheduled to
make a nationwide radio address stressing that the United States must not
become involved in the war. The White House was worried about the
effect of his words and wished him to say nothing. For six months Lindbergh had been on an "inactive active" status with the Air Corps, working
for Hap Arnold on research and development plans.

On the day before he was to speak, Lindbergh discussed his speech with
Arnold, and to assure him there was nothing in it that would embarrass

the Air Corps he showed him a copy of it. Arnold read it and agreed, and wondered whether it should be shown to Secretary of War Woodring. Lindbergh said no, that while he had a great deal of confidence in Arnold and General Marshall, he had very little in Woodring. "I could tell from Arnold's eyes that he was on my side. I like him—think he's the best Chief of the Air Corps we've ever had," Lindbergh noted in his diary.[21]

The next day, while Lindbergh was going over last-minute plans for his address, his good friend and former military attaché in Berlin, Colonel Truman Smith, came to call. Smith brought word that the White House was very worried over what Lindbergh might say. If he did not say anything, or he did not oppose possible U.S. entry into a European war, a secretaryship of air would be offered to him.

The offer had apparently been passed from the White House to Woodring, who, in turn, carried it to Arnold, who called in Smith, knowing the relationship he had with Lindbergh. The latter had asked Arnold, "Do you think for a minute he will accept?" And Arnold had replied, "Of course not."[22]

Now, little more than a year later, the job was reactivated, not as a political payoff but at the insistence of Secretary of War Stimson, who saw the need for the position to be filled. Stimson had been looking for someone with intelligence and energy who also had an appreciation of air power. He knew at once he had found his man in Robert Lovett. A real reorganization of the air arm was to become the first of Lovett's many tasks.

One who returned to the service in the final months of the year was former airman Major Edward S. "Ted" Curtis. A World War I ace who had flown with the 95th Squadron of the 1st Pursuit Group, Ted Curtis bore the added distinction of being the youngest major in the U. S. Army, having just turned twenty-one when he left the service in the fall of 1919. He also had no great love for a fellow major, somewhat his senior, named Tooey Spaatz. Their association had been distant, for Curtis as a flying student had been assigned to Issoudun, France, where Spaatz commanded the Third Flight Instruction Center. There was a notable shortage of planes at Issoudun but an abundance of rocks covering the fields, and while he struggled to obtain the former, Spaatz used the students to get rid of the latter. Curtis and his rock-picking squadron mates did not figure this duty was a part of becoming a *pilote de chasse*. They promptly dubbed the Major and his adjutant, Captain Wiedenbach, "the German spies."

Some months following the Armistice, when Curtis returned to the United States, he served briefly on Billy Mitchell's staff, and found that Spaatz was on it also. That was not the reason he gave up the Army, but he left it no fonder of Spaatz than he had been when he departed from Issoudun for Toul and the front.

There was, however, one member of Mitchell's staff with whom he did keep in touch, and that was Bob Olds. Olds, in the summer of 1940, convinced Ted Curtis that he should take a leave of absence from his job as Sales Manager of the Motion Picture Division of Eastman Kodak and return to the service.

It was November when Curtis accepted Olds' suggestion. He found that after an interim of twenty years he was going to serve under that damned red-headed major, now a brigadier general, again. Spaatz was Chief of Air Corps Plans. His Executive was Lieutenant Colonel Muir "Santy" Fairchild, Ira Eaker's old flying mate, who was one of the better brains in the air arm no matter how large the arm grew. To Curtis, Santy Fairchild was a first-class thinker, and he in turn became Fairchild's Executive. But stepping from the orderly operations of Eastman Kodak to what he saw as "the pretty thoroughly chaotic" inner workings of the fourth-floor, Air Corps wing of the Munitions Building, Curtis had some catching up and some adjusting to do.

In the swirl of disorganization, the pressure of priorities, the tangled lines of authority, the cross-purposes of contradictory orders issued from who the hell knew where, Curtis noted that the only thing that seemed changed about the unflappable Spaatz was the spelling of his name. In the old days it had been spelled with one *a;* now the double *a* gave the correct pronunciation.* Coincidentally, Curtis also knew that following the war Captain Wiedenbach had also changed his name. His father had been an officer in the German Army; his mother's name was Willoughby. He switched to the latter, possibly having learned the epithet he'd picked up at Issoudun.†

Ted Curtis slowly got to know Tooey Spaatz better. It would have been hard not to, under the conditions that existed. There were four desks in the office, Spaatz and Olds side by side, Fairchild and Curtis across the narrow room. Civilian clothes hid rank, and rank was no object and never had been with Spaatz. Lunch, when they had time to eat it, was at an excellent, overcrowded cafeteria, The Allies Inn. After hours, those who still had strength could repair to the tennis court or the fairway. The more serious-minded established a perimeter around the poker table and dug in. But it was here, at the poker table, that Ted Curtis began to appreciate the Spaatz style—his dry humor and daring card playing.

For the moment, Ted Curtis was one of a planning staff of about fifty officers and civilians whose numbers seemed to increase daily but not nearly in proportion to the demands made upon it. Distribution of aircraft and engines was a problem. A shortage of parts and machine tools was a problem. A shortage of skilled labor added to the production problem,

* The spelling of the name was officially changed from Spatz to Spaatz in 1938.

† Later, as a major general, Charles A. Willoughby became General MacArthur's Chief of Intelligence.

which added to half a dozen other problems. There was more: Not only were all recommendations still subject to approval by the War Department General Staff, which was in turn caught in its own upheaval of building a ground army, but it and everything military was also operating under a policy dictated by a President and his closest advisers that was twisting and turning its way ever closer to war.

Near year's end, Secretary Stimson summed up what he saw as the essential problem at the top: "Conferences with the President are difficult matters. His mind does not follow easily a consecutive chain of thought but he is full of stories and incidents and hops about in the discussion from suggestion to suggestion and it is very much like chasing a vagrant beam of sunshine around a vacant room."[23]

Four

The Most Valuable Possession

In the morning, when the weather permitted, it was General Frank Andrews' custom to walk from his home, in Northwest Washington, to his office, in the Munitions Building, on Constitution Avenue. The exercise was good now that so many of his weekends were like weekdays, preventing him from swinging a golf club or riding horseback with his wife, Johnny, in Rock Creek Park. The three-mile jaunt also gave him time to be alone—to think over yesterday's actions and today's probabilities in the hectic acceleration of demands.

Yesterday, November 6, 1940, fifty million Americans had gone to the polls in the largest voter turnout in U.S. history. The weather—at least in the Washington, D.C., area—had been pure Indian summer. This morning it had started out similarly, to the tune of the radio and the newspapers headlining Franklin D. Roosevelt's victory over Republican Wendell L. Willkie. The President had won the election by a plurality of five million votes, giving him a much disputed third term in office.

As a Tennesseean, Andrews was by tradition a nominal Democrat, but his politics, like the canniness of his investments in the business world, was not a subject he discussed at any length. Military officers, for obvious reasons, steered clear of announced political favoritism. There had been a tenuous kind of contact with the White House. Johnny had ridden in the honor guard at Roosevelt's first inaugural, and Mrs. Roosevelt had invited the Andrewses to tea, but Andrews had never talked officially or unofficially to Roosevelt, even though his military fortunes were tied to the President's wishes. During his GHQ Air Force days, several outside efforts had been made to bring Andrews and FDR together for a private discussion on the need for a separate air force. They had not been successful, and some of Andrews' friends believed the President had been behind the airman's exile to Fort Sam Houston, Texas, the previous year.

The strongest evidence to refute this belief had come shortly before the election. General Marshall's recommendation that Andrews be given command of the newly named Panama Canal Department Air Force had been swiftly approved by Roosevelt. The underlying significance of the move was that both FDR and his Chief of Staff viewed the Panama Canal as the most strategically valuable and threatened of all U.S. possessions. As for the Mitchell-type treatment Andrews had received, he knew full well that his reassignment from Commanding General of GHQ Air Force to an innocuous post two grades down the ladder had been manufactured in the War Department and not in the White House.

Only a few of Andrews' closest confidants were aware that he had been given fair warning by the hierarchy of the Army General Staff during a little-known, highly charged encounter two years past. That meeting perhaps more than any other revealed the inner workings of Andrews' character.

Major General Oscar Westover, Chief of the Air Corps, had been killed in a crash at Burbank, California, on September 21, 1938. Andrews had been with Westover at March Field just previously and was still there when the word came. He immediately flew back to his headquarters, at Langley Field, Virginia, and directly thereafter his backup pilot and son-in-law, Lieutenant Hiette "Sonny" Williams, Jr., was alerted to have the General's DC-2 ready for a flight to Bolling Field, near Washington.

Williams, as Andrews' aide, rode with him from Bolling Field to War Department headquarters. The office they were directed to was literally full of brass. Chief of Staff Major General Malin Craig and the four assistant chiefs of staff, the mighty G's of the War Department, greeted Andrews.

Pleasantries over, Lieutenant Williams was asked to wait in an adjoining office. The meeting immediately got down to business. Said Craig, without preliminaries: "Andrews, we are in a position to recommend to the President that you be appointed Chief of the Air Corps. Before we do so, we would like your assurance that you will give up these ideas about large bombers and conform to the policies of the War Department."

To Williams, who was able to overhear the proceedings, the silence was like a violin string being tightened to the snapping point. When Andrews finally spoke, his voice was firm and seemingly relaxed. "Gentlemen, I appreciate your consideration and I want to assure you that if I am appointed I will carry out my duties as I see them to the best of my ability." The accent was on *as I see them*. Craig's flat response—"Thank you for coming; that is all"—was like a cold wind slamming the door shut.[1]

On the return ride to Bolling, Andrews had nothing to say to his son-in-law, who was used to his long silences but knew now there was really nothing to say. On the basis of his convictions, Andrews had rejected the opportunity to compromise. Thus he had relinquished the offer to be Chief of the Air Corps under the War Department's entrenched ground rules.

When they got back on the plane, instead of going forward to do the flying or act as Sonny Williams' copilot—as was his usual custom— Andrews sat down in the rearmost seat. After the flight to Langley, Williams left the cockpit to find his passenger sound asleep.

Several days later, it was announced that Hap Arnold had been named the new Chief of the Air Corps.

Now, as Andrews strode toward his office in the Munitions Building, amid the Washington traffic, he was in the bright autumn of his life. He had been a military officer for nearly thirty-five years, twenty-two of them as an airman. He had once remarked that he would rather be a colonel in the Air Corps than a general of the line. Yet he had been made a general of the line, and for the past fourteen months he had been the *only* Army flyer ever to serve as an assistant chief of staff. But now he was about to return to the air—and the move was much to his liking. His name had been on the promotion list Marshall had brought to Stimson at the end of October, and the increase in rank to major general had been a promotion of substance to fit the new job, rather than one of form and prestige.

As G-3, Andrews had taken part in the Army planning and policy conferences centering on the defense of the western hemisphere, with particular regard to the Panama Canal. Even earlier than that, the Air Corps Board had, in the summer of 1938, quietly elected to begin a study titled *Air Corps Mission Under the Monroe Doctrine.* Considerable impetus for the study had come from Andrews, the Commander of GHQ Air Force. Three of his B-17's, led by Bob Olds, had visited Buenos Aires, Argentina, and other flights into South America had demonstrated the Boeing's strategic potential for defense of the western hemisphere and particularly the Panama Canal. In 1939, Andrews himself had delivered a lecture at the Army War College stressing the need for aircraft of greater range than the B-17 for hemisphere defense.

A War Department board headed by Tooey Spaatz then undertook a study to determine the number and types of aircraft, the bases, and the logistic support needed to defend against German or Italian invasion of South America from bases in West Africa, thus opening the way for attack on the Canal or the U.S. homeland. Adding to their concern was attempted political penetration of several South American countries by the "Nazi-Fascist states" through military missions, propaganda, and the more than twenty thousand miles of air routes Germany's Lufthansa Airways was operating in South America. Given the estimated strength of the potential enemies' military aviation, albeit overestimated, as events were to prove, the study implied clearly that the only defense against a well-organized attack on the hemisphere was strategic air power.

In the fall of 1940, it didn't take a military strategist to recognize that with most of the Fleet in the Pacific and the remaining elements on patrol in the Atlantic, air power more than ever was the major defense of the Canal and its environs.[2]

But if the external threat was understood, the internal military conflicts of command that exacerbated the threat were not. Traditional Army concepts were ingrained, and if the ground officer at the top, no matter how competent an administrator, neither understood the uses of air power nor was equal to the scope of his task, the whole effort suffered. Marshall foresaw that the complexities of the Canal's defense, greatly extended by the acquisition of British bases in the Caribbean, required an officer who was more than an able air commander. He had to be an organizer, a builder, a diplomat, a strategist—withal, a cool thinker under the pressures of political and threatened military attack. In Andrews, Marshall saw that man.

In his new assignment, Andrews would report to Army Lieutenant General Daniel Van Voorhis, the Panama Canal Department Commander. Van Voorhis was a sixty-two-year-old ground officer with a solid general staff background. This was his next to last post before retirement, and until July 1940, when he received his third star, it had been considered somewhat of a cushy assignment, the accent on the social. Andrews knew from personal correspondence with Bert Dargue, who had commanded the Canal's air arm, the 19th Wing, for the past two years, that Van Voorhis, with his infantry-cavalry background, had no real understanding of air power. Dargue, who was returning to the States to be the Air Corps Inspector General, had told Andy Andrews that under Van Voorhis' command the 19th's thin echelons were overworked auxiliaries serving the Coast and the Field Artillery batteries and infantry units, towing targets by day and ducking searchlights by night. The demands of so-called "cooperative missions" left the 19th's squadrons no more than 10 percent of their time to train for their principal missions: defense of the Canal and the Caribbean. To Van Voorhis' way of thinking, artillery—coastal and antiaircraft—was the principal guardian of the waterway.

* * *

However, the defense of the Panama Canal had now become synonymous with Caribbean defense. In that regard, for years airmen had strongly opted for a base in Puerto Rico, but for years the War Department had failed to see any need for it except in time of war. Hitler had changed its way of thinking, and by March 1939 a base at Punta Borinquén was under construction.

The inclusion of an Army Air Corps base in Puerto Rico as a *must* in

U.S. defense plans indicated a growing recognition of just what defending the Canal now entailed. Goering had publicly boasted that the Panama Canal was not invulnerable. "Two of my bombs, dropped on the Culbra [sic] Cut," he declared, "would render the entire waterway unusable in ten minutes."[3]

Although when war came to Europe, in September 1939, air defense in the Canal Zone was seen as the only real answer to the threat of a possible attack. Even so Canal and Caribbean aerial forces continued to be woefully inadequate. A buildup had been approved with a target date for completion of June 30, 1941, but events were outrunning projections. As a stopgap measure, in October 1939, Panama, with U.S. encouragement, convened a conference of all the foreign ministers of the American republics. The conferees issued a declaration establishing a "security zone" around the hemisphere south of Canada which ranged from three hundred to one thousand miles offshore. The combatants were warned not to engage in hostile action within the zone. The declaration was hardly enforceable and was jokingly referred to as the "Chastity Belt." In *sub rosa* fashion Roosevelt shaped the warning to Allied advantage. He had put into action a so-called Navy "neutrality patrol" whose announced purpose was to assure U.S. neutrality by reporting the movement of belligerent ships. The Panama Declaration expanded the area of patrol, and U.S. ships spotting German raiders or submarines were to give their position in the clear in plain English, and to stay in contact as long as possible. This was of obvious benefit to British patrols operating outside the zone and their convoys in it.

Because the bulk of the Fleet was in the far Pacific and the security zone was so vast, the Atlantic patrols were spread extremely thin. Thus it was the Navy that first accepted the wisdom of the Air Corps's long-standing bid for a base in Puerto Rico. The Navy asked Hap Arnold to aid in guarding the sanctity of the Chastity Belt by flying reconnaissance patrols out of Borinquén Field, which must have brought a certain amount of glee. Maybe even Tooey Spaatz cracked a smile. In any case, on December 5, 1939, the 27th Reconnaissance Squadron began its patrols from Puerto Rico, as requested.

Just a week later the credibility of the Panama Declaration was shredded when three British cruisers chased the German pocket battleship *Admiral Graf Spee* through "neutral waters" into the harbor of Montevideo, Uruguay. There her captain scuttled his ship on Hitler's order and then committed suicide. Protests were dispatched to the belligerents, but the example was clear enough.

The fall of France brought a chain reaction in Washington with definite emphasis on the Canal Zone. The sudden shift brought action: everything from the 19th Wing's first weather officer to a rush of equipment to complete the aircraft warning net. By the end of July, the Signal Corps was experimenting with radar on the Pacific side of the Canal. By summer's end there was complete acceptance of the need for heavy bombardment aircraft, a need foreseen months before by Spaatz and his staff of planners.

The announcement by Roosevelt on September 3, 1940, that fifty U.S. destroyers were to be traded for bases on British-owned Caribbean islands greatly expanded the Canal Zone's eastern defenses and meant that more aircraft groups would be allotted to the area. But like nearly everything else at the time, most of it was on paper. Altogether, in September the Air Corps had fewer than thirteen thousand officers, more than half of them undergoing training. In a twelve-month period, about three thousand recruits had been sent to fill the Air Corps's understrength units in the Caribbean, but all of them were in need of training, and while plans in Washington envisioned the Caribbean's becoming a bastion of strength, it was still far from that when Andrews learned he would be taking over to guide the buildup.

* * *

This, then, was generally the military situation in the Panama Canal Department when Andrews was given his new command. If there was time, the problems would be solvable, but no one knew how soon the Canal's defenders might have to face the growing threat. As Arnold had said, "An increase in the range of modern bombers has made the Panama Canal more susceptible to attack from many places."

Were there hostile forces in position to make such an attack in one form or another? Or, as Roosevelt's foes said, had the Administration overreacted to Hitler's victories and exaggerated Germany's capacity to launch even a hit-and-run raid against a far-distant target in order to stimulate the U.S. military and naval buildup? Answers to those questions depended heavily on one's knowledge of internal and external political factors pertinent to the Caribbean and Central and South America.

Through British intelligence sources, Roosevelt was in possession of supposedly authentic German maps dividing South America into four states and one colony and showing how the Panama Canal was to be taken and how Luftwaffe aircraft could be put into position to bomb U.S. cities.[4] That the President and his Secretary of War believed the documents were *bona fide* and not forgeries there is no doubt.

Although the basis for Air Corps plans to defend the Canal was focused on the threat of German long-range bombers, there was a threat much closer at hand emanating from German-owned aircraft operating throughout much of Latin America. For nearly two decades, German and Italian commercial aviation had been hard at it, servicing the southern hemisphere. The German fleet numbered about one hundred planes. Many were Ju-52's—lumbering Junkers trimotors, transports that had been designed as the Luftwaffe's first bomber. Slow and cumbersome, the Junkers nevertheless could be converted for bombing easily enough.

Since early summer 1940, the U. S. State Department had been talking with the government of Ecuador about eliminating Scadta, the oldest German-operated airline in South America. Back in the mid-twenties, Hap Arnold had participated in blocking Scadta's efforts to establish routes in the United States. The line operated in Colombia as well, employing about twenty German pilots, who were rumored to be Luftwaffe reserve officers. The Colombian Government had assured U.S. officials that the copilot on every Scadta flight was a Colombian Army officer.

Brazil was an even more worrisome case. When Marshall had visited there in May, he had seen how woefully inadequate the country's defenses were. Worse, there were strong Axis sympathies within the Brazilian Government and officer corps. Yet President Getulio Vargas wanted no American soldiers on his soil. Arms and equipment, yes, but Yankees in uniform, no. Marshall had precious little of either to offer anyway, even though Roosevelt had issued a directive that a force of one hundred thousand men be readied to go to Brazil immediately.

The Condor line, a subsidiary of Deutsche Lufthansa, was reported to be operating a fleet of twenty-five assorted aircraft with landing and servicing facilities at some fifty locations, many of them along the coast. Since 1934, the island of Fernando de Noronha, about three hundred miles off Brazil, had been a communications control point for both German and Italian air operations from Europe to Latin America. In Peru and Bolivia, German airlines also were operating. These countries, as well as Colombia and Brazil, were in striking distance of the Canal. German and Italian airways also continued to do business in Chile and Argentina. In all these countries there were substantial settlements of Germans and Italians. Many of them were known to be strongly in favor of establishing a firmer connection with the homeland and were working toward that end either openly or secretly.

In Panama and the other Central American countries, there were similar colonies, along with Japanese settlers. The fear of sabotage had increased following the French surrender. Van Voorhis had rounded up eighty-one aliens working in the Canal Zone, and in September he had ordered that all European-born workers employed there by the Army be fired.

U.S. intelligence had no hard proof of plans to bomb the Canal locks or a ship in passage through the forty-mile waterway, but there was plenty of reason to be on the alert. The threat loomed large in the minds of those who had to guard against it, from Stimson and Marshall on down.[5]

Since the mid-thirties, Panama had played unknowing and often uncaring host to a wide assortment of German, Italian, Japanese, and Russian

erals Henry H. Arnold and George C. Marshall
Randolph Field, Texas, 1940. Between them
built the greatest air force in history. (Credit
. Air Force)

Bee Arnold sees her husband, Major General Hap
Arnold, off for London, April 10, 1941. (Credit
U. S. Air Force)

eral Arnold greets his son, Lieutenant Henry
Arnold, Jr., with gifts of home-cooked deli-
es, at Albrook Field, Canal Zone, two months
r Pearl Harbor. The Lieutenant, stationed at
Amador, had not seen his father in nearly a
r. (Credit U. S. Air Force)

utenant General Frank M. Andrews, at the con-
s of his command C-47, and his opposite
ber in the Canal Zone, Rear Admiral Clifford
Van Hook, explore a bit of the wild blue yonder.
edit Jean A. Peterson)

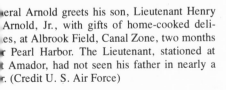

A threesome guarding the Pana Canal: Rear Admiral Van Hook, S retary of the Navy Frank Knox, a Caribbean Defense Command Lieutenant General Frank Andrew (Credit Jean A. Peterson)

Andrews, the diplomat as well soldier, chats with Manuel Prado, President of Peru, after landing Lima for a state visit. (Credit U. Air Force)

President Somoza, of Nicaragu does the honors, awarding Gene Andrews the Presidential Medal Merit, October 2, 1942. Somo thought so highly of the Caribbe Defense Commander that he nam his country's new airport Andre Field in his honor. (Credit U. S. Force)

Brigadier General Carl "Tooey" Spaatz ready to go on the gauges in a Link Instrument Trainer, March 1941. (Credit U. S. Air Force)

ieutenant Colonel Harold Lee George, heavy-bomber ad-
ocate, B-17 pilot, and leader of the team of Army air
lanners who produced AWPD-1, the air projection to defeat
itler through daylight strategic bombardment. (Credit U. S.
ir Force)

ummer 1942. Brigadier General Ira. C. Eaker and friend at
igh Wycombe, Eighth Air Force Bomber Command Head-
uarters, in England. In February 1942, Eaker had been sent
 the United Kingdom with a staff of six to organize and
stablish the "Mighty Eighth." (Credit New York *Times*
hotos)

Top brass of the Eighth Air Force pose with serious-looking "Boss" at a B-17 base in Englan From the left, Brigadier General Robert (Candee; Eighth Fighter Commander Brigadi General Frank O'D. "Monk" Hunter; Brigadi General Newton Longfellow, 1st Air Divisi Commander; Major General Walter "Tony" Fran Service Commander; Lieutenant General Dwig D. Eisenhower, Theater Commander; Major Ge eral "Tooey"Spaatz, Eighth Air Force Comma der, and Brigadier General Ira Eaker, Eigh Bomber Commander. It was this handful of airme whose job it was to carry the air war to German (Credit U. S. Air Force)

A more relaxed moment. "Ike" Eisenhower a Ira Eaker descend. Diplomatically bringing up t rear is Ambassador Anthony J. Drexel Biddl (Credit Sport & General)

On August 17, 1942, the Eighth Air Force launched its first raid against Hitler's Reich. A dozen B-17's from the 97th Group attacked the marshaling yards at Rouen with Bomber Commander Eaker on board *Yankee Doodle*. All planes returned safely. From this small beginning the numbers and the targets would grow. (Credit Russell Bradshaw)

Fortresses above the overcast, heading for the U-boat pens on the Bay of Biscay, while a German FW 190 fighter (upper left) swings in to attack. (Credit U. S. Air Force)

Bombs away over the German submarine base at Lorient. Precision bombing even with the Norden bombsight was no easy task, especially when under heavy attack by flak and fighters. (Credit U. S. Air Force)

Submarine pens at St. Nazaire (Flak City) and other U-boat bases were protected by concrete roofing twelve feet thick. Direct hits bounced off them. Here bombs fall on submarine installations adjacent to lock gates. (Credit U. S. Air Force)

The Germans employed the technique of concealing their vital installations with smoke. In this case, too little and too late. Bombs can be seen hitting the Kiel U-boat construction yards in an attack by B-17's and B-24 Liberators. (Credit U. S. Air Force)

On the money. Nearly one hundred Eighth Air Force heavies pummel the U-boat construction yards at Vegesack, where later photos showed seven submarine hulls severely damaged. In the winter of 1942–43 Hitler's wolf packs were winning the war in the Atlantic. Bombing their pens and construction facilities became a primary responsibility of the Eighth Air Force. (Credit U. S. Air Force)

espionage agents. The Canal's importance made the area a camping ground for spies, none better organized than those directed from the Abwehr offices in Berlin.[6] At the request of the Luftwaffe General Staff as well as German Naval Operations, the German Intelligence Service had been asked to supply a detailed topographical and technical report on the Canal, the ships moving through it, and the strength of the Army garrison and military installation within and without the ten-mile-wide Zone. Two spy rings were established by the Abwehr's Panamanian resident chief, Kurt Lindberg, who had double cover as Panamanian Manager of the Hamburg-America steamship line and German Consul in the Caribbean-coast city of Colón.

Although part of one ring was caught in the act of photographing gun emplacements, Van Voorhis failed to catch the other members, and at the end of 1940 they were still functioning. Known at Abwehr headquarters as Project 14, they were able to supply detailed maps and close-up photographs of all the locks, power stations, and military installations, including pertinent information on each.

The ring's ability to collect the requested information was an indication of the validity of the War and the Navy departments' concern, although at the time the counterintelligence branches of G-2, ONI—the Office of Naval Intelligence—and the FBI were not aware of Project 14 or its mission. However, extreme sensitivity over the Canal's safety in the upper reaches of the War Plans Division was illustrated by the type of evidence that was sometimes used to reach the conclusion that either an attack on or sabotage of the canal was imminent. The alert of U. S. Army forces in Panama and Hawaii signaled by General Marshall in June 1940 was based not only on actions by the Japanese Fleet and Army, but also on unsubstantiated remarks. A nameless German full of strong drink sounded off to a nameless friend in a bar in Eureka, California, maintaining that if it appeared the United States was going to enter the war, he was going to blow up the Canal. Shortly thereafter, the Los Angeles section of the Coast Guard picked up word that Brazilian seamen had been told by members of a Japanese crew that all Japanese ships in the canal area had been ordered to scuttle if the United States mobilized.

On such molehills were mountains built, but that was not to say that espionage in Panama wasn't a highly developed and thriving business. The threat was always there, often obviously so, and no more apparent than at the famous Tivoli Hotel. Built during the Canal's construction, the Tivoli, with its Victorian façade, had an aura of its own—a watering place well known to the military. So was the Countess, a striking blond refugee from somewhere across the sea who held daily court in the Tivoli's fine mahogany barroom. The Countess had a great fondness for flying officers, particularly second lieutenants, whom she was known to invite home to enjoy tea and crumpets in the coolness of her air-conditioned apartment—said to be one of the very few air-conditioned apartments in all of Panama City.

One of the agreements reached at the Panama Conference of October 1939 was that no Central or South American country would permit the establishment of a base on its territory by any of the belligerents. Eight months later, in July 1940, again at the urging of the United States, the foreign ministers of the Latin American countries met in Cuba and came forth with the Act of Havana. The Act, in response to Secretary of State Cordell Hull's call for "Collective Trusteeship," declared that colonial territories in Latin America belonging to European nations—The Netherlands, France, and Britain—and threatened by any hostile force would be taken over and governed jointly by all the American countries until the war was over.

The Act was aimed at the Axis powers—a collective move of support for the Monroe Doctrine. Therefore, by the end of 1940, on the surface at least, it would have seemed that the disparate republics of the Caribbean and of Central and South America were loosely united in a pro-Allied policy. This was not altogether so, and support for the Allied or the Axis side varied not only by country but also in degree.

The Roosevelt administration was intent upon pushing its Good Neighbor policy, seeking to convince suspicious republics from Mexico southward that alliance with the United States meant security and not the domination or disinterest that had marked the earlier part of the century, but political sensitivity remained. State Department resistance to the Air Corps's desire for negotiations with Costa Rica and Ecuador regarding landing strips on the strategic islands of Cocos and the Galápagos was a manifestation of it.

During the week before Roosevelt's election, an incident occurred that illustrated both the sensitivity and the tinderbox quality of the Caribbean as viewed from Washington. Andrews as G-3 had been directly responsible for the training of special detachments, including paratroops, for possible moves into Greenland, Iceland, the Azores, and the Caribbean island of Martinique. On November 1st, five days before the election, a very troubled General Marshall informed Andrews and then Secretary of War Stimson that he had received orders from the State Department to have five thousand troops put on a seventy-two-hour alert in preparation to attack Martinique.

Marshall knew such a move could result in a bloody mess, for the French had an estimated force of six thousand soldiers on the island. No one knew where the order had come from, and Stimson made a hurried visit to the State Department, where Secretary Hull pled ignorance of the dispatch. So, too, did Under Secretary Sumner Welles, who stressed that no action should be taken unless the United States was prepared to blow the French force right off the island. That word of the proposed move had leaked was apparent on election eve, when a Republican-sponsored radio broadcast addressed to the mothers of America proclaimed: "When your boy is dying on some battlefield in Europe—or maybe in Martinique—and he's crying out 'Mother! Mother!'—don't blame Franklin D. Roosevelt because he sent your boy to war—blame yourself, because you sent Franklin D. Roosevelt back to the White House."[7]

There was at least one positive action affecting Andrews' new command. For a number of months, negotiations had been going on between various departments of the government and Pan American Airways in an effort to reach agreement for the Air Corps to use Pan Am stations and facilities throughout Latin America on a long-lease basis. That such agreement had been reached was good news to Andrews. He knew, too, that an effort was underway for the airline quietly to buy up a controlling interest in Scadta, ending any threat it might pose.

On that mild November morning following the reelection of President Roosevelt, Frank Andrews was eager to take command of his new post. Before he and Johnny set sail for the Canal Zone, on the twenty-seventh, there would be many briefings: talks with Marshall and Strong, Hap and Tooey, and others, including Bert Dargue. He would leave Washington believing that he had an accurate picture of what he could expect to find when he arrived. But he would learn, as is so often the case, that realities of the picture seen close up changed the perspective, the lines becoming markedly more harsh.

* * *

Colonel Adlai H. "Gilke" Gilkeson, Commander of the 12th Pursuit Wing, had come to believe that no one in the upper echelons of the War Department would ever recognize the importance of air power—particularly in the defense of the Panama Canal. Gilkeson was a graduate of West Point, class of 1915. He had earned his wings a year later at Rockwell Field, California, in the same class as Tooey Spaatz.

In his opinion the only time military aircraft had been properly employed was when he commanded the 8th Pursuit Group of GHQ Air Force under Major General Frank Andrews. When he heard that Andrews was coming to take over command of the air units in the Canal Zone, his rather dour spirits brightened perceptibly.

At the moment, the 12th Pursuit Wing consisted of thirty-six flyable aircraft. Half of them were eight-year-old Boeing P-26's. The other half were Curtiss P-36's of somewhat newer vintage but undeniably not first-class. The paucity of equipment and personnel was no more disturbing than the paucity of ideas on how to use them.

This was particularly true with regard to the ideas of Gilkeson's *bête noir,* Lieutenant General Daniel Van Voorhis, the commander of the

Panama Canal Department. His knowledge of aircraft was summed up by an incident at Albrook Field. Noting that a number of planes lacked engines, he asked why. When informed that the engines were undergoing overhaul, he suggested that the planes be made flyable by requisitioning truck engines from the motor pool. On another occasion, he observed an oxygen cart beside an aircraft and when informed what it was, he inquired whether the oxygen was for the pilot or for the plane.

Van Voorhis' understanding of the strategic use of air power was on a par with his technical knowledge of it. During training maneuvers, pilots sweated in their cockpits under the fierce tropical sun, waiting interminably for an order to take off and attack a squad of troops dug in on the backside of a jungle hill.

The news that Andrews was leaving Washington for Panama also brightened the day for Gilkeson's Operations Officer Major Thomas C. Darcy. Twenty years Gilkeson's junior, Darcy, from the moment of his graduation from West Point, in 1932, had his course set on a career in military aviation. Unlike many of his compatriots, his interest in flying didn't exclude thinking about how aircraft should be used. He could see around long-standing frustrations and perceive that in a world on the verge of all-out war, air power must come into its own. The fact that Andrews was being sent to Panama indicated to him that Washington was beginning to see the light.

There were many others who shared Darcy's feeling, none more so than Andrews' son-in-law, Lieutenant Sonny Williams. He had recently been assigned to the new, 41st Bomber Group, formed out of the famous 2nd Wing. The Group, commanded by Lieutenant Colonel Caleb Haynes, was to be stationed in Puerto Rico at the yet uncompleted Borinquén Field. To Williams this meant leaving behind his wife, Josie, the Andrewses' eldest daughter. Josie was not physically strong. She had lost her first child, was carrying her second; in November 1940, when Williams flew away piloting a B-18 of the new bomb group, he was not sure when he would see her again.

It was about a month later that he was awakened in the middle of the night by the officer on duty, who informed him that he was to be on board an Army transport seventy miles away, departing from San Juan for Panama the next morning. The only way he could do it was to load all his belongings into his car and drive it right onto the ship, without the foggiest idea who wanted him in Panama or why. Once again he was to become the General's aide and pilot. It was a pleasant surprise and a grand Christmas present.

When the ship that brought Andrews, Johnny, and Josie docked in Colón on December 6, 1940, several officers assigned to Andrews' staff were on hand to greet and accompany them on the fifteen-minute flight to

Albrook Field. One was Lieutenant Colonel Francis Brady, who had been Bert Dargue's Chief of Staff and now would be Andrews'. He also was a GHQ Air Force alumnus. Although Brady was considered by some with whom he served as bombastic, Andrews thought that he had "developed tremendously since the old GHQ Air Force days."

Still another member of the old GHQ Air Force staff to join up was Master Sergeant Theodore C. Totman. Even before Andrews' new appointment was officially announced, he had written to Totman telling him he was leaving New York on November 27 aboard the U. S. Army transport *American Legion* and asking if the Sergeant would like to be his personal secretary. Totman, a quiet, dedicated NCO, had served as Andrews' secretary for nearly four years at Langley. Serving him again, Totman knew, would mean having to leave his wife in the States, at least until there was sufficient housing; yet he immediately accepted.

There was another recruit who attached himself to Andrews' staff. He was a newcomer of mean disposition, a bird of colorful plumage and syntax. He went with the living quarters the Andrews acquired at Albrook Field. George was his name, a macaw of unknown antecedents whose crusty temper was matched only by the discordant sound of his screeching cry stimulated by passing planes. Since the Andrews dwelling was situated close to the end of the principal runway, George's unflagging attempts to harmonize with aircraft at the moment of searing lift-off produced a sound that required steady nerves and a certain degree of lighthearted tolerance.

Although George obviously resented people almost as much as he resented the things they flew, he did have one favorite, and that was the master of the house. Andy Andrews was his pal, and when the General came home for lunch, as was the custom, he would be there to greet him and perch on his shoulder throughout the meal, adding his raucous two cents to the conversation when so inclined. He did not join Andrews in a routine after-lunch Chesterfield, but in the ten-minute catnap that usually followed, he stood guard. To everyone but Andrews, George was a mean bastard, but like the cockroaches which, it was said, kept the house standing on its cement-block stilts by holding hands, he was accepted.

Andrews quickly sized up the combat readiness of his new command. With the exception of the base at Río Hato, whose use was in contention, his air units were restricted to within the ten-mile-wide Zone. A third base, Howard Field, was now under construction. It was just three miles from Albrook, on the other side of the Canal. Access to the field would require driving across the locks or taking a ferry from Balboa. Aside from that, its proximity simply accented the degree of vulnerability the Panama Canal Air Force faced within the narrow confines of the territory. As Andrews noted, facilities for auxiliary fields and bombing and gunnery ranges would have to be negotiated through the State Department in dealing with the less than cooperative government of Arnulfo Arias. A measure of how that relationship was viewed could be seen in a secret study previously prepared by Tom Darcy. One boundary of Albrook Field bordered Panamanian territory, and Darcy's assignment was to come up with a plan to defend the field from sabotage or attack by Panamanians.

Although Andrews would come to know U. S. Ambassador Edwin Wilson and President Arias well, for the time being acquisition of air-base and training locations outside the Canal Zone was a matter to be worked out between Washington and Arias. Andrews considered these additional facilities to be as pressing a problem as the lack of trained personnel. He had just two hundred officers, although the War Department had determined that more than one thousand were required to staff his command. Some newly formed squadrons were activated with a single officer in charge. Hundreds of totally green enlisted men were arriving and had to be given basic training. Housing—even tenting—was in such short supply that five hundred men were quartered temporarily in a hangar at Albrook Field. And at root, all was tied into the continued lack of trained air crews and modern aircraft.

In discussions with Gilkeson, whose interceptors were stationed at Albrook, and with Brigadier General Douglas Netherwood, who commanded the 19th Bombardment Wing and whose bombers were situated at France and at Río Hato, Andrews came to the same irrefutable conclusions that Dargue had reached before him. Andrews wrote to George Brett, his longtime friend and now Chief of the Air Corps, that "under present conditions our pursuit reaction is worth little, and you know the price we would pay in operating B-18's in daylight against anything modern."

"Lousy" was the word Andrews used to describe both ground and air communications. He wanted a couple of Signal Corps radio sending and receiving sets immediately as a stopgap until the scheduled delivery of more extensive communication equipment arrived. "I can't get people down here to realize that we are in a war, and that we must prepare our mental attitude to just that," he added. "Everything here now seems to be planned on what may happen two or three years from now instead of next week or next month."

With that in mind, he sent his observations and recommendations to Van Voorhis and the War Department. "All pursuit equipment in the Zone is obsolete," he wrote. "With a target as vulnerable to damage by aerial attack as the Canal, and with the efforts being made to defend it, the type of pursuit planes here is inexcusable. Due to the importance of the Panama Canal I believe we would be justified in suspending shipments abroad, if necessary, until Caribbean pursuit units are properly equipped."

Andrews judged Netherwood's bombers to be no better than the pursuits. The B-18, which had been a second-rate plane since its acceptance, in 1935, would, said Andrews, "carry on at the cost of great losses until reinforced from the United States by suitable types. By suitable types, he was referring to the B-17.

In his memo to Van Voorhis he made two overall points: "Much thought, energy and money has been and is being expended by the United States, particularly in the present international situation, to prepare the Panama Canal to withstand air raids," and—

Air action (pursuit in reasonable strength) is at least eight times as effective for active defense in stopping air raiders as any other element of defense, even in an area as highly organized for antiaircraft artillery as in the Panama Canal Department. To the results to be expected from pursuit activities must be added the contributions bombardment aviation can make. Therefore, I suggest that every possible means be sought and applied to bring the air units under your command to maximum efficiency: if necessary adopting measures as extreme as temporarily requisitioning labor and equipment engaged in other projects with less pressing priorities, to prepare operating facilities for air units here, or for those which may be sent here. . . .

A month went by and there was neither response nor action from Van Voorhis. Andrews could sum up his relations with the tall, thin, erect Department Commander as being correct and unproductive. Van Voorhis appeared to have his mind focused elsewhere.

In a letter to Arnold describing his unhappiness about the "air situation in Panama," Andrews confided: "I have not been called upon yet by Van Voorhis for any recommendation for an air organization for his new responsibility of Caribbean defense. When he is ready to call on me I sincerely hope that our minds run in the same channels on the basic concepts and missions. But frankly and confidentially, from casual conversations that have already taken place between us, I am uneasy. It is again a matter of education. You know how that is. We have both been through it so many times."

Indeed Arnold did know whereof Andrews spoke, but in his quick response he stressed his number one problem and how it would affect the Panama Canal Air Force. "Frankly, I am worried about aircraft production. As you know we are leaning over backwards to give everything to the British. Very little is coming to us."

He admitted that past policy decisions to hold up on production during the Phony War period, and industrial expansion difficulties since, compounded the problem. But—"Taking everything into consideration, aircraft production insofar as getting airplanes for U.S. units is concerned is more or less of a mess, and no matter what we do in this matter there will be no relief for several months in the future. . . ." And that would be that so far as getting some new aircraft to fill Andrews' aged squadrons was concerned.

* * *

Prior to his departure from Washington, Andrews had discussed with Arnold and his staff, as well as with General Marshall and the War Plans Division, expanding the Panama Canal Air Force into an organization that would be capable of defending the entire Caribbean. The decision for such a defense was derived from the Joint Army-Navy Rainbow Plan No. 4, worked out by Marshall and Stark and approved by the President. After Andrews' departure, however, and before the end of the year, the plan was extended somewhat. Originally it had been concerned with hemisphere defense only. By late fall, defense was still the linchpin, but it was decided also to pursue a more offensive policy in the Atlantic as an ally of Great Britain.

Equally important, the Joint Planning Committee decided on December 21, 1940, that if the United States was forced into a war with Japan, operations against the Japanese would be restricted in order to prepare for a major thrust against Hitler. It had been proposed that the Department Commander of the Panama Canal Zone would become the Commanding General of the Caribbean Theater. Rainbow Plan No. 4 stated: "For the Army, this plan does not call for a major effort." Possibly that point took root in Van Voorhis' mind, for even after Andrews returned from his first inspection tour of Caribbean bases, on January 25, there was no reply waiting for him on his recommendations. Nevertheless, on February 18, he submitted to Van Voorhis a detailed organizational plan for the theater. And again there was silence.

Rainbow 4 defined the Caribbean Theater "to include the islands in and bordering the Caribbean Sea, all or such parts of French Guiana, Dutch Surinam, British Guiana, Venezuela, Colombia, Ecuador and Central America less Mexico, and the sea areas adjacent thereto as may be required for Army and Navy operations."[8] For twenty years, ever since the emergence of Army air power, there had been ambiguity and contention concerning Army Air Corps and Navy responsibilities for control of coastal and offshore areas. The contradictions of a policy that was dictated by tradition and influence and a refusal to cooperate was spelled out in all its lack of clarity in the War Department's Plan P4-40. While Van Voorhis was named Theater Commander, the stated mission of the Army was to support the Navy in controlling the Caribbean Sea and adjacent waters and to support naval operations against shore objectives. There were precious few naval ships in the area on either side of the Isthmus, and in spite of Andrews' obsolescent and understrength equipment, his was the only force that had any real chance to carry out the Navy's objectives.

As Andrews had pointed out to Van Voorhis: "The area of responsibility of the Caribbean Defense Commander extends not only to the geographical limits of the area indicated but to the area included within the range of the weapons at his disposal operating from points within subject area. Accomplishment of the mission indicated in the first sentence above, together with the defense of the Caribbean Defense Command area indicates that bombardment aviation, with such pursuit as is practical, must be prepared to attack any bases—afloat or ashore—within range of modern aviation. This area of responsibility will extend between 750 and 1,000 miles beyond the geographical limits of the Caribbean Defense Command."

Van Voorhis had been named Theater Commander as a result of recommendations made by Hap Arnold and his staff because a buildup of Army air forces was planned and air power would be the dominant factor in the Caribbean. While no airman had thus far been considered qualified to command ground forces as well as air, the opposite had long been standard procedure.

Andrews believed in the concept of unity of command, which meant that whoever commanded the largest segment of forces in an area should command them all. Naval Commander of the 15th Naval District, headquartered in Panama City, was Rear Admiral Frank H. Sadler. He was aptly considered by airmen—both Army and Navy alike—as a Van Voorhis in blues. Sadler's primary mission, in keeping with Plan P4-40, was defense of the Canal, though the responsibility for that defense rested with Van Voorhis. Andrews observed that coordination between the Army and the Navy was absolutely essential and "vital to [the] success" of any defensive strategy and that it could "only be obtained by unity of command."

In his proposal to Van Voorhis, he stressed the folly of waiting until an attack was in progress before deciding who would give the orders. That decision should be made right now and publicly announced. The largest problem, as he knew from long experience, would be coordination and cooperation between his air units and the few ships and patrol planes under Sadler's command. Andrews naturally viewed the Panama Canal Air Force as "the primary element of the Caribbean defense."

But Sadler had already indicated the kind of cooperation that could be expected. During the alert of June 17, 1940, Van Voorhis had sent him a directive to implement joint preparedness. He got back a reply that spoke for himself, the rudeness on a par with the implications.

1. The Fifteenth Naval District not being a part of the command of the Panama Canal, and orders emanating from that source having no authority in said District, enclosed order is returned herewith.

2. If it becomes necessary to communicate important information to the Commandant of the Fifteenth Naval District he may be found through telephone 2-2661 or 2-2662.

Van Voorhis' response to Andrews' proposal concerning who would be in overall command of air defense was to form a six-man board of officers whose purpose was to "study, develop and recommend a coordinated system of control which will insure the maximum contribution to the defense of the Panama Canal." There was no mention of the Caribbean. Serving on this board with Andrews were Sanderford Jarman and Walter Prosser, artillerymen and major generals. The Inspector General's Department was represented by a colonel, the Signal Corps by a lieutenant colonel, and the recorder was a major from the Department General Staff. Andrews was the only airman. He attended one meeting and, as he told Gilkeson, it was suggested that the air defense of the Canal be put under Jarman, the Coast Artillery commander. "I succeeded in avoiding a vote on the subject," he confided to his pursuit commander, "and hope that it does not come up again. We haven't had a meeting now since last Friday. The way things are going in that board I think we should be just as well off if we did not have any more meetings."

In his presentation of "Air Organization for the Caribbean Defense Command," Andrews informed Van Voorhis: "As clearly indicated in operations abroad, main reliance must be placed upon pursuit for air defense. As the Air Warning Service is primarily a source of information for pursuit aviation, its operation should be under the commander of pursuit forces." It was, however, falling under Signal Corps control.

Perhaps of even greater significance, Andrews also informed Van Voorhis—although it should have been thunderously obvious—that his aircraft made up the *only* force at hand with sufficient mobility to affect any military situation. He proposed that:

Bombardment and reconnaissance aviation be grouped under one command for tasks assigned by the Caribbean Defense Area Commander.

Air Defense Commands be established at critical points with minimum pursuit aviation, anti-aircraft artillery, and Aircraft Warning Service personnel and facilities, under unified operational control.

A Pursuit reserve force be organized for such missions as may be assigned by the Caribbean Defense Commander.

Very soon thereafter, a joint Army-Navy exercise illustrated graphically all of Andrews' concerns.

In early February a single ship was used to represent a hostile task force supposedly consisting of an aircraft carrier and a screen of destroyers. Sadler sent out his patrol planes to locate the enemy. Netherwood launched his B-18's to bomb the reported target. Gilkeson's interceptors went forth to escort the bombers home. It sounded good, but the postmortem Andrews held with his wing commanders bore out the substance of his previous evaluation. Communications, the vital linkage between units, was wretched, a combination of antiquated or unsuitable equipment, untrained personnel, poor planning, little cooperation between ground and air units, and perhaps worst of all, poor discipline.

The aircraft warning system was full of holes. Gilkeson felt that by adding visual reporting stations, as the RAF was doing with such success, they could certainly improve the situation. Andrews agreed, but at root there remained two basic problems, problems as old as the peacetime army: lack of training and lack of proper equipment. He foresaw it would take at least a year to correct the first, perhaps longer because of such a serious shortage of housing facilities. Many of the new recruits coming in were put to work building, getting no training.

How long it would take to correct the equipment problem depended on production and the determination in Washington of where that production was going. On the latter, Andrews could urge change and hope that Marshall's influence would bring results.

* * *

In March, Andrews received a visit from his closest confidant, retired Air Corps Colonel Hugh Knerr. They had been friends for more than twenty years, and for three of them Knerr had served as Andrews' indefatigable Chief of Staff. Lean and unyielding, his mind cloaked in stubborn resolve, Knerr had been a dogged proponent of two interwoven causes: a separate air force and the doctrines of strategic air power.[9] He saw a twofold enemy: the Army General Staff and the Navy Department, both determined to crush his twin objectives and all those who espoused them. As a staff officer and planner, as an engineer and logistics expert, there were few airmen who could match his steadiness and zeal. As a plotter in the cause of aerial independence he was tireless, and this last had brought him down.

In 1938 he was removed from Andrews' command and posted to Fort Sam Houston as Air Officer of the VIII Corps Area. It was the exile post to which Billy Mitchell had been sent in 1925 and the one that Andrews would be assigned to in 1939. Knerr's efforts had burned him out emotionally, and that, combined with the recurring physical effects of a crash suffered in the early days, forced his retirement from the Air Corps in January 1939. Since then he had become an executive of the Sperry Gyroscope Corporation. Leaving the service, however, did nothing to blunt his determination to bring about an independent air force. He ghosted articles, stimulated newspapers and magazines to preach the cause, worked to gain aviation supporters everywhere. He labored openly and plotted secretly to build the congressional backing needed to bring about the long-sought legislation.

When he came to Panama with his boss, Bob Lea, however, the purpose of their visit was to check out coast artillery and antiaircraft components made by Sperry. He and Andrews did not talk over the deep-seated issue of air independence but focused instead on the course of the war. Knerr brought news that the British were working on getting their antiaircraft fire up to sixty thousand feet. This meant not only that aircraft would have to fly higher but that cabins would also have to be pressurized, a development they had foreseen years before. Knerr felt the war couldn't be won by the British so long as their main effort was based in the British Isles. The threat was no longer invasion but attrition by submarine blockade and nightly aerial bombardment.

The Lend-Lease bill was coming up for a vote in the Senate, and Knerr correctly believed that it would pass. The issue was one of the most bitterly debated in U.S. history.[10]

To Knerr, Roosevelt was a dictator. Not that he was opposed to Lend-Lease. Quite the contrary. But while Andrews was discussing with him ideas on improving the ever-present bugaboo of aircraft maintenance and supply, an incident occurred that indicated the possibility of hostile action should the Senate vote in favor of the Lend-Lease bill.

Andrews' observation planes as well as naval patrol craft reported that a large Italian vessel, the *Conte Biancarmano,* was in the Canal area near Colón, on the Atlantic side. The twenty-three-thousand-ton ship appeared to be acting suspiciously, and word came through G-2 that if the Lend-Lease bill passed, the ship's captain, acting on orders from Mussolini, would scuttle his vessel while transiting the Canal. This threat took on broader scope when it was learned in Washington that the Italian plan was to sabotage *all* their ships in U.S. harbors, in an effort to block the roadsteads. Marshall sent word to Van Voorhis to seize the *Conte Biancarmano* and a smaller Italian ship also in Panamanian waters.

In the myriad problems of building the Caribbean defenses, Andrews found that Hugh Knerr, as always, offered some valuable suggestions. One was that a large supply depot be set up in southern Florida, far enough away so as not to be open to attack and close enough so materiel could be ferried into the theater quickly. In the early 1930s, Knerr had put together an embryo transport command, the first of its kind. The need for an air freight service equipped with cargo planes designed to carry supplies and personnel was obvious. Converted B-18's weren't much good for the job, and neither were commercial airliners.

Since his arrival in Panama, building a unified air defense had been one of Andrews' major goals. There were four integral parts in such a defense: an early-warning system, an interceptor command, antiaircraft batteries with searchlights and barrage balloons, and a communications network linking all the parts to a central operations headquarters. So far, two major deterrents had prevented its establishment: a lack of equipment, which Andrews felt would be solved in time, and General Van Voorhis' failure to act decisively, particularly on Andrews' proposal that the entire system be placed under a single command.

Andrews had kept Hap apprised of his efforts, but quite apart from them, Arnold's foresight on the overall question of air defense was to be of considerable benefit.

The Army Signal Corps had begun operational testing of radar in 1939. This prompted Arnold to suggest to Marshall that the Air Corps take over from the Coast Artillery all the components of air defense. With Marshall's concurrence, Arnold set up in early 1940 an "Air Defense Command" at Mitchel Field, Long Island, with Brigadier General James E. Chaney in command. Chaney, who was known more for his planning and executive abilities than anything technical, had as his aide a gifted engineering officer, Captain Gordon P. Saville.

With two companies of radar and communications people, they went to work to find ways to integrate all the components of air defense, and within the year they tested two major systems: one to protect an army in the field and the other to protect targets in a large industrial area. In the fall of 1940, accompanied by Bart Yount, Chaney and Saville went to England and learned all they could from the RAF defense against German air attacks. When they returned, at the end of the year, Arnold took them to Marshall, and together the three convinced the Chief that air defense in the United States should be patterned on RAF lines—that the responsibility for repelling air attack should be under air command.

In March, Andrews was informed that a ten-day indoctrination seminar on air defense was going to be held at Mitchel Field, and he was invited to send representatives. Pursuit Commander Gilkeson headed the four-man Air Force contingent. With them were Coast Artillery and Signal Corps officers. Brigadier General Follett Bradley headed the attendees from the Puerto Rican Department.

In all, sixty-seven officers gathered on March 25 to hear Delos Emmons deliver the opening remarks. As a lieutenant general and the ranking officer of the Combat Air Forces, Emmons was officially in command of all air defense in time of peace. Present also were the heads of the four continental air forces: Chaney, of the First; Major General John F. Curry, who commanded the Second Air Force and the northwest air defense sector; Major General Jake E. Fickel, Commanding General of the Fourth Air Force and the southwest air defenses; and Brigadier General Bart Yount, chief of the Third Air Force, whose area of responsibility was the southeastern part of the country.

As it was, after Emmons spoke, Chaney, who possessed somewhat the look and manner of an Indian Chief, arose and gave the assembled a brief background history of air defense. He was followed by Saville, now a major but, when compared with Emmons and the top air brass present, hardly an officer of rank. What he lacked in that department he made up in directness. He told his superiors that none of them really knew much about air defense, and most of what they knew was incorrect, but when he and his fellow lecturers, Lieutenant Colonels Fenton G. Epling and Paul S. Edwards, were done, they would all be better informed.

Everyone but Lucky Emmons took Saville's frankness in the manner intended: to throw out the old ideas, because here were some new and better ones. When the session ended, Emmons went to Chaney and complained. He wanted Saville dismissed from the seminar, reprimanded, and reduced in rank. How dare he address his superiors in such a manner!

Chaney, who wore two stars to Emmons' three but was senior to him in age and class at West Point, told Lucky to calm down. Saville might be a bit brash, but he knew more about his subject than anyone present. They were all here to learn something important, not to test the prerogatives and sensitivity of high and exalted rank. Emmons, seeing that he lacked support, backed off, and the seminar went forward.[11]

As for dispersion and the need for more bases, Andrews commented it was "manifestly impossible to operate one hundred fifty airplanes from Albrook Field."

The number was meaningful, for at last his air force was about to receive some of the aircraft it had long been promised. Further, Howard Field was now operational. Six P-40's would be ferried every day from the depot at Fairfield, Ohio, until the first increment, of eighty, was delivered. The route was no easy jaunt: across the country to Brownsville, Texas, and then down the length of Mexico and Central America. Thirty pilots were sent to Mitchel Field for transition training. The planes were new to them and had a tendency to ground-loop. Navigation was not a strong suit. Andrews assigned Tom Darcy to organize and ramrod the operation under what became known as the Panama Ferrying Command Provisional. As the aerial trail boss, Darcy practically lived in his plane, flying up and down the line and herding his charges on the long flight. One method he used to keep his planes flying in the face of possible Central American bureaucratic delays was to have orders written up festooned with fancy-colored ribbons. Somehow their presence sped the air units southward. As for the weather en route, the rainy season held off.

But Van Voorhis remained the real bottleneck in every phase of organizational planning. Andrews knew that he had to do something special to capture the Department Commander's attention. He began with a "Confidential and Personal" letter to Marshall in which he confessed:

Here in the Caribbean I am not so satisfied. I perhaps have accomplished something, at least I hope so, but drawing upon all the tact and diplomacy that I possess I feel that I have failed to gain Van Voorhis' complete confidence, consequently I have made slow progress in selling him my ideas on the organization and operation of the Air Forces in the Caribbean. Perhaps I am impatient but things seem to move so slowly, and time now is a precious commodity. . . .

He followed his letter to the Chief of Staff with one to his old friend Brigadier General Joseph T. McNarney, in the War Plans Division. Andrews suggested that McNarney come down and take over the Pursuit Wing, since Gilkeson's tour would be up very soon. "It's a tough job," he wrote, "with the organization under which we are now operating, but I know from experience in the GHQ Air Force that you could handle it." McNarney had been his G-4, and Andrews was not flattering the lean, tough-minded veteran. Rather, he was letting him know that in the Canal Zone the Coast Artillery outranked the Air Force in officers and influence, and that the present war plan, which he knew was in McNarney's office, contemplated coordination by cooperation, "which you and I know won't work."

He went on to say that he had recommended the air force in the Caribbean be set up with "a bomber command and an interceptor command under which there would be as many Regional Air Defense Commands as the situation requires—Puerto Rico, Panama, Trinidad. But so far," he concluded, "I haven't been able to sell this idea."

Very shortly thereafter, Colonel William E. Lynd, of the Inspector General's Department, arrived on the scene. An old friend of Andrews', Lynd got a thorough briefing and made a careful survey of what was going on. Soon after he returned to headquarters, he wrote Andrews that "a letter has gone to the C.G. of Panama to the effect that his present air organization does not meet the approval of the War Department and suggested rather pointedly that several things be done."

Van Voorhis asked Andrews to report to him at once and showed him the communication Lynd had referred to. He then issued an order creating the Caribbean Air Force, placed Andrews in command of it, and instructed him to draw up an organizational plan for the force immediately. Andrews was kind enough not to remind Van Voorhis that he had submitted such a plan more than two months before. Instead, he described again what the plan involved and said he was going to implement it as quickly as possible. One of the two barriers blocking defense of the Caribbean had been deftly removed.

In a letter soon after to Knerr, Andrews described the makeup of his new air force, pointing out that he was modeling it along the lines of the air forces in the United States as well as the RAF, with both defensive and offensive units. Then he got down to what he had been mulling over since Knerr's visit. "The Maintenance Command will have under it all base depots, and will be responsible for coordination of service and supply with the projected and planned operations. If you decide to come back in the Air Corps when the war starts how about coming down and running the Maintenance Command? I don't know of anyone who could do it better. If you are interested, drop into the office and talk it over with George Brett. Tell him I said you would have to be made a Brigadier General in order that you would have the proper rank senior to all the base commanders."

As for Joe McNarney, he received travel orders, but not to Panama. He was headed for England as Jim Chaney's Chief of Staff in a continuing round of secret American-British military conferences begun in Washington at the end of January. Chaney had been taken from Air Defense to head the Special Observers Group in London. The talks included representatives from the Army and Navy staffs of both countries, and McNarney was one of the four Army members. On the British side, Jack Slessor, whom Tooey Spaatz had found so helpful during his stay in England, was the RAF representative.

At the opening session of the first conference, which was held on January 29, 1941, both Marshall and Stark spoke briefly, cautioned the utmost secrecy, and took no further part in the discussions. All involved knew if word leaked out the result "might well be disastrous." Should it become known that military discussions on joint Anglo-American war planning were going on in secret, Roosevelt might well face impeachment charges. The four-man British delegation wore civilian clothes and were officially designated as "technical advisors" to the British Purchasing Commission.

When the talks ended, on March 29, the plan drawn up was titled ABC-1—American British Conference No. 1—indicating that more conferences were to follow. The plan outlined a joint grand strategy for war on a global scale. Its basic point, agreed on by Marshall and Stark six months previously, was that if the two Allies became involved in a war with both Germany and Japan, the offensive would be against Germany, while a war of attrition would be fought against the Japanese. For the time being, the British war against Germany would be waged by blockade, by intensified bombing, and through subversion and propaganda, in order, as Churchill phrased it, to "set Europe ablaze."

It was also agreed that in a continuing effort to coordinate plans and exchange information, each country would place a military mission in the other's capital, and it was for this that Joe McNarney went to London to assist Chaney, no one seeming to take much note that both were airmen.

Five

Plus Ça Change

The spring of 1941 was a time of heightened motion and promotion within the Army, and in a telegram congratulating his old polo-playing pal George S. Patton on getting a second star, Andrews summed up the outlook: "If international affairs continue as they are going it looks as if you are going to have an opportunity to satisfy some of your bloodthirsty inclinations."

In March the British, after having won several naval victories against the Italians in the Red Sea and the Gulf of Aden, appeared to have the Eastern Mediterranean under control. That single success at sea, however, had been offset by increasing losses of merchant ships and by the threat of General Erwin Rommel's Afrika Korps's eastward advance across Libya all the way to the Egyptian frontier. This, combined with Hitler's swift occupation of the Balkans and Greece with the entrapment and loss of twelve thousand British troops in the latter place, raised strong doubts in the minds of some War Department strategists.

Colonel Truman Smith, of G-2, brought by Marshall to brief Secretary of War Stimson on the situation, described the British losses in Greece and Africa as "the biggest evidence of disastrous interference by the political body of the country in its military strategy since General Halleck in the Civil War."[1] Stimson was shocked by the bluntness of Smith's report and worried about the adverse effect such criticism of Churchill would have on public opinion, should it reach the press. Stimson called Marshall and told him to round up all those officers in G-2 who concurred with Smith's evaluation and warn them not to repeat it. He felt that the success of U.S. policy depended on the preservation of the Churchill government.

This policy was pushing U.S. naval patrols farther out into the Atlantic —eastward to longitude 26 degrees west—which meant that the U.S.

neutrality zone now encompassed Greenland. Admiral Ernest King's Patrol Force, now designated the Atlantic Fleet, was risking encounters with the German Navy in escorting British Lend-Lease convoys. Besides Greenland-Iceland, the Azores and Martinique were slated for possible U.S. occupation.

In the Far East, China had finally been added to the list of Lend-Lease recipients in an effort to speed up the trickle of supplies reaching the Nationalist government of Chiang Kai-shek via the Burma Road. With the acquiescence of the Vichy government, the Japanese were beginning to move into strategic areas of Indochina. Washington and London feared that the next move would be into the Malay Peninsula, against the oil fields of the Dutch East Indies, and possibly into the Philippines.

At home, Roosevelt ordered a massive increase in heavy-bomber production, calling for five hundred planes a months. At the Boeing plant, strikes and slowdowns, said to be inspired by Communist-controlled unions, had their effect.

From where he sat in Hangar Six, Inc., Jack Lapham, an old flying friend of Andrews' from San Antonio, Texas, described the swelling scene as "more hullabaloo, fuss and feathers than you could shake a stick at. As a matter of fact, I believe we would pay little attention to them should a hostile force land on our shores today, being so completely occupied with our own multitudinous bickerings as we are. Lost motion, extravagance, labor troubles and what not are the order of the day. Everyone has a grand time telling everyone else just how it should be done from top to bottom. Methinks I will get myself a job ferrying airplanes, slow ships over long routes, so I can spend my time peacefully in the air where I will not have to listen or see what goes on."

General George C. Marshall described the hectic situation to Andrews: "The staff, and legislation, and British requirements situation present a tremendously complicated task here in Washington. I spend, seemingly, most of my time before committees of Congress or in meetings outside the War Department, all of rather momentous importance. I made a recent quick inspection trip of about 3,000 miles, and I hope to get off to the West Coast in about two weeks. Heretofore, it has been almost impossible for me to get out of Washington. I wish you could see the Army as it is now developing following your earlier struggle with organization. It is an inspiring spectacle."

In spite of a raft of strikes and slowdowns directly hindering aircraft production, Hap Arnold's fight to keep enough of what was produced in order to build U.S. defenses continued—which meant that his running disagreement with the White House continued. Stimson had recommended to Marshall that Arnold visit England, but it was Bob Lovett and John J. McCloy, Assistant Secretary of War, who suggested the April trip to Stimson. They knew Hap's attitude on sharing aircraft production. To see what was going on in Great Britain, to talk with the leaders there, would broaden Arnold's views and it would also get him clear of the presidential doghouse. Matters had come to a climax of sorts in early March, and although the B-17 was still a bone of contention, the central issue remained an ill-defined policy.

On the last day of 1940, Arnold had brought to Stimson the news that the Judge Advocate General, Major General Emory S. Adams, had finally ruled that it would be a violation of the law for U. S. Air Corps instructors to train RAF crews to fly the B-17. Stimson fumed that the decision was niggling nonsense but cooled off when Arnold gave him a solution worked out by Colonel Bob Olds.

A six-man RAF crew would be trained by Trans World Airlines personnel on its four-engine Boeing Stratoliner, an airline version of the B-17. At the same time, other RAF crews would be given transition training on the ground by Air Corps instructors, then fly as observers in the B-17. When the TWA-trained RAF crew was checked out, in about two weeks, it would go to Sacramento to pick up the first B-17C off the Boeing line. That crew would check out the other crews, some of whom would fly their new B-17's to Canada and then on to England.

The British were to get twenty of the thirty-eight Fortresses originally ordered by the Air Corps. The B-17C was an improvement over the B model. Paneled gun positions had replaced bulging side blisters, and a "bathtub turret" under the fuselage now protected the tail. There was more crew armor, and the plane carried six .50-caliber and one .30-caliber machine guns. The payload was eight 600-pound bombs or a variation thereof, and it was Bob Lovett's belief that the B-17 in RAF hands might well change the course of the war.

But as Arnold was later to point out, "These planes were not the Flying Fortresses with their big, spiny tails and turning turrets, bristling with fourteen .50-caliber guns. . . . They had only four, flexible (hand-held) guns for armament, no computing sights, not even any tail guns (that famous stinger), only a gunner lying on his stomach and firing rearward from a slit in the bathtub where the ball-turret would be on later Forts."[2]

The training plan that Olds proposed was scheduled to begin in early January, at about the same time that presidential confidant Harry Hopkins would leave for London. In the belief that Lend-Lease would get through Congress, the purpose of Hopkins' visit was to find out what the British needed. When he came home, in February, he was, if anything, more determined than Henry Morgenthau to give England *all* it requested. Throughout his stay he had sent Roosevelt a voluminous array of details. Upon his return he put them all together in a fourteen-point secret memo. Marshall passed the memo to Arnold for comment, and Arnold came out spitting tacks.

Item eight was representative of the whole. Hopkins wanted the British to have: "The maximum number of B-17C's or D's in addition to the twenty already agreed upon to be sent to England immediately. Planes should be sent complete, ready for immediate operation, including spare parts, bombs and ammunition. [U.S.] crews urgently needed."[3]

This was March, and a small part of Arnold's frustration was manifested in the knowledge that fifteen of the twenty B-17's the RAF had been clamoring to get were still sitting outside the Boeing plant, of no use to anyone because of a seemingly lackadaisical British attitude in getting flight crews to the United States. But it was the overall meaning of Hopkins' shopping list that raised Arnold's hackles. He responded to the demands with a bluntness that did nothing to conceal his anger:

The carrying out of the provisions of this communication will result in—

a. A piecemeal reinforcement of the British by our airplanes and personnel. This piecemeal reinforcement violates the principles so well established by General Pershing during the last war that Americans must fight in American units under American command.

b. It eliminates the present objectives in building up our air force, and it prevents the forming of a striking force and reduces to the vanishing point the low combat strength of this force.

This again emphasizes the constant changes in our objectives due to the diversion of airplanes planned for the equipping and training of our combat units. If also personnel is now to be diverted it is apparent that a decision must be made whether or not the United States is to be a zone of interior to provide airplanes and personnel to maintain or augment British units, or whether an American air force is to be brought into being.

Conclusion: "Unless a definite program for our air force is established and maintained against pressure, the Chief of Staff should not accept the responsibility for the defense of our National interest in the Western Hemisphere."

Arnold bracketed his conclusion with quotation marks apparently to indicate to Marshall that he was prepared to be quoted on it. He went on to say the world situation demanded that the United States have "a modern equipped air force in being" and in a geographic breakdown—Pacific-Central and South America-Atlantic—gave his reasons. Of the last he said: "The Atlantic situation . . . is based upon an intangible condition, that is the possible fall of England. As long as England holds out, the situation is static. However, with the fall of England the entire Eastern seaboard of the United States may be subject to hostile attacks."

In his recommendation he proposed that the fifty-four-combat-group program be immediately expanded to the one hundred-group plan, but "during the critical period of 1941 and continuing so long as the United

States is not actively engaged in the war," he would be willing to back off and "defer implementing in full the approved 54 Group Program and its proposed subsequent expansion. . . ." Attached graphs indicated how this would be accomplished, and he suggested a joint military mission to be convened to determine the number of additional aircraft the British were to be given. Arnold had thrown down the gauntlet, then picked it up again, knowing that if he did not, he might very quickly be out of a job.

Both the list and Arnold's response to it clearly indicated that in the political desire to aid Great Britain, Harry Hopkins was willing to commit U.S. airmen to the conflict while the Administration maintained the country was still at peace. As Arnold saw it, Hopkins' support for England was blind to U.S. military reality, as was Roosevelt's, and he was bold enough to say so even though he knew he must again compromise.

Arnold was not alone in his stand. The War Plans Division, headed by Brigadier General Leonard T. Gerow, concurred in his evaluation of Harry Hopkins' secret "Memo for the President." How Roosevelt and Hopkins viewed the detailed response from the War Plans Division, Hap Arnold did not know. What he did know was that FDR objected very strenuously to his attitude. Roosevelt, he was told, took extreme umbrage over his position on the need for the United States to have an air force in being. More probably he had been aroused by Arnold's implicit criticism of the all-out policy underlying the Hopkins memo. Certainly Hopkins saw it that way, and as Arnold put it, he "expressed himself in no uncertain terms about me regarding these recommendations."

Arnold had always considered Hopkins his *amicus curiae* at the White House, but for the record he wanted it known that he, as a Deputy Chief of Staff, must make recommendations to Marshall as he saw them. If he could not, he said, he would be of little or no value to the Chief of Staff.

His patience was further tried by British action on item 10 of Hopkins' list, calling for "at least 5 additional civilian flying training schools, completely equipped." He was writing his evaluation for Marshall when an agreement was reached with RAF representatives on the additional schools. Nearly two weeks passed and there was no move by the British to follow through. Arnold mentioned this to Stimson, who got on the phone to Arthur Purvis, Chief of the British Purchasing Mission. The next morning, Air Commodore Pirie came to call on Hap. He explained the problem was economic—a question of money. They were determining what part of their training program could be paid for with Lend-Lease funds.

Arnold suggested the only way to do that was to get a cost breakdown from the schools in question. He offered to have representatives of the two schools that could be operating within a month in his office the next day.

No, declined Pirie, he would prefer to do his inquiring by personal interview with a representative in Miami on Sunday, some four days thence.

"That," noted Arnold privately, "is what I call speed!"

The anti-Administration forces in Congress could delay military expansion programs, but they could not stop them. At the moment it was just one more incident to add to Arnold's impatience. His departure for London in early April turned out to be a good move from every point of view on both sides of the Atlantic. During the brief two weeks he spent in England he spoke with all the major leaders of the British Government—civilian and military, air, land, and sea, even the King. While in London, at the Dorchester, he and his aide, Major Elwood "Pete" Quesada, experienced some of the Luftwaffe's heaviest strikes against the city. During the height of the bombing he and Quesada would go up on the roof of the hotel. There they would watch fires turning the night sky an ugly red, shrapnel from barking antiaircraft batteries falling like rain about them. Like Spaatz and other Air Corps observers before them, they visited RAF bomber bases to watch the missions launched and then, in the dawn's light, talk with returning crews. Quesada, without informing his boss, made arrangements to go on a raid, and when Hap learned about the plan he gave his aide holy hell. "Goddammit," he fumed, "you'll get over there, and you'll get shot down, and you'll go blabbing your big mouth all over Germany what I'm over here for, and you'll create a helluva mess for everybody. You just mind your own business!"

What he was over for, among other things, was to offer one third of all U. S. Air Corps flying schools, equipped with planes and instructors, to train RAF airmen. It was Tooey Spaatz who had conceived the idea, the previous September, while talking with Jack Slessor. Harry Hopkins' recent winter visit revived and expanded the idea, and by spring it was presidential policy, brought by Arnold as a gift on Easter Sunday. His additional offer—to have U.S. crews take over the operation of a transatlantic ferry route via Greenland and Iceland—was also welcomed by the RAF, which could not spare personnel for the undertaking, vital as it was.

It was clear to Arnold that the British leadership, including Churchill and Beaverbrook, with whom he had met, was out to make a convert of him. Now that he was on the scene, Arnold saw that the war was being fought almost exclusively in the air, with tremendous demands being made on the RAF to aid the Army and the Navy while conducting operations against the Continent. He also could better understand the demands being made in Washington, particularly when finding himself a potential target for German bombers overhead.

Yet gentle but persistent RAF efforts to sell him on the strategy of night, rather than daylight, operations got nowhere. He and Mike Scanlon, who was returning home with him to head air intelligence, believed the B-17 and B-24 were far superior to any British bomber they saw. Bomber Command's losses were an added convincer. There were crews for only about half the seven hundred available aircraft, and the Command was losing about two hundred men a week, many due to weather and night landings. It was no wonder Arnold had a higher regard for the German bombing efforts than he did for those of the RAF, but he did not think much of either. Both used area tactics instead of precision targeting, and neither employed the mass firepower of close-formation flying. Another reason for Arnold's negative view of RAF tactics was their decision not to use the Sperry bombsight, since it required too long a straight-and-level run to the release point.

He saw the German bombing of London and the port cities as "simply devastating." The havoc created by one four-thousand-pounder was horrendous: thirty-five houses completely destroyed, over three hundred more severely damaged. Worse, he found the bombing reduced production by one third in many instances. He concluded that "England was going to have a helluva time supplying her own home forces with the seaports being knocked out of commission faster than ever before." Most of the leaders with whom he spoke admitted the Germans probably could establish bridgeheads on the English coast but would not be able to hold them. The RAF, at least by day, controlled the skies above.

When Arnold left England for home on April 27, he recognized that the British were fighting for their very lives. Their courage and morale, he saw, were magnificent, not just that of the leadership but that of the people. As Ben Kelsey had observed earlier, without popular support there could be no chance at all to preserve the British Isles in the immediate future. In the meantime, he believed England could do no more than try to stand off the preponderant German forces. That would be the way of it in Britain and in the Mediterranean and in Africa for a long time to come.

One bright note was that through Beaverbrook's ruthless drive, the RAF had 100 percent fighter replacements, and its fighters, day and night, were superior aircraft. Still, Arnold saw that the overall picture was very much touch and go. The figures painted a grim picture: food growing short, metal for aircraft growing short, huge quantities of supplies lost at sea through submarine and air attack and in the bombing of port warehouses, Germany with 270 divisions, eighteen of them armored, and England with forty-six and not one fully equipped with armor, and the Luftwaffe with a disputed figure of between five and twelve thousand first-line planes.* Even the British military high command did not foresee going on the offensive until 1943, and from close up such a projection looked to be in the nature of a far distant dream that, like the end of the rainbow, keeps moving away.

When Hap Arnold arrived home, he promptly gave his staff a confidential and somber appraisal of Great Britain's uncertain future. Ger-

---

* British Intelligence, with the aid of ULTRA, gave the lower figure. Col. Arthur Vanaman, U.S. air attaché in Berlin, gave the larger, but Vanaman was complaining about not being able to get accurate information.

many's immediate intentions, he thought, were to deny the English their
sea bases and to take over the Mediterranean and the Near East. His only
mention of a possible German move eastward was to relate that his British hosts had told him Hitler could take the Ukraine from Russia any
time he chose, and that Stalin would probably do no more than make a
feeble protest.

One thing Arnold wanted to make clear to his listeners. In first reporting on his visit to Cordell Hull, the Secretary of State had cautioned him
not to let "this dreary picture get out to the public through the press."
Said Arnold to the assembled, "Don't anybody quote me as saying that
England was going to get licked, because I haven't said any such a goddamned thing!"

As a result of what he had seen (his talks with RAF crews and his examination of their strike photos), the long-held Douhet-Mitchell-
Trenchard theory of bombardment was reinforced in his thinking. "My
discussions in England with [Air Chief Marshal Charles 'Peter'] Portal
and Churchill and the others left me with the impression that by air alone
we might bring Germany to her knees, that it might be unnecessary for
the ground forces to make a landing," Arnold wrote. "Certainly destruction by air power could make a landing of ground forces possible. The
Navy could insure the existence of England but air power and air power
alone could carry the war home to central Germany, break down her morale and take away from her the things essential to combat."[4]

It was not just the damage he viewed that convinced Arnold of the
rightness of the theory but also his ability to look ahead. If a mass of several hundred bombers could wreak such havoc on London, what would a
fleet of one thousand or more do to it, particularly if they were carrying
two or three times the amount of explosives, and they were dropping them
on industrial targets by daylight? "Give us one hundred heavy bombers a
month," one air commander told him, "and we'll lick Germany." Arnold
believed that, whatever the number, it could be done. He returned more
amenable to supplying the British with what they needed, but no less determined to build U.S. air power.

On May 6, the day after he briefed his own staff, he was summoned to
brief the President. They met in the White House library. Present were
Hull, Morgenthau, Stimson, Knox, Hopkins, Marshall, and Stark. Roosevelt started the conference by asking Hap to give an account of his trip.
Arnold delivered "an admirable statement—quick, clear and very observing, so much so that when he got through, the President said that was the
best account he'd yet received from anyone of the situation in Great Britain," so reported Stimson.

Privately the Secretary of War noted that he was very glad of this, "because the President has been rather down on Arnold, and I had several

times told him that he was wrong—that Arnold was a fine officer—and I think he proved it."[5]

Stimson claimed he did not know what caused the original enmity, but he knew that Morgenthau was no friend of Hap's either. Now he hoped that Arnold's fine presentation of the British situation had cleared the air. And, in fact, as far as Roosevelt was concerned, it did just that.

* * *

It was shortly after Arnold had made this very positive impression upon the President that his rank of permanent major general was confirmed. In a congratulatory letter, Andrews commented, "It was a good way to clear up what must have been an awkward situation, both to you and George Brett." Hap replied wryly, "The awkward situation hasn't completely cleared up yet, but I still have hopes that it will."

What both were referring to was the yet unresolved clumsy command and staff organization of the air arm. Even if a permanent major general, who was Chief of the Air Corps, was in a firmer position than a temporary lieutenant general (Emmons), there was something wrong with a system that permitted the inequity to be established in the first place. A confusing system of rank, however, was only the top of the smoldering volcano. What lay beneath, now starting to boil up again, was the issue of autonomy: the formation of a separate air force.

Back in February, on a gray Monday, Secretary of War Stimson had sat down with advisers Bob Lovett, John McCloy, and Arthur Palme. They were determined to give the Air Corps and GHQ Air Force a more cohesive relationship and to offer both a greater degree of procurement and tactical independence.

Lovett was in favor of a separate air force, but not at this particular time of upheaval.[6] It was he who had convinced Stimson of the great need for air reorganization, not just to head off the separatists within the Air Corps, the Congress, and the press, but also because he recognized that as things stood, the present organization would never do in times of crisis or war.

The division of authority between the Air Corps and the Combat Air Force had actually been compounded the previous fall with the formation of a triumvirate: Arnold, Emmons, and Brett. Supposedly Arnold spoke for both in the councils of the mighty. Further, the relationship between Brett's command, concerned with training and procurement, and Emmons', concerned with combat operations and under General Staff direction, was as bowlegged as Andrews had termed it five years earlier.

Stimson, having read lengthy memos on RAF organization and operations—one from Chaney, which he found very valuable—understood what Lovett was anxious to attempt. He wrote that "air warfare involved not merely a new auxiliary weapon for the ground troops but it is becom-

ing clear now that it involves independent action quite divorced from land
and sea. The difficulty is finding just how far to go in freeing them but it
seems to be my job now to try to solve that. It is a very big one."[7]

The Secretary of War saw the situation clearly, but he was wrong in his
belief that Marshall, like those around him, remained wedded to the
theory that air power was "merely an auxiliary force." Marshall was too
perceptive to accept that strongly cemented theory, which the Navy was
determined to sell.

Admiral Ernie King, long a foe of Army air power, convinced the air-
minded that he had been at sea too long when he was quoted as saying,
"Air objectives are so nearly non-existent that they are admitted to be
remote of attaining even by the ultra enthusiasts of air power. . . ."

He was seconded by Admiral Clark H. Woodward, who boldly maintained: "A plane will never be able to sink a battleship. The deck armor
of a battleship can easily resist the impact of the most destructive bomb.
Do not misunderstand me: we do think that the air arm is a very efficient
and very necessary adjunct, but it is only an adjunct to the Navy, and it
can do nothing else. Air ships can never win a war; they can never win a
battle."

Unfortunately, as Stimson, Lovett, and others in the War Department
knew, old military viewpoints die hard. Whether proclaimed by admirals
or subscribed to by generals, it was difficult to change such a fixed attitude and bring much-needed reform.

A few days later, military expert Frederick Palmer dropped in to see
Stimson. He, too, was studying the situation, interested in contributing
constructive suggestions. Stimson asked Marshall and Lovett to join them,
and Lovett offered his appraisal of where the problems lay in the present
Air Corps structure. There was no doubt in Stimson's mind that Lovett's
penetrating analysis made a strong impression on Marshall, for the General, in response, gave a detailed background on the issue. He knew the
differing views on air autonomy, the trials and errors made. He knew
what was at stake, and he knew there must be change. The question was,
How?

The Plans Division, under Tooey Spaatz, was also at work on the jig-
saw of reorganization. Leader in this effort was a newly arrived Reserve
Captain, Guido R. Perera. A graduate of Harvard Law School, Perera
found working in an office with Spaatz and Olds, Santy Fairchild and Ted
Curtis a stimulating yet relaxed experience. Bull sessions over lunch at the
Allies Inn with people like Hoyt Vandenberg, Fred Anderson, Ken Walker,
Possum Hansell, and Larry Kuter made him realize that his previous ideas
about the smallness of military minds were far off the mark. He soon
realized, in the office or out of it, over drinks or tennis, that he was working with a unique group of professionals whose unselfishness and dedica-

tion were seldom equaled in the civilian world. The root of the problem, he saw, was how to give the air arm the independence it needed to prepare for war and still remain part of the Army.

Assigned to A-1 Personnel under the affable Major Byron E. "Hungry" Gates, Perera began a study of previous Air Corps legislation. He then sold Gates on the idea of writing a complete legislative history of the Air Corps. Gates showed the result to Santy Fairchild, who passed it to Spaatz. Both were impressed, and Spaatz asked Perera to become his confidential adviser in dealing with the legal and administrative red tape by which his Plans Division was still bound to the General Staff. The question foremost in Perera's mind was, "How could air power come into its own when it did not participate adequately in decisions involving the allocation of national resources or strategic priorities and when all its policies were subject to review and approval by what were described as unsympathetic non-Air Corps superiors?" [8]

He believed the answer lay in Army Regulation 95-5, which encompassed the role of the Air Corps in the Army. Although a regulation could not go beyond the underlying law governing it, Perera felt that AR 95-5 could be modified and still remain within the bounds of the law, giving the Air Corps broader latitude in which to operate. Both Spaatz and Fairchild were quick to agree, and apparently took the thought to Arnold and Lovett, and thence to Marshall. It was Larry Kuter who informed Perera that Marshall favored giving the Air Corps more autonomy in spite of War Department hostility to the idea, and that the General was being kept apprised of the need to rewrite the regulation.

These actions within the Plans Division were going forward at the time Lovett and his staff were wrestling with the same issue. Finally, on May 7, Marshall directed that Arnold revise AR 95-5 to define a command structure that would provide the autonomy necessary to assure proper procurement, training, and operations, and to include a doctrine of strategic bombardment. Spaatz and staff were excited by the prospect, and Perera sat down to make the revisions, knowing that any new air legislation in Congress was going to bring on a donnybrook. The forces seeking complete separation would be there to make their demands.

He was absolutely right, and the leader behind the scenes was Hugh Knerr. Back in the fall of 1938, after he was relieved as Andrews' Chief of Staff and exiled to Fort Sam Houston, Knerr sent a wry letter to Andrews from the base hospital saying, "The hospital here wanted to know if I wanted to retire. Said I had enough arthritis if I did. I said no, so I guess I'll escape. I had in mind also that I'd hold on to this job in case you did want it. So keep in mind if they do you in and don't take care of you properly you can say positively this place is open."

Andrews replied: "It's fine of you to hang on to that job down there for me. I don't know whether I will be expected to have anything as good as that. I have no information from any source as to what my future is to be."

By January of 1939, Knerr was gone from the service and, indeed, Andrews was soon to be assigned to the vacant post, but Knerr continued to work behind the scenes for air independence. There can be little doubt that he was the principal driving force in coalescing public and congressional opinion favoring a separate air force. He was in no position to know of the joint efforts going on in Lovett's office and the Air Corps Plans Division, but knowing would not have changed his mind. Separation was not revision, not compromise.

On a far more covert level, Knerr was out to help Andrews in the organizational difficulties of creating a Caribbean air force worthy of the name. Unable to get an appointment with Marshall, he called on Hap Arnold just prior to Arnold's departure for England. In the course of their discussion, Knerr suggested that the best way to solve Andrews' problem with Van Voorhis was to put Andrews in command of the whole works: ground and air, Panama Canal, Puerto Rican and Trinidad departments.

Much to Knerr's surprise, Arnold confided that was exactly the plan. It couldn't be done at once, because of assignment changes presently going on, but when Van Voorhis was retired, in August, it would happen. In itself this was momentous news, for no airman had ever been given command of both ground and air forces. Aside from its being a signal of Marshall's confidence in Andrews, Knerr should have recognized the full meaning of Arnold's news. Although he passed it to Andrews, most probably he did not accept its validity. He didn't trust Hap, always seeing an ulterior motive in what Arnold said and did. Besides, even if the intention was there, it had nothing really to do with an independent air force.

Knerr continued his behind-the-scenes agitation. He wrote articles and supplied background information for major newspapers and magazines, to organizations such as the American Legion, and to contacts with connections in Congress. His system was to submit the material, which would then be rewritten by staffers and published under some one else's name.

As he was to tell Andrews later, "This time I am trying to get a close personal friend of FDR behind it with the idea that he will be made the Secretary of Air. That is where we fell down before. We had no friend at court to flatter, etc. while grinding his own axe. Dirty business, and I hate it but I have found that it is by such means that things are accomplished now in our unadmitted democratic dictatorship."

Apparently Knerr's choice was Fiorello La Guardia, New York City's popular mayor. The plan for a separate air force with La Guardia as Secretary of Aviation was spelled out in a New York *Daily Mirror* series titled The Mirror's Fight for Air Power, under the byline of Reagan "Tex" McCrary.

In McCrary's articles and in its editorials, the *Mirror,* joined by other newspapers throughout the country, kept up a drumfire for air power managed by airmen.

Joining the fight with Knerr, speaking and writing openly, was Alexander P. de Seversky. The former aircraft designer corresponded with Andrews, sending copies of his provocative articles that pushed air independence and damned the Navy. Andrews considered "Sasha's" piece in the June *Mercury,* "The Twilight of Sea Power," "splendid." But situated where he was, involved in trying to establish a smoothly functioning organization with its far-flung and disparate bases in various stages of building, he had not been aware of the campaign for independence or the mention of his name in it. At least not until Knerr confided to him: "In order that you may not be taken by surprise I better let you know that the old ghost of a separate air arm is walking again. I have been carrying on a quiet campaign for the past year through various agencies, writers, etc., and the thing is rapidly coming to a head. Hearings will start again on the 23rd [June] (not yet revealed) and the material I prepared for the '37 effort is being used as a starter. . . ."[9]

To Knerr, the biggest problem was going to be finding a way to insure that Andrews and not Arnold would become "the first air marshal." The only way it could be done would be to discredit Arnold's leadership while showing that it had been Andrews who fought "for the things that the present war has proven to be essential for victory." But Knerr couldn't bring himself to that, even though he felt that Arnold had not lifted a finger when he needed his aid. Smear tactics, he knew, might discredit the whole movement, because he could be accused of a personal motive. "So looks like the old slicker is sitting pretty again," he observed, and then added, "You better dust off your old ideas and see if they are any good—you may be called on by some politician. When this is out of the way I'll probably look like the pigeon that flew into a badminton game."

Knerr was wrong on all counts. Roosevelt, hearing that a joint Senate-House resolution to create an independent air force was making the rounds and in danger of passing if brought to a vote, moved to block it. On Thursday, June 12, Stimson received a telephone call from Harry Hopkins, who said he was calling for the President. Hopkins wanted the Secretary of War to contact House Speaker Sam Rayburn and give him all the arguments against passage of the resolution. If necessary, he was to tell Rayburn that Roosevelt was personally against an air force independent of the Army and Navy.

Stimson got in touch with Marshall first and gave him the news. Where was the reorganization plan begun four months ago? Marshall immediately contacted Arnold. Lovett was informed, and Spaatz produced Perera's revision of AR 95-5. In a single day the work on reorganization that Stimson noted had been "progressing gradually but very slowly" was completed, and as the Secretary of War wrote, it "gave me something with which to meet the threat of an independent Air Corps created by legislation. . . ."[10]

Finally, Stimson called Rayburn and told him that if there was any danger of a bill's passage he wanted to see him. The Speaker didn't think there was much danger. He hadn't heard of any agitation in the House, and he himself was against it.

The following day, Andrew May, Chairman of the House Military Affairs Committee, called Stimson to say that he concurred with Rayburn. He saw little chance of a bill for a separate and independent air force being forced through the House. Greatly relieved, Stimson prepared to hold a press conference and announce the structure of the newly organized Army Air Forces.

Arnold didn't think things were going all that smoothly. That weekend, he wrote Eaker, "we are going through a crisis, trying to find out how the Air Corps should be organized. Perhaps this one will last for a while and we will have no more growing pains until we can get well started toward completing our organization."

None of this was known to Knerr or to Andrews, whose efforts on Knerr's behalf were confined to getting him back into the service and under his command as a brigadier general. Brett, who appeared to be getting more rigid in his outlook, had already turned down the suggestion that Knerr return to duty with the rank of brigadier. Andrews was continuing to argue the case through the mails when he received Knerr's confession of intrigue. He responded promptly on June 23.

> I am very much interested to hear that the separate Air Corps idea is up again. I still think the recommendation that I made to Craig, when we thought we were going to have hearings before the Military Affairs Committee under Lister Hill's Chairmanship, was essentially the correct one, but perhaps you are right that it will be necessary to go the whole way to give aviation the prestige and power to develop it as our chief line of defense, which I am convinced it will ultimately become, when technical development is not throttled as it has been in the past. I have not been doing much thinking lately on the question of higher organization of air power in our country, except to retain the conviction, which I have long held, that it cannot be developed under an organization which considers it an adjunct of surface forces; even with a man as broad-minded and farseeing as Marshall at the head of the Army. No matter how progressive Marshall may be himself, the rank and file of the Army has not changed materially. I will take your suggestion and begin dusting off my ideas of present requirements. . . .

Having recently been G-3 and now having to deal with the likes of Van Voorhis, who saw the Caribbean Defense Command as an adjunct to the

Panama Canal Department in the same way that he saw his air units as an adjunct to his artillery, Andrews was not saying anything that Knerr would not immediately second. However, on the matter of command, Andrews did offer a more perceptive and equitable point of view. "With reference to your dilemma about HHA [Henry H. Arnold]," he wrote, "don't let that influence you in any degree. Arnold is capable all right. The main objective now is to get started. He is probably the best man available to head it up. He is a much better politician than you or I, as he very clearly demonstrated when he sat back and let us butt our heads against a stone wall and kept in the background. Whoever handles this thing initially has got to be a good politician."[11]

By the time of Andrews' reply to Knerr, the politicians, with FDR in the background, had outflanked the independence forces in and out of the Air Corps led by Hugh Knerr, who was also in the background. On the nineteenth, Stimson had canceled his press conference, knowing the question of an independent air arm would be raised by reporters. The issue had already been leaked by military writer Hanson Baldwin. To the Secretary of War's way of thinking, the matter was being solved in an evolutionary rather than a revolutionary manner. At the moment, however, not all the i's had been dotted and t's crossed. The next day, joined by Lovett, he sent messages to the chairmen of both the House and Senate Military Affairs committees to block any moves taking place for legislation on a separate air force. And on that same day, the War Department released its newest revision of AR 95-5.

The new regulation made several vitally important changes. It created the Army Air Forces, and in so doing put both the Air Corps and the Air Combat Command—the new name for GHQ Air Force—under the AAF, with Arnold as Chief. It was his job to supply policy and plans for all Army aviation. To assist him and to avoid some of the previous War Department control and dictation, he was given his own policy-making staff. He was answerable to Marshall, and in retaining his position of Deputy Chief of Staff he maintained his place as one among equals on the General Staff, while Brett and Emmons in turn reported to him.

In the seven-page regulation setting down the AAF structure, there was much that pleased Arnold and others who thought as he did. Air leaders would no longer be treated as second-class citizens by the War Department. Their organization would have a direct line of command from a single head and not have its combat arm directed by the General Staff or its training policies determined by one branch (the Air Corps) while its combat units were left out of the matter. The changes did not grant autonomy, but they afforded much greater freedom of action to Arnold and his staff. There were still lumps and bumps in the new AR 95-5, but the reorganization was the first real forward movement in over five years. The impetus for the change had been supplied by Stimson, Lovett, and Marshall. Billy Mitchell wouldn't have liked it, but Hap Arnold, Tooey Spaatz, and Ira Eaker were pleased.

Although there was no way of measuring its impact on the reorganization issue, Arnold and Eaker's book *This Winged World,* published in January, had some influence on public opinion. Soon after publication, Eaker had written to Arnold, "There have been several newspaper stories that a Congressional investigation was coming up on the Separate Air Force with you as the star witness. Your statements in the book were quoted on that subject in most of the news stories."

"The general impression among the military personnel here," wrote Arnold to his coauthor, "is that the book is well written and covers the field quite well—further, that we did not err on the side of superenthusiastic support of air to the disadvantage of everything else."

Replied Eaker, "Several people have told me or written to me that the lack of animus or spleen and the calmness and reserve with which we discussed controversial topics such as a separate Air Force is one of the strongest things in the book. I agree that our dedication and foreword disarm those who would normally be critical of it. I still think at least ten thousand copies will sell before July first."

The two had played the volatile question of independence coolly, hewing to a straight and level course despite the growing turbulence. Championing neither side, explaining both, their position helped to support the reorganization.

Others were not so calm about it, some of them vocal in their denunciation of what they saw as yet another War Department "trick." Seversky was quoted in the New York *Post* proclaiming before the New York Advertising Club: "In a panicky attempt to head off the emancipation of air power, to prevent a showdown, certain officials in our War Department have just indicated that they intend to make the Army Air Corps semi-independent. Such half measures in a time of total emergency are an insult to the intelligence of the American people, who I feel will not take the insult lying down."

Seversky's main criticisms were that military aviation would remain artificially split between the Army and the Navy, and that would mean no overall command and air strategy. He also believed the critical function of procurement would still be in the hands of those whom he blamed for the lack of air power.

Knerr, in informing Andrews that he had been collaborating with Seversky, told him that he was the author of the bill for a fully independent air force that Seversky was going to submit to the McCarran hearings.† "Little chance," he added, "because Arnold beat us to it with the

† Senator Patrick A. McCarran, Democrat of Nevada, Chairman of the Senate Military Affairs Committee.

enclosed." Andrews' reaction to AR 95-5, a copy of which Knerr had sent him, was neither shrill nor bitter.

> The new organization of the Air Forces of the United States Army [he wrote Knerr] is, of course, a step in the right direction, but it does not go far enough as it still leaves too much influence on the development of air power in the hands of ground-thinking men. This is particularly true of technical development of equipment in which I am afraid that the support idea of Air Forces rather than their strategic abilities will still dominate. Although I believe that Marshall, as long as he remains Chief of Staff, is progressive and farsighted enough to be more influenced by Arnold's recommendations than he would be by the recommendations of his General Staff, I still believe that the organization I proposed is the correct one and that the next step will be to that organization. . . .

Andrews was not the sort to be influenced by prejudice or rumors. Moreover, Spaatz had written about getting some transports down to Panama "for the use of Infantry in parachute and airborne training." The Service Organization they were planning to set up, he said, was similar to the one Andrews previously proposed. And as for AR 95-5, they were attempting to clarify the regulations, and the first step was the formation of an Air Staff, using the Plans Division and adding more officers. He hoped they could get shaken down into a smoothly working outfit within a month or so.

It was not difficult to see why Hugh Knerr's attempt failed to bring about from the outside what airmen like Knerr himself had been trying to accomplish for over twenty years from the inside. He was quixotic enough to take on all comers, but this time more than the windmill of a powerful administration defeated him. There was no legislative spokesman who could command attention and public support on the issue, no one who could override Roosevelt's opposition. Numbers counted: guns, planes, men. The question of an independent air force, in spite of wide, often colored journalistic support, was seen by many legislators as simply a new source of turmoil and expense. Airmen like Larry Kuter, Possum Hansell, and Santy Fairchild, long champions of separation, now working in the Washington meat grinder, could see the gigantic complication an independent air arm would present.

At root, there simply were not enough trained officers and noncoms to staff a separate air force, or even, for that matter, an air force that could still depend on the Army for communications, ordnance, supply, and a host of other support services. More, they trusted Marshall, saw what he was doing, and were willing to go along, knowing that AR 95-5 was not the whole loaf but a good piece of it to sustain them for now.

Amid the communications filtering down to Panama on the creation of the new Army Air Forces, none was of more interest to Andrews than word from Arnold. Hap had written his congratulations to Andy on becoming Caribbean Defense Commander, and Andrews had responded in kind, also thanking him for arranging for his son Allen's flight to the Zone so the family could have a brief reunion. In his reply, Arnold spoke confidentially:

> With regard to the new organization, I have hopes it will prove to be a success. If it is not a success, all I can say is, God help the Air Corps because the whole entire responsibility for Air Corps preparation is now on our shoulders and in our laps. The General Staff can no longer be blamed and, incidentally, as far as I can see, the Air Corps future in Panama and in the Caribbean area is in your lap and you can't blame the General Staff for anything that happens down there.
>
> The Chief of Staff has been with me 100 percent in creating this new organization. It is not a separate Air Corps, but we are no longer the fifth wheel of a wagon. We have stepped up in importance and in responsibilities in accordance with our value in national defense. Someday—who knows—we may have a separate Air Corps. I have always said it is bound to come but I also say that right now is not the time for it, certainly not in the midst of such an expansion program as we have.

Arnold phrased his explanation to Ira Eaker in a somewhat different syntax but stressing the same conclusion:

> At the present time there are no steps towards a separate promotion list. Our budget is prepared, etc., under the Air Corps budget, and the Deputy Chief of Staff for Air [Arnold] has the final say before it gets to the Secretary of War.
>
> Taking everything into consideration, it looks to be a very sensible thing to let the separate air force drop at this particular moment because, frankly, we are having so much difficulty in completing our expanded air organization that I don't know what we would do were we to try to take on a separate air force at this time.

There was another change in the wind, almost as far-reaching as the new regulation. Andrews had been selected to represent the United States at Argentina's Independence Day celebration when Roosevelt and Stimson decided that General Marshall could not be spared to make the trip. When Andrews returned from the nine-day visit, in mid-July, he was informed that he was to succeed Van Voorhis as commander of the Caribbean defenses. What Arnold had confided to Hugh Knerr several months before had come to pass.

Andrews believed that Arnold's influence was decisive in his appointment to command the Caribbean Theater, and he told him so. There was no doubt that Arnold was all in favor of the Chief of Staff's dramatic decision, but it was Marshall who made it. Neither the public nor the politicians could appreciate the psychological impact the appointment had on military traditionalists. It had been shock enough to make an airman G-3. Now this same airman was to take command of ground and air forces in a vast and strategic theater. It was a signal honor and a huge responsibility.

It would be natural for a Hugh Knerr or a Jan Howard to suspect that in spite of Andrews' capabilities, some part of Marshall's decision and Arnold's approval to give him command of the Caribbean and the defense of the Canal was to keep him away from Washington and the forces supporting a separate air force, as the newspapers indicated. They would have been wrong.

Back in January, Marshall was talking with a friend, Colonel G. de Freest Larner. The subject was unity of command and how it might apply to possible theaters of operation. Marshall brought up the Canal Zone and Andrews. He told Larner that he had first picked the airman to take on the Army's most important training assignment as G-3 and next sent him to Panama purposely so that he could place Andrews in a position of command when the time and the need came.

In Marshall's thinking, the time and the need were now.

Six

Everything Going Hellward

In the summer of 1941, events crowded in on events in a rising tempo.

After crushing Balkan and Greek resistance and conquering Crete in a costly airborne campaign, Hitler hurled his legions, 164 divisions strong, along a two thousand-mile front against the unprepared forces of his erstwhile Soviet ally. He chose June 22, the anniversary of Napoleon's ill-fated Russian campaign, to launch his own. The Comintern faithful in the United States, who for two years had preached and practiced the Moscow line of isolationism and antimilitarism, tacked neatly around and became champions of anti-Fascism. Hap Arnold could stop worrying about Communist-inspired strikes and slowdowns riddling the aircraft and allied industries.

In England, the news of the German attack on the U.S.S.R., spearheaded by a force of thirteen hundred bombers and fighters, was met with a sigh of relief. At least for now the year-long threat of invasion was gone, and with it the nightly air raids had dwindled away. A week before Hitler struck, Churchill sent a message to Roosevelt forecasting the thrust and stating, "Should this new war break out, we shall, of course, give all encouragement and any help we can spare to the Russians, following the principle that Hitler is the foe we have to beat."[1] Or, as he was to say later in a more colorful analogy, "If Hitler invaded Hell I would make at least a favorable mention of the Devil in the House of Commons."

John G. Winant, who replaced Joseph Kennedy as U. S. Ambassador the previous fall, was the Prime Minister's houseguest the weekend the German blow fell on the Soviet Union, and he brought with him Roosevelt's reply that, should the attack come, he would immediately support publicly "any announcement Churchill might make, welcoming Russia as an ally." The British leader spoke on the BBC that Sunday evening, announcing his government's reaction to the dramatic new development, making it clear that he had always been opposed to "the foul baboonery of Bolshevism" but in this case. . . . Almost at once, the British Communist Party, whose line had been anti-war and anti-imperialism, swung around like its American counterpart and began calling for a second front.

In the Atlantic, since the passage of Lend-Lease, tension had been building. Roosevelt made it clear that American warships were not escorting British and Allied convoys. They were, he admitted, acting as scouts and alerting convoys to the movement of German ships, and in so doing patrolling farther and farther eastward, into waters Hitler claimed as a blockaded area and therefore subject to attack. Even though the German dictator had given orders to his U-boat captains not to fire on U.S. naval vessels unless first fired upon, it was obvious to the Navy Department and those close to the scene that someone was going to pull the trigger, and soon.[2]

Against such a possibility, Secretaries Stimson and Knox had for some months been trying to prevail on Roosevelt to shift a large portion of the Fleet from the Pacific to the Atlantic. The President kept weather-vaning on the decision. He had finally given the go-ahead in early April. But then came the jarring announcement that the U.S.S.R. and Japan had signed a five-year neutrality pact, and he felt compelled to rescind the order, much to the disgruntlement of Stimson and Knox. In May he compromised on the number of ships to be transferred, and in the end, about 25 percent of the Pacific force joined the Atlantic Fleet. The ships consisted of three battlewagons, the aircraft carrier *Wasp,* and an assortment of smaller vessels. Search planes on the *Wasp* carried only smoke bombs.

At the end of May, a great sea battle took place southeast of Greenland when the German battleship *Bismarck* was sunk in a three-day running encounter with the planes and ships of a superior Royal Navy task force. Unknown to the American public, the *Bismarck,* which had eluded its pursuers after sinking the cruiser HMS *Hood,* was spotted by a PBY of British Coastal Command flown by U. S. Navy Ensign Leonard Smith.

A few days before the *Bismarck* went down, so did the U.S. merchant ship *Robin Moor.* It was sunk without loss of life by the German submarine U-69. The forty-six passengers and crewmen were rescued in two widely separated groups off the coast of Brazil and off Cape Town, South Africa, in early June. For the first time in the war an unarmed American ship was the victim of hostile attack.

At this juncture, Roosevelt, in a "fireside chat" to the American public, declared an "unlimited national emergency." In 1939, five days after the war began, he had announced a "limited national emergency." The subsequent move greatly increased his power. He ordered all German consulates in the United States closed. Axis-held funds were frozen, and in a warlike message to Congress over the sinking of the *Robin Moor,* he declared, "We are not yielding and we do not propose to yield." Privately, he informed Admiral Stark he wanted Iceland occupied by U.S. marines, and on the seventh of July the first marines landed, relieving the British garrison, which was badly needed elsewhere. Agreement for this move had been reached at the ABC-1 conference, in January, and Roosevelt's action, though long delayed, was in no small part the result of pressure applied by Churchill, Stimson, and Knox.[3]

The President's explanation for this not unexpected move was that Iceland was now in the sphere of U.S. influence. In German hands it would pose an unacceptable threat by sea and air to American shipping carrying badly needed supplies to England. Furthermore, marines were not draftees; they were volunteers. According to the polls, a majority of the public supported the decision, but the people of Iceland were not all that happy to find themselves caught in a potential nutcracker.

Roosevelt next announced an even bolder step—although later he drew back on it somewhat. U.S. naval ships, he said, would begin escorting convoys of "any nationality which may join such U.S. or Icelandic-flag convoys between U.S. ports and bases in Iceland." This stepped-up action was an act of undeclared war (no less so than flying combat aircraft from the United States to Great Britain and to Africa by Air Corps and civilian crews). However, Hitler wanted no problem with the United States until he had destroyed the Russian bear. He ordered that his Commander-in-Chief of naval forces, Admiral Erich Raeder, instruct angry submarine captains to avoid contact with U.S. ships.

In the Pacific, the building tension was no less. The April neutrality pact between the U.S.S.R. and Japan was viewed as a blessing in both capitals. Both felt the agreement left their mutually troubled back doors a bit more secure, the Japanese so they could extend their reach southward, and Stalin so he could concentrate on placating his German ally.

When Hitler struck, in June, he sought without success to persuade the Japanese to break their pact with Stalin and attack also. At the time Admiral King was preparing to land marines in Iceland, a secret meeting of Emperor Hirohito's government under Prime Minister Konoye was convened. Tokyo decided to begin an advance "into the southern region"—southern China, French Indochina, Thailand—all aimed toward "the establishment of the Greater East Asia Co-prosperity Sphere and world peace no matter what international developments took place." Although fruitless U.S.-Japanese diplomatic talks continued in Washington, once the secret decisions were made, the Japanese Army and Navy began operational plans for taking Malaya, Singapore, Java, the Philippines and a surprise attack on Pearl Harbor. Openly, total mobilization was announced.

Directly thereafter the Japanese issued an ultimatum to the French

Vichy government. Japan had previously occupied several air bases in Vietnam. Now it wanted to expand its hold and occupy air and naval bases throughout Indochina, and on July 21 its forces began to do so.

Reaction in Washington was swift. On Friday 25, a Joint Army-Navy Board dispatch put the Hawaiian and Panama Canal departments on alert even though immediate action was not foreseen. The next day, the President announced the freezing of all Japanese assets in the United States, an embargo on the export of oil and cotton goods to Japan, and the closing of the Panama Canal to all ships flying the flag of Nippon. The Administration's terms for removing what the Konoye government considered an unbearable economic straitjacket, was to get out of China, which the Japanese were not about to do. There were more announcements to come on this hot Saturday.

Four years previously, in 1937, General Douglas MacArthur had retired from the U. S. Army, but he had remained the military adviser to Manuel Quezon, President of the Philippine Commonwealth. In January 1941, the G-2 of the Philippine Department recommended to Marshall that an overall high commander of U.S. forces in the Far East be appointed. In April, MacArthur, writing to White House Press Secretary Steve Early, a longtime admirer and friend, suggested he approach Roosevelt with essentially the same idea: a unified Army command in the Far East with MacArthur at its head. He received no answer. In mid-June, Marshall contacted MacArthur on the latter's announced plans to return to the United States and settle down in San Antonio, Texas. The Chief of Staff asked him to sit tight where he was.

On the same day Roosevelt announced his strong actions against the Japanese—joined by the British and the Dutch—he also declared that he was federalizing the Philippine Army, joining it under U. S. Army forces stationed in the islands, and appointing Major General Douglas MacArthur as Chief of the new U. S. Army Forces Far East (USAFFE).*

Up until this time, Rainbow War Plan No. 5—a broad-based scenario indicating how the United States planned to operate in a war against the Axis—did not contemplate holding the Philippine Archipelago against a major Japanese attack. Instead, a delaying action was envisioned, the Fleet supplying protection should evacuation of the Army garrison around Manila be necessary. The reasoning was sound. The islands were seven thousand miles from the U.S. mainland, forty-six hundred miles from the Hawaiian Islands, and only two hundred miles from Japanese Formosa. They lay close to the Japanese mandated islands and lines of supply and were in the roadstead of territories the Japanese wished to acquire. Unless large U.S. reinforcements could be sent to Manila and the principal islands, most planners in the War Department did not believe they could be held.

* MacArthur was quickly promoted to lieutenant general.

Very soon after MacArthur's appointment, however, this section of
RAINBOW 5 was revised to say the Philippines would be defended. The
Commander-in-Chief of the U. S. Asiatic Fleet would be responsible for
the direction of naval forces supporting such defense.

The decision to defend the Philippines, not just Manila Bay and adjacent territory, was a far-reaching shift in U.S. policy. What caused it were
two major considerations: One was the force of MacArthur's personality
and salesmanship, and the other a sudden acceptance of the belief that the
B-17 was a superior weapon, capable, in ample numbers, of repelling any
attacker. In the first instance, although MacArthur's new assignment was
viewed as an "almost insurmountable task," his glowing reports on the
training of his combined U.S.-Filipino forces of over one hundred thousand men—whose number he planned to have doubled by early 1942—
helped to convince Marshall, the War Department, and Secretary Stimson
that he could defend the entire archipelago. This dramatic shift in policy
was, of course, dependent on two essentials: equipment, and the time to
receive it and train his troops in its use. Even as the policy became fixed it
did not appear that he would have either.

Half a world away, on the day after MacArthur learned of his recall to
duty, Harry Hopkins took off from Invergordon, Scotland, on board a
Catalina PBY of the RAF Coastal Command. He was bound for Moscow
by way of Archangel. The end result of his whirlwind week spent as
Roosevelt's surrogate in talks with Stalin and Soviet leaders was that
Roosevelt issued new and more demanding orders to Stimson and Marshall. Even before MacArthur's recall to active duty and Hopkins' journey
to Moscow, the President was asking for nearly two billion dollars' worth
of aid in armament and planes for the badly savaged Red Army.

Although Intelligence did not agree, the White House believed that if
the Russians could hold out until October and the onslaught of winter,
Hitler's armies would be tied down and there would be breathing space
until spring. Therefore, Roosevelt demanded that practically everything
available, even equipment allocated to Great Britain, be dispatched to
Russia. Roosevelt gave Hopkins the job of riding herd on Lend-Lease to
the Soviet Union, and in spite of protests by Stimson—often angry and
disgruntled—and enormous concern by Marshall, Hopkins had greater
power than either of them. One result was that precious time passed and
supplies promised to MacArthur did not arrive, even though theoretically
if not actually† within the War Department the Philippines enjoyed the
highest priority.

A haze of mystery hangs over the estimate of when war with Japan
might begin. Like the sudden switch in the long-held Philippine defense
policy (which actually began within the War Department six months be-

† According to USAFFE personnel.

fore MacArthur's appointment and became fully accepted after he took command) the amount of time remaining somehow became accepted for unspecified reasons. Yet all evidence indicated the projection was far too optimistic and an enormous piece of miscalculation.

In August 1940, Signal Corps cryptologist Colonel William F. Friedman, in an almost superhuman feat of brainpower, broke the most secret Japanese diplomatic code. It was given the code name PURPLE.‡ This permitted certain select individuals within the Administration and the military to know much of the thinking of the Japanese Government in its negotiations with the United States. By August 1941, these negotiations were in a delicate and perilous state. The big question was whether the Japanese would move north or south, and the alert of July 25 sent to the Philippines, Hawaii, and Panama was in this connection. Although the Japanese airwaves were filled with a mass of conflicting coded reports there was little doubt that war could begin at any time.

Yet Stimson, Marshall, MacArthur, and many others in the War Department clung to the date of April 1942 as the point after which hostilities could be expected to commence. Part of this strange piece of misjudgment might be explained by the fact that MacArthur was not privy to the details of U.S.-Japanese negotiations as revealed by PURPLE. Neither, for that matter, was Hap Arnold, who now sat as a sort of junior member of the Joint Army-Navy Board. As he was to say, "When air problems came up, I sat in as a member of the Board. . . . Accordingly, I never had access to all the secret information available to most high-ranking officers in the War and Navy Departments relating to Japanese movements in the Pacific. For instance, I never saw copies of the intercepts of the Japanese cables and radiograms, nor the breakdown of their code messages. . . ."[4]

What Arnold and others, particularly MacArthur, didn't know injected into the overall strategy of holding the Philippines an unrealistic evaluation of time to prepare.

If the time remaining was misjudged, so was the capability of the B-17. For six years, air spokesmen led principally by Frank Andrews had been pushing the strategic superiority of the long-range heavy bomber: the B-17, and now with it the B-24 Liberator. In 1938, Andrews had introduced Marshall to the B-17 and its proposed operational uses. Arnold continued the educational process, and by the time in question, recognition of the plane's potential, enthusiastically endorsed by Lovett and thus Stimson, had grown within the War Department and the Administration. In more than the public mind, the Flying Fortress was an invincible dreadnought of the skies. Models with additional armament and other combat improvements made it seem even more formidable, and when in

‡ All the numerous Japanese codes broken by Army and Navy cryptologists were referred to as MAGIC.

May 1941 Roosevelt announced that heavy-bomber production was to be raised to five hundred planes a month, the only dissenting voices came from a minority in Congress.

Several months before FDR's announcement, the War Department had rejected an Air Corps proposal to establish a ferry route across the Pacific to Far Eastern points, principally Hawaii. War Plans Division saw no need for such an undertaking. By April, minds were changed, and on the eleventh, while Arnold was en route to England, Stimson wrote Knox an official request asking that four naval vessels be stationed at five hundred-mile intervals over the twenty-four hundred miles between San Francisco and Hawaii. The ships would be there in case of emergency and to offer weather information for a mass flight of twenty-one B-17's of the 19th Bombardment Group.

The War Department was concerned about public reaction should the venture turn out to be a failure. There was no such thought in the mind of Lieutenant Colonel Eugene L. "Gene" Eubank, Commanding Officer of the 19th. A long-time bombardment and engineering officer, Eubank was also, like Curt LeMay, an expert navigator. In April he began training his group for the flight from its base at Hamilton Field, California, to Hickam Field, Oahu, Territory of Hawaii. On May 13 he took off in the lead plane, and thirteen hours and ten minutes later, the twenty-one aircraft began landing at Hickam, only five minutes off their estimated time of arrival.

The seeming ease with which the long flight was accomplished made it that much easier to sell the idea that these same heavy bombers could be flown twice as far: from Hawaii to the Philippines. Improved landing facilities would be needed at Midway and Wake islands; and at Port Moresby, New Guinea; and Darwin, Australia, as well.

When MacArthur took command in the Philippines, his air force was hardly worthy of the name. Its numbers were few and their vintage antique. For over a year, Arnold and his staff had been urging that the situation be drastically improved. The Joint Board agreed, and Arnold proposed that four groups, consisting of 340 heavy bombers, and two pursuit groups, of 130 fighters, be dispatched to the newly created Far Eastern Air Force. No one objected. There was only one problem: Total heavy-bomber production at the end of July stood at twenty B-17's and seventeen B-24's—none of them slated for the Philippines. As a result, by September 1941 MacArthur had received just one squadron, of nine B-17's.

Nevertheless, the pioneering flight led by Major Emmett "Rosey" O'Donnell, Jr., from Hawaii—with landings at Wake, Midway, and Port Moresby—proved that land-based bombers could reinforce the Philippines. MacArthur believed, as did Marshall and Stimson, that if the promised aircraft arrived in time, their presence would deter the Japanese, and failing that, they could severely punish any aggressor. As Tooey Spaatz put it, the bombers would not be used for an offensive mission, but to maintain "a strategical defense in Asia."

Of the twenty new B-17C's produced by July, eleven were placed in the hands of the RAF. These were the planes first asked for by the British back in March 1940; the planes over which Secretary of War Henry Woodring had lost his job in June 1940, and the planes that continued to be a sharp bone of contention between the White House and Hap Arnold—the original RAF request for five having quadrupled in the interim.

When Arnold departed from England for home in late April, he was disappointed that none of the B-17's, which the Churchill government insisted it was most anxious to put into action, had been flown in combat. Only five of them were in England. The War Department was equally concerned, eager to learn how the B-17 would stand up under attack and what damage it could wreak upon a target. An angry cable on May 11, from Secretary of War Stimson to Air Chief Marshal Charles Portal, suggesting the RAF get moving, came to rest on Churchill's desk. It was an indication of a sense of growing U.S. impatience over continued delay.

Two months later, on July 8, the Boeing Flying Fortress went to war. Three B-17's of Squadron 90 flew off to bomb the German naval barracks at Wilhelmshaven. One of the three planes had to divert to a secondary target due to engine trouble, and the other two, flying at thirty thousand feet, hit nothing worth mentioning. Apparently, the RAF was not anxious to offer an accurate account of the result, for U. S. Military Attaché Brigadier General Raymond Lee noted in his diary: "The night before last, three of the American B-17's were used, dropping bombs from a height of 30,000 feet without interference by either fighters or anti-aircraft."[5]

Lee had the time wrong; it was a daylight mission. The planes were attacked by German fighters but could not fight back, because their guns froze up. It was not an auspicious debut. Misuse of the B-17 was illustrated at the outset, when the first of the twenty made its inaugural landing in England at West Raynham and ran off the end of the runway. The left leg of the landing gear buckled, and the plane never flew again. Instead, it was cannibalized, becoming a source of spare parts for other Fortresses in need.

It was Bomber Command's plan to use the planes on high-altitude daylight raids, and the B-17's underwent extensive modifications for that purpose. However, Air Corps engineers in the United States and observers in England cautioned that twenty-five thousand feet was the maximum efficient altitude for the B-17C. Equally important, the planes should not be committed at less than squadron strength. They also advised that crews must undergo special training, and with the Sperry bombsights—new to the RAF—at least two hundred practice bombs should be dropped before going after a real target.

The RAF ignored Air Corps recommendations. They were in a war and hard up against it. Crews dropped no more than twenty-five practice bombs before assignment to combat. Planes were flown at thirty thousand feet and above. They were sent against targets in twos and threes, and only once did as many as four go out together. The statistical results offered a sorry conclusion. In a two-month period, twenty-two missions were flown involving a total of thirty-nine planes. Only half of them reached their primary targets. Two B-17's were shot down, two more so badly shot up they were destroyed in crash landings. Four others were eliminated in noncombat crashes. In all, eight, or nearly half of the twenty, were lost, and still others were grounded and unflyable due to faulty maintenance. No target was destroyed, no enemy fighter shot down, and Bomber Command personnel losses were high. The RAF quickly dubbed the B-17's "Flying Targets." Propaganda Minister Joseph Goebbels chortled that they were "Flying Coffins."

Saddest of all to the Air Corps, one of the casualties was Lieutenant Follett Bradley, Jr., son of Major General Follett Bradley, who had taken his first ride in an airplane with Hap Arnold nearly thirty years before. The news came to the senior Bradley in Puerto Rico, where he commanded the air arm. His son had been killed while testing one of the B-17's at very high altitude. Caught in severe turbulence and icing, the plane had fallen into an uncontrollable spin. The RAF turned its remaining B-17's over to Coastal Command for antisubmarine patrol.

This misapplied experiment was accepted by the RAF as further proof that daylight bombing was too costly and would not work. It was a conviction they assiduously sought to sell, and it ran head on into the Air Corps's steadfast doctrine of precision bombing by daylight. To Bomber Command, the accuracy of German antiaircraft fire and the skill of Luftwaffe fighter pilots told the story, and in essence said that the Air Corps should adopt RAF tactics.

Even so, partly in an apparent political attempt to obscure the details and partly in a misunderstanding of them, the story that came back to official Washington gave an altogether different impression. This impression, combined with explanations from Arnold's office, reinforced Secretary Stimson's belief as well as that of Marshall and the War Department in the heavy bomber as a weapon to make the Philippines defensible.

The British publication *The Aeroplane* wrote: "Lavish praise is showered on the Fortresses by their crews. The pilots like their flying characteristics, and the gunners their armament."

On a BBC broadcast to America, one pilot stated, "These Fortresses are wonderful aircraft, perfectly maneuverable, steady as a battleship and incredibly efficient. We thank you, America, for these bombers."

Lee, no believer in the superiority of air power over ground power, nonetheless sent a highly complimentary dispatch to Marshall over the fate of one of the B-17's that crash-landed in Plymouth after an unsuccessful raid over Brest, commenting, "It is an epic story of what went on high in the heavens and as well it proves that the construction of the Flying Fortress will stand all sorts of rough treatment."[6]

Disturbed by contradictory reports, Arnold contacted Brigadier General Ralph Royce, Mike Scanlon's replacement as Air Attaché in London. Royce responded that there were basically two problems: The British Government, for political reasons, wished to indicate to the British public that the United States was becoming a closer partner. This, in turn, forced Bomber Command to commit the B-17's before crew training was completed and maintenance procedures were understood and acceptable.

Colonel Ira Eaker, in England as one of a growing number of Air Corps observers attached to the U. S. Embassy on temporary duty, wrote a personal cautionary letter on the situation to Tooey Spaatz. Eaker's tour in England actually dealt with learning the RAF communications system for vectoring night fighters and reaching a "general agreement on what we should build and what the British should supply." He described this to Tooey, pointing out that the RAF was going to let him test-fly its greatest operational secret, a new type of electronic system allowing night interceptors to home in on attacking bombers.

He then added: "Here is perhaps the real purpose of this letter to you. Don't be too alarmed about what you hear has happened to the Fortresses. I can say with assurance that the same thing would not have happened to our 2nd Bomb Group or to any well trained American outfit. There is quite a story in connection with the use of our planes here. . . . But whatever you do, do not change equipment types or get overconcerned with our training methods and equipment types by the stories which have been sent back of late on:

> Impossibility of Day Bombing;
> Impracticality of altitude bombing;
> Bombardment self-defense, out;
> Uncanny accuracy of anti-aircraft fire;
> Necessity for two hundred plane fighter escort
>   for single bomber formations

"Certainly we have learned a lot about how not to do things; but above all, we cannot afford to go overboard for new untried things and throw out all the old methods and systems by what has been demonstrated here thus far."

Eaker then listed the lessons he had learned from the RAF experiment. Aside from an emphasis on combat crew training and a continuous stress on maintenance under combat conditions, he cited mechanical improvements: heavier armament and armor, and antifrosting devices for guns and windows at high altitude. His conclusion indicated his own degree of balance:

"From the Command and Planning standpoint, the great danger is that we become confused by the pendulum when it swings to its widest arc reach. The clear true picture will always be found in mid-swing. The best example of this is now apparent in the frenzy which has seized everybody over the increased accuracy of anti-aircraft fire. We are very likely to go off chasing fantasies, changing tactics and reworking equipment over these and other wild goose stories."

Hap Arnold scribbled on Eaker's letter to Spaatz, "noted with interest," which, under the circumstances, could be classed as somewhat of an understatement.

The RAF B-17 experiment might have seemed to rate more than a footnote amid the historic events of the summer of 1941. That it didn't was due, ironically, to the various ways in which it was viewed. Army airmen who had fought the War and the Navy departments for two decades, hammering their theories into tentatively accepted doctrine, were not about to buy or to let the Administration accept conclusions that could uproot all they had achieved. They argued with a great deal of validity that Bomber Command had made a complete mess of the entire operation.

Even so, their position might have come under strong attack if Wright Field engineers and Air Force bomber commanders had not been anxious to make combat-proven modifications in the plane. The B-17, like all military aircraft, went through a metamorphosis, with each production model incorporating improvements. Just as the model C was an improvement over the model B, and the D over the C, the model E was a culmination of changes recommended as a result of combat.

On the one hand, Arnold and his staff welcomed the changes in design and equipment brought about by the RAF experiment, while on the other, they deplored and damned what they considered indefensible maintenance procedures and the misbegotten tactics used by Bomber Command.

Conversely, in Jim Chaney the RAF found a strong voice of support. No doubt his evaluation as Chief of the Special Army Observers Group in London influenced War Department thinking. His appraisal, in secret letters to Marshall and Andrews, illustrated the difference in Air Corps and RAF attitudes. As Arnold could have pointed out, Chaney was a staff officer, not an expert on engineering or operations.

There has been considerable impatience on the part of our aviation authorities in the United States with the British for not putting our planes, both bombers and fighters, into action more promptly. They are now carrying out daylight bombing operations with the B-17's at altitudes of about 32,000 feet. Yesterday four went over and bombed from 37,000, 35,000 and 32,000 feet. It has been a problem to operate the B-17's at that altitude and they have had considerable difficulty. We have never done it, that is, carry out simulated bombing missions at that altitude where the crew has to remain at that altitude for from four to seven hours and yet we have been very critical of the British for not starting in immediately. Above 20,000 feet they have had a lot of difficulty with the windows frosting up, with the inner phone communications not working properly, and with the engines throwing oil excessively. Also our oxygen equipment was neither effective nor sufficient. From my observations on the spot, I am inclined to be sympathetic towards the British point of view in not taking planes out on operational missions until they are satisfied with them. Their actual war experience has in most instances demonstrated a military necessity for certain characteristics or special equipment. The fact that the United States has spent five years developing the B-17, for instance, should not prevent operational changes in airplanes allotted to the British even though our engineers, without war experience, feel they are unnecessary or can be overcome by better training. Furthermore, airplanes for the British account should, insofar as possible, have the changes designed by the British made in the United States so as to prevent further delay involved if a completed airplane has to be modified on this side.

As for the RAF's use of the B-24, Chaney was also on the British side of the argument.

Arnold and Brett were also dissatisfied that the British used the first B-24's for Coastal Command long-range reconnaissance purposes in connection with the Battle of the Atlantic. The British modified them to take depth bombs against submarines and cannon against the large German bombers over the Atlantic. However, I believe this use of them was sound, for these first planes had no tail turrets, and furthermore, had no turbo superchargers and therefore could not be used for high daylight bombing over France or Germany. In my opinion, these first B-24's were *by accident* uniquely fitted for just what the British are using them for, i.e. in the Battle of the Atlantic. The next batch of B-24's after about the first thirty, for the British, will have tail gun turrets and can be used for night bombing over Germany, and this is the plan. The third batch will have both tail gun turrets and turbo superchargers and can be used for either night missions over Germany or high daylight bombing missions. So this complaint on our part, which was taken right up to Mr. Churchill, was, in my opinion, completely unjustified. With the two little (semi-flexible) guns in the tail of these first planes it would have been just throwing them away to have sent them over Germany on night bombing missions and I believe the British were much wiser in not doing it than we were in agitating that they so use them. I happened to be out at an airdrome when Mr. Churchill arrived there just after getting this complaint from Washington. He had practically decided to recall them all and put them on bombing missions over Germany which would have been another delay. While it is none of my business he told me about what had happened just because I happened to be out there. I went over the problem as outlined above and recommended that he not recall them. . . .

No doubt there was something to be said on both sides of the ocean, but no one could refute the dismal statistics with regard to the B-17's introduction into the conflict. The civilian officials and the ground officers were diverted from the record by having their attention concentrated on the plane's ruggedness and the strengthening it would undergo. Had it been otherwise, the upheaval could have been volcanic, the consequences irreparable.

That the RAF's verdict was papered over and downplayed for the reasons given was clear enough, but there was yet another reason, more important than all others. It was so woven into the fabric of strategic air philosophy and so fundamental to its past, present, and future that it dwarfed all other considerations in the frenetically paced final months of peace. That it, too, has been given less than its proper recognition—even by some of its principals—is a measure of how furious was the fight of those days.

The genesis of what became known as AWPD-1 lay in the long-expressed complaint by successive Secretaries of War and their key military advisers that the White House did not have a consistent and clear policy with regard to the war. As Stimson viewed the situation, there was a dangerous state of drift, a failure by the President to provide a plan and a stirring call for united action. As he sourly put it: "The President takes his advice from the last person he speaks to."[7]

Marshall expressed his frustration in similar terms: "First the President wants 500 bombers a month and that dislocates the [production] program. Then he says he wants so many tanks and that dislocates the program. The President will never sit down and talk about a complete program and have the whole thing move forward at the same time."[8]

The result, as Secretary of State Cordell Hull continued to repeat wearily, was that "Everything is going Hellward."

The problem at its simplest was that the country had a President who was willing to go to war and a citizenry that was not. The public clung to the belief that the involvement of American forces could be avoided, the attitude best reflected by the August confrontation in the House of Representatives, where by a single vote the draft law was retained.

Although the German invasion of the U.S.S.R. took some of the pressure off the British, as the summer ran on it appeared that both countries were on the brink of disaster, and Roosevelt was anxious to act vigorously on their behalf.

Some months earlier, as a result of Marshall's worry that he could not legally request funds for an Army larger than 2.8 million, Roosevelt had asked both services to make studies of the production and force requirement to defeat the Axis. In May, Marshall and Stark asked their staffs to begin work on strategic estimates for an orderly production expansion, but it was not until the Soviet Union was invaded that any real momentum developed in the endeavor. It began on July 9 with a secret request by Roosevelt to Stimson and Knox asking them to have drawn up "overall production requirements required to defeat our potential enemies."

The following day, in a fateful but seemingly unrelated event, Lieutenant Colonel Harold L. George arrived in Tooey Spaatz's office, atop the Munitions Building. He had relinquished command of the 2nd Bomb Group, at Langley Field, to take over as chief of the newly established Air War Plans Division (AWPD).

During the 1930's, Hal George had spent five years at the Air Corps Tactical School, first as Chief of the Bombardment Section and then as Director of Air Tactics and Strategy. He headed a small cadre of exceptional officers who were refining the air-warfare theories of Douhet, Mitchell, and Trenchard.

The philosophy had long been infused in the minds of Army air leaders, most of whom either had attended the Tactical School before its doors were closed, in 1940, or had served in Frank Andrews' GHQ Air Force. Gradually, the attitude in the War Department, which for years had steadfastly rejected the doctrine of strategic bombing, *had* shifted to a greater awareness of the role strategic air power would play should the United States become involved in the war. Marshall, as noted, was in the forefront of this changing view. Still, the two schools of thought were far apart. Ground officers could argue with pointed accuracy that in France and now in Russia, German air power was tied to the unparalleled sweep of the Wehrmacht and not to bombing far-distant industrial targets. In this latter regard they saw that England had withstood a siege of sixty-seven consecutive nights of bombing while its industry continued to operate and its public remained undaunted.[9]

Prior to the formation of the Army Air Forces and the new Air Staff, the Army's General Staff and its War Plans Division dictated and controlled overall Air Corps policy. Now the principal areas of AAF personnel, intelligence, operations, training, and supply were under the direction of the Air Staff. But what of Air War Plans?

Arnold, as Deputy Chief of Staff for Air, was officially appointed a member of the Joint Army-Navy Board on the same day Roosevelt asked for an assessment of what it would take to win a war. Arnold expected that plans for an air war would be drawn up in the War Plans Division of the War Department, and that is the way it would have been in the momentous weeks that followed had it not been for Hal George. Few realized that the opportunity George was about to grasp would be as important in its ramifications as the reorganization of the air arm itself.

When he reported to Spaatz, Hal George found the largest part of his division was its name. Besides himself, the Air War Plans Division consisted of three officers: Lieutenant Colonel Howard Craig, Chief of the "Projects Group," his assistant, Lieutenant Colonel Orvil Anderson, and Lieutenant Colonel Kenneth N. Walker, who was the sole member of the War Plans Group. Walker, a very close friend, had been a senior instructor at the Air Corps Tactical School when George was a student there. Like George, he was imbued with an abiding—even overwhelming —faith in the doctrine of strategic air power.

They were soon joined by a fourth member cut out of the same strategic mold. He was Major Haywood S. "Possum" Hansell, Jr., former instructor at the Air Corps Tactical School at the same time George and Walker were teaching forbidden theories. Hansell, younger, a crack pursuit pilot in spite of his bombardment convictions, had been serving in the equally small Air Intelligence Division, heading up a section on strategy and analysis. He had just returned from England loaded with RAF Intelligence digests on German industrial targets. George wanted him on his team. In fact, because Craig and Anderson were fully occupied on projects in being, it was a three-man team until it became a foursome through a request that another old friend and colleague from the Tactical School, Major Larry Kuter, be assigned. Kuter had remained with G-3 after Andrews' departure. He and Possum Hansell had been classmates at the Tactical School, and Kuter, having graduated at the head of his class in 1935, was asked to remain as a bombardment instructor.

The President had specified that he wanted the production estimates in a matter of weeks. Under whatever time limit, the order was viewed in the War and the Navy departments as staggering. To begin with, the members of the Joint Army-Navy Board knew that there had to be a military strategy on which to base production and manpower figures. The only guidelines were RAINBOW 5, at best a broad contingency plan, supported by the general agreements reached with the British in the ABC-1 talks back in January, when U.S. and British planners had secretly met to discuss joint strategy. The overall concept was that offensive war would be waged against Germany and Italy while defending against Japan.

Army War Plans Chief Brigadier General Leonard T. Gerow saw the President's directive as an unusual challenge, for this was the first time in U.S. history that a war plan on a global scale had been asked for. To head the group undertaking the massive job, he appointed a very savvy and gifted major, Albert C. Wedemeyer. Wedemeyer, a West Point graduate and career officer, had spent two years (1936–38) at the German War College, in Berlin, and as a result, his insight into German military thinking, particularly with regard to the U.S.S.R., was broader than that of most of his colleagues. Unlike his well-known father-in-law, Lieutenant

General Stanley D. Embick, he had a broad appreciation of air power and an understanding of its strategic use.

The ranking air officer in the War Plans Division was Lieutenant Colonel Clayton Bissell, combat veteran, Billy Mitchell aide, bomber proponent. Wedemeyer expected that Bissell and other air personnel assigned to the Division would prepare an "Air Annex" that would be appended to the Army estimates. But their numbers were few and they needed help. Gerow called Arnold to ask if he could supply assistance. At about the same time, Bissell stopped by to see George and said: Hey, Hal, how about your team coming over and working under us? It's a helluva big job.

George didn't like the idea at all. He went to Tooey Spaatz and told him why. It was obvious the Army would base its estimates on the size of the ground forces it had to defeat. It would do the same when figuring air strength, and it simply couldn't be done that way. There was no record to show how many fighters you needed to shoot down one bomber, how many bombers you needed to destroy a target when the bombers were flying under varying circumstances, in varying numbers, and with differing range and firepower.

The War Plans Division had never undertaken a study of the industrial and economic vulnerability of Germany and Japan from the point of view of aerial attack in order to establish priorities. The Air Corps Tactical School had, and Hansell's intelligence work of the past two years was a continuation of it. Certainly there were those in the War Plans Division who understood all those factors and would attempt to take them into account, but overriding all else was the question: What is the Air Objective?

Spaatz and George were combat veterans of the First World War, and veterans of all the lean, hard years in which they had labored and fought to establish an air objective. Hal didn't have to spell it out for Tooey. If the War Department prepared the Air Annex, the emphasis was bound to be on tactical air strength as an auxiliary support of the troops. Strategic air power would be secondary. If, on the other hand, the Air War Plans Division prepared the estimates, the balance would be there, and for the first time in history the strategic component would become the principal air objective. It was a thunderous opportunity, and Spaatz, not blinking an eye, said they'd better talk it over with Hap.

It might seem that Arnold would automatically accept the idea, but George was worried. Arnold was one of the few early airmen who had not attended the Air Corps Tactical School. That didn't mean he wasn't in favor of what was taught there, but George believed that the impatient Arnold was not excited by long-range plans. That Possum Hansell had been innovative enough to get target information on German power-generating plants by going to New York banks once involved in their financing and asking for blueprints, was the sort of action that made Arnold grin. But contingency plans for far in the future when he was tied up with God-awful production problems right here and now! What the hell, let WPD handle it! Or so thought Hal George and his confederates. Happily, they were wrong.

As it turned out, Arnold cagily suggested to General Gerow that since the War Plans Division was swamped with its task of preparing the requirements for an Army that would number millions, the Air Staff could take over responsibility for drawing up air requirements. Gerow accepted. He asked only that RAINBOW 5 and the ABC-1 agreements be used as guidelines. Later, Hal George was to praise Hap Arnold for having brought off a momentous coup, but it was George who recognized the opportunity and alerted Spaatz and Arnold.

On August 4, George's quartet of airmen went to work on the air war plan. They had exactly a week to do the job.

RAINBOW 5 and ABC-1 called for providing air forces in the western hemisphere; an air offensive against Germany while preparing to invade the Continent; close support for the invasion and subsequent ground operations; and air defense and support for strategic defensive operations in the Pacific.

The imponderables were vast, for as Hansell put it, "There were no commonly accepted formulae for such things as: (1) the method to be employed in the air offensive; (2) the specific objects to be sought; (3) the targets to be attacked; (4) the size and composition of the air forces; (5) the timing of the various major strategic operations, including the mobilization date, the outbreak of war, the buildup of all forces, and the final surface offensive against the Continent. The best we could do was develop our own formulae based on our critical experience at the Air Corps Tactical School, our belief in the potential of strategic bombardment, and our own experience. Perhaps no other military operation in all of history presented such an awesome task without providing a usable past experience and at least a few lessons of history. . . . But if the task was staggering, so too was the opportunity. In a very real way, we sensed that the future of American air power depended, in large part, on what we accomplished. . . ."[10]

At the beginning, they gave their study the somewhat deceptive title "Munitions Requirements of the Army Air Forces to Defeat Our Potential Enemies." A big question was the time left before the United States entered the war, and here again, from some crystal ball in the War Department came the date of April 1942. But, to the air planners, it was as much a matter of *what* as it was *when*. What types of aircraft would be coming off the production line around which they could build the air offensive against Germany? For the immediate future there were the B-17 and the B-24, and beyond them longer-range, more-powerful bombers were in development, the Boeing B-29, the Consolidated B-32. At the very time George and his team were weighing the problem, Robert Lovett was meeting with George Brett and Wright Field engineers to review design studies of a bomber (eventually the Consolidated B-36) with a ten thousand-mile range carrying a ten thousand-pound bomb load. Like the B-29, it would have a pressurized cabin.

The impetus to get going on the plane was stimulated by the realization that if Germany defeated the Soviet Union and then forced England to surrender, the United States would stand alone and in need of a truly intercontinental bomber. But such equipment could not be ready for several years under any circumstance, and the planners knew that in the interim they must base the offensive against Germany and Italy—and the defense of the hemisphere and the Philippines—on the B-17 and the B-24. Even as they labored, the contradictory reports were coming back from England that the B-17 was being clobbered over Europe and the B-24 wasn't capable of even night operations.

Contradictory reports filtering through on the performance of the Fortress and the Liberator could not for one moment dissuade and/or deflect the planners from their determined course. They had no doubts as to the capability of the equipment involved or the tactics that should be employed. Their lives were meshed into the development of one end interwoven into the concepts of the other. They were racing the clock, and their considerations were focused on the future, not on the piecemeal, misapplied expenditure of aircraft on which they were staking the cause of strategic air power. If the negative reports on B-17 operations put furrows in Hap Arnold's brow, they simply bounced off the walls of the improvised Munitions Building war room, where they labored.

Aside from the shortness of time to finish the job, they were faced by another time factor. How soon after U.S. entry into the war would the available forces be ready for operations? They saw as their main objective the destruction of German industrial might. To accomplish this goal they broke down targeting into four major headings: the enemy's electrical power system, transportation system (railroads, highways, canals), oil and petroleum industry, and contiguous with all three, the destruction of German interceptor defenses both on the ground and in the air. In all, 154 targets were selected, but central to the plan was the belief that not until the strategic force reached full strength could its effect be felt, and then only by no less than six months of sustained attack. The tentative date to begin large-scale operations was forecast as July 1943, with the six months of sustained bombing running from April through September 1944. This, predicted the planners, "would in all probability cause the collapse of the German military and civilian establishment." They also believed that its effect might well make it unnecessary for an army to invade the continent of Europe.

The numbers of men and planes arrived at to accomplish the global purpose were huge by any standard. More than 135,000 pilots and crews; nearly nine hundred thousand technicians and ground crews; over sixty thousand nonflying officers. Aircraft in all categories were estimated at close to seventy thousand, with more than half the number designated for training. Replacement aircraft were figured at more than two thousand a month. With these production figures and their breakdown as to location and type were included munitions estimates based on how often each target would have to be hit to keep it out of commission.

In this incredible compilation of production needs, attention was also given not only to the defense of the western hemisphere and the Pacific but also to tactical air support for the Army ground forces. The planners felt this last was the weak point, the Achilles' heel of their plan. They knew they were playing a numbers game. Give the Army what it wanted —tactical air forces in England and the Mediterranean—and perhaps they could get it through the War Department. Further, the Air Annex was supposed to be limited to production estimates. Instead, in making only the estimates, they had seized fortune at the flood and with Hal George leading were attempting to ride the tide to a previously unacceptable air objective.

They knew when they presented the plan the whole thing could be rejected—nullified—called back—canceled out, with the attendant effect on their careers. They did not have to remind themselves that they were proposing that the War Department abandon its prevailing doctrine that the principal use of Army aviation was in support of the troops. What they believed was going for them was the nature of the war, the fact that air power could be used against Germany long before an army would be ready to invade.

War Plans Division was operating flat out, and when AWPD planners officially submitted their massive document to Wedemeyer, his officers took the package, stamped it "Annex 2, Requirements of the Army Air Forces," and added it to their own bundle of papers.[11] Still, the program had to be presented to the high brass, and George decided they would put together a formal explanation of the plan with each of them describing a part of it. They would use maps and charts but no script or notes.

On Tuesday, August 12, the curtain went up for a select audience led by Brigadier General Henry L. Twaddle, Army Assistant Chief of Staff for G-3, and members of his staff. There was a nice Machiavellian touch in making the Army Chief of Operations and Training the first of the General Staff to judge the plan. Twaddle had formerly served under Andrews, and Larry Kuter had served under both. To Kuter, Twaddle was a friendly sort, an infantry officer more interested in self than in selflessness, but worth cultivating, a good man for an ambitious and enterprising major to be on friendly terms with. He obviously thought highly of Kuter's intellect and talents, and through their association knew something about air power. It was he, after all, who had permitted Kuter to join AWPD. Therefore, with the thought that flattery might make Twaddle twinkle, they invited him to hear the war plan first. The presentation took two hours, Hal George acting as the keynoter.

There was little doubt that the assembled were impressed with what they heard, perhaps even a bit overwhelmed. In using the provision of RAINBOW 5 and ABC-1, George knew he was on firm ground when he described the primary air objective "to conduct a sustained, unremitting air offensive against Germany and Italy to destroy the will and capability of Germany and Italy to continue the war; and to make an invasion either unnecessary or feasible without excessive cost."

The first of several more-demanding tests came ten days later, when the plan was presented to a gathering that included General Gerow and Robert Lovett. The four knew they could expect strong support from the Assistant Secretary of War for Air, but Gerow was a big question mark. He, too, was an infantryman and, they figured, with an infantryman's way of looking at aviation. Others thought different. Known as "Gee" to his friends, Gerow, like Ike Eisenhower, was considered by Marshall to be an intelligent and broad-minded officer. To the enormous relief of the air quartet he proved he was just that. Gerow had questions, as did others, but he seemed satisfied by Hal George's answers. When it was over, the planners felt they were past another mighty hurdle, but the biggest jump of all lay ahead.

On a Saturday, August 30, they went before Marshall and Arnold and a mixed General Staff, Air Staff, and civilian audience, including, among others, W. Averell Harriman, Roosevelt's Lend-Lease expediter. This was the critical point. Marshall could flatten them with the shake of his head. He listened intently as they explained. Then the questions from General Staff officers and war-production representatives began. The queries were hard and sharp and contentious. There was no hiding the fact, as Hansell phrased it in retrospect, that "our request was out of all proportion to the requirements brought forth by the Army and the Navy," which meant they were making excessive production demands at the expense of the other services.[12]

When the questions and answers and objections died away, Marshall, who had remained noncommittal, rose and gave the verdict. "Gentlemen," he said, "I think the plan has merit. I would like the Secretary and the Assistant Secretaries to hear it."

Thanks to the perception of George Marshall, a roadblock was to be avoided. By directing that the plan be brought directly to Stimson, Marshall circumnavigated the Joint Army-Navy Board. He knew that if the admirals got their hands on the plan they would automatically reject it. The Navy was thinking in terms of ships and all that it took to build them; it saw no reason for Army Air to be any more than an auxiliary, as Navy Air was.

Marshall asked for a repeat performance and brought Bill Knudsen and his production chiefs. Gerow was there again, as was Arnold. Once more the searching questions, mostly from Knudsen and members of OPM (Office of Production Management), and once more the answers, this time well supported by Lieutenant Colonel Edgar Sorensen's A-4 Division of the Air Staff.

Finally, on Thursday, September 11, the four weary planners accompanied General Marshall to Secretary Stimson's office and described what became known officially as AWPD-1. Said Stimson when they had concluded, "General Marshall and I like the plan. I want you gentlemen to be prepared to present it to the President. I will speak to him about the date. Thank you for coming to my office."[13]

The four departed jubilant. At long last the use of strategic air power had been officially accepted in principle by the Army. It was a thunderous victory! But one thing was sure: There was going to be a helluva fight with the Navy and the production people, not to mention the Lend-Lease eagles, in trying to implement the handiwork of Hal George, Ken Walker, Possum Hansell, and Larry Kuter. The least they could do was take time to hoist a glass in celebration of having accomplished what many would have deemed impossible.

During much of the time Hal George and his assistants were hammering out production estimates and melding them with the air objectives, Hap Arnold was out of town. In the midst of their work, in the midst of the B-17's introduction to combat, he was called away, invited to attend a private party and participate in secret discussions concerning joint U.S.-British policies.

For two years, Roosevelt and Churchill had been corresponding, and with new developments of enormous importance unfolding in the Soviet Union and the Orient, they were anxious to meet and explore common objectives. One of Harry Hopkins' concerns during his July visit to England was to arrange the final details of such a get-together. In the course of his broad inquiry, he attended a meeting at 10 Downing Street which included, besides the Prime Minister, the British chiefs of staff as well as Generals Chaney and Lee.* Hopkins laid out the Administration's view of the British war effort, supported by both officers, and then Churchill and his chiefs responded. It was apparent that there were strongly divergent views on the areas in question: the Atlantic, the Middle East, the Pacific, the chance of German invasion of England, the war in the U.S.S.R.

When the meeting ended, Hopkins decided that both Marshall and Arnold should be invited to the already scheduled Big Two conference

---

* First Lord of the Admiralty Sir Dudley Pound, Chief of the Imperial Staff Sir John F. M. Dill, and Chief of Air Staff Air Marshal Sir Charles Portal.

which would take place in Placentia Bay, off the coast of Argentia, New-foundland. Originally, the major military subject of the conference was to focus on the Battle of the Atlantic, but Hopkins knew from what he had heard that the British would come prepared to cover the globe, and he wanted Marshall, as Army Chief of Staff, and Arnold, as the principal Army airman, present to hear their views.

Arnold's first knowledge that he was wanted for something special came on July 31 as he was flying from Baton Rouge to inspect air bases in Texas. "Return to Washington, arriving not later than 10 P.M., August 2," was Marshall's instruction. On Friday, August 1, Arnold did his inspecting, pleased with what he found, and the next day he flew back to Washington, arriving by teatime. He telephoned Marshall, who told him they were leaving at noon on Sunday from Gravelly Point Airport in Arnold's plane. Arnold had no idea where they were going, only that he should be prepared for a ten-day absence and pack an O.D. uniform with Sam Browne belt.

The ten days from August third to the thirteenth, which included the four-day meeting between Roosevelt and Churchill and their key advisers, made history as the Atlantic Conference. The President arrived aboard Admiral King's flagship, the *Augusta,* on August 7, and Churchill came steaming in two days later on the *Prince of Wales,* still battle-scarred from her action against the *Bismarck.* The public was unaware of the carefully guarded meeting and would best remember it for its publicity value: the heralding of the Four Freedoms. At the height of the occasion, a blend of high-level conferences and social affairs, Arnold noted wryly, "I can't make up my mind as yet whether most of us are window-dressing for the main actors or whether we are playing minor roles in the show."

Hopkins had arrived with Churchill on board the *Prince of Wales,* half dead following an incredible week in Russia. Stalin had impressed him. The Russian land and its people had impressed him. They would not go under, of that he was sure—even if everyone around Hopkins was concerned that he himself was going under. Essentially, however, the Atlantic Conference dealt with British needs and U.S. reaction to them. Arnold gave his own appraisal in retrospect.

From my point of view, realizing that there were many talks and conferences at which I was not present; hence, there may have been many things happening of which I have no knowledge.

General—The British prepared, hurriedly, a strategic estimate of the situation, agreed to by all, as a guide during the conference.

It was drawn up with a view of covering operations—British and ours in various theatres.

It did not include our Army and Air Force playing more than a very secondary role. Hence, it did not mention nor did the British repre-

sentatives bring up point of our building up our Army or Navy for active
participation in war.

The British representatives did not realize the almost impossible load
being placed upon us by Army, Navy, Air Force all asking for what each
wanted—100%—with no funnel or central sieve to coordinate the various demands. They did not appreciate that on top of this load we had to
take care of the needs of China, Russia, British Colonies, Dutch East
Indies. Then we also had to make such military dispositions as to insure
that Japan would think before acting in Far East.

The British as usual asked for everything they wanted regardless of
whether we have or ever will have an Air Force. They never blinked an
eye when they asked for 100% of our production. They would have taken
all the Army, Navy, British, Chinese, Dutch planes and engines.

At the same time they asked that we establish depots from Iceland to
Singapore to repair and maintain all of their American planes.

They wanted us to train their combat crews and be responsible for the
ferrying of their 2 and 4 engine planes across the Atlantic by those trained
crews.

Furthermore, we were to ferry all bombers possible across with our
pilots (P.A.A.).

There was no thought given by the British as to co-ordinating their
Army, Navy, Air requirements or balancing them against production.

They never gave a moment's thought as to what we might be called
upon to do. Philippines—Hawaii—Panama—Iceland—Newfoundland—
Azores—Natal and then perhaps operations in Europe—with what, after
we gave them everything? Then they said—we will give you planes to operate there when you arrive.

They wanted us to send Bomber and Pursuit squadrons complete with
all their equipment to become acquainted with the British Communications and Command systems.

Fortunately we were able to get away without promising or giving away
everything we had. As a matter of fact, we might have lost everything we
owned, including our pants—but we didn't.

I think, however, that the conference was invaluable as it gave the British a much better understanding of our problems and certainly gave us a
better understanding of not only their problems but also their urgent desire
to get everything they can regardless of effect on the other fellow.

I must admit [Air Marshal Sir Wilfred] Freeman accepted our refusal
gracefully.

The conference certainly brought home to Stark—Marshall—Turner
and I believe to Hopkins and Harriman the necessity for setting up a

board to determine up and lay down policies re—allocation of War supplies to not only British but also Russia, China and all other nations.

The meeting will probably be called epoch-making—historical—etc., etc., perhaps the 8 points will make it so but in my mind the estimate prepared by the Chiefs of Staff was hastily prepared and was not followed through—that was the only document I saw outlining the purpose of our meeting but what the President and the Prime Minister had to say when together—I know not.

Certainly the Military Minds seemed to follow the same line after all the demands and requests were forgotten.

This meeting of the Minds certainly became manifest with regard to:

(1) Aid to Russia.
(2) The seizure of the Azores.
(3) The reinforcement of the Philippines.
(4) The handling of Japan if that nation moved further Southward.
(5) Iceland's defense.
(6) Occupation of Canaries and the Cape Verdes.

but not with regard to:

(1) Occupation of Dakar.
(2) Occupation of Morocco.

The conference dragged on for at least two days too long for there was a potential disaster in being just as long as those ships were anchored and assembled in Placentia Bay. Each day that passed increased the risk and hazard. We all breathed a sigh of relief when the Prince of Wales, the Augusta, the Tuscaloosa, and their destroyer escorts pulled out of the harbor.

The conference was well worthwhile.

Took off Quonsett - 6:45.
Arrived Anacostia - 9:00.

It was not long after the War Department's acceptance in principle of AWPD-1 that Arnold let it be known that he was prepared to supply General MacArthur with four groups of heavy bombers which, in total, amounted to the 340 aircraft mentioned earlier. He was also anxious to provide 204 B-17's to strengthen the Hawaiian Air Force, under the command of Major General Fred Martin. In both instances, these figures came from the estimates set down by Hal George and his planners in AWPD-1. They sounded good. They looked good on paper, but they were caught between the nutcracker of too many outside demands and a foreign policy that left too little time.

Seven

Radius of Action

On the day of the grand farewell review for General Van Voorhis, Andrews received a personal radiogram from Hap congratulating him on his promotion to lieutenant general. It was one of a great many, coming in from all over the globe. Perhaps the one from his wife Johnny was the most meaningful: YOU'RE THE BRIGHTEST STAR OF THEM ALL. WHAT TOOK YOU SO LONG?

On September 18, the day Andrews officially took charge of the Caribbean Defense Command, they gave Lieutenant General Daniel Van Voorhis a farewell that would long be remembered. Ordinarily at such occasions, the air's contribution to a final review of the troops was a squadron flyby that was over in seconds. Not this time, thanks to Sonny Williams. Andrews had asked his aide to arrange air force participation in the event, saying it was a good opportunity to exhibit the air arm's mobility. Williams took him literally, and when the troops passed in review, it was not just airplanes that flashed by, but everyone mobile that served them: ranks of marching airmen, followed by trucks, loaders, and all kinds of movable equipment, even oxygen carts, a most unusual display of military might.

Moving past the reviewing stand where Andrews and Van Voorhis and their aides and principal staff members stood resplendent in white uniforms, the parade appeared to go on and on, the contingents of ground troops from the artillery and infantry commands overwhelmed by air representation. The Panamanian sun beamed down. The thick tropical growth remained still and listless. The trumpets blared, the drums boomed. The dust rose and the sweat trickled, and there was a certain embarrassed shifting of feet among the assembled Department brass. They were being outdone on their own parade ground! Andrews, whose

surprise was as great as theirs, threw a quick glance at his aide, who saw
that he was struggling to keep his composure but nevertheless could not
hide a smile. Only an airman could see the humor in Sonny Williams'
sleight-of-hand move to turn out all the air troops and their support
equipment for the departing General.

Van Voorhis gave no sign that the review was anything more than his
just due. As an old campaigner, he knew how to check to the dealer. Beneath that ramrod backbone, that austere and weathered countenance,
there lurked a soldier's sense of humor. It was a damn' good farewell review, no matter who marched in it.

The next day, Andrews issued his first general order to his far-flung
command, which stressed the need for unity and not separateness. They
had been entrusted with the serious and difficult task of organizing and
building within the Theater the necessary defenses and guarding them
against attack. "This responsibility," he told his command, "has meant
hardships, strenuous work under difficult conditions, and personal sacrifice. We must realize that the immediate future offers nothing better,
but you have demonstrated a splendid willingness to accept necessary
conditions—to shoulder *together* the burden for preparing yourselves for
whatever eventuality time may bring. Whatever your job is in the air or
on the ground, it is the spirit of teamwork which has made possible the
progress which has been made and which still must be made. . . ."

Since July, when Andrews received his appointment, he had been more
or less the Acting Defense Commander, and at the time he issued his message to his Theater forces, the progress referred to had been described in
a feature article in the September 1 issue of *Time* magazine. Not many of
Andrews' friends liked the rendition of his face on the cover, but all were
pleased with the magazine account. In offering "a quick grasp of the
reasons why General Andrews' Caribbean task is so big and so important," *Time* explained:

> Before the U.S. can be effectively invaded from the middle Atlantic—or
> from enemy outposts established in Latin America—the Caribbean must be
> taken or penetrated. . . .
> If attack comes through South America, the U.S. will have to move
> swiftly to aid in the defense of its Latin American neighbors before the
> enemy is entrenched there, and Caribbean bases will necessarily be the es-
> sential stepping stones over which such aid is carried.
> Only by having a ring of Caribbean bases and rapidly arming them can
> the U.S. gain insurance against having to go south to defend South
> America itself. . . .
> The Caribbean bases are vital to U.S. defenses in *both* oceans. . . .

On those bases Andrews had forces and installations in various stages
of completion, reaching from Mariguana, in the Bahamas, down to Puerto
Rico and the Windward Islands to Trinidad, off the Venezuelan coast, to

Atkinson Field, in British Guiana. Trinidad and Puerto Rico were being built up as main operating bases, with bombardment, pursuit, and patrol aircraft supported by ground forces. The smaller islands were primarily servicing stations for reconnaissance and submarine patrol planes. On Jamaica, facilities for one heavy bombardment group and a reconnaissance squadron were operational but far short of the necessary aircraft, and there were no heavy bombers. And although Bermuda was not considered to be in the Caribbean area, a base was being established there to accommodate a composite group.

As *Time* phrased it, the Panama Canal was "key to U.S. strategy in the Atlantic and the Pacific, a certain target for any invader," but it was more:

> Most people think of Andy Andrews' Citadel as primarily a place to be defended with the strongest possible local forces, and with all the might of the outlying bases. It is. But it is also a base for any major expedition that it may be necessary to launch against any enemy invasion of Central America, northern South America, or the southernmost U.S.
>
> The precise state of defenses in these Caribbean bases is a military secret. No secret, however, is the general fact that Andy Andrews needs a lot more men and equipment.

That there existed a strong belief in such an invasion possibility made it real and indicated to the public the depth and breadth of Andrews' command responsibilities. While the article dealt with the geography of the Theater, its logistic and personnel needs, it failed to go into the organizational plan Andrews had developed by which the command would now operate. Later, it was a pattern that was adopted in the formation of U.S. air forces everywhere within the four continental air forces, and later in the air forces formed in Europe.

Directly after taking command, Andrews sent an account to Marshall detailing his immediate plans. He was leaving, he said, on September 28 to make an inspection tour of the Theater, and his recommendations concerning personnel would follow. The proposed increases in men and materiel Arnold had brought on his visit were only half the number needed to provide a proper defense. "If the Navy was prepared to perform its function of reconnaissance," Andrews observed, "I think we could safely reduce the air garrison. A somewhat similar situation exists in Puerto Rico," he added.

In responding, Marshall made no mention of the Navy's role, or lack of it, in the Canal Zone and the Caribbean. But if Andrews mentioned the problem in passing—which simply added up to neither service being properly equipped to carry out its duties—Arnold was far more direct in his attitude toward the Navy. Neither he nor any alert airman who had been around awhile was about to turn the other cheek where the Navy was concerned.

At a mid-October meeting of the Joint Army-Navy Board, Admiral Jack Towers was asked how the Navy was planning to operate from Iceland when the ice was in the harbors and fjords. "Smiling" Jack replied, "We had planned on using amphibians, but now we are planning on using twenty land-based bombers. As a matter of fact, the Navy is thinking of utilizing land-based bombers from other stations as well, since we think they are necessary."

Jack Towers was an old friend of Hap Arnold's, but these words sent the alarm bells ringing in Arnold's helmet. He believed that the underlying meaning of Towers' comments—at least as he interpreted them—escaped Marshall. And so he approached the Chief of Staff with "a sore point which has existed for about 22 years in connection with Army-Navy relations. It is one of the best arguments that the Separate Air Force advocates have," he said, "in that it admits that there is really no definite line of demarcation between Army and Navy operations. Patrolling at sea, bombing of ships, bombing of naval bases, bombing of the factories and shipyards which produce the ships, bombing of the factories which make the materials that go into ship construction and bombing of the sources of supply of raw materials, all merge one into the other so there is really no definite line of demarcation between Navy air targets and Army air targets. Accordingly, then, the only real line of demarcation between Army and Navy operations is that in general the Navy operates water-based planes and the Army operates land-based planes."

Arnold was protecting Air Forces interests, enlisting Marshall's support by combining Navy acquisition of land-based bombers with the drive for a separate air force, and at the same time offering a pretty fair description of what strategic bombardment was expected to accomplish.

In order to block the earlier aim of air independence and with a certain amount of unappreciated irony, Arnold and Towers had prepared individual letters which Admiral Stark told Marshall would "probably be more helpful at this time than any other single thing towards quieting the present agitation for a separate Air Force."

Marshall, of course, was well acquainted with Arnold's sensitivity toward the Navy, and their shared feelings on air independence have been noted. The three-page, single-spaced Arnold letter to which Stark referred was sent to, among others, Warren Atherton, Chairman of National Defense for the American Legion. In it Arnold cited some statistics that illustrated a prime reason why he and his closest confidants were against independence:

> In this day and age, we must remember that conditions and facts on which opinions are based are in a constant state of change and what is true

today may not be true tomorrow. However, it is a fact that the Air Forces have expanded from about 2,000 officers and 18,000 enlisted men in 1939 to 13,800 officers and 165,000 enlisted men today. Under present directives it may continue to expand until a total force of some 500,000 officers and enlisted men may be reached. This expansion has been made possible only by the sweat and hard work of every man in the Air Force and the wholehearted cooperation of the men in the affiliated branches of the rest of the Army.

Just imagine what would have happened if the small nucleus of air men had been required to assume not only the work of the purely air expansion but also that of the affiliated arms.

While there was a rare willingness for those who were opposed to a separate air force to enlist support from the Navy, when the issue came to strategic air power, to types of aircraft, to the usurpation of coastal air bases, and to the all-important but very slippery policy of "unity of command," the airmen were not about to trust the Navy.

As Arnold also pointed out to Marshall after the Joint Board meeting at which Towers raised the Navy plan of acquiring land planes, ". . . everything has pointed for some time to the fact that the Navy is afraid of long-range bombers and they are afraid of the effect that the long-range bomber is going to have on the operation of surface vessels. Accordingly, it would not be a surprise to me if they endeavored to start a campaign to take over all long-range bombardment operations."

Arnold saw the problem close up as a somewhat junior member of the Joint Board. Andrews, on the other hand, like Short, in Hawaii, and MacArthur, in the Philippines, faced it operationally. Within Andrews' Caribbean Theater there were two naval districts: the 10th, commanded by Rear Admiral John H. Hoover, in Puerto Rico, and the 15th, in Panama, where Sadler still held sway. Both, due to Roosevelt's increasingly aggressive naval policy in the Atlantic and the Japanese threat in the Pacific, were faced by demands they could not adequately fulfill, particularly in the air. In the former area the Caribbean Air Force, under the command of Brigadier General Davenport "Johnny" Johnson, was called on to assist Hoover.

In describing the arrangement in the Caribbean to Arnold, Andrews pointed to a weakness in Joint Board thinking. "As you know," he explained, "I have a bombardment squadron on each of our bases in the Antilles except Jamaica. These squadrons have only five or six B-18's each, but we want to be in a position to give the Navy any support within our power and give it to them promptly. The directives we received from the War Department on the subject contemplates that all calls for this support will come through Naval District commanders. Apparently they do not visualize any situation which might require quicker action on our part than would be possible with such a roundabout means of communication."

Andrews certainly visualized a need for fast action. He was concerned about the possibility of a hit-and-run raid from either ocean. On the Atlantic side there were valuable oil and bauxite targets, not to mention the Canal. From the Pacific, the Canal would be the primary target. Ecuador still refused to allow the United States to build landing strips on the Galápagos Islands, which would have extended air patrol and reconnaissance a thousand miles more out to sea.

To speed action in support of Admiral Hoover, Andrews suggested, ". . . we could, if the Navy desired it, arrange to have each individual squadron on an isolated base receive and act directly on calls for support in an emergency. Since we are furnishing the support, though, we will do it the way the Navy wants it done." And the way the Navy wanted it done was by the numbers.

In the eyes of seasoned airmen, Hoover was the Navy version of old Major B. Q. Jones—short, spunky, direct, bullheaded, but withal a man who wanted to make things work. He liked Andy Andrews and enjoyed sitting in the copilot's seat with him as Andrews flew them around in his command plane on inspection trips.

The decision over who had paramount interest in the area was a testimonial to the mixed positions of both services in recognizing how air power weighted that interest, particularly when the Army's force was predominant in a coastal frontier. Andrews was very reluctant to have units of the Sixth Air Force fly directly from Panama to Puerto Rico when it became apparent that Hoover, using the unclarified ground rules that applied, wanted to requisition the planes for his own use. Still, Hoover was an officer who would listen, even if he had little with which to act.

Not so Frank Sadler. In Tom Darcy's eyes, the Admiral was a hard shell who automatically put the quietus on any suggestion coming from the Army. Darcy wondered at Andrews' infinite patience and tact in dealing with a commander who was even opposed to sending air patrols out as far as the Galápagos Islands. Yet, here again, until planes attacking from the Pacific were actually over the narrow Isthmus, the paramount interest was the Navy's, and Sadler—not Andrews—would give the commands.

This was October, and Darcy was now close to the problem, for he had recently replaced Sonny Williams as Andrews' aide. Previously, he had acted as Andrews' chief of staff on the state visit to Argentina. Actually, the change was Marshall's doing. In view of Andrews' position, the Chief of Staff did not think it a good idea to have a member of the family as a close and confidential aide—it smacked of nepotism. Andrews hadn't thought of that, but he dryly notified Marshall, "I have changed my aide-

de-camp as you suggested. I told him that he had disqualified himself by
marrying into the family. He recognizes the wisdom of your policy. My
new aide is a bachelor, and I still have an attractive unmarried daughter,
so I have warned him to watch his step."*

Darcy and anyone else in Andrews' command would have little time for
socializing with or without the boss's charming, seventeen-year-old daughter, Jeannie. Very soon after he took up his duties, the whole contentious
question of paramount interest about unity of command came to the fore
with a new war alert.

In mid-October, directly after the fall of the Konoye government in
Japan, and fearing that it would be replaced by a more militaristic one,
the War and the Navy departments alerted commanders in the Pacific
and the Caribbean. In the latter case, the torpedoing of the U.S. destroyer
Kearny, on October 17, by a German U-boat some four hundred miles
south of Iceland heightened the feeling that war was close.[1] The warning
from the War Department, however, was not aimed primarily at a possible Japanese attack against the United States (the Canal had been closed
to their shipping since July) but more in the belief that the Japanese
might attack the U.S.S.R. in concert with the continuing German advance
toward Moscow. G-2's later appraisal of the situation, supported by General Gerow and the War Plans Division, was quite different from that of
the Navy, which warned that hostilities between the United States and
Japan could begin at any time.[2] From the War Department came the
more optimistic intelligence prediction "It seems logical to believe that no
major move will be made before the latter part of November in any direction—with a chance that the great break, if it comes, will not occur before
spring."

Marshall, in evaluating Andrews' position, stressed the very point the
War Department was emphasizing to Short, in Hawaii: "Your new job involves first of all, under present circumstances, security of the Canal
against sabotage, which involves our relationship with the Government
and people of Panama." To a lesser degree than in Hawaii but still in
considerable number, some of the people to whom Marshall referred were
Japanese settlers. But whereas the threat of sabotage meant, to General
Short, bunching Major General Fred Martin's aircraft together for protection, to Andrews it meant exactly the opposite. Dispersal was the answer,
and it was one reason why he had fought for auxiliary fields since his arrival in the Canal Zone.

Marshall also recognized the need "to guard against a surprise or trick
attack from the air, and this involves" he wrote Andrews, "what it seems to
me is one of your most difficult problems—the maintenance of a more or

* Lieutenant Williams became Squadron Commander of the 59th Squadron, at
Howard Field, flying Douglas A-20's.

less continuous alert by a considerable portion of the anti-aircraft artillery. . . .

"Outside the Canal Zone," he added, "you have so many problems it is difficult for me to pick out a particular one for comment."

In his response of October 18 Andrews pictured the state of his command's combat readiness. All antiaircraft guns and searchlights were manned in battle positions. Morale of the men in jungle outposts was excellent. As for the air defenses, ". . . certain units of the pursuit are held on the alert night and day." Interceptor Command Headquarters was operating on a twenty-four-hour basis. The greatest weakness, aside from not enough planes, was in radar equipment. There were only two long-range, one-hundred-fifty-mile detectors in the Canal Zone and none anywhere else. They, of course, were functioning around the clock, although their efficiency did not measure up to their need. His mobile strike force of infantry and airborne troops, Andrews reported, was "alert and active." And so he was as ready as he could be under the circumstances.

And under the circumstances, he had been giving a great deal of thought to "the matter of unity of command in the Caribbean." He admitted to Marshall that he had not yet found a solution to propose to the War Department, but he capsulized the problem neatly enough:

> Our respective organizations [Army and Navy] within this area are fundamentally different. For example, under present instructions we may be called upon by elements of both the Atlantic and Pacific Fleets and by Naval District commanders to support the Navy. We may have to call upon Naval units from several Naval commands, for support for Army forces. Another basic difficulty attending the proposition of unity of command is that we have Army Air Forces and Navy Air Forces located practically side by side at many points, each capable of operating in the same area, but each having different functions within that area. I am of the opinion that where the Army is established it should be responsible for all combat functions of Air Forces operating from shore bases, water or land."

The Navy was not so convinced. Directly thereafter Andrews received the views of Chief of Naval Operations Admiral Stark in his proposed revisions of that portion of the Joint Army-Navy War Plan—RAINBOW 5—that applied to the Caribbean. Andrews did not concur in the changes. "They appear to be based on the Naval phase of the problem only. They do not recognize the magnitude of the Army responsibilities in the matter, and consequently tend to overlook the fundamental purpose of the defense organization in the Caribbean area."

That purpose was to defend the area and its shipping, and the primary weapon to do the job was air defense. In such case ". . . the air decision must stand or fall on the employment of the Caribbean Air Force of the Army," Andrews stated. The Navy simply didn't have the necessary equipment, and what it did have could be more advantageously employed with the Fleet.

When it came to the Navy's organization plan, Andrews argued that Stark would divide the Caribbean into two "apparently unrelated frontiers with separate supply and maintenance systems and separate channels of command." Andrews concluded that the Navy saw the defense of the Caribbean broken down into two possibilities: an attack from the east or from the west, excluding altogether "the likelihood of an attack from the south along the line Trinidad–Panama. Consequently, the very nature of the proposed organization is inconsistent with the requirements of the problem."

He stressed that his present organization of the Caribbean Defense Command was sound and logical in that it provided mutually supporting sectors and bases, prepared to defend the Caribbean against attack from any direction. "Its Air Force is capable of exerting a maximum offensive effort in a minimum time against any threatened point with the execution of a single plan. Its strong points in Panama, Trinidad and Puerto Rico are so organized as to provide local support for the outposts within their respective sphere."

In commenting to Marshall on the Navy's viewpoint as to how unity of command should be applied in the Caribbean, Andrews wrote, "I am inclined to think that their recommendations are based on incomplete estimates. I imagine that you received a similar reaction from Short in Hawaii, although his situation is not entirely similar to that in the Caribbean. It is very difficult to visualize a situation in which a Naval District, in a coastal frontier, could be properly charged with the responsibility of unity of command. Certainly it would be a very rare occasion when the Fleet commander would be given the responsibility, as it would operate to tie the Fleet to a defense job rather than to leave it free for strategic operations. . . ."

Andrews' opinions had no immediate effect on the unresolved issue. Neither side was going to give up what it had always considered to be its prerogatives of command. The Navy's business was guarding the sea approaches, the Army's the land, and if the air was over the water, why, the paramount interest belonged to those who went down to the sea in ships. And so, in a time of growing peril, prerogatives took preference over common sense.

To a lesser or greater degree, the same situation applied in the Philippines and Hawaii. General MacArthur did not see eye to eye with Asiatic Fleet Commander Admiral Thomas C. Hart on much of anything. During the autumn they disagreed, among other things, on who would be responsible for offshore air reconnaissance.[3] On Oahu, General Short and Admiral Kimmel played golf together, but they did not confide their plans or much of their information to one another. Since the Navy had the paramount interest in the Islands, it dominated the offshore patrol situation, its PBY's ranging far out to sea, while Army reconnaissance units were restricted to inshore patrol, extending seaward, according to Martin, no more than four or five miles. This arrangement had been confirmed by the Joint Coastal Defense Plan of April 11, 1941, which detailed the responsibilities of both services at Pearl Harbor. Should Martin's reconnaissance planes have spotted hostile shipping or aircraft, it was estimated that notifying the Navy through the indirect communications system would take about half an hour.

In his mid-October comments to Andrews, Marshall remarked on the complicated political challenge with which the Caribbean Defense Commander was faced. In Panama the politics of the area had undergone a dramatic change. President Arnulfo Arias, tall, thin, and aesthetic, clothed in his usual white, had gone off to Cuba with his mistress, supposedly for a weekend. At its end came word from Havana that he would not be returning; he was retiring from the political scene. A sizable portion of the Panamanian treasury had accompanied him into retirement.

Both Ambassador Wilson and Governor Edgerton, as well as the U. S. State Department, denied having any part in Arias' sudden departure. Nevertheless, he was quickly succeeded by Ricardo Adolfo de la Guardia, a vocally pro-American politician.

Andrews had gotten to know Arias well, for, unlike the Department commanders before him, he had made it a point to know not only the President but also many Panamanians outside the Zone. Arias obviously appreciated Andrews' approach, liking his genuine manner, his willingness to socialize. As a result, he had become more amenable to building auxiliary airfields on Panamanian territory, and their relationship had been a pleasant and profitable one. It removed the need of Roosevelt's earlier suggestion to Hull and Stimson to get tough with Arias.

Andrews' ability to cultivate personal relationships made him an extremely valuable adjunct to U.S. foreign policy throughout Latin America. Through flying visits to Central and South American capitals, invitations to visit his headquarters and base commands, and offers of cooperation and aid, Andrews lowered the Andes-like barrier in the minds of important South Americans who viewed North Americans without warmth and were on the fence with regard to cooperation. One of Andrews' reports to Marshall gave an indication of the reason for such feeling.

> The Peruvian Minister to Panama, Mr. Ortiz de Zevallos, whom I know quite well and who speaks very frankly with me, was in my office on Wednesday last, to tell me of the reaction of his country to the impounding by the United States of the planes which Peru purchased from the Norwegian government. He was of the opinion that it was a pressure move to force Peru to a line of action desired by the United States in the Peruvian-Ecuadorian dispute. One interesting angle of his point of view

was that he considered that the United States was taking advantage of
Peru and not playing fair, inasmuch as the United States had influenced
Peru to join in the seizure of Axis vessels and the Lufthansa airline in
Peru. After Peru by such action had antagonized Germany, the United
States then had the existing government in Peru in a position where it
could do little but protest about the impounding of the Peruvian planes.
He fears the fall of the present government. The interview ended pleas-
antly with an invitation to a party at the Peruvian Minister's house, which
I accepted.

The purpose of Andrews' activities outside the Caribbean Theater was,
of course, the building of a hemispheric defense system, and here, too, cooperation with the Navy was imperative.

These defense plans were taking on both form and substance in the fall
of 1941. In form, there was a joint Army-Navy agreement to supply
armed assistance to Latin American countries in the event of either internal or external attack. In substance, Andrews had a mobile force of two
special infantry battalions—one parachute, one airborne. They were the
only overseas combat-ready units of their kind in the Army. That they
were in being was due in large measure to Andrews' having been G-3.
Should a Latin American neighbor call for help, plans were to move these
battalions by air to strategic points within that country. The Navy's job
was to occupy the threatened seaports. An expeditionary force from the
United States would follow. Though still short of combat aircraft, transport planes to move his airborne infantry were high on Andrews' priority
list.

Andrews considered the island of Martinique an enemy salient on the
fringe of his front line, and he would have liked to immobilize it. He also
viewed the colony of French Guiana, north of Brazil, as a danger point.
His evaluation was based on intelligence reports of his own G-2.[4] He had
an appreciation for the value of espionage that was lacking in most of his
military confreres,† and the imagination to use it properly. His Chief of
G-2 lived at the Tivoli Hotel, where, on the Victorian veranda or in the
bar, easy talk flowed with the drinks.

One of Andrews' most valuable sources of information was newsman
Jules Dubois, the Latin American editor of the Chicago *Tribune*. Dubois,
who spoke Spanish and Portuguese, was an energetic reporter with contacts throughout the region. He was deeply committed to the Allied cause
in spite of his newspaper's isolationist position. But Andrews' most important source in French Guiana was a faceless undercover agent who signed
his messages Blalock. From Cayenne, the agent reported:

† Col. William "Wild Bill" Donovan, Roosevelt's special agent, made a point of
calling on Andrews on his various intelligence-seeking travels. Nelson Rockefeller,
also involved in aiding British Intelligence in Latin America, stopped to see Andrews
as well.

Last week while in the customs warehouse to withdraw gasoline, the customs men were busy unpacking several hundred rifles and sidearms. Their explanation was that the guns had been in the colonies ten years and were obsolete, therefore they were being assembled and made ready to be sold along with several thousand cartridges that had just arrived in the colony.

Another, and more ominous, message read:

Was informed by a government official (anti-Nazi) that should there be any indication of American occupation, that all arrangements are made to quickly bring in several thousand German soldiers that are now working in Brazil.

Was informed by the Governor himself that the naval ship or ships from Martinique would arrive here on the 15th of this month.

Blalock had his eye on a gold prospector who "seems to have plenty of financial backing. He has prospected the entire colony in places that all other gold men say is stupidness because no gold could possibly be in some of the locations. . . . Yesterday this man and a friend of mine pack and load on the French naval boat 1700 bauxite samples. Consigned to 'Kreeger, Berlin.'

"On my recent trip to the north end of the colony," Blalock reported, "we stopped at the prison islands (Devil's Island) to unload rice. There the colony was busy building a dock. Since the rivers are filling with mud so fast, the boats (combined navigation and one from Brazil) will have to disembark all goods there and tow them into Cayenne and St. Laurent. After 200 years, the island needs a dock 900 meters long with a minimum of 18 meters of water on either side. This forces them to make the leg of the T 700 meters long to get out to that much water."

It wasn't difficult to conclude that a dock for submarine servicing was being constructed by the penal colony.

All this information was simply part of a disturbing mosaic extending in Andrews' sphere from Guatemala to Argentina, and he and his staff gathered the pieces where they could, even at a potential enemy's dinner table. On the evening of October 31, Andrews was a dinner guest of the Japanese Minister to Panama.

Some congressmen in Washington and some like-minded editors might scoff at the idea of the Axis attempting to gain a foothold in Latin America, but Andrews, whose job it was to guard the Canal, guard the Caribbean, and repel an attack from any direction, did not. He had good reason to see such threats as real. To Marshall, he listed probable enemy priorities: "(1) first and above all, the Canal itself, followed by (2) the bauxite mines, (3) the oil refineries at Trinidad, Curaçao and Aruba, (4) shipping in the harbor of Port-of-Spain, (5) installations and shipping in Puerto Rico, and (6) installations at the outerlying bases."

And with this evaluation he stressed the fundamental reality: He had precious little with which to fight, and the Navy had even less.

* * *

It was Hap Arnold's belief that the Joint Army-Navy Board, the highest military council in the land, operated under guidelines that were dangerously inefficient. If the members agreed, a plan was adopted. If they could not, the decision was postponed, and no officer on the Board had the power to make a decision if a difference of opinion arose. There was simply no effective means of bringing about the coordination necessary to establish a unified command. This did not make for cohesive operations in the Caribbean, Hawaii, and the Philippines.

During the summer of 1941, both the Navy General Board and the Army War Plans Division had recommended forming a Joint General Staff directly responsible to the President, but agreement could not be reached on how a unified command could be established. The Operational and Concentration plans for RAINBOW 5 accepted by the members of the Joint Board were revised by the Navy in late October. Arnold forwarded these proposed changes to his Air War Plans Division. It was Ken Walker who passed judgment on them, his critique aimed not at finding ways to cooperate but, rather, ways to block the Navy from taking advantage of the Army Air Forces.

He declared in part:

The Army must lose no opportunity to insist upon exercising its right to conduct air operations within the tactical operating radius of its aircraft— as an Army responsibility. It must be shown that the Army does and can operate in lieu of naval forces.

When the full right of the Army to operate in lieu of naval forces is acknowledged, then the Navy will lose one argument to substitute 4-engined bombardment-type airplanes for patrol boats which, if agreed to, may well cut into our organization of our heavy bombardment groups. For example, North Atlantic bases can accommodate only a limited number of heavy bombers. Patrol boats cannot operate in winter months. We cannot give up bases to the Navy for naval land-based bombardment patrol planes in the first instance. In the second instance, the Navy cannot operate in lieu of naval forces.

Referring to the Navy's task of preparing "to occupy the Azores and the Cape Verde Islands," Walker suggested: "This should be followed by, 'until relieved by the Army.' This added statement tied in with par. 28 h. reduces the possibility that the Navy will consider their occupancy a permanent one and thus advance arguments for constructing land-based bombardment planes for operation from such bases."

In commenting on the Navy's view of action in the Pacific, Walker wanted it made clear that there would also be " 'naval support of Army air force operations.' Joint air support plans in the Pacific and Far East area are not confined wholly to the support of the Navy. The operations of the Philippine Air Force will be of paramount importance in securing the Philippines and enabling the conduct of an effective strategic defensive. Under such conditions, the Army could not agree to reducing its air forces to a supporting and subordinate role."

The Army airmen's worry about Navy dominance had gone on for so long it was in the nature of a tradition, a kind of chronic watching for an attack out of the sun that kept a pilot on his toes. Yet, with a steadily worsening war picture—the U.S. destroyer *Reuben James* was torpedoed and sunk in the Atlantic by a German U-boat on October 31, with the loss of 115 lives—the emphasis on both sides should have shifted to the positive. Otherwise, the question might be asked, Who is the real enemy?

While interservice rivalry was a bone of contention on which the nation was soon to choke, within the air arm there was an internal conflict just as long-running, equally fixed, and potentially as dangerous in its outcome.

In September, Air Observer Ira Eaker sent Tooey Spaatz a brief appraisal of the valuable information he was gaining from his investigation of RAF fighter tactics. He also asked to be made a member of a board on future fighter development that Spaatz had spoken of.‡ "I have taken the pains to get the best thought here on the subject up to date and have some definite ideas based on what I have seen and learned here," Eaker wrote.

The board met in October soon after Eaker's return from England. Spaatz was chairman; Eaker and Colonel Monk Hunter were members, as were Lieutenant Colonels Mark Bradley and Ben Kelsey, who was the recorder. One of the board's primary purposes was to examine the need for and the characteristics of an escort fighter to accompany bombers on their deep penetrations of the enemy heartland.

Over a twenty-year span, there had been many boards involved in the same problem. None had come forth with an acceptable recommendation that did more than fuel the fires of debate. Whether an escort fighter was needed was a question that simmered in the engineering section of the Materiel Division, was denigrated by the bomber-over-all theorists at the Air Corps Tactical School, was tested and found wanting in GHQ Air Force maneuvers, and was reflected on in the office of the Chief of the Air Corps. The end result was that when Hal George and his planners tackled AWPD-1, which was to include types of aircraft, there was not even a design of an escort fighter on hand.

George and his planning team were among the most vociferous of all bomber advocates. At the Air Corps Tactical School they had preached a gospel built on the belief that bombers such as the B-17, with its speed and firepower, needed no escorting fighter to protect them from attack, particularly if the bombers flew in massed formation.

‡ The old designation "Pursuit" was officially changed to "Fighter" in May 1941.

During the 1930s this theory had become almost a faith within the Air Corps. At root it was fostered as much by a lack of funds—most of what there was in the budget went into bomber development—as it was by the built-in concepts of national defense that perceived the fighter as an aircraft with great speed which precluded long range.

The wars in Spain and China did little to change this thinking, but the war in Europe—with both RAF and Luftwaffe bomber losses—began to have its effect on the open-minded. By 1940, Hal George, a bomber man from boots to goggles, was telling Hap Arnold that it appeared to him that bombers would definitely need fighter protection. The question then was whether to proceed with a test model of an escort (a long-legged fighter, as it was called) or to do a design study on a type recommended by a previous board. Neither was done. Bomber influence prevailed and, instead, a study was made comparing increased B-17 firepower with that of an interceptor.

Reports coming back from air observers in England tended to give the impression, if not the outright conclusion, that losses of heavily escorted German bombers were a result of improper tactics and equipment. RAF bomber losses were attributed to similar inadequacies. The firmly fixed opinions of Air Corps bomber proponents were not easily or quickly reversed or modified.

Nevertheless, when Hal George and his team drafted AWPD-1, in August, they gave some recognition to the need for a long-range fighter escort, although neither Walker nor Kuter nor Hansell really believed the need existed. They believed that the B-17 and the B-24 were actually long-range fighters capable of carrying a heavy bomb load. In fact, the escort they described was a bomber loaded with armament instead of bombs, capable of higher speed, its single purpose to protect the bomb carriers. No such plane was on the drawing boards, but the planners endorsed the tactical requirements for such a plane and believed a program for its development should not be neglected.

Claire Chennault, a fighter expert who had bitterly opposed the theories of the bomber men at the Air Corps Tactical School, was now using P-40's taken from Ira Eaker's 20th Group to excellent advantage against the Japanese in China. He would have uttered a few choice obscenities at the idea of tying fighter to bombers. So did other fighter specialists closer to home.

When Ben Kelsey had returned from England after his tour with Tooey Spaatz, he knew that one basic weakness of British interceptors was their short range. As Chief of the Fighter Branch in the Production Engineering Section at Wright Field, Kelsey was in favor of building a fighter with greatly increased range. The idea was not all that new, but now it was taken seriously. It had been proposed at Wright Field frequently in the late 1930s, but the ambiguities that prevailed between pursuit and bomber boards and were passed on to the Air Board for reshuffling, produced nothing but reports and memos.

Not until war actually began in Europe did the Air Corps admit that a single-seat aircraft could be used as an escort, but not for offensive action unless there was an improvement in range. Toward that end, Kelsey and Wright Field engineers suggested mounting droppable fuel tanks on the bomb racks of a P-36. Arnold flatly rejected the idea for combat. In the office of the Chief of the Air Corps, any external fuel tank was seen as an added fire hazard.*

This did not mean that Arnold was blind to the problem. Quite the contrary: he had been involved in it since his March Field days. About the time Hal George admitted to him that bombers would have to be protected by fighter escort, Arnold wrote to Delos Emmons taking a left-handed swipe at the bomber theorists: "Reference to reports from air activity in recent wars clearly indicates the necessity for pursuit aviation and the very great role it plays in air combat and anti-aircraft defense. A doctrine which has been widely propounded in certain Air Corps circles for many years to the effect that fighter aircraft cannot shoot down large bombardment planes in formation has now been proven wholly untenable. It has been demonstrated recently beyond a doubt that the best anti-aircraft defense is pursuit aviation."

This said nothing about escort, but if fighters could shoot down bombers, then bombers needed fighter protection. Arnold directed Spaatz and Hunter to come up with a recommendation on the type of fighter needed to protect the bombers. The result was a variation on the old theme. They decided neither to build a prototype nor to do a design investigation but, rather, to propose a repeat: a study comparing bomber firepower with that of escorting fighters.

This stalemate led to a conference with representatives from all the interested Air Corps divisions, including the Ordnance Department. Once again, the necessity for a long-range escort aircraft was accepted in principle. Either the plane must have the necessary speed and range to match the bomber's on its own, be refueled in flight, or be carried by a mother ship and released at the proper time. This last was seen to be no more difficult technically than the first proposal. Until Ben Kelsey made his recommendation on extended range using external tanks, this was the strongest support for an escort the Air Board had considered. However, in reaching a final conclusion, the members managed to negate their own projections by deciding that the B-17 could defend itself without fighter escort.

It took an entirely different need to start feeding range into U.S. fighters. In May 1941, Bob Olds had been given the job of organizing the

---

* Actually, the use of droppable gas tanks dated back to World War I. The first leakproof tanks were installed by the French in DH-4's in November 1918.

ferrying of Lend-Lease planes to the British Isles by the North Atlantic route and to British forces in Africa by a southern route. Naturally, he was in full support of adding range to all fighter aircraft. Out of Kelsey's determined recommendations and Olds's demands, both Lockheed and Republic Aviation were asked to increase the ferrying range of their new fighters, the P-38 and the P-47.

Ironically, this fundamental modification, which would be a vital qualification for any escort fighter, was pushed ahead for an essentially noncombatant reason. When Arnold summoned Kelsey to Washington and told him to start testing external tanks, Kelsey admitted that he had already been doing just that.

"You mean in violation of my orders?" barked Arnold.

"Yes, sir," admitted Kelsey.

"Well, goddammit, the result had better be good."

Thus, through some *sub rosa* testing engineered by Kelsey, Lockheed's plans included using droppable tanks. In September the question was whether the tanks were to be used at high or low altitudes. The answer was the former, which certainly indicated that the emphasis was on ferrying, not escorting, in which the tanks would be dropped at low altitudes. Still, when Spaatz, Eaker, Hunter, and Kelsey sat down to go over the entire fighter question, the problem of extended range was addressed.

In their two weeks of deliberation and evaluation, the five covered the gamut of fighter requirements. Eaker's tour with the RAF had acquainted him with the latest British equipment and tactics. He had flown their newest fighters on both day and night tests, concentrating on the latter, for as yet the United States had no night fighter per se. In November 1940, the Northrop Aviation Company had been given a contract to build two experimental models, and Eaker's input into what was to become the P-61 Black Widow was of major importance.

In April, it will be recalled, FDR had told Hap Arnold that his verbal report on the situation in Great Britain was the best the President had ever received. Hap told Ira essentially the same thing. "Have read your report as thoroughly as my time permitted. I want to let you know it is one of the most all inclusive reports that I have seen from an official observer returning from abroad. It covers in all detail the various subjects and items of equipment outlined for investigation in your directive. You have done your job, and now it is up to us to get some action to take advantage of the information and ideas that you have brought back to us."

But Eaker's ideas were undoubtedly influenced by the RAF's thinking on fighter escort. Arnold's directive to him had specifically required that he look into the matter, and he had been informed by the RAF's leading technical people that they did not believe such a plane could be built. RAF Chief of Staff Air Marshal Portal suggested to Eaker that the only practicable escort for bombers was another bomber, loaded with guns instead of bombs. Spaatz and the Board felt swapping bombs for armor and guns was only a temporary solution at best. They projected the design of a multiplace fighter and recommended that its development begin at once. And then, as done previously, they stepped back and cast aspersions on their own proposal. While they agreed that bombers must be protected, like the RAF, they doubted the aviation industry's ability to build a plane with the required performance. Further, they questioned the feasibility of attempting to do so in the face of production demands being made for other types of aircraft. They were dubious about the practicality of the "convoy defender," and then, in establishing a list of priorities for *six* different fighter projects, they put the escort at the bottom of the list.

Their contradictions reflected all the considerations mentioned earlier as well as the urgency of producing equipment needed right then in England, North Africa, the Soviet Union, China, and the U.S. possessions in the Caribbean and the Pacific, not to mention the home front.

A brief but clear picture of aircraft production problems was given to Hap Arnold by his good friend Dutch Kindelberger, president of North American Aviation:

> We have been having one hell of a time this month getting things clear of here. As you know, the crack-up we had, which killed one of the radio operators and badly injured one of our pilots was due to the failure of a bolt due to strong-arm work stripping the thread. We made an inspection of everything in the field and everything in work here, and found other cases, none of them so serious that they would have been tragic but indicating that with inexperienced personnel, the thinly spread training program, new supervision and inexperienced inspection, it is possible for most anything to happen. I wouldn't let anything go out until every possible connection on all the airplanes had been rechecked which meant disassembly in many cases. Net result is that our month of deliveries is about half what we anticipated, part of which is also due to the fact that the bags for leakproofing made by Goodrich, have been leaking and swelling up and we have had to pull them out of most of the airplanes and replace them, which is a big job, particularly after the airplanes are assembled and out on the ramp. Same thing applies in our pursuit planes. We are catching up on this and hope to have some good bags in here next week. . . .

When Kindelberger wrote to Hap of his problems, his company was in the first stages of producing a new fighter for the British. The RAF, as Chaney had pointed out to Andrews, did not like the Curtiss P-40 any more than they liked the B-17. With the Air Corps concentrating on the P-38 and the P-47, North American, with technical data from Curtiss, went to work for the RAF on the new plane. It was designated the P-51. There was no knowing then that in later models of the P-51 lay the an-

swer to the long-range escort fighter. Had its potential been foreseen
earlier, the lives of thousands of U.S. airmen would have been saved in an
onrushing future.

George Marshall once remarked that before the war began in Europe,
there was plenty of time but no money. Now he said there was plenty of
money but no time. This feeling was present among the members of the
Pursuit Board. All the pressures that sat with them did not excuse their
attitude toward developing a long-range fighter; that attitude simply
resulted in their decision to rate it as the least important consideration
facing them. It was a decision whose burden would later fall most heavily
on Spaatz, Eaker, and Monk Hunter.

There was one additional factor apart from considerations of a long-
range fighter that illustrated with devastating clarity the abysmal lack of
appreciation the War Department had for Japanese aviation. Mark Bradley, as the junior member on the Board, was asked by Spaatz to obtain
from G-2 the Army intelligence file on its appraisal of Japanese aircraft.
Bradley did so and was permitted to examine what he described as a
razor-thin folder. There was nothing in it to indicate the Japanese had
developed a modern air force—Army or Navy. The material in the folder
included some antiquated photos and design drawings, a scattering of
dated newspaper clippings, and in one news dispatch brief mention of a reported new Japanese all-metal interceptor that could climb vertically. It
was called a Zero.[5]

The time was six weeks before Pearl Harbor.

Eight

Day of Reckoning

During Ira Eaker's six-week tour as an RAF observer, his investigation was divided into two parts: The first centered on the latest British technical and tactical advances in both fighter and bomber operations, day and night. He was permitted to fly the Spitfire and the Typhoon, a new RAF night interceptor, with a top-secret device called the Hellmore Light, used to expose enemy bombers tracked by radar.* The brightness of the turbine light would not only expose the bomber but blind its crew as well. He also flew the twin-engine Mosquito, which the RAF was to employ in day and night missions. He got lost, too, flying a Spitfire in typical English weather (fog and more fog), and in the course of his activities he spent time with bomber and fighter squadrons, absorbing information like a blotter.

That was one part of his assignment. The other was politically more significant. He inspected five air bases nearing completion in Northern Ireland and Scotland, flying first to Belfast with the British Air Ministry's Director of Fighter Operations. There he met Air Commodore Lawson, who commanded 82 Group. Lawson escorted him to the Group's various fields, showed him the facilities, and explained the sectors for which each field was responsible both day and night. This was far more than a routine look-see by a visiting fireman. Eaker had switched from the business of things to the realm of ideas. In the report he wrote for General Chaney on the adequacy of these bases, it was obvious that his investigation was the result of a policy decision made at the highest level. The newly built air bases were to be occupied by U.S. personnel, and Eaker recommended "a skeleton group staff and a skeleton sector staff should be sent to North Ireland for training in November:

* Named for its inventor, Group Captain Hellmore.

"The first squadron brought over should occupy the Airdrome at St. Angelo and take over the sector there first, in my opinion. The next Airdrome and sector taken over should be Eglinton, and the last Balley Halbert. This recommendation is made to save the mixing of American and British squadrons on the same airdrome. One fighter group as we know it, of 4 day squadrons and one night squadron and a training squadron, plus air base detachments, can easily be accommodated in Northern Ireland on the Airdromes mentioned. The personnel set-up in your plan are believed to be entirely feasible and desirable for this area."

One point that Eaker stressed to both Chaney and Joe McNarney was that in Ireland and Scotland, after U.S. personnel had received training in the RAF method of coordinating group and air operations, U.S. units would remain independent of British control. "One group of ours as outlined above can be accommodated at Ayr and Turnberry if we get complete control and use of Turnberry. Every effort should be made to secure Turnberry and it should be the first Airdrome occupied in Scotland. . . . No squadron should be put at Turnberry unless we can get complete control and use of the field. . . ."

In July 1941, the American public had generally accepted the announcement that U. S. Marines would be relieving the British garrison in Iceland. In September it knew from press reports that American construction workers were building naval facilities in Northern Ireland and Scotland, supposedly for British use but more likely for U.S. naval ships engaged in convoy duty. However, there was no indication that either the public or the Congress had been made aware of plans to station U.S. pilots and airmen in the British Isles. According to RAINBOW 5 and ABC-1, that move was to occur *only* after M Day (Mobilization Day), which, for the Army, was to be announced by the Secretary of War.

Military Attaché Raymond E. Lee's mid-July letter to Brigadier General Sherman Miles, Chief of Army Intelligence, showed a knowledge of plans for the naval bases, but he apparently knew nothing of the planned U.S. air bases. To Miles he confided, "You may be interested in the following account of an off-the-record interview given by General George C. Marshall, Chief of Staff of the U. S. Army, to a representative of the Associated Press who has just returned to this country.

"Marshall took it for granted that the United States were going to war with Hitler for the protection of the United States. He described the British Isles as his advance base and said he was willing to equip this base fully with materials and men. He mentioned the possibility of establishing bases for the Air Corps, the Navy and the U. S. Army, including newly mechanized divisions. . . ."[1]

It took the Roosevelt-Churchill meeting in Argentia Bay, a month later, to gain secret approval for these projects. The Air Corps plan was given the code name TRIGGER, and it was Eaker who brought back to Spaatz the method by which TRIGGER would be implemented. There were two phases: The first (code-named SHADOW) was to send immediately a small number of officers and men to train with 82 Group. They would return to the United States and set up an operational training unit for additional ground personnel, who, in turn, would form a group and sector staff to train with 82 Group.

As Major Frank Armstrong was to put it: "Air training of U.S. personnel at 82 Group at the present, later at a separate designated station in the United Kingdom, will enable the U. S. Air Force to have available at the earliest possible time, fighter personnel."

Armstrong had served under Eaker during the airmail crisis in 1934 and was an observer in England when Eaker arrived there. They were longtime friends, and Armstrong and Gordon Saville were to become very active in organizing and promoting TRIGGER. It was Eaker's hope that he would command TRIGGER, in whatever form it was finally accepted, and that Armstrong and Saville would be his principal aides.

So far in 1941, there had been two major U.S. war alerts, both of them related to Japanese moves. Undeclared war in the Atlantic between German U-boats and U.S. naval ships had resulted in loss of life. However, it had not brought a break in U.S.-German diplomatic relations. Yet, while concern mounted over new aggressive moves by the Japanese in the Pacific and continued failure to negotiate any mutually agreeable compromise with Nippon, the main thrust of Roosevelt's policy was to aid Britain, and now the U.S.S.R., to the point where not just U.S. seamen but U.S. airmen were bound to become directly involved against Germany.

Thoughts of TRIGGER no doubt were on Eaker's mind during the two weeks he spent on the Pursuit Board deliberating with his close friends on recommendations for new day and night fighters. However, as soon as the Board had completed its deliberations, on the last day of October, Eaker was on his way to Spartanburg, South Carolina. He had been assigned as Interceptor Commander of the 10th Pursuit Wing, the combat air arm of the Blue forces in the major maneuvers and mock war begun in Louisiana during the summer and now continuing in the Carolinas.

The maneuvers that took place that summer and fall were the largest war games on record, the Second and Third armies opposing each other in the Louisiana exercises. The maneuvers were the result of Marshall's unflagging efforts to prepare his largely green and ill-equipped forces for combat.

In the New York *Times* of September 30, military correspondent Hanson Baldwin had described the root of a continuing problem that plagued the Louisiana maneuvers:

Perhaps the chief results [*sic*] of the maneuvers has been the realization by ground generals that air superiority is essential to success in war, mimic or real, and the corresponding realization of air generals that the plane is not the sole instrument of victory, and that the airman, if he is to be of much use in a tactical mission, must be able to do more than fly a plane and drop a bomb.

Despite this mutual understanding, produced by cooperative missions, there is still conflict of authority. The old question of the separate air force may continue to create jealousies and internal Army strife. . . .

Indeed it would, but the use of air power and the attempt to coordinate it with the ground forces led to the war games in the Carolinas. There General Hugh Drum was to command a force of three hundred thousand infantrymen opposing a mechanized army of 100,000 led by Major General O. W. Griswold. Griswold's forces, the Blue, had four hundred aircraft at their disposal, and it was Eaker who had been chosen by Arnold to command the fighters.

When Eaker arrived at Cleveland Park to take command of his wing, which was made up essentially of the 20th Pursuit Group, he found that the Blue air commander was Colonel Asa Duncan. Duncan, a somewhat retiring and thoughtful type, had learned what combat was all about as George Kenney's observer over German lines during World War I. In this case, the principal opponent was another old friend, Colonel Bill Kepner, who was commanding the Red Interceptor forces. Kepner had the advantage, having been on the scene for two weeks getting his command organized. Unlike Eaker, however, he had not been an RAF observer, and in the eight days left before the mock war began, Ira went all-out to institute the same fighter system the British employed.

He signed up a contingent of civilian volunteers, largely women, to act as ground observers, placing most of them near local post offices, where there was a telephone they could use to report their sightings through a filter center to a fighter board. A communications system was installed so that the board had instantaneous contact with Wing Headquarters, which, in turn, was equipped to signal Eaker's squadrons, which numbered about one hundred fifty fighters. Working day and night, Eaker and his staff organized aircraft dispersal pens, camouflaging their bases, honing their tactics. On hand to encourage and make suggestions were two of the RAF's noted Battle of Britain aces, Wing Commodore Stanford Tuck and Group Captain Harry Broadhurst. Eaker had met Tuck in England, and they had discussed the kind of improvements needed in fighters.

Two days before the maneuvers were to begin, Tuck gave his hosts a bit of a scare. He was tooling along in a Republic P-43, following one of Eaker's pilots back from a publicity affair in Charlotte, North Carolina. The day was pure Indian summer, warm and hazy, and when his escort hand-signaled that he was going down to land for fuel, Tuck decided to show him how it was done in the RAF. He peeled off at eight thousand feet and pulled out just above the ground. The only problem was that he lost sight of his guide, who lost sight of him as well, and there was no landing field anywhere about. Tuck began circling, hoping to spot one or the other. All he could see were acres and acres of cotton and corn, and when the fuel gauge indicated he was out of gas, he set the plane down in a cornfield at Cheraw, South Carolina, some sixty miles east-southeast of Charlotte. He was a most chagrined ace, a bloody damn' fool! having gotten lost like a tyro. Since he was long overdue, his wing mate had notified Cleveland Park, and Eaker had dispatched planes on a search. It was the crowd around Tuck's P-43 that helped locate him, and with great relief word of his safety was flashed to headquarters.

Later, Eaker asked him half jokingly, "Why didn't you bail out?"

"I remember you suffered the same experience in England," Tuck said. "You didn't jump; I didn't figure I would."

Which meant, good pilots didn't bail out if there was a chance of setting the bird down in one piece. Eaker, in recounting the tale to Arnold, said, "He made a good landing, no damage done, and we were able to fly the plane out."

But now he had other things on his mind, and a wicked piece of poker-playing up his sleeve. Looking sufficiently stony, he asked for a volunteer to go on a dangerous mission. The result was that on November 14, the night before the "war" officially was to begin, a heavily equipped airman bailed out of one of Asa Duncan's bombers over the Red Army lines and floated down close to Kepner's headquarters. The next morning, a bright-eyed second lieutenant reported with fifty or so other officers to Kepner's regular staff conference. At it, Red fighter plans were discussed and orders given to Red squadron leaders on their assignments for the day. Shortly after the meeting broke up, Eaker's daring spy slipped away into the woods, where he had stashed a new Signal Corps radio transmitter. This became his daily practice, and the wily Blue Interceptor Commander received a rundown on the intentions of his opponent.

Even without his spy, Eaker's knowledge gained from his RAF experience put Kepner at a disadvantage, and the 10th Wing made an impressive showing. Both Marshall and Arnold spent a day and a night at Eaker's headquarters observing his operations. Marshall had told Arnold the maneuvers were a testing ground for officers of Eaker's rank. Should war come, it was those among them who had done well during the maneuvers that would be put in operational commands. Hap later sent Ira a note saying, "Upon returning from my inspection trip I want to tell you I have heard nothing but compliments as to what you have done. I add my congratulations."

He made no mention of the sweet revenge he took on former Deputy Chief of Staff Lieutenant General Hugh Drum while observing the maneuvers: They were in a control tower watching paratroopers making a jump when Drum said, "Say, Hap, where is that transport plane that you're supposed to get for me?" He was referring to the suggestion Marshall had made that all the Army field commanders should have their own planes.

Replied Hap, "That transport is still on the drafting board, just exactly the same place it was three years ago when I asked you to buy it for us." It would be another two months and an admonishment from Marshall saying, "Hap, for godsake send him down a Piper Cub or something," before Drum finally got his plane.

Asa Duncan was also to write and congratulate Eaker "for the superior manner in which you directed operations of our Interceptor Command and the most valuable service you gave me." Asa said he'd learned a lot and enjoyed the whole affair tremendously.

The war game referees gave Eaker high marks too. In five days of concentrated operations, his 141 planes flew 170 missions, putting in two thousand hours and racking up a nearly two-to-one margin of victories over Bill Kepner's Red airmen. All fun and games, but when it was over, Eaker headed back to Washington with TRIGGER on his mind.

* * *

The maneuvers ended on Thursday, November 27, their most important feature said to be the first major use of paratroops and airborne infantry. On that same day, a coded message over Marshall's signature was dispatched to U. S. Army commanders Andrews, Short, and MacArthur. In substance the radiogram said that negotiations with the Japanese Government appeared to be terminated. Japanese moves could not be predicted. Hostile action was possible at any moment. The U. S. Government's desire was that the Japanese strike the first blow, but that wish should not preclude any necessary defense preparations, including "reconnaissance and other measures you deem necessary. Should hostilities occur you will carry out tasks assigned in Rainbow 5 so far as they pertain to Japan."

For Henry Stimson the day was long and very tense. It began with a telephone call to Cordell Hull; he was anxious to know what the Secretary of State's final word had been to the two Japanese envoys, Saburo Kurusu and Kichisaburo Nomura. Had he handed them the new proposal or had he broken off the talks? Hull, dispirited, replied, "I have washed my hands of it and it is now in the hands of you and Knox—the Army and the Navy."

Stimson immediately called the President. Roosevelt was not so pessimistic. He said the talks had ended with "a magnificent statement prepared by Hull" that indicated there was still room for maneuvering. But Stimson quickly learned that the statement was simply a reiteration of the U. S. Ten Point Note.[2]

He was digesting this information when Hap Arnold came in with orders for the movement of two B-24's to Manila. His description of how the planes could fly from San Francisco over the Japanese-mandated Marianas Islands and photograph the military concentration there without fear of being shot down by Japanese fighters was reassuring. But the number of bombers flying out to reinforce MacArthur was not nearly enough, although another two squadrons, a total of fourteen Fortresses, were slated to leave Hamilton Field shortly. There just wasn't enough time. Marshall, who had previously thought there would be, now agreed with Stimson. Diplomacy was the only hope by which the inevitable could be held off, and it appeared Hull had given up. This raised the question whether keeping the plan for fortifying the Philippines secret until the job was done was a wise one. It had been hoped that when Roosevelt revealed MacArthur's full strength, it would impress the moderates in Japan and so prevent war.[3]

While Marshall was in North Carolina at the maneuvers, Knox and Stark came to Stimson's office with General Gerow, and they prepared to draft a message to MacArthur. The Far Eastern Commander had already been sent what Stimson termed a "quasi-alert." In his earlier conversation with Roosevelt, the Secretary had suggested that he now be sent to "final alert; namely, that he should be on the qui vive for any attack and telling him how the situation was."[4]

Stark and Gerow stressed the need to buy time, and Stimson was all in favor of that but not at the cost of humiliation or any show of weakness on the part of the United States. Another telephone call was made to Hull while drafting the alert. Stimson was satisfied that the dispatch was in proper shape, but the talk with Hull toned down the Army's warning, which then began: "Negotiations with Japan appear to be terminated to all practical purposes with only the barest possibilities that the Japanese might come back and offer to continue."[5]

The warning sent to Admirals Kimmel and Hart by the Navy Department was far more direct. It began: "This dispatch is to be considered a war warning. Negotiations with Japan toward stabilization of conditions in the Pacific have ceased."

Three days prior to this message, Admiral Stark had dispatched a similar warning to naval district commanders. It, however, stressed that Japanese attacks might be launched in any direction, particularly against the Philippines and Guam. In Hawaii, Admiral Kimmel neglected to inform his most senior officers of either of these warnings, dated November 24 and November 27. One of these officers was Rear Admiral Patrick Bellinger, Kimmel's principal air officer in command of naval patrol aircraft. Another was Rear Admiral John H. Newton, who was planning to depart on December 5 with a task force led by the carrier *Lexington* and five destroyers, transporting a squadron of twenty-five fighter-bombers to Midway Island, whose defenses were being beefed up partially to protect the movement of B-17's to MacArthur.

Kimmel did inform his War Plans Chief, Captain C. H. McMorris, of the warnings. Together they agreed that Pearl Harbor would not be a target for surprise attack. McMorris weighed the number of patrol planes and available crews against the Navy's training program and came up with an evaluation of the need to conduct long-range reconnaissance: "It was determined that the searches would not be initiated." His opinion was that such searches would only be token in nature and offer limited effectiveness. If they were carried out, "training would suffer heavily," he said, "and if we were called upon to conduct a war we would find a large portion of our planes needing engine overhaul at the time we most required their services."[6]

As for General Short, his interpretation of the November 27 message was no more prescient than Kimmel's. He took it to mean that "the avoidance of war was paramount and the greatest fear of the War Department was that some international incident might occur in Hawaii. . . . There was nothing in the message directing me to be prepared to meet an air raid or an all-out attack." The term "hostile action . . . at any moment" meant to him the War Department was predicting sabotage.

After a half hour of talking over the intent of the message with his Chief of Staff, Colonel Walter C. Phillips, Short, unlike Kimmel, had the warning passed to his principal commanders: to Fred Martin, of the Air Force, to Henry Burgin, Chief of the antiaircraft units, to G-2, and to his two division commanders. His reply to the War Department read: "Report department alerted to prevent sabotage. Liaison with Navy. . . ." The response was not taken note of by Stimson, Marshall, or Gerow.

As for the liaison Short referred to, it was slipshod, confusing, typical. Kimmel, upon receipt of the November 27 message, agreed with his Fleet intelligence officer, Captain Edwin C. Layton, that the Japanese were planning a move into Southeast Asia. He notified Admiral William S. Pye, at sea with the major portion of the Fleet, that war appeared imminent and to take all precautions. From where Kimmel sat, the Navy was on an alert and had been for some time. A quarter of his antiaircraft batteries were manned, and ammunition was ready for the remainder. Short, on the other hand, had been talked into scaling his alerts on a three-level basis under the heading "Standard Operating Procedure." In so doing, he reversed the levels used by the Navy, so that his number *one* was the lowest on the scale—an alert "against acts of sabotage and uprisings within the islands with no threat from without." His number *three* alert called for "the occupation of all field positions by all units prepared for maximum defense of Oahu and the Army installations on outlying islands." While Short had instituted his Number 1 alert, Kimmel considered that his call to arms was analogous to Short's Number 3. But the fact of the matter was neither had really gotten the message.

In Manila, MacArthur agreed with his new Air Chief, Major General

Lewis Brereton, to put his air force on an immediate war footing. "Black-outs were established at all fields and at the depot. A 24-hour alert was established for half the Bombardment and Fighter Force."[7] However, when Brereton asked MacArthur to permit him "to conduct high altitude photo missions of southern Formosa," MacArthur refused. Patrols could fly two thirds of the distance to Formosa but no farther, because the War Department had cautioned against any overt acts.

Philippine Commissioner Francis B. Sayre and Admiral Hart also received the November 27 warning, and met that afternoon with MacArthur. In Sayre's words, "Back and forth, back and forth paced General MacArthur, smoking a black cigar and assuring Admiral Hart and myself in reassuring terms that the existing alignment and movement of Japanese troops convinced him that there would be no Japanese attack before spring. Admiral Hart felt otherwise."[8]

Before his departure from Washington, in mid-October, Brereton had found the assumption "that hostilities, if and when they came, would not begin before 1 April, 1942" permeated the War Department.[9] Since this was the proposed date by which MacArthur would have all his promised air and ground forces in place, the wish had become father to the thought.

Even though MacArthur, unlike Short, was quick to put his forces on a war alert to disperse aircraft—no easy job with thirty-five B-17's and uncompleted fields and installations—and step up reconnaissance patrols, he, too, felt the emphasis of the November 27 warning was on sabotage and not attack.

Inadvertently, Hap Arnold, through the heavy-handed action of Brigadier General Sherman Miles, Chief of Army G-2, reinforced this misconception. On Friday morning, November 28, Arnold informed Miles that bombers coming in from various points to one of the western depots appeared to have been sabotaged; the planes in question were reported to have the same defect, which was not traceable to production error. Arnold told Miles he wanted a warning sent to all his air force commanders instructing them to take every precaution against sabotage. Miles responded that a general warning on this threat had been sent the previous day. This wasn't good enough for Arnold, who wanted a specific, rather than a general, warning. He didn't mind erring on the side of caution, so long as the message was clear.

Arnold told Miles he would have his own intelligence chief, Mike Scanlon, draft a warning and they could discuss it. Scanlon brought in the head of his counterintelligence, Major C. R. Blake, and between them they drew up a message that ordered all air commanders to "initiate forthwith all additional measures necessary to provide for the protection of your establishments and equipment against sabotage, protection of your personnel against subversive propaganda and protection of all activities against espionage."

This message had a preamble that cited the world situation as cause for the warning, and a conclusion that asked for reports on action taken on or before December 5. But certainly there was nothing very specific in it. Miles, who had been upset by what he termed Arnold's proposal "to send out drastic orders" to his air commanders, now objected strongly to such a dispatch going out to air forces only. Further, he considered the directive as written too broad and general for so many commands. The Intelligence director "feared all kinds of drastic measures against civilians which would have disastrous repercussions." He argued that this was how General Marshall felt, as witnessed by the message sent the previous day.

Miles's objections led to a conference late that afternoon in the office of Marshall's chief of staff, Brigadier General William Bryden. Gerow was there too, as well as Scanlon, but not Arnold. A new text drafted by Miles was approved and sent out to all Corps Area and overseas-department commanders that evening over the signature of the Adjutant General. It read as follows:

> Critical situation demands that all precautions be taken immediately against subversive activities within the field of investigative responsibility of the War Department. . . . Also desired that you initiate forthwith all additional measures necessary to provide for the protection of your establishments, property, and equipment against sabotage, protection of your personnel against subversive propaganda and protection of all activities against espionage. This does not repeat does not mean that any illegal measures are authorized. Protective measures should be confined to those essential to security, avoiding unnecessary publicity and alarm. To insure speed of transmission identical telegrams are being sent to all air stations but this does not repeat does not affect your responsibility under existing instructions.

An identical message went out, at Arnold's insistence, to his air commanders. Neither message added anything to what had already been signaled from the War Department. No specifics, just generalities saying watch out for fifth columnists but for God's sake don't rock the boat or offend anyone by doing so. The warning would simply reinforce General Short's focus on internal rather than external threats.

In some significant ways Frank Andrews' position was analogous to that of Walter Short and Douglas MacArthur. Like both Pacific commanders, he had a large, potentially dangerous segment of the population in his midst: German, Japanese, Italian. The area abounded with spies. He hardly needed to be warned on the threat of sabotage, subversion, or espionage. As previously noted, he had organized a very active counterespionage branch. And like the Pacific commanders, he had too little too late. It was not the similarities, however, but the differences that counted.

When Marshall had sent Andrews to Panama, the Chief of Staff believed the Canal and the Caribbean to be the U.S. area most vulnerable to attack, and he saw Andrews as the man he wanted there in command. That was the first difference—one of attitude—for from the moment he arrived, Andrews adopted the belief that attack could come at any moment, and he worked successfully to inculcate that belief in his staff and among his officers and men, particularly his young pilots.

The second difference was that, unlike MacArthur, Andrews did not fall into the trap of making projections on when the enemy would be prepared to move and then base his preparations on such a date.

Andrews had known Walter Short for a good many years and considered him a "top-notcher," but Short, like so many of his military generation, lacked the imagination, knowledge, and real appreciation that went with an understanding of air power, and this was the third difference. Naval strength in the Caribbean and Canal area was, as noted, minimal. Further, Short had the comforting thought of the Fleet as his bulwark to guard against external attack. And so, at the end of November, MacArthur looked to the future, Short looked inward, and Andrews looked to the immediate and in all directions.

From the moment he had assumed command of the Panama Canal Air Force, a year past, Andrews had been faced with possible hostile action from Martinique, nearby Vichy French Guadeloupe, and French Guiana. Guadeloupe, unlike Martinique, was flat and an ideal location for a hostile air base. German submarines were beginning to prowl the Caribbean, taking a heavy toll of Allied shipping. With these immediate threats from the land, air, and sea, Andrews had labored to prepare his forces psychologically as well as militarily.

In 1937, he had proposed in an article that had been rejected for publication by the Army Chief of Staff, Marlin Craig, that the United States should consider making the Caribbean an American lake. Now, four years later, the War Department was out to do just that. It was a lake ringed with new air bases and nests of antiaircraft batteries, but it was thinly manned and nothing was really completed. Andrews had a force of forty-five thousand men and over eleven hundred officers stationed on fields and installations on the tri-sectoral defense he had created in Panama, Puerto Rico, and Trinidad. His combat air strength consisted of 137 fighters, seventy-seven bombers (only six of which were B-17's), and twenty-two attack bombers. As he confided to Marshall, "The air force situation is a matter of much concern to me. Though I feel confident that the strengths established in existing war plans are quite adequate, it must be realized that we are far below our totals. The bombardment equipment now available to us, except for a few B-17's, is decidedly obsolete and lacks sufficient range to perform missions that are required for adequate reconnaissance and naval support. We have no night pursuit." Nor did he have an aircraft warning system installed throughout the Caribbean.

But what Andrews did have, which was possibly more important than all else, was an outlook that his officers and men understood. The Miles/Arnold warnings of November 28 were in the nature of being routine, because Andrews' command was as alert as it could be for attacks, within or without.

* * *

It was Billy Mitchell who first foresaw the possibility of a surprise dawn air attack on Pearl Harbor. In the thirties, at the Air Corps Tactical School, the Young Turks dared to plot such a strike, and beginning in 1936, the Navy war-gamed it. Hap Arnold and others predicted the blow, but apparently few of them really believed it could happen.

Conversely, on January 24, 1941, Secretary of the Navy Frank Knox wrote a secret letter to his opposite number, Secretary of War Henry L. Stimson, in which he opened with the statement:

> The security of the U.S. Pacific Fleet while in Pearl Harbor and of the Pearl Harbor Naval Base itself, has been under renewed study by the Navy Department and forces afloat for the past several weeks. This reexamination has been in part prompted by the increased gravity of the situation with respect to Japan and by reports from abroad of successful bombing and torpedo plane attacks on ships while in bases. If war eventuates with Japan, it is believed easily possible that hostilities would be initiated by a surprise attack upon the Fleet and the Naval Base at Pearl Harbor.
>
> In my opinion, the inherent possibilities of a major disaster to the Fleet or Naval Base warrant taking every step as soon as possible as rapidly as can be done that will increase the joint readiness of the Army and Navy to withstand against a raid of the character mentioned above. . . .

Knox cited six possible forms of attack, the first two being "air bombing attack, air torpedo attack," to which he addressed the remainder of his letter, remarking that both types of attack could occur simultaneously. To guard against the eventuality, he called for a high-priority increase in fighters, antiaircraft guns, barrage balloons, mobile equipment, and an early-warning radar network. He also called for "local joint plans drawn for the effective coordination of naval and military aircraft operating . . . against surprise aircraft raids." The Secretary further proposed that Army and Navy forces agree on a form of joint readiness, and that they hold joint exercises against surprise attack at least once a week.

In his response, Stimson concurred in every respect. He outlined the steps the Army was taking to increase planes and guns and a scheduled arrival of barrage balloons by September. On the matter of joint defense plans, he said he was forwarding Knox's letter to Short and "directing him to cooperate with the local naval authorities in making these measures effective."

The fact that it was an established custom for Stimson, Knox, and Hull to get together every Tuesday afternoon in order to discuss informally their most pressing demands would indicate that they had shared their fears of a surprise attack on Pearl Harbor. The letter that Knox would write in order to stimulate a joint move to strengthen the bastion must have resulted.

In seeking to carry out the Secretaries' instructions, General Short and Admiral Claude C. Bloch, Commandant of the 14th Naval District, on Oahu, signed a document on April 11, 1941, titled "Joint Coastal Frontier Defense Plan." The Plan was a variation of two previous agreements: RAINBOW 1 and a pact drafted in 1935, "Joint Action of the Army and Navy." During the summer, the new agreement was revised, but its linchpin remained fixed in that ". . . the method of coordination will be by mutual cooperation until and if the method of unity of command is involved."

As Andrews had declared to Marshall, in his theater or in any theater, cooperation in time of war simply would not work. There had to be unity of command, which meant that someone must be in overall control. Or, as Arnold was to put it specifically to a congressional investigating committee long after the fact:

> The Navy was to be responsible [in Hawaii] for long-range reconnaissance, for locating attacking forces approaching by sea, and to execute joint attacks upon hostile surface vessels. But the Army also had a responsibility under the same conditions: to cooperate with the Navy in defense of coastal frontiers, to support naval forces, to establish an inshore aerial patrol of the waters of Oahu, to have tactical command of defensive air patrols over and in the immediate vicinity of Oahu. Thus neither the Army nor the Navy could know just where its responsibility started or ended. Both Army and Navy ran air patrols—both there to search for attacking surface craft but neither had full responsibility. What is the difference between "Inshore patrols of the waters of Oahu" and "Patrols in the immediate vicinity of Oahu"?
>
> To make matters more complicated, the Naval Search and Attack Group was to: destroy hostile ships by air attack with priority targets, (1) carriers, (2) large supporting ships. The Army Air Force was to trail attacking type planes to carriers and report the location to commander of the Naval Search and Attack Group. Under those "joint plans" just who was responsible at a distance, close in, or during an air attack? No one person was in command of the defense of Hawaii and efficient defense depended upon the reaching of joint action, mutual agreements between two services.

Arnold told the congressmen, he was not citing an isolated "case of the failure of the Joint Action of mutual cooperative agreement system," and he used as another example the friction in the Philippines between Mac-Arthur and Hart.

Since the days of Billy Mitchell, the Navy had always objected strenuously to "offshore patrols" by the Army. The record was replete with examples, but the prime illustration of this mindless position came not from Hawaii or the Philippines but from Alaska. It was the last overseas department to receive combat planes, and naturally all of them were obsolete. Still, Lieutenant Colonel Everett S. Davis, who commanded Elmendorf Field, at Anchorage, had a dozen B-18's, and with the concurrence of Brigadier General Simon Buckner, Jr., Commanding Officer of the Alaskan Defense Command, he sent them out on offshore patrols.

The Navy learned of these patrols and protested vigorously. This was a Navy responsibility! Never mind that in the fall of 1941 the Navy had *no* planes in Alaska. Air Corps offshore patrols must cease! The protest came to Spaatz, who turned it over to Hal George and his planners to come up with an action paper. The reply, drafted by Ken Walker, pointed out that although offshore patrol was a Navy function, Army pilots were required to carry out overwater reconnaissance to keep up their combat proficiency. In order to avoid offending the Navy, flights out to sea thenceforth would be referred to euphemistically as "tactical reconnaissance" rather than "offshore patrol."

On November 5, General Short issued a directive to his principal commanders concerning his three newly defined types of alert. Number 1 was in force against acts of sabotage during the first week of December. It specifically stated that aircraft would *not* be dispersed or prepared "to ward off an attack," for there was *"no threat from without."* (Emphasis supplied)

Previously, in personal letters to "Happy," Major General Fred Martin, Commanding General of the Hawaiian Air Force, kept his old friend apprised of Short's training and using AAF troops as infantry to guard Army installations and closely clustered planes. In response to Arnold's request for details, Martin, on November 3, recounted Short's misuse of AAF airmen from May maneuvers to the present. He vitiated his entire case by statements such as: "General Short is a very reasonable man of keen perception. It is now my belief that he sees more clearly the training problems confronting the Air Force and realizes its enormous proportions. . . . I am happy to say that this problem of training Air Force troops with Infantry, which has caused me such deep concern, seems now on its way to a satisfactory solution. . . ."

It was nothing of the sort, and two days later, when Short's Standard Operating Procedure (S.O.P.) directive was issued, putting his forces on a No. 1 alert, Martin's airmen went back to doubling as infantrymen and M.P.'s.

Although the attention of Arnold and his staff was more firmly focused on efforts to reinforce MacArthur and Brereton with promised B-17's and P-40's, Short's S.O.P. No. 1 brought quick reaction. It was stimulated by an Air Force Technical Inspector on Oahu who reported that he considered maintenance for a number of fighter squadrons unsatisfactory due to a lack of mechanics, who were dispersed for guard duty. Arnold went directly to Marshall, and the Chief of Staff sent two personal communications to Short suggesting that it was wise to use air troops for air duties. As a result, Martin's airmen were briefly relieved from these infantry functions, but following the November 27 warning, they were ordered back to guard duty.

Several months earlier, in late July, Martin had forwarded to Arnold a reconnaissance defense plan for the Hawaiian Islands. Authored by Colonel William E. Farthing, Commanding Officer of the 5th Bomb Group, and two of his officers, Major Elmer P. Rose and Captain Clinton Coddington, the plan envisioned that with a force of one hundred eighty B-17D's and thirty-six torpedo bombers, Oahu could be guarded from attack by air or sea on an around-the-clock basis. It was a well-conceived plan, but it was pigeonholed for two sound reasons. The total number of B-17's of all models in the United States and its possessions the first week in December was 142. Secondly, since mid-August the strategy of defending the Philippines had reduced the B-17 force in Hawaii to a dozen. Their essential purpose was not for reconnaissance but for training crews preparatory to the long flight to Manila, and of these twelve, only six were operational in early December.

However, Martin did have thirty-three B-18's, and Admiral Bellinger nearly seventy patrol aircraft. Their cooperation was far closer than that of Short and Kimmel. Together they made this joint estimate on the possibility of an attack by sea or air: "In a dawn air attack," they postulated, "there is a high probability that it could be delivered as a complete surprise in spite of any patrols we might be using and that it might find us in a condition of readiness under which pursuit could be slow to start." The action they proposed was to "run daily patrols as far as possible seaward through 360 degrees to reduce the possibility of surface or air surprise. This would be desirable, but only effectively maintained with present personnel and material for a very short period and as a practicable measure cannot therefore be undertaken unless other intelligence indicates that a surprise raid is probable within rather narrow limits."[10]

Bellinger himself did not have the authority to order reconnaissance, only to recommend it to Bloch, who, like Short, was not an airman. Consequently, Bellinger was not made privy to any of the "other intelligence": the war-warning dispatches. His information on U.S.-Japanese relations came from the newspapers. As he was to say, "The information available to me—limited and unofficial as it was—did not indicate that I should recommend to the commander in chief, Pacific Fleet, that distant patrol-plane search for the security of Pearl Harbor be undertaken at that time."[11]

In his January letter to Stimson, Knox had proposed that the two services hold weekly drills, and Martin and Bellinger did attempt to do so. Between April 12 and November 12, they had thirteen combined air-raid dry runs. The one scheduled for November 29 was canceled. Both officers knew that they did not have the aircraft or personnel to conduct sustained long-range reconnaissance. They concentrated on training instead. Martin had the additional responsibility of using his facilities as a staging area for B-17's en route to the Philippines. However, had Bellinger been properly informed of the November 27 warning and those that followed, he might have prevailed on Bloch to approve the joint plan of reconnaissance worked out with Martin.

Short's No. 1 Alert, following the November 27 warning from the War Department, canceled out any gains Martin thought he had made with the Army commander. Frustrated and worried, Martin knew he couldn't go directly over Short's head, so he tried an end run. He hadn't been the leader of the 1924 round-the-world flight for nothing. On December 4, he sent a radiogram to the War Department asking for more troops: "SINCE LARGE PART OF AIR CORPS TROOPS ARE BEING USED IN CLOSE DEFENSE AND AS ANTI-SABOTAGE GUARDS, ADDITIONAL GUARD PERSONNEL WILL BE NEEDED," he cabled, hoping someone in Arnold's office would get the message. The message was not delivered to the War Plans Division of the War Department until December 10, three days after the attack on Pearl Harbor.

In Panama, Andrews had received essentially the same warning messages as the Pacific commanders. His forces were on a full alert. Some antiaircraft units were manned on a twenty-four-hour basis, and his fighters and bombers were dispersed and camouflaged on his three main bases and outlying auxiliary fields. In cooperation with Captain Quinn, who commanded the dozen Navy patrol planes at Coco Solo, daily reconnaissance was being flown over the Caribbean and the Pacific. Ecuador, however, still refused to permit the United States to build landing facilities on the Galápagos Islands, which did nothing to reduce the vulnerability of the coastal area.

No planes were permitted to approach the Canal Zone after dark without clearance. Any plane attempting to do so would be fired upon. All commercial flights, principally Pan American, landed at Albrook Field, so that Andrews' G-2 could keep an eye on travelers moving up and down the continent. Happily, Admiral Sadler now considered himself a task-force commander to the theater commander, or so Andrews informed Marshall.

The alert plan for the Zone had been devised by Gilkeson, and Andrews decided to give it a test. As he had told Marshall, what he must guard against most was a low-level dawn attack. He instructed Ed Lyon secretly to move a squadron of his bombers up to David, close to the Costa Rican border, about two hundred miles west of the Canal. During the early-morning hours of November 25 the bombers took off, heading for a dawn strike on the locks.

Gilkeson, after his air-defense training seminar at Mitchel Field, in April, had perfected a system of Panamanian Ground Corps observers throughout the provinces. Local call-in points had been established with a direct line to Interceptor Headquarters, at Quarry Heights. Calls began coming in from the west, reporting many low-flying aircraft. A jangling phone in his quarters awoke Gilkeson. A startled duty officer reported sightings of an unknown aircraft and wondered what he should do.

"Do! What are you supposed to do?!" roared Gilkeson. "Goddammit, push the button!"

The button was pushed, and air-raid sirens wailed across the Isthmus. Antiaircraft crews rushed to their batteries. Searchlights began fingering the dark above, and fighter engines barked into life as P-40 pilots scrambled and were vectored by ground controllers toward the oncoming attackers. Before contact was made, the interceptors were notified that the approaching bombers were friendlies. And so, although sleep was lost, the citizenry awakened and alarmed, the test proved that the troops were on their toes, and whatever the success of the attack, it would have come as no surprise.

Only Johnny Johnson, Commanding Officer of the Sixth Air Force, seemed displeased. He called in Gilkeson and gave him hell for having scrambled the P-40's at night. They weren't night fighters. "And just who could hit the Canal anyway?" he wanted to know.

Gilkie knew who he'd like to hit, and he stormed out of Johnson's office before doing so. Andrews, who was quietly pleased with the way the exercise had been conducted, heard of Johnson's complaint. In a letter to Hugh Knerr he remarked, "My present Caribbean Air Force Commander is pretty much of a scatterbrain. Lyon is a much sounder man and uses his head a great deal more. . . . Gilkeson is a doer. He has installed and is operating here a very good Interceptor set-up."

The mock attack had not come out of the Pacific, where there were no observers at night and few planes to patrol its vastness during daylight. There was a single, newly installed radar detector station on Point Mala, but its efficiency was questionable. Had the December 7 attack been launched against the Canal instead of Pearl Harbor, the chances are that it would have come as a surprise, but the reaction would have been swift and well directed. As Tom Darcy was to say long after the fact, "The warnings of late November and early December changed nothing in our method of operations, for we had been on an alert for six months."[12]

That was not the case on Oahu. The 55th Coast Artillery Company had a four-gun battery on Sand Island, about an hour away by truck and barge from the crew's tent encampment on Black Point, near Fort Ruger. Following the October 16 alert, the crew moved to Sand Island and established permanent residence in shacks of their own design and construction. An order that came down following the November 27–28 warnings emphasized that the gun crews must guard their equipment against sabotage. Since this was standard practice anyway, neither they nor their Commanding Officer attached any more than routine importance to the order. The troops felt that every time a Japanese fishing boat came within a thousand miles of the islands, an alert was sounded.

Since midsummer they had been on maneuvers twice. They had also practiced firing their three-inch guns at a sea target towed by a Navy tug and at targets towed by aircraft. In none of this training was there a sense of being on a war footing. Everyone knew Oahu had become an Army staging area for the reinforcement of the Philippines. The antiaircraft guns remained covered unless being used, the component parts, range finders, etc. disassembled, ammunition stored in bunkers. Should a real attack come, it would take the gun crews twenty minutes to prepare for action, and the 55th considered itself better-prepared than most. Everybody knew that an entire battalion of mobile antiaircraft guns was parked wheel to wheel, unattended, at Schofield Barracks' motor pool. And, of course, there were always weekend passes for those not on duty. Someday the Japs might try something, but nobody really believed they would.[13]

* * *

On Saturday, December 6, Hap Arnold and Captain Gene Beebe arrived at Hamilton Field, California. Arnold had left Washington with two major purposes in mind. One was to get two squadrons (fourteen B-17's) on their way to the Philippines, and the other was to go quail hunting with his longtime friend aircraft manufacturer Donald W. Douglas. A month previously he had written to "Doug" saying he might be able to sneak away from the Washington turmoil, arrive in Los Angeles late on December 6, and remain until the tenth. His letter gave an indication of how worn out he was: "Heretofore I have been able to get you to romp around the hills out there by Hemet but this year I feel more like operating in the flat country."

If it hadn't been for the supposed delay of the B-17's in taking off to reinforce the thirty-five in Brereton's command, there probably would have been no quail hunting. In the past week the urgency to get as many of the bombers as possible to MacArthur had become so paramount that Arnold had suggested to Marshall that they have Fred Martin send his dozen B-17's to Brereton, which indicated Hap's view of the likelihood of an attack on Pearl Harbor.

The squadrons at Hamilton, the 38th and the 88th, had actually not been delayed in their departure date. The Commanding Officer of the 38th was Major Truman H. Landon, who had participated in the first mass flight of B-17's to Hawaii, in May. When he learned of the intended

The cost was ever high. An Eighth Air Force B-17, hit by flak, goes down in flames over Paris. (Credit U. S. Air Force)

That the Boeing Flying Fortress and the Consolidated Liberator were built to take incredible punishment was proved daily over the skies of Europe and the bases in England to which their equally magnificent crews returned them. First Lieutenant Lawrence M. De Lancey brought this bird back, its nose shot away by flak over Cologne, Germany. The bombardier was killed. (Credit U. S. Air Force)

They said the hole in the wing was big enough to fit four and proved it. (Credit U. S. Air Force)

Looking like a beached whale, this B-24 got back to base, but just. Its crew would fly again, but it wouldn't. (Credit U. S. Air Force)

Miraculously, they walked away from this one. Returning from a mission over Rouen with the brake system of his B-17 shot out, the pilot, in landing, could not avoid another B-17 parked at the end of the runway, and both planes were destroyed but without death or injury. (Credit U. S. Air Force)

British artist Captain Bruce Bairnsfather, creator of the famous World War I cartoon character "Old Bill," stands grimly beside a B-17 bearing the same name. Hit by a frontal attack over Heligoland, the eleven-man crew, nine of them wounded, the navigator mortally, fought off fighters, a 200-mph slipstream through the nose, wing damage, and no hydraulic support, to bring *Old Bill* home again. (Credit U. S. Air Force)

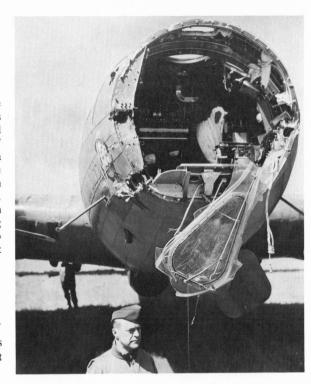

"Death Plunge of Heavy Bomber" reads the identification label of this tragic wartime photograph. (Credit U. S. Air Force)

General Eaker awards the Medal of Honor to Flight Officer John C. Morgan. Morgan, former RAF volunteer, was co-pilot on a raid against Hannover, Germany. Under fierce fighter attack, the intercom system knocked out, and a dying pilot refusing to loosen his grip on the control column, the big Texan flew the B-17 to the target and back with a smashed windshield, one hand, and no way to communicate with the rest of the crew, most of whom were also wounded. (Credit U.S. Air Force)

The success or failure of daylight strategic bombardment rested on the shoulders of the pioneer group commanders. No one had attempted what they were doing. They learned what they knew in combat. RAF Bomber Commander Air Marshal Sir Arthur Harris awards the British Distinguished Flying Cross to Colonel Stanley Wray, Commanding Officer of the 91st Bomber Group. Frank Armstrong, Commander of the 97th Bomber Group, and Colonel Curtis E. LeMay, Commanding Officer of the 305th Bomber Group, have already been decorated. Present but not in the photograph was Colonel James H. Wallace, Commanding Officer of the 303rd Bomber Group. (Credit U. S. Air Force)

Colonel Curt LeMay welcomes Brigadier General Possum Hansell, left, and Captain Allen V. Martini back from an attack on German aircraft factories. It was traditional in the Eighth Air Force for the brass to fly combat missions. (Credit U. S. Air Force)

Command decision. At PINETREE, the code name for Bomber Command headquarters, General Eaker and his operational staff consider a choice of targets. At the far left is Eighth Air Force Intelligence Chief Lieutenant Colonel Harris Hull. Eaker sits at his desk. He will make the final decision. (Credit U. S. Air Force)

With the U.S. invasion of North Africa, in November 1942, Major General Tooey Spaatz became Commanding General of the Northwest African Air Force, and Air Chief Marshal Sir Arthur Tedder Mediterranean Allied Air Forces Commander. In support of General Eisenhower's forces, they had their work cut out, having to overcome bad weather, shortages, and an aggressive, highly skilled Luftwaffe. (Credit U. S. Air Force)

Brigadier General Asa N. Duncan, Spaatz's longtime friend and dependable Chief of Staff, was lost when the B-17 in which he was flying to Africa crashed in the Atlantic Ocean off the coast of France. (Credit Margaret Bourke-White)

Colonel "Ted" Curtis replaced Duncan. Like Duncan and Spaatz, he had been a World War I combat pilot, and like Monk Hunter, an ace. He served as Spaatz's Chief of Staff throughout the war. (Credit Margaret Bourke-White)

Brigadier General Frank O'D. "Monk" Hunter, Fighter Commander of the Eighth Air Force. Demands in North Africa prevented him from building fighter strength when it was badly needed, and shortness of his fighters' range plagued efforts to supply bomber escort. Hunter believed his fighters should sweep far and wide to challenge the Luftwaffe, his tactics being criticized by those who believed that fighters should provide close-in bomber escort. (Credit U. S. Air Force)

After General Spaatz went to North Africa, General Ira Eaker became Commanding General of the Eighth Air Force, and Brigadier General Newton Longfellow took over as Bomber Commander. Here "Newt" chats with a B-17 crew chief at a heavy-bomber base in England. (Credit U. S. Air Force)

The look on Spaatz's face indicates that whatever his old friend Major General George S. Patton is reading, it's not to his liking. This is Constantine, Algeria, at the end of 1942, when the mud was thick, the weather bad, and the fighting hard. (Credit U. S. Air Force)

The Casablanca Conference, of January 1943, was for Allied policy makers one of the most critical meetings of the war. Before assembling, the leaders of the U.S. delegation pose for a photo with President Roosevelt. Standing, from the left, Harry Hopkins, Lieutenant General Arnold, Lieutenant General Brehon B. Somervell, Averell Harriman. Seated from the left, General Marshall, the President, and Admiral Ernest J. King. (Credit U. S. Air Force)

Major differences were ironed out if not fully resolved at the Casablanca Conference. General Marshall here makes a point to his British counterpart Sir Alan Brooke, Chief of the Imperial General Staff. Hap Arnold is at Marshall's left. Lord Louis Mountbatten, fist to chin, and Admiral Sir Dudley Pound, First Sea Lord and Chairman of the British Chiefs of Staff flank Sir Alan Brooke on one side, while on his left are Sir Charles Portal, Chief of the Air Staff, and Field Marshal Sir John G. Dill. (Credit U.S. Air Force)

Arnold enjoyed nothing better than hangar flying with his airmen. In the Western Desert, Egypt, the accommodations weren't so hot, but the "Old Man" was a welcome visitor. (Credit U. S. Air Force)

flight of his squadron to Clark Field, in the Philippines, he was stationed at Albuquerque, New Mexico, with the 19th Group, which was slated for the same destination. This was September, and there were three basic problems: not enough trained pilots and crews, not enough safe aircraft for such an extended mission, not enough equipment, particularly navigation gear. Ordered to supply the 19th with what he had of all three, Landon was then asked by Spaatz's office when the 38th would be ready to go. He replied: in ninety days—by December 6.

Because Landon's Estimated Time of Departure was somehow lost in the rush to aid MacArthur, Arnold used his own impatience and Marshall's as a chance to kill a few birds with the same stone of command. When he arrived at Hamilton Field, it was much to the surprise of Landon, Major Richard N. Carmichael, Commanding Officer of the 88th, and their crews. All the shortages Landon had experienced in September had been remedied, navigators joining the crews that afternoon. So had the planes' machine guns, boxed and packaged in Cosmoline. They were loaded onto the catwalks of the bomb bays, of no immediate use.

Arnold gathered the crews for a farewell briefing. One point he stressed was the feeling among those in authority, including himself, that war with the Axis powers was fast approaching, but he had found little evidence on the West Coast that anyone recognized its imminence. As he saw it, everyone was behaving in peacetime fashion. When he paused, Landon interjected his agreement—at least insofar as their armament was considered. They'd had one helluva time getting the depot to supply the guns at all. The plan now was to remain in Hawaii long enough to clean, mount, and fire them before going on.

Arnold understood the pressure "the youngsters" were operating under. He swung to the positive to pep them up, and then asked Landon if he had anything more to say. The Major did. He went over the problems encountered in manning, equipping, and training a unit for overseas duty. He mentioned that the planes they were flying, the new B-17E's, had a sighting system for the guns that was unfamiliar to everyone. There were no Tech Orders, no S.O.P.'s on its use. Arnold said he knew the problem, and there would be Tech Reps at Clark Field to check the crews out. With the situation as it was, everyone would have to make do.

And so they did. Landon had given December 6 as the day of departure and it was, in spite of the problems encountered. The first of the thirteen planes took off at ten-thirty that night.† Hap watched them go with no premonition of what the morrow would bring. Then he and Gene Beebe headed for Bakersfield, to be met by Don Douglas and his father. The next morning, they were up early, out in the flatlands, gunning for quail.

† The fourteenth plane had mechanical problems, and one plane returned for the same reason.

Arnold was to remember his brief escape "as the best shooting I ever experienced." The Japanese attacking Pearl Harbor might have phrased
their hunting in the same terms.

When the hunters returned to their cabin, they found the elder Douglas
sitting by the car listening to its radio. He broke the shocking news to
them. Arnold didn't say anything. He picked up his gear and they drove
to Bakersfield with the accelerator on the floor. Later, in a thank-you note
to his friend, Arnold described his return home. "Got to Washington 3:50
Monday afternoon where hell was a-poppin' and where it's been poppin'
ever since. Whatever happens and no matter how many wars we get into,
the afternoon spent with you at Bakersfield will be a pleasant memory
which will have to do me I guess until we get this war business over and it
can be repeated."

In Panama the last Saturday night of peace, Frank Andrews had as his
house guest the Army's Chief Signal Corps officer, Major General Dawson Olmstead. A Signal Corps battalion was running a land line from
Albrook to Río Hato, through some very rugged jungle country, and Olmstead was anxious to see how the project was going. He thought he might
drive up to Río Hato the next morning. Andrews said he and Darcy
would fly up and meet Olmstead for lunch, inspecting outlying auxiliary
fields on the way. One of these fields was Chame, lying midway between
Albrook and Río Hato. When they circled it, the area looked completely
abandoned. "Dammit," said Andrews, "I thought I told Gilkie to keep
this place occupied."

As they made their landing approach, Darcy figured Gilkeson's neck
was in the wringer. Nothing of the sort. To Darcy's relief and to Andrews'
pleasure, they found the field was very much in operation, installations
camouflaged and planes so well dispersed that from the air the base appeared vacant.

Later they met Olmstead for lunch at Río Hato and then took off with
him to have a look at Point Mala, the Canal's only radar station on the
Pacific side. While they were circling the installation, Andrews received
an emergency message to return to Albrook Field at once. The news of
the attack on Pearl Harbor was waiting for them. All units were on full
alert. Reconnaissance patrols were ranging far out to sea.

On that Sunday no one would ever forget, Tooey Spaatz was encircled
by a clutter. He and Ruth had bought a colonial house on Duke Street, in
the Old Town section of Alexandria, Virginia. They had moved in on the
first of December, and between then and the seventh, carpenters, plas-
terers, electricians, and plumbers had been hard at it, restoring and mod-
ernizing. When the phone rang early that afternoon, Spaatz fought his way
through the maze to answer it. Upstairs, Ruth heard him exclaim, "Christ
no!" Since she had never heard him swear, she knew it had to be very serious news.

"What's the matter?" she called, coming down the stairs.

He was already headed for the front door. "If you want the car, you'll have to take me to town," he said.

At Air Force Combat Command Headquarters, at Bolling Field, only a skeleton staff was on duty, headed by Colonel Robert L. Walsh. His phone rang; it was Major Lauris Norstad, who said he was picking up garbled accounts of a Japanese attack on the Hawaiian Islands but he thought it must be a hoax. A few minutes later he was back on the phone. The President had gone on the radio to announce that the strike on Pearl Harbor was real.

Walsh was still trying to digest the news when his phone rang again. This time it was Spaatz, calling from his office. He confirmed Roosevelt's words and said, "I have an urgent message for you. I can't give it on an open phone."

"There's a secret phone in Colonel Scanlon's office," Walsh said. "I'll pick up ours here." He did so, but nothing came over the wire. Then an orderly poked his head in the room and reported that General Spaatz was back on the office phone.

There was no doubt in Walsh's mind that Tooey Spaatz was coldly furious. Scanlon's office was locked. No one else had a key. No one knew where the Chief of Air Intelligence was. "The hell with it," snapped Spaatz. "Put Rainbow 5 in effect. That's the message."

Of the blizzard of telephone calls Spaatz received, one came from Ira Eaker. Eaker had planned to leave that evening by train for Hamilton Field, where he would wrap up his official affairs before being transferred to an unnamed assignment at Mitchel Field. When Eaker got through to Spaatz he said, "I think I'd better switch that train ticket for one on a plane."

Tooey said, By all means, and hurry back. Organizing TRIGGER in secrecy had become academic. Yesterday's plans no longer applied.

On Friday, two days earlier, Arnold told Eaker he'd just received a call from the Republic Aviation plant on Long Island informing him that the first P-47 had come off the line. "I want you to go up and put it through its paces," he said. "I want to know if it's as good as the British planes you flew. I want to know how it compares with the German fighters."

Eaker put the fighter through a strenuous series of tests all the way from ground level to thirty-seven thousand feet. He liked its surprising speed and dive characteristics; he was sure it would make one helluvan attack plane. When he returned to Washington that evening he felt as though he had been put through the paces too. When his wife, Ruth, suggested they call the next afternoon on the Arnolds, he begged off, saying he was going to catch up on all the sleep he'd missed during the maneuvers. They were staying at her mother's apartment, and he'd hardly closed his eyes when she was at the door exclaiming excitedly, "The Japanese have attacked Pearl Harbor!"

"You'll have to think of a better one than that" was his weary response.

But then Ruth turned up the radio and that was the end of any thoughts of rest.

Eaker flew west that night with one goal in mind, and that was to get where the fighting was, preferably commanding and flying fighters.

Of all the airmen in command, only Andrews spent a relaxed evening. He and Darcy attended a movie at Quarry Heights. There was a neat touch of psychology in his appearance at the compound's theater. He wanted to be seen unruffled, offering a sense of reassurance to counteract the rumors of a Japanese task force off the coast. He knew the word would spread that if the Boss could go to the movies things must be under control.

There was no time to use psychology in Washington. Spaatz did not leave his office that night. In Arnold's absence he was the center of air operations, working to instill cohesion and calm amid a welter of conflicting demands and reports coming in from every direction, many of them touched with hysteria. From one West Coast base the word was that the officers would have only their .45's to hold off an anticipated Japanese landing. Fighter aircraft were on the move westward, but someone had decided to send their armament by train. At the arsenal in Benicia, the officer on duty was refusing to release bombs for aircraft until he received written orders from Washington. It was a busy night.

Arnold, still on the West Coast, set up temporary headquarters at March Field and alerted personnel there against a possible sneak attack on the Los Angeles area. He spoke to Lieutenant General John L. DeWitt, Commander of the Western Defense Command, at the Presidio, and then to Marshall, in Washington, who wanted him to see DeWitt personally and bring back information on the state of West Coast defenses.

With Beebe at the controls, they took off for San Francisco. Following the conference with DeWitt, they were back over March Field at midnight, but it was blacked out and Arnold said, "All right, let's go to Washington." The flight was as wicked as any he had ever made across the country. Possibly it damaged his heart, because they had no oxygen and were forced to fly at seventeen thousand feet to try to get above the weather. During the flight, he had no time for reflection or evaluation, in what he described as an atmosphere of commotion, disorder, and confusion everywhere—no time to dwell on the results of the past two years.

In that period he had fought as best he could against a political policy that sought to build Allied air strength at the cost of his own forces. His was a proprietary drive. He could appreciate the reason for the policy, but he had to deal in numbers and in the belief that the policy was bound to bring war to the United States. The neck of the bottle was production and all that it entailed, from supplies to skilled workers. Overall, in two years there had been enormous expansion and improvement—the method of allocation, the administration of development, the techniques of research all accelerating. Still, on December 7, 1941, the Army Air Forces complement of combat and transport planes totaled just over thirty-five hundred in a year when aircraft production exceeded twenty thousand planes. Arnold had 148 B-17's, eleven B-24's, and fewer than fifteen hundred fighters, of which 175 were obsolete.

Almost two years earlier, the fifty-four-group program had been accepted by all involved, and tables of organization for eighty-four and one hundred groups had been drafted. Directly after Pearl Harbor, Stimson informed the President that, with the West Coast unprotected, he was hurrying all air forces there except those needed to protect industries in the East such as Pratt & Whitney and Curtiss. "I advised him to take the plane production from Lend-Lease, and, if necessary, from British orders until we had completed the 54 Group program. . . . He acquiesced and subsequently expressed . . . his approval of this policy."

The fact that there were only forty-five first-class interceptors to guard twelve hundred miles of the West Coast, ten heavy bombers to seek out reported Japanese task forces off that Coast, and seventy-five short-range medium bombers with little ammunition to support them, brought no response from Roosevelt. Perhaps he realized what Hap Arnold had been driving at for so long.

Now Arnold would get the planes he needed, but in the meantime his forces would suffer, too few in number, spread too thin everywhere, sustaining heavy losses against an underrated foe who, with stunning success, had proved the value of air attack. In the immediate hours following the Japanese attack, he did receive one piece of good news: The twelve B-17's, whose departure he had speeded, arrived over Oahu in the midst of the Japanese strike. Through some adroit evasive action and cool flying after fourteen hours aloft—one Fort landed on the twelve hundred-foot fairway of a golf course—all the crews survived, with only two wounded, even though five of the planes were no longer fit for duty.‡

If nothing else, the whirlwind reaped at Pearl Harbor chillingly illustrated the failure of the U.S. military mind to adjust its thinking to the meaning of strategic air power: planes neatly lined up on the ramps, wing tip to wing tip, battleships anchored bow to stern. And overhead the early morning sky an empty blue—until it was darkened by aircraft.

‡ Flight Surgeon William R. Shick, a passenger, was killed by strafing Japanese Zeros.

Part II

Nine

Perspective

Since political policy dictates the form military strategy takes, doctrine and tactics are the methods by which that policy is carried out. The Allied policy behind the strategy of RAINBOW 5 and ABC-1 was to go on the offensive against Germany and Italy while fighting a defensive war against Japan. Militarily, to most planners, the strategy was sound, for three reasons: It was reasoned that defeating Japan first would do little harm to Hitler, whereas defeating Germany and Italy would do much to defeat Japan. Geography, combined with Axis victories in the U.S.S.R., North Africa, and the Pacific, reinforced the concept. Finally, in spite of Pearl Harbor and Japan's swift and stunning conquest of the British and Dutch East Indies and the Philippines, Roosevelt, Churchill, and Stalin were determined above all else to crush Hitler.

That was the policy, and RAINBOW 5 fitted it, even though it meant that for the immediate future, General Douglas MacArthur and Admiral Chester Nimitz would be forced to fight defensive actions in their vast Pacific theaters, their forces depleted by skillful Japanese operations, their replacements in men and equipment taking second place to a buildup aimed at Hitler. At the time, the only way the United States could wage war against a Germany in possession of most of Europe and all of the western Soviet Union was by joining the RAF in attacking it from the air. As detailed, this strategy had been foreseen, and even though it would be six months between Pearl Harbor and the first U.S. heavy bombardment raid against a strategic target in Europe, on June 12, 1942, the intended campaign long antedated its launching.

As shown, the acceptance by U. S. Army planners of the doctrine advanced by AWPD-1 was in large measure the hard realization that the only offensive weapon available at the outset of war was the bomber. At least over Europe, it must be utilized against the enemy until it was possible to conduct land operations. In the beginning, aerial bombardment *was* the second front, the drafters of AWPD-1 had gone so far as to claim that if their doctrine was properly employed, there might not be any need to follow it with invading armies. The position was pretty well buried in the fine print, and no War or Navy department planner was about to subscribe to the theory. However, for the moment, the doctrine involving the bomber's strategic use over Europe was accepted.

Conversely, the air war in the Pacific demanded an entirely different approach. Yet, the key to MacArthur's brilliant and unparalleled campaign to retake Japanese-held islands, land masses, archipelagos, and sea lanes was air power. He referred to the "bomber line" as his front line of defense and described his plan to recapture the Philippines as a war of supply protected by the air. "Victory," he told his staff, "depends on the advancement of the bomber line."[1] Bombers, he said, were his long-range artillery. Certainly their use was tactical in that their actions were coordinated to the movement of his ground forces, frequently supplying that movement through the use of C-47 transports, "leap-frogging" mountain ranges, jungles, and seas to outflank and outsmart the enemy.

In fact, MacArthur readily admitted to his indefatigable and innovative air chief, Lieutenant General George C. Kenney, that without air power it would require ten years and heavy losses to accomplish what he succeeded in doing in two years with amazingly low casualties. He also admitted to Kenney that one of the greatest mistakes of his career was to oppose the creation of an independent air force during his tenure as Chief of Staff, in the early 1930s.* At the moment, past mistakes were academic; it was present usage that counted. If those who nailed down the tenets of what strategic air power was all about did not choose to describe Kenney's inspired use of his air forces—skip-bombing by medium bombers, low-level attacks by heavies, greatly extending the range of his fighters, moving masses of men and equipment—as strategic, they would have to describe it as a wonderfully versatile and imaginative development of tactics to suit the unique needs of the time and place.[2]

Most significant of all, although the strategic air planners were thinking of Germany's heartland in their operational projections, it was against Japan that the first strategic air attack by the United States took place. Combined within this action was every ingredient the most zealous promoter of strategic air power could have dreamed up, but because it was a single incident it was never properly evaluated in its strategic context.

The germ of the idea came not from the thinking cap of a U.S. airman, but from the British Chief of the Air Staff, Peter Portal. In a Washington

---

* *A Few Great Captains,* pp. 133–54.

meeting, three weeks after Pearl Harbor, with Hap Arnold and Air Marshal Arthur Harris, Portal asked Arnold what he was going to do about attacking Japan. Hap replied that plans were going forward to mount operations against Japan from China. He was also optimistic that the Russians would soon grant permission for U. S. Army bombers to fly missions out of Vladivostok. Portal couldn't see that happening right away, and he then advanced a theory that immediately attracted Arnold: He suggested that U.S. carriers sneak up on Japan and give them a replay of Pearl Harbor. The carriers, he said, would be taking no more risk than the British carriers had taken at Taranto or the Japanese at Hawaii.

"Your carriers are fast," he added. "The ocean is big. I believe such an attack would cause the Japanese fleet to return to home waters."

Two weeks later, at a White House conference that included Roosevelt and Churchill and the principal members of their military staffs, Arnold made notes on the joint use of carriers and Army bombers. The discussion centered on the possible Allied invasion of French North and West Africa under the code name of SUPER GYMNAST.

Admiral Ernie King had suggested the use of three carriers in the operation, one loaded with Army bombers, and Arnold quickly scribbled, "By transporting these Army bombers on a carrier it will be necessary for us to take off from the carriers, which brings up the question of what kind of planes—B-18 and DC-3 for cargo?

"We will have to try bomber take off from carrier. It has never been done before but we must try out and check out how long it takes."

Usually any good idea is the sum of a number of parts, and it was not from an airman's brow that the final concept flew forth but instead from the depth of the sea, proposed by Captain Francis S. Low, a Navy submarine specialist. In taking off as a passenger from Norfolk, Virginia, Low had observed a couple of Army bombers making a run on a carrier deck outlined on the ground. The outline was used by Navy pilots in practicing landings and takeoffs. By the time Low arrived in Washington, his thoughts had jelled and he was anxious to suggest to King what Portal had suggested to Arnold. That the Admiral was receptive to the idea of Army bombers taking off from the decks of a Navy carrier glistened with irony as sea water glistens in sunlight, for Army air power was an anathema to King.

The plan as it evolved was aptly given the official title "First Aviation Project." It was a first in a number of ways, not the least of which was effective cooperation. Although it had required Japanese bombs to rope the will-o'-the-wisp Unity of Command, Army-Navy collaboration to bring off the April 18, 1942, Doolittle strike on Japan was an exemplar of the two services working together. Admiral William "Bull" Halsey commanded the task force that escorted the carrier *Hornet* through enemy waters to a launch point less than seven hundred miles off the Japanese coast, and Lieutenant Colonel Jimmy Doolittle, with less than five hundred feet of heaving deck on which to take off, led his airmen on a one-way mission to bomb Tokyo, Yokohama, and other Japanese cities.

The selection of Doolittle to train and then lead the squadron of sixteen Mitchell B-25's on the mission was an inspired one. At forty-five, he was the epitome of all that was right in a professional airman. He had earned the first Ph.D. given in aeronautical engineering, from M.I.T. in 1926. He combined a razor-sharp analytical mind with the sort of nerve and confidence that were coolly there in the clutch, exhibiting the kind of airborne leadership that his young pilots were eager to emulate.

The plan was that after Doolittle and his crews had dropped their bombs on industrial and military targets, they would fly eleven hundred miles to bases in China. Thus the mission also utilized for the first time the technique of overflight: taking off from one locale to bomb a target and then continuing on to land at another locale.

In a personal memo to Roosevelt, Arnold described what took place:

> On the 18th of April when the *Hornet* was 668 nautical miles East of Tokyo, the Naval Task Force ran into a Japanese patrol ship. This ship was sunk by the *Nashville*, but not before it had had an opportunity to send a message stating that it was being attacked by hostile enemy ships. It is to be noted that at this point the Task Force was some 150 to 400 miles further away from Tokyo than General Doolittle had planned his take-off. . . .†
>
> At 1:30 P.M., in the midst of an English propaganda broadcast from Japan in which a woman [Tokyo Rose] was telling how safe Japan was from bombing, the broadcast was cut off and another broadcast made giving information that fast, low flying bombers were at that time bombing Japan. A later broadcast told of fires and requested people to pray for rain. It was not until 48 hours later, however, that a broadcast was made stating that the fire was under control. Still later, another broadcast was made which stated casualties amounted to three to four thousand. . . .

Doolittle reported from Chungking on April 30 that "13 B-25's bombed Tokyo's oil refineries, oil reservoirs, steel and munitions plants, naval docks and other military objectives. One bomber attacked with incendiaries the Mitsubishi airplane factory and other military objectives at Nagoya. We all took care to avoid bombing schools and hospitals, churches and other non-military objectives" such as the Emperor's palace.[3]

Although the assigned targets were hit and fires set, material damage was actually minimal. Casualties were not several thousand but several hundred. None of the planes reached the fields in China, Doolittle and his crews having to bail out or crash-land in the rice paddies.

† Doolittle was promoted to Brigadier General directly after the raid.

Yet the raid was a tremendous strategic success in its psychological impact. News of it gave the U.S. home front an enormous shot in the arm after nineteen weeks of retreat and defeat. Of equally important military significance, not only the unexpectedness of the raid but also the fact that Doolittle's planes sullied the sacred air above the imperial palace shook the Japanese high command to its boots. A great deal of all-important face was lost. Neither the Japanese Army nor the Japanese Navy General Staff knew for sure from whence the raiders had come—Roosevelt said from Shangri-La—and as a result hundreds of Japanese fighters that could have been used offensively against the thinly spread American and Australian forces were tied down to defend Tokyo.

Perhaps of even greater magnitude, according to naval historian Samuel Eliot Morison, the first strategic bombing of the war by the United States so infuriated the Japanese that they overreacted in planning their attack on Midway Island. They overextended their forces, which made more devastating their defeat at what later was judged to be the turning point of the Pacific conflict.

It was less than two months after the Doolittle raid that the Army Air Forces carried out its first strategic bombing mission against Hitler's Europe, and it, too, because of its size and limited military effect was not given its proper strategic recognition. On June 12, a dozen B-24's flying out of Fayid, Egypt, made a dawn strike on the Romanian oil fields at Ploesti. None of the twelve planes was shot down: Six landed, as intended, in Iraq, two in Syria, and four were interned in Turkey.

The attack on Ploesti was indirectly tied to the attack on Japan. When Portal had asked Arnold, in December, if he was planning to hit Japan, Arnold had responded in the affirmative, not going into detail, but after the Doolittle raid the decision was made to send twenty-three Liberators from the 376th Bomb Group to do the job. They would have no replacements, no spare parts other than what they could carry. They would fly as many missions as the equipment and longevity of the crews would permit. As for additional bombs and ammunition, they'd be hard to come by too.

Hap put Colonel Harry A. Halverson, longtime friend and longtime airman, in command. Halverson, among other feats, had flown as backup pilot with Spaatz, Eaker, and Quesada in the famous Question Mark endurance flight, of 1929. Short and square-set, a tough old pro whose operation went under the code name HALPRO, he arrived in Egypt in May with his group of B-24's en route to China. There he received orders to hold.

The Japanese, in a major offensive push, took a ghastly vengeance on the Chinese, who had aided most of the downed fliers to escape capture.‡

‡ Of the sixteen U.S. crews, the Chinese rescued thirteen; one was interned in the U.S.S.R.; two were captured. Four U.S. airmen were executed by the Japanese, and two others died in prison camps.

In so doing, they slaughtered an estimated quarter of a million men, women, and children in the eastern provinces and overran and destroyed the field that the HALPRO crews were planning to occupy. More, in North Africa the vital British bastion at Tobruk was under heavy attack by Rommel's Afrika Korps, and the Russians were being hard pressed in their own country. It was felt the B-24's could be put to more immediate use in the hotly contested Mediterranean basin.

Their introduction into combat was the aforementioned raid on Ploesti. Led by Halverson, it was the first but by no means the last such attack on the oil fields. At the time, it came not only as a startling surprise to those in the target area—thirteen hundred miles inside Europe—but also to those in Berlin and Moscow. The purpose of the mission was to cripple fuel supplies reaching the German forces advancing against the Russians. Although a dozen U.S. long-range bombers individually hitting a large target couldn't expect to do all that much damage, the very fact they had reached the target struck a somber note in the German high command and cheered the Russians. Stalin was impressed that the United States was intent upon long-range offensive operations on his behalf, and so the first strategic strike against Hitler from the air, like its Japanese counterpart, had a far more positive effect than either its numbers or bomb damage would indicate. Spaatz had suggested that hitting Ploesti would force the Germans to deploy additional fighters and flak units away from the front, which was the case. Of course, the British and the Germans had been at the same game for over two years, the RAF having launched a raid of over one thousand planes against Cologne the previous month, but both the U.S. attacks were unique—cocky, daring, imaginative, and strategic.

Since the inception of the Churchill government, in May 1940, overall British policy and its grand strategy had undergone few fundamental changes. But by the beginning of 1942 the RAF's use of strategic air power had reached a major turning point.

As previously related, RAF daylight bombardment missions were becoming specialized exceptions to the rule of night operations. This was due to unacceptable losses against dubious results. Even so, by the fall of 1941, night bombardment efforts had come into question as well. Churchill best reflected the change in attitude. During the grim and desperate summer of 1940, he had written to Beaverbrook, his aircraft production czar, that while fighter production must be the prime consideration, the only method England had to strike back at Germany was with "absolutely devastating, exterminating attacks by very heavy bombers from this country upon the Nazi homeland. We must be able to overwhelm him by this means. Without which I do not see a way through."[4]

By mid 1941, Bomber Command was beginning to put into operation much-improved aircraft-Halifaxes and Sterlings, capable of carrying five tons of explosives, able to cruise at two hundred miles per hour. It was about then that the Air Staff, under Air Chief Marshal Portal, came forth with a plan to produce a frontline bomber force of four thousand planes, an unheard of and unreachable production figure. Portal wrote the Prime Minister in September saying that when the number had been reached, his planners estimated, it would take in the neighborhood of six months to crush Germany's industrial capacity.

Churchill's response illustrated the change in his outlook. While he was all in favor of bombing the Third Reich into rubble, he no longer saw the effort in the same light. "It's very disputable," he wrote Portal, "whether the bombing by itself will be a decisive factor in the present war. On the contrary, all that we have learnt since the war began shows its effects both physical and moral are greatly exaggerated. The most that we can say is that it will be a heavy and I trust seriously increasing annoyance."[5]

The seeming switch in appraisal greatly concerned Portal, who had formerly headed Bomber Command and was, in his determined and thoughtful way, a longtime practitioner of strategic air power. Portal had flown over a thousand hours in combat in World War I, and on one occasion had taken on five German planes single-handedly, shooting down three of them. He was not the type to be easily deterred from a chosen course of action, and he replied in kind to Churchill, over whom he had considerable influence on air matters. The Prime Minister went into more detail, outlining his pragmatic view.[6] No doubt, one cause for his view was the Butt report.

D. M. B. Butt was the secretary to Churchill's scientific adviser, Frederick A. Lindemann, Lord Cherwell. The Chief of Scientific Intelligence, R. V. Jones, who had studied under Lindemann, had been bringing to him reports that belied Bomber Command's claims of target accuracy. One example was a raid on the important Skoda munitions works at Pilsen. Jones's evidence indicated that the citizens of Pilsen knew nothing about the attack and that the nearest bomb had fallen fifty miles away.[7] Lindemann decided to investigate by having cameras installed in the bombers that would indicate the time of bomb release. He appointed Butt to make an evaluation of a two-month period—June and July—using over six hundred fifty photographs and interrogating air crews. In this last, since it was recognized that on any given night mission approximately one third of the attacking planes did not reach their primary objective, Butt limited his questioning to those who did. His findings were devastating. He reported that, on an average, only one third of the raiders dropped their bombs within five miles of the target, and over the Ruhr the estimate dropped to one tenth.

The RAF was not about to accept the findings. For one thing, the weather had been notoriously bad during the months in question, but as R. V. Jones noted, the Butt report did convince the air marshals that astronavigation, dead reckoning, and ordinary radio beacons were simply too antiquated for all that was needed, and the drive was on to develop the latest electronic navigational aids.

However, Churchill was disturbed, and he demanded from Portal: "Your most urgent attention. I await your proposals for action." Action came in the aforementioned proposals for a huge increase in bomber production and in scientific improvements. The latter, which shortly led to the employment of Gee, a radio signal aid by which a navigator could determine his exact position by reference to three transmitting stations in England. This brought an advance in tactics that was coupled with a major change in air strategy. The change was to give up the long-held doctrine of precision targeting and switch to area or urban bombing, concentrating on breaking German morale by destroying not just industrial sites but the cities that housed the workers in them as well.

The question of why the morale of the German people was any more likely to crack under aerial bombardment than their British counterparts remained a matter of faith. The German capacity to take such punishment was not as great as that of the British, was one commonly accepted answer, nurtured by a belief in one's own propaganda. To reinforce the change in doctrine, Lindemann sold Churchill on a projection of the bomb destruction of German housing and the psychological impact it would have on the citizenry of the Third Reich. Further, Bomber Command planned to hit German cities with far greater numbers than those used by the Luftwaffe. And so, for reasons that were both technical and strategic, the doctrine of area bombing was officially adopted.

Thus, at the time the United States became a combatant in the war against Hitler, there were two fundamental differences in approach to the use of strategic air power by the Army Air Forces and the RAF. Arnold and his airmen were committed to daylight operations and, as AWPD-1 had pointed out, operations against selected critical German industrial targets. While the RAF was prepared to run special daytime missions against particularly sensitive objectives, the Air Ministry as well as Bomber Command did not believe the U.S. plan could be carried out. Air crews would suffer unacceptable losses. Two years of experience, nearly eight thousand airmen dead or prisoners of war, and mixed opinions on target damage had brought this conclusion.

From every indication, the British bombing experience had had little or no effect on the plans and intentions of U. S. Army air leaders. U.S. policy was opposed to area bombing on humanitarian principles, which privately the British considered sophistry if not downright hypocrisy. Having been the victims of aerial bombardment, their point of view was aimed at retaliation, whatever the form.

Since May 1941, Generals Jim Chaney and Joe McNarney, as Chaney's chief air officer, had been sitting in London heading the Army Special

Observer Group, which consisted of a small, somewhat permanent staff of mostly ground officers and a rotating group of visiting firemen coming over to learn all they could of the British war effort. Chaney's operation was broad and complex, one of liaison with the Churchill government and its military leaders. Before Pearl Harbor it existed under special circumstances. Chaney was, on the one hand, having to prepare for the possible entrance of U.S. air and ground forces into the British Isles, and on the other, he was involved in the allocation of Lend-Lease supplies. He was also an adviser to General Marshall, and in September he accompanied Averell Harriman and Lord Beaverbrook to Moscow to listen to Russian demands for aid and to judge Soviet capacity to repel the German advance. His opinion was that the Russians would not be defeated. In November he had returned to Washington for a briefing and was informed he was going to be Theater Commander of U. S. Army forces in the British Isles, when and if the United States went to war.

During a meeting, Hap Arnold suggested that Chaney adopt the command system Andrews had established in the Caribbean: a composite air force headed by a single commander, with Chaney as Commanding General of the theater.[8] There is nothing to indicate that they discussed the change in RAF bombing policy. Both were enthusiastic about hitting the Germans from the air by whatever method. Apparently, neither was aware of the degree of disagreement within the British Government, particularly on the part of the Admiralty, which was maintaining that Bomber Command's effort was largely a wasted one. The Royal Navy wanted bomber strength parceled out to greatly assist it in its desperate sea war, and the Army wanted more air strength in Africa.

Shortly after Chaney's return to London, Rear Admiral Robert Ghormley, his opposite number in liaison with the Admiralty, sent a cable to Washington denigrating the effectiveness of Bomber Command, saying day or night it was producing heavy losses but not results. He recommended that the plan to produce large numbers of long-range bombers be reexamined. Chaney read this as a typical Navy move, motivated by a desire for the aluminum used in both aircraft and ship building. Not so much a matter of RAF failure as a fight for raw materials was involved. The War Department asked Chaney to sit down with Ghormley to discuss his claim and then submit an opinion.

U. S. Military Attaché Brigadier General Raymond Lee, whose own views on the use of strategic air power were not far from Ghormley's—that daylight operations were "now only a wishful dream" and that "night bombing has done some damage"[9]—was asked more or less to referee the encounter. It was a long, unresolved argument, but it concluded with agreement on the same bottom line reached by the British: Currently, bombardment was the only method available to the British to attack Germany directly. Added to the results, it was not so much a matter of German morale being broken as British public spirit being lifted in the knowledge that the enemy was getting it.

U. S. Assistant Military Attaché for Air to London was Brigadier General Ralph Royce, a blunt, outspoken airman who had known Chaney for over twenty years. He had little respect for him or for British Army methods, and when asked for an opinion by Lee, Royce stated he didn't think the RAF effort was getting very big results. But neither Chaney's opinion nor Royce's nor that of any other U.S. airman in England raised any doubt as to what U.S. air power could accomplish under the same circumstances.

Neither did Lee's evaluations have any influence on the momentum of policies already in motion. Due to leave for Washington in late November, Lee had a talk on the subject with Harriman, Roosevelt's key man in England. Harriman confessed he was very much afraid of the effect on the four-engine-bomber program of the rising official British opinion concerning strategic bombardment. He said he had backed the program, but he admitted B-17's were really luxuries and should not be permitted to interfere with the basic tool of war such as tanks, cannons, Navy fighters, transport planes, and so forth.[10]

Whatever these second thoughts, whatever doubts were rising in some minds over the efficacy of strategic air power, Pearl Harbor and the joint high-level U.S.-British conferences in Washington that swiftly followed, determined that the bomber program as generally promulgated by AWPD-1 would go forward.

Ten

The Point Man

By the end of December, Ira Eaker was beginning to wonder if Hap Arnold had decided to save him for the Junior Prom. Or so he said in a congratulatory letter to his good friend Major General Walter R. Weaver, the new Acting Chief of the Air Corps. In explaining his situation, he told Weaver how he had arrived at Hamilton Field on the afternoon of December 8 prepared to clear the post and return to Mitchel Field for assignment. But when he'd entered Fourth Air Force headquarters, his plans were swiftly changed.

Commanding General Jake Fickel was on the phone with Combat Air Force Commander Delos Emmons, and when he spotted Ira he said, "Eaker has just walked in. I want to keep him here." And that took care of that. When Fickel finished his conversation with Emmons, he said, "Ira, go over and report to General Ryan. I want you to coordinate pursuit activity."

In the swirling three weeks that followed, there was no time for reflection. It was all action amid a blizzard of alarms and excursions: whales that got bombed for Japanese submarines; ferry boats reported as Japanese battleships; industrial smoke mistaken for the results of Japanese attack; P-40's of the 77th Squadron of the 20th Pursuit Group that nearly attacked P-40's of the 55th Squadron of the 20th Pursuit Group because against the setting sun the insignia on the 55th's planes looked like the rising sun of Nippon. Over this near miss Eaker had made a direct call to Arnold. As a result, the red circle within the insignia of all U. S. Army aircraft was swiftly painted over.[1]

Near the end of the month, Eaker got off a quick position report to Tooey. He was in command of the Fourth's Northern Region—the Bay Area—with headquarters at the Information Center in San Francisco. His duties kept him going day and night, his office more the cockpit of his Republic P-35 than in the Stock Exchange Building. His group was based on four fields. Flying P-40's, the 20th was one of the two combat-ready groups in the United States.

While in the weeks directly following Pearl Harbor there was an underlying air of confusion combined with a sense of shock (it was believed that the same Japanese task force that had struck Oahu was steaming to strike vital West Coast factories) Eaker exhibited a sense of firmness and a quality of leadership that transmitted itself to his staff and eager pilots. Others might rant and shout over all the things that were lacking in the sudden emergency—parts, ammunition, equipment, trained personnel— but Ira, puffing calmly on his new Christmas pipe sent by longtime friend Harris Hull, of Sperry Gyroscope, gave orders quietly and went about his business of improving combat readiness through training, sending reconnaissance patrols a hundred miles out to sea—with no objections from the Navy now.

He told Weaver, "The work is interesting and I'm anxious to stay this close to the war front in the hope that I may get to the scene of hostilities." But as time passed it began to seem to him that everyone was heading toward the actual fighting but him. And tragically, less than a week after the attack on Hawaii, there was one old friend who didn't make it.

To Army airmen, Marshall's choice of Major General Bert Dargue to replace Lieutenant General Short in the Hawaiian Department was yet another indication of how highly the Chief of Staff thought of the top leadership in the air arm. Andrews in the Caribbean, now Dargue to take command of ground and air forces in Hawaii.

Bert Dargue had acquired his wings flying a Wright B in the Philippines back in 1913. Now, on Friday, December 12, 1941, he was flying a B-18 en route to Hamilton Field with a planeload of staff and critically needed crew chiefs, all heading for the Pacific. Eaker was at March Field refueling, and checking the weather, having flown in from San Diego headed for San Francisco. The tower operator reported that Dargue had heard Eaker conversing with him and asked that, when Eaker got north a ways, he contact Dargue in flight and report on the weather situation. Eaker took off, and the farther he flew the worse the conditions, the overcast coming down on the telephone poles. He grabbed some sky and found he was battling wind. He began calling the General on an assigned frequency. Dargue picked up his call somewhere west of Tucson, en route to Hamilton. "General, the fog is on the ground," Eaker reported. "If you're planning to go through Cajon Pass, don't. You'll have to stay high. If you have to fly in the overcast be very careful. There's an extremely strong wind blowing from the west."

Dargue thanked him, and Eaker descended in the hope that he could sneak through in spite of the fog. He recalled that the General was the kind of old-time pilot who liked to pick an altitude and stay at it, regardless of what lay ahead. What lay ahead for Eaker were zero-zero conditions, and he turned back and landed at Fresno. From there he traveled by bus to San Francisco. When he walked into the Information Center, on Sansome Street, at nine o'clock that evening there was a message waiting informing him that General Dargue was unreported and long overdue.

A week later, when Eaker wrote to Weaver, he informed him, "We are still searching for General Dargue."* Bert, who long before had been Ira's commander on the Pan American Goodwill Flight, of 1926, was the first of the old pros to be claimed during the war.

Dargue's immediate replacement was Lieutenant General Delos Emmons. Whether he was selected through Arnold's recommendation to Marshall is not known, but the choice did two things: It reiterated the Chief of Staff's preference for an airman with his feet on the ground, and it removed a source of possible competition from Arnold's back. Hap was now a permanent major general and very soon to be a temporary lieutenant general, like Emmons, but still, having Lucky stationed in Hawaii helped to clear not just the air but the chain of command as well.

Such considerations were far from Eaker's mind at this time. It seemed to him that all his old buddies were passing through on their way to the Pacific—Clarence Tinker and Monk Hunter among others. In his eagerness to join the exodus he wrote to Major General Walter "Tony" Frank, Commanding General of the Third Air Force, in Tampa, Florida. Supposedly the purpose of his letter was to send belated thanks for all of Frank's help during the Carolina maneuvers. But, more to the point, he had written to say, "Naturally, I would like to stick with fighter aviation if that is at all possible, and, of course, I am also very anxious to get to the war. I have a feeling, however, that there is no better way of getting to the war than to stick with you."

Or maybe by letting hard-pressed Louie Brereton, in the Philippines, know that Ira Eaker was ready and available, for at the same time he wrote Tony Frank, he dropped a line to another old *compadre,* Brigadier General Francis "Ray" Brady, Brereton's Chief of Staff. He told Ray, "If you need pursuit reinforcements over there let me know. I am crazy to get in shooting distance of this war and to get there in a single seater."

His appetite for combat was further whetted two days before Christmas by a letter from Frank Armstrong. It informed him that Gordon Saville had returned from England with two new proposals for setting up TRIGGER and the SHADOW project. Armstrong included personnel figures and said they had been coordinated with high-ranking British officials. But all the figures, projects, and proposals didn't amount to a bucket of prop wash without the necessary orders.

---

* The wreckage of the missing plane and its eight passengers was not found until March 1942.

And then suddenly it appeared that opportunity was knocking, not from Washington but from Chungking. Over ten years before, when Eaker had been aide to Assistant Secretary of War for Air Trubee Davison, he had gotten to know Chiang Kai-shek's Military Attaché, Colonel Yu Pak-chuen. The Colonel, now a general, was on the phone with an offer that spelled plenty of action. Yu told Eaker that the Generalissimo was look-ing for an airman he could trust, someone who could advise him on just what kind of air operations the Chinese could mount against the Japa-nese. The most pertinent information Eaker had about Allied air strength in China was that Claire Chennault had managed to pretty well clean out the 20th's P-40's the past summer. Chennault, however, at the moment was not on active duty with the U. S. Army, having been made a Briga-dier General in the Chinese Air Force. Yu wanted to know if he could make a request to the War Department that Eaker be appointed as Chiang's special U.S. air adviser.

Those who knew Eaker well, knew that at the poker table he took his time. Because the offer sounded as though it would take him to war quickly he was immediately attracted, but then he backed off a bit. Would the General give him his phone number? He'd like to think it over and would call with his answer in the morning. During the night he debated the proposition. As a student at Southeastern Teachers' College, in Durant, Oklahoma, many years before, he'd been the debating team's star. Now he was up against himself, and the simple but far-reaching question was to go or not to go.

There was something in the offer that was remindful of the past: It was 1919, and he was on the verge of leaving the service to pursue a career in the law. Then he had learned there was a plan afoot to send two aero squadrons out to the Philippines. The offer was that if he could raise enough recruits he could command one of them. At age twenty-three, to Eaker the Philippines sounded like the clarion call to adventure. The law would have to wait a bit.

He located most of his sixty recruits among Indian tribes in Arizona and New Mexico by dropping out of the sky in his Jenny, awing the reser-vation inhabitants. In spite of the fact that his braves found the California climate too cold and nearly burned up a barracks in an effort to keep warm before Eaker was able to get them aboard ship, and in spite of the fact that the nervy Lieutenant came within a propellor blade of being court-martialed for having commandeered for his famished troops food from the commissary of an absent artillery company on Corregidor—the Commanding General predicting that the culprit would either end up in jail or become a general, like himself—Eaker never regretted his decision to go to the Philippines. It had been the right choice at the right time. Now, twenty-two years later, he must determine whether this was the same clarion call in a different guise.

More than logic, however, it was an inner sense that told him China, exciting as it sounded, could put him in the wrong place at the wrong time. The next day, he conveyed his thanks and regrets to General Yu. Almost immediately thereafter he received a radiogram from the Adjutant General ordering him to report to the Chief of the Army Air Forces preparatory to overseas duty. It looked like the Junior Prom had finally arrived! He was on a United Airlines DC-3 heading east as fast as he could hand over his duties, thoughts of TRIGGER or some other fighter command dancing like sugarplums in his head.

In his twenty-five years as an Army airman, Ira Eaker had learned a few worthwhile military axioms, most of them early in his career. The first concerned his introduction to the airplane. It was October 1917, and as a newly minted ninety-day wonder, Second Lieutenant Eaker was drilling his platoon on the hot and dusty parade ground at Fort Bliss, Texas, when down out of the sky fluttered an ailing Jenny. Close to, the Curtiss JN-4 intrigued Eaker. The pilot, Lieutenant Scott, said he was on a recruiting tour, headed for Deming, New Mexico, but, alas and alack, the Jenny's OX5 engine wouldn't develop enough power to get him over the mountains. Eaker was totally unmechanical but very observant. He noted a spark-plug lead lying in the engine bed, saw the way the other leads were attached, and refastened it. This act promptly restored full power to the restarted Jenny. Lieutenant Scott was mightily impressed. He thought the aeronautical genius should give up drilling doughboys and join the Aviation Section. Before he took off, he gave Eaker an application form that would make the change possible.

Battalion Commander Major Charles H. Danforth, with slab face and beaky nose, had observed the aerial doings from the vantage point of his horse's back. When the day's travail was ended, and Eaker as Danforth's adjutant accompanied him back to the stables, riding three paces to the rear, the commander remarked, "I saw you talking to that aviator this morning."

"Yes, sir," replied Eaker. "He gave me an application form to fill out. If I pass the physical I'm going into the Aviation Section."

"Let me see that form," said Danforth over his shoulder.

And that was the last Lieutenant Eaker ever saw of it, although he later saw a lot of Danny, who somehow managed to transfer to the Aviation Section before he did. Out of the incident a lesson was learned: *Don't ever tell superior officers anything you don't have to.*

It was big Jim Fechet, Chief of the Air Corps from 1927 to 1931, who, Polonius-like, passed on to Eaker, whom he looked upon almost as a son, another truism that "Iree" never forgot. Said Fechet, "Influence is like money in the bank. But once you spend it, it's gone forever."

A third axiom, known and practiced by every good officer, was, Take care of your men *first*. From the time he'd assembled his Indian recruits for the Philippines, that had been Eaker's method of going, and everyone who served under him knew it.

As he flew eastward on January 17, 1942, he had no way of knowing that all three of these engrained precepts were to stand him in good stead. Neither did he have any inkling of what awaited him in Arnold's office. Long-range, he and "the Boss" had been attempting to finish up on their third book, *Army Flyer,* a volume geared to informing the newly commissioned air officer of what Army life was all about—the idea born on a flight to Alaska several years previously. Of late, there had been no time for book writing at either end of the country, but winging above it, Eaker settled down to do just that. Yet in all the miles and all the hours it took to reach Washington, a single question rode with him: What was his new job to be?

When he finally learned the answer, he was flabbergasted. "You're going over to England," said Arnold, "to understudy British bomber operations and take command of our bombers as soon as I can get you some planes and crews."

"Bombers, hell!" Eaker shot back. "I've been in fighters all my service!" The words came out in an astonished rush, a reaction to the possibilities considered on the long flight. The words were no sooner spoken than Eaker knew if he'd been in Arnold's place, he'd have said, *Evidently I've got the wrong man.*

But Hap ignored the outburst, in fact smiled at it, and said mildly, "Well, you can put some of that spirit into your bomber crews." And then he added, "I'm going to a dinner at Walter Weaver's tonight for Peter Portal and Bert Harris. I want you to be there."

And so he was, still trying to get used to the abrupt change in the direction of his career, while Elizabeth and Walter Weaver were happy to make him welcome.

He had never met Bert Harris before, an RAF Air Marshal quite the opposite in looks and personality from the tall, intellectual RAF chief with his long nose and quiet, pipe-smoking manner. Stocky, blunt-faced and blunt-spoken, Harris had first come to the United States as a member of the British Purchasing Commission in the late 1930s. He left an impression within the War Department of being an independent-minded, outspoken bomber advocate—articulate, forceful, sure of the correctness of his views, and wickedly critical of those high or low who differed with him. His earthy metaphors were often offensive to the delicate-minded, his attitude toward the British Army and Navy on a par with some of his U.S. aerial cousins'. He was often quoted as saying that the Army would never understand tanks until they could be modified to "eat hay and shit."[2] Early in the war, he had served under Portal as Commander of Bomber Group 5, the RAF's premier bomber unit. Now, as an Air Marshal and soon to be Sir Arthur Harris, he was in Washington as head of the RAF's permanent delegation.

He had arrived in June of 1941 with his lovely young wife, Jill—"Jillie"—and their eighteen-month-old daughter, Nancy. He had known Arnold previously, but now he got to know him better, along with Bob Lovett and other high U.S. officials. But, of greater importance to the Churchill government, he became a frequent and welcome visitor at the White House, where his fierce determination to bring down Hitler at all costs appealed to Roosevelt and Hopkins. Often, he would huddle with Hopkins in the latter's office bedroom—which had once been Abraham Lincoln's—or in the Harris suite at the Shoreham Hotel, and plot how to get more planes and equipment for the RAF, skirting behind the War Department, Congress, and Hap Arnold's aching back.

Upon one occasion, Roosevelt asked Harris if there was anything more he could do for him within reason—meaning without risking impeachment. Short of ferry pilots on the Atlantic run, Harris responded, and explained the problem. FDR said he would speak to Hap about it, and soon thereafter Harris received a supposedly angry call from Arnold, wanting to know where Bert got off, trying to steal pilots both of them knew he didn't have. Harris said it wasn't military pilots he was after, but civilian. Arnold, of course, knew all about the problem and said he would see if he could find someone who might be able to help. Harris was bowled over when a very attractive blond lady walked into his office and said she'd been sent by Hap Arnold. She was Jacqueline Cochran, one of America's most accomplished aviators, and after the Air Marshal had recovered sufficiently, she offered to enlist the best women pilots in the country to fly the Atlantic for him. He promptly accepted.[3]

Coincidentally, Eaker and Harris were to begin what was to become a close association and a lasting friendship with a point in common. Portal had just informed Harris that he wanted him to take over as Bomber Commander. He needed an aggressive, tough-minded, go-to-hell leader who saw eye to eye with him. Someone to ramrod the new policy of area bombardment and make it felt in Germany, someone quick enough in thought and hard enough in temperament to hold off the demands of the hard-pressed Admiralty. With his piercing eyes, his fearlessness in making decisions and carrying them out against the criticisms of powerful detractors, Harris was the right man for the task. Churchill would nickname him Buccaneer.

Eaker took to Bert immediately, finding his directness more American in its flavor than English, probably due in part to Harris' having spent his early youth in the Rhodesian outback in various rugged jobs.

Now, over Weaver's brandy and cigars, Arnold filled Portal and Harris in on the mission he had given Eaker. There were two parts to it. First, the logistics: This involved the acquiring and building of air bases, the establishment of a communications system tied into the RAF's, and the setting up of an all-important supply-and-maintenance-depot network for the bomber groups once they began to arrive. The second part was that Eaker would be in command of bomber operations. Both Portal and Harris already knew the general policy behind the plan for sending Eaker to England. It had developed as a result of the meetings of the newly formed Combined Joint Chiefs of Staff, which included Arnold and Portal. The meetings were still going on, with accompanying conferences at the White House. In fact, at the moment, Portal and Harris knew a lot more about the forces at work in the formulation of such policy than did Eaker.

At the first official Anglo-U. S. White House meeting, on December 23, Arnold, Portal, and Harris had been present. There the President told the assembled that he had already discussed with Churchill, who was present, the need to get a small number of U.S. bombers to England. They both agreed the move would have an important effect on the French attitude as well as the German. Later, when Portal asked Arnold how large a bomber force he was planning to send, Arnold replied not less than a group (forty planes), because the group was the smallest unit that was self-sustaining and self-contained. When Portal asked when, Arnold replied, By March.

In the passage of two weeks, that estimation had been greatly expanded, partially through Churchill's persuasion, partially as a result of changing policy. On January 4, Harry Hopkins had summoned Arnold to the White House for a private discussion on the air situation. Among other things, he wanted to know about the Air Forces expansion program, with particular emphasis on heavy bombers. Hap told him that General Marshall was all in favor of the overall one-million-man, 115-group estimate, which would include thirty-four groups of the heavies, the strength of the latter to be reached by the end of the year. Out of this strength, the plan was to have a force of eight hundred bombers in England by the end-of-December target date. There was also a plan to have four fighter groups, two based in England and two in Northern Ireland, or three hundred twenty aircraft.† It was obvious Hopkins was anxious to push the program hard.

After they finished their discussion, Hopkins told Arnold the President wanted to talk to him, but on finding that Roosevelt was tied up, he took him instead to see Churchill, for the Prime Minister was also eager to have the benefit of a few private words.

Right from the outset of the combined conferences, the British leader had been pushing the strategy that no matter how bad things looked in the Pacific, Germany was the foe to beat. Among other things, Churchill was interested to know how soon Arnold could get an air staff to London to

† A fighter group numbered eighty aircraft.

get acquainted with RAF methods and procedures. Arnold said it would be done very shortly (it was a matter of weeks). Churchill was most pleased to have the assurance.

In his subsequent meeting with Roosevelt, Arnold briefed the President on the same points he had gone over with Hopkins: expansion, the problems in reaching the agreed-on goals. Could they be reached? FDR wanted to know. What were the obstacles in the way? How many planes were going to be sent to England and Ireland? "How are you getting along with Portal?" he asked.

"One hundred percent," Arnold said, and then told Roosevelt of the agreement he had made with the RAF Chief: that no combat aircraft would be held back waiting for something to happen, but all would be sent across to fight.

"That's an excellent thing to do," the President agreed.

Following Arnold's one-on-one at the White House, another two weeks would pass before he summoned Eaker. Like the preceding two weeks, it was a period of constant flux and contained turmoil, of determinations made and unmade, of continuing battle losses in the Pacific, and a groping to solidify differing Allied viewpoints on a course of global action. The feeling out between the two staffs encompassed everything from unity of command—to which Churchill was then opposed—to insuring that the vital link in the South Atlantic-African ferry route at Natal, Brazil, remained secure.

Amid this day-and-night effort to gear up for total war, Arnold had to have taken the time to deliberate on whom he was going to send to England to organize the tricky preparations for a bomber force and then to command it. Although there is no record to prove how his choice came about, it is almost certain that he did some of his deliberating on the matter with Tooey Spaatz. This is so for at least two reasons: Above all, Spaatz was the friend whose judgment he valued more than any other. Spaatz was to be his number-one airman, his first among equals. No association within the air arm was more closely knit.

Moving Delos Emmons to Hawaii made it possible for Arnold to shift Tooey from Chief of the Air Staff to Combat Commander, but in either post, he was a principal voice in the determination of how air units were to be utilized. Originally the newly formed Eighth Air Force was to be employed in supporting an invasion of northwest Africa. The invasion plan was dropped and the question was, Where best to use the Eighth? The answer was in England, with Spaatz as commanding general.

And who would command the Eighth's fighters? The obvious answer was Monk Hunter. Bring him back from the Pacific.

And the bombers? The air was full of bomber experts: Bob Olds, Hal George, Gene Eubank, George Kenney, to name a few.

No one can prove that Tooey recommended Ira, nor when he did that

Hap voiced Eaker's own reaction: a preference for fighters. But if he had, Spaatz would have replied, *What the hell difference does that make?*

And indeed it would have made no difference. What was wanted was an airman who could plan and organize, who could be diplomatic and tough-minded at the same time, someone who could get along with the British but not be snowed by them, someone who could stand up to all the rigors involved, who could stand firm against the ever-present critics within and the cruel realities of war without, a thinking officer, determined, percep-tive, able to visualize a very dimly formed future . . . withal, a rock of a man. Certainly in what lay ahead he would need to be that.

Spaatz would sum it all up years later in one of his famous short, short speeches. "I've known Ira Eaker for forty years," he said at an honoring celebration. "He's a good man." Arnold thought so too, and proved it in a gesture of warm support. He had recommended Eaker for promotion to brigadier general, and when the appointment was announced, he gave Ira the stars Bee had pinned on his own shoulders six years before, saying, "Herewith a couple of stars for you to wear. Incidentally, they were my original stars as BG and perhaps they will bring you luck. I don't know whether they have brought me luck or not. They certainly have put a lot more stars on my shoulders, but that doesn't always mean luck. Anyhow here's wishing you the best in the world."

Around the Weavers' table that evening of January 18 as Arnold outlined Eaker's tasks, Ira was forming his own impressions of the two air marshals. He already knew that the RAF's dream, once the Yanks were in the war, was to absorb within their own command U.S. fighter and bomber units. It was agreed that cooperation in combat training and the integration of a communications system was going to have to be very close, as was the setting up of a supply system, but absorption was not ne-gotiable. Portal was too circumspect and too canny by half to raise the question; deft and subtle persuasion was his style. Not Harris, whose bluntness was laced with pungent humor. When the discussion got around to the kind of operations Eaker was intending—daylight precision bom-bardment—Harris had no reluctance in speaking out. "I bloody well don't think you can do it." His words were clipped and crisp. "We've tried it. We know. We've even tried it with your Fortresses."

"Sure. You tried it with one or two B-17's at a time," Arnold said. "We don't plan to do it that way. We're going to send them out in mass forma-tion."

"It doesn't matter a tinker's dam what you send them out in," Harris argued. "The Boche have too many fighters, too much flak, too much bloody power against that West Wall to make it worth the losses. God knows, I hope you can do it, but I don't think you can." He grinned at Eaker. "Come join us at night. Together we'll lick them."

"Yes," Eaker agreed, picking up a theme he would hold to. "We'll bomb them by day. You bomb them by night. We'll hit them right around the clock."

It would be a very short two weeks before Eaker departed for England. In that brief period of preparation, he was given a time schedule within which he could expect aircraft and crews to start arriving, beginning in May. This meant he would have about ninety days to set up shop: to establish his own headquarters and that of Spaatz; to acquire fields and installations; to learn just how the British Bomber Command operated, from the squadron level to the top; to organize training facilities for the crews coming over untutored as to combat operations.

Portal and Harris had assured him that he would have their complete cooperation, and he anticipated receiving similar support from Major General Jim Chaney in London. He would also have with him a small, skeleton staff, a nucleus to assist in a task that by any method of measure must be described as Herculean and unprecedented.

The five objectives laid down in his initial directive were couched in military language. Read one: "Prepare training schedule for American units arriving in England to insure their readiness for combat in the minimum time." Behind such matter-of-fact instructions an enormous gamble was riding—twenty years of gamble whose contentious genesis lay in Billy Mitchell's bombing of the battleships in 1921.

There were few, if any, Army airmen who did not either devoutly believe in or accept the doctrine of daylight precision bombardment. Granted, the theory had never been tested in combat using the tactics the bomber advocates foresaw. As already noted, there was a great deal of hard evidence to show that the attempt would end in costly failure. Yet the handmaidens of faith and stubborn resolve could not be denied.

The very fact that combat crews would be arriving untrained for what lay ahead, primarily because there was no body of record to base their training on, illustrated the degree of the gamble right at the point where it was to be taken. It marked the tenuous course to which Eaker must hew. Not only would combat training be necessary in England to get crews familiarized with the generally awful flying weather, but it would also be required because of the need for haste. Some crews would be coming over never having fired their weaponry or done any practice bombing. In short, Ira Eaker was the point man in an experiment that had been twenty years in the making, and now was being dangerously hurried because of adversaries whose power was undented and whose victories continued to mount.

Eaker was not one to concern himself with the overall meanings of what was at stake. He only knew he had a job to do, and he'd let the all-knowing hindsighters argue the merits of the plan. His assignment was to carry it out as best he could. At the outset, to aid him, he needed a staff.

On that score, Arnold said, "We have a limited number of first-class officers. You know them, and I know them, and I'm going to keep them. You pick your people from the lower ranks and civilian life and I'll promote them accordingly." He also observed that he'd found you could make a good officer out of a business executive, but you couldn't make a good officer out of a dumb one.

Eaker took the advice. In forming a nucleus staff of six to accompany him, he selected half from the reserve corps and half from newly commissioned civilians. He did manage to enlist Lieutenant Colonel Frank Armstrong, who had been slated to join him on TRIGGER as his Chief of Operations. He had also previously approached Harris Hull on joining the TRIGGER operation. Now he had no trouble signing him on as his G-2. Hull, the son of a former congressman, was a veteran air reserve officer specializing in intelligence. As a civilian he had been a Washington-based newspaper and radio correspondent. Before coming on active duty, in November 1941, he had been employed by the Sperry Gyroscope Corporation, in New York City.

Also working for the firm, as assistant to the president, was Hull's good friend, Frederick W. Castle. Castle's father had been a classmate of Hap Arnold's, and the son, crowned as the class baby, graduated from the Academy in 1930. He joined the Air Corps, earning his wings in 1931, and before switching from regular to reserve status, in 1934, served in the 1st Pursuit Group, under Frank Andrews. Eaker did not know him, but at Hull's suggestion they met, and Castle, whose specialty was logistics, joined "Eaker's Amateurs."

So did Peter Beasley, new to military life but not to the multitudinous ways of aircraft maintenance. Aircraft manufacturing was his forte, and Eaker enlisted him as his G-4.

Another past associate Ira literally snared on the run was Lieutenant Beirne Lay. They passed in a corridor as Eaker was hurrying to a meeting. "Beirne, you want to come with me?" he called. "Yes, sir," was Lay's immediate reply, although he had no idea where his answer meant he was going.

A Yale graduate, Air Corps reserve pilot since 1933, successful film and magazine writer, Lay had first gotten to know Eaker when the latter was serving as Chief of the Air Corps Information Division, in 1937. Eaker had read an article by the Lieutenant titled "Night Flight." A writer and journalism graduate himself, Eaker was impressed by Lay's obvious talent. He made a point of meeting him and was equally impressed with his outgoing manner and quick-witted style. The following year, in serving as Andrews' G-2 for the famous East Coast maneuvers of 1938, Eaker enlisted both Lay and Hull (on Reserve duty) as his assistants. Now they were going to be his assistants in a far greater venture.

In all the hustle and bustle of departure, the accelerating movement of airmen out of the country to far-distant war fronts, the mission took precedence over all else. It took precedence over private lives, over the wives left to mind hearth and home. All their married lives, they had had to share their husbands with the dispassionate siren of flight, the years full of good-byes, knowing that any day could be the last day. Now would come a good-bye longer than any previously experienced—for some, final. Yet, without fuss or fanfare, these women of airmen gone to the wars would adapt and endure against that long-distant day of return. They would join together to aid the war effort, concealing their loneliness and fear in joint occupations. After all, they were married to soldiers, some for over twenty years, some since last week. What more could they expect? They would rally around and protect each other whatever came. And whatever came, it was they, quietly, unseen, unsung, with no medals for bravery, who would sustain their far-distant men.

On Wednesday afternoon, February 4, Ruth Eaker bid her husband good-bye. During his six weeks in England, followed by the maneuvers in South Carolina, she had been living with her mother in the District of Columbia. Up until Pearl Harbor she was under the impression that she and Ira would be together at Mitchel Field—at least temporarily. Everything was preceded by the adjective *temporary*. When she learned that he was returning to England for an *indefinite* period, the reality of his going took some getting used to. She already knew how poor a correspondent he was.

When Eaker departed from Washington, it was not to head directly for England. Instead, with Ruth he went up to New York to turn over the manuscript of *Army Flyer* to his publisher. Somehow, in spite of everything that had to be done, he had managed to finish the book, whose authorship he and Arnold would share. They had felt it important to get the project finished, not only because there would be no time for such side interests once Eaker arrived overseas but also because they believed the book would serve as an important guide to the newly commissioned officer. Eaker's editor, George W. Jones, predicted *Army Flyer* would enjoy "a steady sale for a long time—as long as the war lasts at any rate." Whatever the book earned, Arnold had decided that the proceeds would go to the Army Air Forces Aid Fund to assist widows and children of officers and enlisted men who gave their lives.‡

In a farewell letter to Arnold explaining the publishing details, Ira concluded: "General, before departure, I want to thank you again for all the things you have done for me. Again I want to say how much it means to me to be wearing your stars. Here's looking forward to the time when we can go to that village in Oregon and begin doing some things we have neglected for so long. In the meantime, please remember that it is going to be my aim to show you that you did not pick the wrong guy on this job I am about to undertake.

‡ The book, published in April, went into a second printing in August and by year's end had earned nearly $1,500 for the Aid Fund.

"Give my love to Mrs. Arnold and David. I shall write to them both from the other side."

Getting to the other side wasn't all that easy. Eaker met with his select half dozen in New York, and after bidding his wife farewell, on the evening of February 4 they boarded a Pan American Clipper for a five-hour flight to Bermuda. The group now included Eaker's aide, Lieutenant William S. Cowart, Jr., who had served under him in the 20th Pursuit, and Major Cecil P. Lessig. Lessig, a former sergeant major, was an administrative officer.

The anticipated brief stopover in Bermuda stretched out for twelve days. During the winter months there was as yet no regular Army Atlantic ferry service to England. Pan Am and BOAC flights were dependent on weather and enemy aerial activity. Golf and bridge became the order of the day, and Eaker noted, "Rest and relaxation greatly improved personnel."

It was not until the nineteenth that they finally reached Lisbon, Portugal. There the pace quickened. They were airborne at seven the next morning and back on the ground again an hour later at Porto, on the northern coast of Portugal. Supposedly the need was for fuel, but actually the pilot of the KLM DC-3 realized that unidentified aircraft off the shore were tracking them, and he did not like the sensation.

That the Dutch airline was permitted to operate by the occupiers of the Netherlands, flying out of Amsterdam to European cities and points in England, was on the surface an irony, but actually it was a way to collect foreign exchange and a method by which German intelligence could keep track of who was going where. Shooting down an occasional KLM flight if it served the Third Reich's war aims was a part of the game. The windows of KLM planes were covered over in order to prevent passengers from taking pictures or giving any indication of the course being flown.

When the pilot decided to land at Porto, he summoned Eaker to the cockpit to explain why. Not long after they had taken off the second time, he asked Eaker to come forward again. They were over the Bay of Biscay, and he pointed to an aircraft. It was a German Ju-88 boring in on them. There were no clouds to escape into, and Eaker had a very cold feeling that his new command was apt to be a very short one. As the German attack bomber drew closer, a sense of being trapped flew with its approach. Then suddenly one of its engines began to spew black smoke, and directly thereafter it swung about and headed back toward the far-distant French coast, continuing to trail smoke. There was no need to say anything but *amen!*

It was a long flight in any case, and they did not touch down at Bristol, England, until midafternoon. Another, much briefer and safer flight brought them to Hendon, near London, at teatime. There they were welcomed by Eaker's old *compadre* Colonel Ralph A. Snavely, of Chaney's staff, and Air Marshal John Baldwin, who had been serving as the Acting Head of Bomber Command. The welcoming committee escorted them to the Strand Palace Hotel, and after dining at the Dorchester with Snavely and Lieutenant Colonel de Freest Larner, a longtime friend of Ira's, they felt as though they had really arrived.

If Ira Eaker had stopped to reflect on the most difficult aspect of his mission, outside of the mechanics of establishing the vast ground work for and solid structure of an air force, he would probably have considered his relations with the British, and particularly the RAF, as the greatest part of his challenge. Diplomacy and a firm course of action had to go hand in hand. From Arnold, from his own observations, from the dinner with Portal and Harris, he knew they were out to woo him. With guile and subtlety and gentle persuasion, his hosts would seek to impress him with the soundness of their strategy. This was their country; they'd been at war for two years. *Meld your units with ours; join us in night bombing,* was their theme song. Eaker was quietly alert to any stratagem they might seek to employ. What he was not altogether ready for was the type of reception he received from Major General Chaney, Commanding General of U. S. Forces in the British Isles and most of his staff.

What Chaney envisioned was what RAINBOW 5 and ABC-1 had earlier proposed: token U.S. ground forces to aid in the defense of Great Britain; air and antiaircraft defense for U.S. naval bases in the Isles; and a bomber force to operate in coordination with the RAF. He saw himself commanding all these forces, which also included troops in Iceland. He also believed that U.S. interceptor and antiaircraft units should be an operational part of RAF Fighter Command. In none of this, he stressed, was there need for separate U. S. Air, Ground, or Service commands.

This kind of thinking might be okay in peacetime, Arnold had advised Chaney shortly before Eaker's departure, but not now. Not with three infantry divisions and one armored division and an air support command already slated for Northern Ireland. Instead, he had proposed that Chaney become theater commander and Spaatz commander of all U.S. air forces in the U.K. Think in terms of a major headquarters, he was saying, of an air commander and his staff who would be on separate but equal footing with the British Air Ministry.

Chaney bluntly turned down Arnold's proposal, sending his rejection home with Joe McNarney, his right-hand man in the Special Army Observers Group (SPOBS). He found Arnold's projections "quite undesirable" and stated flatly, "I do not concur in adopting this plan." His reasons were that the British theater required special circumstances and that to parallel the British organization with one of our own would be a serious mistake. Further, the Army Air Forces did not have enough experienced staff officers to handle such a scheme. This last sounded like an old General Staff refrain, and the fact, as Arnold pointed out, that Frank Andrews in the Caribbean was successfully implementing such a command structure made no difference to Chaney.

Arnold's response had been twofold. He dispatched an old friend from March Field days, Lieutenant Colonel Claude E. Duncan, as a kind of advance man for Eaker to test the air turbulence at Chaney's Grosvenor Square headquarters and to act in liaison with the RAF.

Arnold's second move was to send a copy of the directive he had given to Eaker on ahead with his own rejection of Chaney's plan. He followed it with a cable that not only stressed his fear of the RAF's attempting to control U.S. air units but, of equally significant importance, indicated his position on the role of fighter aircraft in England:

> Our bombers must be utilized by us in accordance with standard U.S. doctrine. This makes necessary U.S. pursuit support for our bombing operations. If our pursuit units are part of the British Fighter Command, then such support cannot be given. . . .

None of his letters or cables did anything to change Chaney's mind. He had never been an Arnold confidant, and in Hap's proposal that Tooey Spaatz be made chief of all U.S. air forces in England, he could easily foresee an unbreakable chain of command being formed: Arnold, Spaatz, Eaker, and Hunter. Whether this obvious backfield influenced Chaney's stand, whether it made him feel that indeed he would become a rubber stamp where air matters were concerned, is not known. That the British had had a strong influence on him, there is no doubt; he was anxious not to hurt English pride by using their facilities while setting up a very large independent operation. He appeared unable to adapt to the swift changes that were afoot. He had become a traditionalist surrounded by traditional Army types.

As to Eaker's reception, by mischance he did not find an opportunity to talk with Claude Duncan before he reported to Chaney's headquarters, at 20 Grosvenor Square. Had they met, he would have been forewarned. It was Saturday morning and Chaney was not in as yet. Eaker delivered his directive, hoping to get to work immediately. Instead, at the conference that followed, he quickly realized he had come up against Army concrete. It was suddenly like the old days that he had thought were bygone days. Of the thirty-five members of Chaney's staff, only four were air officers, and when he presented Arnold's organizational plan to the key members, they rejected it out of hand. They were "absolutely dead set against an Air Force Headquarters being established." Spaatz, they said, would not be coming over to head anything in England.

As Ira described the meeting to Tooey in a letter: "They had made up their minds and no argument would change them in the slightest. I presented the arguments as strongly as I could but without the slightest effect. They are unalterably opposed to an Army Air Force in Britain.

They say that they are perfectly able to handle this in addition to their other duties and such an organization would make of them merely rubber stamps. They consider that function their primary mission here and are not willing to surrender it. . . ."

There were two colonels on Chaney's staff, John E. Dalquist, the G-1, and George W. Griner, the G-4, who to Eaker summed up the atmosphere in which he found himself. The pair made it a habit to return to Ralph Snavely and Al Lyon all staff papers which mentioned "Army Air Forces," demanding the material be rewritten excluding the word "Air."

Of Chaney, Eaker wrote to Hal George, "I could not believe any man did not wish to be pushed to a higher job, but I found one. They [Chaney's staff] are the Air Force Headquarters as they see it and are reconciled and even believe in being subordinate to the British. . . ."

Chaney's authority came from the War Department, not from Arnold, and although General Marshall had tentatively accepted Hap's proposed organizational revisions, a much broader and more profound plan of reorganization was taking place, about which Chaney knew very little and Arnold knew a lot.

Joe McNarney, who had arrived home from England directly after Pearl Harbor, apparently took little part in any attempt to reconcile the immediate differences, for after serving on the Roberts Board (investigating Pearl Harbor), he was tapped by Marshall for a much bigger job. He was to reorganize the entire command structure of the U. S. Army and to rebuild in the place of entrenched bureaucracies—filled with byzantine bureaus where it took a month to move an order from one office to another—an administrative and command system geared to fighting a global war. It was to be a revolutionary undertaking, and McNarney, incisive, direct, tough, was the right man for the job. So were his two assistant revolutionaries, Brigadier Generals Larry Kuter and Otto Nelson.

Kuter in particular was well suited. On February 2, he'd been a lieutenant colonel for just six weeks when Marshall called him into his office and told him his name had gone over to the President for promotion to brigadier general. Kuter promptly called his wife, Ethel, and suggested she sit down while he gave her the glad tidings. At age thirty-six he was to become the youngest general officer in the U. S. Army, and it was nationwide news.

Some months earlier, Marshall had told Arnold it was time he started giving big promotions to some of his younger officers. Since it was going to be a big air force, he said, it was going to need fresh talent to make it fly. Hap never argued with Marshall, but he did nothing to implement the suggestion because of the effect it would have on a great many highly experienced oldsters whose dates of service went back to World War I and whose rank was not above colonel. So Marshall made the move himself, and the shock waves nearly collapsed the Munitions Building and all its

War Department additions into Constitution Avenue. Hap's old buddies blamed him for Kuter's gazelle-like leap over their heads, but Marshall knew he had made no mistake in his choice. He not only thought well of the new brigadier's intellect, he also liked the way he wore his brass. On the telephone with Roosevelt one morning, he summoned Kuter. "The President has been speaking to the Dutch Ambassador," he said. "The Ambassador says our bomber commander is a coward. He's a man named Eubank. I believe you know him."

"I know him very well, sir," snapped Kuter, "and the man who says he's a coward is a liar!"

"Keep your shirt on. He's evacuated base after base."

"Yes, sir, that's exactly what he's done. He's kept the few B-17's we still have out there in Java in our possession so they can fly, and bases they can fly from. The Dutch have provided no defense around those bases. Eubank has not let the Japanese march in and take the airplanes. He's flying offensive missions in those B-17's as often as he can get them off the ground. And I want to know who says he's a coward."

Marshall swung around and addressed himself to the President. "I have a flying officer who knows Eubank and knows his performance, and he speaks pretty violently on your letting anybody call one of your commanders a coward."

Kuter stood there and listened to the Chief of Staff really put it to Roosevelt, telling him that his loyalty was to his subordinates and not some frantic ambassador ten thousand miles from the scene.

None of this, of course, made any direct difference to Ira Eaker, a somewhat lesser distance from the center of what Marshall frequently termed "the madhouse," but the fact that both McNarney and Kuter were among the brainiest air officers around couldn't hurt. As Eaker put it to Hal George not long after the Saturday conference with Chaney: "The only information available here is that organization here is delayed pending the reorganization there. The sooner the organization is fixed upon and published and the sooner General Spaatz and staff get here, the sooner we can start toward real offensive combat operations."

That was his goal, and that was what he started toward immediately upon leaving Grosvenor Square. Chaney and staff had suggested that he fit his small group in with theirs; they'd make room for him. He politely begged off. Instead, as a result of Claude Duncan's having been in London for three weeks, they were able to set up temporary headquarters at nearby Cranmer Court.

Duncan was a quiet, reserved officer who spoke little, but Ira was most anxious to learn what kind of cooperation he could expect from the RAF, having run into rough weather with his own side. He had known Claude since March Field, where Duncan had served as Arnold's G-4. Later they had gone to Command and General Staff School together, and when Eaker became Arnold's Executive, Claude was his assistant. Administration was his forte, not command, although Arnold had failed to see this; Eaker, who was too shorthanded to make changes, sensed it. In the meantime, Duncan assured him he could count on the British. They were truly anxious to cooperate in every way.

The next morning, Eaker received a clear signal of the correctness of Claude's evaluation. He arrived at Chaney's headquarters and there was Air Marshal Bert Harris, waiting to greet him so they could walk to church together. They had something in common and something to celebrate. Harris' appointment as Bomber Commander had just been officially announced.

In the gray, sunless days that followed, swiftly merging into weeks, Eaker and his staff—which gradually increased in numbers—accomplished with the full support of the British Air Ministry what they had come to do. Eight bases were acquired in the Huntingdon area to receive the anticipated first groups. Like so much else, the projection of numbers and dates of arrival far outran expectations. Bombers and fighters originally scheduled by Arnold to start arriving by mid-March—then May—would not be on the scene before July. Delay was an axiom of military life, and one simply adapted and went ahead preparing for what was to follow. The airfields had names that would become indelible in the lives of thousands of young airmen: Polebrook, Chelveston, Thurleigh, Molesworth. . . .

Harris suggested, and Arnold had previously concurred, that it might be wise to select and build airdromes more eastward, in York. It was a question of proximity to enemy targets and a matter of less congestion in the crowded English skies, but since Chaney, on the recommendation of the Air Ministry, had accepted Huntingdon, Huntingdon it was. York would come later. In all, Eaker was planning to establish the Eighth's forces on sixty-one airfields—some built, most to be built—to accommodate the thirty groups scheduled to be in England, Scotland, and Northern Ireland before year's end.

RAF Bomber Command headquarters was at High Wycombe, about thirty miles west of London, and it was in this same locale that Eaker wanted his own headquarters. Chaney would have preferred that Ira and his staff remain in London, but as Eaker pointed out, they could not understudy Bomber Command at Grosvenor Square. Chaney had already commented on what he viewed as the inexperience and low rank of the Eighth's original half dozen, and he did not press the point when Eaker outlined the experience that would be gained in working with the RAF. Harris pressed the point from another direction. He immediately turned over temporary office space at his own headquarters. Then, sitting in his office with Eaker, he drew a tight circle of the area on a map and said, "Try to find something within this radius and I'll do what I can to help you get it."

What was quickly found was Wycombe Abbey, about four miles away, at Daws Hill. It was an imposing manor house, capable of housing a staff of several hundred, overlooking four hundred park-like acres where additional Nissen huts could be implanted. Once the domain of nobility, now a posh girls' school, it was therefore not available. At least it hadn't been available to RAF Bomber Command. When Eaker asked that Chaney's office put in a bid for the site with the Air Ministry, his request was ignored. The day after eight new members of his staff arrived, he sat down with Chaney's Chief of Staff, Brigadier General Charles L. Bolte, and stressed the need for action. Soon thereafter several representatives of the Air Ministry came calling. Their purpose was to explain why Wycombe Abbey would not be attainable. The girls attending the school, they explained, came from British dominions and couldn't be sent home because of the submarine danger. The suggestion was that a new site be found.

Eaker, who seldom raised his voice but knew how to make himself clearly understood, replied crisply, "If you're more interested in educating your daughters than in winning this war, I'm glad you told us."

The Air Ministry got the message, and Eaker was informed that as soon as arrangements could be made, Wycombe Abbey was to become 8th Bomber Command headquarters. In the interim, first Harris and then his gracious wife, Jill, invited him to come and live with them at their conveniently situated official residence, Springfield House. There was plenty of room, and Harris' Deputy Air Vice Marshal, Sir Robert "Sandy" Saundby, was also a resident. Eaker's ration card would help provide additional food, and if his socks needed darning Jill was adept with a needle. How could he refuse? His staff, meanwhile, was billeted at the officer's mess at Bomber Command, each member assigned his specialty in learning the facets and methods of command operations.

Although Eaker realized that the offer from Bert and Jill Harris was one of genuine courtesy, he had few illusions that Harris wouldn't use every opportunity to convince him that setting up an independent air force, with all the enormous logistical and administrative problems entailing months of time and thousands of troops, was a bloody mistake. Eaker quickly came to recognize that one of the reasons Chaney was so adamantly opposed to a separate Eighth Air Force Headquarters and Fighter Command was due to his acceptance and sympathy with the British viewpoint. Neither knew at the time that the reorganization worked out by McNarney & Company was to be of great benefit to Eaker. Moreover, air forces, wherever situated, would thenceforth be on a par with ground and service forces. Arnold's plan as he had described it to Chaney was now accepted. Chaney failed to see that what had been reorganized in Washington was going to have a direct effect on what was to be established in Great Britain. This was partly so because just before the reorganization went into effect he received word that *his* plan had been upheld and Arnold's rejected. The decision had been made by the new War Plans Division Chief, Brigadier General Dwight D. Eisenhower.*

In a memo dated March 4 to Hap Arnold titled "Establishment of United States Army Air Forces in the United Kingdom," Eisenhower's explanation for supporting Chaney's position indicates a delaying action more than an outright turndown. Yet, the general vagueness of its reasoning and seeming reluctance to act decisively suggests a contradiction born out of a lack of accurate information. Eisenhower agreed with Arnold that Great Britain should become the "bridgehead" to launch combined attacks against Europe, and the sooner the better, to aid the Russians. This, of course, would require complete agreement by the British, which they are "probably not yet willing to give." That being the case, Ike reasoned, to attempt to impose an American system of a totally different type would result in confusion and misunderstanding, and this could delay the basic objective. The disclaimer was in the final sentence: "This action will not prevent revision in the directive under which General Chaney is operating, if such action is considered desirable."

The argument drafted by OPD appeared to be a rather weak-kneed response to Arnold's hard-driving, aggressive determination to wage war in a manner that was direct and forceful. The system Eaker was working to establish was *not* that different from the RAF's, and his understudying the British would make it ever less so. In a week's time Arnold dispatched two memos to Marshall, possibly written by Larry Kuter or Hal George. One was on the employment of Army air forces and the other in reply to Eisenhower. Both were very concise and extremely well thought out, the one on the use of air forces concluding:

> Germany's military strength as well as her resources for war have been strained by the costly Russian campaign in which she is still engaged. In order to take advantage of this condition I strongly recommend that we immediately adopt the policy of building an effective air force in the British Isles for offensive action against Germany proper.

A few days later, Roosevelt dispatched a long cable to Churchill in which he spoke of "plans for establishment of a new front on the European Continent." Directly thereafter Harry Hopkins wrote a memo to the President titled "Matters of Immediate Military Concern." Item 3. read in part:

* On March 9, 1942, when the reorganization took place, the War Plan's Division's title was changed to Operations Division (OPD).

England. I believe Arnold's plan in England should be pressed home. There is nothing to lose. The bridgehead does not need to be established unless air superiority is complete. . . .

During this period Eisenhower and OPD were at work on the plan FDR had mentioned to Churchill: an invasion of northern France. The plan went under the code name ROUNDUP, its preparation being called BOLERO. The target date was set for spring 1943. A possible limited operation to grab a foothold and establish Hopkins' bridgehead on the Continent bore the name SLEDGEHAMMER; it was scheduled for mid-September 1942. The plan had to be sold to the British Government and its military chiefs; the principal salesmen would be Harry Hopkins and George Marshall.

All of this had to be known to Eisenhower, and most of it to Arnold. None of it was known to Chaney or, of course, Eaker. But with so much in the works, a definite plan of action going forward, spurred by a paramount interest in aiding the Russians, one has to question the unnecessary delaying action, on Eisenhower's part, of the essential force structure of the plan: air power.[4] The answer could be that at the time he simply didn't understand or appreciate all that was involved in putting together an air force.†

On the same day Roosevelt sent news of invasion plans in the making to Churchill, Eaker wrote a six-page personal report of his progress and his needs to Arnold. It was the first of a great many letters. Mostly it dealt with his mission: The eight airdromes would be satisfactory for accommodating three heavy groups, two photo squadrons, and two mobile air depots. They'd be ready for occupancy in April.

He repeated what was to become a continuing RAF theme as enunciated to him nightly by Harris:

> The British are skeptical of our ability to conduct day raids deep into Germany. They think our losses from enemy fighters will force us to abandon this ambitious scheme. I believe their pessimism is based on their knowledge of the state of training of their crews and their methods of conducting such operations. I personally believe we can do daylight bombing with our crews and equipment. We shall see who is right when we get to work. They will cheer loudly for us if we can do it, as our day bombing and their night bombing will give the enemy no rest, and the air space around bases will not be so cluttered up as if we were both working at night.

In his queries concerning equipment, Eaker demonstrated his own lack of information on details that were fundamentally important and could spell the difference between British skepticism and Yankee success. He indicated that Arnold had better know the answers, too. Will our bombers

† See Eaker's comments on this page.

be equipped with cameras? Will our supercharged bombers have flame dampers? (This to conceal exhaust flames, permitting approach to and return from the target in darkness.) Will our bombers take both British and American bombs? What is the status of the bomb supply? Will ample two thousand- and four thousand-pound bombs be available to provide continuity of effort?

"What radio equipment will our bombers have upon reaching this theater? Either they must have British radio equipment or our radios must be able to reach all the British wave lengths used in homing, rescue, fixing, etc. This subject has occasioned some of the delay in getting American-made bombers into combat in the past."

It was under his heading of "Organization" that he brought up the Chaney impasse: "As a result of my studies here I am more convinced than ever that the organization General Marshall tentatively approved for this theater, including an Army Air Force, is absolutely sound. I am not willing to admit that running our air effort in the months to come is not a full time job. The Theater Commander and staff can devote but part of their time to it. I have plenty to do to run the bomber effort. Definitely there should be an Air Force Commander to sit at the R.A.F. level, see that we get replacements, bombs, fuel, spares, ample overhaul, etc., and to co-ordinate the fighter and bomber effort."

He was saying as much as he could, and in describing his accomplishments and the magnitude of what was required, giving Arnold as much ammunition as he could to push for what was so obvious.

In closing, he reported: "The London papers carried front page stories yesterday on the Army re-organization at home. British Broadcasting Corporation also carried the story. All comment was favourable. Naturally we are anxious to know its details and how it will affect our effort here."

All to the good, Arnold could have replied. His title was now changed from Chief of the AAF to Commanding General of the Army Air Forces. In the change, the office of Chief of the Air Corps and that of GHQ (Combat) Air Force were abolished. Once and for all, this removed the schism of divided command which had been put into operation with the blessing of Chief of Staff Douglas MacArthur in 1935. However, in his new position theoretically Hap Arnold had absolutely no combat function; he was the commander of a training and supply agency and that was supposed to be all. Theoretically, but not for one second in actuality. He continued to wear the hat of a deputy chief of staff and was a member of the Joint Chiefs of Staff, which, of course, gave him a voice in military policy and strategic planning. Those who would command the air forces, particularly in North Africa and Europe, were old friends, and so there was personal linkage as well. However Arnold's responsibilities were described on paper, there was no doubt that he would play a very direct role in the use of strategic air power.

Overall, the reorganization meant that the foresight of George Marshall had given to the air arm a new level of autonomy, greater and more cohesive than that of the previous June. It was not the structure of independence Andrews, Knerr, and like-minded believers sought, but it was what Marshall wanted and Arnold was happy to accept. In a later exchange of letters between Arnold and Andrews, the difference in their philosophies on the subject was neatly expressed. Wrote Arnold:

> For some time, it has been apparent that the Navy is making every effort to get land based long range bombing planes. So far, we have been able to hold our own because we have not enough of these planes for our own mission, much less supply the Navy any. This seems to be the irony of fate considering that the Navy fought the procurement of large numbers of these planes for such a long period.
>
> It has been quite apparent to me for some time that while in time of war we can do almost anything, when the peace treaty is signed, there is going to be so much overlapping a complete reorganization will become a necessity. . . .

To which Andy replied to Hap:

> I agree with the basic thesis outlined . . . in connection with reorganization of our national defense, but I am not quite with you on the timing. Organization is merely a means to an end and when it becomes apparent that the existing organization is not doing the job satisfactorily, there is no reason that I can see for waiting to change the organization.

How the two viewed the broad approach was of no direct concern to Ira Eaker. What was more to the point was a heartening communication from Arnold telling him to be of good cheer; he would be sending what was needed, and in not too long a time Tooey and Monk would be coming over.

In those first, formative months Eaker not only came to live with the Harris family, he also spent a good deal of time with Harris at Bomber Command, learning. As Sandy Saundby was to note, a firm personal friendship grew between the two that was vitally important to the course of the war. Each could clearly understand and support the other's position without compromising his own. At root, they had some basic problems in common that helped strengthen the bond between them.

Eaker knew soon enough that as the new Commanding General of Bomber Command, Harris had his back to the wall. He had a total force of 378 operational aircraft, of which only sixty-nine were classed as heavy bombers. In the Atlantic, sinkings by German U-boats had reached a catastrophic level. In February alone, seventy-one ships were sunk, the largest number so far in the war, and it was soon to be exceeded. On February 11–12 three German cruisers, *Scharnhorst, Gneisenau,* and *Prinz Eugen,* departed from Brest after nearly a year of being under surveillance and bombing attacks by the RAF. The ships, with their destroyer flotilla and massive air protection, sailed up the English Channel and past the Cliffs of Dover to berths in Germany. Neither the Royal Navy nor Bomber Command halted their passage, not knowing their whereabouts until noon of the twelfth. Their independent attacks did little damage, and their losses were heavy. The British public was dumfounded, outraged, and as Harris took over, Bomber Command was coming in for fierce partisan attacks.

Internally, the harshest critics were found in the Royal Navy, which, like its American counterpart, was bitterly fighting for a greater share of industrial resources and much greater use of the end product: the long-range bomber for use in antisubmarine warfare.

Professor Patrick M. S. Blackett, Nobel Prize winner and prestigious scientific wizard, who was to become Director of Naval Operational Research, was to write on February 18: "I say emphatically that a calm dispassionate review of the facts will reveal that our present policy of bombing Germany is wrong; that we must put our maximum effort first into destroying the enemy's sea communications and preserving our own; that we can only do so by operating aircraft over the sea on a very much larger scale than we have done heretofore, and we shall be forced to use much longer range aircraft . . ."[5]

To which Harris is reputed to have replied, earthily, "Bullshit!"

Blackett's official opinion, and others like it, was not for public consumption, but voices speaking out against Bomber Command's operations in the House of Commons were. The most notable was Sir Stafford Cripps, the Lord Privy Seal, who three days after Harris had assumed command made a highly critical speech in which he questioned the policy "as to the continued use of heavy bombers and the bombing of Germany."

His words were reported by the New York *Times,* and the RAF delegation in Washington hit the panic button. A cable was sent to Portal maintaining, "Unless authoritative reaffirmation of our belief in bomber offensive is supplied immediately, effect on both strategic and production planning here may well be irremediable." Translated, this meant, unless you make a strong counterstatement, those in the Roosevelt administration and in the Congress who believe the United States should focus its war effort on defeating Japan may succeed in reversing overall strategy.

Harris could and did write a biting, vigorous defense of Bomber Command's past operations, pointing out that nearly 50 percent of its effort between April 1941 and March 1942 was directed against Germany's sea power and that for a single long-range bomber to sink one submarine would take an estimated seven thousand hours of flying. He also pointed out that Bomber Command had done almost all air-sea mining since the war began, accounting for over three hundred enemy ships sunk—and a great many more damaged, such as the *Scharnhorst* and the *Gneisenau*. But even with the ammunition he brought to bear, ridiculing his detractors who wished to parcel out his thirty-six squadrons to Coastal and Army commands, comparing them to "amateur politicians who believe the millennium will arrive by dividing available cash among all," he had to prove himself fast or his opponents might well succeed in whittling away his forces faster than German flak and night fighters.

Harris had four primary areas he could go after in Germany employing Gee as well as a number of targets outside of Gee range. He could also attack a nearer target, the Renault works at Billancourt, close to Paris. The plant produced fourteen thousand tanks and motorized vehicles annually plus armaments—all needed at the Russian front. On the night of March 3, Harris sent off his bombers in the opening raid of his campaign of mass bombardment. Eaker wrote Arnold the results:

> Night before last the C-in-C sent 240 bombers against the Renault factory on the outskirts of Paris. Last night he showed me the pictures obtained by P.R.U. [Photo Reconnaissance Unit] under a 200 foot ceiling yesterday with low visibility. The pictures are excellent and show unmistakably that this plant was badly messed up and will build no more trucks or tanks for the Germans for a long time. Forty 4,000 lb. bombs were included in the bomb loads dropped on this plant. The photos show clearly the advantage of such bombs as compared with lighter ones. British information indicated that a large portion of German trucks came from this plant.

What Eaker did not say was that he had viewed the photographs through a stereoscopic device in Harris' den, his so-called "conversion room." It was here that the two held many nightly sessions, Harris trying to convert Eaker into night bombing while they studied the results of his campaign of raids against Ruhr and Baltic-port targets. Gee was the guiding instrument. Aircraft equipped with it were divided between those dropping flares and those dropping incendiaries. The main striking force followed them over the target. In his rapid-fire attacks, Harris was putting up a force of more than two hundred planes a raid, experimenting with new tactics, finally making an impact on the German citizenry.

He and Churchill would have been pleased to read Propaganda Minister Joseph Goebbels' diary after "an exceptionally heavy air raid by the R.A.F. on Lübeck. . . . The damage is really enormous. . . . We can't get away from the fact that the English air raids have increased in scope and importance; if they can be continued for weeks on these lines, they might conceivably have a demoralizing effect on the population."

Across the Channel, Churchill was enormously pleased with the photographic evidence, and he wrote Roosevelt accordingly, saying only the weather was holding back "continuous heavy bombing attacks." Bomber

Command's new methods were paying off. Essen, Cologne, Lübeck—all were on the Coventry scale. "I am sure it is most important to keep this up all summer, blasting Hitler from behind while he is grappling with the bear."

Roosevelt agreed, but he stressed the submarine threat, suggesting that Harris send his bombers against U-boat bases and their building and repair yards. On the latter, this had long been Harris' own position. He thought it asinine to send bombers out over the ocean—"Navy fashion"— rather than going after the problem at its source, "Air fashion." And in "air fashion" he attacked the problem.

Closer to home, a similar type of cooperation between Air and Navy was doing little to halt the massive sinking of badly needed shipping in the Atlantic. Major General Follett Bradley was the Commanding General of the First Air Force, and Major General Hugh Drum was Commander of the Eastern Defense Command. Bradley's bomber command had a special sub-hunting task force, but it was under Navy direction at the point of contact. On a fine clear morning an Army reconnaissance plane, flying out of Morrison Field, Florida, came on a dream sight: a German submarine aground. The plane began circling, calling for action. The word was passed to Bradley, but since the destruction of submarines and use of Army planes off the shore were a Navy and not an Army matter, he called Navy Deputy Chief of Staff Admiral Richard S. Edwards, in Washington, who, after some conversation, rang up Admiral Russell S. Crenshaw, at Key West, who, after some conversation, then got on the horn to Hugh Drum, who repeated that the use of Army bombers was a Navy function.

Meanwhile the Army plane was still circling, watching the German U-boat work itself free after twenty-five minutes of struggle. At Morrison Field, aside from a squadron of bombers, there was an ample supply of bombs and depth charges. Hap Arnold, in his anguish on reporting the incident to Marshall, went so far as to list the numbers and poundage of each. It was not the sort of unity of command that contributed to winning the war. Nor was the fact that in a three-month period the First Air Force submarine task force racked up a score of fifty-four attacks and zero kills.

Arnold would have been in complete agreement with Harris' position of "attacking the kernel of the problem at the center." All very well, but the Admiralty's response was that wherever the kernel was being attacked, the number of German submarines was growing at an alarming rate.

The issue was one of targeting, and it was one on which the two bomber commanders were in complete agreement. Eaker, at Harris' suggestion, had written a critique on RAF bomber operations, and in the conversion room, amid the haze of pipe and cigarette smoke, they debated British and U.S. tactics.

On the latter, the question of fighter escort loomed large. Arnold had

written, not just to Chaney and Marshall, that "the basic role of fighter
units should be that of providing close support for the operation of
bomber units, for which they are barely adequate." This last observation
was, of course, the nub of the problem, and Eaker, in discussing it with
Harris, was able to define what was at stake in clearer terms.

In examining RAF methods, he and his staff had become acquainted
with techniques that could be used in daylight operations. The big problem was the location of the kind of profitable targets cited in AWPD-1.
How difficult were they going to be to find under conditions of haze
and weather, and once found, could bombing be done without fighter escort? The answer was yes, because it had to be. Yes, if there were enough
bombers in massed formation with enough firepower to hold off the
fighters; and yes because, as noted, there was no escort with range and
speed necessary to accompany the bombers to targets deep in Germany's
heartland. As Eaker knew, it would be a serious weakness on the part of
any commander to base his strategy on weapons that were not in being.
He could only plan on what was available. The P-38 and P-39 would be
available, and the P-47 would follow. Each could supply bomber protection for some of the way; none could supply it all the way to distant targets.

And so his determined advocacy of the long-range daylight bomber was
built on the three legs: mass, firepower, and the Norden bombsight.
Weather and navigation were indeterminates to be surmounted, the first
by scientific means, the other through training and practice. In the beginning, the raids would be of shallow penetration with fighter escort and
then, as experience and confidence and numbers were gained, of deeper
degree until all of Hitler's war-making potential was vulnerable to attack.

Harris couldn't buy it. The immediacy of his need was paramount. His
was the only force that was drawing German fighters and flak guns and
the personnel to man both away from the Russian front. And his force
was just too small. There were problems with the new, Lancaster bomber.
The Germans had developed a counter to Gee with an electronic system
that aided their fighters in homing in on the bombers. In the Ruhr they
had implanted a searchlight belt that illuminated the bellies of the attackers. In the month of March, Harris lost one hundred aircraft. In
April, that number would be nearly doubled. If in the beginning, when
Eaker began to receive his groups, they could temporarily be fed into the
RAF's night raids, it would make all the difference. Months would be
saved and. . . .

And Eaker could only shake his head and repeat the same arguments,
the bottom line being, I don't make the policy, Bert. You take it up with
the Combined Chiefs.

The U.S. half of the Combined Chiefs was wrestling with a broader
problem, Arnold now informed Chaney. The recent deterioration of the

Far Eastern Theater had brought the need to reevaluate plans. We can't be strong everywhere, he said, but we simply must use our available forces to the best possible advantage. He described the most vital factor in the decision, aside from guarding the United States, as the perseverance of the Russians. "Our intelligence people tell us that, unless Russia has immediate assistance this summer in the form of a Western Front to divert German forces, the end of Russian resistance may be expected—either from military defeat or by a separate peace. . . ."

He then got to the heart of the matter: The major bombing effort already planned must go through, but he did not feel that it could be operational in time to be of real assistance to the Russians in 1942. Instead, an offensive against Western Europe must be mounted "which carries with it the threat of actual invasion. We must pave the way by vigorous air offensives against the German air force, and we must create the air conditions which will make landing on the continent possible. Then we must bend every effort toward effecting a large scale operation in France."

With this letter of March 9 he enclosed a copy of a more lengthy one to Portal, saying the same thing but in more detail, pointing out that, until autumn at least, the RAF would have to carry most of the fight. In describing his plan for an "all-out air offensive across the Channel," he felt that initially daylight action should be limited "to the radius of operation of the mass of our fighters, and require a large fighter force operating with the bombers apart from the fighter defenses of England." But, aside from the details, what he was really trying to get through to Chaney, in spite of Eisenhower's support, was that Chaney's limited plan for the utilization of U.S. forces in England had been outdated, not just by events alone but by a new approach to them.

Whatever Chaney thought, shortly thereafter, in shorter but more specific terms, he received a cable from General Marshall that said:

> Current organization of your command set-up should permit and facilitate the eventual employment of large forces both ground and air in major offensive operations when these can be made available. Air forces in these eventual operations will include bombardment and the necessary supporting pursuit aviation. . . .

The message was clear enough, but to make it even clearer five salesmen came calling. They were A. H. Hones, C. G. Mell (who through forgetfulness was in uniform), A. L. Foss, J. H. Case, and J. E. White. They traveled via Pan American Boeing B-14 flying boat under the code name MODICUM, arriving in England on April 8. Hones was Harry Hopkins, Mell was George Marshall, and the three officers accompanying them were their Army, Navy and Air Forces advisers—the first being Lieutenant Colonel Albert C. Wedemeyer.

The primary purpose of the top-security visit was to sell the British on

the plan for BOLERO, ROUNDUP, and possibly SLEDGEHAMMER, the outline
of which Arnold had been trying to impress upon Chaney, who now, because of his position, became a member of the sales group.

The arrival of Hopkins and Marshall for their eight-day stay was of importance and benefit to Eaker. On that day, he drove into London and
lunched at the Army Officers Club, where he met J. H. Case, who was old
friend Colonel Howard Craig, Marshall's Air Forces adviser. Craig had
much to fill him in on, and they had tea that afternoon in Eaker's room at
Claridge's, and in the evening dinner at the R.A.F. Club with Major Peter
Beasley and Colonel Al Lyon. The bull session that followed was divided
between plans and problems. There were many of both, but the best news,
though unofficial, was that Arnold's stand on organization was to take
precedence over Chaney's.

While the salesmen were at work, in the week that followed, hoping to
convince the British chiefs of the soundness of U.S. strategic policy
against Hitler, Eaker was at work commuting between High Wycombe
and London, acquainting the visitors with the state of his progress and in-
troducing them to his hardworking staff. In London he had met with
Marshall briefly, inviting him to come out to his headquarters at Bomber
Command. Harris arranged for a joint reception, and when Marshall arrived, at 10 A.M. on Saturday, Eaker had his staff present to be introduced. It had grown in number to twenty-two, plus a dozen RAF
WAAF's loaned by Harris. Marshall spoke to the assembled at some
length on the importance of their task.

Peter Portal came calling too, and later, over lunch at Springfield
House, the four spent several hours conferring on present conditions and
future expectations. Marshall did a lot of listening and, as Eaker phrased
it, made "many searching enquiries." This was still a getting-to-know-you
period. For over two years the British had been supplicants at the U.S.
production table. Now they were allies in fact, not exactly equals, because
they had been fighting the enemy since 1939. Their experience at the time
was a large counterweight against the forces that the United States would
one day put into the conflict. But, every day, the British had their Empire
to safeguard; it came before all else. The United States had the Four
Freedoms and no thoughts for future political policy beyond the defeat of
the Axis powers.

Arnold had described British intent laid down by Portal as "nibbling at
the periphery" of Hitler's Reich, when he, like Marshall, wished to go for
the jugular. Their desire to aid Russia was purely military. The Russian
political system and Stalin's previous alliance with Hitler were of no matter. To Churchill and his government, the political and the military were
bound together, and so was everything that concerned the future of the
Empire, particularly the manner in which the war was to be waged in the
Middle East, India, and Burma. The differences in viewpoint were there,

and Marshall perceived them more clearly than Hopkins, although outside the conference room the British were generally charming and cooperative, wonderful hosts.

Eaker could vouch for that, particularly after they all drove to Chequers for dinner with Churchill and a mélange of other notable British and American guests, including Hopkins and Harriman.

Spring had finally come to the English countryside. The sun was out for the first time in two months. Hopkins in later reflection waxed poetic, observing, "It's only when you see that country in Spring that you begin to understand why the English write the best goddamned poetry in the world."[6]

For the moment, it was a different kind of poetry that Eaker enjoyed. Chequers, the Prime Minister's Elizabethan-style country estate, shaped like the letter "E," with its spacious grounds and gardens without, its huge dining and living rooms within, was a grand setting for the lively evening that followed, Winston dominating the stage. To Eaker, who did not know the reason for the Hopkins/Marshall mission, the central question around the dinner table was whether the Allies were going to go on the offensive or remain on the defensive. His own thinking: If it was to be the former, then send over the trained bomber groups he was preparing for, along with the fighters to escort them; and if it was the latter, why, send over fighters.

It was Harriman who asked him how soon he anticipated receiving some bombers. He replied that Colonel Craig had brought word that the first two groups would not be arriving before July. "Why don't you borrow some B-24's and Fortresses from the British?" Harriman wanted to know.

"They belong to Coastal Command, not Bomber Command," Eaker explained. "Air Marshall Harris is using all the bombers he has available for his own operations. There would be nothing gained by his lending us any of his force, which has already been diminished by the demands of Coastal Command."

Harris, seeing a chance to score a point against the Admiralty, gave his statistics on the very long odds against long-range bombers finding submarines at sea. Send them after the subs where they're made and berthed, he said. To which Admiral Sir Dudley Pound agreed, but then added that such operations would do little damage to the U-boats already at sea.

Later, in a letter to Arnold, Eaker responded to Pound's criticism by making the comparison of having guns in England that could fire eleven hundred miles. "We wouldn't shoot them out to sea in the hope of hitting a submarine in the vast expanses of the Atlantic," whereas "we would aim them at nearby interior or coastal targets and destroy the munitions industry."

Along the same line, Harris said to Churchill, "The destruction of the

Renault factory destroyed tanks and mechanized equipment of five motorized divisions in six hours of bombardment operations. This was more
tank destruction than has been effected by both sides in all the campaigns
in Africa." It sounded like boasting and no doubt to some extent it was.
Bomber Harris was never one to paint the scene in pastels. He believed in
what he was doing and, unlike others, was not afraid to speak out on any
occasion.

After they rose from the table, Eaker had a few minutes to talk privately to Marshall. He informed him that he and his staff were going to
follow a policy of flying a number of combat missions in order that they
would know exactly what the crews were facing. Previously he had told
Chaney that he thought it was time for an American general to stick with
his fighting men in every situation. Marshall was in complete agreement;
it would be an added morale factor.

That, for the moment, was enough of the serious talk. Churchill led the
way to the next order of business. With all the servants present, the guests
gathered for a showing of the swashbuckling film *The Prisoner of Zenda,*
which featured Ronald Coleman and lovely Madeleine Carroll. Before
dinner, the curator of Chequers had shown Eaker Cromwell's death mask
and a ring worn by Good Queen Bess. For Eaker, the ghosts of yesteryear
were all about. Following the movie, the conversation and the whisky
flowed before a crackling fire, while from the shadowed walls the portraits
of those who had made history in other times looked down on those who
were making it now. Past and present were closely entwined as the guests
listened to Churchill wax eloquent on the American Civil War while they
all considered the uncertain fortunes of the morrow.

Actually, the morrow was not just Ira Eaker's birthday—he was forty-
six—it was also Bertie Harris', who was two years older. Eaker's staff gave
him a surprise party at which he cut the cake, and that evening Jill Harris
had a gala reception for both the airmen. They could at least toast each
other and their plans for the future.

When Marshall and Hopkins and their small party departed for home,
on April 16, believing they had sold the British on the American plan of
action, Eaker took the opportunity of sending a personal letter to Arnold
through Howard Craig. He included in it photographs Harris had given
him of the bomb damage to the Renault factory and of Lübeck.

"I note that you are continually harassed by a certain school which
would minimize the effect of bombing," he said, "and I believe this gives
ammunition for you, and which you will know how to use better than
anyone."

It was a thorough letter, as always, two and one half pages single-
spaced, covering a wide range of activity and preparation. Colonel Al
Lyon was returning to the States, and Eaker had given him a plan for the
reception of the early groups. "He will represent my view that the highest

priority for immediate action should be given to the establishment of repair facilities for aircraft and replacement facilities for combat crews. The volume and continuity of our operations are absolutely circumscribed by these two factors. . . ." Also, he made clear that before he could launch and maintain effective bombing operations, he must have in being the essential depots for supplies—ordnance, signal, engineering, and quartermaster.

In a follow-on letter to Hap, Bert Harris was much more effusive. "Come on over and let's clean up!" he sang. "1000 Bombers per raid, instead of 2–300 as now, and we've got the Boche by the short hairs." He mentioned Ira's sending the Lübeck photos and added: "He and I see eye to eye in all such matters—and indeed in all matters. He's a great man. I do not thereby infer that I am also! But I find myself in invariable agreement with him—except perhaps that I think he will find it necessary to go easy with the daylight stuff until he has felt his way.

"The Boche is squalling over Lübeck, and the sooner we give him 100 Lübecks the more he will have to squall about. . . .

"Ira lives with us but spends most of his time rushing around. My rushing around was done by my predecessors. . . . We both much look forward to Tooey's arrival. He also has a bed in our house and Jill has her darning needle poised ready—for his socks, not his posterior, tell him. I think he should stay with us for at least a month even if he has to shift to London later."

Harris went on to push the advocacy of *Big* bombs and incendiaries as the only things that mattered. Nothing less than five hundred pounds, preferably over one thousand. They had dropped an eight thousand-pounder the other night. "Your Tokyo bombing was great," he cheered, "and we rather like our Augsburg show. . . ." He continued full of enthusiasm and praise for Ira's staff and for the dinner at Chequers, and then concluded with his old refrain: "The weather improves and if they would only stop bleeding me for crews and aircraft overseas we could really get down to it. Extraordinary how many people can think of how many ways of employing air power except the right one! I know you have your troubles, too. Frightening codfish all over the wide ocean spaces will never win a war. Bombing Germany and Japan will win this one—or else.

"Jill sends her love to you and Bee, in which I most heartily join. My very best regards also to Bob Lovett and to all old friends. Come on over!"

Eleven

A Small Beginning

The message Howard "Pinky" Craig had brought to Eaker, that he would not begin to receive the first of his promised long-range bombers until July, was correct. In the interim, Hap Arnold *did* come over, the major purpose of his visit not to reply to Harris' invitation but to deal with the knotty problem of aircraft allocation, which in turn had a direct bearing on Eaker's expectations.

The issue had been raised by the Navy through the voice of Admiral King, who, soon after Pearl Harbor, had been given by Roosevelt the dual appointment of Chief of Naval Operations and Commander in Chief of the U. S. Fleet. Said King in one point of a five-point memo to his colleagues on the U. S. Joint Chiefs of Staff:

> 3. The basic strategic plan on which we are now operating is to hold in the Pacific. I am not convinced that the forces now there or allocated to that theater are sufficient to "hold" against a determined attack in force by the Japanese, an attack which they can initiate very soon. The mounting of BOLERO must not be permitted to interfere with our vital needs in the Pacific. I am convinced that the Japanese are not going to allow us to "hold" but are going to drive and drive hard.

These words and their supporting arguments, political as well as military, caused Roosevelt to act, and on May 1 he issued a directive calling for an increase in air combat strength in Australia to one thousand aircraft, and ground troops to be raised to one hundred thousand.

Marshall, while on an inspection trip in the South, heard of Roosevelt's decision and hurried back to Washington to oppose it. As he phrased it to the President, "While I agree that we must *hold* in the Pacific, I do not concur that this is *our basic strategic plan*. My view, and I understood it to be your decision prior to my visit to England, was that our major effort would be to concentrate immediately for offensive action against Germany from the British Isles."

Arnold, in a requested response to Marshall, tore into King, declaring that his position "emphasizes again the fundamental error under which he and the whole Navy seems to be laboring, to wit, that our first priority objective is the Pacific. This concept unless rectified will eventually consume the major part of our military effort and render us impotent in what we have before considered the decisive theater. . . ."

Military considerations aside—and certainly they had to be the determining factor—what lay beneath the surface of Arnold's spleen was the unresolvable friction, the undying contention between senior Army airmen and the Navy. Arnold went so far as to draw an analogy between King and General McClellan defending Washington at the beginning of the Civil War: "—more men, more guns, more training, etc.—always striving for a higher degree of perfection, but never a fight." It was hardly an apt comparison. The root of the bitterness was the long-range bomber, whose development the Navy had sought to deter throughout two decades of peace and now, at war, wanted in large supply, which would certainly further delay plans to carry out the strategic bombardment of the Third Reich.

Actually, what King, Nimitz, Emmons, and MacArthur had prevailed upon Roosevelt to grant (above agreed-on figures) was twenty-five thousand soldiers and three hundred forty combat aircraft for the South Pacific and Hawaii. It did not seem like all that much, but at the time it was, and Marshall put it bluntly to Roosevelt that such a move would scotch the plans he and Hopkins had carried to the British: "The increases in U. S. Army Air Forces suggested for Australia and the South Pacific Islands, if executed this summer," he said, "would have the effect of postponing, by more than two months, the initiation of an American offensive in Western Europe."[1] The troop increase to Australia, he added, would mean the United States would not be able to participate "in the most difficult and vital phase of BOLERO, the landing operations." In short, if Roosevelt insisted on supporting the King request it was Marshall's recommendation that he abandon BOLERO.

Arnold had lived with, faced, and fought one source of the allocation problem since before the war: the demands of allies for aircraft, particularly the British. Now he and his advisory council reasoned there was one way to cut the aircraft-production pie in a way that would afford a larger piece to the seven Pacific areas that King and his commanders felt were in dire need: *reduce the British slice.* This would be no small task, for the RAF was urgently calling for nearly five hundred U.S. fighters and one hundred heavy bombers in Africa and the Near East, and 244 Fortresses and Liberators for Coastal Command's antisubmarine campaign.

Portal's idea was to parcel out aircraft to those theaters whose security was in doubt, and therefore his thinking was somewhat similar to King's. He was currently sending two thirds of U.S. fighters allocated to the RAF on to Russia, and Arnold and his planners knew that the changes to be suggested must be sold to the British not on the basis of need in the Pacific but under the banner of BOLERO. Roosevelt approved the approach and wrote Churchill accordingly, not going into detail. He'd let Hap do that. However, even before Arnold's departure there were complications illustrating how decisions made at the top for good and sound reasons could bring delay to the best of plans.

In his response to the President on Admiral King's position, Marshall had also made brief reference regarding "the hazard we are accepting in the Alaskan-Aleutian theater now under threat." The Chief of Staff said he was willing to gamble on that hazard "in order to stage an early offensive on the Continent of Europe." Willing to gamble, but not without drawing a card or two.

On May 22, Arnold, Tooey Spaatz, and Major General Millard "Miff" Harmon, Chief of the Air Staff, sat down to lunch. Hap told them he was leaving for England the next day, that he was taking with him letters of instruction defining the role of the U. S. Air Forces in BOLERO. Spaatz would be in command. The Eighth Air Force would at all times be an autonomous force.

All very well, as far as Tooey was concerned, but he was damned annoyed by the ordered withdrawal of four of his B-17's, shunted out to Alaska. It was bad enough to have his force dissipated by such withdrawals, but worse, the loss was going to delay the "Movement Plan." The plan was a unique and daring one. Spaatz, Hunter, and their staffs, working in conjunction with Hal George, who had just taken over as Commanding General of the Ferry Command,* were organizing a first-of-its-kind joint movement of bombers and fighters from the United States to England via the northern route. For safety's sake, Spaatz wanted no more than four fighters accompanying each bomber, which would act as a navigational guide. Now, with the loss of four B-17's, the plan was going to have to be reworked. The planes involved were the B-17's of the 97th Group, and the 1st and 31st Fighter Groups, flying Lockheed P-38's and Bell P-39's. Monk Hunter and his headquarters were in charge of organizing and directing the mass movement, which would encompass nearly three thousand miles from Presque Isle, Maine, to Prestwick, Scotland, including three intermediate stops. It was a venture that would save time and shipping, and in its current planning, involve one hundred eighty aircraft, many of them flown by very inexperienced crews.

* The Ferry Command became in June 1942 the Air Transport Command. Hal George replaced Bob Olds as its Chief when Olds became Commanding General of the Second Air Force.

Hap told Tooey he regretted the diversion of the Fortresses. Certain pressure had been brought that he couldn't override, but Spaatz could be sure it wouldn't happen again. That it had happened, Spaatz replied, would mean that some of the bombers would have to return to accompany the remainder of the fighters. It was a lousy solution, because it would mean added delay and greater risk. But the three of them agreed it was the only way.

The following day, Hap and a party of ten others, including his principal assistant, Colonel Hoyt S. Vandenberg, as well as OPD Chief Ike Eisenhower and Major General Mark V. Clark, took off from Bolling Field. Two days later they were in England.

Eisenhower's journey was at the request of Marshall. Overtly, it was for the purpose of discussing with the British the training and staging areas for the two and one half divisions the United States would be contributing to BOLERO and possibly SLEDGEHAMMER, the proposed mid-September cross-Channel attack to secure a bridgehead in France. Additionally it was to bring back recommendations on the restructuring of the U. S. Army command organization in England. Underlying this last was the question of Chaney's capability to head such a command. The answer to that, in Arnold's thinking, privately at least, was that Chaney should be removed. As he was to note cryptically near the conclusion of his visit, "Learned today that I brought with me the Arnold guillotine."

Eisenhower, in his reflections, offered excuses for Chaney and his staff, saying they "had been given no opportunity to familiarize themselves with the revolutionary changes" that had taken place in the United States "and were completely at a loss in their earnest attempts to further the war effort."[2]

One of Chaney's reactions to change pretty well summed up the problem: When he learned that there were WAAF's working at Eaker's headquarters, now code-named PINETREE, he objected. He didn't think the proximity of the sexes working together in such an atmosphere was conducive to sound military operations. This was one objection that Eaker ignored, but he was anxious to return the borrowed WAAF's to Harris, who needed their services badly. So he asked Arnold if he would see about getting him a company of WAAC's. Hap mentioned the idea to Chaney, who immediately rejected it. He wanted no Army women in his theater; it would cause a morals problem. Eaker responded flatly, "If I were you, General, I'd get some anyway." As Harris told him, and he had observed himself, women in the office did a thorough job, and out of it, far more than men, could be depended upon to keep their mouths shut concerning their work.

Although much of Arnold's visit was spent in conferences with Portal and Slessor and other RAF and Air Ministry officials, wrestling with the thorny question of who was to get what and where, he did manage to spend some time with Ira. They lunched the day of his arrival, and the following morning, after a stop to see Harris at Bomber Command, he and Bert drove over to PINETREE, where Arnold was duly impressed. It was a fine place. Ira had his staff "well trained and functioning." The visitor had a chance to say hello to old friends Claude Duncan and Woggie Towle and to interrupt Fred Castle, whom he had known since he was a baby, at a touch football game, but mostly he was absorbed in playing his own game of football. Or was it cricket?

Whatever the game, there were three goals: The reallocation of aircraft to the British was one—Churchill had said at their initial meeting that out of the sixty thousand planes produced in the United States he couldn't understand why an issue was being raised over a mere five thousand planes to the RAF; the second was the reiteration of the U.S. air contribution to BOLERO—daylight precision bombardment; and the third was the question of Chaney's remaining as Theater Commander. All three considerations had him running, debating "Portal and his henchmen," assigning Vandenberg to negotiations with Slessor over the differing viewpoints—"They gave him [Vandenberg] a thorough going over but he finally came through okay"—and sounding out Chaney, who did not think the P-38 and P-39 were effective combat aircraft: "He doubted their efficiency. He was fearful that I was committing the Army Air Forces when such commitment should be decided by Spaatz and Hunter."

In a conference at the Air Ministry, Arnold did not feel that Admiral Jack Towers was aiding the reallocation cause one bit. The Navy, Towers said, could not help out Coastal Command. The solution for more transport planes was to stop building B-17's, and as to what the Navy might give up, his answer was, "Nothing, as nothing the Navy could give up would help."

Arnold did have two meetings outside the scope of his visit that were informative and pleasurable. He talked with scientist Sir Henry Tizard and learned about a new, low-level radar able to track aircraft under one hundred feet, and he also discussed British progress on jet propulsion. The RAF had one jet ready to test-fly. The other meeting was with Jackie Cochran, who was working to establish a women's ferry command, as she had promised Bert Harris. Hap had a better idea. How about coming home and starting one for the AAF? Jackie decided that was a grand thought.†

The prime thought, however, that Arnold pushed right from the start, as he had assured Spaatz he would, was the air independence of U.S. units. He told Churchill that exceptional young men, the cream of the nation, would be flying those bombers and fighters and they could fly them

† In September 1942 the WASPs—Women's Air Force Service Pilots—began ferrying aircraft.

better than any other youngsters. The American public knew that, wanted a U.S. air force, and wanted action in Europe just as soon as possible. He had met with Air Marshal Sholto Douglas, Chief of the British Fighter Command, and explained that while Monk Hunter would command U.S. fighters, Douglas would be in charge of all operations until U.S. squadrons were fully indoctrinated, but it was Spaatz who would head and direct the Eighth Air Force.

As for Bomber Command, Bert had shown him photos of raids on Rostock and Augsburg, indicating great destruction, particularly at the Heinkel works, but, according to Harris' figures, while he had four hundred fifty operational aircraft he had only three hundred eighty crews to man them. On that score Churchill remarked, when Arnold insisted he would have seven hundred planes and crews in England by year's end, "Perhaps your program is too ambitious. You are trying to do, within a few months, what we have been unable to accomplish in two or more years." He then reminded Arnold of promises made previously that U.S. units would begin arriving by April. Here it was the end of May and none were on the scene. Because of the U-boat scourge, Churchill added, "shipping may be your real bottleneck in meeting your program and getting the units in action." Which brought up the question of Coastal Command allocations and the war against the submarines. It was all a vicious circle or maybe a wicked jigsaw puzzle with sharp points and square holes and nothing really fitting properly, because in Russia and North Africa and China and Burma, in the Atlantic and the Pacific oceans, the enemy was on the move, and there were not enough men or ships or planes to oppose him everywhere.

On this score Arnold took his strategy from Frederick the Great, whom he quoted whenever the occasion suited: "Small minds want to defend everything. Intelligent men concentrate on the main issue, parry the heavy blows and tolerate small evils to avoid greater ones. He who wants to defend everything saves nothing."

On the weekend of May 30, Arnold was a guest of the Prime Minister's at Chequers. Saturday evening, Eaker was present as well as Harris, Ambassador Winant, Harriman, Portal, General Hastings "Pug" Ismay, and Admiral Towers. Hap thought he might attempt some proselytizing on the cause and effect of daylight precision bombardment. Instead, he was completely upstaged by Harris, who reported on a dramatic display of RAF air power taking place while they met—the first one-thousand-plane raid of the war. It was partly a psychological maneuver with strong overtones of canny PR and partly an example of splendid organizational direction.

Actually, 1,046 aircraft took part, 376 of them borrowed from training units, over 700 of the raiders twin-engine types. The target was Cologne. Harris gathered together just about everything that would fly, including Oxford trainers that didn't have the range to make a round trip to the target. Only the Admiralty failed to cooperate, refusing to permit a loan of any bombers from Coastal Command. Nevertheless, the attack was a monumental success. Forty aircraft were lost, but the damage wreaked upon Cologne was staggering to its inhabitants. In less than two hours, forty-five thousand residents lost their homes and over three hundred factories were destroyed or damaged. The city was devastated, all its services in a shambles, some of its transportation facilities put out of commission for months. To the British it was sweet revenge; to the Germans, shock. To Arnold, it was not the night to preach what havoc daylight operations would also reap. Nevertheless, he took comfort from the dynamism of Bomber Harris, and later saw the attack "as the real beginning in the world's eyes and in German eyes . . . of round the clock destruction of Germany from the air."[3]

There were two unwarlike but unique highlights to Arnold's weekend in the country. Colonel Gene Beebe, his aide, got to sleep in a pair of Churchill's pj's, because he had none of his own; and Admiral Towers got stuck in a downstairs lavatory and made his exit via the window, abandoning ship posterior first. Mrs. Churchill, walking in the garden with Arnold, observed the escape and remarked: "My, what an extraordinary way to leave the house!"[4]

Before his departure, Arnold managed to spend a good part of a day and an evening with his bomber commander, including dinner and the theater. He was pleased with Eaker's progress, the diplomatic manner in which he had gotten along with the British, and the adroitness with which he had cooperated with Chaney and staff. Arnold knew there was little he and Chaney could see eye to eye on. In fact, he had already privately discussed Chaney's replacement with Ike's Chief of Plans, Major General Mark Clark. Both agreed it should be Eisenhower, and Arnold was prepared personally to make the recommendation to Marshall as soon as he arrived home.

But, for now, he and Ira did not talk personalities. They talked over their new book, a promised supply of cigars for Eaker, and Major General Jim Fechet's new wings. The retired Air Corps Chief had been awarded a pair of command wings, and was elated with them. On the serious side, they had met with Lord Louis Mountbatten, the Chief of Combined Operations—which meant commando raids—going over the part air power would play in establishing a beachhead on the Continent.

Mountbatten was planning to accompany Arnold to Washington for talks with Roosevelt, Hopkins, and the U. S. Chiefs; not, ironically, about the establishment of a bridgehead in France, but possibly in Norway or North Africa. Thus the real purpose of Mountbatten's journey was to signal a shift in British policy of which neither Arnold nor Eaker was aware. Otherwise, Arnold would not have departed from England so optimistic.

The night of the Cologne raid, Arnold had spoken by transatlantic telephone to Hopkins, informing him that he was coming home at once. He and Portal had signed a new allocation agreement he was bringing for approval. The point in it that most directly affected Eaker was that the United States would furnish three hundred heavy bombers and crews for BOLERO; this meant before mid-September. Arnold had gone over the airbase situation, the depot and supply situation, even the public morale situation, noting there were no dogs on the streets in London, and that "now men, women and children have lost that expression of dreaded expectancy. They have a cheerful look on their faces. They smile and walk with a determined air. That look of almost fearful bewilderment is gone. The shops are open but with very little in stock. . . . No glass—debris—broken water mains—gas fires—unexploded bombs.

"In fact the Huns have not been here for about a year. Last May they were still coming. Pianos are playing—men are whistling—London is changed." Earlier he had been told by two ranking "brass hats" that if the blitz had gone on another week, both London and Liverpool would have folded up.

Arnold went home smiling, feeling he had accomplished his task, that "in general, the air strength in all theaters would be maintained or increased." At least, that was what the intent was and the words said.

Eaker had originally approved 61 airdromes to accommodate his bomber strength. This number had been increased to 75, most of the bases to be built in East Anglia, with an overall total of 127 installations for all elements of the Eighth Air Force, including a training command in Northern Ireland. Arnold had presented to Portal a schedule of arrival that foresaw, by March of 1943, a force of 66 combat groups, 19 of which would be heavy bombers, 12 medium and 12 light, 15 fighter groups and 8 transport, for a total of over 3,600 aircraft and 195,000 men. The first fifteen groups were to arrive by the end of July, but when Hap departed, on June 2, there were fewer than 2,000 Eighth Air Force troops in England, and none of its aircraft.

Ira bid the Boss good-bye at Northholt Aerodrome, assured that the picture was about to change. Accompanying Arnold and Eisenhower on their return, along with Mountbatten, were Air Marshal Jack Slessor, the RAF Chief of Plans, and Averell Harriman. The movement to Washington indicated to Eaker that the pace was quickening. It had to be, because the good word was that Tooey and some of his staff were already en route.

They had taken off on June 1 from the bomber staging area at Grenier Field, New Hampshire, in a Ferry Command B-24 bound for Prestwick, Scotland. But as Scottish poet Robbie Burns once observed, "The best laid plans of mice and men gang aft a-gley . . . ," particularly in war. Spaatz and group arrived in the afternoon at Presque Isle, Maine, and at six-thirty, in the midst of a conference with Hal George and Pinky Craig,

Tooey received a telephone call from Larry Kuter, in Washington. Kuter's message from Marshall was brief: "Move nothing to the north and east. Further orders will follow within two hours."

Spaatz immediately contacted Monk Hunter at Grenier, gave him the word, and told him to stand by for another call at eight-thirty.

To Spaatz and Hunter the call came in the form of a large monkey wrench. "All existing orders pertaining to the movement of the Eighth Air Force are suspended," announced Kuter. "It is directed that the 1st, 31st, 97th and 60th [Groups] be prepared to take off at 8 A.M. tomorrow or at six hours' notice for destination over itineraries to be announced later."

The destinations for the 97th Heavy Bombardment Group, under the command of Colonel Cornelius Cousland, were McChord Field, in Washington State, and Hammer Field, at Fresno, California. The 1st Fighter Group went south to North Carolina, it, too, ordered to the West Coast. The 31st was to continue on to England, but the crews were to leave their planes and go by boat instead where, at their English bases, Atcham and High Ercall, they would inherit RAF Spitfires. The 60th, a C-47 transportation group at Presque Isle, was also ordered west, but first eighty thousand pounds of supplies for the Eighth Air Force and Hal George's Ferry Command bases along the route had to be off-loaded.

As Spaatz's aide, Major Sy Bartlett, noted, "This order emanating from Washington had the effect of completely disrupting the highly organized movement of Eighth Air Force men and materiel to England."

And what was the cause for the sudden disruption? As Tooey put it to Ira, "Several Japanese fishing and other boats moving in the general direction of our west coast from Japan scared everyone to death."

It was a little more serious than that, as indicated by Admiral King's demand on May 20 for four of Spaatz's B-17's to be diverted to Alaska. Earlier in the month, U. S. Naval Intelligence had determined that the Japanese were preparing for a major offensive whose overall purpose was the annihilation of Admiral Nimitz's Pacific Fleet and whose specific goal was the seizure of Midway Island and the occupation of strategic points in the western Aleutians. Coupled with this intelligence was the fear of a Pearl Harbor-type strike against the thinly defended West Coast. By the time the 97th's B-17's had arrived in Washington and California and the 1st's P-38's had reached North Carolina, the Battle of Midway was over, the main Japanese thrust defeated, the stunning U.S. victory later recognized as a major turning point in the Pacific war. The Japanese had successfully bombed Dutch Harbor, in the Aleutians, and landed token forces on two islands in the chain, but the threat to the West Coast was greatly diminished. As a result, the 1st Fighter Group was back at Presque Isle, Maine by June 6 and the 97th in position to cross the Atlantic with the 60th by the eighteenth.

In letters, memos, diaries, and cables back and forth, the movement of men and equipment to England was referrred to as "the Bolero move." In fact, Tooey's Chief of Staff, Asa Duncan, used the phrase "the Bolero theater." The usage was an indication of Army airmen's thinking, from Arnold on down; an acceptance of the belief that BOLERO—the buildup—was aimed toward air supremacy and a twofold goal.

A month earlier, at Bolling Field, Spaatz and his staff had briefed Secretary of War Stimson on how they viewed this basic concept. In so doing, Spaatz outlined target selection, which left Stimson a bit puzzled. The strategic targets seemed different to him from those originally planned. Spaatz explained that initially the idea had been for the Eighth Air Force, supported by ground forces in England, to concentrate wholly on enemy industrial targets. Now, with BOLERO as the platform from which SLEDGEHAMMER and/or ROUNDUP was to be launched, the new concept was that ultimately the Eighth's air power would be *both* tactical *and* strategic.

Spaatz divided operations into two expeditionary forces, the first using heavy bombers to hit vital industrial and interior installations and the second to gain air supremacy over a limited area where the proposed bridgehead was to be established. Or, as Spaatz phrased it, "permitting ground forces a necessary latitude to carry out the mission." It was this tactical aspect of the plan that brought the inclusion of medium and light bombardment groups into the Eighth's tables of organization.

There were two critical points of caution that Tooey Spaatz stressed to Stimson. He wanted no exaggeration of U.S. air strength. Until he could be assured of a steady flow of replacements, he was going to operate on the basis of 100 percent reserves. A P-38 squadron of twenty-five planes would operate as a dozen with thirteen in reserve. He must have that safety factor, and he would flatly oppose any effort to limit it. Of equal importance, he told the Secretary of War, he did not want political pressure from home to force the commitment of his units into battle prematurely. Hasty action to grab headlines could bring severe losses, he warned, not to mention damage to prestige and a blow to morale. Stimson assured him he understood and that no such pressure would be forthcoming.

Yet, unbeknownst to Spaatz and Eaker and probably Stimson, in a thank-you letter to Churchill written on June 10, Hap Arnold promised the British leader, "We will be fighting with you on July 4th." On this same day, he had also written to Eaker and Jim Chaney. To Ira, he said nothing of significance, and to Chaney he gave no hint of a possible change in command, and in fact offered the opposite impression, commenting, "It's a big job we all have ahead of us, and if I can help you out in your end at any time, let me know and I will do my darnedest."

There was no doubt that Arnold was fiercely anxious to get U.S. air units into combat. Churchill had goaded him with his remarks concerning earlier promises. Directly upon his return to Washington he had passed to Marshall his own account of the Prime Minister's comments, suggesting that Marshall take note of Churchill's attitude relative to U.S. air operations, advising that "he [Churchill] apparently was very doubtful as to our ability to get fighting units to England."

Arnold had always possessed a penchant for painting the scene with oils rather than pastels. It was a characteristic born of a time when everything was in short supply. Then a carefully honed sense of exaggeration was a weapon in the fight to keep the Air Corps flying. Part of the technique was an equally developed public-relations awareness. Ira Eaker had it too. Any thinking airman did. However, its use was a matter both of exploitation and fear: Knowing when to take advantage of a public-relations opportunity to gain public support was one thing; at the same time, possessing the sensitivity and judgment against exploitation at the wrong time with the attendant damaging results was another.

Whether Arnold got the idea of inaugurating Eighth Air Force combat operations on the Fourth of July while he was in England or en route back to the United States or directly after he arrived home is not known.[5] Possibly it was a suggestion made by Arnold's special Advisory Council, which had been formed as a result of the Army's reorganization. The reorganization had given to the Army Air Forces its own large, autonomous staff, but Arnold was used to doing business with a few closely attuned advisers on whom he would depend. As his forte had always been the gleaning and pursuit of better ideas and the less administration the better, the new air staff was too unwieldy for him—and he to it, with his free-flying pet projects. This led to the forming of the Advisory Council, few in numbers—never over four—but chosen exclusively for the purpose of batting around new ideas with the Boss. Its originator, Larry Kuter, Deputy Chief of the Air Staff, described the council as one consisting of carefully selected officers. "They were picked as men with far above average potential and with a wide spread in recent experience. These were the men Arnold could and did talk to freely and easily."[6]

At the time Arnold returned from England the Council had two members, Colonels Charles "Pre" Cabell as Chief, and Lauris Norstad. Before his departure, Arnold informed them that at a meeting of the Joint Chiefs, the possibility of additional bombing raids over Japan was brought up. "I explained that we were thinking about this," Arnold said, "but distances for the moment had us licked unless we could go to Siberia. You fellows use your imagination and see what ideas on the subject you can present me. I realize that the distance from the Aleutian Islands probably makes that prohibited but there might be some other way to get at this proposition."

The thinkers came up with several standard suggestions: a repetition of the Doolittle raid; operations from Russian bases; a modified HALPRO; plus consideration of the placement of airdromes on Attu and Agattu, in the Aleutians. But to this they added one fairly fancy thought: the development of fuel-carrying gliders. If the gliders could carry a thousand gallons of gas, operations could be conducted from Alaska or maybe even from Hawaii against Japan with landings in Siberia or China.

That was a representative response from the Advisory Council. Later other members would suggest putting thermite bombs on bats and dropping them from B-29's over Japan. There, it was reasoned, the bats would take refuge in Japanese houses and burn them all down. The thinkers in this case failed to take into account that at thirty thousand feet the bats would need oxygen masks and fur-lined clothing. In any case, the suggestion by the Advisory Council that the Eighth Air Force begin combat operations on Independence Day does not seem all that remote, although it could have come out of the White House or the Secretary of War's office just as easily, for both were in full support of it. The public-relations appeal was obvious, the fact that Harry Halverson's HALPRO squadrons were already flying regular combat missions against North African and Italian targets notwithstanding. The only question remaining for the Fourth of July celebration was, Who was going to fly the mission? It was not a question as yet that had been asked of either Spaatz or Eaker.

On Thursday morning, June 18, Major General Spaatz, accompanied by two of his staff, Majors Harry Berliner, his A-5 chief of plans,‡ and Sy Bartlett, his aide, departed from Reykjavik, Iceland, on the final leg of the flight to Prestwick. Their aircraft was a B-24, and because German fighter planes had been snooping around the neighborhood the day before, the Liberator's pilot, Captain Chapman, was concerned that the enemy was out hunting for Tooey. Spaatz's remedy was that he do some of the flying and that Berliner and Bartlett take turns manning the tail-gun station. The only other aircraft they saw on the eight hundred fifty-mile flight were three Spitfires that came up to look them over as they made the approach to Prestwick. Awaiting their arrival were Ira Eaker and his pilot-aide Captain Bill Cowart. As Bartlett noted, it was a happy reunion.

The ensuing two weeks passed in a blur of activity, their swiftness paralleled by meaningful changes in organization and command. Upon his arrival, Spaatz went with Eaker to High Wycombe for the evening. The next morning they drove to London to pay an informal call on Jim Chaney. The Theater Commander was not in. Perhaps he was home packing, for word had just come that he was being relieved of his command. Less than two weeks earlier he had been officially informed that he was to be Commanding General of the European Theater of Operations, the designation replacing U. S. Army Forces, British Isles. As such, his mission was to have been the preparation for and the carrying out of operations

‡ Berliner was a longtime friend of Spaatz, an aircraft designer and aviation expert. Bartlett was a former magazine and film writer.

against the Axis powers in Europe. Instead, he was going home to command the First Air Force, replaced by Major General—soon to be Lieutenant General—Dwight D. Eisenhower.

Eisenhower, upon his return from England with Arnold in early June, had recommended to Marshall that Joe McNarney be made Commanding General of the European Theater, but McNarney was the new Deputy Chief of Staff for the War Department. On June 8, Ike submitted to Marshall his inspection report and plan for a unified command of all U.S. forces in Europe. On the same day, Chaney received word from the War Department that he was to be head man. Three days later, Marshall informed Eisenhower that the job was his.

That there were some crossed signals somewhere, there can be no doubt, and it could be that Chaney felt a certain amount of animosity toward Arnold and friends over the sudden, and obviously shattering, reversal of his fortunes. It wasn't that he was being returned to an inconsequential command. Quite the opposite, for at the time the waters off the eastern seaboard of the United States were a battleground against the German wolf packs. But Chaney had been the principal U. S. Army officer in England since the Battle of Britain. He had accompanied Harry Hopkins to the Soviet Union, given Churchill advice, been at the center of U.S.-British military planning, and now, when those plans foresaw going on the offensive, he was ordered home, his career eclipsed. A bitter pill, whatever the circumstances. Whether his failure to greet Spaatz and Eaker was inadvertent or intended is not known, but Spaatz did not see him before his departure.

Spaatz did see Ambassador Winant that day, and invited him to visit Eighth Air Force installations, such as they were. He also saw the press in an off-the-record briefing of U.S. and British newsmen. The conference took place in Public Relations Officer Lieutenant Colonel Harold B. Hinton's office. After stating, "I will be rather a disappointing person," Spaatz said, "I can't give you very much but I will answer such questions as I can." In so doing he stressed that his presence for the time being was not to be announced. Also, he borrowed a theme that Eaker had used when unexpectedly asked to address a large gathering of British service men and women. "We won't do much talking until we've done some fighting," Ira had said. "We hope when we leave you'll be glad we came." As Spaatz phrased it, "I believe in making a point first and discussing it afterwards, rather than talk about it and anticipate the action. In other words, I believe in delivering the punch first and doing the talking afterwards. The reverse does no harm to the enemy and no good to ourselves."

In the course of the questioning, Spaatz unknowingly revealed an essential tactical weakness of the air plan. "If and when we can establish the effect of daylight bombing," he said in answer to a question, "it might mean the beginning of the end—with massed attacks by night and bombing in the daytime."

"That means a continuous day-and-night attack to go on and on?" asked a reporter.

"Yes."

"You mean raids right into the heart of Germany?"

"Yes—right into their territory."

"Will that mean new tactics?"

"Some—combined with those also at present proved successful."

"That means a lot of fighters?"

"No. This will have to be done without fighters. The fighter planes cannot make the distance, although there is a type which could."

"What type of long-range fighter?"

"Well. . . ." Spaatz paused and then backpedaled, admitting, "There is no type which really has *that* long a range."

It was obvious the gathering liked his no-nonsense, unadorned approach. His words were as spare and to the point as were his craggy looks.

Within the next few days he moved into WIDEWINGS, the Eighth Air Force headquarters at Bushy Park, in Teddington, a London suburb. He met with Air Minister Sir Archibald Sinclair, Air Chief Portal, and other RAF brass, with officers of both the British and the U.S. navies; the latter he found were more interested in talking about war against Japan than war against Germany. All of them attended a large welcoming dinner given in his honor at Claridge's.

They sat him next to Air Marshal Sholto Douglas, Chief of RAF Fighter Command. Douglas, like Spaatz, was noted for his taciturn nature, and to those who didn't know him, his dour aspect. He had replaced Dowding following the Battle of Britain, and was the same kind of aggressive air leader as Bomber Harris. His pale blue eyes were said to have been fashioned of steel, at least by those who earned his displeasure. As Fighter Commander, he wanted U.S. fighter units under RAF direction. Arnold had agreed, at least to begin with. But the issue was a touchy one with Spaatz, and a great deal depended on how the two airmen hit it off.

Throughout the long meal neither man spoke to the other. When the eating was done and the dishes cleared, the port wine was passed. Tooey received the bottle and did the honors for Douglas, remarking, "I hear you're a mean son-of-a-bitch, and that I'm going to have trouble with you."

Sir Sholto nearly dropped his glass. "Oh, I say, old boy! I hope not!" he exclaimed. "I hope this isn't so!" And then he saw the glint of humor in Spaatz's eye and knew it wasn't so.

It was the following afternoon that Spaatz and Eaker called on Douglas and his principal assistants at Stanmore, headquarters of British Fighter Command. The ice had been broken and informality prevailed in the discussion that ensued. Tooey made it clear that the primary function of the Eighth's fighters was to support the Eighth's bombers. However, they would be trained in defense operations so that in an emergency they could be used for that purpose.

Douglas said: Fair enough, but the quickest way to accomplish that was to blend U.S. squadrons into British wings until they had learned the procedure. Spaatz said he wanted more time to think it over. It was obvious that he, like Eaker, was extremely leery of U.S. fighter units becoming absorbed by the RAF. When Sir Sholto suggested that U.S. forces might take over an entire sector, which had actually been envisioned in the TRIGGER plan, Tooey shied away, saying that would mean having to defend the sector. What would the RAF do about that? RAF defense was purely offense, replied Douglas, but he admitted that the Eighth's fighters might be called on to supply Fleet Arm protection in the Channel. Spaatz again deferred a decision. However, the mood remained relaxed as the two airmen sounded each other out on the delicate business of working out an agreeable tactical relationship on British home turf.

On that same Tuesday, Lieutenant General Eisenhower arrived in London, and on Friday the twenty-sixth Spaatz met with him. They discussed the use of U.S. fighters vis-à-vis the RAF, and Spaatz once again made his position clear: "Our fighters' primary function," he told Ike, "is to support our bombers in an effort to secure air supremacy and not for the defense of England. They will, however, be trained in defense procedure, so that in an emergency they can be used for defensive purposes."

This was Monk Hunter's bailiwick, he pointed out, and before Eisenhower sought approval from the top, Spaatz suggested it would be best for Hunter to determine just what Douglas was willing to accept.

Of the many points they discussed, Eisenhower stressed that he wanted plenty of lead time in knowing when U.S. air units were going into combat. They agreed on a week's notice, and Spaatz said he would call Ike, day or night, when that time came.

It came sooner than they expected, but, in the interim, at High Wycombe, Eaker threw his own welcoming dinner for Tooey, which included Ambassador Winant, Bert Harris, and Saundby as guests. When it was over, they repaired to Ira's quarters for a bull session. During it, Spaatz's pragmatism did battle with Harris' unyielding faith in air bombardment.

Harris believed that if they could put one thousand bombers over Germany every night for three months the war would be over.

Not unless the night raids were followed by daylight missions against specific targets, argued Tooey.

Suppose you had five thousand bombers, Winant asked, wouldn't that do the trick?

Indeed it would and then some, Spaatz and Harris both agreed. Five thousand would be more than enough.

Well, in view of present production figures, the Ambassador said, he could see no reason for not being able to obtain the required number.

Not that easy, Spaatz explained. There were commitments to other theaters, plus training, plus attrition to be considered.

Winant, tall and somewhat Lincolnesque, was an air enthusiast, eager to be of help and to be involved in all that was to come. One-time Governor of New Hampshire and a longtime government official, he, no more than Spaatz or Eaker, caught the underlying significance of the argument Harris presented against attempting to gain a foothold on the Continent. Spaatz maintained that the war couldn't be won until that was done—until it was possible to operate from such a bridgehead. Amid the haze of cigarette and cigar smoke and the taste of good brandy, Harris said no. To put troops in enemy territory meant supporting them. To do that would prevent equipment from going to theaters such as Egypt, where it was so badly needed. To attempt gaining a foothold in France now could mean another Dunkirk. No. Bombing the Hun's vital cities and industries —that was the only way to finish the job.

Spaatz's insistence that ground troops would be necessary to win the war against Germany, at least enough divisions to hold an area so that Allied air power could be launched from within it, indicated two beliefs. Unlike the architects of AWPD-1, the bomber-over-all champions, he was not cemented to the absolute that Harris was preaching. No bridgehead could be established without air supremacy, he said, but the reason for its establishment was in order to put his bombers closer to the intended targets and to give them a greater degree of fighter protection. Thus his thinking was both pragmatic and adaptable to the strategic plans that foresaw a landing in Europe. However, the RAF chieftain's adamancy against a cross-Channel operation was a hint of something more than a characteristic stubbornness.

There had been other hints. That same morning, Colonel Douglas Williams had arrived from Washington with a hand-carried letter from Asa Duncan. Williams was a communications expert who was being assigned, with Colonel Ruben Kyle, to Commando headquarters, to act as liaison for an upcoming combined operation code-named RUTTER or HORSE SOLDIER.

Duncan's letter informed Tooey: "Mr. Churchill arrived unexpectedly, and Miff Harmon told me confidentially that he made a very impassioned plea for a lot of assistance in the Middle East, and succeeded in selling the President on the idea. However, General Marshall and General Ar-

nold et al. put up a very determined and solid front against Mr. Churchill's proposal." Asa went on to say that a compromise was reached on
what would be sent, but apparently it would have very little effect on the
Eighth Air Force. Events would prove him wrong.[7]

Spaatz, like Eisenhower, was aware of the events, as was everyone else.
One was the fall of Tobruk to Rommel's Afrika Korps and the very grave
threat it posed of German occupation of the entire Middle East and its oil
fields. Right on top of this defeat came word that Sevastopol, under siege
for nearly a year and the last Soviet bastion in the Crimea, had also been
taken. The question was, Would the Russians make a separate peace? The
cry was for a second front.

Eisenhower had arrived in England in the week between these two de-
feats. It was he who had drafted the plans for the cross-Channel attack,
but he promptly learned the British had no plan of their own for
SLEDGEHAMMER. Further, at the very time he left home, Churchill and
Roosevelt were locked in debate with their military chiefs considering a
wrenching shift in course from the agreed BOLERO buildup to an invasion
of North Africa. Nothing was settled at the time. Neither Eisenhower nor
Spaatz was immediately privy to the shifts. It was a season of uncertainty
at the top, internal and external pressures building, and they would definitely have their effect on the Eighth Air Force.

On June 28, Spaatz received two messages. One was a birthday greeting
from Marshall, "with great confidence in your ability to carry out the mission," and the other instructed him to begin combat operations on the
Fourth of July. This was exactly what Tooey had warned Secretary Stimson against in their meeting before his departure, but Hap Arnold's idea
of celebrating Independence Day with some Eighth Air Force fireworks
had been enthusiastically accepted at the White House. It could be
reasoned that this was the kind of publicity the home front—not to mention the Russians and the British—needed at such a crucial hour.

It could also be viewed as an indication of Arnold's supposedly unau-
thorized direction of the Eighth, and his finely honed sense of public relations. Neither Spaatz nor Eaker liked the idea worth a damn.

It was Colonel Harold Hinton, Spaatz's PRO chief, who brought the
word to Harris Hull at PINETREE. Hull, now a major, had been involved
since his arrival, in February, in learning the air intelligence trade under
the guidance of the RAF. The Eighth had no intelligence service to begin
with, and it was Hull's job to establish one. He had attended the RAF
intelligence school at Harrow and was now working with Group Captain
Laurie Pendred, Harris' principal intelligence officer.

When Hinton, a former newspaper colleague, brought Hull the word,
saying, "You guys are going to have to fly a mission the Fourth of July,"
Hull's response was, "You're going to have to tell that to General Eaker.
We don't have any planes." They went at once to see him.

Eaker's first reaction to the news was that someone must have gotten April Fool mixed up with Independence Day. "You're out of your mind," he said. Hull handed him the order from Arnold.

The rationale for the urgent directive was to let the Germans know the Yanks had really arrived and to give the British a badly needed lift. Fine, if the Eighth had at least one group of B-17's with crews ready for combat; the RAF could provide fighter escort. But the first B-17 of the 97th Group was yet to land in England, and as for fighters, the pilots of the 31st Group had just begun transition training on RAF Spitfires. In the entire Eighth Air Force of that moment, there was only one unit available for combat duty. It was the 15th Light Bombardment Squadron, attached to the Air Support Command, which meant that its intended eventual use was tactical and not strategic.

The squadron had arrived in England in May. Originally slated to operate as a night fighter unit, it was switched back to light bombardment and began training with RAF 226 Squadron, flying twin-engine Douglas A-20's, Havocs which the British called Bostons. It was from this squadron that crews would have to be selected to fly the Eighth's first combat mission.

If Spaatz was tight-lipped and monosyllabic about the unexpected directive, Eaker was more voluble. It was his Bomber Command that must carry out the order. It was not what he had anticipated. He recommended against it. The gimmick was totally against his better judgment. He did not think the crews were ready. A low-level sweep against heavily defended coastal targets was not his idea of strategic bombardment. As he was to say, "Any Commander that had to commit forces to combat with equipment which was not suitable and with a minimum of training faced very tough decisions." He sensed disaster. But, of course, it made no difference. From the point of view of the uninitiated, which included Eisenhower, the debut made good sense: the RAF and the Yanks together attacking the enemy on the Glorious Fourth. Although Bomber Command operations had not planned an attack by No. 226 Squadron for the Fourth, one was quickly laid on, the targets to be four Luftwaffe airfields in Holland. Six American crews would join six British in the twelve-plane sweep.

On July 3 Harris Hull went to the grass field at Swanton Morely, in Norfolk, where the 15th was based, and carried out his first briefing job, going over the targeting, supplying the details of what to expect. Eisenhower, Spaatz, and Eaker also paid visits, on the second and the third, checking readiness, talking informally with the eager airmen. Certainly youth and enthusiasm were there. Captain Charlie Kegelman and his crew had already flown a mission with the RAF, bombing the Hazebrouck marshaling yard. Maybe it world work all right, but Ira had a cold feeling in his bones.

The next morning, he took off at seven for Swanton Morely, anxious to be on hand when the raiding planes of the 15th returned. The six A-20's had been taking off in the misty morning at the same time, their aircraft bearing the RAF roundels. The dozen attackers assembled into four flights of three planes each and, at treetop level, headed out over the North Sea. The plan was to stay low and avoid enemy radar, but German "squealer" ships spotted them and flashed a warning to coastal defenses. The result was a fierce reception. Even as the four units split up to head for their assigned targets, intense flak and other ground fire were thrown up at them. As they approached the De Kooy airfield, the plane of Kegelman's wing man, Lieutenant Frank L. Loehrl, was hit, and he saw it go down crashing in flames. Flak slammed into Kegelman's right engine, tearing the propellor off and starting a fire. With the wrenching impact, he lost control, the starboard wing tip furrowing the ground, the rear of the fuselage carooming into the earth, ripping a hole in the metal. Kegelman fought to keep his plane in the air. He jettisoned his bombs, and that helped. "Give 'em hell, Captain!" shouted his rear gunner, Sergeant Bennie Cunningham. Machine guns in a flak tower opened up on the plane, and Kegelman angled toward them, firing his nose guns, extinguishing the threat, and raising his battered wing over the tower's roof. The engine fire had gone out, and he headed for home on the wave tops. Others weren't so lucky.

At nine-thirty, Eaker called Spaatz from Swanton Morely to report the loss of two American crews—Lieutenant William G. Lynn's plane had also been shot down. Two others had failed to reach their targets. The RAF had also lost a plane, the flight leader claiming the flak was the worst he'd encountered. Eaker congratulated the returnees, and Hull carried out the debriefing. It was a helluva way to celebrate the Fourth. The price, it appeared, was eight American lives, one third of those engaged.* Eaker knew the press would now take over, and indeed it did.

"U.S. Bombers in Action—First Raid from England," clarioned the London *Daily Express*. Its front-page account gave details of how the unescorted attack was pressed home at Haamstede, Alkmaar, and Valkenburg, where "bombs were seen to burst on hangars, administrative buildings and dispersal points" and where considerable damage was done to aircraft and personnel. As important as the glowing report of the mission, the *Express* featured the announcement that Captain Kegelman (soon to be Major) was to be awarded the Distinguished Service Cross by Eisenhower, and his crew the Distinguished Flying Cross.† It was Hull who brought the written report of the raid to Eisenhower, the first combat

---

* Lieut. Marshall Draper survived the crash of Lieutenant Lynn's plane, which went down in the water, close to the shore. Draper became the Eighth's first POW.

† Spaatz and Eaker made the awards. On July 25, one of the crewmen who took part in the raid committed suicide.

action under the General's command. Regardless of news reports, it could hardly be called a success. The heavy loss plus the fact that four of the six U.S. crews had failed to drop their bombs on their assigned targets was not exactly a victory. But on reading the details of Kegelman's action, Ike wrote in pencil across the page, "This officer is hereby awarded the Distinguished Service Cross" (the nation's second-highest award for gallantry). And then he asked Hull a question: "Are all of the reports going to be like this one?"

In the United States, the headline news stories were even more glowing. In the Washington *Post,* YANKS RAID NAZIS IN HOLLAND shared equal front-page billing with BRITISH DRIVE AGAINST ROMMEL and REDS FALL BACK ON KURSK FRONT. Kegelman's photograph was featured, as was that of his pretty wife, Marian, from El Reno, Oklahoma. One hundred fifty German airmen had been caught flat-footed by the raid, wrote Wes Gallagher, of the AP, who also reported the losses were the heaviest since the British had sent an equal number of planes against Augsburg. However, it was Raymond Daniell, of the New York *Times,* who gave Hap Arnold the disclaimer he probably wanted most: "After months of preparation the units of the U. S. Army Air Force in Britain struck their first blow at the Axis in Europe," was Daniell's lead. In describing the attack that "plowed up Nazi airfields, blasted enemy planes and gunned German personnel," he declared: "The attack was no holiday stunt. Perhaps by coincidence, it took place on Independence Day." The British were comparing it to the Fourth, he stated, "Yet it is not fair to the officers commanding the U. S. Air Force here to liken this first token or practice operation to a holiday stunt. It was not a mere gesture for publicity or propaganda purposes."

To which Eaker and Spaatz might have added a few pungent observations, and perhaps did.

*   *   *

Hap Arnold celebrated the Fourth of July in Dayton, Ohio, in the company of Generals Marshall, Andy Andrews, Oliver Echols, and a number of other Materiel Command officers. They had flown out from Washington to Wright-Patterson to have a look at the newest planes in the pipeline, Arnold anxious for the Chief of Staff to see the advances made. The Boeing B-29 was an inspiring sight. Gliders were coming into the picture. There was a mock-up of the XB-35, a radically designed flying wing under construction by Northrop, as well as other impressive experimental models. Beneath the surface, however, there was more than show and tell on the Glorious Fourth. Andrews' presence was other than routine. He had come up from the Caribbean at Marshall's request, stopping briefly in Key West to see wife Johnny, daughter Josie, and granddaughter Allen. With him flew his aide, Colonel Tom Darcy.

Until the Battle of Midway, a month past, Andrews' theater had been considered a prime target for Japanese attack. He had seventeen B-17's now, flying reconnaissance out of Guatemala, Ecuador, and the Galápagos, making sweeps a thousand miles seaward. While he also had a strong complement of P-40's, he still had no night fighters, and although detection equipment was on the increase, it remained inadequate. In the Caribbean he had been on the island of Aruba in February when a German submarine shelled the oil-refining installations, without much effect. Supposedly this was an area in which the Navy had jurisdiction in case of attack, but the Navy had nothing to attack with, and Andrews assumed Admiral Hoover's responsibility for the island's defense, launching bombers that he felt may have sunk a sub. At Balboa, Admiral Sadler had been replaced by a far more cooperative and ingratiating officer, Admiral Charlie Van Hook. When Hugh Knerr had written a wicked article for the *American Mercury* magazine on the Navy's lack of cooperation in the Caribbean, Van Hook had protested to both Andrews and Knerr, declaring it wasn't so. Hugh replied with half of an apology, intoning, "You are damned by the sins of your predecessors."

The medium bombers, the old B-18's of Andrews' command, were utilized for antisubmarine warfare with little real success. In the seven months between Pearl Harbor and Andrews' visit to Washington, 337 ships were sunk by U-boats in the Atlantic and the Caribbean. But with the move to fulfill BOLERO in Great Britain, and the close engagement with the Japanese in the Pacific, Andrews' hemispheric command, although still considered vulnerable and liable to attack, was no longer viewed in Washington with the same degree of concern. Secretary Stimson had paid a recent visit and come home tremendously impressed with the manner in which Andrews utilized his ground and air forces for the defense of the region.

Andrews answered Marshall's summons, not knowing the cause for it, arriving in the Capital on July 2. When he went to see Marshall, Tom Darcy waited in the outer room. As Andrews' close confidant, Darcy was permitted to read all his incoming and outgoing communications, no matter how secret, and he knew of the special relationship that existed between Andrews and the Chief of Staff. But when Andrews came out of Marshall's office, Darcy realized from the look on his face and the clipped manner in which he spoke that he was furious. They went immediately to Arnold's office, and again Darcy waited while his boss talked behind closed doors. It was only after the encounter ended and they'd left the building that Andrews confided to Darcy what his anger was all about.

It concerned General MacArthur. Since his arrival in Australia, in March, following his presidentially ordered escape from the Philippines, MacArthur's principal airman had been Major General George Brett, Andrews' old and valued friend. MacArthur, for undeclared reasons, disliked Brett from the outset of their relationship and was now demanding that he be replaced. According to Marshall, Hap's recommendation for the job was Andrews, which infuriated Andrews for two reasons.

Arnold was fully aware of Andy's long-held unfriendly feelings toward MacArthur; and Andrews, as a theater commander, not only ranked Arnold but was also outside his jurisdiction. Undoubtedly he did not know the details behind MacArthur's desire to get rid of Brett, nor that it was MacArthur in the first place who was said to have recommended him as Brett's replacement.‡ But he did know he wanted no part of the assignment and felt that Arnold knew that too and therefore was doing him a disservice. This he had told Hap, with the admonition to stay out of his business. It was uncharacteristic, and to Darcy his anger illustrated just how deep his personal feelings toward MacArthur went.[8] The fact that Major General Jonathan M. "Skinny" Wainwright, who had been Andrews' roommate at West Point, was now in a Japanese prison camp, having taken over MacArthur's command following the latter's departure from the Philippines, did nothing to soothe Andrews' unusually aroused feelings.

No doubt Hap apologized and insisted that he was simply thinking of the best man for the position, but to Andrews it was a piece of artfulness he wouldn't tolerate. Under the surface was the smoldering of air independence, publicly and militarily held in check, concealed for the moment by reorganization, but still unanswered and still there. Arnold had a reputation, whether justified in whole or in part, for cutting off the heads of those he felt were not in his camp and might be in a position to upstage him. His mention of the "Arnold guillotine" with regard to Chaney was a case in point. That he admired and genuinely liked Andy Andrews was true enough, but that somewhere down the road he saw him as a possible threat to his own ascendancy is probably also valid. He must have known that Andrews under MacArthur would have worked out no better than Brett, and the result would have been to Andrews' detriment. In fact, when Larry Kuter shortly afterward suggested spunky, independent-minded George Kenney as Brett's replacement, Arnold's reaction was that Kenney wouldn't last long either. To which Kuter responded that at least they'd find out quickly. Additionally, Kenney had long been a staunch Andrews supporter, but much to everyone's surprise, he became, as noted, MacArthur's highly praised, all-important premier airman.

It has also been suggested that Marshall had other plans for Andrews at the time, but if he did, he did not divulge them either to Andrews or to Arnold. Instead, he accompanied them to Dayton and spent the Fourth of July with them looking over new aircraft. That evening, joined by a dozen

‡ This according to Forrest Pogue, in *George C. Marshall, Ordeal and Hope, 1939–1942* (New York: Viking Press, 1965), pp. 376–77.

or so others, they dined in a private room of the old Biltmore Hotel, long a favorite watering place for airmen.

On one side of the room, Hap held forth painting the big picture, ebulliently describing for Marshall and his listeners how, soon, swarms of planes would be flying over Germany bombing the hell out of the place. Seated across the room was Andrews, talking with Oliver Echols about the requirements and details for organizing and building air bases and supply depots in England so that planes could fly over Germany. He was stressing exactly what Ira Eaker had been engaged in working to do, pointing out that until it was done no swarms of U.S. planes would be attacking the enemy. Marshall, overhearing Andrews, got up and crossed the room, sitting down beside him, where he spent the remainder of the evening listening to what he had to say.

In England, Eaker sat down with Spaatz and reported in detail the results of the Eighth Air Force's first mission, which the Germans described as being an inconsequential sortie, causing no appreciable damage.

Twelve

Deflection

In the six weeks that followed, two wholly divergent but closely related developments took shape. The second had a profound and irrevocable effect on the first, which was the continued buildup and preparation for sustained action by the Eighth Air Force. The second was a wrenching switch in strategic policy signaled by Churchill and ambivalently supported by Roosevelt in June.

When Marshall accompanied Arnold and Andrews to Dayton, he was privately very upset by what he perceived as presidential indecision. He found that the White House was prepared to support the British postponement and deflection of SLEDGEHAMMER and ROUNDUP. Three months earlier, Eisenhower had proposed that if a cross-Channel attempt was not to be made before the end of 1942, then the United States should shift the preponderance of its effort against Japan. King was all in favor, of course, particularly in view of the victory at Midway. Upon his return from Dayton, Marshall made this recommendation to Stimson and to the Joint Chiefs, and then presented it to Roosevelt.

Among other things, Roosevelt saw the proposal as an ultimatum to the British, and he rejected it. He was still committed to putting troops on the continent of Europe, he said, but he was not going to abandon Churchill in his hour of great need in the Middle East. He admitted he was tending toward GYMNAST, the North African proposal. Ironically, his major objection to concentrating on the defeat of Japan was exactly that of his military leaders in being against a North African venture: Neither strategy would bring Germany down. Marshall's determined position was that an attack in the Middle East would be even more risky than one against French-held Algeria and Morocco—but he and the Joint Chiefs recognized "that apparently our political leader would require major military operations this year in Africa."[1] Throughout White House seesawing, the President insisted that he was still committed to BOLERO. However, he admitted that in considering North Africa and the Middle East, BOLERO would require a substantial reduction for at least three months. Following an inconclusive meeting with Marshall, King, and Hopkins, which was described "as a very tense day in the White House," FDR determined to send the three of them to England to get a common policy worked out with the British for the third time in six months.[2]

In his instructions to the three, Roosevelt outlined several courses of action based on the option of either proceeding with or canceling SLEDGEHAMMER for 1942. If the decision was to proceed, BOLERO must be speeded up to prepare for an invasion of France by April 1943, and if not, BOLERO would be slowed, in which case, the President suggested, all planes now allocated to England and the Eighth Air Force be diverted to the Middle East and Egypt. One thing he knew he wanted was U.S. ground troops in action against Germany before year's end. He also knew that his military leaders, Army, Navy, and Air Forces, were not in sympathy with his shifting strategy, which was partially influenced by political as well as military considerations. There were important congressional elections coming up in the fall.

Chief British representative Field Marshal Sir John Dill, aware of what was going on, sent a private message to Field Marshal Alan Brooke, warning him that Marshall was almost at the end of his patience. Brooke wrote in his diary, "It will be a queer party as Harry Hopkins is for operating in Africa, Marshall wants to operate in Europe, and King is determined to stick to the Pacific."[3] He added, following a meeting with his own Chiefs in preparation for the visitors' impending arrival: "They have come over as they are not satisfied that we are adhering sufficiently definitely to plans for the invasion of France in 1943 and possibly in 1942. In my mind 1942 is dead off and without the slightest hope . . ."[4]

The plane bearing the American visitors landed at Prestwick on Saturday evening, July 18. The weather being typically bad, the Prime Minister's private train took them the rest of the way to London. There Eisenhower, Clark, Ambassador Winant, Brooke, and other British officers were on hand to greet them. But once welcoming protocol was observed, Marshall was anxious to sit down with his own surrogates. They went immediately to Claridge's to hammer out position papers to present to the British. Churchill had invited Marshall and his staff for the weekend at Chequers, but Marshall and King declined the invitation, Brooke remarking that Marshall & Co. were "determined to avoid temptation from the great 'diversionist.'" Their refusal threw Sir Winston into a fit of pique. *He* was the mighty panjandrum, not the Army-Navy staffs who worked for him! He should be met with first, or so he told Harry Hopkins in no uncertain terms, pacing the floor at Chequers, orating from a book of war laws, tearing away each page as he read it and throwing it on the floor. Hopkins, dubbed by Churchill as "Lord Root of the Matter," got to the root of the matter by letting the Prime Minister work off his spleen and assuring him no rudeness was intended.

Meanwhile, throughout the weekend Marshall and his planners went over their proposals, which foresaw the capture of Cherbourg and the Cotentin Peninsula before mid-October. A primary consideration for the attack was the assistance it would give to the hard-pressed Russians. Spaatz told the assembled that he believed such an attack could be made with a fair degree of success. The Luftwaffe was concentrated on the Eastern Front. The time might not be so favorable later to gain control of the air, particularly should the Russians be defeated. Marshall asked him to prepare an air plan for the invasion. Spaatz summoned Eaker and selected him to head a seven-man committee to draft the plan right away.

Since the Fourth of July, all of Eaker's energies had continued to go into combat preparations for his Bomber Command. On the day he and Spaatz flew to Molesworth Field to decorate Major Kegelman and his crew, total Eighth Air Force heavy-bomber strength was three B-17's. Now, ten days later, that number had been greatly increased as the mass movement of aircraft proceeded with minor losses of planes but not of crews. On the eighteenth, the day Marshall and Hopkins arrived, Monk Hunter and his staff departed from Dow Field, bringing up the rear with eight P-38's and two B-17's to complete the movement of one hundred eighty aircraft, forty of which were heavy bombers.

So it was, as the physical buildup of the Eighth and all its components moved forward, that Ira Eaker was asked to switch his thinking from organizational requirements to operational employment. He and the committee, which included Asa Duncan and Harris Hull, worked through the night and into the next day in preparing an outline. Eaker presented it to Spaatz, who went off to show the Second Front Committee's handiwork to Marshall, who then gave instructions to draw up the plan in detail. This was done, the drafters offering a four-phase air offensive, the first phase to begin immediately, concentrating on "the destruction of the communication and transportation systems between France and Germany."

But the plan in any form was all for naught. Admiral Stark, U. S. Navy Commander in European waters, was not in favor, because the Channel waters would be too dangerous by autumn, while Churchill and his Chiefs were not in favor under any conditions, absolutely adamant in their refusal to go along. Brooke believed the attempt would mean the elimination of six Allied divisions, the risk of a tactical disaster, and "no hope of our being in Cherbourg by next spring." Hopkins sent word to Roosevelt of the not unexpected rejection. The President responded with instructions to find agreement on some other location for U.S. troops to fight, which Hopkins believed would be an "expanded GYMNAST," swiftly rechristened by Churchill as TORCH.

The change in policy changed the course of the war. Whether it lengthened or shortened it is a matter of conjecture and conflicting opinion. But the reaction at the time indicated, if nothing else, the disparate viewpoints held by those who did the negotiating. Marshall's fight to preserve SLEDGEHAMMER was in recognition that it probably would never be launched but that the impetus deriving from its preparation would make an invasion of Europe by the spring of 1943 practicable. Thus he was out to save ROUNDUP. "Otherwise U.S. forces would be dispersed to the Pacific and the Mediterranean and the main objective would be lost."[5] Eisenhower considered the decision might well go down as "the blackest day in history." He and Mark Clark were deeply disappointed. Admiral King was far less so, his thinking more in line with Marshall's, but also fixed in the Pacific. On the British side, Churchill couldn't have been happier, for as Brooke noted, "it is satisfactory to feel that we have got just what we wanted out of the U. S. Chiefs."[6]

Spaatz's thinking was summed up by Hoyt Vandenberg in a position paper in which he said, "Whether SLEDGEHAMMER is abandoned at this time, the fact remains that since Germany cannot be defeated in any other theater, the major part of our air effort should be used in Western Europe."

To Eaker, this was the purpose of his being in England in the first place. He arrived at WIDEWINGS for a conference on the fateful day at about the same time as Vandenberg, who came from the joint meetings and announced cryptically, "Somebody upset the apple cart. The plan for SLEDGEHAMMER is out." Later, when Spaatz filled Eaker in, Ira recognized he had a new and bigger worry to add to all the rest. Was he going to receive the promised buildup, or was it all going down to North Africa? Spaatz was to suggest in a subsequent staff meeting with Eisenhower that perhaps it should.

A month earlier, Arnold had given orders for two additional heavy-bomber groups, the 301st and the 92nd, to prepare for movement to England, and with them the 14th and 52nd fighter groups. It was his plan, he told Tooey, to send units over as fast as he could get them started. When Marshall returned from England, at the end of July, and briefed him on what had transpired, Arnold continued to believe for the moment that along with the mounting of TORCH he would still be able to build air strength in Britain. This was welcome news to Spaatz and Eaker. He also advised Tooey that in connection with planning, he was sending over some top-notch men: Vandenberg (who was making a quick turnaround) and Colonels Lauris Norstad and Max F. Schneider. Possum Hansell was on his way too. "He has some very good ideas about the employment of air," wrote Arnold. "Get his ideas, and all of you whenever possible talk the same language covering the real role of the American Air Forces in Europe."

What that real role was remained unfixed, fluid. Had SLEDGEHAMMER gone forward, three phases of the air plan would have been tactical in nature. Not until the Cotentin Peninsula was secure would Eaker's bombers have been released, in the final phase, to attack strategic targets in Germany. Now, with SLEDGEHAMMER out, Spaatz's planners went back to square one, declaring, "The European Theater becomes an Air Theater, as visualized, more or less, in AWPD-1."

Before his departure from England at the end of July, Marshall had informed Eisenhower that he was naming him to command TORCH but that he also wished him to remain as Commanding General of the ETO and to continue preparations for ROUNDUP. This meant maintaining three separate staffs, and Eisenhower began complaining that he had no one to head his Air Section on any one of them. Colonel Pinky Craig recommended Possum Hansel for the job, and Eisenhower personally requested his services. Hansel had moved from Air War Plans to the Joint Strategic Survey Committee of the Joint Chiefs of Staff. There, with Colonel Albert Wedemeyer, he had fought and finally won the battle against the Navy representatives, keeping Europe as the key theater for offensive operations.

Spaatz was to tell Arnold after Hansell arrived, in early August, that Possum would be the top planner for air and, as such, Eisenhower's Air Planner. "He is responsible for seeing that his [Eisenhower's] planning reflects my views," Tooey added, "and to maintain the closest possible tie-in; he is living in the same house with me and a number of the key officers of the Eighth Air Force. Norstad is the planner on ROUNDUP and Vandenberg on the new GYMNAST [TORCH], all assigned to Theater Headquarters."

Hansell had a far higher regard for Spaatz than he did for Arnold, whom he saw as more of a driver than a leader, a boss who constantly conveyed the unspoken belief that there was someone outside his staff who could do a better job than those who served on it. As for Eisenhower, his original letter of instruction prepared by OPD, which he then headed, made no mention of how a strategic air offensive would be conducted. Neither, specifically, did Spaatz's instructions from Arnold, although both accepted the unwritten strategic meaning behind the approved production goals of AWPD-1. In assuming his dual role, the big question in Hansell's mind was whether Eisenhower would ignore the strategic use of heavy bombers and employ them only tactically in support of his ground forces.

Although Eisenhower would quickly recommend Hansell for promotion to brigadier general, there is nothing to indicate that Eisenhower's somewhat doctrinaire attitude on the use of air power was modified by his

newly appointed chief of the Air Section. In the first place, there was just
no time for contemplation on the pros and cons of the question, for as Eisenhower said:

> The decision to invade North Africa necessitated a complete reversal in
> our thinking and drastic revision in our planning and preparation. Where
> we had been counting on many months of orderly buildup we now had
> only weeks. . . . Our target was no longer a restricted front where we
> knew accurately terrain, facilities, and people as they affected military op-
> erations, but the rim of a continent where no major military campaign had
> been conducted for centuries. We were not to have the air power we had
> planned to use against Europe and what we did have would be largely con-
> centrated at a single highly vulnerable base—Gibraltar—and immediate
> substantial success would have to be achieved in the first engagements. A
> beachhead could be held in Normandy and expanded, however slowly; a
> beachhead on the African coast might be impossible to maintain.[7]

To Hansell, and other planners of a like mind, the Roosevelt-Churchill
decision to overrule their military leaders and invade North Africa made
them fear that their long-sought use of strategic air power was going to go
by the boards, vitiated and weakened by diversions that were missing the
point altogether.

Spaatz was too much of a pragmatist, too hard-bitten a realist to be
thrown by any change in plans. He would keep his own counsel, adapt and
work for his own goals within the structure, whatever it was. Arnold fully
understood this last. He wouldn't have been where he was if he hadn't. He
had advised Tooey, at the time of the change, "I would like to have you
see Eisenhower and get him to accept your headquarters as his air planning unit. Get him to use you in that way as he is the head of all U. S.
Army forces in Europe. I want him to recognize you as the top airman in
all Europe."

This last was to be Hap's recurrent theme with Spaatz: *I want you to be
the number one airman in all Europe.* Number one because the bond was
so close. Number one because Arnold was really number one, and
through Spaatz his connection with Eisenhower would be made more
secure, and through Spaatz he would know that the use of U.S. air power
would not be misdirected by ground commanders.

There was something about Tooey Spaatz's presence that left an unde-
niable impression. The press liked him, although they couldn't write about
him at the time. Eisenhower sensed his dependability, valued the
directness and cogency of his thought. His key staff people—Asa Duncan,
Ted Curtis, Harry Berliner, Cookie Stovall—knew what he wanted done
and did what he wanted. Some officers had to play poker with him before
they could get behind the seeming remoteness of his personality. Others
had to be present on a special occasion to observe his wry deftness—such
as the time the King and Queen of England came to High Ercall to wit-

ness an air demonstration. Spaatz was presented to the royal couple, and as they stood watching the show it began to drizzle. Spaatz quickly took off his raincoat and draped it over the Queen's shoulders, saying, "You are now a Major General in the U. S. Air Forces." She was delighted by the gesture, as was the King.

He had the ability of getting down to basics with eager young pilots as well. On a Sunday in late July, he arrived at Tangmere, a principal RAF fighter base. Pilots of the 31st Fighter Group were in training at the field under RAF direction, and seven of them were about to take off on their first operational mission, the first U.S. fighter pilots to do so. He was there to wish them good hunting. This was to be a sortie over Abbeville for the purpose of drawing the Germans into combat, and unlike the July 4 mission, it was not a public-relations event.

Spaatz, in the company of Group Captain Appleton, went to the Operations Room to follow the action. There was plenty of it. Focke-Wulf 190's, aircraft the U.S. pilots knew nothing about, came up to tangle. One got shot down for sure, and so did one of the Spitfires. It was piloted by Lieutenant Colonel Albert P. "Red" Clark, the Group's popular Executive Officer. His wingman believed he managed to crash-land. Word that a downed pilot had been picked up in the Channel momentarily raised hopes that Red would be buying the drinks that night, but it turned out to be a German pilot who was rescued.*

In the debriefing that followed, Spaatz took a very active part. He questioned the half dozen pilots at length. They were eager to repeat the performance and requested that after they had a few more sweeps under their belts, their squadron mates should be moved to Tangmere and they would take over and train them as they had been trained. They had no trouble talking to Spaatz and Hunter, a couple of vintage fighter pilots who, if they'd had their druthers, would have liked nothing better than to be flying with them. Ten days later, the 31st, under the command of Colonel John R. Hawkins, would have the distinction of putting the first U.S. fighter squadron of the Eighth Air Force into combat.

Getting fighters and light bombers into operation was, of course, an important step forward, but Ira Eaker's heavies were what it was all about. The 97th's thirty-five B-17's were on hand, two of its squadrons at Polebrook and two at Grafton Underwood. Eleven of its crews were considered combat ready, and it was felt the remainder would be by the first of August. The 301st was on its way over, flying the northern ferry route. But now, suddenly, there came a hitch of a personal nature.

On July 29, Eaker had sent a recommendation to Spaatz for promotion to brigadier general for three of his key officers: Colonels Claude Duncan, whom he had placed in command of what was to be the Eighth's 1st

---

* Clark was taken prisoner and suffered the dubious distinction of being the first Eighth Air Force fighter pilot to become a POW.

Wing; Charles B. "Jingle" Bubb, his Chief of Staff; and Newton Long-fellow, who would command the 2nd Wing. The three were, among other things, old friends, and it was natural in a time when experience was in short supply to want to use and to promote old buddies. Duncan and Longfellow each had over twenty-four years of service, and Bubb, who had left the Air Corps ten years past because of TB, had been found fit to return.

As Eaker said in his recommendation: "These are the officers best suited to the Command and assignments involved. They have demon-strated unmistakably their qualifications for the assignments."

Two days later Ira was ready to take it all back where Duncan was con-cerned. Previously he had invited Eisenhower and Spaatz to inspect his headquarters, a B-17 unit, and to be taken on a gunnery mission. The guests arrived on Friday, August 1. Ike was most taken by what he saw at PINETREE. "I was especially impressed by the thoroughness of the staff or-ganization and functioning demonstrated at General Eaker's head-quarters," he later told Spaatz. He liked the enthusiasm, the morale, the efficiency, and Eaker's obvious grasp. "Everything I noted there," he added, "was highly pleasing in its promise that our future bomber battle tasks would be skillfully conducted."

Ira wouldn't have agreed with this last for a minute. In fact, he was fu-rious with what he told Duncan was "a disgraceful performance." "I per-sonally advised you several days in advance of the anticipated inspection that plans be prepared so that they [Eisenhower and Spaatz] could be taken on a gunnery mission. I . . . stated that time was limited and that I wanted them to see a crew at work. I recall distinctly that I stated to you that I would expect the organization involved to 'put their best foot for-ward.' You were asked if you could carry out these plans and gave an affirmative answer."

What had happened was that when Eisenhower and Spaatz, accompa-nied by Eaker, reached the selected squadron, they were assigned to a crew that had never fired on tow targets before, was recently arrived, and as yet had received no combat training. Although Ike was a private pilot through his own efforts, it is possible that he was not fully aware of the wretched performance, for he made no mention of the debacle, which Eaker told Duncan had wasted their time and given an erroneous idea of the status of the heavy-bomber crews.

The goof-up was reflective of a number of factors, all centered on get-ting the mission launched. Because of the combined military and political rush to get the Fortresses into combat, partially to prove the skeptics wrong and partially to put an American presence in the fight against Ger-many, the crews were not properly trained. They had done little flying at high altitude, little on oxygen—which was a must. Some gunners had never fired at a target in the air, some radio operators didn't know a dit from a dah. Pilots were just as inexperienced on the all-important technique of formation flying. What could be said about the deficiencies of the 97th could also be said about the 301st. Many crews had been together only a short time. Help was needed from the RAF, and it was forthcoming in all departments, thanks to Bomber Harris and the willingness of his subordinates.

More worrisome than anything else—a condition the RAF could do nothing to change—was the weather. Over England it was notoriously and consistently rotten, particularly for bombers taking off, assembling in the air, and landing. It caused accidents, and the 97th suffered its first fatality when a B-17 of the 304th Squadron flew into a mountain in Wales, killing all on board. Over Europe, conditions weren't going to be much better and were bound to limit the number of days when targets could be hit by precision bombing. In fact, weather scrubbed the 97th's first mission.

In the interim, Duncan was not working out as Eaker had hoped, and the 97th's Commander, Colonel Cornelius "Connie" Cousland, did not have what it took to muscle the Group into a state of readiness. Eaker knew that, as never before, he needed someone on whom he could depend in the clutch, someone who could pull all the loose pieces of the four squadrons together and, through toughness and by example, inspire the crews to the required level of performance. He asked Frank Armstrong, the first of his original six staff members, to step in and take command. Neither Eaker nor the Eighth Air Force was to regret the selection. Practice missions were stepped up, the crews in the air from dawn to dark. The RAF, with its new Spitfire Mark 9's, acted as both escort and attacker, and the B-17E, although it lacked straight-ahead firepower, appeared ready to go.

On August 8, Eaker sent an enthusiastic and detailed letter to Arnold, making no mention of personnel and mechanical problems, stressing the positive. "The tempo is stepping up as we approach the zero hour," he announced. "Tooey's and my theory that day bombardment is feasible is about to be tested where men's lives are put at stake." The wording indicated exactly what was at issue. Saying that the theory was his and Tooey's did not mean it wasn't the theory of a good many others, but he was quick to point out that a great many people who had previously championed the cause of daylight bombardment had grown lukewarm or now, "with the chips down," had deserted the camp altogether. He did not say who they were, only that he and Tooey remained steadfast in their belief. He then listed six familiar reasons for daylight operations, all of them heavily coated in optimism.[8]

Next, he described flying on a gunnery- and bombing-practice mission, wishing Hap could have been there to see the way the youngsters cut up tow targets one thousand yards away. This obviously was not the mission he had flown with Ike and Tooey on board, nor was he thinking of Duncan and some others when he gave "thanks for all the good people you have sent to this theater. We not only now have the best collection of officers I have ever seen assembled in one place, but they are all working like one congenial happy family. Your solution has been perfect; from the higher echelon to the lowest there is complete accord and harmony and the fiercest enthusiasm I have ever seen."

He was not laying it on all that much, for his way of operating inspired the kind of enthusiasm of which he spoke. Most of those who worked for him were anxious to do their best, because there was something in his quiet confidence that made them want to. Aside from Spaatz, he was out-ranked by Major General Walter "Tony" Frank, whom Arnold had named to head up the Eighth's all-important Service Command. This was the organization that would keep Bomber Command flying, but it was not a post Frank was all that eager to assume, for various reasons. He was se-nior to Tooey by date of service and, of course, there was even a greater gap between Eaker and himself. Back in the twenties, when Ira was a cap-tain, Frank had been General Mason Patrick's Executive Officer and Eaker had been Major Frank's assistant. Now Frank felt himself relegated to something less than his position and knowledge deserved, particularly because his last duty had been Commanding General of the Third Air Force. Heading the Service Command was not a glory post, but as any thinking airman knew, the rapid repair, overhaul, and return to duty of battle-damaged aircraft was a must. And so Frank swallowed his pride and, as Asa Duncan put it, gave the job "the Tony Frank push," which was all to Ira's benefit.

In concluding his letter to Arnold, Eaker offered a forecast of things to come. Should the Russians fail to stop the Germans, the Luftwaffe would spend the winter recouping, preparing "for the battle of its life," across the Channel. Should the Germans find an inferior air force, they would "get on with the war—with the invasion," predicted Eaker "The air battle is primary and maybe the decisive or near decisive phase. It is certain that the sailors and the soldiers cannot fight their land and sea battles until this air thing is decided." This left six months to do three things, he said: build air strength, prove effective in combat, and reduce German air power through bombing and combat.

Eaker wasn't telling Arnold anything he didn't already know, but in ret-rospect he was indicating several points that were significant. In view of the situation in Russia, considerations of an invasion attempt by the Wehrmacht in the coming year was indeed valid. Further, Eaker, unlike the planners of AWPD-1, saw the destruction of the Luftwaffe as his number-one priority, whereas they had considered it an "intermediate ob-jective," although of overriding importance. The primary objective, in their thinking, was targets that supported the Third Reich's ability to wage war: electric power, transportation, fuel, metals.

In his conclusion, Eaker made note of "all the discouragements—slow arrival of equipment; small numbers; bad weather and the necessity for more training. . . ." He wasn't making excuses, but he wanted Arnold to know that the problems he faced on his side of the ocean were not a result of his own performance.

Arnold passed the letter to his new Chief of Staff, Major General George Stratemeyer, and to Deputy Chief Larry Kuter. On it he wrote, "Note and *then destroy* [emphasis mine]," an instruction that was not carried out.

For his own part, he wrote to Tooey, sending the letter by courier so that it arrived four days later. It began: "I am personally gravely concerned over the apparent extension of the time period which you had anticipated necessary to complete the training of our units prior to their actual entry into combat."

The paragraph and much of what followed could be cited as the opening gun in Arnold's home-front desire to run the Eighth Air Force from his office in the Munitions Building and then from the newly built Pentagon. His impatience was understandable in that he had just been hit with TORCH, which meant among other things that he was going to have to build a new air force out of units previously allocated to the Eighth. Worse, the White House had agreed to send nine additional air groups to the Pacific,† which had also been slated for BOLERO, and he feared that if the Eighth didn't get into combat right away, it would come unstuck altogether. More than that, his impatience was incurable. He wanted action not tomorrow but today, and he'd brook no excuses. Another thing was that he'd never held a combat command, and so he could never really understand what that was like—what Eaker meant when he said men's lives were at stake, what it was to give orders, knowing that by those orders men were going to die, and so trying to give orders that would bring the greatest success at the smallest cost.

After stating his grave concern to Spaatz, Arnold then tried to show that he understood the difficulty of the decision and the danger of committing crews to combat who were not properly trained for it. "I realize that this procedure could result in a vicious cycle," he wrote, "which might set back our air offensive many many months. In making this decision, you have my sympathy and understanding."

Maybe so, but then he hopped on his favorite General McClellan analogy, citing the Civil War leader's "fundamental error in military judgment" by overemphasizing preparation. In so doing, he contradicted what he'd said above, urging Spaatz not to make the same error, declaring, "Where doubt exists as to the ability of our units to acquit themselves adequately, I urge that you do not be overconservative." Operational Train-

† Originally the figure had been fifteen groups.

ing Units—OTU's—had been set up, but he felt that crews going to them should be ready for combat after very brief indoctrination. He went on to stress the speed with which they both knew the German Air Force could recuperate, and "the apparent lethargy" of the British in similar matters. He would rather have Tooey suit the actions of his own forces to German lines than to those of the Allies.

A single sentence with an underlying meaning telegraphed his considered need for writing the letter: "The strategic necessity for the immediate or early initiation of effective, aggressive American Air Force offensive operations becomes more and more apparent here daily."

A few days previously, he had written a memo to Marshall on the subject of "Air Force Employment." In it, the figures he gave explained the root of his concern:

> Fifty-four (54) Air Force groups were required under the Bolero-Roundup plan and were allotted for that purpose. Of these nine (9) have subsequently been assigned to the Middle East and eleven (11) are now necessary to implement the Torch plan, leaving a total of thirty-four (34). The further allocation of nine (9) groups to the southwest Pacific would reduce the number available in the United Kingdom to twenty-five (25).

As to what this was going to mean, he offered some cold arithmetic:

> Under the terms of the latest plan, Western Europe becomes virtually an air theater. Our air strength in that theater, however, has been reduced to less than half the strength available under the combined air-ground plan. Comparison with the original concept of this as an air theater, AWPD-1, shows a greater discrepancy.

Spaatz, in his reply to Hap, also delivered by courier, was all in favor of prompt action, confessing he was having difficulty in controlling his impatience for "getting our first units into battle." Then he neatly parried the McClellan lunge, reminding Hap with a riposte that the name "recalls to my mind that there was also a Burnside." He then explained all the factors aside from training that had to be taken into consideration, not the least of which was the weather. It had now held up the first mission for ten days. Five additional missions were already planned, but Spaatz's evaluation was that since his arrival, in June, there had been no more than a half dozen days when accurate bombing from twenty-five thousand feet could have been carried out—due to the weather.

He then threw the ball back to Arnold, remarking that since they were going into combat immediately the promised replacement crews had not arrived. He was figuring a 5 percent loss per mission, and the flow of replacements would affect the number of missions that could be flown.

There was yet another matter troubling Arnold. From the planning material coming back from Eisenhower's headquarters, he was not satisfied that Ike was using Spaatz and his staff in the manner hoped. Hansell had been assigned as the connecting link, acting as Air Planner for Eisenhower and Deputy Theater Air Officer for Spaatz, but Arnold in his impatience felt that Eisenhower was making decisions that indicated he was not getting the advice and air counsel of Spaatz's command. He was considering suggesting the same to Ike, that the Theater Commander should always have a high order of air talent at his elbow. More, he also was considering offering him as his Chief of Staff any air officer he might choose. He knew that Ike's choice for the job was Brigadier General Walter Bedell Smith, who was serving as the U. S. Secretary of the Combined Chiefs of Staff. Not only did Arnold want an airman next to Ike, but he also did not believe that "Beetle" Smith really understood the proper use of strategic air power.[9]

Arnold's concern over the matter was reflected by his request to Spaatz: "If we are to seriously consider an Air Chief of Staff for Ike, I must have your answer by courier on the first possible airplane returning to the States."

He got it. And with it, a copy of a letter Spaatz had sent to Ike that sought to clarify Possum Hansell's dual position and at the same time prevent the building of two large, possibly competing air staffs. As for an Air officer becoming Ike's Chief of Staff, this was a delicate business, and Spaatz did not think he could make the suggestion unless Ike asked for his advice. The War Department could advance the thought more diplomatically, he said. "In an assignment of this kind, personalities are bound to play an important part," he noted. Pinky Craig was already on Eisenhower's staff. He had been made a general officer, and Spaatz considered him highly qualified for assignment as Ike's Chief.

In another month, Smith would join Eisenhower and remain his loyal, indefatigable Chief of Staff throughout the war. So if Arnold attempted what he was considering and followed Spaatz's suggestion of working through the War Department to get Craig or another air officer into the job, he was not successful. What is left is the question of how differently the war might have been conducted had Arnold succeeded. At the time, he and Spaatz were not thinking of TORCH as much as they were thinking of getting bombers over Europe.

Spaatz believed that Luftwaffe strength in the West at that time was such that if he had two hundred B-17's he could cripple German air power and ensure supremacy by the next spring. He was also anxious to determine whether a formation of Fortresses could take care of itself against a fighter attack. "If we are right," he told Arnold, "then the depth of daylight penetration would be limited only by the firepower of the formation." But the answer was too vital to the success of the war, he said, to jump to hasty conclusions from a few missions flown by a handful of planes. Twenty-five crews of the 97th were ready to go, and the 301st would be operational a week after its ground echelon arrived. The first missions would be shallow penetrations against railroad yards, round-houses, power plants, and several important factories. They would have strong RAF fighter protection, and simulated practice runs with the Spitfires were being carried out daily. So if Hap would just calm down, back off, and lay aside his Civil War history, they'd get to it.

No one was more eager to do that than the Eighth's Bomber Commander. On August 2, Tooey had handed Eaker a disappointment by saying that he was going to go on the first mission, and certainly it wouldn't be wise for both of them to go.

Two days later, at Eisenhower's headquarters, Eaker, unlike far-distant Arnold, in Washington, "was tremendously impressed with [the General's] keenness for air operations and his evident interest in our personnel." Ike approved Spaatz's decision to go on the first mission and Ira to go on the second, also agreeing that it would be all right for Ira to fly a mission with the British. "Who is going to succeed you if anything happens?" he asked Tooey.

"General Eaker," said Tooey.

"And whom do you recommend succeed you?" he asked Eaker.

"Colonel Longfellow," was Eaker's response.

The question of flying missions loomed large in Eaker's mind, not just for himself but also for members of his staff. He knew that Harris Hull, Beirne Lay, Fred Castle, Bill Cowart, and the others were eager to sign on, but beyond that there were two sound reasons for instituting such a program. One was so that staff members would get to know the problems of combat crews firsthand and therefore be sympathetic to their needs. The other was morale. If the troops knew that the head man and his aides were willing to fly with them and fight with them and risk their lives with them, they were going to appreciate that kind of support more than any other. Toward this end, Eaker wrote a memo in which he outlined methods by which his people could fly in combat. Anyone who went had to be qualified as an aerial gunner, and no one going was to replace a regular crew member. As observers, they'd be the extra man.

There was also the question of the psychological impact of air combat upon the individual. Not all would be able to withstand its rigors: under ground and air attack five miles up, manning guns in subzero temperatures, holding course and formation against a blizzard of cannon and machine-gun fire, long hours of stress to and from the target in which the weather was always an enemy. These were conditions that added up to the grinding physical and mental ordeal of air combat. And to assuage the latter, Eaker and Spaatz had a facility established to instruct flight surgeons and medical officers on how to handle the traumas of combat fatigue suffered by airmen.

On the evening of August 9, crews of the 97th were alerted for a mission to be flown the following morning. That night, weather moved in and scrubbed the plan for a solid week, much to the annoyance, impatience, and frustration of everyone concerned, Arnold's letter of the ninth notwithstanding. On the eleventh, Eaker attended a four-hour meeting at WIDEWINGS chaired by Spaatz. The subject was future operations—the forces required and the equipment needed to mount them. Hansell and Vandenberg were among those present, and a cable was drafted to Arnold citing figures and asking for a schedule of arrival.

At the same time, Arnold came through with another critical query, this one directed at Harris and Bomber Command. A statement by Admiral Leahy, Arnold said, indicated that the Renault plant, supposedly put out of commission by the RAF in April, was back in operation. Eaker called on Harris and showed him Arnold's letter. Not so at all, responded Bertie. He gave Ira a recent reconnaissance photo of the works plus intelligence information that showed Renault was still unable to produce tanks. Truck fabrication was at only 60 percent of capacity. Eaker then went up to London to confer with Tooey on Arnold's letter of complaint over the failure to mount a combat mission. There really wasn't a helluva lot they could do about it. The East Anglia weather was clinging to the treetops as though it would never come unstuck.

But as far as Eaker was concerned, one good thing came out of the delay: Portal, Harris, Douglas, and other RAF brass heard about the plans of the two commanders to fly combat missions and protested. In RAF thinking, the experience and knowledge of the pair was far too important to be needlessly jeopardized. Further, the two were privy to important intelligence, and if they were shot down and taken prisoner that information could be compromised. Spaatz, in his position, accepted this reasoning. Eaker accepted it too, but when he weighed it against the psychological importance of one of them taking part in the first mission, he came down on the side of going. After all, he reasoned, he didn't want it thought that he'd send his airmen where he feared to fly himself.

The RAF attitude on the anticipated campaign was best expressed by Portal in an internal policy paper. He observed that Eaker and Harris were close friends and that they would have no problems working out their joint day and night operations. Spaatz, he thought, might tend to interfere with Eaker at first but he'd soon discover that there was no need and Eaker would be left with the same freedom as Harris. Astute as he was, Portal partially misread the Spaatz-Eaker relationship. Officially, Tooey was always recognized as the senior member of their partnership, but this never prevented Ira from telling Tooey just what he thought, and very often what he thought had a direct influence on the decisions Spaatz made. Additionally, Spaatz recognized that Eaker was a far more articulate diplomat than he, and he was quick to use Eaker in talking to the press and to the inquiring brass, particularly on the question of daylight bombardment.

But Portal, like Harris, continued to feel that daylight operations were going to be too costly. Harris was sure his American friends were in for some bad casualties, but he thought they'd better give it a try, because the Americans knew more about daylight operations than they could learn about night bombing in several years.

And so the day to begin finally came: Monday, August 17. The weather broke, clearing fast. Eaker called his first operational conference at 11:00 A.M. and gave orders for the mission to take place that afternoon. The target was the railroad marshaling yards at Sotteville-lès-Rouen, France, thirty-five miles in from the English Channel, a shallow penetration. Eaker flew to Polebrook, where the twelve crews for the assigned raid had been waiting to take off for a week. Collectively, they were as fed up and anxious as Arnold to get on with it. Eaker was impressed by their nonchalance and pleased at their evident enthusiasm that he would be flying with them. Generals were very rare birds in their lives, and here was the old man himself ready to come risk his ass with the least of them.

It was close to three-thirty when Colonel Frank Armstrong lifted *Butcher Shop* off the runway. Eleven B-17's followed, Eaker riding in *Yankee Doodle,* the lead ship in the second element of six planes. They were three minutes early at the rendezvous point over Beachy Head at twenty-two thousand feet. They circled twice before four squadrons of Air Vice Marshal Leigh-Mallory's 11 Group wheeled up and tacked on by prearranged plan. The sky was clear, visibility excellent. Halfway across the Channel, Eaker could see the French coast coming up. He observed that the planes were in good formation, though not quite as tight as he would have liked for the best fighter protection. Station keeping was also good. Neither he nor the radio operator, with whom he took turns manning the single .50-caliber, saw any sign of enemy fighters as they made landfall. The formation flew straight to a point three miles north of Rouen and then turned slightly to make the bomb run. So far there had been no flak, no enemy air attack.

One problem was the shortness of the oxygen hose, which restricted movement and hindered free use of the machine gun. Eaker's hose pulled loose, and it took him about a minute to replug it. Also, the masks were clumsy, and as he moved about he noted that some of the crew had taken them off. Another problem was the cold above fifteen thousand feet. It affected men and equipment, the gunners testing and working their guns frequently. Eaker found it took both hands to charge the weapon.

When the bombing run began, he moved to the door of the bomb compartment, and with the bomb bays open watched the target coming up. He saw the bend in the Seine and the village of Sotteville, and then the closely joined spider web of the marshaling yards. He saw the five 600-pounders fall singly, and then, disconnecting his oxygen hose, he moved to the waist gunner's compartment so that he could see the bombs hit. The pilot turned right, passing over the target, and Eaker could look down and watch the collective bursts, which made long, mushroomlike configurations of smoke and debris. Most bursts were within the target, exploding amid the tracks and roundhouse and shops. A few were wide, and he was afraid some of the misses had fallen among the homes of the French workers. But, for a first mission, he considered the overall results good.

It was then he saw the German fighters. There were three of them, FW 190's. They went after the number-two plane in the formation, attacking from below, closing to within about a thousand yards, then rolling over and diving away as bottom-turret gunners returned their fire. They made only one pass, and Eaker moved to the other side of the waist gunner's station and saw at least a dozen puffs of flak dirtying the sky. The gunners below were deadly accurate as to altitude but their tracking was off.

On the run back to the coast, Eaker observed that there was considerable fighter activity between their RAF escorts and German interceptors. He continued to move about the plane, and from the radio gunner's station he could see that all the B-17's were accounted for, although one was lagging, trailing black smoke from its left outboard engine. There were a half dozen Spitfires shepherding it. Flak poked at the formation, and Eaker was able to spot two antiaircraft batteries firing at them, but the B-17's swiftly reached the Channel, and the remainder of the flight was uneventful.

Those who had seen the mission off—ranking air officers, disappointed airmen not assigned to the raid, ground crews, and a large contingent of the U.S. and British press—had spent a restless and anxious three hours waiting for the return of the dozen.‡ Perhaps only Spaatz and the members of his and Eaker's staffs understood all that was riding on this small, first step. The pressure had been building on both sides of the Atlantic for action, best signaled by Arnold's outcry to Spaatz. The British press was politely but pointedly indicating that it was certainly taking a long time for the Yanks to get into the fight. The skeptics, mostly ground and naval officers, were predicting grim results.

It was close to seven o'clock when watchers on the control tower spotted a cluster of specks in the soft evening sky. A moment of breathlessness prevailed as the count began, and then a great sigh of relief was expelled as the number reached twelve. No losses.

An elated throng greeted the combat crews, the newsmen particularly anxious to get the story. One of them, Peter Masefield, of the London *Times,* an authoritative aviation writer, had just published a highly critical

‡ Another six Fortresses flew a diversionary mission over the Channel attacking no target, their purpose to confuse German fighter control.

piece on both the B-17 and the B-24, maintaining they were not capable of carrying out their assigned missions. Masefield declared, "Their bomb loads are small, their armour and armament are not up to the standard now found necessary and their speeds are low." Not only had Arnold seen the article, but so had the President, and he wanted to know what it meant. The Rouen raid, small as it was, was the first answer.

Bert Harris wired his congratulations, proclaiming, "Yankee Doodle certainly went to town and can stick another well deserved feather in his cap." Eaker responded cryptically to the praise in general, "One swallow doesn't make a summer." Directly upon landing, he had quietly told Tooey, "I think we killed some Frenchmen today." Almost immediately, they contacted General Charles de Gaulle's headquarters and expressed apologies for bombs that had hit dwellings outside the target area. *As long as you are bombing the boches, c'est la guerre,* was the French reaction.

Eisenhower was about to sit down to dinner when Spaatz called to report on the mission. Ike was most relieved to hear the news; he had been particularly worried over Eaker's safety. Naval aide to Ike Captain Harry Butcher gave some insight into how Eisenhower's headquarters viewed the use of strategic air power. "We are experimenting with our ideas on bombing operations," wrote Butcher. "If our conception works, British can bomb at night and we in the daytime or both. Fact that all twelve are back safely, despite attack by German fighters including Focke-Wulfs, indicates American ideas on the subject may not be so haywire as has been indicated. . . ."[10]

In his own, detailed critique of the mission, Eaker stressed the need for a greater degree of sharpness in all phases of the operation, from gunnery to pilotage, but he was "very favorably impressed with the B-17 as a daylight bomber with its excellent defensive firepower." However, he did observe, "It is too early in our experiments in actual operations to say that it can definitely make deep penetrations without fighter escort and without excessive losses." (Seventy-five Spitfires had accompanied the dozen bombers to Rouen.)

The next day, with Spaatz and Hunter, he met with Portal's Deputy, Air Marshal Norman Bottomley, and they agreed on a joint operating policy. The bombers would have fighter escort for the time being but eventually would go it alone in attempting to extend the tactical range, which Spaatz believed they could do. The mission of the fighters would change from that of flushing the enemy to that of protecting the bombers. Until the 8th Fighter Command was built up, bomber escort would be supplied by the RAF.

In the next ten days the Eighth Air Force flew a remarkable seven missions, remarkable due to their results and that the weather permitted. On the nineteenth, as part of the air operations of the disastrous Dieppe raid, twenty-two B-17's unloaded thirty-four tons of bombs on the Abbeville-Drucat Air Base, home of Gruppe 11/J.G. 26 and the famous "Abbeville Kids." These were Goering's elite fighter pilots, who flew yellow-nosed interceptors and were noted for their daring and skill. They were not at home, engaged instead over the bloody beaches of Dieppe in the largest air battle of the war to date. The 97th's bombers left a grand assortment of holes in the field and eliminated several hangars before returning, without loss.

Above Dieppe, where five thousand Allied troops, mostly Canadian with fifty American Rangers, were being decimated in an unsuccessful combined operation whose code name had been changed from RUTTER to JUBILEE, Eighth Air Force fighter pilots were in the thick of the battle. As Tooey described the action to George Stratemeyer: "The 31st Spitfire Group got a real baptism of fire during the Dieppe raid and handled themselves like veterans. All three squadrons were in and out all day long, and the final score now is four missing, one dead, and one wounded. There is a good chance of at least two of the missing getting back. The boys think they got 3 F.W. 190's surely, damaged three other 190's and a Dornier 217."[11] The wounded man was Second Lieutenant Sam Junkin, who got credit for being the first Eighth Air Force fighter pilot to shoot down a German plane.

While the pluses and minuses of JUBILEE were being weighed, on the twentieth, Eaker sent out twelve of his B-17's to hit the Longeau marshaling yards, at Amiens, a key rail junction between France and Germany. Again, it was a no-sweat mission, although Possum Hansell froze his hand. At the last minute, he had gotten permission from Eisenhower to go on the mission, and he arrived at the field only a half hour before takeoff. In the rush, he wasn't issued the proper clothing, and when he found his oxygen mask wasn't functioning properly he tried to fix it with his gloves off. The result was that he paid a visit to the flight surgeon after landing, and for a time he flew no more missions. A few days later, Newt Longfellow saved his pilot's life, on a raid over the shipyards of Le Trait, when a piece of flak punctured an artery and Longfellow quickly applied a tourniquet.

But perhaps a dangerous bit of euphoria crept into the oxygen supply, for the next day a dozen B-17's took off from their base at Grafton Underwood headed for the docks of Rotterdam, but they were slow in getting into formation and three of their number had to abort due to mechanical failure. This made the remaining nine too late for their rendezvous with three Spitfire squadrons, one of which was the 31st. The result was that the escort had to leave the bombers halfway across the North Sea. They flew on and had just reached the Dutch coast when Bomber Command sent a signal to return.

German Fighter Control had been sending signals too, and as the

Fortresses wheeled about they were jumped by about twenty-five FW 190's and Me 109's. A twenty-minute running battle followed, and for the first time the supposedly inadequate firepower of B-17's was put to the test. It passed, but not without hurt. Five of the attackers ganged up on lagging *Johnny Reb,* and a 20-mm shell exploded on one side of the cockpit windshield, mortally wounding the copilot and burning the hands of the pilot so badly that he couldn't fly the plane. Bombardier Lieutenant Edward T. Sconiers, a washed-out flying cadet, took over. With two engines knocked out and *Johnny Reb*'s gunners holding off the attackers, he brought the plane home, crash-landing it at the first RAF base he could find.

The mission was a failure, but the group was given credit for downing two German fighters. Later the number of attackers was questioned, for the numbers game in the sky was always a difficult one to judge. Five planes attacking could seem like twenty-five, and one plane going down in flames could be counted as a dozen when each of those firing on it thought it was his personal kill.

In the four additional missions the 97th flew before the end of the month, their numbers were never over a dozen, their penetrations shallow, and their escorts ample. They struck at shipyards in the Netherlands and France, and at an airplane factory, a fighter repair depot, and an FW 190 base. In none of these raids were they attacked by interceptors, and they suffered no losses, but in the aggregate their material effect was minimal.

In the meantime, the 301st Group had about completed its combat training and the 92nd had made the North Atlantic ferry hop and was ready to move into Eaker's first specially established Combat Crew Replacement and Training Center—CCRC—at Bovingdon. Since the 92nd had brought the new B-17F over, its many design changes making it a better combat aircraft than the E, Eaker decided to have the 92nd swap their planes with Armstrong's battle-tested Group. The 97th had been having maintenance problems as well, and these problems were a continuing part of the growing pains that would plague Eaker in particular and Spaatz in general. Tony Frank was not the easiest service commander to get along with, and the tick beneath his right eye was speeded up by the demands made on the key Burtonwood Depot for supplies which were slow in arriving. "Such supplies have been obtained and delivered by organizations [groups] themselves rather than by the Service Command," noted Eaker. As a result he and Spaatz and Hunter met with Frank informally to try to straighten out what was becoming a large mess due to a lack of Service Command organization. Frank gave little satisfaction. His attitude was that whatever was wrong, 100 percent of the problem rested with the three of them and not with him. "The matter was dropped," wrote Eaker, but certainly not the problem.

At the same time, Major General Oliver Echols, Chief of the Materiel Division, and Colonel Ben Chidlaw, Chief of the Experimental Engineering Branch, paid a visit, and Eaker had a chance to talk to them about a half dozen B-17 improvements he had in mind: everything from improved oxygen equipment to bulletproof windows for pilot and copilot.

Maintenance, supply, and improvements were the nuts and bolts of the operation. Without them, all the rest was meaningless. Yet, even as the Eighth chalked up its eighth mission in ten days, all the rest became imperiled, not by enemy action but by combined Allied policy.

When Marshall came home and briefed Arnold on TORCH—which Hap at first referred to as "The Special Operation"—he also told him that he expected Eisenhower was going to command the operation. This was fine with Arnold, but it was another reason why he wanted Tooey to become Ike's number one airman. As noted, few Allied leaders were in favor of TORCH, Arnold confiding to Spaatz he had done everything he could to oppose and block it. To his way of thinking, the strategy was not only a deflection from what had become fixed in the minds of Army airmen as the main target, but it also meant having to build another air force in a war that would now require official air superiority in nine theaters. There was only one source to draw on in building air support for TORCH. The equipment and personnel would have to be taken from BOLERO, which meant the Eighth Air Force. Here was Ira Eaker, all his energies and talents focused on getting his first crews and planes into combat, he and Spaatz holding off pressures from Washington to Whitehall, from the press, even from Goebbels' Propaganda Ministry. Here he was, out to prove what his closest RAF friend and ally, Bert Harris, did not think workable, and suddenly came the word that anticipated bomber and fighter groups were to be used elsewhere. He protested as vigorously as he could, but what did that mean? It meant even less than Arnold's outcry. Sympathy from everyone concerned was of no benefit, and for the time being while Eaker concentrated on his major task, the air was filled with more confusion than with aircraft.

Nothing better points up this period of bruising planning changes and the manifest doubts raised around them than the exchanges between the principals involved.

On August 19, Arnold sent a "for you and you alone" message to Tooey by special messenger. In it he covered familiar ground, ". . . the tendency of the Strategic Planners to take aircraft away from the European Theater and throw it in the South Pacific." In the doing, there and elsewhere, he complained, "we are so dispersing our effort that we will have an overwhelming [air] superiority in no theater." Then, having carried the theme for a page and a half, he proposed a course of action. Wouldn't it be possible for Spaatz, Ike, and Portal to join together and get "everybody

over there to stand up on their hind legs for the Air Force that is needed"
and thus let the American people know that they were out to "hammer at
the innards of Germany," putting forth a maximum effort every day?

If nothing else, his three-step suggestion "to support any offensive—to
constantly attack Germany—to build an air force" capable of taking on
the Luftwaffe under any conditions, showed the degree of his influence in
matters of overall policy. Unlike Portal he was not an equal among
equals, although Portal treated him as one, but instead a kind of minority
member of the Combined Chiefs. Air Power was the one power that the
United States could bring against Europe during that dark summer of
German triumph. Yet, when Marshall and Hopkins sat down to knock
heads with the British on changes that would have a profound affect on its
use, Arnold wasn't even there. Now, having put Spaatz and Eaker and
Hunter in the position of proving that twenty years of strategic theory was
correct, he was calling on them for support, for, aside from Bob Lovett,
he was essentially by himself. Outside the minds of a few vintage airmen
—U.S. and RAF—there were no military or political leaders who
believed Hitler could be overcome by air bombardment alone, although
all recognized the vital importance of air superiority. That basic difference
made all the difference in the conduct of the war.

As to its immediate conduct, Arnold felt that by fall the Germans
would be closing up shop in Russia, coming back determined to wipe England off the map.

In his response to Hap, Tooey said he couldn't add much to what he'd
already said. When his advice was requested, and often when it wasn't, he
had "reiterated the folly of attempting to fight the war all over the world."
In his opinion, if the powers that be didn't get it through their heads that
a concentration of air forces was necessary in the ETO, they stood an excellent chance of losing the war. Both he and Arnold tended to see the
situation in absolutes.

Portal told Arnold he was also concerned about the effect of TORCH. He
quoted a statement by the Combined Chiefs on the strategy of hitting the
enemy from the air day and night while his forces were concentrated in
the East. Yet he repeated the British line of asking for no cutback in the
air detachments for the Middle East in the fight against Rommel. He
thought it unwise to accept any reduction in the planned strength there,
for they might soon be called on to support the Russians in the Caucasus
and to cover the Persian oil fields. There was nothing that he said that
added anything to what Arnold already knew, and nothing that he proposed that offered any alleviation to the problems they faced.

Eaker received a personal, hand-carried letter from Arnold as well.
Aside from praise and the statement that he had stripped the office in
Washington to give Ira the best possible staff, he repeated what he'd said
to Spaatz.

The decision to mount TORCH had been taken in July, but the end of August plans for the operation had gone through a considerable metamorphosis. Even though, from a purely military standpoint, the risks were considered so great as to condemn it, the undertaking, through Roosevelt's suggestion, became almost entirely American. Three invasion forces would strike—at Oran, Algiers, and Casablanca, Major General George Patton commanding the latter force, the purpose to sweep eastward while the British drove westward and so secure all of North Africa. Roosevelt believed the French forces in Algeria and Morocco would not fight against U.S. troops, and so, except for British naval units and limited RAF support, TORCH had evolved into a combined operation that was, by and large, American.

Eisenhower's breakdown of aircraft for the triple invasion foresaw the need for nearly twelve hundred planes at the outset, one third of which would be contributed by the RAF, most of them fighters. In all, recommendations were made for more than three hundred U.S. bombers, most of them mediums, but included would be two groups of heavies, a figure that would soon double. Naturally, all of Eisenhower's energies were directed toward the Herculean hurry-up job of organizing and preparing for the combined land, sea, and air operation under strict security. He appreciated the Eighth Air Force's ongoing pinprick missions against targets in France and the Low Countries, but that effort had to be very secondary to the main thrust.

Fully aware of this and struggling to keep the Eighth Air Force a viable entity in the face of the dissolution of its strategic purpose, Arnold made several shrewd moves. They may have evolved in part from the thinking of his Advisory Council, or possibly from proposals by Larry Kuter or Hoyt Vandenberg. Aside from his recommendation to Ike that he make Tooey his overall air commander, he attempted to sell both Marshall and Eisenhower on the idea that the invasion of North Africa and the bomber operations of the Eighth Air Force and the RAF were complementary to one another and therefore directly linked.

To Marshall, he argued: "If decisive results are ever to be attained in this war, offensive operations against the center of strength, *industrial Germany,* must be continued relentlessly *from now on* and from every possible base. At the moment only the British Isles are available as a base. The bombing offensive of the British Isles and the action in North Africa, therefore, are basically complementary."

To Spaatz, he stressed the importance of getting this concept accepted and that Tooey "bombard the War Department by cables and letters signed Eisenhower to Marshall and signed Eisenhower for Arnold from Spaatz," making it clear that "the bombing offensive from the United Kingdom and the Middle Eastern operations are inseparable . . ." and that "regardless of the success of the North African operations, the only way to bring any direct pressure to bear upon Germany with present weapons, is to amplify the bombing offensive from the U.K. . . ."

He and his Chief of Staff, George Stratemeyer, warned that if this message was not sent back from London, particularly one from Eisenhower outlining the success of the bombing effort to date, air strength in England would be so dissipated by diversions that it would become a token effort at best.

Spaatz went forth to convince both Eisenhower and Major General George Patton that, important as it was to build a tactical air force quickly to support TORCH, daylight strategic bombardment must not be relegated to the back burner. He also put together a series of letters, documents, news stories, and photographs of bomb damage to help buttress Arnold's position. But even as he did so, Arnold moved again in reaction to presidential worries and demands.

The Marines had landed on Guadalcanal and Tulagi, in the Solomon Islands, on August 7 and were locked in vicious battle with the Japanese. Sea and air power were hotly engaged, and Roosevelt sent a handwritten note to his Chiefs of Staff saying that there must be adequate air support not only in the South Pacific but also for TORCH, "even though it means delay in our other commitments particularly to England. . . ."

Because of his worries in the Pacific, in the Soviet Union, in the Middle and Far East, and over the fact that "we will soon find ourselves engaged in two active fronts," he asked Arnold for an immediate estimate of aircraft needs. Just how many combat planes should be produced for the Army and Allies in 1943 to gain air ascendancy over the enemy?

At midnight on August 26, Possum Hansell awoke Spaatz to tell him that he had received a cable requesting that he return to Washington immediately for an important conference. He was to bring all supportive data on the bombing so far, and the assumption was that this was another method Arnold was using to convince the War Department of the correctness of his position. To aid him, Hansell asked that Major Harris Hull, Eaker's Intelligence Chief, and Group Captain Robert "Bobbie" Sharp, an invaluable RAF liaison officer, be permitted to accompany him. Spaatz went one better and requested that Eaker go too. He trusted that Ira would not be detained for over a week, but realizing the importance of what was transpiring he thought it of "vital importance" that he be there. "Eaker's ideas exactly parallel mine," he told Arnold. "In our discussion of the entire situation with Ike this a.m. I emphasized the vital necessity of continuing our present operations in this theater with H.B.'s and P-38's."

Their salesmanship had its effect, and as Arnold had fervently hoped, Eisenhower sent a cable to Marshall in which he gave praise to "high altitude daylight precision bombing," saying that by increasing the attack "effective results can be obtained." He made clear, however, that he in-

tended to use if necessary "all of the US air force now in the United Kingdom in Torch." But he added that it was "imperative that a strong air
force particularly in heavy bombers be built up quickly" in England not
only for possible use in TORCH for a limited period, but also to "fix the
GAF [German Air Force] in Western France and the low countries."
Thus he gave implicit support to Arnold's idea of two theaters of operation in one.

He went on to urge that the Eighth Air Force be built up to a strength
of ten heavy and five fighter groups by mid-October, and that by January
1 the figure be doubled with ten medium groups added.

His conclusion read as though it had been dictated by Spaatz or Eaker,
stressing that the U.K. was one of the few places in the world adequately
organized to support the air forces he had in mind and at the same time
"strike at the heart of the principal enemy . . . where a continuity of action is obtained through the air operations of our Allies."

Arnold was so gratified that he immediately told Marshall he believed
the cable was of such great and immediate importance that it should be
shown to the President and the Joint Chiefs. He felt that the impact would
be greater if Marshall, not he, made the presentation. He then signaled
Tooey his congratulations, saying that Ike's communication to Marshall
was of "inestimable help" and to keep it up. He also was all for the idea
of releasing photos to the press showing bomb damage, because people
more readily believe what they see than what they hear.

Meantime, Eaker, Hansell, and aides had arrived, and Possum found
himself in a repeat situation of the previous year. He had just eleven days
to come up with a new air-war plan. Only now, Hal George was commanding ATC; Ken Walker was Commanding General of the 5th Bomber
Command, in New Guinea, and Larry Kuter, as noted, was Deputy Chief
of the Air Staff. Nevertheless, he, Santy Fairchild, Lieutenant Colonel
Malcolm Moss, all of whom had contributed to the original plan, plus
members of the Air Staff were made available to update AWPD-1. The
figures changed, but the basic air strategy remained the same: to undermine and destroy "the capability and will of Germany to wage war by destroying its war-supporting industries and systems."

When AWPD-1 had been drafted, the Russian war had just begun.
Now the fate of the U.S.S.R. loomed large in the position developed by
Hansell and his planners. They stressed the strong possibility that by the
time the aircraft in question were produced, Hitler's armies would have
defeated the Red Army and the Wehrmacht would outnumber the ground
forces of the Allies. Therefore, strategic air power was the one weapon
that would reverse the imbalance, aid the Soviet Union if it could survive,
and at the same time materially weaken the enemy.

A second point, which threatened to dominate all others, was the German submarine campaign. In cold figures, more Allied tonnage was being

sunk than could be produced. Nearly two hundred U-boats were preying on shipping in the Atlantic and the Caribbean, and the immediate question was, Could the sinkings defeat TORCH, which foresaw the movement of more than six hundred ships to North Africa from both the United States and England? In seeking for the answer, the planners of AWPD-42 cited as their secondary strategic purpose air support for both the Mediterranean and the Pacific. Whereas the number one aim of the air offensive was to knock out the Luftwaffe, the second was to destroy the sources of German submarine construction, while the third priority was to "undermine the German war-making capacity."

Aside from numbers—the final estimate for the 1943 total was 127,000 planes—there were some fundamental differences in the new Air War Plan versus AWPD-1. The air offensive against Germany now included the RAF. But, most significantly, the planners were no longer saying that the war could be won by strategic bombing alone. Its purpose now was to so soften up Germany that an invasion could be undertaken with light losses. The new plan took note of a strategic air offensive against Japan after the defeat of Germany, noting that it would have to be carried out by new long-range bombers not expected to be available until late 1944. While transportation, electric power, and oil remained priority targets in Germany, aluminum and rubber were added to the list, nine systems in all, with aircraft the overriding priority.

However, in the estimates of what could be done and how, the results of the Eighth Air Force initial raids created entirely too much optimism with regard to attrition and the superiority of the heavy bomber over German fighters. Also, as Hansell was to point out later, no reference was made to the need for an escort fighter. He was to consider it one of the greatest faults of the plan, although he pointed out that AWPD-42 was a requirement for production in 1943 and there were no escort fighters in existence then. "It was not considered possible to design and produce such aircraft in such a short time," he wrote. "Insufficient attention was given to the possibility of adapting existing types by extending their range."[12]

There was one major wrinkle in the plan. The Navy refused to accept it. When Arnold presented AWPD-42 to Admiral King, he declared it completely unacceptable. The surface reason was that the Navy had not participated in the preparation. The real reason was as old as the Army airmen's struggle against Navy encroachment on its vested position of maintaining land-based aircraft. The Navy wanted B-24's to use as patrol bombers; it also had a large program for land-based fighters. In drawing up the estimates for the air plan, the planners included B-24's in the numbers the Navy wanted, but they assigned them to Army Air Forces units, many to be used against submarines in the same guise as RAF Coastal Command. Because of King's adamant rejection, AWPD-42 was never accepted by the Joint Chiefs, but Harry Hopkins bought it minus the Navy's requirements, and so, too, did Stimson and the President.

While Hansell and the Air Staff were working overtime to present a program that by its very nature would reinforce the Army airmen's position on the use of strategic air power from England, Eaker, during his very brief visit, was quietly working to convince fence-sitters, doubters, and antagonists that the strategy was viable. He had brought bomb photos and intelligence reports, which Arnold considered most valuable and convincing, ". . . the kind that . . . demonstrates beyond a doubt the effectiveness of our bombing efforts." He arranged for Eaker to talk to the President. The Bomber Commander also sat down with Stimson and Marshall and other War Department brass. To Spaatz, Arnold reported, "Ira has made a very valuable impression on everybody with whom he has talked here, and in accordance with your recommendation, I am forwarding his nomination for Major General. Hope it goes through."*

More important, Arnold was hoping that Hansell and his crew were going to be able to come up with an air plan that would be accepted and would remain unchanged. But he wasn't all that sanguine. He felt the major program of hitting Germany was bogged down due to diversity of interest. "It has been dispersion, dispersion and more dispersion in our unity of thought for the main effort," he told Spaatz, remarking plaintively that democratic forms of government didn't seem to lend themselves to continuity of effort. Ira was leaving on Friday and would give Tooey "all the lowdown."

Eaker made good time, arriving back in London the next day, Saturday, September 5. He came directly to Park House, where Tooey lived, and they went over the current picture on both sides of the Atlantic. The 97th, Tooey told him, had gone back to Rouen that morning along with the newly operational 301st, thirty aircraft in all. Bombing accuracy hadn't been all that good, and the Germans were reporting 140 civilians killed and many more wounded. But again all the Fortresses had returned safely.

That evening, Spaatz gave a small dinner which included Bert Harris and his wife, RAF Coastal Commander Air Marshal Sir Philip Joubert and his wife, Tony Frank, Ira, and several important press contacts: the Walter Lippmanns; Ed Beattie, of UP; and Wes Gallagher, of AP. Seeking a good press simply made good sense, but in this case the stories newsmen filed on the actions of the Eighth were considered crucial.

Most senior Army airmen were acutely tuned to the value of public relations. In war it was a weapon of immeasurable influence. Eaker's sharp new aide, Captain James Parton, had come from *Time-Life,* and most of the ranking press officers in Eisenhower's headquarters and the

---

* It did. Eaker became a major general on September 14, 1942.

Eighth had been newsmen just yesterday. As such, they had an immediate knowledge of and a rapport with their former colleagues. Moreover, Eaker, as a journalism graduate and writer, had a solid news sense. He, like Spaatz, was genuinely appreciated by the press. Handling newsmen wasn't just a matter of wining and dining and all pals together. Much was off the record. The organizing and planning of TORCH was top secret. What was released had to be tightly controlled, but enough had to go out to tell the story in a way that would gain and keep public support.

Marshall had complained recently over what he considered too much publicity featuring high-ranking officers in England, and Spaatz had given orders to downplay such coverage. *Time* magazine was planning to put him on its cover, and he canceled that, suggesting his Chief of Staff, Asa Duncan, instead. Yet, several days later, when he flew to PINETREE and Polebrook to decorate Ira and Frank Armstrong with the Silver Star, Arthur Sulzberger, New York *Times* publisher, accompanied him.

The big story that windy afternoon, however, had nothing to do with awards but, rather, centered on Bill Cowart's pilotage. He was flying the party in a twin-engine British PQ 6, and when he came in to land at Bovingdon, he misjudged the strength of the crosswind. The result was a vicious ground loop, which wiped out the landing gear and pretzeled both props. There were no injuries, and publisher Sulzberger walked away from his first crack-up with a new experience to write about.

One story that couldn't be reported went to the bedrock of all that Eaker and Spaatz had been assigned to prove through daylight operations. It was the formation of the Twelfth Tactical Air Force, the U.S. air arm that Eisenhower would need for TORCH. Most of its strength would have to be drawn from the Eighth. When Eisenhower had sent his cable to Marshall on the need to build up the latter, while saying in contradiction that he'd take all of it if necessary, there were four heavy groups in England and five on the way in one form or another. Two were already slated for TORCH. So were three medium groups, and the 15th Group, of July 4 fame.

To Eaker the move was nothing more or less than disembowelment. How in the name of strategic air power could he build a force to support the concept when, right at the outset, the 97th and the 301st—the two combat-trained groups that he had—were being taken from him? Asa Duncan had pointed out to Eisenhower's headquarters that these groups could not be operational and reorganizing for movement to another theater at the same time. Which was to have priority?

From where Eisenhower sat, the question was simply one of a thousand with which he had to contend. As he was to write: "The venture was new —it was almost new in conception. Up to the moment no government had ever attempted to carry out an overseas expedition involving a journey of thousands of miles from its bases and terminating in a major attack."[13] As to the size and logistical support of TORCH, from which everything had to be improvised on short notice, he added that they were existing "in a state of scarcity with no such thing as plenty of anything." He observed, "The situation was vague, the amount of resources unknown, the final objective indeterminate, and the only firm factor in the whole business our instructions to attack."[14]

Under such circumstances, it took a strong degree of steadiness on the part of everyone concerned. The pressures came like a blizzard of arrows, high and low, but the answer to Duncan's question, which was number one with Eaker, was that operations would continue while staff work on tables of organization went forward in organizing JUNIOR—the Twelfth Air Force.

Actually, the Twelfth had first been established at Bolling Field in early August. Arnold had recommended its commander to Marshall at the same time General Patton was recommended to Ike as his principal field commander. Hap's choice to command JUNIOR was Brigadier General Jimmy Doolittle. Previously the only force Doolittle had ever led was the Tokyo Raiders, but Arnold knew Doolittle's capabilities went beyond his expertise in aeronautical engineering and aircraft troubleshooting, and the American public knew him as its most distinguished air hero. Eisenhower didn't know him at all, and when he arrived in England on August 6 with Patton, Ike was anxious to meet him.

The introduction took place the following day, with Spaatz, Patton, and Hansell present. It was an unqualified disaster. In Doolittle's view the Theater Commander took an instantaneous dislike to him. Patton, an old friend and well known to Ike, first outlined how he would utilize his ground forces during the invasion. When he'd finished, Eisenhower turned to Doolittle and asked, "Now, what would you do with your air?"

By his own reckoning, Jimmy Doolittle then pulled one of the stupidest things he'd ever done. "General Eisenhower," he answered, "I can't do anything with my air until the ground troops have cleared and occupied the air bases, have brought in ammunition, fuel and spare parts. At that time I'd send in my ground troops followed very quickly by air troops and aircraft."

What he had said was correct, but it was so patently obvious that it implied that Eisenhower had to be told how to run a war. He nodded curtly, and Doolittle realized that in his eagerness he had made a dreadful gaffe.

That night, Eisenhower sent a cable to Marshall accepting Patton but asking for Spaatz, Frank, or Eaker—in that order—to command his air forces. He promptly received a reply from Marshall and Arnold saying he could have anyone he wanted but they still recommended Doolittle.

This did nothing to enhance Eisenhower's opinion of the airman, whom he felt was being forced on him. If he insisted on a change and things went wrong with the air effort, the blame would be on him. In the days that followed, life was not easy for Jimmy Doolittle, for whenever he was called on to make a presentation he could read the antagonism in Eisenhower's glance. It would take a solid year of trying and an awful lot of war in between before Doolittle would get to know the warmth of Ike's curling grin, with the added recommendation that he be awarded the Distinguished Service Medal. In the meantime, it was a tough autumn for everyone.

Doolittle, as Shell Oil's Aviation Manager, had proved himself a man of many parts, even though the public saw him as a daredevil aviator out to break speed records if not his neck. As a global traveler for Shell, coordinating aerial activities in Latin America and Europe, he had not only supplied valuable reports to Hap Arnold on Germany's aerial growth and intentions, but he had also developed organizational capabilities that were of benefit in his new position of command.

Eisenhower probably didn't know, and at the time would have been too busy to care, but it was Doolittle's aeronautical vision that had been in large measure responsible for the development of 100-octane gasoline, which powered the aircraft that would support TORCH. Without it, there would have been no TORCH.

At the time that Doolittle had sold Shell Oil on putting a million and a half dollars into an iso-octane plant, nobody wanted to make an engine that required a better fuel, because nobody had the fuel and nobody wanted to make the fuel while there was no engine that could use it. In doggedly pursuing what seemed like the chicken chasing the egg, the experiment came to be known as "Doolittle's Folly." But in working with Sam Herron and Captain Frank Klein, of the Engineering Development Lab at Wright Field, a great deal more than an egg was laid. An engine was produced to use the higher-performance fuel, and once it was tested the Materiel Division recognized that a giant step up in performance was in the making. Without it, U.S. aircraft would have gone into combat at a killing disadvantage.[15]

Now, however, in spite of Doolittle's many talents, he'd never put an air force together, and when he set up temporary headquarters at Claridge's, Spaatz gave him three of his best officers: Colonels Norstad for operations, Max Schneider for supply, and Hoyt Vandenberg as Chief of Staff. Both Arnold and Spaatz knew that Vandenberg had been slated for promotion to brigadier general, but in order to get to England and participate in the planning there, he had bypassed the opportunity.

For Doolittle, organizing JUNIOR meant stealing personnel and aircraft from Ira Eaker. He felt bad about it, but no more so than Eaker. They had known each other since the days at Rockwell Field, directly after the end of World War I, but they had not been close friends, simply because they followed divergent courses: Doolittle, testing and engineering; Eaker, staff and command. Though their personalities differed, Doolittle quick, electric, extroverted, and Eaker quiet, contained, introspective, they had an essential toughness in common. It was the aviator's quality of alertness, a capability of following a determined course, yet with the flexibility to make sudden changes in the face of the unexpected.

Eaker understood the position Doolittle was in, but his own position was far more delicate. On Sunday, the day after he returned from Washington, he launched the Eighth's largest mission to date. Forty-one B-17's went forth to attack the Avion Potez aircraft works at Méaulte, near Amiens, thirty-three of them reaching the target. The 97th Group led the 92nd on its first foray into combat, while the 301st, in a diversion, struck at two airfields at St.-Omer.

In all previous raids, RAF fighter escort had been more than substantial, 118 Spitfires accompanying the 37 bombers that had hit Sotteville-lès-Rouen the day before. This time, although the Spitfires were again out in force, the target was beyond their range, and the yellow-nosed German fighters swept in. According to Spaatz's headquarters, the Luftwaffe dispatched their largest force, with the exception of Dieppe, in the past year of operations. They pressed home the attack, and a B-17 of the 97th Group went down over Flasselles, three FW 190's hounding it. Four chutes were seen to open. A Fort of the 92nd fell out of formation and was last seen near Beachy Head trailing smoke, trying in vain to reach Dover. British Air Sea Rescue found no trace of it or its ten-man crew.

And so, on that bright September Sunday the Eighth Air Force suffered its first heavy-bomber losses. Still, the returning crews claimed to have shot down five of their attackers, with thirteen probables and twenty-five damaged. If nothing else, the figures indicated the strength of the opposition.

"This obviously marks a turning point," was the comment in the Eighth's Daily Diary. In one respect, certainly, Eaker's reaction was anything but laconic. He sent an "Attention to Duty" memo to all his General and Special Staff section heads in which he told them they, too, were at war:

1. Yesterday, Sunday, September 6, the Eighth Bomber Command participated in the largest mission it has yet executed. Two of its aircraft were lost; two airplanes were seriously damaged; one returning aircraft had one dead and several injured aboard. During the progress of this mission I was impressed with the following facts which deeply concern you:

a. Many of the offices had no officer on duty; several of the offices had no individual on duty and their telephones did not answer.

b. No interest or concern was manifest on the part of a great many officers and individuals of this Headquarters concerning the operation.

c. Many of the officers in some of the departments performed in a typical peacetime manner, treating Sunday as a complete holiday and day of recreation.

2. I am well aware that one of the reasons for some of above conditions lies in the fact that many individuals in some departments did not know that a mission was in progress. Obviously, for reasons of security, it is not possible widely to broadcast the initiation of combat missions. On the other hand, there is not a department and there should not be an officer in this Headquarters, who is not vitally interested and deeply concerned with the success of our operations. Our bombers and their crews are doing more than just fighting the enemy during this critical phase. They are determining methods of combat and deciding strategic tactical and even political factors of tremendous import to all of us individually and to the outcome of this war. Some of these factors now in the balance, which this small organization will be greatly instrumental in deciding, are:

a. The feasibility of daylight bombing.

b. The Air Forces which will be built up in this theater.

c. The feasibility of independent Air Force operations.

d. Future plans for winning the war—the major theater—the principal enemy—the destruction of vital enemy objectives.

He concluded by warning that anyone who didn't do whatever he could to support daylight bombing operations was not going to remain in his command and didn't deserve to be in the Army Air Forces. He was not satisfied with the effort or attitude of his headquarters as demonstrated by its behavior on Sunday. In his warning, he saw a necessity for a closer application to duty and for a more alert and intelligent operation by everyone. He had spoken and the message was clear. There would be no need to speak of the problem again.

Thirteen

An Endangered Strategy

Tooey Spaatz was unable to sleep. He had a cold. The weather was unflyable and had been for more than two weeks. It was but one of his concerns. In a letter to Arnold's Chief of Staff, George "Strat" Stratemeyer, he expressed others. Their friendship dated back to flying school at Rockwell Field in 1916, when all the world had been young, and now, in the small hours of a September night, he had no hesitation in giving his thoughts free rein.

Like Ira, he was hung up on the physical and strategic inroads the formation of the Twelfth was making and was going to make on the Eighth. They had fastened JUNIOR to the Eighth like a patient needing a transfusion, and now it was busily draining away in personnel and materiel too much of the Eighth's lifeblood.

He had weather-vaned back and forth on whether to halt the bomber offensive for at least two months. He had drafted such a cable to Arnold, and Ike had advised against sending it. In it he had said that it was his opinion that the North African operation was going to jeopardize their gaining air supremacy over Germany. At the same time, he had told Ira they would continue operations. But, of course, JUNIOR must have priority, and the standing joke was, "You can't have that; it's for Junior." Only it wasn't all that funny, because not only was the movement by air of the Twelfth—all its units and personnel—the responsibility of the Eighth, but so also was its training, with the exception of the medium-bomber crews, which the RAF took over.

He was also a bit annoyed at what seemed to be an increasing U.S. habit of belittling British bombing missions in the face of a handful of shallow, heavily escorted raids on the Eighth's part. He told Strat the only times the Germans had been stopped anywhere were by the RAF. They were the ones who were doing the pounding, and although he wasn't an enthusiastic supporter of all their activities, particularly their attitude about daylight bombing, everyone had benefited a helluva lot from their experience.

That day, he had sent to Hap a copy of a joint RAF-Eighth Air Force operations agreement which was simple and direct enough but whose main strength illustrated the close degree of cooperation between the two services. Yet, unbeknownst to him, while he was burning the midnight oil defending the RAF, powerful critics in it were rising to the fore mounting an attack against his own efforts. The issue had been and would continue to be daylight versus night bombardment.

Sir Archibald Sinclair, Churchill's Secretary of State for Air, not at all impressed by the U.S. bombing record to date, wrote an impatient query to Air Marshal Jack Slessor asking, "What are the Americans doing? What do they intend to do?" He knew the number of planes they had in England, but how many officers and men did they have? He understood they hadn't dropped a single bomb on Germany. Wasn't it also true "that they have not dropped a single bomb outside the range of our single-seater fighter cover?" He went on with a series of questions, sounding perturbed and obviously not that well informed on U.S. plans.

Slessor answered each of Sinclair's nineteen questions in precise detail, and in so doing gave a clear picture of the position Spaatz and Eaker were caught in. His replies also illustrated that they had a good friend in the British court of high command. He informed the Secretary that the Americans had six heavy-bomber groups and a dozen pursuit groups, half of which were Spitfires and half P-38's. The latter were having trouble getting into action because their radio antennas were cracking under stress, preventing proper communications. More, since they were preparing for "a certain operation" (TORCH), they were severely restricted. Wrote Slessor:

> General Spaatz has suffered a setback by having to set aside his first units operational for the certain operation. He has now to start again at the beginning breaking in new units as they arrive. He is wisely doing this gradually, profiting by our experience and not attempting to put operationally inexperienced units straight into action. . . . Operational training in America is not as yet up to standard.

Slessor then added, "I think it is worth remembering that they have been severely hampered in the past in this respect by the fact that they gave us many aircraft which they badly needed for their own operational training."

There are at the present time, the Assistant Chief of the Air Staff then told Sinclair, 54,644, officers and men of the USAAF in the U.K. and

Northern Ireland. He then described their intent to bomb Germany by daylight using precision bombing, believing that armament and numbers would assure success. Their early operations, he observed, "lend some support to this belief. . . ." The question remained as to whether they could carry the war deep into Germany. He was personally inclined to agree that it could be done, "once they get really adequate numbers," and this proviso he underlined.

Slessor then gave an account of AWPD-42, not aware that the Navy had rejected it and that Marshall was displeased with the manner in which Hansell and his planner had shifted numbers from the Navy to the Army column without informing him. He called the plan a "war winner," providing it was found possible to bomb Germany by day. It foresaw a force of three thousand heavy and one thousand medium U.S. bombers in the U.K. by the end of 1943, with between fifteen hundred and two thousand RAF bombers. By June 1, 1943, there should be a combined force of about twenty-five hundred.

He then described targets and made the point that even with the drain of TORCH, Spaatz expected to have something over two hundred aircraft operational by the end of November. "They recognize that their casualties are likely to be heavy to begin with, but they reckon that they should be much lighter subsequently if they can really seriously reduce enemy fighter production."

"Meanwhile," said Slessor, "they are quite rightly feeling their way. They keep in closest touch with us and we have a weekly meeting to discuss current operational problems. They are dividing their operations into 3 Phases: (1) short-range raids under British fighter protection, (2) longer-range raids, using the longer-range American fighter escort, (3) the long-range raids, including those into Germany, developing the technique and tactics of getting the bombers in through the enemy fighter crust with fighter collaboration and 'scooping them out' on their return."

A point Slessor did not make in his mention of Phase 1 was the fact that a substantial share of the British fighter protection was supplied by the three Eagle Squadrons, made up of American pilots who had been flying in combat with the RAF since 1940. At the time, the Eagles were in a state of transition, for while Hap Arnold was out "beating the bushes" for experienced pilots at home, Spaatz and Hunter were working out a transfer with Air Marshal Sholto Douglas for the Eagles to form an Eighth Air Force fighter group.[1]

Called irreverent, unmanageable, and temperamental by Allied brass, the three squadrons looked upon the B-17 missions of August and September as "public relations" exercises. To fighter pilots who had flown three and four sorties in the wild melee over Dieppe, escorting "the poor Fortress guys" was something of a joke. Observed Squadron Leader Red

McColpin,* ". . . they were inexperienced, they carried only token numbers of bombs, they were sent to nonessential targets to gain experience, and they were commanded by inexperienced colonels and generals. . . . I was told by the RAF to 'guard those B-17's with your lives.' The missions were a laugh. The bombers shot at us, their escort, whenever we came within range—within sight, that is. Then that night we would hear their great claims of destroyed enemy fighters—which were us—with never a German in view."[2]

In recounting the Eighth's mission to date, Slessor remarked, "I think Generals Spaatz and Eaker are good sound commanders who know their business. Through no fault of their own it is taking longer to get going than they hoped." His guess was that by mid-December Spaatz would be making his first raid into Germany with one hundred-plus aircraft. But it was all "very much a matter of conjecture," because they were faced with a number of unpredictable variables bound up in production, the demands made upon it, and the policies influencing the war's course.

Where Slessor's explanation to Sinclair dealt with what was, he was on sure ground. Where he gave his opinion on the future timetable of the Eighth, he was correct at least on the matter of conjecture. The unpredictables like the English weather were . . . wet, foggy and unflyable.

Whether Slessor's account to Sir Archibald changed his view or whether it was Churchill's suggesting the Secretary curb his criticism, by early October Sinclair was speaking out in strong support, proclaiming "the prodigies of daylight bombing which the U.S. Bomber Air Force had already begun to achieve."

No doubt the view was colored by where you stood or what cockpit you sat in with what degree of experience, and how much you knew of all that was involved in what McColpin blithely described as the U.S. and Great Britain garnering publicity in European warfare.

From where Spaatz sat, nursing his cold, the British attitude as seen from the top of the Air Ministry or from an Eagle Squadron Spitfire at twenty-five thousand feet did not carry the same importance as his other, immediate problems. The climate was one: On Saturday, September 26, just three days before the Eagle Squadrons were formally transferred to the AAF in the autumn rain at Debden, their base, an attempt by the Eighth to bomb German airfields in the Cherbourg Peninsula with a force of sixty-two B-17's was aborted by the wretched weather, and due to a gross error by a weather officer escorting, Eagle Squadron 133 lost a numbing twelve pilots.[3]

During this three-week period of daily morning fogs and heavy downpours, Eaker was worried that the powers in Washington were going to get the impression that they were sitting on their hands, and while Arnold

* Later Maj. Gen. Carroll Warren McColpin, USAF.

was on a whirlwind tour of the Pacific theaters, Ira wrote Strat accordingly. He stressed that his trained bomber force was being taken from him and the new force at his command was about ready to go. On October 9, it finally went, the target Lille. It was a combined force totaling 108 aircraft, including the 93rd Group flying B-24 Liberators under the command of Colonel Edward "Ted" Timberlake. There were over two hundred escort fighters, three squadrons of them P-38's from the 1st Group. They, like the B-24 crews, were entering combat for the first time. But in the perilously clear October sky, the German fighters stayed clear of them and struck at the heavies. They got four, one of them a B-24; happily two of the crews were rescued from the Channel. Flak over the important steel and engineering works of the Compagnie de Fives and the locomotive and freight-car works at Lille was heavy. Nearly half the attacking bombers were battered by hits, some severely. Bombing was generally poor, and the Germans announced heavy civilian casualties.

Although fourteen of the Liberators had to abort due to mechanical problems, those that reached their targets came home with claims of having shot down fifty-six German fighters with twenty-six probables and twenty damaged. Since these figures totaled half the entire German fighter force stationed along the West Wall, they were a bit hard to accept. Even when scaled down to about half, the British couldn't swallow them. The press called the raid a great victory, but the claims were quietly chalked up to "Yankee big talk."

There were, however, several more realistic factors concerning the mission. In less than two months, Eaker, who had begun combat operations with only a dozen bombers, had now launched over one hundred—from a conglomeration of five groups. The targets at and around Lille, although far distant from Germany, were of definite strategic value, and German fighter units had responded in kind, pressing home sustained attacks. As one crewman put it, "Lille was our first real brawl." As a brawl, even though the bombing had not been good and the aborts many—thirty-three in all—the mission had shown that the long-held theory of daylight bombardment appeared valid. The mass firepower of a large complement of bombers had been powerful enough to sustain the bombing attack over a well-defended target with losses that were acceptable. It was reasoned by Spaatz and Eaker and their subordinates that the problems of precision and operational control would come with combat experience. Optimistically, Lille was seen as the proof of the pudding, although the pudding was nothing to rave about.

There were two additional points that had a direct bearing on the first: Eaker did not know it at the time, but due to the requirements of TORCH, the demands from other theaters, and a failure fully to recognize and support what his bomber crews were fighting to prove over Lille, it would be another five months before he would again have as many aircraft to send

out on a mission. The other point was the role of escort fighters. Sometimes the heavies were accompanied by as many as several hundred. Both
Spaatz and Eaker had said at various times, verbally and in writing, that
the bombers could do it alone, *providing* their numbers were great
enough. Three hundred was the figure Eaker gave. Meantime, the P-38
had more range than the new Mark IX Spitfire; the long awaited P-47
would have more than that. But none would have enough range, even
with drop-tanks, to accompany Ira Eaker's bombers into Germany.

Eaker felt that the Lille mission concluded the first phase of his bombing plan, and now he was ready to take on phase two, which he described
as "deeper penetration with general fighter cover through the fighter belt,"
coming and going, but with no fighter cover to the target. This could be
accomplished, he said, with ten heavy groups, using one hundred aircraft
per mission. Currently he had five heavy groups, half of them belonging
to the Twelfth and on loan for only one mission a week. He was losing
the P-38's to TORCH as well, but he was confident that the RAF would
continue to supply escort just as they had been doing. Then, quite suddenly, a major shift in targeting took place and the Eighth Air Force was
thrust into phase two without the necessary aircraft or crews or effective
ordnance.

During his return to Washington, in late August, Eaker with Arnold
had met the President in a brief conference. During it, Roosevelt had
asked him if it would be possible for his bombers to knock out German
submarine bases on the Bay of Biscay. Eaker said yes, if he had ten heavy
groups. Hap supported him. It was Eaker's personal feeling that with the
necessary strength he could attack the five U-boat ports on the Bay and
"reduce the German submarine effort in the Atlantic by more than 60
percent." He said his estimate was based on considerable study of the
problem and the nature of the targets.

Over six million tons of Allied shipping had been sunk by Admiral
Dönitz's wolf packs since the beginning of the year. Their success posed
not only a continuing and perilous threat to the British Government's
ability to feed its people adequately, but also a threat to TORCH—its
supplies and its invasion fleet of six hundred ships. Eaker's optimistic
forecast of what he could do if given what he needed—backstopped by
Arnold—was in a sense typical not only of his own character but also of
the attitude of vintage airmen in general. The "can-do" approach was
built into their psyches during the years of having accomplished so much
with so little. The President, however, was not concerned with Eaker's
motivations, only with what he said he could do. The matter of ships sunk
in the Atlantic—119 in the month of October—was of paramount importance to everyone concerned, and now particularly to General Eisenhower. His convoys, coming across the North Atlantic to rendezvous off

the coast of North Africa, most to pass through the narrow Strait of Gibraltar, would be fair game for the wolf packs prowling the sea lanes.

On October 13, Ike sent a brief memo to Tooey, following several discussions of the subject. In it he said, "I want you to know that I consider the defeat of the submarine to be one of the basic requirements to the winning of the war." While he recognized that pounding the German Air Force was a number one priority, nothing should rank above the need to defeat the German subs. As a specific target he wanted "effective action against the submarine ports in the Bay of Biscay." Would Tooey give him an idea of what he could expect with regard to the scale of attack and the degree of British cooperation?

Tooey called Ira, and the next day Eaker submitted a four-page, detailed plan of operations. He pointed out that there were two reasons why the five principal U-boat bases hadn't been hit so far. One was a matter of gaining experience through Phase 1, and the other a prescient forecast:

> There has not been available to this organization a sufficient force to do the job properly. If undertaken prior to the availability of such a force, destruction could not be guaranteed and the German reaction would be to assemble heavier defenses which would cost us greater losses when sufficient force was assembled and the subsequent attack in force were made.

One hundred planes a mission was what Eaker wanted, the idea to knock out one target with repeated raids before moving on to the next.

"Whether the pens themselves, with their 11½ ft. thick reinforced concrete roofs and heavily reinforced sides can be cracked by 1600 lbs. Ap and 2,000 lbs. Gp bombs remains to be seen," Eaker wrote, and then added, "It is unnecessary, however, to demolish these sheds in order to render these bases unusable."

That same day, Spaatz and Eisenhower discussed Eaker's plan with Air Marshals Portal, Harris, and Joubert, of the Coastal Command. The RAF was not equipped to attack the bases by day, and by night as yet they wouldn't hit much of anything. Instead Harris would send his bombers against submarine-manufacturing and -launching targets in Germany. They were in agreement that submarines and all their components would for the time being have number one priority.

At the outset, the decision to go after the U-boat pens appealed to almost everyone concerned. Destroying the closely linked submarine turn-around ports was an Allied must. To reach them did not require deep penetration. A direct flight in and back was estimated at no more than three hours, and Eaker could foresee attacking three times a day, although coming in from the sea to avoid radar would take considerably longer.

Due to weather, it was another week before the first raid on the sub pens took place. Four groups set out, led by Frank Armstrong and the 97th. At 22,000 feet over the target of Lorient, there was solid overcast and three of the groups turned back. Armstrong, spotting a hole in the cloud mass, led his force down and came in over the target at 17,500 feet. The bombing wasn't too bad, but the opposition was. An estimated thirty-five yellow-nosed FW 190's came zinging in on the fifteen Forts like a swarm of hornets. The B-17's fought their way home and lost three of their number in the process. It was the highest percentage of losses so far and only a foretaste of things to come. Photo reconnaissance indicated that several of the submarine pens had sustained direct hits but suffered no damage, the bombs unable to penetrate the layer-cake concrete roofing. Previously, the crews had tended to denigrate German fighter opposition. They would no longer.

In the next two and a half months there would be ten raids on four of the ports. The largest number of planes actually to bomb the target, which in this case was St. Nazaire, was sixty-eight, on January 3, 1943. Ten aircraft were lost to flak and fighters and many others were damaged. Photo reconnaissance indicated that 14 percent of the bombs dropped hit the target but caused no lasting effect. In the ten operations, seven of which were flown in November, twenty-eight aircraft were lost; most of the more than two hundred airmen missing were believed killed. This was against claims of eighty-one German fighters destroyed, forty-nine probables, and thirty-eight damaged. If nothing else, such exaggerated figures helped to sustain the morale of bomber crews.

The Germans, realizing that their ports of Lorient, Brest, St. Nazaire and La Pallice were Ira Eaker's number one targets, moved in over one hundred flak batteries and alerted fighter components accordingly. St. Nazaire, which was the target in five of the missions, was renamed Flak City by the bomber crews. The antiaircraft brigades developed a new strategy: Batteries closest to the target would track the bombers from the IP—Initial Point—and throw up a box barrage as the grouped aircraft came in on the target. German interceptor pilots were also developing new tactics, making daring, straight-in approaches, singling out a lagging plane or concentrating their efforts on a single plane in the element.

Because bombing results of the first two raids on the pens—Lorient and Brest—seemed to indicate nothing positive accomplished, Spaatz suggested to Eaker that new tactics be tried during the upcoming mission, the first against St. Nazaire. The lead group, instead of going in at twenty-three thousand feet, would go in at ten thousand, and the last group of the three would go in at eight thousand. The German .88-mm flak guns quickly reversed that strategy. Every B-17 but one in the lead group was hit, although all made it back to base. Not so the last group. Four of its number went down, three over the target and one in a crash landing, for a 10 percent loss of the total.

In all, the Bay of Biscay ports had the capacity to shelter and refit about one hundred submarines at a time out of a total fleet at sea of two hundred forty. The RAF, having agreed to go after the construction yards and the launching slips of an additional two hundred fifty submarines in various stages of completion, had by year's end flown only three inconsequential missions against them. Previously, during a fifteen-month period, Bomber Command had devastated the major port areas of Rostock, Lübeck, and Emden, but still, the Germans were in the process of doubling their undersea fleet, and if the Eighth Air Force could not disrupt the marauders at their nesting sites, its determination and sacrifice were for naught.

This proved to be the case. That there weren't more missions mounted against the pens was due to the weather and perhaps a blessing in disguise. That the number of planes attacking the targets ranged from eleven to sixty-eight was essentially the result of the Twelfth Air Force, which took away twenty-seven thousand men, or half the Eighth's manpower, and nearly eleven hundred of its aircraft. This, in turn, reduced Ira Eaker's Bomber Command to fewer than one hundred fifty planes, with less than that number of crews to man them. There were two simultaneous primary assignments—to support the Twelfth with replacements, materiel, and planes, and to strike at the jugular of the U-boat menace— and carrying out the first effort helped to defeat the second, as well as the overall purpose of daylight bombardment. In a four-and-a-half-month period, only twenty-seven missions were flown by his bombers, and none into Germany. And whereas weather played a large part in the number of missions, the paucity in numbers of planes sent on the missions was due to TORCH and the demands of other theaters.

From his position of command at PINETREE, Ira Eaker could send cables and reports on the problems with which he was faced in fighting to keep daylight bombardment alive, but down at the group level numbers and cold statistics took on life and were translated into flesh and blood.

In late October, Colonel Curtis E. LeMay was at Syracuse, New York, with the thirty-five B-17's of his 305th Group. He was on his way to England—or so he thought. His ground echelon had departed aboard ship three weeks past, and he was anxious to lead his group in the northern route to Prestwick. However, there were modifications to be made on the ball-turret guns, and his crews had only summer wear to face the British climate. Suffering from Bell's palsy, a painful nerve inflammation of the face, which did nothing to enhance his normally bleak expression, LeMay invaded a nearby quartermaster depot to requisition clothing. He had no more authority than the look in his eye and the sound of his voice. The combination was enough. He departed with a couple of truckloads of heavy clothing, feeling somewhat proud of himself. Then an old buddy, Colonel Fred L. Anderson, showed up, bringing anything but glad tidings.

Anderson, a West Point graduate, class of 1928, had taken flight training with LeMay at Kelly Field. Bombardment had been his forte, and he
had established the first instructor's school for bombardiers, in 1940.
Later, he had been in England studying RAF bombing tactics, and now
he was in Hap Arnold's office as Assistant to Muir Fairchild, Director of
Requirements. His coming to Syracuse was not to advise Curt on how
best to hit the target, but on getting the hell over to it.

George Kenney was yelling for more heavy bomb groups. Hap had just
been out in the Pacific, promising him the same. "They're thinking of
sending you," Anderson told LeMay.

"Old Iron Ass," as his crews called him, was flummoxed. He gave Fred
all the good reasons why such a move would be asinine—all his ground
equipment and personnel gone one way, and now he was supposed to turn
around and go the other. Fred couldn't have agreed more, "But they're
yelling their heads off for a heavy bomb group out there in the Pacific,"
he said. "And at the moment you're more ready to go than anyone else."

LeMay couldn't argue with that. He was more ready to go than he'd
ever been, but to Blighty, not to New Guinea. "Stall them, as much as you
can, will you?" was his plea. While Anderson went back to Washington to
stall, LeMay and his group climbed on board and got moving north to
Presque Isle and Gander.[4]

A couple of days later at Prestwick, Scotland, he met up with another
old buddy, Frank Armstrong, on his way back to the States. Curt literally
grabbed Armstrong and said, "Look, you've been in combat; tell us what
we've got to know." The man who'd been there had a few minutes and
LeMay gathered his crews for a fast Q and A. Armstrong left them with
some grim tidings. "The flak is murder," he said. "If you fly straight and
level through it for more than ten seconds, you're a dead duck."

On the flight from Prestwick to Grafton-Underwood, where the 305th
was to be temporarily and wetly stationed, where the fog rolled in and the
runways weren't long enough and the food was as bad as the mud, LeMay
was transfixed by Armstrong's warning. If what he'd said was so, if you
couldn't fly straight and level for more than ten seconds . . . how in the
hell could you hit the target while taking evasive action? The Norden
bombsight, for all its wonders, wasn't that good. Nothing was. And if you
had to change course and altitude while trying to bomb, daylight precision
bombardment, for all the splendid theories and highfalutin, brass-hat projections on what it was going to do to Hitler, was so much oatmeal.

It would be three weeks before LeMay would lead his group on its first
combat mission, the target St. Nazaire. In that period he made some dis-
coveries. It was a form of pioneering for which he received no medals.
First, he learned that other combat-experienced groups and squadron
leaders agreed with Armstrong's contention. Next, he managed to have a
look at the slim photo reconnaissance evidence—the during and after

shots. They were few in number, due to weather and lack of preparation, but when LeMay examined them he couldn't believe his eyes. There was no telling where half the bombs landed, and most of the rest failed to fall within the target area. He didn't sleep well, trying to figure a way around the problem. Just before the St. Nazaire raid, his concentration paid off. He got out of bed one night and extracted from his footlocker a dog-eared ROTC manual on artillery. Using a French 75-mm cannon as a model, he calibrated its fire against a target the size of a B-17 at twenty-five thousand feet. From his logarithms, he determined that the German flak batteries firing their .88's would score one hit out of every 273 rounds. Those were fair enough odds, he reckoned, to fly straight and level from the IP to the AP, the Aiming Point, and it could take longer than ten seconds to get properly lined up. He dozed off that night with one worry laid to rest. There were, however, others.

One was the formations in which the attacking group flew. Each commander was free to devise his own tactics. Wing Command headquarters sent orders down on the rallying point, but beyond that it was up to the groups to link up and proceed to the target. LeMay's four squadrons had never had the opportunity to fly in formation together, and the first attempt was a complete debacle. The eager but green young pilots were all over the sky, simply too inexperienced to manage what was intended. It was back to the drawing board for Curt and another sleepless night. The next time they took off he was in the top turret of the lead plane, mike in hand. Like a ringmaster, he placed each plane in the formation: one fifty feet to the rear above, one the same distance below, and then another three-ship element behind the first. This made up the lead squadron. Behind it and above, the second squadron, and below and behind it the third, eighteen planes in all. It was a box formation, not only easy for inexperienced crews to fly, but also—more important—tight and effective in its defensive firepower. Its one drawback was that, with staggered elements, each aircraft would be maneuvering to come in on the target, and the formation would lose its cohesion. LeMay had the answer to that, too, although it took longer to work out. All aircraft would drop their bombs on a signal from the lead aircraft of the group. The argument was that if he missed, then they'd all miss, but LeMay's counter was to put the most experienced crew and best bombardiers with the lead element.

On November 17, LeMay led his group in its box formation to Flak City, his crews holding straight and level from the IP to the target. The flak was heavy, but all eighteen planes returned safely. It was soon thereafter that Curt sat down with the new Wing Commander, Larry Kuter, to discuss some of his ideas.

Kuter had arrived in England about ten days after LeMay. He was coming over because Hap Arnold wanted him to get some operational command experience in a combat theater and Spaatz had offered to supply same. Kuter made the flight across in a B-24 replacement, arriving on Saturday, November 7.

Three days earlier, Generals Eisenhower, Mark Clark, Jimmy Doolittle, and aides had left London by train for Bournemouth and a flight to Gibraltar in preparation for the North African landings. Doolittle's Fortress, however, was delayed by mechanical trouble and departed the following day. Off Cape Finisterre it was picked up and attacked by four Ju-88's. They knocked out the number 3 engine and wounded the copilot, Lieutenant Thomas F. Lohr. Doolittle, who happened to be in the cockpit, took over for the wounded airman, while Brigadier General Lyman L. Lemnitzer saw to the Lieutenant's hurts with some good scotch whisky. Meantime the pilot, Lieutenant John C. Summers, took adroit evasive action, and the German pilots, low on fuel, gave it up.

None of this at the time was known to Spaatz, who made Kuter welcome and gave him a bedroom at his domicile, where Possum Hansell, Asa Duncan, and Ted Curtis were also living. Tooey kept him there for several days while they pumped him on what was going on in the minds of those back in Washington. One thing he could tell them in detail was the attempt the Navy had made to shoot down AWPD-42. Through Admiral Leahy, Ernie King had sent a blistering letter to Roosevelt rejecting the air plan. He maintained that by eliminating medium and heavy land-based bombers from the Navy's allocations, the Army Air Forces were attempting to take control of antisubmarine and convoy operations. Marshall believed the airmen had pulled a fast one on him, and even Joe McNarney's attempt to explain had not removed the suspicion. In Kuter's words, Marshall had written an "appeasing letter" to Admiral King. But Bob Lovett, briefed by Kuter, had gone around left end to sell the plan to Harry Hopkins.

Kuter's rationale was that AWPD-1 was an American plan to win the war accepted by the President. AWPD-42 was more than an update, for, having failed to adhere to the first plan with forces scattered all over the world, it was now necessary for Roosevelt to make this new effort "the Bible and the only Bible." The implementation of the "Bible," said Kuter, should be labeled "air priority." It was his belief that by getting away from numbers and letters when it came to priorities and by using the almighty word *air,* it might eliminate the tanks and the battleships being added later.

Lurking behind such thinking if not tied directly to it was the ever-smoldering concept of a separate air force, and Larry Kuter was far from being alone in his thoughts on the subject. Shortly before his departure, Colonel Earle E. Partridge, serving on the Army Section of the Joint Strategic Committee of the Joint Chiefs of Staff, informed Kuter that the Committee was considering a plan for a separate air force. It was Partridge's belief that AWPD-42's acceptance would add impetus to the idea.

Kuter agreed and wrote a draft of the proposition, which he took to Stratemeyer, recommending that Strat take up the proposal with Bob Lovett. If Lovett said okay, they'd seek Marshall's approval on giving the Air Staff permission to prepare a plan for a separate air force, just in case the long-sought dream was forced into the open by congressional action or by pressures arising from the conduct of the war. Lovett, although in favor of a separate air force someday, was not in favor of it now, and he said no. It was too tricky and complicated a move to entertain at this point, and Marshall, who was annoyed and embarrassed by maneuvering airmen, would hardly be inclined to approve what could only be viewed as more of the same.

Whether Frank Andrews was privy to the moves attempted by Kuter and Partridge can only be surmised. He had come to Washington on October 20 in answer to a cable from Secretary of War Stimson ordering him to report to Marshall. Andrews had served in the Caribbean now for two years, and he had converted a once-threatened and weakly defended territory into a well-organized, efficiently run theater. U-boats were continuing to create havoc in the sea lanes, but neither the Canal nor any land mass within Andrews' command was any longer in danger.

Andrews arrived in Washington knowing full well he was going to be reassigned. Apart from this important consideration, he was anxious to talk to Stimson about Hugh Knerr. He had learned that the Secretary had moved to silence Knerr's speaking out. In fact, in order to take reprisal for Knerr's continuing attacks in magazines, from the speaking platform, and through the guise of author W. Bradford Huie's popular book *The Fight for Air Power,* the Navy had forced him from his position with the Sperry Company. Much of Sperry's business was with the Navy, and the admirals were damned if they were going to work with a gadfly who dared to proclaim their battleships were obsolescent and their thinking on air power was impeding the war effort.

Tom Gillmor, of Sperry, got around the Navy's insistence that he fire Knerr by rehiring him as a part-time consultant. This was fine with Knerr, because it gave him even more time to continue his crusade for a separate unified air force with most of its eggs in the daylight-bomber basket. But the Navy wasn't going to stand for such heresy, and Secretary Knox called on Secretary Stimson. Although faceless brass in the War Department had prevented Knerr's numerous attempts to return to active duty, he was a reserve officer and Andrews learned in a letter from Johnny, with accompanying news story, that Colonel Hugh J. Knerr had been given orders to cease and desist his inflammatory talk or he would find himself facing very serious charges.

On the day before he departed from Panama, Andrews wrote to Knerr saying he was keenly disappointed at the action taken to silence him. "I consider our main defects in military organization for the successful prosecution of the war: the dispersal and subordination of Air Power," he told Hugh. Recently he had said the same to Marshall, pointing out "that a unified air organization coequal with ground and sea was insurance against otherwise almost certain grievous errors in strategy and in the production of types of airplanes." Like Arnold and Spaatz, Andrews also informed Marshall, "I am much disturbed by what seems to me to be the recent trend in our national air policies—that is, dispersal of our air effort."

Some months earlier Andrews, through his friend Major General Walter Weaver, had been trying to push the idea of a unified air force into the Oval Office, at the White House. Weaver's former West Point roommate and longtime buddy, Pa Watson, Roosevelt's Military Aide, was the point of contact. Through Weaver the word came back for Andrews to lay off unless he wanted to endanger his career. This did not stop him from expressing himself to Marshall on the twin-pronged issue of consolidation and unity of command, and there is every reason to believe that when he arrived in Washington in October he had occasion to talk to Larry Kuter, who regarded his former boss in G-3 as the most brilliant officer in their midst. Stimulated by Andrews' presence and what he had to say on a subject close to their hearts, Kuter and Partridge may have been inspired to attempt an end-run contingency plan for a separate air force, which Bob Lovett stopped.

As for Hugh Knerr, Andrews found that it wouldn't be necessary for him to speak on his behalf to Stimson. Old Foxy Hugh had finally outwitted the hounds.

He was in Minneapolis preparing to make a town-hall speech when a telegram arrived from Stimson telling him he was to make no more public appearances and that he was to stop writing articles on American policy and the conduct of the war. The telegram was worded in such a manner that Knerr saw a way around it. He did nothing to change his speech but simply gave it from the point of view of Adolf Hitler speaking.

When Knerr arrived back in Washington he received a telephone call asking him to come to Under Secretary of War Patterson's office. The meeting was brief. Patterson asked Knerr if he was going to stop making public appearances. Knerr said, "I am not." The next day he received another call. This one was to report to Joe McNarney's office, and Knerr figured he was on his way to hear he was going to be court-martialed. When he entered, McNarney was standing behind his desk, a faint smile flickering on his usually dour countenance. "Well, would you like to come back on active duty?" he asked.

"I certainly would," Knerr replied. "That's what this is all about."

"Come on," McNarney said, leading the way to Arnold's office. "Well, I've got him," he greeted Hap as they went through the batwing doors.

Major General Jimmy Doolittle, Commanding General of the Twelfth Air Force, in North Africa, seated in the "office" he liked best, the cockpit of a B-25. His flying combat missions with the Twelfth worried Eisenhower, but Doolittle did as Doolittle said, and Ike came to appreciate Jimmy's command abilities, as did the pilots and crews of the Twelfth. (Credit U. S. Air Force)

After Casablanca, Hap Arnold stopped in Cairo, Egypt, to talk future plans with his longtime friend and colleague "Andy" Andrews. Andrews had departed the Caribbean in November 1942 to take over as commander of all U.S. forces in the Middle East. (Credit U. S. Air Force)

Three Yanks and a Limey equal four top Allied airmen at headquarters in Cairo. Arnold, Andrews, RAF Air Marshal Sir Sholto Douglas, and Major General Lewis H. Brereton, Commanding General of the Ninth Air Force. (Credit U. S. Air Force)

Brigadier General Laurence S. Kuter, after serving as 1st Bomb Wing Commander of the Eighth Air Force, went to North Africa as Deputy Commander of Allied Tactical Air Forces. With victory in Tunisia, Arnold requested that Kuter be returned to his staff and welcomed him with the Legion of Merit for his services in the air war against Rommel's forces. (Credit U. S. Air Force)

One decision made at Casablanca was that Lieutenant General Frank M. Andrews would become U. S. Commanding General of the European Theater of Operations. Andrews set up his headquarters at the Dorchester Hotel, in London, his principal task being to organize and direct the buildup for a cross-Channel invasion of France. (Credit Jean A. Peterson)

Army Air Forces Chief of Staff Lieutenant General George Stratemeyer pays a call on the 44th Bomb Group, "The Flying Eight Balls," at Shipdam. The B-24 group, under the command of Colonel Leon W. Johnson, would soon depart for Libya and its part in the Ploesti raid. For his leadership in the low-level attacks, Johnson would receive the Medal of Honor. (Credit U. S. Air Force)

Cooperation between Allied military leaders was essential to winning the war against Hitler. Nowhere was such cooperation closer than among airmen, and particularly so with RAF Chief "Peter" Portal and U. S. Air Forces Chief in England Ira Eaker. (Credit U.S. Air Force)

Prime Minister Winston Churchill and Lieutenant General Frank Andrews greet each other following sunrise Easter services on April 25, 1943. Lord Mountbatten at the far left, British Chief of the Imperial Staff Field Marshal Alan Brooke, and others observe the handshake which was in fact a farewell. Eight days later, Andrews died in a crash in Iceland. (Credit Jean A. Peterson)

Gone with Andrews were key members of his staff, including his Chief of Staff, Brigadier General Charles H. Barth, left, who, but a few days before the fatal flight, joined Bomber Commander Longfellow to visit a B-24 base with Brigadier General James P. Hodges, right, 2nd Bomb Wing (later 2nd Division) Commander. (Credit U. S. Air Force)

Lieutenant General Jacob L. Devers was selected to replace Andrews as commanding general of the U.S. forces in the European Theater. Addressing Eighth Air Force combat officers, he lets them know that he is impressed with their record and is in full support of their needs. U.S. Ambassador John G. Winant is seated at the left next to Brigadier General Frank Armstrong. Brigadier General Longfellow listens as Ira Eaker, right, mulls over his own thoughts. (Credit U.S. Air Force)

General Devers wishing Captain Robert K. Morgan, pilot of the *Memphis Belle,* and his crew a fast flight home. Having completed twenty-five combat missions, they prepare to depart from Bovingdon for the good old U.S.A. General Eaker waits his turn at the farewell send-off. (Credit U. S. Air Force)

Royalty pays a visit to the 78th Fighter Group, at Duxford. On the operations tower, the King and Queen of England await a review in their honor. The King chats with Eighth Air Force Fighter Commander Brigadier General Monk Hunter, the Queen with Group Commander Colonel Arman Petersen, downed in combat over Holland a few weeks later. (Credit U. S. Air Force)

The royal couple also visit an Eighth Air Force heavy-bomber base at Basingbourne. Of interest to the Queen are the members of the combat crew. She talks with them as Brigadier General Haywood Hansell, First Bomb Wing Commander, looks on, joined by Brigadier General Frederick K. Anderson, 4th Bomb Wing Commander. (Credit U. S. Air Force)

Others came to call. British Foreign Minister Sir Anthony Eden mans a waist gun of a Flying Fortress and takes practice aim. (Credit U. S. Air Force)

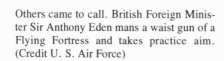

Of great military significance for the Eighth Air Force was the inspection made in late spring 1943 by the Assistant Secretary of War for Air, Robert A. Lovett. He listens while Colonel Ted Timberlake, Commanding Officer of the 93rd Bomb Group, discusses a mission with one of his Liberator pilots. (Credit U. S. Air Force)

Regensburg, on the Danube, where the Germans produced the Me 109. On August 17, 1943, a two-pronged strike was launched against it and the vital ball-bearing works at Schweinfurt. Brigadier General Curtis LeMay led 147 aircraft of the 4th Bombardment Wing, hitting the Messerschmitt installations, then flying on to bases in North Africa. The mission was a stunning success, the cost fiercely high: twenty-three B-17's shot down, another sixty unable to return to England from Africa. (Credit U. S. Air Force)

On August 17, the attack on Schweinfurt was even more costly: thirty-six B-17's downed, twenty-seven too badly damaged to fly again, and the question of target damage not clear. A second attack, by 227 B-17's, followed on October 14. Sixty aircraft failed to return, but five hundred tons of bombs struck the four main factories outlined in the photo and temporarily eliminated 60 percent of ball-bearing production. (Credit U. S. Air Force)

Major General William E. "Bill" Kepner became Fighter Commander of the Eighth Air Force. World War I infantry veteran, Air Corps balloonist, and pursuit specialist, his task was to provide close escort for the bombers and to seek out the Luftwaffe. He personally flew twenty-four combat missions. (Credit U. S. Air Force)

Major General Frederick L. Anderson, planner and strategic bomber expert, was made Eighth Air Force Bomber Commander. He mounted second Schweinfurt and knew the air war hung in the balance. (Credit U. S. Air Force)

Arnold was wearing his biggest grin. "That's fine," he said to Knerr, sticking out his hand. "We're glad to have you back."

It was mutual. Four years of Mitchell-like proselytizing were ended, but Knerr was back where he most wanted to be and where he would render great service, first as Tony Frank's assistant in the Air Service Command.

And so, although Andrews did talk to Stimson, it was not about Hugh Knerr but about the course of the war in general and the new command he was to assume, that of Commanding General of all U. S. Army Forces in the Middle East. It was rather a hodgepodge, gerrymander collection, consisting of air units and four service commands: Persian, Eritrea, Delta, and Levant. The conglomeration was to be lumped under a heading of Services of Supply USAFIME.

Since June, beginning with the HALPRO Group, the United States Air Forces in the Middle East had been flying missions against enemy targets in the Mediterranean basin. Their numbers were few, the heavy bombers a mixed bag of B-24's and B-17's. When Major General Louie Brereton came from India, in late June, to take command, he brought with him the 9th Bomb Squadron, and there had been other additions, a P-40 fighter group, some B-25's, and later more B-17's. In all, by the time Andrews took command these forces had flown seventy-five tactical missions against shipping, port facilities and, since late October, in support of General Montgomery's desert campaign against Rommel.

With TORCH about ready to be launched, Marshall was anxious to have an officer of Andrews' caliber in overall command of U. S. Middle Eastern forces, whose territory involved an even vaster area than the Caribbean Defense Command. It extended from Cairo and the Nile all the way to the Tigris and Euphrates rivers and the Persian Gulf at Abadan. Within his new theater Andrews would be responsible among other tasks for the utilization of his air power against the Germans and Italians and at the same time for seeing to the swift supply of aircraft to the Russians via the Persian Gulf.

When he departed from Albrook Field, on October 30, to make the ocean crossing, learning to fly a B-24 en route, he took with him a number of his trusted staff officers: Tom Darcy, Ted Trotman, and Major Fred A. Chapman, who had become an aide; and Sergeants Gustav Fehrn and O. T. Smith. Sadly, he left behind his eighteen-year-old daughter, Jeannie, who had remained in Panama after Pearl Harbor to work at the Air Depot. They hoped that perhaps she would be able to rejoin him at some future station, but for now it was good-bye and write often.

As Commander of GHQ Air Force in the late 1930s, Andrews had fought the War Department in an effort to build a strategic strike force. As Marshall's G-3, he had backed Arnold and done all he could to induce training and production to bring such a force into being. As Caribbean Defense Commander, he had never had enough modern equipment to guard his theater from a concentrated air attack. Fortunately, it had never come. Now he was taking over a theater in which the air emphasis was on tactical, not strategic, air power. He was to support in every way he could the drama begun with Montgomery's attack from Egypt, to be followed by Eisenhower's North Africa venture. This was Marshall's doing. He was moving Andrews from one difficult organizational post to the next.

Conversely, Arnold was set on the idea of a supreme air commander to have overall direction of air operations "from Iraq to the U.K." As Arnold had told Tooey, it was his opinion that the whole problem of air operations in Europe must be controlled and planned by one man—and Spaatz was that man. From where Arnold sat, Ike was down in Gibraltar, with Doolittle commanding the air units, but Spaatz was sidetracked, acting as a part of the Service of Supply, funneling equipment and personnel to them, and not as a strategic air commander.

Before his departure, Spaatz had discussed the issue with Ike, who had also been hearing from Arnold on the subject and was in tentative agreement. It was Eisenhower's position that after TORCH became operational, he would probably return to England—"in about a month"—to concentrate on ROUNDUP, the cross-Channel invasion. If nothing else, his supposition indicated how unwise it was to make such projections prior to a major campaign. Arnold's continuing, repeatedly expressed worry was that "we will find our air effort in Europe dispersed the same way we are now dispersed all around the world. We will find as many different bases of operations operating under as many different directives and commanders as there are land commanders. This must be prevented. . . . It appears to me," he wrote Spaatz directly after Kuter's arrival, "that if something is not done we will find the air being used more as a support for the ground arms than it should be, particularly so, when if there ever was a time to use it strategically that time is now."

All well and good, and Kuter had brought with him a new flow chart, an estimate of the replacements that would be forthcoming. But Hansell had brought a similar estimate in September, and Strat had previously sent not one but two, and none of them tallied, none of them were realistic, and none of them had been signed or authenticated by Arnold or Marshall.

Two weeks before Kuter's arrival, Spaatz had sent a blunt reply to a cable from Arnold criticizing the lack of operations. In it he had emphasized the need "for a full understanding of conditions of operations in this theater, as well as the necessity for a topside policy as to what is the goal of the air force operating in this theatre, and what will be the means placed at its disposal to include replacements." He warned that combat attrition might prevent the buildup of an adequate strike force of at least

two hundred bombers in the near future. He added that if TORCH succeeded, Eisenhower was considering using *all* of the Eighth Air Force, operating from bases in North Africa.

None of this spoke well for the future of strategic bombardment, and
Arnold could exhort, preach, and project on the theme of the need for a
supreme air commander, but without an influx of crews and planes, what
would there be to command?

The North African invasion of November 6, 1942 was an amazing and
unexpected success. Landings at Casablanca, Oran and Algiers were
lightly opposed by French forces and the fighting quickly ceased. Arnold
had told Kuter that once TORCH was launched he was anxious to have
Spaatz go down to Gibraltar and talk to Ike about a unified air command.
This Spaatz was intending to do, and early Tuesday morning, November
17, he set out. Eaker had provided a B-17 and crew from the 92nd
Group. Asa Duncan, Kuter, Possum Hansell, and Colonel Charlie Booth
were to accompany him. Asa Duncan was to fly down in the courier plane
with a duplicate set of all the necessary papers, Hansell carrying the
originals—in a heavily weighted briefcase attached to his wrist. Finding
that the second squadron of the 97th Group was heading for Gibraltar at
the same time and there would be no courier plane, Hansell stayed with
Spaatz, and the others were assigned to three of the seven planes in the
squadron, Duncan in the lead plane, with the squadron commander and
Kuter with the second-in-command.

About an hour and a half after takeoff, flying low over the water amid
rain squalls seventy-five miles off the French coast, Kuter was alerted by
his pilot that the squadron leader's plane was in trouble. The number 3
engine was trailing white smoke. The smoke became flame and the entire
engine was engulfed, the wing starting to burn. Helpless to aid, the others
in the formation saw the engine tear loose and drop into the water. The
plane quickly followed as the pilot attempted to ditch. It was not a good
landing in the rough sea, and the B-17 broke up in flame before it sank.
Kuter's pilot dropped low and circled. Through the rain they could spot
debris and bodies and saw a yellow life raft drifting off in the murk. It appeared that someone was in it. When Kuter, who had taken over the
copilot's seat learned the flight leader had no instructions for an emergency, he ordered radio silence broken, instructing the planes in the second element to drop a yellow raft. His plane, having done so, climbed to
fifteen thousand feet and radioed the details to coastal rescue in the U.K.
One B-17 remained over the crash site until it was low on gas and then
returned to Land's End. There others flew on to Gibraltar.

Upon landing, Kuter reported to Spaatz, who was momentarily devastated by the news. Asa North Duncan, more than his trusted chief of staff,
had been a close friend and compatriot since they had served in France
during the First World War. Now, unless he was the survivor in the

dinghy, he was gone.† "If North's time had arrived," Spaatz wrote to "Dearest Al," Duncan's wife, "I know that he went the way all of us would prefer to go, that is, in line of duty and in the face of the enemy. I shall miss North sorely." And so would many others, particularly Ted Curtis, who had been Duncan's assistant and would now become Spaatz's Chief of Staff.

Before Spaatz sat down with Eisenhower to discuss the organization of the Air Forces, they both decided it would be a good idea for him to have a look around. At Oran with Doolittle he found operations moving in an orderly fashion. Not so at Algiers, particularly at Maison Blanche Airport, where some of the 97th Bomb Group were based. Spaatz felt they were too far forward and that the whole operation lacked organization. He returned to Gibraltar and talked over the situation with Doolittle and Ike. Doolittle wanted to move his bombers and the P-38's of Colonel Thayer S. Olds's 14th Fighter Group eastward to get at the Germans in Tunisia. He also wanted to operate from Maison Blanche to get away from the mud of Tarfaraoui, near Oran. But Spaatz warned that Doolittle's forces were badly exposed, and the Germans proved the point, coming over at night and bombing hell out of the field, forcing a pullback of the B-17's to Tarfaraoui.

At Casablanca, Spaatz checked things out with "Uncle Joe" Cannon, Commanding General of the 12th Air Support Command for Patton's Western Task Force.‡ As Doolittle had reported, Joe had the situation well in hand—except for the mud. It was the rainy season, and Spaatz watched a P-40 break through the sod crust while attempting to taxi. When Doolittle landed a short time later in a B-17, it took four of Patton's tanks to haul it free. Spaatz sent word to Arnold that the field would require some type of cover—"any type!"—but on the whole his impression of Casablanca was favorable, particularly as to American-made machine tools and skillful, friendly Frenchmen to operate them.

He returned to Gibraltar, whose air base he considered poorly suited to the purpose it had served. Their success in moving so many aircraft via the Rock he saw as a combination of luck and efficiency. Part of that luck was due to Hitler's failure to get Spain's Franco at least to shell the exposed airfield.

During his inspection, Spaatz had detailed Kuter and Hansell to draft a plan for air reorganization. This they did, and at the same time Kuter conveyed to Eisenhower a message he had brought over from Arnold. The gist of it was that Ike should send more official requests for planes and units. This would give Arnold and Marshall ammunition in replying to continuing pressure to disperse same to indecisive areas.

The conference Spaatz held with Eisenhower and his staff lasted all

† An extensive air search was made for the dinghy, but it was never found.
‡ Brig. Gen. John K. Cannon.

through Saturday. Out of it came agreement that there would be a unified command of all air forces in the ETO. Its chief would advise the theater commander on all air force matters, coordinate strategic air operations with the RAF, and prepare future air plans.

At first Ike was hesitant. He wanted to defer action until Tunisia had been taken from the Germans. He didn't think that would take long, with Field Marshal Montgomery and his hard-driving Eighth Army pushing westward. He foresaw his own forces moving eastward swiftly, catching the Afrika Korps in a vise. However, a new letter from Arnold, arriving by happenstance at the conclusion of the conference, persuaded him to act. Spaatz would return to England and then rejoin Eisenhower on a more or less permanent basis with a small staff consisting of Craig Curtis, Charlie Booth, and Everett Cook. Spaatz would add a few others, but as he informed Arnold, he was keeping his staff down to a very small number. As for the Eighth Air Force, Ira would be the Acting Commander "until formal orders are published." It was Eisenhower's recommendation, seconded by Spaatz and approved by Arnold and Marshall, that Eaker move from PINETREE to WIDEWINGS to assume command of the Eighth Air Force.

In most of his communications to Arnold and Stratemeyer, Eaker made it apparent that he and Tooey saw eye to eye on everything. Tooey's plans were their plans. Tooey's pronouncements on the use of the Eighth Air Force—either build it up and use it strategically as intended or send it all to Africa—reflected a joint opinion, although neither really wished to pursue the latter course. While Spaatz had no hesitation in answering Arnold's or anyone else's criticism on the Eighth's lack of missions bluntly with a *get off my back* admonition, Eaker both by nature and by rank was diplomatic and detailed in his explanations. "The weather during the past month has been, by long odds, the most prominent reason for the small number of missions. . . . The directive under which we have operated limited target selection to one small geographical area. . . . Units of the Twelfth Air Force have been given first priority on organizational equipment, spare parts, personnel replacements and aircraft replacements. . . . In order to do a take-off at dawn or in the early morning hours before dawn, it is necessary to leave the planes parked at the end of the runway overnight, since the perimeter track is too narrow to taxi aircraft during the hours of darkness. . . . No single aircraft or combat crew has been received as replacement. . . . Nearly 100 of the heavy aircraft now available to this command are in the hands of units not yet operational. . . . The 44th Group has been here three weeks and it has not yet received any of its transport or bombing handling equipment and is still short of much of its administrative organizational equipment. . . ."

Eaker's recitation of facts was fully understood by Spaatz and those on the scene, whereas those far distant were apt to be harsher in their judgment, impatient to prove in action what they had been preaching in the councils of the mighty. In a personal letter to Arnold, Ira admitted that he and Tooey could load up bombers as fast as they arrived and send them out, but it would be suicide, he said, and daylight bombardment would be ruined forever. "Please don't let anyone get the idea we are hesitant, fearful, laggard or lazy," he advised. "Every human thing is being done every day to make this pace as fast as possible."

Anxious as he was, Arnold backed off for the moment. Unable to send the personnel and equipment Eaker so badly needed, he focused on a subject they both knew well: public relations. He was sending over First Lieutenant Tex McCrary, former editorial chief of the New York *Daily Mirror,* to aid in selling the potentials of air power. He suggested that Ira go on the air once a week in a broadcast to the folks at home to give a roundup of the air war. He felt such a weekly report would attract more attention than any news commentator. His sole desire, he said, was to present facts. If nothing else, the suggestion illustrated how far Washington was from the realities facing Eaker in England.

Shortly after Kuter's arrival, Spaatz had taken him out to High Wycombe to talk with Eaker and Harris, and now, upon his return from Gibraltar, Kuter again sat down with Ira. They discussed the state of combat operations and the part Kuter was to play in them. Eaker confided that he had given a great deal of thought to speeding up operations by sending his meager forces out in bad weather, but measured against doubtful results and obviously higher losses, he was determined to hew to a step-by-step policy. He was convinced that the course being followed was the correct one. He could not brush aside the limiting factors, and he was convinced that his group commanders and his reduced staff were working at maximum. He repeated that he didn't think it was very wise to try to conduct operations from Washington. As long as he was left in command, he would use his best judgment, and that was that.

As for Kuter, he was checked out in B-17's, and bombardment was his specialty. Ira was going to send him up to Brampton Grange to take over from Newt Longfellow as Commanding Officer of the 1st Wing. Longfellow was going to become Bomber Commander. This, then, was where Kuter would get the combat command experience Arnold was anxious for him to receive.

In spite of all that Kuter had been told about the difficulties at hand, he found them worse than anything he had anticipated. What he had at his command were five understrength groups—a squadron of B-24's loaned to RAF Coastal Command, another squadron detached for intruder operations. Three of the groups were living under less than ideal conditions. Only Colonel Stanley L. Wray's 91st Group, at Bassingbourn, had decent accommodations. The fall and winter rains had coated all else—inside and out—in mud. Mud was the cake frosting on the goddamned English weather!

The tower would call to the pilot, "Can you see the runway lights?"

"See them, Hell! I can't even see the copilot," was the standard reply.

Kuter was naturally anxious to start sending his units to hit strategic targets in Germany, but for all the optimistic projections put down on paper, it was out of the question, and not only because the submarine pens were the principal target. From where he viewed his command, the bomber crews had been "very very poorly trained." When he visited bases and watched squadrons and groups try to fly in formation, he had trouble knowing they were in formation. It was necessary for him to meet with RAF Fighter Command on several occasions over complaints that Spitfire pilots were being shot down and shot at by the bomber crews, who in turn maintained they were being shot at by their escorts. Feelings ran strong and hard, and he also found it necessary to get bomber and fighter commanding officers together, preferably over a bottle.

His five group commanders were Curtiss LeMay, Stanley Wray, Jimmy Wallace, Frank Robinson, and Chip Overacker. Overacker's 306th Group was the most experienced of them, having flown its first mission on October 9. Wray's 91st had gotten its baptism a month later at ten thousand feet over St. Nazaire, all but one of its aircraft suffering flak damage. LeMay and Wallace had led their groups against the same target on November 17. Since then only three missions had been flown, all against the submarine pens.

In the regular sessions Kuter held with his commanders and their staffs, each put forward his own ideas on methods to improve defenses and bombing capabilities, but it was LeMay's experiments on building formations that could beat back German fighter attacks that appealed to him most. The staggered three-plane unit within the squadron and staggered squadrons within the group made good sense, as did LeMay's idea of all bombs being dropped on signal from the lead bombardier. The others were not so keen on the latter idea, arguing at length that if the leader's bombs were off target, all bombs would be off target. The converse was that if the leader's bombs were *on* target, the result would be total, the devastation concentrated.

Because of the weather, they had plenty of time to debate the idea and ponder ways to fight off the German tactic of the head-on attack, pioneered by Egon Mayer, a noted fighter ace commanding Gruppe III of Jagdgeschwader. Mayer recognized that both the B-17 and the B-24, with all their firepower, were vulnerable to a head-on approach, and although it was an extremely dicey way to come in, with the closure rate so fast it took split-second timing and only an instant to fire, he put his plan to work with harsh effect.

On November 23, for the fifth time in two weeks, St. Nazaire was the primary target. A force of fifty-eight heavies from three groups set out, and due to weather and aborts only thirty-six reached the target area. Here Mayer and his *Gruppe* were waiting. They struck in elements of three, coming straight in, their cannon fire ripping through the small formations. In all, they downed five aircraft, taking with them two squadron leaders as well as Wray's chief bombardier, lead navigator, and gunnery officer. Most of the other aircraft suffered battle damage; only LeMay's units returned to Chelveston unscarred.

All knew that the answer to repelling Mayer's tactics was to install a power-operated gun turret in the nose. Word was sent home accordingly with the knowledge that it was going to be a helluva long time before they could expect the needed modification. Meantime, they must improvise with what they had, and Kuter encouraged each group to go at it. Because of the plane's construction, the best that could be hoped for was the installation of a single .50-caliber to replace one of the less than efficient hand-held twin .30's. Two enterprising staff sergeants in Overacker's 367th Squadron, Jim Green and Ben Marcilonis, came up with that welcome answer. It was adopted by the Eighth's Air Service Command with Eaker's approval, so that eventually all B-17's were modified accordingly. This was not the answer, of course, only a method of fighting back.

The cockpit was terribly vulnerable, and so were the engines; Kuter learned that pilots were developing their own avoidance technique. It, too, was a matter of split-second timing. As the FW's bored in, seen as no more than a needle-like glint in the sky, a flame-pointed arrow, the pilot sharply dropped the nose of his aircraft, losing enough altitude, if timed correctly, to throw off the attacker's aim. Timing was everything while the contestants gathered within them the sum total of their energies in equal determination to outwit each other in their brief and deadly encounters.

Monk Hunter, Fighter Commander, World War I ace, pursuit specialist, with magnificent black mustache, observed the ballet from the flight deck of a B-17. He was there because he wanted to know what a bomber mission was like and because he wanted the bomber boys to know that the head man of the fighters was with them in body as well as in spirit. At one point he wasn't so sure about the former. Through the windshield he saw the FW's come knifing in, saw the ugly, bright wink of their fire, felt the Fort dip evasively, and then felt as though all the sound and fury of the nether regions had been unleashed upon him five miles in the air.

There was a thunderous roar, a rushing and a howling and a tugging. Maps and unanchored papers and objects went swirling upward, and he was hanging on to keep from swirling upward too, sure they had taken a cannon shot in the cockpit. Overhead, through a large, furrowing rent, he glimpsed the blue above. The pilot pulled off his mask and filled the windblown flight deck with some blue of his own. The copilot observed the damage and shook his head in wonder. And then Hunter realized they were not suffering the work of the enemy but that of the top turret gunner, who, in his eagerness, had somehow managed to shoot the top off the cockpit.

Upon landing at Molesworth, Monk Hunter went back to his command with a new sense of admiration for the men who flew the bombers.

In the long month that Larry Kuter headed the 1st Wing, he developed a similar respect, but it went deeper, so deep that he was always to remember this period as a special time, unlike any other he experienced throughout the war. Part of the impact was due to the fact that he was an intellectual, a gifted planner who had dealt in recent years with aerial concepts, not with the nitty-gritty of operational command. As a staff officer, his environment had been the office, the conference room, the neatly prescribed planning papers and vaguely worded directives, the production and personnel figures of AWPD-1 or -42—whatever would prove in words what he and others had been preaching for years. Washington headquarters was a world unto itself, where work pressures could kill a man and sometimes did but usually left nothing more painful than an ulcer, where pecking order and social custom prevailed, and where frustration over the stupidity of others was the common complaint, and a less than excellent efficiency rating was the only real danger.

The world of combat operations was different. Like the mud on the barracks and mess-hall floors, it encompassed only cold realities. And although from his somewhat remote position of command Kuter did not face the ultimate reality of flying on a combat mission, his perception was such that he could sense the gut-empty feelings that rode with the crews out to the hard stands on an undigested breakfast of powdered eggs. He could see them climb on board the waiting bird . . . or he could see them not climb on board at all but see them simply waiting . . . waiting . . . waiting.

December was a month of waiting. Crews awakened at 0300, getting steamed up for a six o'clock takeoff. . . . Briefing. The cigarette smoke forms its own cloud layers in the closely packed Quonset hut. The Weather Officer, flushed with the importance of his isobars, declares the targets obscured by cloud . . . by ice . . . by fog. At the squadron level Ira Eaker's words of explanation to higher authority do not intrude, but attempt to give reasons: "At present time our aircraft are being used for daylight missions only. This means when a target is four hours distant, that we have but about two hours daylight during which it can be struck."

Cancel the mission. Unload the bombs, the guns. . . . Next day, try again.

Kuter saw mission after mission called, briefed, scrubbed, and knew the psychological impact upon the men—the flight crews, the ground crews, all those concerned—of being yo-yoed by the weather day after day. It was brutal. In a sense it was harder than combat, because once you were engaged the icy grip of fear was husked away in the slipstream, and the mind and spirit became locked on the ultimate reality.

"We were getting along all right until the flak caught up with us and a fragment sliced through the fuselage into the ankle of our navigator. The pilot called me on the interphone to come and administer first aid to the navigator, but I was too busy fighting off enemy planes that were attacking from the rear. As soon as I had a chance, I crawled forward to the nose and found the navigator sitting on an ammunition box cheerfully spotting fighters for the bombardier, who was leaping from one side of the nose to the other, manning both guns.

"I applied a tourniquet to the navigator's leg, gave him some sulfa pills, and sprinkled the wound with sulfa powder. Three times I had to stop to take a gun and help the bombardier ward off attacks from dead ahead.

"Then the lead ship of our element was hit in the No. 1 engine and began to fall back. We dropped back too, holding position on our leader's wing. Just then an FW flashed in like a barracuda, came right between the two Fortresses, and raked our ship with cannon fire. I could feel the hits slamming into us. Word came through that the tail gunner was hit, and then just afterward the interphone went dead.

"The wounded navigator seemed all right, so I crawled back to the tail gunner. He was intact, but he told me that the ball turret had received a direct hit. I went back to take a look and found it completely wrecked. The gunner was crumpled in the wreckage. I tried to do what I could for him, but it was no use. I don't think he ever knew what hit him. I reached into the turret and fixed the broken connection of the interphone, then I went back to the nose and gave the navigator a shot of morphine to ease his pain. Then I went back to the radio compartment to man my own gun again."[5]

There was nothing unique about it, for the action was routine, variations of it played over and over again on the same selfless theme on every mission.

And Kuter, the thinker, the planner, felt an inner sense of helplessness and frustration. There were only four missions flown in December, all of them costly, the losses averaging 10 percent, the damage to aircraft much higher, their ruggedness phenomenal:

"Ten hits with cannon shells were sustained by the B-17. . . . Both elevators were hit and virtually shot away. The rudder was rendered useless. Flaps, oxygen system and radio were put out of commission. The No. 3 fuel tank was holed, the No. 2 engine went out and could not be feathered, two holes the size of a living room table were shot out of the right wing, a dangerous fire was started in the radio compartment and holes were shot in various parts of the fuselage. . . . Captain Robert C. Williams, the pilot, flying his first mission, and the co-pilot Lt. Warren

George, Jr. braced their feet and knees against the control column to hold the nose down, the pressure required calling for all their strength. . . ."

And while their crew fought off a horde of FW's, putting out the fire and seeing to their wounded and dead, the pair brought the savaged bird home with skin peeled off its wings and fabric ripped from the elevators and made a safe landing with no flaps.

To Kuter it was agonizing, for from the time of his arrival in England he believed that the submarine pens were not a war-winning objective. They were too small to hit and too heavily protected to destroy with the available ordnance. He believed spraying bombs all over France while losing aircraft that smashed little could only boost German morale. From Brampton Grange, seventy miles from London, he felt the high command was utterly disregarding the capacity of the forces available. He saw three basic errors: In the two years of frantic growth before Pearl Harbor, there had been almost no chance to develop operational training, and the crews that were valiantly battling the Germans over the submarine pens, over Lille, over Rouen, over Romilly-sur-Seine, were learning on the job.

Replacements. There were none, and the loss rate kept climbing. The empty places in the mess, the empty bunks in the barracks were a hollow, jarring daily reminder of those "who no longer felt dawn or saw sunset glow." A crew figured that at that rate of loss none of them had long to live. And yet, on every mission, off they went, and to their Wing Commander it was the greatest example of raw courage he had ever witnessed.

The third error was the primary target, and although he recognized all the reasons for its selection, he struggled to have it shifted to submarine-building yards in Germany. A team had come from Washington to work with the RAF on an analysis of operations, and he brought them to his headquarters and gave them the whys and wherefores of his opposition to wasting men and planes on U-boat pens. "They can't hit their damned targets, and if they hit them they can't hurt them. And even if they could blast one clear out of the sea they'd only destroy two submarines."

Kuter wrongly blamed the Navy and Admiral Ernie King for exerting the influence and pressure necessary to make the pens a number one priority. The acceptance had been total, and it was only now, under the conditions cited, that realization of the wrongness of the strategy was beginning to sift upward. Eaker, who had officially become Acting Eighth Air Force Commander on December 1, had told the President in September what he could do if he had a force of three hundred long-range bombers. Now, at year's end, Kuter as Wing Commander could dispatch less than a third of that number, and the last raid of the month was still against the pens. On December 30, Lorient was the target.

The decision to hit Lorient had come down from Bomber Command at PINETREE to Kuter's headquarters at three o'clock the previous afternoon. The bomb-loading order was passed by telephone, followed by a teletype field order. Kuter's staff evaluated all that was involved, prepared Wing instructions, and at ten that night the teletypes began to chatter in the group headquarters. At each group the Commanding Officer, with his operations officer, principal navigator, and bombardier, gathered to arrange briefing details to be given to the crews. Times were set for wake-up, mess, briefing, transportation, and takeoff—weather permitting! The group operations officers were on the phone to each other, agreeing on method and place of assembling, rendezvous point with the fighters, route out and back, plan of attack, and the IP's. It was all a fixed routine, its rhythm paced by the impersonal clack-clack-clack of the teletype machine.

Effective strength of the Eighth Air Force Bomber Command on this final mission of the year was 112 aircraft, 77 of which were operationally fit. Of that number, due to weather and mechanical problems only 40 reached the target, but they reached it flying the box formation devised by LeMay.

On board one of the 305th's Forts was Major Harris Hull. As Intelligence Chief for the Eighth Air Force, Hull was flying the mission to get a bomber's-eye view of the effectiveness of the effort. He needed first-hand information because by Eaker's recommendation and Arnold's order he was going back to Washington to brief the Air Staff on the feasibility of continuing a strategy Larry Kuter and others believed was wrong and wasteful.

For a time, Hull wasn't sure he was going to get to brief anyone. The interceptors came out of the sun from straight ahead and both sides. A Fort from the 91st went down in flames with a squadron commander. When one of LeMay's bombers pulled away from the formation after dropping its bombs, it was pounced on by FW's. Another plane broke LeMay's rule to stay in formation and not to aid the cripple, and they both were shot down. A fourth, badly hit B-17 made it home on two engines with one dead and two wounded. In all, casualties were two known dead, eighteen wounded, and thirty missing. To what effect?

Photo reconnaissance following the raid indicated that only 9 percent of the nearly eighty tons of bombs dropped hit the target. In the ten raids from October to January the average was 6 percent. When Hull arrived in Washington, he carried with him an impressive display of statistics, but like the report drafted by the A-5 Section of the Eighth Air Force, his presentation was caught between the need and the means with which to do the job. Writers could wrestle with wording trying to satisfy the decisions of the policy makers, trying to fit all the variables into acceptable syntax that would say *yes, no, maybe, and if,* so that if their judgment was wrong and their recommendations faulty they could still point to the imponderables:

Recommendation was requested as to the relative value of anti-submarine patrol and attack operations as compared to the same number of planes in direct attacks against submarine construction, maintenance and supply bases. The relative value of those operations depends on a constantly changing situation and is based on the whole background of the war effort.

Careful evaluation has led to the conviction that it would be impossible to paralyse the Axis submarine effort within the next 12 to 18 months by attempting to *destroy* submarines from the air. This applies whether the attempt is made by attacking the submarines at the building yards, operating bases, at sea, or two or more of these concurrently. The problem thus becomes one of control.

It is believed that effective control may be obtained and maintained by convoy air protection, supplemented by air attacks on submarines in transit and regular air attacks on the operating bases. . . .

Our recommended weight of attack is 50 aircraft per week against each operating base, a total weekly effort of 250 sorties. It is believed that this is ample to secure a very material decrease in the operating efficiency of these installations within a reasonable time. There are new blind-bombing devices which will shortly come into use and these should enable us to make attacks independent of weather at the target. Since British Coastal Command believes that they will be able to cope with the submarine menace in the Northeast Atlantic with their contemplated force and since they value most highly the even partial neutralization of the Brest bases it is believed that the combined progress will insure a drastic curtailment of the enemy's submarine effort.

To Eaker, Longfellow, Kuter, and his group commanders the figures were pie in the sky. They didn't have fifty aircraft to send out five times a week, and even if they had and they were equipped with the new blind bombing devices, where were the trained crews to fly them? The evaluation had to be aimed at some future time, for as the year ended, the campaign against the pens had not been a success, and the underlying fear was that its failure would be perceived as proof that daylight strategic bombardment was a costly myth.

The problem for the moment would no longer prey on Larry Kuter. At month's end he had received word from Eaker that Spaatz wanted him to join his staff in North Africa.* Possum Hansell took over Kuter's command and began the New Year, 1943, by going along on the costly raid against St. Nazaire on January 3. It was a bitter day with a strong wind blowing directly in the face of the attacking force of four groups. They were trying out LeMay's theory of holding a straight and level course

---

* Kuter was to become Deputy Commander of the Allied Tactical Air Forces in North Africa.

from the IP to the target. With a 115-mph headwind it was a nine-minute ordeal as the flak batteries fired their salvos in well-aimed box patterns. Three aircraft took direct hits. Over half of the aircraft involved—sixty-eight planes—suffered flak damage. In the cloudless winter sky, the German fighters had been waiting for the RAF escorts to turn back, and as the stacked-up formations approached the target, they struck, coming in head on. The two wing planes in Hansell's flight were shot down in flames. Another five were to fall, all others to battle their way home, some performing incredible feats of daring and sacrifice.

Hansell arrived back at Brampton Grange shaken by the ordeal. He considered the bombing to have been erratic, and he knew that heroism was not enough to bring destruction to submarine pens. The next day, he called a meeting of his group commanders. Out of it came the determination to establish a doctrine of standard tactics that everyone would follow. No deviation would be permitted. They must field a striking force aimed first at mutual defense, and the key to that was a single type of formation.

They decided on a variation of LeMay's configuration which included eighteen planes in a combat box, boxes staggered as to altitude and numbers. They also adopted LeMay's method of targeting, although with some improvements. Only the lead plane and the deputy carried the Norden bombsight. All would drop their bombs in salvo with the leader, and after bombs away all planes would hold their formation. They developed other defensive methods, and Hansell characterized their new doctrine "Flexible Rigidity," because they all knew the enemy would seek to counter whatever they developed. They agreed to examine their tactics after every mission, and make changes if necessary, but from now on there must be consistency and cohesion and concurrence in all their actions. They agreed, too, that a wing of four groups was too large for a single leader to command efficiently, and as Kuter had already suggested and Eaker had authorized, Hansell divided the four groups into two combat wings, with LeMay commanding one and Frank Armstrong, who had relieved Overacker, the other.[6]

There was a final consideration. Hansell, like Eaker, believed that those commanding should fly missions. Since every group commander had four principal staff officers, each would fly every fifth raid. The reasoning was that to improve tactics you had to be there, and if you were there you added that extra sense of confidence to those who were going too.

Hansell was there ten days later on the next mission, this one against the locomotive works at Lille, but using the new, uniform tactics. He was in the lead plane. The Focke-Wulfs struck on the bomb run, trying to spoil the bombardier's aim. A cannon shell blasted into the cockpit, killing the pilot. The copilot took over. The closely linked formations held together and put up a wall of fire. Only one Fort was lost against six of the attackers, with thirteen probables. The bombing looked good. All things considered, from a point of view of tactics a step forward had been made.

* * *

Larry Kuter, in his brief tenure as Wing Commander, could and did speak out on the wrongness of the bombing objective. Possum Hansell, who would command the Wing and then the 1st Bombardment Division for seven months, could and did improve on the combat tactics of the costly effort.

Newt Longfellow, as Bomber Commander, was having to operate at little more than 50 percent of assigned strength. He saw his mission as self-defeating. For lack of replacements, his dual missions to bomb Germany and at the same time build up his strength were mutually opposed. An officer with a short fuse—his men called him the "Screaming Eagle"—he could rant and rave, and did at the endless frustrations he faced.

Monk Hunter was not the type to rant about anything. When the Eagle Squadrons were making the transfer to become the 4th Fighter Group, there was the question of what U.S. rank each pilot should receive. Don Blakeslee, considered by the Eagles to be their finest fighter tactician, had been broken from squadron leader to flying officer—or from major to first lieutenant. Hunter wanted to know why, and when he was informed that during an unexpected inspection, not one but two WAAF charmers had had to bail out of Blakeslee's window, his response was, "Did you say two women? And you suggest that he become a major? Hell, I'll make him a colonel."[7]

That was Monk Hunter, but at year's end the 4th, with its three squadrons, was the only operational fighter group he had to his name. Five other groups had been taken by Doolittle off to Africa. The 78th and its three squadrons had arrived in November, with long-awaited P-47's showing up the day before Christmas. Equipped with only UHF radios and a plethora of mechanical bugs, they wouldn't fly in combat until April. Meanwhile, Hunter's very limited forces remained under the flying control of RAF Fighter Command, a condition that carried its own sense of frustration.

But it was Ira Eaker, as the Eighth's new Commanding General, on whose shoulders the aggregate of all the diverse and manifold command problems rested. It was he who had to approve or disapprove or modify the contentions and actions of his subordinates. When he had said farewell to his staff officers at High Wycombe on the first of December, he indicated that he recognized the remoteness of high command and that he was getting too far away from the troops. Certainly as Bomber Commander the distance was great; no enlisted man or junior officer was ever going to feel comfortable in the presence of a two-star general, no matter how many hours the "Old Man" had flown or how well he understood their problems. But as Bomber Commander, he had made regular visits to his bases, and he knew from past experience and what his crews were facing that in combat operations the Group Commander was the key figure in the performance, and even the survival, of the unit.

Colonel Charlie "Chip" Overacker, commanding the 306th, had all the attributes of a good group commander but one. He was too soft-hearted. He felt like a father to his crews, and they in turn thought he was a great guy. He took each loss to heart and responded by letting discipline slide, by easing up and not demanding a rigorous training program between the missions. The losses on those missions began to mount. A B-17 that had pulled out of formation and was shot down over Flak City was from the 306th. Two Forts from the 306th had a midair collision in clear skies.

With Newt Longfellow, Eaker paid a visit to Thurleigh, where Overacker's group was based. From the entrance gate, where the guard failed to rise and salute, he noted the laxness, the sloppy attire. It was more a campus atmosphere than that of an operational base. It wouldn't do. Much as he disliked doing so, because he had known Overacker personally for a number of years and liked him, he relieved him and replaced him with tough, dependable Frank Armstrong. Armstrong was the right man in the right place, and he whipped things into shape.[8]

Curt LeMay, of course, was the antithesis of Chip Overacker—the kind of "Iron Ass" who would lock his navigators and bombardiers in a room with a photographic wall panorama of industrial target areas from twenty-five thousand feet and not let them out until they had memorized every salient feature of the topography into and out of the target areas.

It was the Armstrongs and LeMays on whom Eaker's career depended, and as far distant as WIDEWINGS might seem from Thurleigh, Chelveston, Molesworth, Bassingbourn, and all the other bases, he knew it. He also knew that basic to any mission his two groups of Forts and Liberators would be called on to fly was the Air Service Command. Tony Frank, never happy in the job, had been replaced by Major General Henry J. F. Miller, a far more genial and relaxed officer.

Spaatz had confessed to Henry, who was an old and trusted friend, "I would be very concerned about departing from the U.K. and leaving the Eighth Air Force did I not have complete confidence that you and Eaker will work together in complete harmony. You have grown up on the materiel side, and as you well know, I am most happy that you are coming here to run the Air Service Command. There is no more important task to be performed in this theater."

Repairing and getting battle-torn aircraft back into the fight was Henry's job, and like Bomber Command, he was plagued by the same fundamental problems: untrained personnel and not enough of anything to get the job done on time. Miller had been a classmate of Ike's at West

Point and was eight years Eaker's senior, but Spaatz's confidence was rewarded in that their relationship was a solid one.[9]

In moving from Bomber Command, Eaker had lost one Chief of Staff,
Charlie Bubb, and gained another in Brigadier General Charles C.
Chauncey. Bubb he had known since he'd had a forced landing in San
Francisco Bay, back in the twenties. Chauncey he had known in the same
time period, when they served on the Air Service staff in Washington.
Like Miller, Chauncey was considerably older than Eaker. Unlike him or
Bubb, he was quiet and reserved, a workaholic, who had commanded the
OTU—training units—in Northern Ireland. Eaker found him to be an
ideal chief of staff.

Even though Spaatz fully expected to be returning to the U.K. in a
month or so, Eaker needed all the support he could get at the moment.
Sitting in the hot seat, as he called it, he could feel the pressure as never
before. In November he had written a confidential letter to Arnold on his
belief that the missions against the sub pens were going to be successful.
He expressed the need for the ten groups, as already stated, but intelligence reports indicated they were making progress even with the small
force at hand. He enclosed a supportive comment from Sir Dudley Pound,
the First Lord of the Admiralty, to the same effect.

By the end of December, Eaker knew it wasn't so, knew that Kuter was
right, knew that Hansell was right when he said that a major failure had
been in Ordnance, that while the bombs they dropped could destroy any
industrial target, they were incapable of knocking out the pens. He knew
also in his close relations with the RAF that criticism of the American
effort was mounting at the Air Ministry, and at 10 Downing Street. Portal
and Slessor would rally to his defense, but Bert Harris was sending out
several hundred bombers a mission to hit German targets and the deepest
raid the Eighth Air Force had managed was to Méaulte.

Eaker's sensitivity was reflected in an angry letter to Arnold in which
he described a matter he termed "a matter of grave concern to you." A
group of U.S. manufacturers had come to England, Eaker guessed at the
invitation of the British Ministry of Aircraft Production. They were wined
and dined and shown what the English were producing. During their stay,
they visited no U.S. installations or headquarters, and what really infuriated Eaker was not so much their rudeness, but their comments. When
one of the visitors arrived home he was quoted as saying that "the B-17
was not quite suited to combat in this theater and that the Lancaster was
a better bomber for use here." To Eaker this sounded like Peter Masefield
talking, for as a British aviation writer, Masefield reflected the Production
Ministry's viewpoint, "which was naturally 'thumping the drum' for their
products."

Eaker then went into a defense of the B-17 and B-24 as compared with
the Lancaster, maintaining that once the Liberator had its bottom turret

installed it should prove just as rugged as the Fortress. What galled him was that American manufacturers on a "get rich quick visit" could be "led up the garden path" by their British hosts and, without so much as a peek at anything the Eighth Air Force had, go home and criticize its equipment. He had gone to both Ambassador Winant and Eisenhower to protest, suggesting that from now on all such junkets be handled by his command.

His lengthy account to Arnold pointed up the underlying delicacy that lay beneath the surface in relations between the two allies. It worked both ways, and he gave an account of the shoe being on the other foot due to a gaffe from Washington "which makes our position here difficult." The Air Ministry had received a report put out by Arnold's intelligence people which Eaker termed "most unfortunate." He had looked it over and concurred with his own staff that it was a faulty presentation and very unfair to the British effort, its conclusions unsound. Such spearpoints needed to be blunted, and Eaker reminded Arnold that at Spaatz's suggestion Eisenhower had sent back a list of British officers recommended for the Medal of Honor. He thought it would do much to help if the awards were made.

On the combat front, Eaker told Arnold he was sending twenty-four Liberators of Ted Timberlake's 93rd Group in Spaatz's direction on ten days' temporary duty to help in the battle in North Africa. Spaatz did not send them back for nearly three months, and Eaker's entire B-24 strength thus consisted of just three squadrons—twenty-seven aircraft—of the 44th Group, based at Shipdham.

It was two of the 93rd's squadrons that had been loaned to Coastal Command for antisubmarine and convoy-protection work for a month during the critical stages of the North African landings. They flew long, essentially fruitless missions out over the Bay of Biscay. On one routine patrol, a bomber of the 330th Squadron piloted by Captain Ramsey Potts was attacked by five Ju-88's. Potts's gunners knocked down two of the attackers and damaged a third. The bomber returned to base full of holes. The RAF de-briefing officers refused to believe the crew's account, and Potts's C.O., Major Kenneth Cool, was furious with the Captain because he'd been jumped by the Germans as a result of carelessness in failing to follow orders Potts himself had written with regard to flying close to the base of the overcast. However, the young pilot's long day was made when he received in the mess that evening a cable of congratulations from Air Marshal Joubert, Commander of RAF Coastal Command, confirming the claims. Cool said the message meant Joubert didn't know his ass from his elbow, but the London press thought otherwise and gave the story a big play.

When the 330th returned to Group in late November, the 93rd joined the 44th, the two units making up the Eighth's 2nd Wing, under the command of Brigadier General James F. Hodges. Finally, with three squadrons of the 93rd, which became known as "The Travelling Circus," gone south to Africa, the 44th, "The Flying Eightballs," was the only Liberator Group remaining to Eaker.

The 44th, under the command of Colonel Frank H. Robinson, had flown its first operational mission, a diversion, on November 7, and by the end of the year had taken part in half a dozen missions. Its three squadrons had been badgered by a host of gremlins: inadequate flying gear, mechanical bugs causing a high abort rate, casualties, and combat damage. But it was the January 3 raid on St. Nazaire that topped the hard-luck list. Only eight of the 44th's planes reached the target. They escaped the flak, and on the return followed a B-17 group out to sea. It was too far out, the B-17 navigators off course, and the B-24's were low on fuel, purposely reduced in order to hold formation with the lighter, faster Fortresses. The result was that three of the eight were forced to crashland on the English coast at the cost of two killed and others injured. To the 44th, the worst part of the snafu was that Colonel Robinson, who, like Overacker, was extremely popular with his men, was relieved by Longfellow with Eaker's approval and replaced by Colonel Leon W. Johnson, who was not at all welcome.†[10]

B-24 crews had the feeling that they were considered poor relations to the B-17's by both the American and the British press. Fortress attacks received a big play, with scarcely a mention of the Liberators, so few in number and so beset by misfortune that the 44th was referred to by the B-17 crews as "that hard-luck group."

From where Eaker sat, their hard luck was his, their losses his, the need to improve combat effectiveness his. Toward this last, he had in late November assigned a squadron of B-24's to work with the RAF in equipping their aircraft with the electronic device Gee. With training, Gee would make it possible for the B-24's to conduct bombing raids in bad weather. These were called intruder, or moling, missions, and bad weather was a must. Because each mission was flown by a single aircraft, its primary purpose was not so much to destroy a target as it was to disrupt industrial production by alerting German warning systems and forcing the workers off their jobs.

Captain Bill Cowart, who had happily handed over his job as Eaker's aide to Captain Jim Parton, was assigned to command the intruder squadron, and by mid-December was ready to try some moling. But then, incredibly enough, the weather refused to cooperate. While cloud cover was less than satisfactory for daylight bombing, it was not sufficient to risk secret electronic navigational equipment over Europe, and the three attempts to fly intruder missions in January were all canceled due to im-

† Colonel Johnson won the Medal of Honor for leading the raid on Ploesti on Aug. 1, 1943.

proving weather conditions. To Cowart and his fellow moles, as well as to Eaker, the irony was wicked.‡

But Eaker was particularly interested in a more sophisticated British invention, called H2S. It was in fact the first airborne radar, and through the overcast its cathode ray could reflect the shadowy image of the earth below. It meant, of course, a giant step had been taken toward bombing through cloud cover. Added to it was Oboe, a twin-beam device similar to but far more advanced than the beam the Germans had used over England. The beams were transmitted from ground stations, and where they intersected, bombs were dropped. The RAF proved Oboe's accuracy in night raids over Lorient and St. Nazaire during December. Its major drawback was that, due to the earth's curvature, the beams were limited in length and only extended as far as the Ruhr.[11]

Eaker was extremely interested in both H2S and Oboe, and in response to a paper submitted to Longfellow by Hansell on future bombing operations, he indicated his thinking:

> . . . I believe we must carefully husband our forces until our flow of replacement aircraft and crews is greatly increased. On the other hand I am quite certain that we cannot discontinue operations. This means that we must, not only in target selection, but by the employment of surprise and improvement in operational methods, accomplish this economy of force. I am concerned that we fly better formations, varying the altitude to the target, employ to a greater extent evasive actions, approach our targets unobserved or undetected from the sea, at low altitude, climbing as late as possible to a proper bombing altitude; and that we employ to the fullest extent as soon as possible all the late instrument navigational and bombing devices so that we can operate in a wider range of weather than has been possible in the past.

He instructed Longfellow to investigate at once the use of H2S, so that bombers equipped with it could act as formation leaders above the overcast. Both Portal and Harris had told him they would do all they could to help in getting the equipment on the Eighth's bombers, and he directed the staff to support Longfellow in getting it done as a number one priority.

Just before Christmas, Arnold wrote to Ira thanking him for his letters and telling him to keep sending same. He was glad Ira had seen his eldest son, Hank, who was off eagerly to join Ike's staff. Arnold admitted he was worried about operations in North Africa, because he felt the Luftwaffe was going to assemble a force of about two thousand planes and U.S. air forces were liable to "get the hell licked out of us since we do not have a comparable force." He wanted to know what Ira and Bert Harris and Tooey thought about this possibility. "Perhaps your vision along this line

‡ Moling was given up in Mar. 1943.

will be clearer than mine. Perhaps you can come closer to a logical determination of what will happen in the future than I can from my position over here," he wrote. None of them had a crystal ball, but Eaker knew one thing: Arnold had repeated himself twice in his letter on the number of enemy aircraft, and in all things it was numbers that counted.

Tooey, in a year-end message to Arnold, approached numbers from a different but equally important side: the number of combat missions a crew must fly before its tour was ended. The 97th had already flown more than twenty, other groups more than fifteen. "All of us who have visited these units were immediately impressed with their weariness and the first question the crew asks is, what will be the yardstick?" Spaatz had discussed the question with Eaker and Doolittle and the numbers they came up with were thirty missions and two hundred hours on the high side, twenty-five missions and one hundred fifty hours on the low. Spaatz predicted a decided lift in aircrew morale once the numbers were declared. He pointed out that the British had long since seen the necessity for a yardstick, and that they would have done the same thing a lot earlier, but it had taken time and missions and losses to know just what the yardstick should be.

His being engaged in North Africa had not changed his earlier view: "The one way to win this war in the shortest time and with the greatest economy is by the maximum application of the Heavy Bomber force from the fixed bases in the U.K.," he said. But, as he had pointed out earlier to Arnold, the lack of a clear-cut directive as to what the mission of the Eighth Air Force was to be, the absence of any continuity in the program, and the delay in replacements were undoubtedly prolonging the war.

Arnold was somewhat more optimistic, or at least he was in his end-of-the-year message to Eaker. He sent holiday greetings and congratulations on the good work being done. "Ira, we have got a big year ahead of us," he said, "one that will in my opinion bring about the fall of the axis." He then described the grinding down of the German war machine in quite a different context from that in which he had described in his before-Christmas letter. Now he put the burden on Eaker's shoulders to prove his *pro forma* contention: "Your bombing raids will determine to a large extent how long it will be before the morale of the German people is broken and the German Army loses its will to fight," he said. It sounded like something out of Douhet, and it illustrated again just how far distant Washington was from a B-17 or a B-24 base, where there were a total of 123 heavy bombers and not enough crews to man them, and aside from promises no replacements in sight.

A characteristic Arnold, Spaatz, and Eaker all had in common was a facility for painting the picture brighter than it really was and the distant horizon in glowing colors. That their predictions were often wrong didn't matter that much, because in having the courage of their convictions and faith in their ability to lead, lead they did. They were professionals, struggling to configure fact out of theory in the face of merciless combat and political maneuvering. While their written words might express their hopes, their actions were what counted. Early in the New Year, they and Frank Andrews would prove the point, as all they were fighting for hung in the balance.

Fourteen

Symbol

In late November 1942, Franklin Roosevelt sent a long cable to Former Naval Person in which he suggested that once the Germans had been defeated in Tunisia, "a military conference should be held between Great Britain, Russia and the U.S." He was sure Stalin would be willing to meet with them and make plans for the future.

In reply, Churchill agreed, admitting, "At present we have no plan for 1943 which is in the scale or up to the level of events."

During the next month, arrangements went forward for an Allied conference code-named SYMBOL. However, it was soon apparent that two of Roosevelt's wishes were not going to be met. In spite of Field Marshal Montgomery's continued successes against Rommel's forces and Eisenhower's getting ashore in North Africa, the Germans refused to give up their positions in Libya and Tunisia all that easily; Hitler was having reinforcements rushed in, and the Luftwaffe was knocking down a great many Allied planes. Wretched weather was another unforeseen factor. The campaign would not be over in a month or six weeks, as Eisenhower, Marshall, and the War Department had originally believed. Of more significant political importance, Stalin declined the invitation to meet with his wartime partners. He was too busy driving the Germans out of Stalingrad, he said.

Churchill was not unhappy over "Uncle Joe's" decision to stay home, for as he told the President, the Soviet view would be "How many German divisions will you be engaging in the summer of 1943? How many have you engaged in 1942?"

Marshall and his military chiefs were anxious to supply an answer to the first question while doing the best they could to fulfill the Russian demands of the second, in North Africa if not in Europe.

Numerous suggestions of sites for the conference were exchanged before Casablanca was selected. It was not a choice Eisenhower would have
made. He, too, was busy fighting a war, and the locale was well within
range of German bombers. More, there were hostile groups within the
city's population willing to undertake an assassination attempt. The day
before Christmas, Admiral Jean François Darlan, who had been cooperating with Eisenhower in an effort to assure French colonial military support for the Allies, was murdered. This, with the conference scheduled to
begin on January 14, required, as Eisenhower was to say, "anxious care
and a very considerable amount of work, not the least of which was spent
to preserve secrecy."

The conference setting was in the suburb of Anfa, several miles southwest of the city, a mile inland from the ocean. The central point was a
hotel bearing the same name, with stylish villas scattered about for the
principals, the enclave surrounded by barbed wire and closely guarded by
General Patton's troops.

Hap Arnold, traveling with Marshall, Sir John Dill, and others, arrived
in Casablanca the morning of the thirteenth. Previously they had landed
at Bathhurst, in Gambia, where Hap had a chance to visit with Brigadier
General C. R. Smith, who, in spite of military and diplomatic obstacles,
was doing an exemplary job in establishing African air transport routes.
However, when Arnold's plane came in under a low ceiling and touched
down at Casablanca, there was a lot more on his mind than C.R.'s problems in setting up ATC bases at Dakar and elsewhere. Being met at the
airport by Generals Mark Clark and Al Gruenther did nothing to alleviate
his concerns, and although finding his son Hank on duty at the Anfa was
a most pleasant surprise, his worries remained. The arrival of the British
delegation only heightened them. With Churchill were Portal, Brooke,
Ismay, Pound, Mountbatten, and Slessor, attended by what seemed like an
army of aides. For the moment, Arnold looked upon them almost as he
would the Navy backfield at an Army-Navy football game.

Since Arnold's first visit to wartime England, eighteen months earlier,
he had been vigorously wooed to give up the doctrine of daylight bombardment and join the RAF in night forays. As noted, RAF commanders,
Air Ministry leaders, members of the British War Cabinet, and Churchill
himself had sought through various indirect means to convince U.S. military and political chiefs to make the switch. Upon arriving in Casablanca,
Arnold was sure that the biggest fight he had on his hands now was to
save daylight strategic operations against a renewed British onslaught led
by Churchill. He was under the mistaken impression that Sinclair, Portal,
and Slessor had convinced the Prime Minister that the cost and results of
such operations were not worth the losses. Moreover, he was aware that
the Prime Minister had already taken up the matter with Roosevelt in
written communications.

He could foresee that, face to face, the President would accept Churchill's arguments and then bring pressure to bear on Stimson and Marshall to convert the Eighth Air Force from daylight to nighttime strategy—not precision bombing but area bombing. He saw his only course of action was to change Churchill's mind before it was too late, and he knew he needed the strongest support available. That afternoon, directly after an informal meeting with Admiral King and General Marshall, he sent word to Eisenhower asking that Ira Eaker be ordered to come to Casablanca.

While Arnold's fears as to the Prime Minister's intentions were correct, his suspicions as to RAF leaders having recently stimulated them were not. Eaker could have told him that. When he received the call from Eisenhower's headquarters on the scrambler phone, he was not aware that Arnold was at Casablanca or that a high-level conference was taking place there. But he realized the summons to come at once could only mean that the bomber program was in trouble. Actually, in a sense he had been forewarned and was able to draw the right conclusion. In his most recent message to Spaatz, he had referred to "terrific pressure" building up. He had been shown evidence of it by Sir Archibald Sinclair, at the Air Ministry. The Minister had queried him on how soon the Eighth Air Force would be hitting German targets. He then showed Eaker a paper defending the Eighth's operations to date. Eaker deeply appreciated the defense of his command, but he recognized that it must have been mounted to refute powerful forces.

Arnold's suspicions, once arrived at, were not easily removed. They were fed by more than British press reports, including the obvious conclusion that if Churchill was soured on U.S. efforts it had to be because his own people had influenced his thinking. A month earlier, Arnold had written to Portal on the need for a supreme air commander. He argued that operations in North Africa had convinced him that trying to carry on an air war against Germany and Italy through unrelated air operations from three locales was no good. A single air chief would be in a position to utilize air units from two or more areas against a primary objective. Otherwise the shotgun technique was being employed, resulting in not enough force used anywhere with enough effect, and concomitant losses.

Arnold informed Portal he was submitting his views to the Joint Chiefs, which he did, where in turn the idea was passed about and commented on. However, Sir Charles made no response, and Arnold came to Casablanca believing that neither Portal nor the British had ever bothered to develop a definite bombing program. He made this point at the first Joint Chiefs meeting at the Anfa Hotel on the morning of the fourteenth. He also stressed that in view of the planned U.S. buildup in the U.K., the Combined Chiefs should establish a priority bombing program. There was considerable discussion, and Marshall and King generally approved the idea. To assure British support, Arnold suggested that Air Marshal Harris be put in command of the program.

There were, of course, other strategic issues at stake at the Anfa Hotel, and their resolution had to have a direct bearing on Arnold's fears. The British came to Casablanca with a carefully devised plan supported, documented, and backed by a vast array of material obtained through their monopoly on intelligence. They even brought a ship, the *Bulolo,* a special communications vessel staffed with combined-operations experts. The overall purpose of the gathering was to agree on the best method to defeat first Germany and Italy and then Japan; that goal had not changed. But General Alan Brooke, who presented the British position, was as dead set against a 1943 invasion as he had been against one in 1942. What he offered was a six-point plan whose central thrust was to take Sicily once the Axis forces in North Africa had been defeated. The strategy was to open up the Mediterranean not only to shorten the sea-lanes drastically in order to aid in supplying Russia, India, and China, but also to undermine the Axis in the Balkans, remove Italy from the war, and possibly bring Turkey in on the side of the Allies.

Marshall, Arnold, King, and their handful of planners—which included Brigadier General Al Wedemeyer, Rear Admiral C. M. "Savy" Cooke, and Colonel Jacob E. Smart—had come to the conference believing that with the completion of TORCH, efforts would once more be focused on the original plan of BOLERO followed by ROUNDUP: an invasion of France by August 1943. Wedemeyer saw at once how the American team had been outmaneuvered, and referred to the British negotiators as "locusts" swarming down on them. "They had us on the defensive practically all the time," he wrote, and he attributed the British expertise to "generations and generations of experience in committee work and rationalizing points of view."

Wedemeyer recognized that since the first U.S.-British military conference, at Argentia in August 1941, the British always presented a united front backed by a wall of preparation, behind which was the unspoken strategy of assuring the continuance of the Empire. With such knowledge aforethought, the American Chiefs might have been better prepared to counter the smooth British move to dictate the strategic course of the war.

However, they had been misled by the White House into believing this was going to be a small, secret enclave: the two heads and a handful of their chief military leaders. (One original stipulation was that neither Secretary of State Cordell Hull nor Foreign Minister Anthony Eden was to be present.) The result was that Marshall, King, and Arnold—Admiral Leahy was left in Trinidad with the flu—arrived with few aides and a very small staff. As Arnold's planner Colonel Jake Smart put it, "We felt we had been duped." This, of course, was another reason why Arnold sent for Eaker, and then Spaatz while Marshall sent for Andrews.

Eaker received his orders to report to Arnold and set out the following evening in his faithful Humber. It was an all night drive to Portreath Airdrome, at Land's End, and a dawn takeoff. With him was his aide, Captain James Parton. At Eaker's request, Parton had obtained from Lieutenant Colonel Harris Hull, the Eighth's Intelligence Chief, a survey of the bombing record to date. Thus he was prepared to supply answers to all operational questions. However, Arnold's day was one of consecutive meetings, and it wasn't until they dined with Averell Harriman, that evening, that he had a chance to inform the Eighth's Commander fully on why he had sent for him.

At an informal dinner the night before, attended by Roosevelt and Churchill and the principal players, the Prime Minister had said, "This is the most important meeting so far. We must not relinquish initiative now that we have it. You men are the ones who have the facts and who will make plans for the future." Maybe so, but in talking to Harriman and Hopkins, Arnold was reinforced in his belief that Churchill was set to make the case against daylight bombing. Then, fortuitously, shortly before joining Eaker and Harriman, Arnold went for a solitary walk to take some air and mull his thoughts. He ran into another solitary walker, the Prime Minister. They walked together in the twilight and Arnold sought to impress on the British leader the need to continue daylight bombardment. Churchill did not appear to be convinced, although he was nowhere near as blunt as he had been but a few days before in a response to the Air Staff.

Sinclair had then sent to Sir Winston what the Prime Minister considered a weak reply to his critical view of Eighth Air Force operations, and he answered with a sarcastic counterattack. The Air Staff, including Portal, Slessor, and Harris, had said it believed that both the Eighth Air Force and RAF Bomber Command would be able to hit Germany by day, "given sufficient strength to saturate defenses."

"What is meant by 'given sufficient strength to saturate the defenses'?" asked Churchill. "This is quite a meaningless condition unless some idea of numbers is attached to it. By 'defenses' do you mean flak or enemy fighters? Then again, take the statement 'no one can say for certain until it has been tried and tried repeatedly.' So far they [the Americans] have not tried it at all [the bombing of Germany]. Even when they begin, the weather will make the chances of experiment few and far between. Thus it may be four or five months before the Americans are convinced one way or the other.

"Meanwhile I have never suggested that they should be 'discouraged' by us, that is to say, that we should argue against their policy, but only that they should not be encouraged to persist obstinately and also that they should be actively urged to become capable of night bombing. What I'm going to discourage actively is the sending over of large quantities of these

daylight bombers and their enormous ground staffs until the matter is settled one way or the other. It is much better for them to work in Africa."

The Prime Minister's response was full of petulance and contradiction.
He wasn't going to argue against the U.S. policy of daylight bombing, but
he was going to do everything he could to change it. He wrongly believed
there were five hundred U.S. bombers "all laid out in East Anglia," as he
described it, and after a year of building up their air power the Americans
had not bombed Germany once. This was what he stressed to Hap Arnold, but as Wedemeyer later pointed out, there was sophistry in the British leader's position, as there was error in his figures. That the Eighth Air
Force had not been able to bomb the Third Reich was due to a policy
which had compelled and was continuing to demand the dispatch of
bombers and fighters away from target Germany to North Africa.

Still, as Arnold and the Prime Minister walked and talked, Churchill
backed off a bit and agreed at least to listen to a full-scale defense of the
American position. Later, over dinner with Harriman and Eaker, Arnold
briefed Ira on the delicacy of the situation.

As Eaker had been saying for a year, a switch to night operations
would be a complete disaster. It would preclude destruction of targets of
great value to the enemy. Day bombing meant that with the RAF bombing at night, the enemy had to be on the alert twenty-four hours a day,
resulting in lost man-hours of production. U.S. combat crews were neither
equipped nor trained for night bombing, and the process would cause un-
thinkable delay. Eaker estimated that losses from crashes during such
night training would probably exceed present combat losses. In addition,
ground, air, and communications congestion in launching both forces at
night would make for an unholy mess, and one that would grow as their
strength grew.

Offensively, day bombing was aimed at destroying not only Germany's
industrial capacity but also the fighter strength of the Luftwaffe. If that
strength could not be broken, a cross-Channel invasion would not have
much chance of succeeding. If daylight bombing was canceled, then the
hundreds, even thousands, of flak batteries and all the troops organized
for daylight defense of the Third Reich could be shifted to the Russian
front and perhaps spell the difference there. Finally, day bombing, as
Eaker pointed out, was one half of a coin in which the RAF was the other
half. They were complementary. Each helped to strengthen the other and
jointly weaken the enemy. This was the way to mount joint operations,
not by cluttering the fog-shrouded night skies of England with two differing forces. Eaker's recital was familiar enough, but the delivery was what
counted, and Arnold told Ira he was going to try to arrange for him to
meet privately with Churchill, so he'd better put his thoughts in order.
The future of strategic air power could lie with the way in which he
presented the case to the Prime Minister.

The next morning, ensconced in Arnold's small villa, Eaker and Parton went to work, drawing up the case for daylight bombing, Parton supplying Hull's information, Eaker doing the writing. They had no privacy. Visitors such as Harry Hopkins and British Field Marshal Earl Alexander wandered through to pass the time of day, unaware of the urgency of Eaker's task. Actually, he had two assignments, the second to prepare for Arnold a series of reports, the most important titled "Why Have U.S. Bombers Not Bombed Germany?"* It was a very fundamental question, and Arnold needed the answers to reinforce his position in the meetings to follow.

There wasn't much Eaker could add to the reasons why. For those who were hostile to the strategy in the first place, the reasons were simply excuses for projections made and not kept. And no matter how valid the reasons, they had been caused at least in part by those who were unenthusiastic to begin with. Churchill could talk about five hundred bombers when Eaker had barely one fifth the number. And Admiral King could deride Arnold's effort to increase Eaker's bomber strength while he demanded more bomber groups for the Pacific and that the Eighth go after submarine pens that existing ordnance couldn't destroy. However, all the reasons why Eaker's bombers had not yet reached German targets by day would become academic if Churchill's mind could not be changed. Toward that end, and to present to the Combined Chiefs, Eaker wrote seventeen pages of reasons to continue his mission.

Meantime at the conference table, the overall concept of military strategy was debated. Again it appeared, as it had six months previously, that the two sides were at loggerheads. Acrimony and the smell of gunpowder were in the air. But after four days of wrangling, outmaneuvered and lacking the unified front the British put up, the American side acquiesced. There would be no second front in northern Europe in 1943—although lip service was paid to one. Marshall, who considered the Mediterranean an area to avoid, a "kind of dark hole," came around to supporting HUSKY —code name for the attack on Sicily—and the decision to penetrate the "soft underbelly of Europe," which he recognized was not soft at all. The British side, for its part, had halfheartedly agreed to ANAKIM—a full-scale operation to capture Burma from the Japanese.

Of the six points in the joint military agreement finally worked out on January 18, three were of the utmost importance to Arnold in his concern for the future of daylight bombardment. When Brooke had first offered the British proposals, he had cited the defeat of the German submarine fleet as the number one priority. On this, both sides were in full agreement. There were now nearly four hundred U-boats in Admiral

* Eaker wrote five additional reports on critical questions concerning the efficacy of daylight strategic bombardment.

Dönitz's undersea force. In 1942 they had sunk 1,665 ships, or nearly eight million tons. If sinkings continued at this rate—an average of five ships a day—it would be pointless to argue about the year a second front would be attempted.

In December, Jack Slessor had written to Arnold saying, "I suppose we must face the fact that the sub is now our most dangerous enemy, and that if we can reduce the sinkings, we are indirectly helping the bomber offensive against Germany." To which Hap replied, "The submarine right now is a terrible menace, and it must be a target for our bombers. Their destruction is one of our primary problems." He then listed four target areas: component parts, assembly yards, operating bases, the open sea. He added that Spaatz was already hitting them at their bases.

Several days before the Casablanca conference convened and a week after the costly raid on St. Nazaire, Eaker had informed Spaatz, "We are in the nutcracker for fair on this submarine shed bombing. The Admiralty, as you know, is most enthusiastic about the result. The RAF when asked by Washington were rather lukewarm." He believed the RAF attitude was to protect itself against being diverted to such targets, adding, "I do not question their sincerity in being lukewarm about submarine shed bombing, but they do think the primary task is to bomb material objectives in Germany." He, too, said he was going to do everything possible to get some worthwhile missions into Germany and that pressure from both sides of the Atlantic to do so was terrific.

And, of course, it was, and the reasons were obvious. Therefore there was no disagreement on either side of the conference table that bombing operations against Germany should be stepped up, and it became Point Four in the agreement.

Point Five addressed itself to the deferred BOLERO buildup preparatory to an invasion of Western Europe in the late spring of 1944. That invasion couldn't take place without air supremacy, and Arnold had Eaker present to argue forcefully and effectively before the Combined Chiefs that supremacy could not be gained without daylight attacks on key German industries.

Unknown to Arnold, several months earlier Portal had written a memo which he had given to Slessor. He said the time had come to work out a joint policy with the United States to defeat Germany, and that unless something very unexpected cropped up, it should be adhered to. He cited three possible policies: *A* was to build up the necessary strength to invade Europe *before* German industry and economic power had been broken. *B* was to shatter German resistance from the air before making the landing. And *C* was simply to build up strength without any clear objective or time to strike in mind.[1]

At Casablanca the conferees accepted *B*, which supported Arnold's goal but did nothing to alleviate his fears of how Churchill might now sit down with Roosevelt and wreck the fundamental concept on which U.S. strategic air power was based.

Before Arnold was able to arrange for Eaker to have a private session with the Prime Minister, Ira sat in on two gatherings—afternoon and evening—at which only airmen were present, including Portal, Tedder, Slessor, and Arnold's planner from the Advisory Council, Jake Smart. Arnold was to characterize the meeting as concentrating on operations in the Mediterranean, discussions on strategy, and the air command of the European Theater, "which had many serious phases." Afterward, he wrote in his daily diary, "Eaker here, and a big help." He would add to that point after his very determined Eighth Air Force Commander met with Churchill. The encounter took place in the Prime Minister's villa on the morning of the eighteenth, and their private discussion lasted a half hour.

Both men knew where the other stood on the matter, and both had a high regard for the opinions and beliefs of the other, but it was Eaker's job as a subordinate to convince a world leader whose mind appeared to be stubbornly made up that it was made up incorrectly. Later, in describing their debate—and as a college student debating had been one of Ira Eaker's strong suits—Churchill talked about his opponent as having presented his position with "skill and tenacity." His own position was that if Eaker joined with Bert Harris, they could drop a great many more tons of bombs on Germany and, with the development of new scientific aids, they would be able to do so accurately. The Prime Minister's second point was one he had stressed to Sinclair: that with all the months of buildup and promises by Arnold to hit Germany six months previously, not a single bomb had yet been thrown on the Third Reich, and with the weather, few were going to be.

Eaker did not attempt to refute Churchill's arguments directly. Instead, he explained how the proposed change would bring incalculable delay, all to the enemy's advantage. As things stood now, he could promise that before the end of the month his bombers would be hitting targets in Germany and with fewer casualties than the RAF was suffering. Churchill was to say of Eaker, "He stated the case for the daylight Fortress bomber with powerful earnestness and pointed out what immense preparations had already been made in England." There was no doubt the British leader was impressed even if he wasn't totally sold.

However, now it wasn't only Eaker, Arnold had to aid him in the selling, for both Spaatz and Andrews had arrived on the scene. In Spaatz's case, it was Ira who flew to Algiers to fetch him. They came back on the nineteenth, Tooey to attend a Combined Chiefs meeting to confer on the proposed implementation of a new, integrated command structure.

Andrews was asked by Marshall to be present on the same day. He had received his "Eyes Alone" message on Sunday the seventeenth at his villa on the island of Gezira, in the shadow of the pyramids. From previous communications with Marshall, he had anticipated the invitation and took off shortly thereafter. The journey was not without incident. At Gambut, a desert field, Andrews and his party switched to a B-24, with bomb-bay tanks in order to have plenty of fuel for the long, nonstop night flight. There was only one problem: The fuel pumps, whose job it was to pump gas from the bomb bay to the wing tanks, had been installed in reverse order. The result was that Andrews made a straight-in emergency landing at Oran, the gauges reading empty. He and his aides paused for a refill and breakfast, and then went on.

When Andrews reported to Marshall at the Anfa Hotel, he was still wearing his flight jacket, and the Chief of Staff's first question was, "Were you flying a combat plane?"

"Yes, sir," Andrews replied. "It was the only way we could get here in the time allowed."

For security's sake and with such a shortage of combat planes, Marshall didn't like seeing them used for anything but their intended purpose.

Much of Andrews' time was spent with Marshall. They had dinner with Arnold the first night, and the second evening they spent with Andrews' old polo-playing comrade Georgie Patton. But in between they were hard at it, nailing down the main purpose for Andrews' being at the conference to take over the command and buildup of U.S. forces in Europe. This was a decision of great importance to U. S. Army airmen—in some eyes, no doubt, greater than the future of daylight bombardment, because it had to do with the importance and immediacy of command.

As noted, Arnold, with Spaatz's agreement, had originally believed that from the standpoint of air power, operations from England, North Africa, and the Middle East could be lumped into one theater. They now knew it wouldn't work. The demands on Eisenhower in North Africa, were too great for him to also command and oversee strategical air operations from the U.K., plus the promised buildup and training of ground and air forces for ROUNDUP. Marshall wanted Andrews to take over as European Theater Commander, and at the Joint Chiefs meeting the previous Saturday he had informed the assembled that Eisenhower was agreeable to the change. Louie Brereton would take over Andrews' command in Cairo.

On the day of his arrival in Casablanca, Andrews met with Churchill and Portal. Their discussion centered not on day versus night bombing, but on the directive under which Eisenhower had operated, the one in fact he had drafted when Chief of OPD. They felt no immediate need to make changes in it. But the following day Andrews wrote a personal memo to Marshall. He repeated his stand on unity of command and described what must evolve from such unity:

> I am a firm believer in unity of command and shall work as rapidly as possible to a practical application of this principle. To this end I consider that, both for the prestige of the United States and to properly guide the

form of future action, all American forces in the European Theater should be initially under the command of a single United States commander. Within the directive to be issued to this commander can be included such general instructions as are necessary to insure full and complete unity with the British. The manner of securing this unity of action should be preferably left to the United States Commander. In this way the principle will be established that in whatever future operation is undertaken from the United Kingdom as a base, all American troops participating therein will operate under an American commander as a unit under the supreme command of whoever is selected.

Andrews also sat down with Arnold and they reviewed all points of mutual interest. Hap told him of his concerns over the future of daylight bombing and of Eaker's efforts and assistance. Later, with Arnold, Eaker, and Spaatz present, Andrews asked Portal a direct question as to the RAF's position on U.S. strategic bombing. Was there agreement on operational control? Portal replied that the RAF was entirely satisfied, that Eaker and Harris were "in each other's pockets," their coordination as close as possible.

Since Arnold was under the mistaken impression that the basis for Churchill's objections to daylight bombing had come from his RAF chiefs, he was not entirely convinced by the statement of support. Part of his doubts may have been a matter of communication. Portal was by nature a very reserved and private man. Slessor worked for him for two years and they never had lunch or dinner together, where they could have let their hair down and talked off the record. Portal did not believe that bombers could defeat Germany alone. He was sure an invasion would be necessary. It is possible that Arnold misunderstood this position as well and interpreted it to mean that the British air leader was also opposed to daylight operations.

At the time, Arnold indicated that both Andrews and Spaatz spoke with Churchill on the subject as well. This may have been on January 19, when Andrews, Spaatz, and Eaker came in to see Arnold, and afterward he had lunch with Churchill, during which they discussed operations in England. Churchill was later to relate, in considering all that had been staked on daylight bombardment: "I decided to back Eaker and his theme (which was—we'll bomb the devils round the clock) and I turned around completely and withdrew all my opposition to the daylight bombing by the Fortresses."[2] He was also to say that Eaker gave him credit for saving the Fortresses from abandonment by the United States at the moment they were about to come into their own. "If this is true," he observed, "I saved them by leaving off opposing them."[3] But he still thought he was right.

Arnold was to write: "We had won a major victory, for we would bomb in accordance with American principles, using methods for which our planes were designed." Late that afternoon, in another twilight, Arnold, Andrews, Spaatz, and Eaker strolled the beach front together for an hour, no doubt Hap thanking them, particularly Ira, for the support they had given in winning this grave and so important battle. It was a rare moment not only because of the victory but because seldom, over the years, had the four of them been together in such a fashion. And it was a fleeting moment, because never again would the four be alone together.

Spaatz had come to Casablanca to meet with Arnold and participate in essentially the same conferences that Andrews attended. Arnold had long bombarded Tooey with the aim that he be appointed Eisenhower's supreme air commander. Now Spaatz was informed that in the first long-range step toward an integrated U.S.-British command structure, Air Chief Marshal Sir Arthur Tedder was to be Eisenhower's Commander-in-Chief of Air and Spaatz would be Commander-in-Chief of the Northwest African Air Forces. Spaatz's deputy would be Air Vice Marshal J. M. Robb, and his Chief of Staff would continue to be Ted Curtis.

Privately, Spaatz did not want the command. Prior to his return to Algiers, he asked Arnold if it would not be possible for him to return to England and reassume command of the Eighth Air Force. Arnold was sorry, but the answer was no. The organizational melding had been worked out at the highest level and agreed to by Roosevelt and Churchill, and this was no time to ask for an unexpected change. What was being attempted was the "guinea pig" of combined U.S.-British operations. The result was not what either he or Spaatz had planned, but if it worked it was a step forward that a year previously not many of those at the conference would have entertained. It would mean the forging of a military cohesiveness that theretofore had been lacking.

There was another decision made at Casablanca which was to have a profound effect on the course of the war. At least it would always be so in the eyes of the airmen who helped to forge it, both American and British. Somehow the shade of Billy Mitchell should have been there when the Combined Chiefs, on January 21, approved a brief, seven-point policy directive addressed jointly to the Eighth Air Force and RAF Bomber Command.

It began: "Your primary object will be the progressive destruction of the German military, industrial and economic system and the undermining of the morale of the German people to a point where their armed resistance is fatally weakened."

To Eaker, item five had to be more meaningful than all else: "You should take every opportunity to attack Germany by day to destroy objectives that are unsuitable for night attack, to sustain continuous pressure on German morale, to impose heavy losses on the German fighter force and to contain German fighter strength away from the Russian and Mediterranean theaters of war."

Arnold's announced belief that the British had never really had a definite bombing program was disproved by the fact that the directive itself was drawn from a previously written position paper authored by Slessor. It named German submarine construction yards as the number one target and said that day and night attacks should continue on the Bay of Biscay bases so that an assessment of their success—or lack of it—could be made as soon as possible. Kuter, Hansell, LeMay—the handful of group commanders and the crews who had flown the missions against the bases—already knew the answer, but policy, once set, dies hard with acceptance from the top. However, there was now enough flexibility in the wording of the directive to permit a broad latitude in target selection, which included aircraft industries, transportation, oil, and other targets. The directive was also flexible with regard to the future. Item six stated to the airmen: "When the Allied Armies re-enter the Continent, you will afford them all possible support in the manner most effective." This left open the use of air power for tactical or strategic employment or both.

Before Eaker returned to Britain, he and Tooey departed for a four-day conference of their own at picturesque Marrakesh. Monk Hunter flew in, and in the shade of the Atlas Mountains they went over what had been and what was to be.

Back at WIDEWINGS, Eaker received a letter from Arnold with a copy of the all-important bombing directive. Arnold stressed the latitude in it and said he thought it was of the utmost importance that Eaker start hitting targets in Germany. "Was awfully glad to have the opportunity of talking with you down in Casablanca," he said, "and I think I have a much better idea as to your problems than I had before." He then added that while the conference "was more or less a rat race . . . out of it I think there is a definite understanding between the British and ourselves as to the conduct of the war in the future. . . ." Shortly thereafter he dropped a line to Tooey as well in which he reiterated, "You and Ira were both a great help to me at Casablanca. I don't know what I should have done without you." When he stopped in Cairo on his way to Chungking to see Chennault and Chiang Kai-shek, he told Andy Andrews as much. It had been a real team effort, and its significance was lost amid the ongoing, day-to-day demands of the war.

Just a year past, Ira Eaker's thinking and command experience had been on fighters, not bombers, nor had he been concerned with the ever-contentious issue of strategic bombardment. Now, against high odds, he had adroitly and convincingly defended the latter in its moment of great peril. The strong support of Andrews and Spaatz had also helped to win the day. Only by hindsight could this double victory at Casablanca—daylight bombing and the establishment of a joint bombing program—be viewed as a turning point in the war for Army airmen. That is not to say that the use of daylight strategic operations from then on enjoyed clear sailing—it certainly didn't—nor that the operations weren't misused and misdirected, which they certainly were. But through the determination and skill of a quartet of very professional airmen, the patient was saved from execution, and once saved was bound to survive and grow.[4]

* * *

If the high point of the Casablanca Conference for airmen was the go-ahead for a combined bomber offensive, the direction it ultimately took was prescribed by Roosevelt's supposedly off-the-cuff declaration of "unconditional surrender" against the Axis.

The President's son Colonel Elliott Roosevelt, who headed the 3rd Photo Reconnaissance Wing of the Twelfth Air Force, and was with his father at Casablanca, was to say that the idea for unconditional surrender came out of the blue at a luncheon just prior to a much-awaited gathering with the press. At the luncheon were Roosevelt, Churchill, Hopkins, and Elliott. The President unfurled the phrase as though trying it out. Hopkins approved, although he was still unhappy about the delay in ROUNDUP for 1943, which would now become OVERLORD, in 1944. The Prime Minister, after mulling over the thought, had announced, "Perfect!"[5]

And so the supposedly spur-of-the-moment concept of an overall policy toward the enemy of overwhelming importance was announced to the press. But the idea was not all that sudden and certainly not off the cuff, for Roosevelt had discussed the policy idea with his Chiefs of Staff at the White House a week before the Casablanca Conference began. None of those present, including Arnold, had anything to say one way or the other. They saw the decision to make unconditional surrender a policy as a political matter and therefore not within their area of expertise. At a subsequent Chiefs of Staff meeting at Casablanca, Marshall brought up the question again. Having heard from Brigadier General John Dean, secretary to the Chiefs, that General Wedemeyer was strongly opposed to the policy—as was Dean—Marshall asked him to speak out. This Wedemeyer did "with great earnestness and considerable emphasis." He felt that his first-hand knowledge of Germany might influence the assembled in realizing that such a political decision was tied directly to military action, and that the announcement of a demand for unconditional surrender would not only deter resistance to Hitler in Germany but would also only play into Hitler's hands in convincing a disheartened people that they must unite and fight on.[6] Evidently Wedemeyer's position, if repeated to Roosevelt by Marshall, made no impression, and the Chiefs left no views on the subject for the record.

Others besides Wedemeyer and Dean did not think it was so perfect. Sir Stewart Menzies, Churchill's Chief of Intelligence, was particularly disturbed. He said unless the terms were toned down, the German Army would fight with "the despairing ferocity of cornered rats." Eisenhower phrased it a bit differently—but long after the fact: "If you were given two choices, one to mount the scaffold and the other to charge twenty bayonets, you might as well charge twenty bayonets."[7]

Hanson Baldwin, the New York *Times* military expert, termed unconditional surrender "perhaps the biggest political mistake of the war." Roosevelt was to claim the thought, for it popped into his head at the press conference, but obviously it was no such spur-of-the-moment utterance. One reason for it was to reassure Stalin that there would be no compromise—no separate peace—with Hitler. The crowning irony was that Stalin rejected the policy, using political astuteness to distinguish between Hitlerism and the German people.[8]

As for Churchill's acceptance, which he was to defend later in a lukewarm manner, he claimed that at the press conference after Roosevelt had made his historic announcement, "I of course supported him and concurred in what he had said. Any divergence between us, even by omission, would on such an occasion and at such a time have been damaging or even dangerous to our war effort. I certainly take my share of the responsibility, together with the British War Cabinet."[9]

There is evidence to indicate that Churchill's lack of recall concerning the decision was prompted by something more than surprise at the President's declaration. Privately, it has been reported, he made a deal with Roosevelt that Great Britain would have authority to control and command Eastern European and Eastern Mediterranean operations in exchange for support for unconditional surrender.[10]

In whatever way and through whatever arrangement Roosevelt's decision became Allied political policy, it was Air Marshal Jack Slessor, soon to take over Coastal Command, who best described the general reaction of U.S. and British air leaders: "It is by no means certain that, had we been consulted, we would have foreseen its [unconditional surrender's] implications and advised against it, though that is not impossible. But as far as I remember the use of the words in the President's address to the press conference on the 24th made no particular impact on our minds at the time—any more than they seem to have done on the minds of the War Cabinet when considering Mr. Churchill's message. That the actual influence of the phrase on the outcome of the war, and particularly on the bomber offensive, was unfortunate, I have no doubt. . . ."[11]

In his daily diary kept during the Conference, Hap Arnold made no mention of Roosevelt's announcement, nor did Andrews, Spaatz, or Eaker in any of their written exchanges at the time. Soldiers, long accustomed to keeping clear of political entanglements whatever they thought the policy would mean to the war effort, were not inclined to comment for the record. Most agreed with Eisenhower, who, upon hearing the formula, said that, to him, of more immediate importance was the uniting of British and American troops. The airmen were concentrating not on what unconditional surrender might mean but on how best to implement the policy of Combined Bomber Offensive.

Yet when the announcement made by Roosevelt and seconded by Churchill was conveyed to an ongoing meeting of the Joint Chiefs of Staff, the news brought dead silence. As Jake Smart was to observe in an old but apt cliché, "You could have heard a pin drop."

Fifteen

Season of Doubt

Ira Eaker had a rough return from North Africa and was forced to land in Northern Ireland with less than an hour's gas—which was at least that much more than Andrews had had when he landed at Oran. Back at WIDEWINGS on Tuesday, January 26, he carried out his promise to Churchill the following day. He gave the go signal for the Eighth Air Force's first raid on Germany.

Of the fifty-three attacking planes, eighteen were Liberators. Two were lost, as well as one B-17. Frank Armstrong led the attack, flying in the lead ship of the 306th Group. The primary target, Bremen, was cloud-covered and he took the force to the U-boat yards at Wilhelmshaven. It, too, was almost obscured, but they bombed anyway, and from the after-strike photos Eaker considered the results "fairly satisfactory."

But aside from showing Churchill that his bombers could indeed hit Germany, there were factors concerning the raid that he felt were not satisfactory at all. "We are bombing Germany now," he wrote Spaatz, "with less than a hundred heavies—something you and I both agree should not be done." His total strength was 91 operational aircraft. Returning from Casablanca, he had been hit by the unexpected news that Spaatz was taking two more of his heavy groups and all 129 of his P-38's, plus the pilots to ferry them. "We had the 78th Group ready to accompany our bombers by about February 1, if this had not happened. Obviously our bombers will have to go alone for at least another six weeks, " he told Spaatz, and then added: "I think this was the most serious blunder we have made in a long time, and I have a sneaking hunch that you agree. However, when we get a bad order, we carry it out with the same diligence we would a good order." There really wasn't any choice in the matter, and Spaatz's only response was that his losses were so high that it was absolutely essential that he take the planes and pilots of the 78th Group.

There was a more cheering response to the attack on Wilhelmshaven from other sources. Bomber Harris sent congratulations, as did Andrews from Cairo, where he was now in the process of preparing to assume his new command. Arnold had told Eaker that Andrews' arrival in England would be a blessing, the kind he badly needed. Before his departure from Cairo, on January 30, Andrews had had a chance to spend an evening with Arnold, who was on his way eastward. They talked over the decisions made at Casablanca and what lay ahead. Less than a week later, on Thursday, February 4, the day after his fifty-ninth birthday, Andrews and members of his staff landed at Northholt Aerodrome, in Middlesex. Eaker was waiting with Major General Russell P. Hartle to greet them. Hartle had remained in the U.K. as Eisenhower's second-in-command and for the time being would act as Andrews' very competent Chief of Staff.

It was a wet day, and after a quick reception and lunch they drove through the gloom of English winter to the Dorchester Hotel, in London, where Andrews would establish headquarters and residence. That night he and Eaker dined together, and he learned some of the hard facts of the Eighth Air Force. The loss of the P-38's to Spaatz, said Ira, was going to mean the loss of many bombers and their fine crews. Monk Hunter was going to have to start building his fighter forces from the ground up again. They might have one new group of P-47's ready by March 1. But the real problem, Eaker said—and he said it to Arnold, too—was that they were being bled to death by the African operation. In every mission, including the one that went to Emden that very day, they were expending crews and planes at a far faster rate than they were being replaced. Of the thirty-nine planes that bombed Emden, five were lost, or 8 percent, and due to weather that froze guns and bomb bays, plus continuing mechanical problems, more than half of the planes that took off never reached the target.

Andrews, who had come away from Casablanca believing that a buildup in air power in the ETO was a top priority, moved swiftly. The next afternoon, following a scheduled press conference at which the news correspondents got their first impression of him—"He never says, 'I want so and so.' Instead his slow drawl suggests, 'We'll do so and so.'"—he sent a cable to Marshall for Arnold:

Please transmit message to Arnold important he visit this headquarters for discussion on buildup of Eight Air Force before his return to U.S. Bomber strength deteriorating rapidly to point where raids cannot be made in sufficient strength to disperse antiaircraft strength of enemy. Unless better results can be obtained US Air Forces adversely involved. Improved results are possible with more general support from fighters and larger sorties in my opinion. Press conference today showed marked interest in night versus day bombardment. Bomber raid of fourth February was not successful. Would like information of approximate arrival date.

In a follow-up cable to Arnold, Marshall told him that Stratemeyer strongly recommended against his stopping to see Andrews, that no useful purpose would be served. Instead, a reply to Andrews drafted under Stratemeyer's direction said:

> We fully concur with your viewpoint to employ present insufficient forces on daylight missions deep into enemy territory is too costly and accomplishes too little. Any decision made either to postpone effort until adequate forces become available or to use present force against targets in France and low countries or to try out light bombing will be supported here. Bombers have been allocated as directed by Combined Chiefs of Staff. Bulk of force which was set up for England and Joint U.S., British agreement resulted in sending to North Africa. Since further diversion to Africa, Asia, Pacific is considered necessary and has been agreed to, many months will elapse before sufficient force for deep penetration against objectives in Germany can be built up.

In other words, while daylight bombardment against Germany had been saved, and the directive for a combined bomber offensive made grand reading for airmen, the means to carry out the attack would not be forthcoming now, because, in the order of importance, war carried out by strategic bombardment was at the bottom of the list. The situation was at best contradictory and at worst a match for the wretched weather. Nevertheless, in the seven missions that were flown in February, four were against German targets, one against Flak City and one against Brest. Ninety-three was the largest number Newt Longfellow, the "Screaming Eagle," could put up on a single mission, and sixty-five was the largest force that reached one of the seven targets. In all, twenty-two bombers were lost, an acceptable figure if there were replacements, but there weren't any. What there were were simultaneous reaction and some famous Arnold pique, which illustrated that unceasing pressure was getting to him.

On the twenty-seventh he wrote a "Dear Andy" letter apologizing for not visiting the U.K. as requested. He said, ". . . the 'powers that be' indicated" that he return directly from his meetings with Chiang Kai-shek, Stilwell, and Chennault. He didn't think such a visit would have solved much, for he already knew from Ira what the picture was. But he didn't, not really. The day before, he had sent an angry memo to Stratemeyer which may have been a reflection of his real feelings about Andrews' cable and the situation in general:

"During the Casablanca conference," he wrote, "I was put on the defensive by both the British and the United States for not having our heavy bombers bombard Germany. First the matter was taken up by Portal, then by the Prime Minister and finally by the President. The matter became so serious that I called for Eaker and Spaatz, both of whom gave the usual and expected reasons for not operating against Germany.* Their reasons for not operating more frequently, however, seemed very weak."

This criticism hardly jibed with the compliments he had paid to both men, nor did it jibe with the facts and figures he then cited. His feeling was that "We are doing practically nothing with our heavy bombers in England" while already in February the RAF had flown seventeen raids over Germany. He felt a search of the record would show that the Eighth Air Force had made no more than two or three raids in any direction. Further, his records showed that as of February 24, Eaker had a force of 207 B-17's and B-24's at his command. With this in mind, he was wondering whether he might cable Andrews giving the comparison and saying: "I realize full well your total of 207 heavy bombers will not permit you to carry out missions which you would like but this number of airplanes cannot, repeat not, be held on the ground for periods of weeks at a time without subjecting us to severe criticism."

The cable was not sent, quite possibly because Stratemeyer was able to produce numbers that were closer to the mark. It was Eaker who informed Arnold on that same day that his total number of replacements since operations had begun were twenty-four crews and sixty-three aircraft against a total loss of seventy-five planes. The figure did not include those aircraft that had crash-landed in England or were too badly shot up to be repaired. Eaker added that there was no question "that our bomber losses will be greatly reduced when our fighters are ready to accompany us." As he had told Andrews, he thought one squadron of P-47's would be operational in the coming week, but again he was overoptimistic, as he was about the Thunderbolt's performance, maintaining that the anticipated long-range tanks "will give us the needed range for these P-47's in general support of our bombers all the way to and from the targets."

However, in his letter, Eaker demolished Arnold's criticism in his bluntest statement to date:

> The only theory upon which the failure to build up the force here is supportable, is on the ground that they can be used to better advantage elsewhere, or there is some reason why heavy bombers are not effective from this theater against Germany. As I have pointed out so many times, drawing the conclusion from our present bomber effort against Germany that heavy bombers are ineffective against them, is comparable to sending a company of infantry to attack an entrenched battalion, and then deciding from the result that the infantry attack is ineffective. There is only one thing that we require here to do the job—the job that will hurt the enemy the most, and that is, an adequate force. We have all other essentials: the

* According to Arnold's daily diary kept during the Conference, this was not the sequence of events. He sent for Eaker *before* meeting with any of the British delegation. See p. 343.

airdromes, the organization to operate them; the units; the communications; the technique and tactical employment well worked out and proven; and the proven ability of heavy bombers to survive against the fighter and antiaircraft defenses.

As to the number of heavy bombers available to attack German targets, what counted was how many did the bombing. On Longfellow's largest operation to date, one third of the total aborted because of weather and mechanical failure. This was the second raid against Wilhelmshaven, with the primary target again cloud-covered. And this time the Germans employed two new tactics: Their fighters attempted to bomb the bombers, and their flak batteries fired shells that descended amid the bombers in parachutes. Seven of the sixty-three heavies were lost.

Coincidentally, as Arnold was preparing to send his critical cable to Andrews, Andrews was writing a far more dispassionate but equally critical letter to Arnold. He began by saying he was sorry Hap had been unable to pay the requested visit. "Our air here certainly needs help. I was going to prove it to you on the ground." He then reminded Arnold that it was Hap who had once convinced the President that if air operations could be mounted against Germany on a large enough scale, they would go a long way toward winning the war. "But we are not making much of a contribution . . . when we can only send out 75 or 80 bombers about once a week. Consequently, it was with great disappointment that we received the news about the shipping situation for the next three months. . . ."

His suggestion for an immediate solution must have given Arnold and the Air Staff pause. At Casablanca, Eaker had told them that indeed two squadrons of B-17's had been modified and their crews trained for special night operations. Now Andrews went further, saying he was convinced that due to the unflyable daylight weather "we must train our personnel and have our equipment adjusted for night operations."

If nothing else, the shift in Andrews' thinking showed that when it came to hitting the enemy he was flexible as to strategy, method, and time, just so long as the bombing could be done, not only around the clock but around the year, "for night as well as day bombing."

Some days earlier, Andrews and Eaker had been invited to attend the House of Commons session in which Winston Churchill made his report on the Casablanca Conference. During it, the Prime Minister used the phrase "round-the-clock bombing," which Eaker had employed in his arguments to save the daylight side of the strategy. Now Andrews was saying, Let's do both. But a week before, Andrews had asked Eaker to give a statement to *Newsweek* magazine in response to a book highly critical of daylight bombardment. *The Air Offensive Against Germany* was the title, the author correspondent Allan A. Michie. Michie's position was, as the

New York *Herald Tribune* phrased it, "that the American Air Force in Britain is failing to pull its weight because of an obstinate refusal to abandon its dogmatic insistence on day bombing."

Eaker's response to *Newsweek* was that "well-meaning individuals who argue against day bombing are more dangerous to the Allied cause than any fifth column operating anywhere in the world."

The timing was the thing, for the War Department had Eaker's statement ready for distribution along with the reviews of Michie's book. The *Herald Tribune* was so exercised it wrote an editorial blast attacking the War Department, the Air Forces, Eaker, and daylight strategy. Robert Lovett, having read the editorial, contacted Hap suggesting that "one of the ways to spike certain of the unfair inaccuracies in this kind of talk would be to have a statement by Air Chief Marshal Portal or Air Marshal Harris or some other high ranking officer of the RAF." He added, "I am afraid the chatter may increase as Michie's book becomes more widely read."

On his own, Andrews moved to counteract the Michie attack, having Eaker meet with Portal, who in turn had his chief public relations officer, Air Marshal Peck, call a press conference at which he reiterated full RAF support for U.S. operational methods. Eaker sent the resulting news stories home to Arnold by the same courier who was carrying Andrews' letter proposing that the Eighth Air Force get into the night bombing business as well. Since Andrews had a very subtle and dry sense of humor, it could be that he made the suggestion of a switch because he knew it would raise Hap's hackles and possibly result in the action he sought. In any case, the underlying implication was clear: If you can't send us the promised men and planes, we'll be forced to change to a strategy the Michies of the world are preaching—and my God, what a fall that would be! It could have been half that and half the conviction that whatever way could be found to strike at Germany was the best way. And indeed Eaker had two more squadrons of Liberators slated for night training and operations.

In the same communication to Arnold, Andrews brought up a personal matter that would have later significance. Earlier, Eisenhower had suggested to him a trade: Eaker for Doolittle. Ike said he wanted Eaker to serve as Tedder's number one, but it was really Spaatz who was behind the move. He was not at all happy about the new chain of command, and he had gone to "Beetle" Smith and convinced him of the need "for having a high powered Air Force officer as Deputy to Tedder." He knew that he and Ira working together would assure a strong U.S. air presence, and he wrongly feared that the brilliant, low-key British Air Marshal was out to establish total operating control over the Northwest African Air Command. But Andrews was not in favor of the switch, and he asked Eisenhower not to press for it, because he wanted an air commander whom the

British knew and liked and whom he knew possessed keen organizational and administrative abilities. Ike backed off and Andrews recommended his old friend Hugh Knerr to Arnold for the job.

Spaatz had also approached Eaker on the change, and Eaker replied: "It makes me very sad that you and I got separated in this war. I do hope, however, that I can stay here for reasons which you well understand and with which I know you fully agree. Actually, there are no three people in the world I would rather work for than Air Chief Marshal Tedder, General Eisenhower and yourself. You know that. I do believe, however, that I am of most use to the Service in this theater. On the other hand, if it works out so that you can come back here to head the Eighth Air Force, nobody will be happier than I. I hope, however, to get my old job back as VIII Bomber Commander in that eventuality."

It would not be an eventuality, for Andrews had already recommended to Marshall that Eaker be made Commanding General of the Eighth Air Force and a major general as well.

From the time of his arrival in England, the bleak winter days of Andrews' command were filled with a seemingly unending schedule of high-level meetings with U.S. and Allied military and political chiefs; of inspection tours at U.S. and British ground and air installations; of luncheon after luncheon and evening after evening at social affairs—dinners of honor and the like—which had their military and diplomatic importance because they exposed him to the limelight of official scrutiny and, through the press, to the public. It was getting-to-know-you time, for he was swiftly recognized as the most important U.S. military officer in the United Kingdom, his job to head up the yet undefined and unclarified preparations for the distant day of invasion. His quiet style and relaxed manner made themselves felt, his old custom of carrying a riding crop a kind of signature.

Staff Sergeant Don Hutton, a *Stars and Stripes* reporter, would always view the Commanding General as a soldier's general. He had attended Andrews' first press conference. When the Q and A concluded, Andrews requested he remain. The newspaper, just a year old, was staffed exclusively by enlisted men, and neither Hutton nor his colleague had even been asked by an officer if there was anything they needed or lacked. After questioning the young reporter at length about the paper, Andrews smiled and said, "You come and see me if you ever have a problem," and Hutton knew he meant it.

On his first inspection tour of a dozen widely spread installations, during which his aide Major Fred Chapman proudly took note that "the airports being constructed by American engineers are built much more quickly than those done with English labor," Andrews visited Chelveston, bomber base for the 305th Group. Present to greet him and his party was 1st Wing Commander Brigadier General Haywood Hansell. Possum had heard a great deal about Andrews from Hal George, but this was his first command encounter with the General, and under the tenting of the field bakery they munched a muffin and talked bombing tactics. There would be other meetings at Andrews' headquarters and at Brampton Grange, but the effect Andrews left on him was immediate: no wasted motion, sagacious inquiry, warmth, and ease that stimulated confidence. And after the caller departed his impression remained.

Andrews evidently made an impression on a pair of young princesses as well. He was invited to Buckingham Palace to attend an afternoon party, and he arrived at the affair with Admiral Harold Stark and Averell Harriman. He enjoyed meeting the King and Queen and particularly their daughters, Elizabeth and Margaret. Because rations were short and the food being served was plentiful, he asked the children how they managed it all. "We kinda saved it up," was the reply.

In dining that same evening with Lord and Lady Trenchard, he also learned that title no longer kept you out of the kitchen, for the servants had gone to war, like everyone else.

No one could go through an English winter and not get hit by something ugly, and Andrews went down with bronchitis for eight days, Hartle and Chapman and other staff members having to take his place at the social functions. He had no desire to be ill, but huge luncheons followed by lofty evening banquets were not his style and never had been. The routine might be called the third front of the war, which the British were winning. The affairs were special to those who had the rank and position. Perhaps socializing over teacups and brandy was one way to victory, but his own preference was to see whomever he must see, and talk with whomever it was necessary to in his office or at the other's place of business. In this regard, he kept in very close contact with Ira Eaker.

At the outset Andrews had pledged an immediate intensification of the air war against Germany. "My first job," he said to the press, "is to increase the bombing of the enemy." When asked who chose the targets, he replied, "Targets are selected for us by high authority," and then added with a smile, "and I'm the higher authority."

As such, he was with Eaker at WIDEWINGS when the second raid on the marshaling yards at Hamm, 160 miles inside Germany, was the target. The network of railroad tracks at Hamm was the funnel out of which production in the Ruhr Valley traveled to centers in the North and East of the Reich. Bomber Harris was planning to plaster the Ruhr the following night, and what was involved was a one-two punch. But the weather was involved also, and the reports coming in to WIDEWINGS were that of the seventy-one bombers in the attacking force, only fourteen had made it to the difficult target, most of the others hitting Rotterdam. A twenty-two-year-old squadron commander led the small group, and later, reconnaissance photos showed that bombing accuracy made up for lack of numbers. It didn't make up, however, for enemy fighters and flak. Five of the fourteen Forts went down, against a claim of sixteen Luftwaffe interceptors destroyed.

But the raid had another plus side. Right from the beginning, improvements in crew protection had been given a high priority. In his late-February letter to Arnold, Andrews had spoken about the need to remodel the electrically heated gloves the gunners wore. Take off one and the heat was cut off from the other. Such technical problems, he felt, restricted efficiency. Oxygen equipment was still freezing up at high altitudes and there was bottom-turret failure in the Liberators. His suggestion was to send Hugh Knerr over for about six weeks. However, crew protection against shot, shell, and flak was a more basic concern, and Air Surgeon Colonel Malcolm C. Grow had come up with a flak vest, which the crews wore for the first time that day over Hamm. The vest saved at least two lives, absorbing the effects of 20-mm shell fragments with no injury to the wearers.

Two days later, Andrews was at High Wycombe with Newt Longfellow when sixty-three heavies sneaked in out of the Bay of Biscay and clobbered the port area of Lorient. A simultaneous diversion of fifteen aircraft toward Brest caught the defenders off guard. The bombing was good and only three of the force hitting Lorient were lost.

On that same day, Andrews stopped in to see Monk Hunter at Bushey Hall. Hunter's headquarters was in a converted hotel, not nearly so elegant as High Wycombe. The area was surrounded, however, by a golf course that even in the wet of early March caught Andrews' eye. Monk was not a golfer and said the course was closed. Fishing was more to his liking, and from some source he had previously sent Andy a delicious salmon. Their talk did not dwell on either sport but on the lack of fighters. Hunter, like Eaker, had lost most of his command to the Twelfth Air Force. At the beginning of the year only the 4th Group remained and, with its thirty-six Spitfires, most of its sorties out of its base at Debden were in cross-Channel sweeps with RAF squadrons or as escort to RAF light bombers. The 78th Group, which had been all but eliminated by the needs of Spaatz and Doolittle, was to be rebuilt under the command of Lieutenant Colonel Arman Peterson and joined by the 56th Group, under Major Hubert Zemke. Neither the Spitfire pilots of the 4th Group nor the P-38 pilots of the 78th were happy about having to switch to the Thunderbolt. They dubbed it "the Jug"—fifteen thousand pounds of plow horse, and after Hunter had had it tested against a captured FW 190, the saying was, "Above twenty thousand feet, maybe. Below fifteen thousand feet, never!"†

Nevertheless, Hunter planned to have the 4th ready for operations by

† This attitude changed with experience, time, and improvements.

March 1, the 56th by mid-March, and the 78th before the end of the month. But when Andrews came to call on March 6, Hunter was shaking his head. Two days earlier, Lieutenant Colonel Chesley Peterson, Commanding Officer of the 78th and former Eagle Squadron commander, had taken off with his wingman to make a sweep at thirty thousand feet. The P-47's engines caused so much radio interference that they could not communicate and they returned happy not to have met up with the enemy. The problem had to be solved before 8th Fighter Command could return to combat and start escorting the bombers.

Prior to TORCH, Hunter's pilots had flown a scattering of escort missions, accompanying the Eighth's heavies on shallow penetration raids. At the time, there had been no clear-cut formula worked out for fighter escort on deep-penetration missions. This was partially because of the fighter's range problem, partially because of the paucity of daylight fighter defenses deep inside Germany, and partially because neither Spaatz nor Eaker believed the escorts all that necessary. Even after Spaatz went to North Africa, Eaker continued with a stubborn kind of optimism to hold to this concept. Certainly he wasn't alone in his thinking, and certainly the evidence at the time seemed to support the mistaken contention that German fighters were no match for close formations of B-17's and B-24's.

In spite of the fact that there had been no bomber losses while escorts were along, an 8th Bomber Command review used the additional factors of timing and predictable weather to indicate that escorting was an impractical tactic. Contradictorily, Monk Hunter's plan, of offering support to and from the target in relays, was looked upon as hazardous, because bomber groups arriving late at the rendezvous point would be unprotected. The review stressed heavy enemy losses with few bomber casualties and generally downplayed the fighters, stating condescendingly, "This should not be construed as an adverse reflection on the importance of fighter cover in reducing bomber wastage, but it suggests that the use of sufficient numbers, say 500, or more . . . would make possible the dispatch of unescorted bombers without excessive average loss. . . . One salient fact emerges from any study of German fighter tactics against missions flown to date: no tactics have been evolved capable of inflicting uneconomical losses on units of 12 or more B-17's or B-24's when flown in close formation."[1] Although the review, which reflected Eaker's thinking, recognized that the Luftwaffe would improve on its tactics and weaponry, the conclusion was that the bombers could hold their own.

In November, Eaker had written to Arnold assuring him of the feasibility of bombing Germany without fighter cover, *providing the strength was there* (emphasis added). It was a point he consistently stressed: "Three hundred heavy bombers can attack any target in Germany by daylight with less than four percent losses." Since then percentages had begun to prove otherwise, although he lacked the numbers to really test the claim. The error in his thinking and that of Spaatz was to equate too quickly early resistance on shallow raids as opposed to deep-penetration targets that had not yet been attacked. And perhaps the greatest irony was that with growing realization of the real need for escort, the P-38 pilots who had been trained to supply it were now doing just that for Jimmy Doolittle and Joe Cannon in North Africa.

By the end of November, Doolittle's bombers, mediums and heavies, had flown sixteen missions. On all but one strike, when the P-38's were "mudded down," they had supplied escort. On that one mission, two bombers were lost. None were lost on the others. Fighter-bomber escort was made standard operating procedure in North Africa, and from Doolittle's point of view, as he told Arnold, there were not enough P-38's to do the job, and it didn't appear there ever would be.

Monk Hunter would have seconded that for any type of fighter. Now, in March, he and Andrews discussed what Air Service Command was suggesting be done to remove the Thunderbolt's bugs, and how drop tanks would appreciably increase the plane's range. Some months previously, a board back in the United States had considered the development of a new fighter, but like the board that Hunter and Eaker and Spaatz had sat on two years earlier, they had walked around the idea of an escort but reached no decision. There were mixed views about belly tanks, because dropping them at the coast of France would defeat the purpose of a long-legged escort, and they still did not believe a fighter could be designed to go the great distances the bombers were planning to fly.

By the time Andrews was on the scene, Eaker's outlook had been influenced by a lack of bombers, and he was anxious to have as many P-47's as Arnold could send him. When the first of the planes began arriving, he and Longfellow and Hunter had been assured that with a belly tank, the Jug would be able to supply escort two hundred miles beyond the enemy coast. But the Jugs arrived without belly tanks. This cut their range by at least a third and meant, until droppable fuel tanks were received, the planes could not be used for long-range escort.

For more than twenty-five years Monk Hunter had been a practitioner of fighters. Whatever else he knew, pursuit planes had been the focus of his life. And while he told Andrews that he felt the Jug could be best used in supplying high cover over the bombers, the numbers he would need to do the job—twenty groups by August—should be determined not by the size of the force to be protected but by the enemy's strength. Where that strength lay with regard to range, and just how well the P-47 performed against the German opposition, were parts of the equation. But Jimmy Doolittle had demonstrated that you got the best results when enough fighters went along with the bombers. Monk Hunter agreed with Jimmy but also believed that the way to neutralize the Luftwaffe was by sheer weight of numbers of fighters, which he did not have.

And that was the fluid situation that Andrews had to weigh in the fading days of a raw, wet winter. At the moment, no one had enough of anything anywhere. Changing moods and ideas shifted with the pressure of each mission, the tallying of losses and claims, the need to get battle-damaged aircraft back into action because replacements were as empty a promise as the empty bunks in the Quonset huts. In a letter to his son Allen, Andrews wrote: "From a combat point of view this is the toughest air theater in the business. These Germans are really first class airmen. It is the varsity team we are up against all right, every time we take a crack at the Continent. If we had more bombers here our losses would be lower."

* * *

While Andrews and Hunter were going over fighter command problems, a thousand miles to the south Tooey Spaatz was taking his ease at Marrakesh, "in a setting," he said, "which might be Palm Springs except for the filth and squalor of the old town itself." This was the first day since he had left the United States, nearly a year before, that he had "lolled about with the idea that nothing was important except rest, relaxation, and a bit of letter writing," or so he wrote to his wife, Ruth. (And to save time and energy, the letter was meant for daughters Tatty and Becky as well.)

Of Marrakesh he observed, "The conditions under which the Arabs have lived for centuries are almost the only proof necessary that the human being can adjust itself to any condition. Horses' hooves, sheeps' entrails, and an occasional slab of an edible piece of meat, handled by filthy Arab hands, and the whole mass covered with flies, are an indication that you are passing what might be called a butcher shop. Nice heads of lettuce being washed at the occasional water tap together with the weekly laundry indicate that you are passing a vegetable market. The streets are all barely wide enough for a carriage to pass through without grinding a few Arabs against the walls on either side. An occasional deflection off the street into one of the show places indicates an artistic development dating back to the year 1000, which is not only far in advance of anything the Anglo-Saxons produced at that period or even now."

More to the point, in noting geographic similarities and racial incongruities, he took stock of his outlook toward the business in which he was engaged. Nothing in the past year had changed his "idea of the air, its use, and its effect." Privately he would admit that it had taken considerable mental adjustment to switch from his "original idea of winning the war by aerial bombardment operated from bases in the U.K. to the campaign in Africa." Or the switch from the strategic to the tactical use of air power: "The successful outcome of the former," he believed, "meant the end of

the war in Europe, and of the latter, the beginning of the end." The way
he saw it, the war in the air had been successful so far from both places,
and as he took his ease, he postulated that "if air superiority or supremacy is the criterion which decides the war, then the outcome is not questionable, but a matter of time." To him this was "the belief of every aviator."

No doubt, but Andrews, Eaker, Hunter, and Longfellow had no time
for reflection on the long haul. They were caught up in the *now* of the
moment, and it, too, was filled with its own incongruities.

At Casablanca the conferees had agreed in writing that the air war
against Germany and Italy was of primary importance. Arnold had promised that new groups would be coming.

But as of mid-March they were not coming. It was a shipping problem.
It was a priority problem. It was a Navy problem. It was a problem of
supplying eight theaters. It was a George Kenney sneak play.

It was a Hap Arnold problem, because when he got back from China
and the Pacific, even though he said that Eaker and Chennault were the
only ones hitting the enemy, the diversions of aircraft and personnel had
already taken place. Also, there were those in the War Department who
did not believe in the Casablanca Directive, and they were a long-running,
everlasting problem.

A heart attack is an unexpected problem. Arnold's first hit him around
mid-March, and he had to spend two weeks in Coral Gables, Florida, recuperating. Added to these problems were the ongoing daily ones of production, training, and allocations, all fed through a pipeline with the ten-
tacles of an octopus and the bottlenecks of a clogged water system.

In England it was Andrews who set the priorities of everything that was
to come by boat, and in Washington it was Stratemeyer who was indirectly blaming him for the delays because Andrews was demanding what
was necessary to continue air operations and it couldn't be sent because it
wasn't available. As Eaker viewed it from the loss rate, "If I send over 70
and lose 7 that's 10%. If I send over 140 my losses may be 7 or 8 and the
percentage rate is cut in half."

Amid the difficulties, there were a few rays of light. Hap received his
fourth star, and in response to Andy's cable of congratulations he wrote
from Coral Gables after a round of golf with Bob Lovett:

> I know you realize what I've been telling everybody else, and that is that
> I am only the symbol which gives to the Air Forces the rank consistent
> with the organization. Toward that, you and every other individual in the
> Air Forces have contributed immeasurably—you perhaps more than any-
> one else—so in accepting your congratulations, let me pass a few your way
> too.
>
> By God, Andy, after all these years it was almost too much—I don't
> imagine any of us, even in our most optimistic moments, dreamed that the

Air Corps would ever build up the way it has. I know damned well I never did.

Anyhow, as always the best of luck to you.

The Washington *Post,* in an editorial titled "Coming of Age," gave the full meaning of Hap's letter in its lead: "The promotion of Henry H. Arnold, chief of the Army Air Forces, to the rank of full general—making him a peer of Marshall, Eisenhower and MacArthur, and for that matter of Washington, Grant and Pershing—is an official acknowledgement of the cardinal role of air power in the present war. This acknowledgement is, indeed, somewhat belated. . . ."

Additional congratulations were in order. Spaatz, upon his return from the view at Marrakesh, received word that he was now a lieutenant general, and Arnold sent his felicitations, saying he was tickled to death.

On that same mid-March day that Ira wired his congratulations to Tooey, Churchill invited him to lunch, and Eaker brought along the strike photos of the raid on Hamm. He came away from the meal feeling that "the P.M. was reconciled to the continuation of our day effort." But Churchill did say that he wanted the Eighth to bomb at night as well when the weather improved, so as not to be limited entirely to day operations. Eaker agreed, and told him that he was pressing night training and the installation of flame dampers on the bombers' exhaust stacks. In spite of Andrews' suggestion to Arnold that night operations should be greatly increased (to which Hap made no written comment), the entire effort was in the nature of a diversionary mission: few in number and meant to draw off the opposition—in this case Churchill and the naysayers. The Eighth's night operations would be largely limited to a leaflet dropping.‡

At their luncheon Eaker spoke to Churchill on forthcoming plans. The god-awful winter weather had broken, and although of the five raids flown so far in the month, four had been against French locales, the main target, of course, was Germany.

On March 18, Andrews joined Eaker at his headquarters and they flew to 1st Wing headquarters, where with Hansell they awaited the reports on the attack against the important Bremer Vulkan submarine yards at Vegesack. Actually Vegesack had been the primary target on the Eighth's first foray into Germany. It had been completely cloud-covered that day. It wasn't on this try, and ninety-seven bombers—the largest number to date—did their work. The yards were major to the U-boat effort, and the 268 tons of bombs the Forts and Liberators dropped caused "extremely heavy damage." Flak was heavy too, and FW 190's and Me 109's bored in. Yet only two aircraft were downed, against claims of fifty-two enemy fighters. The Luftwaffe tallied its own loss at seven. Nevertheless, the bombing of Vegesack, followed two days later by the third attack on

‡ The total force was two squadrons.

Wilhelmshaven, was considered by Eaker a turning point of sorts. He told the press the operation was "a successful conclusion to long months of experimentation in daytime high-level precision bombing. After Vegesack comes a new chapter."

Churchill sent a congratulatory message to Andrews, stating, "All my compliments to you and your officers and men on your brilliant exploit of yesterday, the effectiveness of which the photographs already reveal." Andrews responded with thanks, and sent his own message to Eaker saying for public consumption, "Yesterday justified our faith in strategic air action." Sinclair, Harris, and Portal telephoned Eaker their compliments on an excellent piece of work, Portal maintaining the raid was "the complete answer to the critics." And Eaker in his report to Arnold that same day gave an estimate that the submarine yard would be out of commission for three to four months at the earliest if not bombed again. There had been sixteen submarines in various stages of construction, and the PRU photographs showed it would be a long time, if ever, before they joined the German fleet.

Everyone could and did take heart from the victory. They knew it was badly needed, and if their conclusions were overoptimistic it was because they were dealing with the immediate results, and they believed that promises of growth would be kept.

At the beginning of the month, Portal had sent Arnold a reiteration of his belief in the day-and-night offensive and its strategic importance. He felt the effects of the bomber offensive were cumulative, and if they could be increased obvious military successes would accrue. He said he fully agreed with Eaker's principal philosophy in rapidly wearing down the initial scale of opposition and to press home the advantage with ever-increasing numbers against an ever-weakening fighter defense. "But it just will not work without the numbers," he stressed. In fact, that was the purpose of his message, to warn by implication: "You know how much I should regret it after all the efforts you have made and in spite of the admirable keenness and efficiency of the 8th Air Force if their efforts came to nothing solely through lack of numbers."

The major problem, everyone knew, was lack of shipping space for personnel, and Portal recalled for Arnold that, at Casablanca, Hap had suggested that despite winter weather they might go back to flying over the new groups. Undoubtedly, some of Portal's ideas were encouraged by Andrews and Eaker. In his report to Arnold on the Vegesack bombing, Eaker touched on the worry, admitting that he was a little concerned that the personnel of the three heavy groups promised for March were not en route. He had everything ready to receive the units as fast as they arrived and said he would put them into the fight in less than two weeks. But the three groups were not coming, all the letters, reports, and cables from

Andrews, Eaker, and Portal notwithstanding. They were going to North
Africa and the Pacific instead.

As Eaker saw it, Arnold had called him to Casablanca to save strategic
daylight bombardment. Although, unknown to him, Churchill was still
complaining to Portal about the lack of results, when he dined with the
Prime Minister he was reassured of Churchill's support. Where the support was lacking was in Washington, and his notable calm began to fray.
At the beginning of the month, Arnold had sent him a proposed flow
chart that foresaw a buildup to nineteen heavy groups by June 30, and
thirty-seven groups by the end of the year, but Arnold cautioned, "They
cannot and positively must not be used as definite commitments." And
that at least was a fact. Near the end of the month, over Andrews' signature, Eaker dispatched a cable warning that if the B-24 allocation promised, of three groups, was not received he would be forced to ground his
two remaining Liberator groups.

On the evening of March 26, Andrews with Eaker attended Bomber
Night at High Wycombe. Churchill was present with his daughter Mary as
the honored guests. Aside from squadron commanders, there were Eaker's
veteran group commanders: Hodges, Wallace, LeMay, Timberlake,
Marion, Putnam. Andrews decorated them with the Silver Star. Air Marshal Bottomley awarded them the RAF Legion of Merit. Sir Winston gave
a stirring talk. Eaker presented him, on behalf of 8th Bomber Command,
a gold-headed stick which he described as "a big stick" without reference
to Teddy Roosevelt. The noted British actor Lieutenant Commander
Ralph Richardson gave an impressive reading of the poem *Don't Wake
the Dead*. At dinner, singing broke out and the Prime Minister joined in.
It was a jolly good evening, but beneath the surface lay the greater need,
and Churchill phrased it in a cable which Eaker sent in a letter to Arnold.
It read: "We are dining together, smoking your cigars and waiting for
more of your heavy bombers." It was signed Churchill, Andrews, Harris,
Eaker. A not too subtle plea sent winging amid all the voices raised in
song and laughter.

It took more than that, however, to get the proper attention, and it was
Ira Eaker who picked up the two-by-four of his pen, slammed his career
down on the page, and in quiet fury attacked Arnold and the War Department with a slashing *J'accuse*. The epistle could have finished him as an
air-force commander, for aside from picturing the wretched state of his air
force, he included a bitter critique of what he saw as the misguided
policies that were affecting it:

> The current position of the Eighth Air Force is not a credit to the
> American Army. After sixteen months in the war, we are not yet able to
> dispatch more than 123 bombers toward an enemy target. Many of the
> crews who fly this pitiful number have been on battle duty for eight

months. They understand the law of averages. They have seen it work on
their friends.

The crews know why this command has never dared to set a limit of operational tours until recently. They know that we have been promised replacement crews as often as we have been promised more planes. They
have seen the number of planes dwindle until its scarcity has restricted
most of our raiding to relatively futile forays on the coast of France.

They have seen our precision bombing improve, in bloody lessons, until
they know with confidence what they can do, or could do, if they had
enough planes to run the increasing gauntlet of enemy fighters to important targets. As it is they know that we have not enough. They know that
they will have to continue battle duty even after the limit of thirty missions lately set. And they know the reason which is that after eight months
in this theater, the Eighth Air Force is still an unkept promise.

This is written in no apprehension of trouble with the crews. They are
American and they will pay for the mistakes of their superiors as un-
complainingly as the men of Wake and Bataan did. This is written as a
statement of our critical need of planes and crews with which to redeem
the promise of the Eighth Air Force while there is still time. The time is
short.

The purpose of the Eighth Air Force was, and is, to strike the chief Axis
enemy in his heart. No other American military or naval force was capable of this at the outset of the war. No other will be capable of it this year.
Nor is any other Allied force except Bomber Command of the R.A.F. capable of it.

On these two forces alone rest our hopes of bringing this war home to
civilian, economic and political Germany. On these two forces alone rest
our chances of crippling or destroying the sources of submarines and
Panzer divisions.

The Eighth Air Force was the one tangible combat partner we could
offer England and Russia. This offer was not charity. It was self interest.
For the Eighth Air Force was our one hope of helping to disorganize and
delay German integration of the fortress of Europe until we can storm the
fortress in combined operations.

This, then, was the purpose and the promise of the Eighth Air Force. It
was our commitment to the offensive idea, to strike the enemy early, with
all we had, where it would hurt most until, with our gathering strength, we
could strike him everywhere. And as it was with us the commitment to an
idea it was for our Allies a tacit pledge that this would be our contribution.

The Eighth Air Force carried in its first Fortress one more implication.
By bitter irony that one implication, that one portent of things to come has
been the best understood and the most resourcefully acted upon. That por-

tent was a warning to the enemy. He of all parties involved in the concept of the Eighth Air Force has most benefitted by its promise. For he, as we shall presently see, has made use of the sixteen months which were to have created an American striking force in Europe.

We have stated briefly the promise of the Eighth Air Force. One look at its operations board tells such a bitter story of its current strength that it is not worth wasting ink on the three digits necessary to print it here. It is, however, well worth reflecting upon some of the consequences both present and potential of this unkept promise.

To consider ourselves first, the delay in our receipt of promised planes and crews means that present crews will have to stay on still longer to break in the new ones.

For many of the individual men this will be fatal. For the larger scope of the whole enterprise it is gravely injurious. These men are the seed stock of our future aerial offensive. They are battle tested. They have made mistakes and overcome them. They have, in their last few missions, fulfilled the technical promise on which our air force is built, the concept of high altitude, daylight precision bombing.

These men should be returning now, to pass on the lessons and bring back squadrons trained in our bloodily bought experience. Instead they will have to remain, in dwindling numbers, until replacements as green as they once were arrive to relieve them. This is the most serious intrinsic consequence of our failure to receive the promised replacements. Every passing day and every lost plane adds to its gravity.

To consider the consequence of our unkept promise upon our English ally is to consider another grave misfortune of our plight. The dream of round the clock bombing remains, thanks to our numerical weakness in places, a dream. The division of work between us and the R.A.F. that was to have been chronological is in fact still geographical. They bomb Germany and we bomb France.

The few exceptions to this humiliating history only accentuate the bitter limitations of our present force. For we have bombed the fringes of Germany with gratifying success. The R.A.F. has been as generous in appreciation of our work as in the guidance and help that have made it possible. But the R.A.F. knows as we know that we cannot conduct sustained operations over Germany with our present strength. They know that we have been promised a vastly greater force. They know, too, how to read the calendar and count.

It is not only the deferment of round the clock bombing that hurts. Round the clock bombing itself would have been but one stage of the proper aerial offensive. With the German fighter strength substantially reduced (and bombing its production roots is the only course to this) round the clock bombing could give way to the final phase of employing both air forces in the admittedly more favorable hours of daylight.

With enough Fortresses to chaperone the rising tonnages of Bomber Command through a thinned out fighter belt, our combined forces could make the German look back on the SchneiderCreusot raid as a quiet day. But in sixteen months we have not been given strength enough to light a beacon fire for the R.A.F. in Germany.

To consider the consequences of our unkept promise upon our enigmatic Russian ally is not more comfortable. The Russian made no secret of his disgust at our failure to open a second front in Europe in 1942. Diplomatic secrecy like military secrecy covers many things. But whoever told Russia we weren't invading Europe last summer must have encountered some awkward conversational gaps. It doesn't strain the imagination to conjecture that he filled them with not very small talk about the bombing of Germany which we would substitute for the invasion.

Since that time the Russian has had much to think about. And he has had a spectacle to stimulate his thinking. That spectacle is the million odd tons of shipping, the thousand odd combat planes and the half million odd men who have spent five months trying to conquer Rommel.

What he thinks of this nobody knows but the Russian. But it must have occurred to him that that much energy would have dumped a lot of bombs into Germany. Within the next few months someone is going to have to tell Russia we aren't invading Europe in 1943. The Eighth Air Force is still a small consolation prize. And what the Russian will think of this nobody knows. But what the Russian does, when he is sufficiently disgusted, everyone who can remember August of 1939 knows well.

To consider the consequence of this unkept promise upon our enemy is to consider another aspect of a situation that is favorable only to him. The ill winds that have blown our bombers to every part of the compass, except the source of our troubles, have blown Germany a windfall of the most precious element of warfare. That element is time.

With every day that the western sky has shown us only the sunset of another hope, the German has strengthened the fortress of Europe.

In the last sixteen months the German has more than doubled the signal facilities and plane detection apparatus in western Europe. The fighter planes these watchdogs launch against us on the western front have increased from 420 to 831. The total operational strength of his fighter force has increased from 1185 to 1704 planes. The production facilities that have hummed without interruption beyond the reach of our bombing effort have increased their monthly output from less than five hundred to an average of seven hundred and sixty-three fighter planes for the last recorded seven months.

These are formidable details but they are only parts of the whole forfeit, the whole tragic price we have yet to pay for headlines on Casablanca and delay in England. The full and sickening name of that price is Aerial Supremacy over Europe.

Someday the Navy and Ground forces are going to ask us for that supremacy. When they have mastered the uncontested parts of the earth to their hearts' content, they may even give us back our planes to pave the way for their well covered approach to the heart of the enemy.

But neither they nor anyone else can give us back the time with which the German has tightened his stubborn grip on the Aerial Supremacy over Europe. That is the rising price, the daily increasing forfeit we have yet to pay for the unkept promise of the Eighth Air Force.

So much for the consequences of our past mistakes. The purpose of the Eighth Air Force was to strike the chief Axis enemy in his heart. It is still our purpose. With every passing day, it becomes a harder task. But the Eighth Air Force, what there is of it, is harder, too. It has learned on adversity.

It has proved that it can cope with fighter opposition in proportion to its own strength. It has proved that it can find and hit precision targets. It has proved that it can get a higher proportion of its planes back from battle, maintain morale, restore serviceability and sent them to battle again. It has proved that its intention of striking the enemy in his heart is feasible in exactly the proportion of the strength which is given to use.

These proofs are available in the records of the Eighth Air Force. With them is the plan of action for an expanded force. The plan is still on paper, as are the original promises which would have made planning at this time unnecessary. It is on paper yet for only one reason. That reason is that we have never been given enough planes to translate it into action. But this plan, unlike any of its predecessors, carries with it the authority of experience, the proof of what we have already done.

This proof has been won by the blood and guts of the 1500 odd crew men who have fought for eight months against the most formidable enemy on the globe to keep the promise of the Eighth Air Force. There have not been enough of them to keep it. There are still enough left to redeem it if we are given reinforcements in time. The time is short. The enemy is using it resourcefully. Our allies are waiting.

It is respectfully requested that the Eighth Air Force be given sufficient planes to redeem its unkept promise.

Considering the nature of Eaker's indictment, Arnold's response was on the mild side. He passed the paper to Lieutenant General Thomas Handy, Chief of OPD, with the comment, "From this you can see that apparently General Eaker thinks that I personally am responsible for taking all the airplanes that he didn't get and sending them down to North Africa. Ideas are also expressed with regard to replacements and losses." He then cited the record on planes and crews Eaker had received since November and, neglecting to subtract the groups that Eisenhower and Spaatz had taken and borrowed, concluded: "It is possible that General Eaker, even though he has 281 airplanes, thinks that he has been badly treated." To which Handy added, "Actually Eaker has more heavies than anyone. He should have them but he certainly shouldn't feel badly treated." Neither Arnold nor Handy addressed themselves to what "the heavies" were supposed to accomplish.

In replying to Eaker, Arnold reminded him that he knew full well "that I have eight youngsters mouths to feed, and that we are pushing airplanes out to all eight theaters as fast as they are ready." He patted Ira on the back, sent him a copy of the chart he had given Handy, and wrote a personal message to the "Officers and Men of the Eighth Air Force," praising their courageous efforts and their pioneering spirit. At the moment, recuperating from five unparalleled years of unceasing pressure, it was the best he could do, knowing, too, that Eaker's situation was going to improve in time. Incorrectly, he told him that fifty-nine heavies for the month of March had already arrived in the U.K. There may have been an additional reason for Arnold's reaction. He knew full well that Eaker's blunt, infuriated position report on the Eighth had to have been read and approved by Andrews, possibly encouraged by him.

In January, Eaker had moved into a fine estate called Castle Coombe, found for him by his aide, Captain Jim Parton. Outside of London, it was bordered on three sides by Coombe Hill golf course, and with the sudden wondrous improvement in the weather, on Sundays Eaker and Andrews strode the fairways, conspiring between shots. Arnold knew, and was not at all unhappy, that Andrews was a great boon to Ira.

So, too, was Averell Harriman. Roosevelt's expediter of Lend-Lease in London, the fifty-two-year-old diplomat was something more than that, for although Winant remained U. S. Ambassador to the Court of St. James's, Harriman wielded more influence and was the most direct line to the White House.

When Eaker arrived at Casablanca and dined his first night there with Arnold, Harriman was present. When Andrews arrived from Cairo and dined his first night in London with Eaker, Harriman was there. When Eaker gave a large reception for Andrews to introduce him to the RAF hierarchy, the only other American present was Harriman. Both Andrews and Eaker saw him often, and often alone. They knew that what they had to say to him was going to the right place.

That Harriman had very strong feelings in support of strategic air power was clearly evident in his reaction to a number of critical articles appearing in the magazine *Newsweek*. They questioned, as Michie had, the wisdom of the U.S. air policy and those who supported it. The wealthy administrator angrily informed Bob Lovett, "I have not supported

Newsweek for ten years through its grave difficulties to allow our hired men now to use the Magazine to express their narrow, uninformed or insidious ideas."

He was insisting, he said, "on a complete showdown with the editorial staff." Either it could accept his policies as he set them down or get out. "I do not care how valuable the man who objects may appear to be from a business standpoint, he is to be given his week's pay and assisted out of the office."

There were four overall points of acceptance Harriman insisted on. Among them, he wanted "the now proven fact that U.S. and British day and night bombing of Germany is an essential and effective part of the strategy for the defeat of Germany. Full support of our combined operations in this should be given."

He wasn't attempting to dictate from London, he said, but by God, his philosophies had better be followed!

Eaker had trouble of a similar nature at the same time. He had come to believe that the single most important trait in any subordinate was loyalty. Pessimism, criticism which reflected on the accepted policies of command, even describing the negative aspects of combat operations was not showing loyalty. He saw it as more in the nature of a stab in the back.

When Colonels Chip Overacker and Frank Robinson had been relieved as group commanders, Eaker asked them to make a study and then prepare a report for him showing the deficiencies in the equipment and training of Fortress and Liberator crews, recommending improvements in both. His plan was to send the pair back to the States to give their report to Gene Eubank, the Director of Bombardment, and to Bob Olds, who headed the Second Air Force and was in command of training bomber crews. They would then return to England, Overacker to head up the B-17 Combat Crew Replacement Center, and Robinson the B-24 CCRC.

As related, Eaker had known Overacker a good many years, and Ruth, his wife, was friendly with Overacker's wife and daughter. Aside from the personal, he had no reason to believe that either man would offer criticisms that would reflect on his command. Yet when they returned to Washington and spoke to a group of ranking officers in the Air Room at Army Air Forces headquarters, they presented a harsh picture which did not accentuate the positive and, to Eaker, was badly distorted. A third group commander, Colonel McGuire, who had been operating in Cairo in support of the British since May, concurred with all that was said. The two stressed a large formation of negatives: poor bombing accuracy; the effectiveness of enemy ground and air defenses; the imbalance in speed between U.S. bombers and German fighters; the greatly exaggerated claims of enemy planes shot down; skepticism toward heavily armed and armored B-17's to act as escort; lack of training as a fundamental reason for lack of bombing success combined with unflyable weather; even with adequate training, 8–10 percent losses; squadron commanders being lost daily due to a lack of replacements; neither day nor night attacks on sub pens successful, the proper ordnance still lacking; equipment lacking for operating at minus-45-degree temperatures; under present conditions, of thirty-five combat crews that begin operations, only five would survive. They recommended the number of combat missions be cut to fifteen. Finally, both Overacker and Robinson believed "the most successful way of making daylight bombing raids over . . . Europe is to use a thousand light plywood planes such as the Mosquito in fast low level attacks."

Whatever they believed, when their remarks reached Eaker, he was infuriated. In his reaction to Gene Eubank he said he had not realized how "completely licked, demoralized and scared the two were." He called them "isolated cases" and told the story of how Frank Armstrong in taking over Overacker's group considered its morale so low he didn't think it could be saved, but how in less than six weeks he had worked an astounding change. Eaker further told Eubank he not only didn't want the pair back, he was also asking that they have "no contact with any groups coming here."

His reaction, which some might have viewed as overreaction, was understandable. Naturally, he was defensive, as evidenced by his response to Colonel Malcolm Grow, of his staff, who had requested Flight Surgeon Captain Donald W. Hastings to make an investigation into the morale of the combat crews. Hastings had also recommended that combat missions be reduced to fifteen, which Eaker said would be "tantamount to discontinuing operations." He was sharply critical of the doctor, remarking that he might know his medicine but he didn't know his military, and the next time Grow sent someone to do an inspection into such a sensitive area, he should make sure of the inspector's qualifications.

Whereas Hastings reported that most of the original combat crews had been lost, Eaker put the figure at "some 46 percent," and then told Grow he had always been greatly concerned in the welfare of the combat units. He was making regular visits to bases, assuring himself that living conditions and flying tactics were sound. The average loss factor he cited, of 4.6 percent per mission, was not only less than anticipated, it was also less than the RAF figure. Moreover, he had found the leadership of his tactical units excellent. There was only one kick in the teeth to high morale: "the failure to provide units with replacements to match their losses. This is beyond our control," he admitted, but he was doing all he could to change that.

To Eaker's way of thinking there were two kinds of courage: the kind the young men of his combat crews were called on to exhibit and the kind a commander must possess in sending them out knowing full well that some would never return. The question of how many that "some" meant loomed ever larger in his mind. And no matter how remote WIDEWINGS was from the squadron briefing room or how far distant personally his rank and age placed him from the crew members, his concern was a constant weight in the night whose heaviness could be measured in numbers of airmen lost. It was a figure that could only rise, and if the other figures did not rise with it—the number of planes going out, the tons of bombs dropped, the percentage of hits, the overall results—then the lives lost were forfeit to poor judgment. Only a commander could experience this kind of unceasing pressure. He could suffer decision fatigue just as pilots could suffer battle fatigue, and he must have the inner resolve to keep the effects under control.

Eaker knew that at all costs he must keep personal depression from showing. Like the flu, it was very contagious and spread rapidly. Whether things were good or bad, he must be upbeat, positive, and when he heard what he considered were negative voices rising, he reacted swiftly, fiercely, as he had with Overacker and Robinson and, to a lesser degree, Hastings. Three promised groups were lost to him in March, and at the beginning of April he learned that the 157 replacement crews assigned for the month were to be reduced to twenty-five. However, he did not despair now, for through Andrews he knew a real change was in the wind. It would be up to him and to his most astute planners to make it meaningful.

Near the end of March, Colonel Charles Pre Cabell, of Arnold's Advisory Council, had personally delivered to Andrews a two-page letter whose significance was basic. It had been prepared by the Council during Arnold's recuperation, its focus on targeting and air strength. The latter projection was in essence a refinement of discussions on the subject Arnold had held with Andrews, Eaker, and Spaatz at Casablanca. They all knew that while a great deal of lip service had been paid to building up a large bomber force in England, no finalized numbers had ever been nailed down to accomplish the objective. As Arnold and Andrews recognized, both the Joint and Combined Chiefs of Staff had looked upon the Eighth Air Force "as a reservoir from which the demands of other theaters could be met." The way to change this "untenable view" was to design a definite program of operations from the U.K., get it approved, and then allocate the number of airplanes necessary to do the job. The Good Lord knew there was nothing new or unique in Arnold's suggestion—Eaker could recite it in his sleep, as they all could—but to get through Navy thinking and Army ground consideration on the Joint Chiefs of Staff was like trying to bomb Berlin with a group of B-18's. And Arnold well knew the value of putting everything down on paper, as did the recipients, no matter at what length it had already been hashed over.

Arnold had already informed his colleagues on the Joint Chiefs of Staff that three hundred heavies was the absolute minimum "that must be in the air within supporting distance of each other on any penetration deep into Germany." This number, he told them, to be really effective must be followed up by a second force of three hundred, and to keep six hundred aircraft operational, Eaker should have a reserve of another six hundred, giving him a total of twelve hundred bombers.

What Arnold wanted Andrews and Eaker to do was to make a study of his Council's estimates and come up with a recommendation. "It is entirely possible that your study of this report may result in air action that will prove the decisive factor in the European conflict," he wrote, asking Andrews to give the matter his immediate personal attention and to discuss it thoroughly with Eaker, Portal, and Harris.

The main portion of Arnold's letter, however, dealt with targeting, and with it was a report drawn up by the Committee of Operations Analysts (COA), which offered a detailed estimate of strategic targets in Europe. The Committee included civilians—businessmen and professionals—who knew a great deal about Germany's industrial components. Thomas W. Lamont was one member, Elihu Root, Jr., another. Organizing the Committee was Arnold's doing as the result of a recommendation by Major General Santy Fairchild, who posed the question: How can Germany be so damaged by air attack that an invasion of the Continent may be made possible within the shortest period, say one year? Arnold sent the COA's report not only to Andrews but to Portal and Spaatz as well. The report indicated that German industry could "be paralyzed by the destruction of no more than sixty targets." Arnold asked Andrews to work with the RAF in reviewing the estimates to decide whether the proposed force would be adequate to destroy the targets and thus make an invasion of the Continent feasible.

He particulary asked Andrews to consider the ball-bearing industry. "This system of targets specially appeals to me," he said, "because its destruction would virtually paralyze all German industry, and secondly, it may well be within our capabilities to destroy this industry with the size Air Force that we hope to have in the U.K. in 1943. If we could destroy the ball bearing industry, it would be unnecessary to destroy airplane or airplane engine manufacturing establishments, or, for that matter, the submarine manufacturing installations, for in a very short time their operations would be vitally affected."

It was an *if* of historic proportions. At the time, however, the Advisory Council believed that coordination of the Eighth Air Force and RAF Bomber Command could virtually eliminate the industry "in one, two or three attacks." The key target was Schweinfurt, four hundred miles from the English coast, in southeastern Germany.

The genesis of Schweinfurt as a fateful target most probably occurred at an informal gathering in Washington shortly before Christmas 1942. It was held at the home of Colonel Guido Perera's father-in-law, the Swedish Ambassador. Present was Mr. Sexton-Wolman, vice-president of

SKF Co., producer of ball bearings in the United States. Said Wolman to Perera, "I see you are now in the Air Corps. Why doesn't the Air Corps knock out the ball bearing plants at Schweinfurt? Germany could not get along without them."[2] The questioner did not know that Perera was the Director of the COA, and the suggestion took deep root. The next day Perera spoke to Dr. Eric Oberg, Editor of *Machinery* magazine, who had been assigned to the Machine Tools section of the Committee. Perera suggested that antifriction bearings should be given close study. Oberg agreed. He had been considering the same idea.

Ira Eaker had already met Colonel Perera and some of his colleagues, directly after his return from Casablanca. In January they had come to call on him at WIDEWINGS. They feared they would be received as interlopers, seen as hotshots from Washington sticking their noses into a business about which they knew little. As spokesman, the Colonel was nervous when he and his party were escorted into Eaker's office. He greeted them courteously, asked them to be seated, and said he had heard about their committee; he would like to inquire into its work.

Perera gave the background and concluded that they had not come to tell anyone what to do but to check data and gather first-hand information. Eaker, impressed with the Colonel and his attitude, said he would be only too glad to cooperate in every way. He would make all Eighth Air Force material available, as well as additional material from the RAF. This was done, and the team returned to Washington as completely informed as possible.

Elihu Root, Jr., a man of enormous corporate background, a director of AT&T, the Carnegie Foundation, insurance companies, and banks, was to record later some of what the visitors learned and some of what they determined to do. "We found to our surprise that while the British had studied the vulnerability of individual plants they had not really considered economic systems of targets. . . . The enemy economy was far too large—thousands of times too large—to blast it all. We had to choose vital points where small physical damage would cause great industrial disruption. We had to choose things which would give results within the time limit set, and we had to choose things that were within the operating possibilities. . . .

"Certainly we very early came to the sense which the British had not yet come to, that it was better to destroy a great deal of a few things than a little of a great many. We came to the sense that the program should be simple and concentrated and that once laid down it should be adhered to with grim determination and pressed forward with inexorable energy, because there was bound to be a race between destruction on the one hand and repair and evasion on the other. . . ."[3]

Eaker, who had considered the COA a nuisance, possibly dangerous, until he listened to Perera in January, had by April come to recognize the

COA's value, knowing that whatever it might recommend, he and Andrews would have the option to approve.

As soon as Andrews digested Arnold's letter and talked over its content with Pre Cabell, who immediately impressed him with his sharpness, he asked Eaker to come see him. They went over what Arnold was anxious to have them supply and the method they would use to do so. The result was that Eaker organized a small planning team. He brought Possum Hansell in from the 1st Wing to be chairman, Fred Anderson from his command of the 4th Wing, Colonel Richard Hughes from the Strategic Intelligence Section, and two additional members of his staff, Lieutenant Colonel "Sailor" Agan and Major John Hardy. Finally, he asked Cabell to join the group.

Both Andrews and Eaker talked the approach over with Portal and Harris, and the RAF chief assigned Air Commodore Sidney O. Bufton, Director of Bomber Operations at the Air Ministry, as well as Group Captain Arthur Morely to the team. Bufton, a bomber veteran and a strong believer in precision as opposed to area bombing, was often at loggerheads with Harris on the subject.

At the first meeting, on April 3, Eaker got things started by reading a letter from Andrews to the group, saying that he would like to see no fewer than two bomber raids of one hundred planes each attacking on a daily basis. Having two such forces would permit simultaneous raids on divergent targets and, when necessary, the total force would go against a single objective. What Eaker wanted from the team was an opinion of the COA's report, and then an estimate of what it would take to destroy the chosen targets in a reasonable time during the present year. He added, "I have always shot at a force of five hundred bombers per mission." Cabell said, "We cannot get five hundred airplanes in the air for this purpose this year. We can get eighteen groups. This will furnish six hundred airplanes and will permit three hundred airplanes in the air in a single day. We should approach the problem from the viewpoint that we ask for a force that can definitely be furnished."

They would go with that figure, but Eaker wanted them to keep in mind that of equal importance was how their case was presented to the Combined Chiefs. Who presented it was going to be just as crucial as how best to present it. "We should tell them in preference to furnishing a paper for them to read," he said.

To which Cabell responded, "General Arnold will read the report. He needs no presentation."

Eaker shook his head. "General Arnold is not the person we need to convince. As I cannot go back at this time, the person who goes back must be someone who has been in the theater and who is acquainted with our operations here. General Anderson may need to go back."

In all the rest of their deliberation, the presentation was uppermost in

Eaker's mind. All who participated in what became the sum and substance of a Combined Bomber Offensive saw their work as the redefining
of what had been generally agreed on in the Casablanca Directive. But as
Andrews pointed out when he attended one of their meetings, there must
be a change in the target priorities set up at Casablanca.

The COA had come up with nineteen target systems, listing them in the
order of their priority. Hansell, who had participated in the formulation
and drafting of AWPD-1 and AWPD-42, found much that was similar in
the selection. However, the previous plans had dealt with what would be
required, and the plan they would now produce would indicate what
could be done with a force in being. As Eaker pointed out, "There are
two troubles with AWPD-42. We said we were going to win the war by
air power. We can do this but people unfamiliar with air activities will say
that it will take ten years. Further, the plan was too theoretical in stating
the force required." He also felt that "the number one target for us this
summer should be the aircraft industry."

The British Air Ministry and the Ministry of Economic Warfare concurred. Of the half dozen major target systems, the team concentrated on
the order of priority shifted a bit, but there was only one major change
that was to bring strong criticism from some quarters after the fact.
Theretofore, Germany's electric power system had ranked high on the list
of prime targets. The COA dropped it to thirteenth place, which for all
practical purposes eliminated it from attack. As Hansell said, this came as
a shock to the planning team. However, they did not challenge the drastic
switch, essentially because they were reluctant to question the vital and
broadly supported intelligence structure on which the target selection was
based. They reasoned, "If the credibility of that intelligence base were
seriously impaired the entire structure of the Air Offensive might be
brought down."[4]

Additionally, Eaker had come to believe that electric power plants, gen-
erators, and transmitters were too small and costly objectives for the results obtained. This had to be a result of RAF influence, most likely
preached by Harris. The RAF believed that German electric generating
plants were too widely dispersed and cleverly constructed to go after. Yet,
even as Hansell and his team looked askance at the wisdom of removing
the German electric power system from its former high priority, the RAF
was preparing for a daring raid against the Möhne and Sorpe dams, the
keys to the Ruhr Valley water supplies, whose power plants supplied elec-
tricity to vital Ruhr industries.[5]

Aside from whatever cross-purposes existed within the RAF and between it and the Economic Ministry of Warfare on the always contentious
issue of targeting, there was a more fundamental reason for COA's decision to downgrade electric power. In his directive to Colonel Guido
Perera, General Fairchild asked for an analysis that would show the rate

of progressive deterioration of the German war effort as a result of increased air operations, so that they would have "as accurate an estimate as can be arrived at as to the date when this deterioration will have progressed to a point to *permit a successful invasion of Western Europe.*" (emphasis added) In other words, as Perera put it, this was not a plan to show how much havoc could be wreaked on German economic production but one that would make it possible to invade the Continent. Otherwise, electric power would have remained in the strategic picture.

As it was, the COA's projections and Eaker's planning team's acceptance of them removed any lingering doubts on the proposition that strategic air power was aimed at bringing Germany down alone. The winged will-o'-the-wisp of victory through air power in Europe remained just that. Preparation for invasion became the raison d'être of the Combined Bomber Offensive. And visions of air power winning the war single-handedly were dropped once and for all, without fanfare and with little recognition that a long-waged theoretical battle had been lost, the retreat easily made. There was no discernible outcry.

Hansell and his team had their plan ready in a week. It listed seven key target priorities, number one being the German Air Force: factories, engine plants, attrition in combat. Number two was now submarine yards and bases, and number three ball bearings. The other systems were oil, rubber, and military transportation industries, a total of seventy-six targets, the all-out attack to begin by fall, with a total force of thirty-five hundred U.S. and RAF aircraft. Hansell brought the CBO Plan to Eaker, who listened and then said, "Let's go."

They gathered in Andrews' office at the Dorchester on April 8 and, in Hansell's opinion, clumsily executed what they had so carefully worked out. Andrews made no comment on that aspect for the moment. "I want you to draw up a letter for my signature," he said, "stating that I'm very optimistic as to our ability to carry out the plan, as the projections are based entirely on factual matter acquired from experience against German targets well defended by flak and fighters. Make it clear that fighter protection for our bombers will be available in the very near future and this will permit better bombing at less cost. Also make it clear that this plan must be a preliminary to any invasion of the Continent."

He went on to say that Arnold was continuing to push on two points, simultaneous raids on different targets and a continuity of action. The weather, of course, was the bugaboo on the second, and Eaker said, "By this winter we'll have Oboe and with it we'll be able to bomb as accurately as the RAF does on many days the weather now grounds us."

Another point Andrews wanted made clear was that the plan must be based on a truly combined method of operations, that the Eighth and RAF Bomber Command would be working not just in cooperation but on joint targeting as well. Further, apart from the plan itself, he wanted an

intensive and continuous search maintained to seek out a system critical
to the German economic structure that could be hit with maximum
effect, time and again if necessary. Finally, he said, it should be stressed
that the proposed bomber force was the minimum needed to do the job.

On Thursday he welcomed Major Generals Thomas J. Handy, Chief of
OPD, and George Stratemeyer, Arnold's Chief of Staff. Both were old
friends and he was anxious to have their thinking on a host of matters, the
most important of which was the Combined Bomber Offensive. Before
hosting a dinner for them, he had a first meting with De Gaulle's right-
hand man in the Levant, General Georges Catroux. Present also was Admiral Stark.

Finally, on Friday morning, he held a full-scale conference in which he
had Eaker with the CBO team deliver the plan to Handy and Stratemeyer. In the interim, Eaker had gone over the final draft of the proposal with Portal, who in turn had written to Arnold saying he was all in
favor but cautioning, "The German fighter strength is increasing and
every week's delay will make the task more difficult to accomplish. We
cannot afford to miss the good bombing weather which will soon be due.
We cannot exploit to the full the great potentialities of the daylight bombing technique if the requisite numbers are not available."

Both Handy and Stratemeyer were in agreement with the plan, particularly Strat, who was intimately acquainted with Arnold's desires and problems, not to mention his damaged health.

Andrews announced only one significant change: During the past week,
in spite of the onrush of affairs, he had reached an important decision:
Much as Eaker was needed in England, he wanted him to return to Washington to present the Combined Bomber Offensive verbally to the Joint
Chiefs. It was both a wise and a logical move. Who was better prepared
to present the CBO, who was better qualified to detail it, with all the
ramifications, past and present? The next day, at Castle Coombe, they
went over it on the fairways, and Andrews then sent a cable to Arnold
saying that Ira would be departing shortly and he hoped to have him back
in about a week.

In a letter to Spaatz, directly after receiving the cable, Arnold commented, "Eaker is due back here in the next couple of days to talk over
his proposition. He seems to be laboring under the belief, and correctly
so, that he has been the 'forgotten man.' Unfortunately, this had to be.
Now we are once more building up the Eighth Air Force, and if I can be
left alone I will get a decent-sized air force over there by fall."

With his "proposition," Eaker brought home among other things a personal letter from Averell Harriman to Bob Lovett, which was also passed
to Arnold and his Advisory Council. It was an overall view as seen from
London, and its purpose was to offer additional support. Its most important paragraph read:

Lastly, but perhaps most important, the Prime Minister in spite of early advices to the contrary and his own prejudice, has accepted the effectiveness of daylight bombing without reservations. This has been a tough job but Ira has finally done it. This goes, too, for the Air Staff and Harris, of course. If there are a few people down the line who have not learned the gospel, don't let it worry you. I hope we can get increasing public expression by the top people here to lay for all time the ghost of the past when there was scepticism.

There was still skepticism in Washington. Even after Eaker went before the Joint Chiefs, on April 29, and did a masterful job of presenting the CBO in its entirety, speaking without notes and with impressive authority —Arnold called his presentation "superb"—there were the doubters, led openly by Admiral King. King raised the twin problems of supply and shipping space. Or, as Hap put it to Andy, "Of course, there are certain individuals asking questions as to where the airplanes will come from, and whether, if we meet the requirements in England, there will be sufficient available to also meet emergency situations in the Pacific. I believe that we have satisfied them on that point. As you know, however," he cautioned, "the battle has not yet been won for there will always be attempts made to send these planes elsewhere up to the time they actually arrive in England. . . ."

Although Arnold gave Andrews past examples of this being done while he was out of the country, he was referring not to Eisenhower's, Kenney's and King's demands, but to Marshall's private questions put to him in a memo following Eaker's presentation, beginning with: "Should we accept without qualification the full estimates?" The questions asked by Marshall were fundamental to the strategic conduct of the war in both Europe and the Pacific.[6]

To supply the answer, Arnold passed to his staff two brief queries that demanded immediate and convincing answers: "Why send bombers to England? Why not to Burma and Kenney?"

They gave him a four-page answer that satisfied Marshall and his advisers and, among other things, addressed the Chief of Staff's worry concerning the effect of poor weather on curtailing operations during the winter months. Six missions a month was the yardstick Eaker had used, and he spoke of how those numbers would be more than doubled once his planes were equipped with new overcast bombing devices. Arnold, through his staff's reply, assured Marshall that the figures were correct. Yet, almost exactly at the same time he was writing Andy a petulant complaint about the lack of Eighth Air Force combat operations. It was a somewhat irrational letter, comparing Spaatz's operation with Eaker's, attacking just about everything in the Eighth Air Force: its fighter and bomber commanders, its tactics, its pilots, and its leadership. Someone was evidently sending back nasty criticisms. "Has Monk Hunter lost his spirit—his dash?" he asked. "I know he isn't the Monk I used to know. He seems to be playing safe on most of his missions. . . . Is not the same thing true of the Bomber Command? Does it not lack an aggressive leader? Is the staff what it should be?"

Although admitting his position was three thousand miles away from the scene, he singled out the raid against Bremen on April 17 for particular criticism, second-guessing the method of attack, not really knowing what he was talking about. How could he? The distance was not only one of miles but also one of combat knowledge.

It was the largest raid to date that Eaker and Longfellow had launched. One hundred fifteen aircraft had risen from their fields in East Anglia, and 106 of them reached the target: the Focke-Wulf works on the outskirts of Bremen. The plant was one of Germany's most important in the production of FW 190 fighters. Why, Arnold wanted to know, had the bombers flown in one long column so that the lead element could be destroyed by attacking fighters? Why hadn't they split up and come in from different directions to confuse the opposition? There were two immediate answers: the policy of strength in numbers, and timing. The force wasn't strung out in a long column, as Arnold visualized it, but in well-organized protective formations. The problem was that an extra aircraft joined the attackers shortly after they left England were over the North Sea. It was a German reconnaissance plane, which signaled their approach, alerting fighter defenses along the entire coastal area and inland as well. As a result, the unescorted bombers were met by "the most vicious and concentrated series of attacks they had as yet encountered." Sixteen of their number fell, forty-six suffered damage. The fighters concentrated on the lead ships on the bomb run, which could not take evasive action. The flak was so heavy over the target that it looked like a storm cloud. Nevertheless, the bombing was on the mark, the target hit, production halted. The plant had been struck several times previously by the RAF but never with such damaging effect, and the German decision was to move the works deeper into Germany, to Marienburg.

But the cost! It was greater than 14 percent, and the realization, coming at the time it did, must have jarred Arnold badly and caused him to react as he did. In cold blood, it came down to a matter of profit and loss. The plan of attack had been well laid out and determinedly and ably executed, but so had the enemy's plan of defense. It was becoming a case of move and countermove as each side sought to utilize a combination of scientific devices and tactical techniques in a strategic contest of aerial blindman's buff. The cost in lives and treasure could only mount. Measured by numbers and losses, all missions prior to Bremen could be classed as skirmishes. Bremen was the first U.S.-German air battle. It was a harbinger of things to come, and Arnold's letter of complaint to Andrews, even while Eaker was in Washington preparing to sell the Joint Chiefs on the importance of the Combined Bomber Offensive (which came to be called the Eaker Plan), was to be but the first reaction to it.

That Arnold was driving himself and everyone around him relentlessly there was no doubt. Shortly, he would have another heart flare-up and be forced to take some needed rest in Oregon. It was in his nature to needle and goad his subordinates, not out of maliciousness but in the belief that by his arousing them they would do a better job. He liked nothing better than having a commander stand up and defend his position, and this was one reason why he had summoned Eaker to Casablanca. Now, directly after sending his letter of misguided complaint to Andy, he dispatched a follow-up congratulating him on his "most excellent" idea "of returning Ira to Washington to make the CBO presentation." He admitted that more than his long-distance view of combat operations was eating at him. Staffs could either make or break a commander, he warned. He knew the job in England was complex and difficult. "You will all need the best brains you can get and emotion and friendship must not in any way be allowed to enter into the picture," he cautioned. But there was more to it than that and, concerning the fate of the CBO, he confessed to Andrews, "I am fearful of the political implications at the present. It would be a shame if political rather than military judgment guided us at this most important time in our military effort, and this particularly applies at the moment."

What he was referring to at the moment was his fear of the British, the influence he felt Churchill had over Roosevelt in deflecting what he was sure must be the main thrust to win the war. He observed darkly:

It is becoming more and more apparent that the British have no intention of invading France or [the] continent of Europe. It is also becoming evident that they have made up their minds to give lip service to our endeavors and at the same time, trying to direct operations to other theaters. A good example of this is the North African operation and present endeavors to keep us occupied after North Africa is completed so that we will not have anything left to operate out of England.

It would seem that the British fear Russia more than they do Germany, but they want to maintain Germany as a buffer between Russia and Western Europe; that by bombing Germany they will be able to have Germany sue for peace with U.S. and England and thus keep Russia out of Germany. Pending that time, all they desire to do is maintain a ring around Germany to keep her within the blockaded area.

* * *

Andrews was unable to respond to either of the aforementioned letters. In the three months he had been in England, he had made an impact on allies and subordinates—ground and air—alike. Churchill, whenever he saw Andrews, kept telling him, "You must come down to Chequers," but as Andrews commented dryly, "he never says when." American and British political leaders in London—Winant, Harriman, Sinclair, Alexander, et al.—were in frequent consultation with him, inviting him to attend social functions which he abhorred, sounding him out on the organizational plans of BOLERO and POINTBLANK. Field Marshal Sir Alan Brooke, Churchill's military chief, who had no high regard for American leadership, found Andrews to be an exception. They met privately or dined with a few colleagues at Brooke's place.

Once the weather improved, Andrews tried to spend some part of the weekend at Castle Coombe with Ira and his guests, getting in some fresh air and exercise. He had stopped smoking to get rid of a cough, and he felt he was putting on too much weight. He was still stuck in the Dorchester Hotel, as his aide, Fred Chapman, had been unable to find a residence that was satisfactory.

Andrews had hoped that daughter Jeannie, whom he had left in Panama, would be coming to London, assigned to another job. Everything seemed set. She had her papers, her ticket, and was about to board the Clipper when orders came from the War Department preventing her departure. It was a cruel blow to her and puzzling to her father, but they had all been soldiers too long to mourn disappointments; they simply adjusted to them. It was Marshall or someone in his office who had blocked the journey, apparently deciding that two members of the same family should not be serving in the same theater. It didn't make much sense under the circumstances, and it was not a regulation that was followed with any consistency.* However, Andrews told Jeannie to be patient and in time perhaps something could be worked out. As for time, he indicated he was looking forward to the day when the war was ended and the three of them—Mom, she and himself—could go vagabonding. He would take them to Egypt, where he knew the ropes but had not had a chance to see the sights, and they would see them all.

To his son, Lieutenant Allen Andrews, who was working on a transfer to the Air Forces, anxious also to serve in the U.K., he reported, "Mom seems to be quite a social butterfly at Miami Beach. She seems to have definitely relinquished claims to Allen Rivas"—which was in reference to his granddaughter and the fact that the baby's grandmother had wisely decided to let the baby's mother, Josie, do the child-rearing.

What little time he had for private thoughts was shared with those he loved. "As I sit writing this letter," he told his son, "I am looking at Hyde Park from my hotel window and though it is 8:35 p.m., the sun is shining

---

* When Spaatz became Commanding General of the United States Strategic Air Force, in London, his daughter Tatty was assigned to the U.K. by the Red Cross.

in. We have double double daylight saving." A glimpse, then, of him in his surroundings at eventide in the English spring.

* * *

As yet no date had been fixed or decision made by the Allies as to when an invasion of France would take place. At the Casablanca Conference it had been decided to deceive Hitler into believing that an invasion was going to be attempted during the summer of 1943 and by doing so keep German ground and air forces, that might otherwise be sent to the Russian front, in the West. An Allied interservice staff, headed by a British officer, was organized both to plan for an invasion and to keep the enemy guessing as to when. Lieutenant General Frederick E. Morgan, an artillery and tank expert, was chosen to head the group. His acronym was COSSAC—Chief of Staff, Supreme Allied Commander—and his headquarters was in Norfolk House, at St. James's Square. Hap Arnold had assigned Brigadier General Robert C. Candee, head of Eighth Air Force Support Command, to COSSAC, and directly after his arrival in England, Andrews was introduced by Candee to Morgan. The Britisher, noted for his good humor and wit, took an instantaneous liking to the new theater commander, and in the ensuing months they were in close touch, Andrews informed of the plans that were evolving, all doors on every level open to him.

Although it was accepted in the upper reaches of the War Department that General Marshall anticipated being appointed Supreme Allied Commander, when the time came to lead the actual invasion forces, U. S. Army airmen believed that Andrews would be the officer chosen. They saw his commands—G-3, Panama, Cairo, London—as stepping-stones to the pinnacle of the yet unformed SHAEF. They believed that was what Marshall had in mind, and they would always believe it. Just where Andrews saw his future lie, he did not say. The job at hand occupied him fully.

Prior to Eaker's departure for Washington, on Good Friday, April 23, they had a sherry together at the British Army and Navy Club. Naturally their conversation centered on the bombing plan that Eaker must sell, and Andrews began to reminisce about the old days and past bomber problems. Did Ira remember how LeMay and the others had found the *Rex* seven hundred miles out, and the next day at the staff meeting Chief of Staff Malin Craig had called sore as hell and said, No more B-17's flying out to sea. One hundred miles was the limit!

Ira would never forget it. It was Harris Hull's idea that he had sold to Andrews during the May 1938 maneuvers. "Didn't you ask General Craig to put it in writing?"

"I did, and he did. Matter of fact, I've always kept that order as a sort of memento. I've got it in my files here." And then he smiled that slow, curling smile that lit up his face. "Anything ever happens to me, Ira, you'll know where to find it. You can keep it for posterity."[7]

Two days later, on a bright Easter Sunday, he attended a sunrise service in Hyde Park. Churchill, Brooke, Mountbatten, and other dignitaries were there. The following Sunday, he was playing golf, using his own clubs, which his wife, Johnny, had managed to send over. He hoped to play every Sunday, but tomorrow he was going on a journey, and he wasn't sure when he'd be back.

In a three-month period, from February to May Andrews had inspected the various segments of his command in England and Northern Ireland. Aside from air-force components, they were largely supply and storage installations, but in Iceland were air units and the 5th Division, under his old friend Major General Charlie Bonesteel. This, too, was a part of his command, and he was anxious to pay the strategically placed island a visit. At the end of the month he put plans in motion to do so.

Major Ramsey Potts—newly made squadron commander in Colonel Timberlake's veteran 93rd Group, lately returned from North Africa—received the order verbally. He was to send a B-24 crew that had finished its twenty-five missions to Bovingdon. There was only one such crew in the Group, maybe in the entire Eighth Air Force. Its commander was Captain Robert H. Shannon, a highly regarded combat veteran of the 330th Squadron who had flown his Liberator across the Atlantic in September 1942 and on most of his missions in North Africa. Now his friends reasoned he was going home to sell bonds and enjoy the good life he and his crew had earned. Potts knew that as a pilot Shannon was tops and as a commander he had kept the morale of his crew high in the worst of times. He had only one aeronautical weakness: When flying under instrument conditions and bracketing a beam he had a habit of getting his A's ($\cdot-$) and N's ($-\cdot$) mixed.

On Saturday, May 1, Fred Chapman, Andrews' aide, dropped in at Air Transport Command headquarters at Bovingdon. He said he wanted to see if the General's flight to Iceland could not be cleared directly from Bovingdon to Meeks Field, in Iceland, bypassing Prestwick, Scotland, and the additional briefing that would take place there. Chapman was told "no" in no uncertain terms right up the line through the Wing Operations Chief to Colonel Burrows, the Commanding Officer himself. Burrows personally explained to Chapman the danger of avoiding the prescribed communications channels, pointing out that all the weather and briefing information was concentrated under TransAtlantic Control, at Prestwick. Chapman listened to the explanation politely—an Alabama boy whose military background was Field Artillery and not aviation, as the ATC people thought. He said simply the decision would be up to the General, and departed.

After his golf game Sunday, Andrews wrote to his son telling him, "I am going on an inspection trip tomorrow to a part of my command and will mail this letter from there on May 3rd. Will be interested to know how long it takes to reach you."

He also confided: "Our air build-up is coming along nicely now but we continue to have a tough time with our daylight bombing. It is quite evident that we have not yet found just exactly the right combination. We should grow better at a faster clip. I am looking for the answer. Our losses are running too high. Leadership and experience are two of the troubles. We will work it out."

The next morning at Bovingdon, Shannon and his crew met the General and his party. It included six members of his staff, among them Ted Trotman, now a major, who had served the General since GHQ Air Force days, in the mid-thirties, Brigadier General Charlie Barth and Colonel Marlow Krum, who had been with him since Panama, and of course, Fred Chapman. One might say they carried special protection, because some days earlier Andrews in the course of his duties had met with Methodist Bishop Adna Wright Leonard. The Bishop was touring the war fronts and was anxious to visit his G.I. parishioners in Iceland. Andrews, hearing of his desire, invited him to come along.

In all, fifteen crew and passengers boarded Liberator 123728. The only members of the regular crew left behind were a waist gunner and copilot Lieutenant J. H. Lentz, Andrews taking the latter's place. Shannon's clearance was for Prestwick, about an hour and a half flying time. Again the point was stressed that they must land there to get a proper weather briefing. It was Andrews, sitting in the pilot's seat, who made the takeoff from Bovingdon. He was, at that moment, where he enjoyed being most.

Andrews' B-24 contacted Prestwick about eleven-fifteen, the approximate time of Shannon's ETA. Weather for Iceland was requested. At that moment the transmitter at Prestwick failed and contact was lost. British control at Stornoway was asked to pass on the weather and request that the plane land at Prestwick, where all flights for Iceland were being held. Ceiling was given as eight hundred feet with clear ice, visibility one mile. This was acknowledged, but the prerogative of rank prevailed and they flew on westward. Weather conditions had never fazed Andy Andrews; flying on instruments was his specialty. But was there another factor in his decision not to land?

Thirty miles east of Iceland's southern coast, the weather deteriorated fast. So did radio reception, and they came down under the low overcast, trying to make contact with Meeks Field. There was no contact, for due to the atmospheric conditions—blowing rain, snow, and sleet—the static was so bad that radio communication was almost impossible either from the ground or aloft.

At less than five hundred feet and edging ever lower they flew on westward, hugging the southern coast. Shannon was doing the flying now; his tail gunner, Staff Sergeant George A. Eisel, was sure of that. They spotted a runway and circled it twice. It was the RAF base at Kaldadarnes. Navigator Captain J. H. Gott fired a double red flare, but visibility was so poor they failed to see the tower's green Aldis light blinking, signaling them to land. Shannon continued along the coast. On the intercom, Eisel heard him ask Gott if sixty feet was enough altitude. Gott said forty would be ample. They reached the southwestern tip of the island, and Shannon turned northward, bracketing the west coast, hoping to make a hedgehopping swing into Meeks. It couldn't be done with the ceiling and visibility nearly zero and radio reception impossible. Eisel heard Shannon tell Gott he was going back to Kaldadarnes. Gott acknowledged, saying the radio beam at Meeks was not dependable. They were unaware of continuous efforts on the ground to make contact with them.

Shannon now began to retrace his course by doing steep turns over the water, a technique of his flying that Eisel recognized. He was in such a turn when he lost sight of the coastline and, at about nine hundred feet, drifted in over the land. There was a 25-mph wind from the south, blowing saturated air against an 1100-foot elevation ahead. It formed a cloud lower than the ceiling and concealed the promontory. The Liberator, in a 45-degree turn, slammed into the unseen hill. There was no warning, no anticipation, just the shattering thunder of impact.

Amid the strewn wreckage and bodies flung across the barren hillside, the swirling mist was a shroud covering the awful finality of the act. Lieutenant Colonel Harris Hull, whose job it had been to brief Andrews on Eighth Air Force intelligence, had said "there was a sense of splendor about him." Now in an instant of miscalculation the splendor was gone, and in the hearts of all those who had been close to him it would be replaced by a lasting emptiness—as empty as the windswept rock fields of Iceland.†

At Lieutenant General Frank M. Andrews' memorial service at Fort Myers, Virginia, General Marshall, before a packed chapel, gave the eulogy. He said of him that no Army produces more than a few great captains, and Andrews was most assuredly one of them.

Johnny Andrews, the family, and friends knew that Andy had often remarked he hoped when he departed this vale of tears he would be in the cockpit and not in a bed. Everyone believed he had been doing the flying at the moment of impact, but Staff Sergeant Eisel, the tail gunner, who miraculously survived, said no, he knew it was Captain Shannon at the controls. Andrews' friends, particularly those who had flown with him and knew how much he prided himself on his ability to fly on the gauges, would never accept that. Eaker was to tell Arnold that investigation of the

† General Andrews' wrist watch was not damaged in the crash.

accident indicated that when the crash occurred, Andrews was doing the flying, working the Meeks Field beam, making a procedure letdown; but Eaker was misinformed, as noted, and Andrews was in the copilot's seat.[8]

There was yet another question left hanging. Had he insisted upon bypassing Prestwick simply because he didn't want to be bothered having to land there and possibly face a long delay, confident he could handle any weather situation he met? Or was there another meaning to his being in such a hurry?

According to Johnny Andrews, there was. She told Allen that General Marshall had confided to her privately that at the time Andrews was planning to visit Iceland, he had sent a message to her husband requesting him to return to Washington secretly. Marshall did not give her the reason for wanting Andrews to return, nor did anyone ever ask him the reason for the order.[9] Ira Eaker, en route back to England at the time of the crash, knew nothing of such a plan. Neither, apparently, did Hap Arnold. Major Ramsey Potts and the men of the 330th Squadron fully believed Shannon and his crew were going home, because Andrews had specifically requested a crew that was through flying combat and was being held for reassignment to the States. They did not know, however, the General was heading for Iceland on an inspection tour. It could have been his first stop in the journey. Instead, all too tragically, it became his last stop in a longer journey, and while the questions might linger, the loss was permanent.[10]

Sixteen

Summer of Discontent

On the day of Frank Andrews' last flight, Ira Eaker cabled him that he would be on his way back to England on the fourth. Accompanying him were Major General Follett Bradley and Colonel Hugh Knerr. Their joining Eaker was a result of Andrews' suggestion that a well-organized and balanced plan for the buildup of the Eighth Air Force in all its component parts from manpower to equipment be undertaken. Andrews knew that Bradley and Knerr were the men to produce the kind of organization and manning tables necessary for orderly growth.* But Andrews and Knerr had an ulterior motive in that Andrews planned to keep Hugh in England and make him a member of his staff, at some point possibly his chief of staff. That the powers that be had not yet forgiven Knerr for his fight for a separate air force was marked by his rank. He didn't give a damn whether there were eagles or stars on his shoulders. He had a job to do, and at long last he believed he was going to be doing it for Andy.

The flight from Bolling to Prestwick took eighteen hours, and when they landed, on Wednesday morning, and were given the news, it was absolutely shattering. Nothing like this had hit Knerr since the death of his son in a bicycle accident years before. Bradley, like Knerr, had known Andrews since the early days and had served on his staff in both GHQ Air Force and the Caribbean. To their thinking, Andy was more than a longtime close friend, he was the proof of all that their lives and careers stood for. Only the special few like themselves could feel that and in feeling it know the awful sense of irreparable loss.

Bert Dargue had plowed into the Sierras, Tink Tinker had gone into the sea at the Battle of Midway. In February, Ken Walker, a bomber cham-

* The Bradley Plan, providing for expanding a strategic air force from 45,000 to 140,000 officers and men by June 1944.

pion, had been shot down over Rabul disobeying Kenney's orders to remove himself from combat. And Bob Olds was soon to die of some wretched disease. All disheartening and meaningful losses. But Andy Andrews killed in Iceland! It couldn't be! But it was.

Two days later, in Algiers, Eisenhower received word of Andrews' death. He was getting ready to fly to Oujda to visit headquarters of General Mark Clark's Fifth Army, and his aide Sergeant Mickey Kay said meaningfully, "I will pray you have a safe trip, sir." With Andrews gone, there were other considerations, such as, Would strategy now be changed? Eisenhower did not think it should be, with regard to the planned buildup in England. To him, going after Sicily was only nibbling at the edges, but the central question was, Who would succeed Andrews?[1]

On that score, in London Eaker swiftly assured Arnold that the Theater Deputy Commander, Major General Harry C. Ingles, who had formerly served as Andrews' G-3 in the Caribbean, had things under control. But he had some recommendations: "I cannot tell you how strongly I feel that an airman is essential to command this theater, at least for the next year," he advised. "I know, of course, that you and General Marshall have probably already determined on this commander. In view of my personal grave concern I hope that you will forgive the suggestion that General Spaatz or General Emmons are the best we have, in my opinion, if you yourself cannot come, and of course, I know this latter is impossible." As indeed it was.

Four days later the announcement was made that Andrews' successor was not to be an airman but an armored commander, Lieutenant General Jacob L. Devers. This did nothing to lift the spirits of airmen in England until they heard that Devers' chief of staff was to be Major General Idwal H. Edwards, an Army airman since 1918, Marshall's G-3, and a longtime friend of Eaker's. As Follett Bradley was to tell Arnold, "When Devers' appointment as Andy's successor was announced, we were all so low it didn't seem possible we could ever recover. However, the announcement of Edwards as his Chief of Staff helped a little. . . ." It helped a very great deal, as Eaker quickly found out.

The new Theater Commander's journey to England had nearly ended in an embarrassing fiasco. The plane's navigator got lost and the landing was made in southern Ireland (Eire), where Devers and his party faced internment for the duration. Some very fast talk and the Irish sense of humor let them go, but Devers, dark and saturnine in looks, arrived at his headquarters in London radiating storm clouds. Eaker called his old friend Idwal to welcome him and said, "I'd like to come in and pay my respects to the Commanding General."

"Come in at six," said Edwards, "but you want to be very careful. The General is eating airmen raw. You'll be no exception," and he explained why.

Eaker arrived at the appointed hour, and Devers, looking withdrawn and forbidding, greeted him coldly, saying, "Let me tell you what your air people did to me."

Eaker listened to what they had done and replied solemnly, "I can sympathize, sir. They did exactly the same thing to me just a year ago."

Devers said nothing for a moment, scowling. Then suddenly he grinned and laughed, and the ice was broken. Very shortly thereafter Eaker invited Jake Devers to visit his headquarters, took him to wing and group headquarters, and then put on a parade for him at WIDEWINGS that made its own impression. Follett Bradley was to inform Arnold before departing for Tooey Spaatz's headquarters that "Devers had announced himself publicly on several occasions as being one hundred percent back of the heavy bomber offensive" and that once again morale was high.† "I think that Devers really means what he says," Bradley told Hap, "and unless, as others have done before him, he gets the idea that running an air force is so easy he can do it himself, he will be quite satisfactory. He even went so far as to tell Ira, 'If anybody criticizes you, tell them you're working for Devers and he likes it that way.'" Bradley added that he thought Ira was "doing a superb job" and that he needed all the backing Arnold and the War Department could give him. "He needs no needling," he cautioned. "The British admire and respect him but put nothing over on him. They have almost stopped trying, in fact. He should be given three stars without delay."‡

At the moment, Arnold's feeling about the British was that they had been trying to put things over on him for years. Due to his health he had not been able to attend the TRIDENT Conference, which convened in Washington, D.C., on May 12. Its outcome didn't please him, because again, as at Casablanca, he felt the British view dominated strategic policy. The British Chiefs, led by Churchill, came well prepared, after an ocean voyage, to sell their plan for the invasion of Italy once Sicily was in Allied hands. The North African campaign, which was to have been wound up in six weeks, had taken six months, and Marshall was anxious to prepare for OVERLORD, the cross-Channel thrust. He did agree that to knock Italy out of the war would benefit the Russians, but he felt it could be done with air power. Portal, the airman, said, No, it would take ground forces as well. At the time, no firm decision was made on the matter. The issue was left to smolder while preparations went forward to mount HUSKY, the invasion of Sicily.

There was one decision made at TRIDENT with which Arnold was in full accord. In fact, he would have presented the paper on it himself had he been well enough. Instead, Joe McNarney did the honors and the Combined Chiefs were in complete agreement. Portal summed it up by saying

† Bradley suffered a serious heart attack on June 7, 1943.
‡ Eaker was promoted to lieutenant general on Sept. 13, 1943.

he was "one hundred percent behind the plan." It was Eaker's plan for the Combined Bomber Offensive. What had been generally agreed to at Casablanca had, through Eaker's updating and broadening, been accepted as strategic air policy at TRIDENT.

But if there was approval at the top for the Eighth Air Force Command, and support in the field by officers like Bradley and Devers, the praise did not deflect the needling criticism coming from Air Forces headquarters in Washington. It was about to take on a more contentious tone, rising, it would seem, as the number of bombers rose, the number of missions increased, and the losses mounted.

In May there were nine missions, seven of them flown against two or more targets, with several attacks numbering over a hundred aircraft. Eight raids were flown against major German targets: Kiel twice, Flensburg twice, Emden twice, with the accent on the U-boat yards. Also, something new was added. On May 4, for the first time, sixty-five heavies hitting motor transport targets at Antwerp were escorted by P-47's. The bombers returned without loss, and ten days later, in a repeat performance over the same target, of the thirty-eight attacking B-17's, only one was downed by fighters. There were no more escort missions flown during the month but, in all, seventy-one bombers went down. For the number of sorties flown—over twelve hundred—the loss rate was about 6 percent. Eaker wrote Arnold what was an almost euphoric letter about improving conditions. His tone was influenced somewhat by word brought over by Bob Lovett of Arnold's "indisposition." Eaker enclosed photos of the Kiel attack of May 14 whose accuracy had brought praise from the British Admiralty. "Our bombing has been superior," he said, "and our crews are gaining more confidence and a higher morale with each succeeding mission." The P-47's were coming along great. Their score against the FW 190's was now better than two to one. Bob Lovett's visit was working out very well indeed. He was "making a tremendous impression" with everyone—U.S. and RAF alike. The only bad news was the disastrous loss of a medium bombardment squadron on May 17.

Two days previously, a dozen B-26's, at RAF request, had made a tree-level attack on two power stations on the Dutch coast. All had returned, but all but one had been hit by flak. On the repeat raid, one plane couldn't take off and another had to abort. Ten went after the same targets, having failed to hit them on the first strike. They carried delayed-action bombs in order to give the civilian population a chance to get clear. None of the ten returned. Possum Hansell would never forget the feeling of waiting with others at the field in the fading light, knowing they were never coming back. As Eaker matter-of-factly noted to Arnold, "You cannot fly up and down this coast in a bomber at fifty feet and survive." Then he guessed, "They may have been destroyed by their own bombs. This half-hour delayed fuse is a trick one—Rube Goldberg at best!"[2]

He closed his letter on a light note, saying that although he couldn't issue Arnold an Oregon fishing license, he could get the President of the Piscatorial Society to take him out to catch a salmon. "Don't worry about us," he added, "we're doing all right and all of us are pulling for you to be back on the tightrope with your big umbrella again in the very near future." Arnold would return to his tightrope in June, not with an umbrella in hand but a battle-ax.

He began the month with a harsh query on the theme: Now that I've given you the aircraft and crews you've asked for, why aren't you using them? Devers supported Eaker's response, and approved the quality of toughness in the detailed reply. He might have seen Arnold's criticism as being indirectly aimed at him. New as he was to the job, he had sized up Eaker's command in a month and was in full support of it.

Said Eaker, in essence, through Devers to Arnold: You're not counting correctly. Yes, we have a total of 664 heavy bombers, but 123 are nonoperational or in reserve, and of the remaining 541, 65.5 percent, or 355, are ready for combat. The figure would be higher, but five groups are operating without their ground personnel or organizational equipment, because neither have arrived, and that means doubling up, which means ground crews having to service their own aircraft and the new groups as well. In the former case, Eaker declared, there are other considerations: "It is to be noted that during the previous nine days, eight target missions were carried out." He explained what that meant as far as battle damage and maintenance were concerned, and he said it should be borne in mind that "We have generally been able to keep in commission as many airplanes as we have had crews to operate them." In the area of maintenance, he suggested that if Arnold approved the Bradley Plan, which would mean additional personnel and equipment, including mobile units, to repair battle damage, the increase would do much to satisfy Arnold's criticism.

It did not, and the temperature in Arnold's office at the Pentagon and in Eaker's at WIDEWINGS began to rise.

Arnold: "Your cablegram relative to maintenance of your airplanes and the number being operated was not entirely what I had expected. I am perfectly willing to take the blame for anything, but that does not correct the existing situation. . . ."

Eaker: "You are not satisfied with conditions here. Neither am I and I am not satisfied with the support I have had. A few failures: failure to supply organizations, men and material requisitioned, shortage of organizational equipment, planes sent not ready for combat; crews need more training, maintenance echelon arrives often weeks behind combat; no tools and men for Warton Depot, etc. But I understand reasons and credit you with doing all you can to help us. Neither of us has been able to accomplish the ideal for reasons both should appreciate. We get nowhere with recrimination. I can do this job if I get the same support from you I am getting from Theater Commander. Nobody can do it without that."

In stepping in to support Eaker, Devers reminded Hap, "When I was in Washington, both you and McNarney indicated that all was not being done from this side," the negative information obviously being brought back by transient observers. "This is not true," he said. All that was needed was genuine help. Lovett and Bradley would bring the details but, above all, get the ground crews and organizational equipment over.

Major General Barney Giles attempted to step in and mediate what he saw as a growing dispute, detrimental to all. Giles, who had been on the Air Staff as Assistant Chief of the Office of Operations, Commitments and Requirements before replacing George Stratemeyer as Arnold's Chief of Staff, was a well-balanced pro. He knew engineering, he knew administration, he knew bombing and pursuit—he'd been pilot of the Air Corps's first B-17—and as important as all the rest, he knew people. Eaker spoke to him on a regular basis via the scrambler phone, and Barney cautioned from the bowels of the Pentagon, "Look, Ira, you've got to be more patient with the boss." And conversely, he attempted to tone down Arnold, pointing out that the combat crews coming out of Johnny Johnson's Second Air Force—Johnson having succeeded Bob Olds—were not fully trained and there were bound to be delays.

But Arnold did not agree. It was not Eaker's abilities that troubled him ("I want you to come out of this as a real commander . . ."), but the lack of ability of those who served him. When Eaker was in Washington to present the plan for the Combined Bomber Offensive, Arnold had mentioned his concern. Monk Hunter was doing nothing. Newt Longfellow's nerves were shot and his voice was hoarse from screaming. Charlie Bubb was not a capable chief of staff, and even though Andrews had recommended his promotion to brigadier general, Arnold was not going to approve it. Finally, if Henry Miller, the Eighth's Air Service Command Chief, couldn't handle the maintenance problems at this stage, how was he going to handle them as the buildup continued? At the time, Eaker had put up a strong defense on behalf of his principal officers. Loyalty to his men was the stubborn bedrock of his code. If they weren't doing well or needed relieving, he would know it—or so he thought. However, like Andrews, he was inclined to overlook the personality shortcomings of his friends. Arnold had told him, "I am willing to do anything possible to build up your forces but you must play your part. My wire was sent to you to get you to toughen up—to can these fellows who can't produce—to put in youngsters who can carry the ball. . . . Just who you want to take charge of maintenance, I don't know. I might suggest Carl Cover or Hugh Knerr, as a starter. Maybe the combination of the two of them is what you need. In any event, a definite change seems in order but you have to be tough to handle the situation."

To clarify the situation before their relationship really got out of hand, Eaker had an idea: "I would like to make a suggestion; it grows out of our experience at Casablanca. On arrival there you were assailed by a series of questions thrown at you by people in high places. When I arrived you threw those questions at me and asked me to supply the answers. Suppose we do the same now: when embarrassing questions are put to you about this Air Force, will you pass these queries on to me and let me give my answers to you? You may not always agree with the answers; I don't expect you to because we're looking at this Air Force from a different perspective, but I do believe it will help for you to have my answers available to you." *Perspective* was the operative word.

It was not written answers that Arnold wanted—excuses, to his way of thinking—but action. And it must come through a change in personnel, and friendship, like the close one he had with Monk Hunter, had to be forgotten.

Barney Giles, who, unlike Stratemeyer, knew how to take direct and hard action, believed it was his own initiative that brought Hunter's relief. The reason: on a recent occasion, German fighters shot down nine bombers returning from a raid on Kiel as they were approaching the English coast. The reasoning was if they had been properly escorted, the loss would not have occurred. Maybe so, but what was not known in Washington was that the bombers' gunners had already disarmed their own weapons. No doubt, this loss was a contributory factor in Hunter's relief, but it was a memo to Arnold from his new Advisory Council chief, Colonel Emmett "Rosey" O'Donnell, that finished Monk. Its title was "Ineffective Fighter Support to Bombardment in U.K." There were six highly critical paragraphs, but the first accusation said it all. "Scrutiny of combat reports from U.K. reveals that fighters are not escorting our heavy bombers to the full extent of their capabilities. They have been in very little combat, have few operational losses and have knocked down very few enemy aircraft."

O'Donnell was a gifted, aggressive bomber man with an outstanding combat record earned in the Pacific in the first bitter months after Pearl Harbor, but any P-47 pilot in the Eighth Air Force would have gladly told him he didn't know what he was talking about when he got onto the subject of belly tanks and the dropping thereof. What concerned O'Donnell most was the range of the Thunderbolt. "If the P-47 airplane does not actually have the ability to escort on fairly deep penetrations, we have been badly fooled and our planning has been extremely faulty. We have a lot of eggs in that basket. It will be the only American fighter-type airplane in the U.K. until December, 1943." Which was not exactly Hunter's fault. But apparently he was to blame for the slowness with which the bugs were being worked out of the plane; first no auxiliary tanks, then tanks in short supply, so it was necessary to turn to inefficient paper ones manufactured by the British. It was no excuse that it takes time for green fighter pilots to become seasoned in order to overcome the desire to drop their belly tanks when still half full of gas in order to be better prepared for combat. The real crusher, however, was that in a six-week period, while 8th Bomber Command had flown a dozen missions, the fighters had provided escort only three times. So Monk Hunter was going to be returned to the States and a new command, and Major General William Kepner, who had been Commanding General of the Fourth Air Force, in San Francisco, and was an old buddy of Ira's, was going to replace him. That was fine with Eaker, who had originally asked for Barney Giles to fill the slot.

Arnold and his staff had other suggestions on command replacements that were not so fine, to Eaker's way of thinking, and he responded accordingly:

"Consideration of Bomber Commander. I am well aware of the officers named in your cable. There is not one of them who has yet had an experience in this theater to justify his immediate assignment as Bomber Commander, with the exception of Hansell and the possible exception of [Fred] Anderson. Hansell has been First Wing Commander, immediately charged with the operation and maintenance of all the old groups. He more than Longfellow is directly responsible for the combat effectiveness and maintenance supervision. He has been carefully considered for eventual bomber commander. He is nervous and highly strung, and it is very doubtful whether he would physically stand the trials and responsibilities of the Bomber Commander task. . . ."

Eaker went on at length, saying that he was bringing Anderson along, that newly arrived Brigadier General Nathan Forrest would be taking over the 4th Wing when he had a bit more experience, that LeMay was now an acting Wing Commander and should be promoted, as Andrews and he had recommended two months previously. He added, "It would be a grave error to put any of the others you name as Bomber Commander," and then in answer to Arnold's query: What did he plan to do? said he would relieve Longfellow and Hansell by July 1 and replace them with Anderson and LeMay.

To Johnny Johnson, Eaker confided his feeling about Newt Longfellow. "He has done an excellent job. . . . He understands better than anybody I know the whole problem of the bombardment operation in this Theater. He is a tireless worker . . . working or carrying the responsibility for twenty-four hours a day, seven days a week. . . . There never was a more loyal officer than Newt. . . ." But that wasn't enough. His subordinates would say his nerves were shot; he was worn out and hell to be around.

Certainly the drumbeat of Arnold's attack on the major components of Eaker's command and thus on Eaker was special unto itself. It is wholly unlikely that he would have gone after his other combat leaders in the same fashion—Spaatz or Kenney, Brereton or Chennault—even if the situation had been similar. In a fit of anger over General Chaney's failure to follow orders to keep the planes of the First Air Force flying constantly when not on the ground for servicing, or sitting air defense duty, Arnold sought to have the veteran airman not only relieved of his command but demoted from major general to colonel.* When the accident rate of Johnny Johnson's Second Air Force, charged with training bomber crews, skyrocketed, Arnold fired him and put Billy Streett in command. Johnson, in a good-soldier letter, said he did not blame the boss, he understood the hard ball game of responsibility. In his reply, Arnold revealed the agony of his own position:

> Your letter touched a responsive chord in me. It is awfully hard in cases like this not to allow the personal element to enter into it. I find it very difficult to run this show on an impersonal basis. It would be so easy for me to say this guy or the other guy is a friend of mine, therefore I must give him another chance. As you know, you are all friends of mine and I like you all, and in addition, I am not naturally at heart an S.O.B. I am trying my damnedest to get this war over in the shortest space of time so that we can all go back to a normal way of living.

He repeated he was not picking on Johnny when he fired him. Instead, he was doing his damnedest "to get the maximum efficiency out of an organization."

It was different with Eaker: The long and close relationship was divided not only by the invisible but ever-present lines of age and rank but also by the psychological forces involved. Arnold telling Ira he wanted to make him a good commander, that he must toughen up, was entirely gratuitous. Eaker already was a good commander, and everyone around him—Andrews, Devers, Bradley, Knerr, Harriman, Portal, Harris, and even Churchill—had told Arnold so. As for toughening up, Arnold was referring to wielding the ax among subordinates, which he himself was busy doing. Arnold was, in fact, seeking to dominate the scene from Washington.

The rising tide of complaint was a reflection of internal stresses. His failing health stimulated his impatience, his feeling of isolation on the Joint and the Combined Chiefs of Staff, the belief that the Army Air Forces were being directly controlled by both bodies more and more each day. There were those around him who were seeking to exert their influence, for whatever their personal reasons. Larry Kuter had come back from Africa with a commendation from Spaatz. He was now Arnold's Deputy Chief of Staff, and it was he who was drafting most of the critical cables from "the Old Man." And last but foremost, Arnold's

---

* Through some deft maneuvering by Barney Giles, who acquainted Marshall with the situation, Chaney, who was a permanent brigadier general, was not demoted. However, his fighter commander, Willis Taylor, lost his star and his job.

greatest concern was the number of bombers in England not flying missions, for whatever unacceptable reason, as opposed to the number of bombers flying missions that were being shot down against mounting German fighter and ground defenses.

* * *

When the Allied victory in North Africa was sealed with the surrender of a quarter of a million of Rommel's Afrika Korps veterans in early May, Spaatz wrote to Hap what for him was a long and reflective letter on all that had transpired in the long year. He made several major points with regard to the air war: "The impact of the well-flown B-17 formation into the European air picture has been tremendous and, in my opinion, will be the decisive factor unless the Germans find some means of opposing it better than they have now." But he quickly added that because of the policies of the past year, which prevented throwing the full weight of bomber production against Germany, he thought it was reasonable to believe the Germans would "solve the problem of meeting the B-17," and when they did the Allied side would suffer a serious setback.

In his evaluation of what the B-17 and the B-24 could accomplish he said, "We feel that any area can be completely neutralized, even blown to oblivion, by these high-altitude attacks."

He proved the point at Pantelleria. The island lay in the path to Sicily, its German and Italian air units a decided threat to the success of HUSKY. Eisenhower determined to take the island by amphibious assault. The objective was viewed as a miniature Gibraltar, and there was recognition that the attack would be difficult and costly, some feeling it would be too costly. Under the code name HOBGOBLIN, Eisenhower prepared the assault. It began with air bombardment, and Tedder, Spaatz, and Doolittle fed in everything from B-17's to dive-bombing P-38's. The result was that after three weeks of softening up, the defending force of fifteen thousand surrendered without the loss of a single G.I., just as the latter were making the run toward the island in their landing craft.

"Surrender of Pantelleria marks the end of an important experiment for the Air Force," noted Ike's diarist, adding that all types of bombs had been used to test their effectiveness. What he didn't say was that the bombing of Pantelleria was proof positive of what Spaatz and other airmen had been preaching since the days of Billy Mitchell. Over Europe, however, the skies were fiercely defended, and as Spaatz had already warned, the Luftwaffe was finding a way to solve its problem.

Following the triple strike of May 29—the 1st Wing going against St. Nazaire and La Pallice and the 4th hitting the important rail yards at Rennes—bad weather kept the bombers on the ground until June 11. The respite which came after the eight consecutive missions Eaker had mentioned to Arnold gave the new crews a chance to adjust their thinking to the stark reality of war in the skies. To those who had been there before, it offered time to figure the odds against reaching the promised land of twenty-five missions.

They all knew about the lucky guys in the *Memphis Belle,* the first crew in the 91st to reach that golden number. They didn't know it was the big boss, General Eaker, who had suggested to Washington that the *Memphis Belle* fly back to the States to show the home folks what a combat B-17 and her heroes looked like. They did know Captain Morgan and his crew had left a couple of days before, going home to kiss the girls hello. To all those left behind it was a far-distant dream.

Unseen by them, the group and wing commanders, the photo interpreters and the intelligence gatherers, the operations planners, the target selectors, and ultimately, Ira Eaker struggled with the search for the formula of the ever-present problem of how to get there, blast the target, and get back in one piece. As with the alchemist searching for the philosopher's stone, the answer was always just beyond.

On the twenty-ninth, the 4th Wing's job had been to knock out the rail center that supplied the Brest U-boat ports. Two groups of P-47's escorted the seventy-two B-17's partway, but they didn't have the range to go all the way, and when they were forced to break off, the waiting Me 109's and the FW 190's, fitted with drop tanks to increase their air time, came barreling in.

Before their escorts had picked them up on the return flight, six Forts had gone down, including a squadron commander from the 95th Group. The 1st Wing attack fared no better, and again it was mostly a matter of no fighter protection, the P-47's and RAF Spitfires not having the range. The German fighters, on the other hand, were able to refuel and were directed by sharp ground control. The 379th Group, flying its first mission out of Kimbolton, lost five aircraft, two of them to flak.

Bremen was the target on June 11. Cloud covered it, and nearby Wilhelmshaven was hit instead. The flak was intense. So were the attacking fighters, coming in head on, risking collision, and in one case making shattering contact. The bombing was poor, and the 379th took a frightful beating, losing six of its crews—a complete squadron destroyed in just two missions.

Still, three targets had been bombed, the U-boat yards at Wilhelmshaven for the second time in three weeks, and the loss of eight aircraft out of a total of 218 was not prohibitive.

The raid that followed two days later again utilized both the 1st and the 4th wings. There were two principal targets: the U-boat yards at Bremen and Kiel, in northwestern Germany. The plan was for the two forces to hit the targets almost simultaneously, thus splitting the Luftwaffe defenders.

The B-17 leading the attack on Kiel carried General Nathan Forrest as an observer. The fighters were waiting, and they came in, using javelin formations, head on, singling out the lead Fortress. Those in the sixteen-plane group saw the General's plane riddled with cannon fire, falling in a spiral, its tail surfaces practically shot away, one engine in flames. Before the vicious attack was over, nine more of the 95th's B-17's were gone and one of the surviving half dozen had to crash-land. The Wing would claim thirty-nine enemy fighters shot down, five possible and fourteen damaged. The actual score was eight German fighters.

Eaker's headquarters would declare that the Kiel mission was the single greatest air battle of the war, and Anderson would claim that not only had the 4th Wing blasted the Kiel yards but in doing so it had drawn the Luftwaffe away from Bremen so that the 1st Wing could do its work against little opposition.[3] Public relations aside, the bombing had not been all that good and the losses set a new record, 26 out of an attacking force of 182, 22 from the 4th Wing, or about 14 percent altogether.

In writing to "Johnny" Johnson, Eaker commented on the death of Nathan Bedford Forrest, named for his hard-riding grandfather, the noted Confederate cavalry leader. Said Eaker, "[His death] was a tragic loss to us. I worry all the more about it, knowing the great sacrifice you made to get him over to us. He was proceeding exactly according to pattern, as I knew him when he was a young fighter pilot, flight commander, and operations officer. He was to be assigned on June 15th as the Commanding General of the 4th Wing. He was understudying Brigadier General Frederick Anderson. In the meantime, in that capacity, as we knew he would, he insisted that participation with his Wing in combat was one of the essential parts of that program." Forrest, at thirty-eight, was the highest-ranking air officer to have been killed in combat thus far. Another observer of note had been lost earlier. This was New York *Times* correspondent Robert B. Post, shot down in a B-24 over Wilhelmshaven.[4]

The Eighth Air Force carried out six more missions in June, all of them against two or more targets: the bombing of the synthetic rubber plant at Hüls, in the Ruhr Valley, the most accurate and effective to date. But in the two-week period fifty-six bombers were lost to fighters and flak. Many more suffered battle wounds, and in the new groups—there were now eleven operational in all—there were many casualties in the returning aircraft.

Part of Hap Arnold's determination to clean Eaker's house was his anguish over these losses. Underneath the criticism, the bark and drive, the desire to shake up the command structure, believing that new faces would bring new ideas in combating the enemy, he had a sympathetic heart. He had never been a combat commander, he had always wanted to be one, but he most probably would not have been a good one for this reason.

Eaker had a different outlook, a different level of acceptance; his view was forward, not inward. He was to write a month later:

We have been going at a great rate with our heavies during the past seven days, having operated in Germany with large formations on six of these seven days. It has been a tough battle but I do not share your discouragement over the loss ratio. There has never been so encouraging a period for this Air Force as the past week of activity. . . . The combat crews share this view as well as all echelons of command and staff. We have definite evidence from our own photographs and eyewitness accounts of excellent bombing results against vital targets, many deep into Germany, two of them but twenty minutes' flying time from Berlin. . . .

He went on to paint an optimistic picture, citing rising German fighter loss, the increased recovery of downed crews, P-47's now with auxiliary tanks meeting the returning bombers on the edge of the Ruhr Valley. "We lost 11 bombers out of 180, but two of the crews have already been picked up. These losses are not uneconomical in view of the targets we have destroyed. We look upon this as a phase we must go through. We cannot destroy this great German Air Force and get away unscarred ourselves."

Several weeks prior to Eaker's account of progress of phase one of the Combined Bomber Offensive, which concentrated heavily on submarine destruction in Germany and aircraft plants in France, his differences with Arnold had reached if not total resolution at least a calmer level of exchange. It had taken a climax of sorts to bring a truce.

When "Ira" received a letter from Arnold criticizing his system of command through combat wings, claiming they delayed "the prosecution of our missions," he had to wonder just who was actually drafting these foul balls. Arnold was now lecturing him as though he were some kind of newly minted second lieutenant, maintaining "there is an actual delay in hours between making a decision in the bomber command and receiving that same information at the squadron," whereas the British took only forty-five minutes to accomplish the same end. The reason for this, Arnold claimed, had been the creation of Wing headquarters. He said he was not criticizing Eaker personally but the American method of doing business, compounding one headquarters upon another, "just to get promotions." And for that reason—which was incorrect to begin with—he was withholding the promotions of Colonels LeMay and Timberlake until such time as Eaker convinced him that the system he was using was sound.

Before receiving Arnold's letter, Eaker met with Averell Harriman, who had just returned from Washington. While there, Averell had talked with Hap twice, and on both occasions Ira's command performance had been brought up, and Harriman returned to London believing the relationship was in danger. The result was that Eaker got off a four-page, single-space personal account, covering all the items of Arnold's displeasure and what he planned to do to resolve them. It was the opening and closing paragraphs of his letter that put his position in perspective.

> Regarding our personal relationship, I have always felt the closest bond of friendship between us as two individuals. I have never thought that you placed quite the confidence in me officially as an officer, as you did as a friend. I sometimes thought you were tough on me officially in order to make certain that nobody had a feeling that I got positions I held through our personal friendship, and to make double sure that you did not allow that friendship to influence you unduly toward me officially.

From there he went into detail on the personalities involved in Bomber, Fighter, Air Service Command. He described the strategic task of the Combined Bomber Offensive and his fear of aircraft and crews being diverted from it. He confessed his worry over official supporters', as well as the supporting public's, not being able to stand the losses in combat. "I want you to know that we can stand them and that we are doing everything possible to keep them at a minimum." He stressed that they were pulling German aviation away from the Russians and "pinning it on the Western Front," and that the Germans saw daylight bombing as their principal threat. "We may as well frankly admit that it is going to be a bloody battle. The side will win which can make good its losses. . . ."

At the end he got back to the personal: "I want to close with this thought: I shall always accept gladly and in the proper spirit any advice, counsel or criticism from you. I do not feel, however, that my past service which has come under your observation indicates that I am a horse which needs to be ridden with spurs. . . ." He praised the support of Devers and Edwards and ended with ". . . we will make the grade in one of the toughest spots imaginable if I can maintain your confidence and backing."

Hard on the heels of his *mea culpa* came Arnold's turndown of the promotions of LeMay and Timberlake over the organization of combat wings, which Eaker had instituted for good and sound reasons. As he had previously pointed out to Arnold and to "each of the visiting officials," the Eighth Air Force command system paralleled the RAF Bomber Command system, not only for reasons of communication but also because handling large numbers of aircraft required a combat wing to ensure proper control and leadership. Now that Anderson had become Bomber Commander, LeMay was handling operational groups, which, with the supporting services, numbered fifteen thousand officers and men. Timberlake was in command of a provisional wing of three groups of one hundred B-24's on temporary duty in Africa. Both men had earned and deserved promotion.

Maybe it was true nobody knew "Old Iron Ass" LeMay ever laughed, but Ted Timberlake was something else again. Everyone knew the story of the time he was leading his "Flying Circus" back from the sub pens, when a squadron of Spitfires, flown by Czechoslovakian pilots, made a playful pass. For their playfulness they got thoroughly shot at, the 93rd's gunners not recognizing them as friendlies. Shortly after landing, Timberlake was approached by the Czech squadron commander, who was not feeling playful any more. He had arrived at base headquarters accompanied by his seconds, where he threw down the gage, challenging Timberlake to a duel. Since Ted had the choice of weapons he wisely chose two highly regarded bottles of scotch. His strategy avoided an international incident and more, for when the contents of the bottles had been emptied, the Squadron Commander returned to his own base and announced that from now on he and his men would be honored to supply fighter cover to the 93rd on all its missions.

How could Hap Arnold reject the promotion of such a diplomatic combat leader?† When he received Eaker's effort to change his mind and grant the promotions, he passed the letter to Bob Lovett, noting on it: "I received this after my last letter to Ira in which I suggested that Wing Headquarters be eliminated—What next?"

This implied that the original criticism had originated with Lovett, who had recently returned from England. If so, it illustrated that visiting firemen, no matter how well-intentioned or supportive, can inadvertently start unnecessary fires.

It was shortly thereafter that Eaker received Arnold's reply to his lengthy personal message. The Boss took only a page to spell out his feelings, but it was obvious that Ira's words had gotten home to him, and by indirection he admitted that not all the flak had been coming directly from him.

"You were quite frank in your discussion of our relationship," he wrote, "and I want you to get this firmly in your mind that had I not had confidence in you—confidence in your ability—I would never have built you up for the job you now have. I give you full credit for having the inherent ability—the knowledge and judgment that goes with the command that you now hold. That being the case, I see no reason in the world for any fears or suspicion as to our relationship entering your mind. But you must know me well enough by this time to know that I am very outspoken. I say what I think and do what I think best, so when you hear these rumors, comments, criticisms, or what have you, always remember that if there is anything serious you will be the first one to hear of it and it will come from me direct.

"I hope that the above will be reassuring to you and will eliminate any doubt or apprehension that you may have as to your status with me."

He closed saying he had seen Ira's wife, Ruth, for the first time in a long time and she looked grand.

† Both LeMay and Timberlake were promoted to brigadier general in Sept. 1943.

For the time being, that put an end to the matter, but Eaker, though reassured, knew there were other critical forces close to the Boss with which he had to contend. In a "for your eyes only" letter of congratulations to Barney Giles on the official announcement of Giles's becoming Arnold's Chief of Staff, he spelled them out. Commenting on the size and caliber of Arnold's wartime staff, he said, ". . . there must be a lot of ardent 'Messiahs' with special hobbies who are riding them hard, each one to the exclusion of and without any regard to the general pattern." One result was having to receive "amateurish" and "screwball" cablegrams, radiograms, and letters bearing Arnold's signature "which can come under no other head than 'needling.' It develops the same spirit as a shrewish wife or a scolding mother will develop in a family. People who are working their heads off, who have done an outstanding job and who have every reason to expect recognition for it, suddenly get a querulous, scolding message as to why they did not do this or that." Such communiqués, he declared, simply illustrate that the person who wrote them didn't know what the hell he was talking about. Without mentioning names, he gave as an example Rosey O'Donnell's June 12 critique of Monk Hunter's use of the P-47. Bill Kepner had brought the memo over with him, and Eaker pointed out to Giles that at the time O'Donnell was faulting the dropping of half-filled belly tanks, 8th Fighter Command didn't have any such tanks to drop.

He cited another case that had come in the day before over Arnold's signature, referring to a supposedly new device the British had developed to confuse German ground controllers in directing their night fighters against RAF bombers. Supposedly Arnold was suggesting that Eaker try it out on his bombers. Ira pointed out he had brought back information on the development over a year ago. "Several of your people, including General McClelland, know all about it. An American parallel development is now in the process of manufacture." Incidentally, his Signal Officer had returned yesterday with a piece of this new equipment. However, at the present time it could not be employed because while it confused German night fighters in their effort to intercept, German day fighters made visual interceptions—which was a fact of life every eager Air Forces boy should know. Eaker explained that when his planes were equipped with through-the-overcast and in-the-clouds aids, then they would give this new gadget a try.

He gave, as the basis of his complaint, fear of a parallel situation to that which had arisen between Generals Pershing and March during the First World War, "where the people in the combat zone became bitter antagonists of the leaders in the zone of the interior and the whole mess eventually to be spread before the American public as each side tells its story." Giles realized Eaker had another fear, far more personal.

In offering a solution to the problem, Eaker suggested a method that

Andrews had instituted "which had a very wholesome effect, changing the whole staff attitude." No critical communication to an Air Force Commander from a subordinate commander was to be sent "without being personally cleared by him"—in this case by Giles.

The new Chief of Staff was well aware of Ira's discomfort—of being attacked from the rear. It was a traditional hazard any military commander must learn to live with: fighting a two-front war, one against the enemy and one against "friends" at home.

* * *

When Secretary Robert Lovett returned from his June investigation into how the U.S. air effort was being conducted from England, he reported to Arnold, among other things, that the need for a long-range fighter must be given immediate attention. The increase in bomber losses strongly indicated this, in Lovett's estimation. The P-47, once it had a proper auxiliary tank, was good for supplying top cover, but Hunter and the people to whom he had talked wanted P-38's, or possibly the P-51 Mustang, which had greater range. Hunter had previously informed Arnold that he needed at least twenty groups of Thunderbolts to do the job of providing escort and for conducting fighter sweeps. He had four groups of P-47's, and Lovett recommended that he be given an additional five to eight groups consisting of P-38's and P-51's.

Although Eaker had always sought fighter escorts for his bombers going to and from the target, he had, as noted, at least until mid-July, hewed to the theme that given the necessary strength, his bombers could go deep into Germany to hit their targets and return without suffering unacceptable losses. At the time, Spaatz was of a like mind, although Jimmy Doolittle had proved over the skies of North Africa that fighter escort was an essential to bomber longevity. Following the June 13 encounter over Kiel in which General Forrest and twenty-six B-17's were lost, Eaker notified Arnold that his greatest needs were more replacements, depot facilities for repair, and only lastly, long-range tanks for his fighters.

Unlike Eaker or Spaatz or Andrews, or for that matter any of his senior commanders with the possible exception of George Kenney, Hap Arnold had always been genuinely interested in scientific development. Since the earliest days of his career, he had pushed such exploration, and the fact that he had stuck to aviation was in some measure due to his sense of scientific inquiry.

Scientists like Robert A. Millikan, Vannevar Bush, and Theodor von Karman knew of Arnold's dedication to this cause, because he had hired them even in the very thin years and turned them loose on a host of projects to advance the state of the aeronautical art. Arnold liked to tell the story of how at the beginning of the war he had had to make a decision whether to recommend the all-out production of the heavy bomber or whether the money and effort should be put into the Kettering Flying Bomb, whose development he had been in on during World War I. Because the range of the latter was limited, he had reluctantly recommended against it. In the workings of his mind, Arnold had a questing nature, always seeking, always looking for a better way or a new way to improve on what was at hand, mechanical, tactical, or strategic. His flexibility of thought kept him from becoming cemented to accepted theoretical concepts, so that when evidence began to work against them, he was quicker than those around him to foresee the meaning and make the necessary decisions to bring change.

Conversely, Eaker's tenacity, his bullish determination, the fact that he was at heart a fighter and therefore affirmative in both thought and action, prevented him from seeing what by hindsight would be obvious. More, with few exceptions right up until the end of July the evidence supported him. Heavy bombers in strength could do it alone, and the percentage of losses overall was still less than the RAF's and still less than 5 percent. That by the middle of July he did recognize that a time factor was now involved was apparent when he wrote to Arnold, "During this immediate present, before the enemy has discovered a way of making our bombing uneconomical, we must press it home, and we must destroy the principal means he has for stopping our bombers, namely, his fighter force." The way to do that, Eaker said, was to keep all the bomber strength that could be scraped together and bomb his fighter factories while shooting down his fighters. If that was done, there was nothing to fear. "The point I hope to make with you is that time is exceedingly precious," he reiterated.

Arnold knew that, but he saw the answer to the problem differently. Just as he had never totally fixed himself to the airmen's belief in the Bomber Supreme, neither he had sat on pursuit boards with Spaatz and Eaker and Hunter and others who could not foresee an escort fighter going all the way. After all, officially, the Engineering Branch at Wright-Patterson didn't believe it could be done.

At the end of June, after talking to Lovett and reading his reports, after going over Eaker's detailed mission reports, he decided it was damn' well going to be done!

He sat down and wrote a memo to Barney Giles. It was the most important memo he wrote during the course of the war, a command decision in the nature of an ultimatum:

Attached are Mr. Lovett's comments on the P-47 situation in England. This brings to my mind very clearly the absolute necessity for building a fighter airplane that can go in and out with the bombers. Moreover, this fighter has got to go into Germany. Perhaps we can modify some existing type to do the job. The P-38 has been doing a fine job from North Africa in escorting our B-17's 400 miles or more. Whether this airplane can furnish the same close escort against the GAF on the Western Front is debatable. Our fighter people in the U.K. claim that they can't stay with the bombers because they are too slow and because they [the fighters] must have a top speed by the time they hit the coast. The P-38 is not able for its poor acceleration, so perhaps it will not be able to furnish close escort and be able to meet the FW 190's. About six months remain before deep penetration of Germany begins. Within this next six months, you have got to get a fighter that can protect our bombers. Whether you use an existing type or have to start from scratch is your problem. Get to work on this right away because by January '44, I want a fighter escort for all our bombers from the U.K. into Germany.

There was only one error in Arnold's projection, and that was a matter of timing. The escort he demanded was going to be needed long before January.

While Hap Arnold was rightly concerned with the development of a long-range bomber escort, Eaker, whose planning was fixed on target Germany, was somewhat miffed and not all that enthusiastic about one approved mission of great daring which did not include fighter escort. It had first been approved at the Casablanca Conference and then again in Washington at the TRIDENT Conference. The target was the oil fields at Ploesti, Romania. Since Major General Lewis Brereton's Ninth Air Force had established bases in Benghazi, Libya, Ploesti was in range of a concentrated B-24 attack involving a twenty-three-hundred-mile round-trip flight.

Eaker's displeasure derived from having to loan two of his veteran, highly experienced B-24 groups and one due to arrive—the 389th—to Brereton for the mission. His reference to Arnold about keeping all the bomber strength that could be scraped together reflected his attitude.

He was stubbornly against any plan that he felt detracted from the main thrust of the Combined Bomber Offensive—"We [Devers and himself] are firmly convinced that the employment of our heavy bombers against German industry is the greatest contribution we can make to the war." He considered the plan to bomb Ploesti an attractive one, as he did other adventurous schemes coming out of the Pentagon, but when viewed against the destruction of "the fighter aircraft industry, submarine-building establishments, the synthetic oil and rubber plants and other industrial and transport targets," he was not in favor. "We are also compelled to reiterate that we do not now have sufficient force to undertake both tasks," he said.

Arnold didn't agree, and neither did a great many others who had approved the strike. The code name was changed from SOAPSUDS to the more euphonious TIDAL WAVE. Colonel Jake Smart was TIDAL WAVE's chief planner, and no mission before or after was put together with such care, forethought, and training. Smart had come to Arnold's Advisory

At the Cairo and Teheran conferences (November–December 1943), Arnold in discussions with FDR, Harry Hopkins, and other Allied leaders had plans for a major shift in air command structure. (Credit U. S. Air Force)

As a key move in the command restructuring, Lieutenant General Tooey Spaatz would come to England to head the United States Strategic Air Forces. (Credit U. S. Air Force)

Spaatz's close friend and confidant Lieutenant General Ira Eaker (in the background) would go south to become Commanding General of the Mediterranean Allied Air Forces, which included the Twelfth Tactical and the Fifteenth Strategic air forces. Spaatz and Eaker would work as a team, the Eighth and the Fifteenth hitting strategic targets in Germany and Italy. (Credit U. S. Air Force)

The fighter everyone was waiting for: the North American Mustang P-51. When Goering saw the bombers' "Little Friends" over Berlin, he knew the war was lost. Here the 375th Fighter Squadron of the 361st Fighter Group returns from a raid over Germany. (Credit U. S. Air Force)

Spaatz and three of his principal officers in the air planning for the invasion of Normandy. From the left, Major General Ralph C. Royce, standing; Major General Hoyt S. Vandenberg, Deputy Chief for the Allied Expeditionary Air Forces; and Major General Hugh J. Knerr, USSTAF's Deputy for Service and Supply. (Credit U. S. Air Force)

Lieutenant General Jimmy Doolittle, new Commanding General of the Eighth Air Force, doesn't seem to have the boss sold as Major General Fred Anderson, Spaatz's new Deputy for Operations, waits for the punch line. (Credit U. S. Air Force)

Debriefing. General Spaatz, with his back to the camera; Lieutenant General Nathan F. Twining, Commanding General of the Fifteenth Air Force, with cigarette; and Lieutenant General Eaker, Commanding General of MAAF, listen as a Fifteenth Air Force bomber pilot answers questions on bombing results over the Messerschmitt factory at Wiener-Neustadt, Austria. (Credit U. S. Air Force)

Shortly after D day, the all-black 99th Squadron, which had flown five hundred combat missions, was joined by three other black fighter squadrons to form the 332nd Group. Transferred from the Twelfth Air Force to the Fifteenth, the 332nd, in their red-tailed P-51's, escorted the heavies on many missions and won a Distinguished Unit Citation for action over Berlin. Captain Charles W. Hall was the first pilot of the 99th to shoot down two enemy fighters in one day. (Credit U. S. Air Force)

On June 2, 1944, Lieutenant General Ira C. Eaker flew on the first shuttle bombing mission from Fifteenth Air Force bases in Italy to three bases in the Soviet Union. The 105 B-17's bombed German targets in Hungary along the twelve-hundred-mile route. At Poltava, General Eaker discusses the flight, through an interpreter, with Russian Air Force Major General Perminov, in command of the Russian bases. (Credit Lieutenant General Ira C. Eaker)

On the home front, General of the Army Hap Arnold, in spite of serious illness, was ever on the move in his efforts to speed the war's end. Here he inspects the Air Technical Service Command in Miami. (Credit U. S. Air Force)

They received no citations for their voluntary efforts in aiding the wives and children of airmen. Seated together, Bee Arnold, right, and Ruth Spaatz. Standing, from the left, Mmes. Kuter, Grant, Hodwood, Eaker, Benedict, Kauch, Brentnall, and Streett. (Credit Ruth Eaker)

Strategic bombardment by the Eighth and the Fifteenth air forces laid waste to the industrial heartland of Germany. The important shipyards of Wilhelmshaven lie in ruins, the cruiser *Köln* sits on the bottom, another ship on its side. Only the church remains untouched. (Credit U. S. Air Force)

The wreckage of Hitler's Reich. (Credit U. S. Air Force)

May 11, 1945: the victors and the vanquished. Generals Spaatz and Vandenberg listen to POW Air Marshal Hermann Goering explain how it was. General Eisenhower quickly put an end to such gentility. (Credit U. S. Air Force)

General Eaker said that General Robert E. Lee had his "lieutenants" but Hap Arnold had only one, Tooey Spaatz. Secretary of War Henry L. Stimson awards the second oak-leaf cluster to Spaatz's Distinguished Service Medal while Arnold looks on. Spaatz was the only American general to be present at both the German and the Japanese surrenders. (Credit U. S. Air Force)

President Harry S Truman signs a proclamation designating August 1, 1946, Air Force Day. It was another step toward the goal of independence, which came in September 1947, when General Spaatz was named the first Air Force Chief of Staff and General Eaker his deputy. Together, they realized the airman's long-held dream. (Credit U. S. Air Force)

Council after serving as Director of Flying Training. He replaced Lauris Norstad on the Council, joining Pre Cabell and Pat Partridge. As recounted, Ploesti had been bombed previously by Colonel Harry Halverson and his HALPRO group in June 1942.

Although Smart's job as a "thinker" was to advance new ideas, it was also to review all previous documents containing information that would be of concern to the Joint and the Combined Chiefs of Staff, thus being able to present to Arnold an unbiased and informed view on any particular consideration. Such a continuing consideration was how best to bleed the heartland of the Third Reich. Hitting Ploesti would cause such a hemorrhage, for it provided a third of Germany's aviation and diesel fuels, and it was generally believed that destroying it could shorten the war by six months.

Smart's plan of attack was the antithesis of a high-altitude precision raid: a massed coordinated strike at extremely low level. He reasoned that coming in at treetop level would surprise the enemy; flak guns would not be effective; the air gunners could attack flak crews; enemy fighters would find it difficult to get at the bombers; the attackers would be too low to be picked up on radar; every aircraft would have a chosen spot to hit; battle-damaged aircraft would have a better survival chance in crash-landing.[5] The attacking force would consist of five groups of Liberators, or nearly two hundred aircraft. They would be releasing their bombs at altitudes ranging from two hundred to six hundred feet.

In late May, Smart and a small staff went to North Africa to present the plan to Eisenhower, Tedder, and Spaatz. Ike was generally in favor. He was in the midst of organizing the invasion of Sicily, and he could see such a strike benefiting the overall effort, although he did not believe one raid would do the job. He set a tentative target date of June 23, but it was soon advanced.

Tedder estimated there was a 10 percent chance of eliminating 50 percent of the target and suffering a 40 percent bomber loss. Still, he recommended the undertaking, for there was much to be gained if it succeeded. Spaatz concurred.

Smart's next stop was Eighth Air Force Headquarters, in London, where he wrote Arnold in mid-June. Privately Eaker might not be in favor of TIDAL WAVE, but he was bending over backwards to be of help. "General Eaker has given me everything I have asked for and more," reported Smart. The two veteran groups he was borrowing, the 44th and the 93rd, would be built up to forty planes and forty crews apiece, and the 389th Group would have at least forty-eight planes. Said Smart, Generals Devers, Edwards, Longfellow, and Hodges were also helping in every way possible. "Models of the target have been made. Target folders are being printed. A movie for briefing is being filmed from the models,

maps, photographs and perspective drawings." British navigation aids
were being installed on the Liberators, and crews were being trained in
low-altitude bombing.

For two months the crews trained in England and Libya, rehearsing
with dummy bombs against a full-scale mock-up of the extensive Ploesti
complex constructed in the desert south of Benghazi, which included
seven refining installations. As Smart told Arnold, "Everything that we
can think of is being done to make the operation successful. Armored
suits for the crews and armor plate for the nose of the planes." Smart
wanted Washington to send five hundred 2–6-minute delay fuses for the
bombs so that those planes attacking in the last wave wouldn't be blown
up by the bombs of those in the waves ahead. But with all the very secret
and careful strategic planning going forward, Jake Smart understood
Eaker's unhappiness. "It is necessary that the U.K. groups be returned
here at the earliest possible date," he informed Arnold. "We people in the
States cannot fully appreciate the importance of maintaining air attacks
against Germany at an ever-increasing tempo. Nor can we begin to appreciate the valor and courage displayed on every mission by every combat
crew member. Not one single airplane has ever turned from the attack
until bombs were away. Not one crew member has abandoned his position
except to aid a wounded man. Words cannot describe the feeling of min-
gled pride and pathos displayed by Fred Anderson as he told the experiences of his men on the Kiel and Bremen raids. One is filled with pride to
hear him describe how a young captain took over the lead and continued
the attack when his leader and deputy leader were successively shot
down."

If, when the 178 B-24's lifted off from their desert fields on Sunday,
August 1, the courage Smart was describing to Arnold could have determined the success of the fourteen-hour mission that followed, the Ploesti
oil fields would have been wiped out. As it was, due to underestimated
German defenses, poor intelligence, and the decision not to send photo
reconnaissance planes over the target for several months before the attack, Tedder's estimation of the loss rate turned out to be close to correct: fifty-three aircraft out of an attacking force of 164, including 8
interned in Turkey. Of those that returned to their bases, another fifty-
three were battle-damaged, most of them unsalvageable. As for the destruction they had caused, two out of the seven refineries were finished,
three were untouched, and the other two were soon repaired. However,
Ploesti refining capacity had been reduced by 40 percent and although the
fields had been operating at only 60 percent capacity, serious attrition
against the Luftwaffe's fuel supplies had begun.[6]

The decision not to photograph Ploesti's defenses over a period of several months was so as not to alert the enemy to the coming attack. Had
photographs been taken, they would have revealed a very heavily de-

fended target with more flak guns than those protecting Berlin and a fighter strength of nearly two hundred fifty first-line aircraft. Unknown to the planners also, the German early warning net was far-flung and efficient.[7]

Jake Smart's greatest personal disappointment was that he did not get to go on the raid, Brigadier General Uzal G. Ent, Commanding General of 9th Bomber Command commandeering his place.

Eaker was greatly disappointed too. He had heard on a radio broadcast featuring Arnold's "bell-ringing, whip-cracking voice," as he described it, that Ploesti had been hit. But no credit had been given by Brereton to the Eighth Air Force groups, and three days later, Eaker still didn't know what shape they were in. It was not until ten days after the fact that he received "a clear picture" of the operation, brought to him by Smart. The details did not please him. To Arnold he expressed his criticism "of the basic decisions which were made and some of the handicaps which were thrown in [the] way by bad decisions on top." He wasn't specific on what handicaps, and he didn't say whether he was referring to Ent or Brereton as to decisions, but he did add, "I'm absolutely certain that if Timberlake had been allowed to lead his Combat Wing which we sent from here, the attack would have been entirely successful." It was a dubious piece of second-guessing at best, which indicated how angry he was at having had to loan Brereton the Wing. He wanted the groups back right now. They were invaluable to him, he said, for in the units were all his trained and experienced B-24 personnel. "With them," he claimed, "it is also certain that we can average the destruction of one enemy fighter aircraft factory a week. . . ."

One positive result of Ploesti for Eaker was that he had gotten to know thirty-five-year-old Jake Smart, whose name was a fair description of the impression he made. He wondered if Arnold could spare him. "Smart would prove of great value to this Air Force," Eaker advised. "I have not had a suitable officer I could spare from combat leadership to serve as A-3 and badly need an officer of Smart's type and ability."‡ But Arnold was not letting Colonel Smart go.

Eaker's less than enthusiastic response to the most carefully planned and daring strategic bombing attack against Germany thus far was compounded of several underlying parts. The fact that he did not control the forces involved, although he had been required to contribute the major portion of them, was obviously galling. He stressed their loss at a time his own strength was growing, but so was the enemy opposition and its weaponry, including fighters with long-range cannon fire and rockets. None of these systems, he felt, had been tried with sufficient force or skill to be

‡ About January 1, he would bring in Timberlake as A-3 and give Smart command of the Wing. It was a request whose time would come later.

alarming. But, he warned Arnold, there was grave danger they soon would be. He recommended two courses of action: experiments be conducted at the tactical school, studying the four methods of attack the Germans were using, and, as he had already stressed and would do so repeatedly, go after the Luftwaffe—factories, bases, and in the air.

During the heavily overcast month of July, he had been sending his bombers to do that, splitting most of the missions between aircraft factories and U-boat yards, the former mostly in France. Ten missions were flown in the month against thirty-one targets, on three raids, over two hundred aircraft dropping bombs. The P-47's were now accompanying the heavies at least part of the way, as well as the newly activated medium groups all of the way. The fighters' presence and the growing ability of their pilots made an appreciable difference. But on the long raids, the deep penetration into northwestern Germany, where the Thunderbolts could not go, the losses mounted in the fierce encounters. During the last week of July, there were six missions. They called it "BLITZ WEEK." On the twenty-fourth, the targets were a brand-new magnesium and aluminum factory at Heroya, Norway, and a U-boat base at Trondheim, in all a nineteen-hundred-mile mission, the longest to date. Both were hit hard by a force of two hundred eight B-17's. The attack was beautifully planned and a complete surprise, the only casualty a Fort that made a forced landing in Sweden. One veteran observer who went along for the ride was a black cocker spaniel named Skipper. RAF photo reconnaissance sent congratulations for the "wizard bombings" and asked for more.

There were more, but unfortunately surprise was not an element in them.

On the twenty-sixth, over the extensive Blohm and Voss shipyards, at Hamburg, and Germany's largest tire factory, at Hanover, 24 out of 199 bombers were lost.

"When the fighters hit us, the wing swelled up like a balloon and then burst into flames, and we went into a dive. I didn't give the order to bail out because I thought I might pull out of it. I got it under control only 150 feet above the water, just in time to ditch. . . ."[8]

Air Sea Rescue picked up sixty-five downed airmen that day.

Two days later, over the aircraft factories of Kassel and Oschersleben, 22, or nearly a quarter of a strike force of 95, went down against the concentrated fighter attacks which used all the kill techniques Eaker had mentioned to Arnold. Everyone knew that had the returning units not been met by protective P-47 squadrons, the loss figure would have been much higher.

Over the aircraft factories at Warnemunde and the shipyards at Kiel, losses were less: 10 out of a force of 193, and on July 30, a dozen B-17's of 134 attackers went down over Kassel.

The tally sheet at the end of BLITZ WEEK stood at eighty-eight B-17's and their crews gone—dead, POW's, or in the hands of the underground seeking to spirit them back to England. This against claims by the bomber crews of 179 German fighters destroyed. The many tons of bombs dropped, the damage done to the German war machine, was an estimate, and like the German loss rate it was overblown though honestly stated. The fury of the Luftwaffe's defense, however, was a measure of the fact that the "Eaker Plan" was having a mounting effect on Hitler's war effort. But not exactly in the manner in which it was primarily viewed by its perpetrators. Industrial havoc being reaped, yes. Cities being pulverized by Bomber Harris' night raids, yes. But Albert Speer, Hitler's production genius, viewed the "real importance" of the air war in a different light. To him, "[the raids] opened a second front long before the invasion of Europe. That front was the skies over Germany. The fleets of bombers might appear at any time over any large German city or important factory. The unpredictability of the attacks made this front gigantic; every square meter of the territory we controlled was a kind of front line. Defense against air attacks required the production of thousands of antiaircraft guns, the stockpiling of tremendous quantities of ammunition all over the country, and holding in readiness hundreds of thousands of soldiers . . . often totally inactive for months at a time."

To Speer, this became the greatest lost battle of the Third Reich, greater than the loss of Stalingrad and the retreats in Russia. He believed that the twenty thousand antiaircraft guns distributed throughout the homeland would have doubled the antitank defenses on the Eastern Front and reversed the tide of battle there.[9]

Allied Intelligence, through photo reconnaissance, ULTRA, and other sources, was the measure of Eaker's knowledge of what his bombers were doing to Germany. In cold statistics, which he sought to keep out of the forefront of his thinking, he knew, however, exactly what German defenses were doing to his forces. The loss rate for BLITZ WEEK was over 8 percent, and as every newly arrived combat crewman could figure, with twenty-five missions to fly, those odds meant he wasn't going to make it.

While Eaker sought to calm Arnold's alarm over these rising figures, they had to have laid their pressure on him, and it was another reason for his unhappiness over the loss of his Ploesti units. Since mid-July he had been planning a double strike on two vitally important aircraft factories: the aircraft plant at Regensburg, five hundred miles inside Europe, and the Messerschmitt factories at Wiener-Neustadt, near Vienna, Austria. He had sent Possum Hansell home to Arnold with the plan, saying, "Portal feels that this has a much higher priority than the oil attack, and General Devers and I do, also." Wiener-Neustadt was considered too far distant for a B-17 raid from England but not from bases in Africa. He had contacted Tooey and told him, "There are two fighter factories which produce 48 percent of all the fighters available to Germany, and let's go get 'em. I believe the best way for us to do this is for us to take on one and you the other, each wiping out the one closest to him." His primary idea was to reduce German fighter production right now, this summer. He knew the factories were well dispersed, so it was going to take a big force and deep penetration to do the job. And that was why "we need to get back as soon as possible our three Liberator groups now with you. They were lent against our best judgment." He said this to Spaatz two weeks before Ploesti and maintained if he didn't have them back by August 1, it would simply mean "that certain German aircraft factories are being spared."

At the time Eaker was working to get approval for his two-pronged mission, which he code-named STILETTO, he had important visitors: Secretary of War Henry L. Stimson and his old friend Lieutenant General Delos Emmons. Stimson had come for a look-see, and was impressed with all he was shown: the bases, the crews, the planes—a formidable-looking and efficiently operated force.

Emmons, on the other hand, had been given a special assignment by Arnold, who knew that he had hoped to be made European Theater Commander, right after Andrews' death. Instead, Delos had been posted from his Army command in Hawaii to become Commanding General of the Western Defense Command. He and Arnold had met at a conference at the Presidio, and when Hap learned that Emmons was scheduled to make a trip to the United Kingdom, he asked him if he would look into the Eighth's air operations, acquaint himself with all details, so they could discuss same on his return. Before Emmons' departure, Arnold wrote to Jake Devers and said, "I hope you'll have no objection to his talking to Eaker or Anderson and other air officers."

Certainly Ira had no objection. His friendship with "Lucky" dated back to a really lucky day in the twenties. He was flying Emmons in a DH-4 from Dayton to Bolling Field in a mess of unfriendly weather, and when Eaker somehow found the ground at Moundsville, they were carrying an unflyable frosting of ice on wings and fuselage, about four hundred pounds, they figured. It was a story Emmons never tired of telling. Now, however, when he cabled Arnold on July 22, he and Eaker had another type of plane in mind. "Recommend that the P-51 with Merlin engine be supplied this theater," advised Emmons. He was backing an earlier message from Ira which said, "Request P-51 groups to limit of availability for September–November. Anticipate these airplanes will be very effective complement to P-47's in support of bomber effort."

Thus, several weeks after Arnold had given Barney Giles an ultimatum on finding a long-legged escort, both Eaker and Emmons were recommending that the Mustang be sent to the Theater to complement the

Thunderbolt, even though it was not then the long-legged plane Arnold had in mind.

Just as the creation and development of the Boeing B-17, back in 1933, was the result of thought, cooperation, and effort among a number of like-minded individuals, so, too, ten years later was the emergence of the greatest fighter plane of the war.

In 1940, a British purchasing commission approached Dutch Kindelberger, president of North American Aviation, on placing a large order for Curtiss P-40's. Kindelberger showed them instead the design drawings for a new fighter, the Mustang, which had been rendered by his engineering chief, Lee Atwood. The British said go, just as the Battle of Britain was heating up. At the end of October, the P-51, using an AT-6 landing gear, made its first test flight. Several months later, a model arrived in Liverpool aboard ship. Following a demonstration flight, RAF observers refused to believe the performance data, and the tests were rerun. As one pilot was to say, "You don't fly this plane, you wear it." But there were problems.

The Materiel Command, at Dayton, which had placed its money on the P-38 and the P-47, was not all that interested in the Mustang, although it asked for two production models in order to conduct its own tests. Somewhere within the Command there was a pigheaded military blindness that saw the Mustang as a "foreign" aircraft and therefore of no real interest— that and the fact that the Engineering Branch was devoting round-the-clock energies to the Lightning and the Thunderbolt. Besides, at Dayton it was found the Mustang didn't perform all that well above twenty-two thousand feet, although below it, officially it was admitted the P-51 "has the best all-round fighting qualities of any fighter."

Ira Eaker thought so when Dutch Kindelberger invited him to test-fly a Mustang at Inglewood, California, in December 1941, when Ira was still looking forward to commanding fighters. He found it to be a sweet-flying aircraft but with not enough power at high altitudes. Still, he sang the P-51's praises to Arnold, who soon thereafter paid a call on his salty old friend Dutch to have a look at the North American production line. Arnold was impressed further when he saw the performance data on the plane's flight tests at Wright and Eglin fields.

In the spring of 1942, when Spaatz was organizing the Eighth Air Force at Bolling Field, Arnold described the P-51 to him, and Tooey remarked, "That's the plane I want." To which Hap replied, "If that's what you really want, you'll get it." Toward that end, he later overruled a Materiel Command recommendation on procurement, the only time he did so during the war, and saw to the placing of a large order of Mustangs.[10] He was further encouraged by reports coming from Major Tommy Hitchcock, Assistant Military Attaché in London. Hitchcock, a famous polo-playing horseman in civilian life, was an accomplished pilot and had fallen in love with the P-51. In September 1942, he recommended the "development of the Mustang as a high-altitude fighter, crossbreeding it with the Merlin 61 engine." Following additional tests, the Packard-Merlin V-1650 was adopted by the British.*

The Materiel Command's attitude that a liquid-cooled engine presented a definite disadvantage in combat was as inexplicable as it was wrong. It was as though the minds at work at Wright Field were unaware of the Spitfire and the Me 109. There is no doubt that this error in judgment turned out to be an extremely costly one. Nevertheless, in November, Hap Arnold sent President Roosevelt a memo on the Mustang, telling him the British were very keen on the fighter and that it would be "a highly successful plane for 1943. We think so much of it we have given orders for 2200." Arnold then added: "They are similar in design to the Focke-Wulf 190 but we believe them to be a very much better airplane on account of their ruggedness, superior armament and equal, if not better, performance."

He made no mention of the P-51's range, for, as already detailed, at the time the general air outlook expressed so strongly by Hugh Knerr, via the pen of author Bradford Huie, was, "American bombardment doctrine does not call for fighter escort. Why should a fighter go with a fortress when the fortress is better equipped to defend itself from the fighter?" The answer was becoming all too apparent over Kiel and Bremen and Hamburg and other German targets.

Even before recognition of the problem began to alarm Arnold, other methods of bomber support were underway. It was Air Chief Marshal Portal who had suggested long before that the best escort for a heavy bomber was another heavy bomber loaded with guns instead of bombs. The Pursuit Board, chaired by Spaatz shortly before Pearl Harbor, had called it a "convoy defender." Such a plane was produced, and later, in May 1943, the B-17 gun ship, designated YB-40, made its first combat appearance. Seven of them escorted nearly one hundred fifty heavies to Flak City. Each carried fourteen .50-caliber machine guns, compared to nine in a standard B-17F. As such, the YB-40 was designated a "secret weapon." In any guise it was a dud. The plane carried too much armor and armament to keep up, once the other B-17's had dropped their bombs, and it flew tail-heavy in whatever mode. It was not the answer to long-range escort.

Colonel Mark E. Bradley, Chief of Aircraft Projects at Wright Field, had spent the spring and early summer of 1943 on a troubleshooting assignment in England, working to get the bugs out of the P-47 and to extend its range. General Monk Hunter was to find Bradley's services "in-

* Hitchcock was killed in November 1943 while test-flying a Mustang.

valuable." He credited him with eliminating many of the Thunderbolt's technical difficulties so that it could get into combat. Bradley wanted to get into combat too, and he was training with Colonel Arman "Pete" Peterson's 78th Group toward that end when word came for him to return to Wright Field. In his capacity as Chief of Aircraft Projects, he had also gotten to know the P-51 well. Further, as an engineer and pilot he was intimately aware of the need to extend fighter range, and he went home with some definite thoughts on how this could be done with the Mustang. What he found waiting instead was the P-75, a Wright Field gerrymandered creation.

Built by General Motors, the P-75's wings came from a P-40, its center section from a Navy Vought Corsair FU-9, and the tail from a Douglas A-24. Up front it boasted a 24-cylinder Allison engine with contrarotating propellers. Bradley was anxious to test-fly the big bird, and when he did, he found it to be more of a dog—a dangerous one at that. After he'd landed the thing he went to see his boss, General Orval Cook, chief of the Production Division.

"Orval," he said, "I'm just back from flying the P-75, and I can't believe what I've heard! We've ordered two thousand of them?"

"That's right. We have to escort those bombers," replied Cook.

"But, Orval, the P-75 won't hack it! It's too slow. It won't be maneuverable enough. And it's so unstable I'd be afraid to fly the damn' thing again. It couldn't even protect *itself,* let alone a bomber!"

The General was not at all happy at what he was hearing. "O.K., Bradley," he said. "What's your solution?"

"We can make the P-51 do it."

"The P-51? How?"

Bradley explained that they could put an extra gas tank behind the pilot. Cook listened to the Colonel's explanation and then picked up the phone on his desk. "Give me General Echols," he said. Then he handed the phone to Bradley and ordered, "Tell him."

Him was Lieutenant General Oliver Echols, Chief of the Air Materiel Command. He sounded even less happy to hear Bradley's report on the P-75, and when the Colonel explained the plane's lack of maneuverability, Echols indicated his own understanding of the problem by arguing, "We don't want it to go so fast. We want it to play around near the bombers. What they're trying to get is something that will actually go and fly right over, or right under the bombers."

Bradley could only say, "Yes, sir." But when Echols added, "That is my information from the Navy," he was momentarily speechless. He brought the conversation back to the things that could be done to the P-51 to convert it to the type of plane that was needed, and the General finally said: "Well, go ahead and try it, and it's ultracritical. In fact, the whole result of the war may depend on it. Every time this is proposed, lots of people find a lot of things wrong with it. We've got to get an answer some way or other."

Bradley agreed wholeheartedly, and as soon as he'd hung up he was on the phone to Dutch Kindelberger, discussing the modifications he had in mind for the Mustang.[11]

It was about this same time that Arnold gave Barney Giles his marching orders on finding a long-range escort, and after reading Bradley's proposal on what should be done, Giles came out to see Kindelberger also. They strolled out on the ramp to look the P-51's over, and Barney said, "I would like to have two hundred more gallons of gas put into these fighters."

"Impossible, can't do it. The landing gear won't hold it," said Dutch.

"Well, you never know until you try."

And after a bit more debate on what could or could not be done, they began to try.

Seventeen

The Bitter Skies

The plan to make a double strike against Regensburg and Wiener-Neustadt, which Eaker had sent Possum Hansell to Washington to sell, was tentatively approved by Marshall on July 19. Since the force attacking Regensburg would not attempt the long return flight back to bases in East Anglia but go on to fields in North Africa, Eaker had proposed to Spaatz that two representatives be sent to talk over the timing and logistics involved. Marshall approved this idea as well but also advised that Portal be informed on the operation. As a result, a party of three flew down to Africa to confer with Spaatz and his staff on the mission. The most important of the visitors was Colonel Curtis LeMay. Several days earlier, Eaker had driven to LeMay's headquarters at Elveden Hall and briefed him on the proposed mission; "Iron Pants," as Commander of the 4th Wing (soon to be called the 3rd Air Division), would lead the Regensburg strike. Colonel Robert Hughes, an intelligence specialist on target data, and RAF Squadron Leader Allom, an expert on German fighter production, accompanied LeMay to Africa to make the necessary arrangements. In Tunis, LeMay met with Spaatz's chief of operations, Brigadier General Larry Norstad, who assured him that arrangements would be made to handle the incoming B-17's, consisting of seven groups, or about 145 aircraft—less those that didn't make it. Telergma was to be the principal field, as it was both a combat operational base and a depot. LeMay returned to England assured that in this first shuttle operation, and the longest bombing mission so far, his crews and their aircraft would be well cared for at the other end.

The rationale for the two-pronged strike, as Eaker expressed it to Arnold, was that "It will be absolutely impossible to execute a successful invasion next year unless we break up the German air force." He believed,

"There is absolutely no question but that we can reduce the German air force to impotence this year if we allow nothing to interfere with this program."

But the always doubtful and unpredictable element of weather did interfere. The tentative date for the mission, now called JUGGLER, was August 7. In the interim and between the hard missions of BLITZ WEEK, LeMay had his crews working on instrument takeoffs and flight procedures. He, more than any combat commander in the Eighth Air Force, recognized just what English weather in the damp, warm days of August could do to kill his part in the crucial plan.

Conversely, bad weather can also be a healer, and from the end of July until August 12, there were no missions because of it. This gave the battle-fatigued crews of BLITZ WEEK a chance to rest and regain their balance, and the ground and maintenance crews the opportunity to service and repair aircraft.

The weather also canceled JUGGLER as originally proposed, but on Friday the thirteenth, Spaatz did launch the Wiener-Neustadt segment of the attack. Sixty-nine of the Ploesti B-24's from the three groups Eaker was so anxious to have returned did bomb the Messerschmitt complex. Due to cloud cover, the results were not at all conclusive. The one good factor was that the strike obviously came as a surprise to the Germans and both ground and air defenses were weak and there were only two losses.

However, between August 7 and August 13, a new target, long in the process of development for attack, was selected. It was Schweinfurt, where an estimated 50 percent of Germany's ball bearings were produced. The strategy that Bomber Commander Fred Anderson now discussed with Eaker at PINETREE foresaw the double strike as planned, substituting Schweinfurt for Wiener-Neustadt, both forces taking off from England. The tactic was that LeMay's three combat wings would penetrate European air space about ten minutes ahead of Brigadier General Robert B. Williams' 1st Bomb Division, of nine groups, or two hundred thirty Fortresses. LeMay's heavily escorted force, it was reasoned, would draw off the German interceptors. Williams' nine groups would be heavily escorted as well, and at the same time, to further divide the opposition, medium bombers and additional fighters would be making a number of diversionary attacks on German airfields and installations in the occupied countries. Timing and weather were keys to the success of the mission, and on Tuesday, the morning of the mission, August 17—the anniversary of the Eighth Air Force's first strategic bombing mission—both were on the side of the enemy.

Thick fog blanketed East Anglia, where most of the bomber bases lay. LeMay's word for it was "stinking." Anderson, at PINETREE, was wrestling with another word that began with s: scrub. Should he scrub the mission? It was his choice to make, since on the preceding Saturday, General Eaker had flown to Africa to be present when LeMay's force arrived. Anderson's phone rang. It was LeMay suggesting an hour's delay. The weather might break. It didn't. Anderson and LeMay talked again and agreed on another half-hour wait. But that would be it, because, as LeMay pointed out, he couldn't risk leading his crews into strange fields in North Africa after dark. What kept Anderson from canceling the mission were reports that the weather over Europe and the targets was the best that had been forecast in two weeks. At the end of the half hour, Anderson gave the word to go. The fog was still so thick B-17's had to be led from their hardstands out to the runway with flashlights and lanterns. LeMay described the air as being "like dark gray jellied madrilene." His pilots had been trained to take off in it, but Williams' pilots had not, and that meant the critical timing factor of the operation was finished before it began. Most of the 146 crews of LeMay's groups, who had been sweating it out since the dawn hours, were sure the mission was going to be called off. But as the word came down to go, and the silence of the viscous morning air was torn by the cough and bark of starting engines, the question remained: Why wasn't it?

Across the Channel, German radio monitors were aware of preparations for a major mission. Headquarters of the German 1st Division, at Deelen, Holland, forecast correctly that at attack was going to be aimed at southern or central Germany. Fighter *Gruppen* on the North Sea coast were ordered to fields near Rheims, and all other fighter units as far north as Hamburg and as far east as Berlin were alerted.

It was shortly after 10 A.M. that the Regensburg force, led by the 96th Group, in which LeMay rode, crossed the Dutch coast. The three combat wings were escorted by a host of Thunderbolts and RAF Spitfires. The weather aloft was clear, and the FW 190's that came up to have a look stayed clear too. Then, close to the German border, the escorts, low on gas, were forced to turn back. It was then the German fighter pilots pounced, Focke-Wulfs and Me 109's slamming in from all angles, coordinated so that when one *Gruppe* ran out of ammunition, another came boring in. The battle raged up and down the sky for an hour and a half without pause, and anybody who was in it had never been in anything like it before. Fourteen Fortresses went down before the remaining 132 unloaded their bombs with remarkable accuracy on the Messerschmitt works at Regensburg: Prufening. Then the formation swung south, briefly surprising Luftwaffe Fighter Control preparing its fighters to hand out the same treatment on the return leg of the mission. Instead, a new opportunity awaited them.

Not ten minutes, but more than three hours, after LeMay's division had crossed the Dutch coast, Williams' force of 229 Fortresses crossed the mouth of the Scheldt headed for Schweinfurt. They, too, were accompanied by protective P-47's and Spitfires, but now German fighter strength, numbering an estimated three hundred aircraft, took on both escorts and bombers and, in any case, soon the escorts had to turn back. No one who fought his way to Schweinfurt that day expected to return, and thirty-six B-17's and three hundred seventy crewmen did not. Some of the Me 109's carried rockets under the wings, and they would come in behind a formation and, out of machine-gun range, would release them. There weren't many hits, but when contact was made, the Fortress blew up. In both the Regensburg and Schweinfurt battles, the Luftwaffe threw in one *Staffel* after another, including twin-engine Me 110's and Ju-88 night fighters. Many of the B-17's that fought their way to and from Schweinfurt came back never to fly again, carrying their dead and wounded.

LeMay's battered groups bound for Africa were under continuing attack for another hour after leaving the target area. They lost ten more aircraft. Two made forced landings in Switzerland, and several ditched in the Mediterranean. Finally, at the tag end of a day of air war that defied description, with fuel tanks registering empty, the 124 surviving B-17's came thudding in on three inadequate and scattered bases. Exhausted to the point of shock, they found that General Norstad's promise to LeMay of accommodations had somehow blown away in the desert wind. They slept under the wings of their planes, ate K rations, refueled the B-17's with hand pumps, and cursed every goddamned brass hat from Telergma to Gebru! But one thing, above all, they were shatteringly thankful they were alive. They had never expected to be.

In all, sixty aircraft had been lost and more than one hundred damaged against the two targets. Over six hundred officers and men had been killed, wounded, or captured. It had been the largest and most sustained air battle in history, and the question in the upper echelons in London and Washington was, did the results outweigh the cost?

LeMay believed his bombardiers had done an excellent job and he was correct. The Messerschmitt works at its bend in the Danube was badly damaged and would be out of production for at least three months. Williams was not all that sure about the bombing accuracy at the three ball-bearing factories at Schweinfurt. Neither he nor Allied Intelligence was aware that an estimated 38 percent of production had been halted, at least temporarily. Had the bombs been heavier and packed more wallop, the devastation would have been greater, but still, the effect was of great concern to Albert Speer. He feared the attackers were smart enough to follow up directly with another raid, and if they did, the German war effort would be in dire peril. To try to move the damaged plants would disrupt everything. But the Eighth Air Force, even if the target planners recognized Schweinfurt's vulnerability, could not have mounted an immediate return. On just two missions into Germany in August—the strike on the twelfth against five targets in the Ruhr and the double strike—eighty-five bombers had been lost since BLITZ WEEK. So severely depleted were the Eighth's reserves that Operations would not send a mission into Germany again for three weeks.

As to the effect of the double strike of August 17, Anderson was quoted for public consumption: "Although we cannot say that the end is actually in sight, the ultimate collapse of German resistance is obvious and inevitable. Our airmen go into the battle of Germany knowing that each airman lost saves thousands in ultimate cost on the ground. They realize that the very savagery of the German opposition indicates the extent of the hurt from our attacks."

In the double encounter, bomber crews claimed to have shot down 288 attackers, and the P-47's and Spitfires, nineteen. The total added up to about the actual number of German fighters engaged. No one would have believed the actual score was only twenty-seven, and it was just as well no one knew it. In spite of Eaker's letters to Arnold citing the high morale of combat crews, there were those who knew better. On some bases where losses were high, morale was pretty ragged.

In keeping with the Combined Bomber Offensive, Eaker had hoped to convince Bert Harris that he should launch a follow-up raid on Schweinfurt on the night of August 17–18. Harris had a low opinion of the importance of the target to begin with. Any target that was smaller than half the size of a city he referred to as a "panacea." His further excuse was that the moon would be full and his bombers would be sitting ducks for the German night fighters.

Actually, moon or no moon, he had been called on to hit a target on the Baltic coast, its importance so critical it remained secret even to the 579 RAF bomber crews that were to attack it. It was Peenemünde, the long-sought research-and-development site for Hitler's V-weapons, which he planned to rain down on England. The timing and strategy of the RAF strike worked out by Harris and his staff was far superior to that of the Eighth Air Force on the same day. To lull German air controllers, Harris had been sending on nightly forays a handful of fast, high-flying Mosquito bombers to hit Berlin. These were nuisance raids, but, as RAF Intelligence reasoned, the Germans would think they were the prelude to a massive attack on their capital. The Mosquitoes flew approximately the same course on each sortie, passing close to Peenemünde. Once this pattern became a regular routine, air defenses in and around the secret site became relaxed. On the night of the attack, the Mosquitoes flew to Berlin and dropped marker flares to outline the supposed target for the main force. Luftwaffe pilots were scrambled to the Berlin area. Meanwhile the heavy bombers, carrying 2,000 tons of high explosives and fire bombs, came in low over the North Sea, avoiding German radar, and then climbed up to seven thousand feet to practically wipe out Peenemünde. Nearly seven hundred fifty scientists and technicians important to the development of the V-weapons were killed.* The site was abandoned and a new one established in Poland, near Cracow. The manufacturing component of the operation was transferred underground into the Harz Mountains, where sixteen thousand slave laborers and two thousand technicians continued work on the missiles.¹ The destruction of Peenemünde by the RAF was considered one of the most important bombing raids of the war, because it delayed the use of the V-weapons by six months and, under the code name CROSSBOW, launched the continued search for and bombing of additional V-1 and V-2 sites.

Ira Eaker set in motion the conclusion of the raids of August 17–18. He came to see LeMay at Telergma to find out what kind of shape Curt's crews and planes were in. Except for about twenty of his B-17's, LeMay said they were in good shape and ready to bomb whatever Eaker had in mind. The result was that, just a week after Regensburg, the remaining eighty-four B-17's of 3rd Wing took off from their African fields and, on their return to home bases in England, bombed with pleasure and accuracy the Bordeaux-Mérignac air base, home of the FW 200, the Luftwaffe's four-engine reconnaissance bomber. In all, it was an eleven-hour flight, and the force lost three planes in passage.

Most of the crews of the damaged B-17's left in the desert sands—perhaps as a reminder to Larry Norstad for all his assistance—came back to England by ship.

With all the pronouncements that were made in the press as to the meaning of Regensburg-Schweinfurt—Hal George predicting, "The economic structure of Germany is going to fall by the end of the year"—it was pilot Lieutenant Owen "Cowboy" Roane, of the 100th Group, who left the most memorable quote. On board his aircraft he carried an extra crew member, a donkey named Mohammed acquired in an Arab marketplace. As Roane came into the traffic pattern of Thorpe Abbotts, he called the tower and said, "I'm coming in with a frozen ass!" The ambulance was there to meet the plane.²

* * *

Hap Arnold arrived in London on September 1, fresh from the deliberations of the QUADRANT Conference, held in Quebec. Militarily, QUADRANT was concerned with how best to remove Italy politically and physically from the war; the reaffirmation of the May 1, 1944, target date for OVERLORD; and the formation of a Southeast Asia Command, headed by Lord Louis Mountbatten with Major General Vinegar Joe Stilwell as deputy commander. There was no doubt that Churchill was still opposed to the invasion of Normandy and to a simultaneous invasion of southern France, code-named ANVIL (later DRAGOON):

* General Hans Jeschonnek, Chief of the General Staff of the Luftwaffe, committed suicide directly following the raid.

"When I think of the beaches of Normandy choked with the flower of American and British youth, and when, in my mind's eye, I see the tides running red with their blood, I have my doubts . . . I have my doubts."

However, there were no doubts on either side for the continued support of POINTBLANK, the Combined Bomber Offensive. When Arnold landed he greeted Eaker with a grin and said of the Conference, "Don't worry, you didn't lose anything."

Eaker's losses, of course, were of a different sort, and once on the scene he saw to it that Arnold got a clear picture of what he was up against. In short order Arnold fired off three significant cables to Marshall: MY VISIT HERE HAS BROUGHT OUT THE NECESSITY FOR SENDING THE 200 B-17's AS PLANNED AT THE EARLIEST PRACTICAL MOMENT. . . . He said if they weren't sent, the Eighth wouldn't be able to maintain constant operations.

His second message reiterated the now obvious need for long-range fighters to escort the bombers, and his third cable was a recommendation that Eisenhower's request for P-38 groups originally allocated for Eaker be denied: I REALIZE THE DESIRE OF EISENHOWER TO GET AS MANY PLANES AS POSSIBLE BUT STRONGLY RECOMMEND THAT THE ANSWER TO HIS REQUEST FOR P-38's BE NO. REPEAT, NO.

At that moment, Eisenhower was on the verge of invading Italy, and his wish, no doubt sponsored by Tedder and Spaatz, was understandable. It was Eaker's hard-held position that just as TORCH had been a diversion that had prevented an all-out air attack on Germany, so, too, was the thrust into Italy. It was Arnold's position that Allied air power in the Mediterranean was now five times greater than the entire German Air Force. Previously, Eisenhower's request for a "loan" of an additional four groups of heavy bombers had been rejected by the Combined Chiefs of Staff. Marshall had suggested the sending of medium bombers in their place, and Eaker and Devers had dug in their heels on that one too.

In one day, Arnold's presence had shored up Eaker's defenses. Since August 17, the Eighth had flown six missions, all against multiple targets, essentially German airfields in France, the Netherlands, and Belgium. And while part of the reason for these heavily escorted, relatively shallow penetrations was a result of a need to recoup and reflect on the tactics and effect of Regensburg-Schweinfurt, there was a strategic reason for them that was secret and therefore could not be used to answer the rising queries of ever-present critics.

When COSSAC had been created, early in the year, and it had been determined that an invastion of the Continent would not take place that summer, Allied Intelligence decided to put into operation a plan of deception to convince the Germans an invasion was about to be launched. The plan was called STARKEY, and it went into operation on the memorable day of August 17, which also saw Allied victory in Sicily. STARKEY was described as "an amphibious feint to force the Luftwaffe to engage in in-

tensive fighting over a period of about fourteen days, by building up a
threat of an imminent large-scale British landing in the Pas-de-Calais."³
Two of the intentions of the deception were to convince the Germans that
when an invasion did come it would be in the Pas-de-Calais region, and
secondly, to engage the Luftwaffe in a war of attrition. The first worked;
the second did not.

As Eaker told Arnold, and Devers later informed Marshall, the German opposition was feeble. Their fighters refused to come up and fight
even when the odds were three and four to one in their favor. Eaker felt
two conclusions could be drawn from the results of the Eighth's attacks
on a total of fourteen targets, nearly half of them fighter bases. Either
there was a breakdown in communications in the German air command
or Goering had decided to conserve his air strength to defend the homeland. It was this last that was the more likely, and it was proved on September 6, when Anderson sent his bombers back into Germany for the
first time in three weeks. The target was ball bearings again, this time the
SKF works at Stuttgart. New B-17's with chin turrets in the nose to discourage head-on attacks had been arriving in England, and at the same
time, back from Africa came the three B-24 groups that had been borrowed for the Ploesti raid. With a force of nearly four hundred bombers,
Eaker and Anderson were anxious to show the Boss what the Eighth
could do.

It turned out to be a bad-luck day all around; only the B-24's, on a diversionary sweep, returned without loss. Of the 338 B-17's that rose from
their bases in England to hit the main target, seventy-six were forced to
abort. The main force got tangled up in heavy cloud. Only one wing, of
forty-six planes, managed to bomb the target, and not very accurately. Between German fighters, flak, and misjudgment, at least twenty bombers
were down in the Channel. The loss was forty-five aircraft. Arnold saw
the mission as a complete failure, the results, in spite of glowing newspaper accounts, again playing into the hands of critics.

Arnold had come to England for two reasons: One was to have a close
look at what he couldn't see from his office in the Pentagon, and the other
was to discuss a matter he had broached to Portal in Quebec. Although
the results of the Stuttgart mission were disappointing, he knew from Portal that Goering had issued orders that the Fortress must be destroyed regardless of everything else. German pilots, on pain of court-martial, were
to lay off the stragglers and concentrate on the main formation to prevent
it from bombing the target. From this news, and from all else he saw and
heard from his airmen, from Devers, and from Edwards, for the moment
he was able to appreciate the realities. Being with Ira, listening to his
calm and measured account of all the complexities involved, was reassuring. Incredibly, with all else each was called on to accomplish, they were

revising and updating two of their previously published books, this connection alone an unseen part of their relationship.

On the evening following the Stuttgart raid, Eaker threw a grand dinner at Castle Coombe, the honored guest Lord Trenchard. Present to drink his health were a host of Allied airmen and some naval types, including Admiral Stark. Portal, Harris, and Slessor were on hand, and Arnold had already spoken to them on the proposition he had raised during the QUAD-RANT Conference.

Looking ahead—as well as backward—Arnold could see developing a situation in which he felt there would be a need to appoint a supreme strategical air commander, just as there would be a need for an air commander-in-chief to control the combined tactical air forces engaged in OVERLORD. The first of the two proposals was the more delicate, for several reasons. Once there were bases in Italy, Arnold foresaw a second strategic air force to join with the Eighth in the mounting attack on Germany, and because of the English weather, particularly during the winter months, these bases would be available to Eighth Air Force units. In his thinking, both air forces would be under a strategic commander. This, from a practical point of view, would require careful cooperation on all levels, but when looked at from the present position of command, it presented a different set of problems, not the least of which were the personalities involved and the positions they held. Sir Charles Portal, as Chief of the Air Staff, was the overall director of the Combined Bomber Offensive. Bomber Harris, as head of RAF Bomber Command, was a power unto himself, supported by Churchill, fiercely independent, cooperating with the CBO as long as he made the target selection. Ira Eaker was commander of a growing air force that would soon outnumber RAF Bomber Command.

During Arnold's visit it was announced, by order of the President, that Eaker would now wear a new hat: Commander of all U. S. Air Forces in the ETO. This was the result of moving what was left of Lewis Brereton's Ninth Air Force to England to build it up as a tactical air arm to support OVERLORD. It was now Eaker's responsibility, working with Brereton, to accomplish this shift but, unlike the building of the Twelfth Air Force, not by the diminution of his own forces.† This, then, added to Eaker's stature, as did his promotion that same month to lieutenant general. Both moves indicated Arnold's support.

Down in the Mediterranean, there was the opinions of Tedder and Spaatz to be considered, Tedder as commander of the air forces there and Spaatz as his deputy.

Arnold went over the idea at length, not just with Eaker, Portal, and

† The Eighth Air Force Support Command, made up of medium and light bombers, became a part of the Ninth Air Force.

Harris, but with Devers and Idwal Edwards as well. His reasoning, he said, was "that with one person directing all operations, night and day, regardless of who the man was, we would get better results."[4] Bert Harris didn't think so and told him straight out, knowing that if any such commander was appointed, he wouldn't be the one and might therefore lose the freedom of action he now enjoyed.

Arnold didn't press the point, but he made it clear and asked for written appraisals from the aforementioned. There was nothing he said that alerted Eaker to any danger signal as to his own position. Quite the contrary, he had been promoted, given greater responsibility and, in a conversation with Arnold and Devers, the Boss had raised the suggestion that in view of the growth of the Eighth Air Force, Eaker might soon need a deputy commander to aid him.

The fact was there was nothing new in Arnold's thinking concerning a supreme strategic air leader. He had tried to press the idea repeatedly on Tooey Spaatz a year before. Since he could not assume the command himself, behind his thinking was the desire to see Spaatz become the number one Allied airman in the war against Germany. What was not possible a year ago might have a better chance now, particularly with the growth of U.S. air power.

At Castle Coombe, the night hoary old "Boom" Trenchard had been the honored guest, Monk Hunter was also among the invited. For two months he had been breaking Bill Kepner in to take over as 8th Fighter Commander, and he was quietly furious at his longtime friend Hap Arnold. He bided his time and finally, as the evening wore on, he managed to maneuver the Boss into a room where they were alone. He backed Arnold up against a wall and cut loose, "Look, goddammit," he swore, knowing he was way out of line and way out of order, "Kepner doesn't know a blasted thing about fighter planes that I haven't taught him! For you to relieve me of a combat command in time of war is a bloody insult! What you're going to do is bring me back to the States, pin some medal on my chest and kick me upstairs! Goddammit, why?"

Arnold only grinned at Monk's outburst, patted him on the shoulder and took no umbrage. It was a good question as to whether Hunter's relief had been inspired by "experts" too far from the scene, plus production difficulties over which he had no control. Giles was quick to admit that when he had called Kepner and asked him what he thought about fighters escorting bombers, his reply had been, "Whatever you do, Barney."

That Arnold had come to recognize that Monk Hunter's disappointment and anger were not without some justification was forthcoming next day when he sent a cable to Marshall: AFTER CONFERRING WITH DEVERS AND EAKER, BELIEVE HUNTER HAS DONE EXCELLENT ORGANIZATION

AND EXECUTIVE JOB AND THAT HE IS BEST QUALIFIED MAN TO HEAD 1ST AIR FORCE. AM SENDING HIM HOME AS SOON AS HE CAN LEAVE.

Monk was wrong about one thing. When it came time, Hap didn't pin one medal on his chest, he pinned two.

Arnold spent little more than a week in England, and when he took off from Bovingdon on his way back to Washington, his greatest concern remained the high casualties the Eighth Air Force was suffering. There was no argument on the steps that must be taken in an effort to lower them, but the variables in air war were unlike any other, and he was looking for greater innovation in their resolution. The foul-up on the Stuttgart raid had not been reassuring, and he was also worried about the morale of the combat crews. The Eighth Air Force Intelligence Chief, Lieutenant Colonel Harris Hull, was on the flight home with him, and Hull, articulate and informed, managed to allay his fears with concrete examples that illustrated that indeed the bomber crews and the men who serviced them were the pick of the crop. On the last score, Hugh Knerr, finally a brigadier general, was on the flight as far as Prestwick, and his description of the new system of repair and maintenance also satisfied Arnold.

As for Eaker's morale, he knew having the Boss on the scene, going one-on-one with him, not having to be concerned with the faceless kingmakers on the Air Staff, was the best way to mend any holes in the fence.[5] But now, with Arnold's departure, the new proposal had left a hole of a different sort, and Eaker quickly contacted Tooey. He told him of the discussions with Devers and Portal on "the desirability of having a supreme Strategical Allied Air Force Commander to coordinate the heavy bombardment of Axis objectives by the RAF, the Eighth Air Force and the Twelfth Air Force from any and all European bases." He informed Spaatz that, directly after Arnold had left, he had sat down with Portal and suggested they all get together—Tedder and Harris included—and talk it over and come up with "a common recommendation to the Combined Chiefs of Staff as against a piecemeal one." He didn't know if Portal would call such a meeting. If he didn't, then Ira suggested it was important he and Tooey get together in order to come up with a united front on the question. He proposed they meet as soon as possible, preferably before October 1, either in London or in Gibraltar.

Spaatz's response was, "I feel very strongly that nothing should be done about the overall organization of the Air without giving Tedder and me a chance to comment on our ideas of the organization insofar as this neck of the woods is concerned." His plans were to return to the States for about a week early in October, and he would stop to see Ira either going or coming and they would also talk with Portal. But the meeting did not work out.

Before Eaker sent his reply to Arnold, over a month later, he not only had the benefit of the RAF point of view but also that of his own senior commanders, such as Fred Anderson. The approach he finally took focused not on whether there should be a supreme strategical air commander but on the effect such an appointment would have on the Allied relationships involved. He also played back to Arnold the advantages Arnold had stressed to him in such an appointment: proper coordination in selecting the objectives of strategic air forces, ensuring the preparation of strategic bases in Italy and elsewhere, shuttling forces between one base and another to take advantage of the weather. He pointed out that already the Combined Chiefs of Staff had designated a British officer as a Supreme Tactical Air Force Commander, so naturally the person named to the strategical post should be an American. But that raised the point of rank, for Bert Harris was senior to any U.S. officer that might be named. He said he didn't know what the reaction would be from the British side, but he pointed out that since Casablanca, the method they had been operating under—from the Combined Chiefs of Staff to Portal—had worked out fine. "The coordination between the Eighth Air Force and the RAF Bomber Command is so close and has been conducted with such thorough amity, good will and accord that little necessity has developed for any other form of single command." He quickly added, however, that the air situation would change as soon as OVERLORD was launched and a beachhead established. By then there would be strategic bases in Italy, and then, repeating one of Arnold's own reasons for the idea in the first place—the need for close coordination between the air forces in the U.K. and the Mediterranean—he concluded: "This can be accomplished by a common directive from the Combined Chiefs of Staff or by the appointment of a Supreme Commander," which was really no conclusion at all. His recommendations did not deal with whether he thought the appointment was a good idea or not but instead with what to do if the British would not agree to a U.S. officer's being selected: either the formation of a committee made up of Portal, Tedder, Harris, Spaatz, and Eaker, or the formation of a smaller committee made up of Devers, Portal, Eisenhower, and whoever was made Supreme Allied Commander of OVERLORD. Both possibilities would, of course, be arrived at through a directive from the Combined Chiefs of Staff.

How Eaker's response affected Arnold is not known. He was looking for new ways to do things better. Acceptance of the status quo, no matter how well it was working, was not about to please him. His regard for the British was not on a par with Eaker's. He knew they had wooed any number of his officers into their camp without their ever knowing it. It is probable that he believed the CBO was working as well as it was more through Eaker's cooperation with Harris and Portal than vice versa. In that regard, he could not have been surprised at Portal's evaluation of his proposal.

Portal said his views had been arrived at after consultation with

Tedder, and what they added up to was, *Let's not rock the boat for now.*
Portal noted that his opinions and recommendations agreed in a considerable measure with the directives for the creation of the new, Fifteenth
Air Force, in Foggia, Italy, sent to Eisenhower by the Combined Chiefs,
which, in essence, accepted that for now it was better to keep the command structure as it was presently constituted, operating from the U.K.
and Italy. Portal closed his letter saying, "I should very much like to discuss the whole question with you when we meet, which I hope will be in
the not too distant future." His hope was to be realized.

It appeared that Arnold was no sooner back in Washington than he
began to pepper Devers and Eaker with cables and letters on the same old
theme: "We obviously must send the maximum number of airplanes
against targets within Germany, now that the German Air Force appears
to be at a critical stage. . . . We must indoctrinate our personnel through
all ranks with this principle so as to cut down the time required to put the
planes back in operation, . . ." etc.

And then: "To us here in the United States, it looks as if the employment of large numbers of heavy bombers has not been followed through
by your headquarters and staff. We have always said that with the employment of large numbers of heavy bombers, the percentage of losses per
mission would correspondingly decrease. However, since my visit to England and the impression in my mind is that you still figure on employing
small numbers of 300 or maybe 400 at a time, followed by another wave
of 300 or 400, or maybe a third of 300 or 400. . . ." He then went on to
lecture Eaker on "the necessity of an entirely new technique—planning
technique, airdrome technique, and actual air operations technique. . . ."
He said he was looking forward to the time when there would be 1800
heavy bombers in England with 900 in reserve and expecting to see 1500
of them being used on every day of bombing, and how could this be done
if Eaker didn't have a better way of getting his planes over Germany?

And Eaker might well ponder who was goading the Boss within the Air
Staff, or was all the pressure coming from without and Arnold's reaction
signaling the state of his nerves and problems with his heart? It had to be
something of both, for if Arnold didn't know the statistical facts, there
were those around him who did—or should have.

At the end of September, Eaker had 604 operational bombers, but he
had only *450* operational crews. In July, he had received 159 new crews
but he'd lost 171. In August, the losses had been 120 against 164 replacement crews, and in September, new crews added up to more than double
the losses of 104. Since Arnold's departure, eight missions had been
flown, six of them against as many as five targets at a time: airfields and
aircraft industries, mostly in France, some in support of STARKEY. Losses
were few and numbers of bombers substantial, with ample escort. On the
twenty-seventh, Anderson sent his bombers back to Emden, and then

again five days later. Out of the 585 heavies that dropped their tons of high explosives and incendiaries on aircraft and shipping, only nine were lost in the two raids, and regardless of the criticisms brought by special messenger from the Pentagon, the figures told their own story.

On October 4, Eaker cabled Arnold on a successful attack against Frankfurt, reporting that photo reconnaissance indicated the city was still burning after 282 B-17's had unloaded 555 tons of bombs and 290 tons of incendiaries on it.

Just as the fury of the Combined Bomber Offensive began to build, Arnold sent a member of his staff to Bushy Park to get from Eaker, "with the least practical delay, your general plan for the employment of your heavy bombers. It should include, among other items, sufficient detail to let me know: 1. How many airplanes per base (operation and reserve). 2. Technique in take-off, assembly, approach, bombing, return and landing to include time allowance. 3. Missions per month per airplane. 4. Tactics whereby the proportion of our bombers to enemy fighter losses may be reduced, to include size of formation attacking objectives." The communication, which did not bear any signature, said the information was needed not only in relation to the ultimate buildup but to the bomber force during it.

All of these points had been explained and detailed many times, as they would be again, but Eaker's patience remained phenomenal. It was his job to explain, or attempt to explain, the actions of his command, but he had to know the two-front war was heating up.

On October 8, 9, and 10, the Eighth Air Force struck eight vital German targets, two of them in Poland. The Luftwaffe came up to fight, and without escort inside Germany, the bomber losses were heavy. The battles were fierce, the skies streaked with flame and falling aircraft, the formations presenting a geometric pattern knifed and torn by the rocket and cannon fire of the angling fighters. But they could not be turned back, and the wreckage and destruction they visited on their targets was felt throughout the Reich.

This brought a reversal in the tone of Arnold's communications. He informed Ira of plans to establish the Fifteenth Strategic Air Force in Italy, which would be under Eisenhower's command. Then he praised him for the very successful raids of October 8 on Bremen and Vegesack.‡ "I believe that the continuation of such raids will produce the desired results that you and I have discussed so many times. When the Germans refer to these missions as 'terror raids,' we know that the effect produced is all that we could wish." He sent his congratulations to Ira and all involved, plus his "anticipation of bigger and better [raids] in the future."

‡ The targets for the raids of Oct. 8–10 were in Germany: Bremen (twice), Vegesack, Anklam, Marienburg, Muenster; in Poland, Danzig-Gdynia, twice.

Several days later he admitted, "Candidly, I think your whole bomber effort is picking up. As you know, I was worried because, in my opinion, you were not getting enough airplanes [into combat] out of the total number we had in the 8th Air Force."

On Tuesday, October 12, the fog was as thick as it had been the day before. The weather was equally bad over the Continent. There would be no mission today; possibly it would be clear enough tomorrow. Much of Eaker's day had been taken up in meetings with Major General Louie Brereton and his staff. Brereton had just come back from Washington, and in conference they had decided that on the fifteenth they would officially activate the Ninth Air Force. Important as the establishment of the new tactical Air Force was, Eaker had at the moment an even more important consideration on his mind. Late that afternoon, he met with Portal and Harris to discuss it. Eighth Bomber Command was going back to Schweinfurt. Careful study of reconnaissance photos, plus intelligence information, had convinced the planners that the Germans were furiously at work putting the plants back into operation while at the same time frantically scrambling around looking for outside sources of ball bearings, neutral Sweden being their principal market, and Hitler was demanding a speedup in production. This recognition, plus the realization that General Bob Williams' fears of not too accurate bombing on August 17 were correct, brought the determination to go back and do it again. They would have to do so knowing that Luftwaffe fighter *Gruppen* were now practically established along whatever target route was selected. Welcome as the very newly arrived P-38's were, neither they nor the P-47's, both with their auxiliary fuel tanks, could accompany the bombers very far into Germany.

Eaker, in his daily letter to Arnold, blandly said, "Prospects are fair for another good demonstration tomorrow," and that his talk with Portal and Harris was on the subject "of how to speed up the knockdown of the G.A.F. and its supporting establishment." But he was apprehensive, as was Anderson. Eaker and Anderson agreed that if the cost of a second Schweinfurt was too high and the ball-bearing plants were not put out of action, the effort would be classed as a catastrophe. And whatever else happened, the hue and cry would be raised again on both sides of the ocean, probably led by Churchill, to drop daylight bombing. With members of his staff he had pondered the value of delay and rejected it. Delay would not break the back of the Luftwaffe. Portal and his people estimated that from the damage the Eighth had visited on Germany so far this month, its aircraft production for November would be half of what had been scheduled. Knock out the ball bearings, and it and a lot of other transportation needs would be a damn sight less.

Fred Anderson, resolute, untiring, a workaholic who kept a cot in his office, was also strongly determined not to delay further. "Go and go now," he said. They could send nearly three hundred B-17's, many with the chin turret.

Eaker had also been encouraged by Churchill's reaction to the October raids. He knew the Prime Minister had sent a congratulatory message to Arnold conveying the thanks of the British War Cabinet and himself "for the magnificent achievements of the Eighth Air Force in the Battle of Germany in recent day, culminating in the remarkable success as of last week."

Now the hope was to add to that record. On Wednesday, it appeared the weather might improve over Germany by Thursday, and that after-noon the teletype machines began to clatter, alerting the bases to the de-tails of Mission 115.

For the crews awakened in the darkness that morning of October 14, the day dawned as it had on August 17: with fog. Many thought the mis-sion would be scrubbed. Many thought, as they climbed up through the overcast and sought to join up in tight formations, that it should be.

Lieutenant Colonel T. Ross Milton, who had been given his first airplane ride by Hap Arnold back in 1926, was Operations Officer for the 91st Group. He had not been on first Schweinfurt, and it didn't look like he was going to be on second. "The weather was terrible. I was sure they were going to scrub it, absolutely sure. I was sitting out at the end of the run-way, and all of a sudden we get the green light to go. We didn't break out until 12 thousand. It was solid until about ten. Then we tried to pick up our formation and a lot of people decided that they weren't going to be enough to make it worthwhile going in, and what we did was sort of collect an ad hoc group. Weather was fine over the Channel and perfect over Europe, so once we were launched a lot of us decided we might as well go. Nobody recalled us, so we went, and I ended up in the lead over the Channel because the designated leader turned around and started back for England. Then he turned again and got into the column."[6]

Actually, 320 planes had taken off. The B-24's never did join up, and twenty-nine of them were sent on a diversionary sweep. Of the rest, sixty-two aborted, and Ross Milton led a force of 229 Forts into Germany. The bombing, he reported afterward, was good, much better than the first time. They left Schweinfurt in flames. But, like the first time, if the bomb-ing was good so too was the hunting on the part of the Luftwaffe. German pilots referred to the B-17 and the B-24 as *der dicker Hund,* the fat hound.

Afterward on that bright fall day, from the air the burnt-out wrecks of *der dicker Hund* marked a trail hundreds of miles long, soiling the au-tumn landscape. The coordinated attacks of over 300 Luftwaffe defenders had shot down sixty B-17's. Another seventeen, which fought their way back to England, would never fly again.

That night, Eaker did not sleep. He spent it with Fred Anderson at

Bushy Park, going over the combat reports, waiting for reconnaissance photos and damage-to-target assessments. He already knew the reaction was going to be unfavorable. The losses were the highest yet, really unacceptable. In some groups, whole squadrons had been decimated. Shock waves had to be running through those bases hardest hit. He would not accept defeat. This was not defeat, it was just one battle in a fight to the finish, and he knew who was going to finish on top. Whatever doubts he might have felt, he suppressed. His steadiness had its own effect on reassuring Anderson and the staff people around him.

The next morning, he drafted a cable to Arnold that began, YESTERDAY THE HUN SPRANG HIS TRAP. He sought to convey that this was the Luftwaffe's last gasp, HIS FINAL COUNTERMEASURE. He used the metaphor of a play, with Schweinfurt A FULL-SCALE DRESS REHEARSAL, but not unexpected, because the Germans had practiced SINGLE ACTS IN THE PLAY BEFORE but now perfectly timed and executed: A SCREEN OF SINGLE-ENGINE FIGHTERS FLEW IN FROM THE FRONT VERY CLOSE, FIRING NORMAL 20 MM CANNON AND MACHINE GUNS. THESE CLOSELY FOLLOWED BY LARGE FORMATIONS OF TWIN-ENGINE FIGHTERS IN WAVES, EACH FIRING LARGE NUMBERS OF ROCKETS SUSPENDED UNDER WINGS. And he went on to describe the action and the effect of seven hundred different attacks made on the bombers, with one combat wing being practically wiped out, the others not seriously damaged, their bombing excellent, all three factories destroyed. He cited one hundred thirty German fighters destroyed or probably so before he mentioned the loss of sixty bombers. He then gave a description of the measures to be taken to defeat such an onslaught, and what they added up to was the very urgent need for long-range fighters and replacements. He must have two hundred fifty replacements before the end of the month, because he was estimating a loss of at least two hundred. WE MUST GROW BIGGER, NOT SMALLER. SEND EVERY POSSIBLE FIGHTER HERE AS SOON AS POSSIBLE. . . .

In a following letter to Arnold in which his statements on Schweinfurt were almost matter-of-fact, he remarked, "There is not the slightest question but that we now have our teeth in the Hun Air Force's neck." To those who flew Mission 115 the metaphor might have sounded more accurate if it had been reversed.

Marshall, however, knew what Eaker was saying, particularly at the conclusion of his detailed cable, which stated: WE MUST SHOW THE ENEMY WE CAN REPLACE OUR LOSSES; HE KNOWS HE CANNOT REPLACE HIS; WE MUST CONTINUE THE BATTLE WITH UNRELENTING FURY. THIS WE SHALL DO. THERE IS NO DISCOURAGEMENT HERE. WE ARE CONVINCED THAT WHEN THE TOTALS ARE STRUCK YESTERDAY'S LOSSES WILL BE FAR OUTWEIGHED BY THE VALUE OF THE ENEMY MATERIAL DESTROYED.

The Chief of Staff responded with a personal communication. He said he was "tremendously impressed with the apparent complete destruction

of the Schweinfurt Ball-Bearing Plant," but, more to the point of all that
was involved, he added, "I like the tone of your message.[7] *No* great battle
is won without heavy fighting and inevitable losses." He was sure the continued gallantry and skill of the Eighth Air Force would finish off the
German fighter force, demonstrating "the awful power of precision bombing with your fine personnel, the pick of America."

Arnold, who had been so strongly attracted to Schweinfurt as a vital
German target, dispatched a letter of support in which he said he was
highly gratified that morale and enthusiasm were holding up in spite of
the heavy losses. He stressed again the versatility of bombing technique
"if we are going to continue these operations with any degree of success."

> We must not only show them we intend to replace our losses but will
> send our bombers into Germany with an ever-increasing strength; that
> with our numbers and determination there is nothing the Germans can do
> which will stop our precision daylight bombing; that we will change our
> ideas, our technique, our equipment just as often as is necessary to secure
> the maximum effort from the airplanes we have available.

Like Eaker, Arnold now turned to metaphor in asking that a message
from him be conveyed to "your command: That the cornered wolf fights
hardest and that the German Air Force has been driven into its last
corner."

German fighter pilots flying over France and Belgium, Luxembourg and
the homeland, following the trail of *der dicker Hund,* might not have
agreed, and combat crews on their bases in England, those who had been
to Schweinfurt and back, would have had no quotable comment, nor
would the maintenance crews working to repair 117 battle-torn B-17's.

Arnold followed with a long cable in which he postulated that the
Luftwaffe might be on the verge of collapse, that the "frantic employment" of all its fighter aircraft was an indication. He asked Eaker to sit
back a moment and view the whole situation with Anderson, Kepner, and
Knerr, to seek out Portal and Harris to see if they could come up with
any substantial evidence to show that the assumption was correct.

While on the surface a rapid flow of messages of support was exchanged between Washington and London, each seeking to reassure the
other, there is no doubt that consternation and doubt lay just beneath it.
Ross Milton, who had unexpectedly led the raid, was called the next day
to headquarters to attend a critique on the mission. He had never been in
the presence of so much top brass. When he was asked to report on why
he had taken over as leader, an argument broke out with Colonel
Budd Peaslee, who had made the turnaround, not to give up leadership
of the mission but to herd in the strays. That tempers and nerves were
frayed was understandable. Milton and Peaslee and all the others had
fought a battle that had extended over a total of eight hundred miles and

had lasted for over three hours, in which the enemy had brought into play every type of fighter he could put into the air, including the old Stuka and the new twin-engine Me 210. As Peaslee later described the conflict: "I think of the Middle Ages. I see myself strolling across an open plain with a group of friends. Suddenly we are beset by many scoundrels on horseback. They come from every direction shooting their arrows. We defend ourselves as best we can with slings and swords and crouch behind our leather shields. We cannot run, we cannot dodge, we cannot hide—the plain has no growth, no rocks, no holes. And it seems endless. There is no way out—then, or now."[8]

Ross Milton was not so graphic in his description, but he believed, from all that was said, that when he left the critique, the whole program of daylight bombing was in great jeopardy.

To guard against such a reality, Eaker gathered with his press officers and much care was taken in getting out official releases on the mission.

On the next day a statement by Eaker gave details on the damage assessment. This was followed in the morning with the first strike photos and then a claim that the entire Schweinfurt works was out of action and possibly only a quarter of it would ever resume production. Then came excerpts from cables of congratulations sent by Stimson, Marshall, and Arnold "which stress completeness of destruction and justify our losses." Eaker felt that his press releases dramatized the importance of Schweinfurt to show that the entire German war machine had been badly hurt and that the attack was ordered knowing the cost would be high.[9]

His press coverage was in answer to Goebbels' cries of victory and also to paper over the rising shock and consternation in high places at losses that in the aggregate simply could not be sustained: 116 crews in two weeks. From visiting the bases that had been hardest hit, Eaker believed morale was far higher among the crews than among those at the top. Then Hap Arnold, at his own press conference, nearly pulled the rug out.

He addressed a gathering of writers, editors, and news broadcasters at the Pentagon. His theme was the destruction of the German Air Force, but when it came to the question-and-answer period, some of his statements shook Eaker and infuriated Anderson and the division commanders. The newsmen were most interested in Schweinfurt, and the British press picked up Arnold's admission that on some missions a 25 percent loss could be expected. "In this connection," Eaker wrote to Arnold with great forbearance, "it seems to me well to remember that our overall losses are still below 5 percent. From the standpoint of maintaining crew morale I am anxious that our crews do not feel that their leaders anticipate enormous losses."

Arnold had also made an additional blunder, hinting that the Germans had been tipped off to the attack. They had not. He was attempting to plant an implied excuse for the high casualties. The fact was that

Luftwaffe controllers had first thought the attack was going to be against Frankfurt, but the statement, Eaker and his command knew, could only put added doubt in the minds of the bomber crews. If the Germans knew the point of attack beforehand, what chance did they have? The press conference was not Hap Arnold at his best.

Whatever else Schweinfurt proved, if it still needed proving, was that the bombers could *not* go it alone. It was a recognition hard to come by, because the opposite view had been held so long, sustained in part by Eaker's unyielding optimism. But, as Anderson bluntly told his wing commanders, "we can afford to come up only when we have our fighters with us." The P-47, even with its 108-gallon auxiliary tank, had a range of only three hundred fifty miles, the P-38 a hundred miles more. There would be no more deep penetrations into Germany until the modified long-range P-51 arrived.

Between mid-October and year's end, the Eighth Air Force would fly twenty-three missions and bomb forty-seven targets, half of them in Germany and two in Norway, but on almost every mission they would be escorted. They would use new radar devices to bomb through the overcast, drop metal particles called "chaff" to confuse German radar controllers, and employ the fast-flying Mosquito bombers as pathfinders to lead and mark the attack on numerous targets. Their losses would no longer be catastrophic, their escorts, "the little friends," being there to take on the Luftwaffe, but the thrust of the daylight campaign of the CBO had been seriously blunted. They could not go deep to hit the vital aircraft factories, and German aircraft production was growing. The new combat techniques that Arnold was calling for were worked out, but there were two things that did not change after mid-October: the atrocious weather and Arnold's yo-yo manner with Eaker—one day patting him on the back and the next kicking him lower down.

* * *

Tooey Spaatz arrived in Washington shortly before second Schweinfurt and was there during reaction to it. No doubt his laconic remarks helped to calm the panic-stricken and perhaps had a modifying influence on Hap Arnold, whom he did not think looked well. Spaatz was home to talk airforce reorganization, in particular the establishment of the Fifteenth Air Force. It was to be set up with six heavy bomb and two P-38 groups, seven fighter and one reconnaissance groups. Although the Fifteenth was called a "Strategic Air Force" until air-base objectives north of Rome were secured, it was also to be utilized against tactical targets. In going over the plan, Arnold undoubtedly detailed his strategic-air-commander concept. Coordination between the Eighth and the Fifteenth was the cornerstone of the latter's creation. Spaatz, as Commanding General of the U. S. Army Air Forces in Africa, would have overall command of the

Twelfth as well as the Fifteenth, plus five service commands and the 90th Photo Reconnaissance Wing. Arnold's thinking on a single head for the strategic air aspect of the war was full of variables, and if Spaatz was to be the head, there were certain conditions he would demand.

At the QUADRANT Conference, in Quebec, it had been generally agreed that General George Marshall would command OVERLORD but would still be Chief of Staff, with Eisenhower coming home to be Acting Chief. This raised a raft of questions as to who would then command what? and where? The decision to select Marshall had not pleased Arnold at all, for he strongly believed that the Chief of Staff was needed to head the Joint Chiefs and manage the total war effort, particularly in battles with the British. For once, Admirals King and Leahy agreed, because, as King put it to Roosevelt, "Why break up a good thing?"

As for his strategic-command ideas, Arnold had taken them to both Hopkins and Marshall. In a memo to the President on October 4, Hopkins observed: "It is essential that there be one strategic air force and that our bombers not be frozen either in England, Italy or Africa. It is only human nature for a theater commander to want to hang on to his airplanes."

Marshall's response to Arnold a month later would have been in keeping with Spaatz's approach:

> You propose vigorous organizational and operational steps for pressing the air war against Germany. Unifying the American strategic air forces in North Africa and the United Kingdom is certainly a step in the proper direction. However, at the moment I think it unwise to press the question of unification of U.S. and British air commands until the more vital problem of unified command in the Mediterranean as now proposed by the British Chiefs of Staff, and also the overall command in Europe problem, have been settled. If the decisions in these matters are made in accordance with our present views, then the problem of unified air command and overall air command will probably be settled automatically.

Marshall was correct in that the problems of unified command would be settled, but not all that automatically.

In late November, Roosevelt and Churchill, their key political advisers, and the Combined Chiefs of Staff met first in Cairo, Egypt, with Chinese leader Chiang Kai-shek, then in Tehran, Iran, with Stalin. Then the two met again in Cairo to settle the outstanding political and military issues confronting them, which included the ticklish question of command. All was not sweetness and light between the Allied commanders when they gathered at the Mena House, by the Nile, on November 21. One very major difference was the British reluctance to commit itself to OVERLORD, Churchill determinedly anxious to push operations into the Balkans, the eastern Mediterranean, and Norway.

Both Marshall and Arnold had pointed out to Roosevelt, during the

voyage from Plymouth Roads aboard the battleship *Iowa,* that there were
now more American troops in England than British, and by January 1,
U.S. aircraft would outnumber the RAF by four thousand. All of which
meant that the buildup was not going to be for naught and the Joint
Chiefs were no longer going to be dominated by their English cousins. At
one combined session, which General Alan Brooke was chairing, he got in
a very nasty argument with Admiral Ernie King. Of the encounter, General Joe Stilwell wrote in his diary, "God, he [King] was mad. I wish he
had socked him!" And Arnold was to comment in his notes that a Combined Chiefs of Staff meeting on the unsettled European campaign "almost ended in a brawl." Brooke penned in his account that he had had "the
father and mother of a row" with Marshall. But then Arnold was to add,
"We finally almost reached an agreement."

This was on November 26, the day after a Thanksgiving dinner which
Roosevelt had hosted, carving the festive bird himself, and some of those
assembled would probably have enjoyed carving each other. Privately,
Arnold talked with Portal on his plan for a single strategic air commander, but the British Air Chief remained unconvinced. On one point
there was joint acceptance, and that was the general understanding that
Marshall was going to be named as Supreme Commander for OVERLORD,
but even this was not firmly decided when they all flew off to Tehran to
meet with "good old Uncle Joe." The selection was the President's choice,
and he was having second thoughts. In this unsettled atmosphere, Arnold,
like the President, played his cards close to the chest, and in his talks with
Portal and Tedder he did not indicate who his choice might be to head a
strategic air command. But Portal could perceive the form of what Arnold
had in mind, and he could see that the major command changes in the
wind might well establish U.S. air as well as ground command for both
POINTBLANK and OVERLORD. Through the Combined Chiefs he was the
Air Forces head and he wished to remain so. Directly after talking to Arnold he sent a cable to his Vice-Chief, Air Marshal Sir Douglas Evill,
asking him to contact Eaker immediately to discuss with him his position
on the appointment of "a combined supreme strategic air force commander."

Eaker promptly took the matter up with Devers, showing him the cable,
and it was agreed that Eaker would meet with Evill at three o'clock that
afternoon and arrive at a response. Eaker, unaware of the contention at
Cairo but fully aware of Arnold's position, must have recognized the delicacy of his own. It was not Arnold asking for his opinion on the matter
but the Chief of the British Air Staff. In the past, Portal had given him
strong support in his running battle with Washington. Now Sir Charles
was asking for his view, already knowing full well where he stood.

Eaker responded: "The status quo is working admirably and the most
efficient policy would be to have it continue in effect as it now is, with

Eaker and Spaatz coordinating the activities of the Fifteenth and Eighth Air Forces and Eaker and Harris coordinating the activities of the Eighth Air Force and the RAF Bomber Command, all being under the Combined Chiefs of Staff who pass their directives through the C.A.S. [Portal], the latter being in effect, therefore, overlord or supervisor of all strategic operations against Axis objectives." If this system was to be changed, then Eaker agreed with the countersuggestion that Portal had mentioned in his cable: that an American deputy commander to the Chief of the Air Staff be named by the Combined Chiefs and that this deputy "should be the senior Strategic Air Force Commander in the U.K." By name, Ira Eaker.

Most probably Portal showed this reply to Arnold, for through him, Eaker was to be asked other questions. But the answers would have made no difference, for there can be no doubt that Arnold's mind had been made up for some time, second Schweinfurt notwithstanding.

It wasn't until the Allied leaders returned from Tehran that the overriding question of who was going to command OVERLORD was finally settled. Arnold noted cheerfully in his diary on December 4: "Marshall had lunch with President. He doesn't get Overlord. Ike does." Against the advice of his political and military chiefs—and the British, too—Roosevelt decided that he needed Marshall in Washington to manage the entire war far more than he needed him to command the European end of it. His choice of Eisenhower was acceptable to all concerned.

He was acceptable to Arnold, not only because Hap believed Marshall to be the greatest Chairman of the Joint Chiefs of Staff and Army Chief of Staff that ever lived, but also he knew that what he had in mind would go down easily with Eisenhower, whereas with Marshall there was no telling.

On the second anniversary of Pearl Harbor, the Combined Chiefs reached agreement or, as Hap phrased it, "many knotty and controversial problems solved!" He lunched with Arthur Tedder and for the first time discussed not just the new air organization that had been agreed on at the conference but the specific personalities involved.

The next day he was in Sicily, and there he met with Eisenhower and Bedell Smith. In his diary he wrote, "Both agree Spaatz was man for job. Wouldn't take anyone else, not even Tedder." Eisenhower was to say of their meeting that it was very brief and that he was all in favor of Ira Eaker being shifted to the Mediterranean to command the air forces there, but, as he was to tell General Marshall, both Spaatz and Eaker were acceptable to him as commander of the "American Strategic Air Force," an assignment which left him "somewhat puzzled as to purpose and position."

Whatever rationalizations or even-handed statements Eisenhower was to make on the shift, he made it obvious in a subsequent letter to

Marshall where he really stood on Arnold's desire to put Spaatz where he wanted him. "With regard to air commanders for Overlord, I am anxious to have there a few senior individuals that are experienced in air support of ground troops. This technique is one that is not, repeat not, widely understood and it takes men of some vision and broad understanding to do the job right. Otherwise a commander is forever fighting with those air officers who, regardless of the ground situation, want to send big bombers on missions that have nothing to do with the critical effort." Had he seen an earlier comment from Spaatz to Arnold, he might have been shocked. Said Tooey regarding relationships with the ground Army: "I would say that the 'situation is normal.' If it were not for the disturbance which would ensue, I would probably announce the urgent necessity of a separate Air Force. The best will, understanding, and intentions topside cannot overcome the basic difference between ground and air which permeates the entire structure."

The day after his brief talk with Eisenhower, Arnold met with Spaatz, Doolittle, Cannon, and other officers to give them the implications of the Cairo and Tehran conferences. Privately, Spaatz outlined the conditions under which he would accept his new role.

After Hap had further talks with Eisenhower and Tedder (who was to relinquish command of the joint Allied air units in the Mediterranean and become Ike's Deputy and later Supreme Air Commander), he flew to Foggia, Italy. There he was met by his son Hank, who drove him through the ruins of the city to Spaatz's house. Or, as Tooey put it in a letter to his wife, Ruth: "While Hap was here we moved bag and baggage over into Italy and entertained him in our handsome Fascist villa—he was in fine spirits and looked much better than he has for some time."

Indeed he did. Arnold had gotten pretty much what he had come for. He was certain the changes he had in mind and those that had emerged from the SEXTANT Conference, at Cairo, were going to bring an improvement in the air war. On December 15 he was back in Washington, all but one part of his mission accomplished.

On the previous day, Portal had asked Eaker to come to see him. He told him that while he was with Arnold in Cairo, Arnold had been extremely critical. He wanted to know why, with thirteen hundred heavy bombers, the most used on any mission had been fewer than six hundred. Why was Eaker not hitting precision targets in Germany, such as aircraft factories, and bombing coastal cities instead? Eaker might have wondered why these questions were addressed to him through Portal and not directly by Arnold himself, except that they had been, *ad infinitum,* through the drafting expertise of Larry Kuter. He informed Portal that, to begin with, the numbers were incorrect. He had twenty-one Heavy Bomber groups, thirty-five aircraft to the group, or a total of 735 aircraft. He had asked for authority to raise the number to forty-eight in each group with twelve in reserve, but so far permission had not been given. On no day since October 16 had weather conditions permitted visual bombing; therefore bombing had to be done using radio aids. He had only a dozen aircraft equipped with H2X radar, of which ten were operational. It took two H2X planes to guide a force of one hundred in bombing through the overcast, and that was why he had been unable to put up more than five hundred bombers in all. As for attacking coastal cities, H2X was not all that efficient, but it worked best where the coastline registered on the radarscope.

To Arnold, Portal reported, "I found Eaker thoroughly alive to the need for earliest possible attack on *Pointblank* targets and to importance of using maximum force available. I am confident you will see great achievements as soon as weather gives him a chance."

At that point it wouldn't have mattered what Eaker had to say in his own defense or how highly both his American and British colleagues regarded him.

The news of change of command when it came, on December 18, was a thunderous and shattering shock to him. He felt as though he had been gutted. Arnold had assured him if he ever reached the point of being dissatisfied, Ira would be the first to know. But this was different, far more subtle. Not being fired; in fact, being given a larger command, but shorn of the air force he had built from scratch and moved downward one rung on the ladder of strategic command.

It was said the news was brought to him verbally first, because they didn't dare put it on the wire, but, officially on the eighteenth, the cable came from Arnold to Eaker through Devers. The slant was away from the obvious, the gist that SEXTANT PROVIDED FOR CHANGES IN COMMAND IN THE MEDITERRANEAN THEATER AND A COMMANDER FOR OVERLORD. If the changes went through, an American would take command of the Allied Air Force in the Mediterranean, the position Tedder now held. AS A RESULT OF YOUR LONG PERIOD OF SUCCESSFUL OPERATIONS AND THE EXCEPTIONAL RESULTS OF YOUR ENDEAVORS AS COMMANDER OF THE AIR FORCE IN ENGLAND YOU HAVE BEEN RECOMMENDED FOR THIS POSITION. To Eaker, the sugar coating on the bitter pill. The other changes: SPAATZ TO COMMAND THE UNITED STATES STRATEGIC AIR FORCES IN EUROPE—DOOLITTLE TO COMMAND THE EIGHTH AIR FORCE—TWINING TO COMMAND THE FIFTEENTH. The cable concluded with a question as to whom Eaker would like as his Deputy IF THE ABOVE GOES THROUGH.

If! It had not gone through as yet, and he simply could not take what he perceived as an enormous betrayal of trust without fighting back. No doubt he was too close to it, too close to all he had given in the quiet agony of command, in the building of a powerful weapon of war and the awful cost in mind and heart burdened by the deaths of all the young men he had sent into the sky to wield it. The Eighth Air Force was his! And he would not be stripped of it like a chicken of its feathers, without a fight.

He drafted a handwritten reply to Arnold, protesting that it was in the best interest of the war for him to stay; otherwise his two years of experience in the theater would be wasted. "If I am allowed any personal preference, having started with the Eighth and seen it organized for a major task in this theater, it would be heartbreaking to leave just before climax." If his services were satisfactory to those above, he requested that he be permitted to remain.

Next he went to Jake Devers, who was to be replaced by Eisenhower but was unaware of it. Devers immediately fired off a cable to Arnold stressing the need for Eaker to stay right where he was. By the new, direct Redline communications system between their headquarters, Eaker cabled Spaatz, informing him that he was stating his preference to keep command of the Eighth, and was this agreeable to Tooey? He repeated his reasons, saying "would like to see the thing through to the finish in this job."

That afternoon, Eaker called on Ambassador Winant to enlist his aid, and then he went to see Portal. All were dismayed by the news, and Bert Harris doubly so. The same could be said for the entire RAF hierarchy with whom Eaker had worked and cooperated for so long. His own close headquarters staff was flabbergasted.

In his message to Eisenhower, similar to the one he had sent to Arnold, in which he used the word "heartbreaking" again, he went even farther and recommended that if he could not keep command of the Eighth, then Idwal Edwards should have it and Doolittle remain where he was.

In Arnold's replies, authored by Kuter, to both Portal and Devers, the high regard and qualities of character they praised in Eaker were used as reasons for Eaker's shift "to the High Command in the Mediterranean." The other reason was that "the dictates of worldwide air operations force the major changes now in progress." Arnold's response to Eaker used the same theme of high praise, worldwide air operations, and the sure belief that he would receive Eaker's loyalty and support but that he could not see his way clear to make any further changes now.

Spaatz's reply to Eaker, two days later—which was also sent to Arnold —stressed the need for an American in command of the Mediterranean Allied Air Force, and establishing a U.S. strategic air command in the U.K., which Eaker was in favor of too. "Believe that command of an air force is of relatively less importance compared to overall requirements and particularly since Eighth Air Force under new setup will function as an operating headquarters more nearly approximating Eighth Bomber Command."

This was not convincing to Eaker. He was willing to serve under Tooey in any capacity just so long as he stayed with his air force. His great error was that he had become too emotionally attached to his command. But now others had become involved in the wrenching shift, particularly Marshall, and he was not pleased with the way the reorganization was being handled.

Two days before Christmas, Spaatz talked with Bedell Smith, who told him that strong objections were being raised to the transfer of Eaker. Tooey told him that unless the change was made he would not consider the overall Strategic Command with headquarters in England. Smith said he would prepare a message from Eisenhower to Marshall making this point clear.

Spaatz was annoyed and disturbed by the reaction from Washington, and he wrote in his diary: "Feel Arnold has slipped out from his original decisions so that he has not stated them firmly to Marshall but has thrown it all into the lap of Eisenhower. My original estimation of Eisenhower's fairness has been strengthened by the way he is taking this, and the way he is standing by my decisions."

What were these decisions? The key one concerning Eaker was that if Eaker remained in command in England, Spaatz would remain in command in the Mediterranean and they would work as a team, utilizing the Eighth and the Fifteenth Air Forces in carrying out POINTBLANK directives. If Spaatz was to go to England as the strategic commander, he would insist upon dealing directly with Eaker on all strategic matters and not with Twining. His purpose was to assure that Eaker's great knowledge on strategic operations would be available to him, and they would work as a team. This he felt Arnold had failed to put across to Marshall, and the Chief of Staff was disturbed because it apppeared to him that Spaatz and Tedder were demanding Eaker's change of command. He was further upset over Eisenhower's plans to transfer all his top ground and air staff people to England, which would leave a serious vacuum in fighting the war in the Mediterranean Theater.

In Spaatz's thinking, Hap Arnold had not only let him down but let down Eaker as well. On the day after Christmas, Spaatz received a message from Marshall accusing him of being both selfish and ambitious in asking for Eaker's release and transfer to his theater. Spaatz told Ike he would send an explanation but then decided he wouldn't. It was best to ignore it. Arnold had made the mess, Tooey wasn't going to try to clean it up, but he repeated to Ike that he was going to deal directly with Ira and not with the Fifteenth Air Force.

By the time Spaatz departed for England, on December 28, taking Smith with him, Eaker had himself tightly under control. He knew the battle was lost. He would do the best he could with the new job, as he had done with every job. With some of his staff members he drove to Paddington Station to pick up Tooey and Beetle and take them to Castle Coombe, "where," Spaatz noted, "too many people did not help speed recuperation from a most tiring trip."

On that same day, Robert Lovett, Under Secretary of War for Air, wrote Eaker a letter of praise and consolation, stating the President had just announced the new commands made at Cairo. "I write, therefore, to congratulate you . . . and to commiserate with you privately in leaving the VIII after you have seen the baby through rickets, croup and measles and just at the time when it grows up into a strong, healthy warrior. I suppose that's the penalty of rank under a military organization but I confess that the military system in many respects does not make a great deal of sense to me." In complimenting Eaker for the important relationship he had built with the RAF, Lovett mentioned that Marshall had made a particular point of this to him that morning "and to the debt we all owe you." It was apparent that the Chief of Staff was not all that pleased by Hap Arnold's use of the "military system."

Eaker indicated some of his bitterness in his answer:

> I wish I could adequately express to you the consolation I derived from your letter. I never had any misgivings that you had participated in my undoing. I wish, also, to hasten to reassure you that my personal disappointment will be allowed in no way to interfere with my vigorous and wholehearted efforts in the new assignment.
>
> There is another thing which I shall hope to make very clear to you. General Spaatz has had no part in rooting me out of here. He is a warm and personal friend who never threw a curve in his life. . . .

But to Ira Eaker, Hap Arnold had, and although in time he would come to realize that the importance of his new command was indeed a larger responsibility and more important to the total war effort than he had imagined, their relationship would never be quite the same again—a casualty of the hard decisions of war.

Eighteen

Resolution

When Tooey Spaatz officially took command of the United States Strategic Air Forces in Europe, on January 6, 1944, there were fifteen months of air bombardment remaining in the war against Hitler's Germany. The period could be divided on the one side into the brief, hectic five-month span leading up to June 6, the D day of OVERLORD, and on the other, all that followed it. Whichever side of the mark, air power was the decisive military force that made the invasion possible and then sustained the armies both tactically and strategically as they slugged their bloody way across Europe into Germany. At the outset, Spaatz's command was a growing force, but it was beset by three problems, two organizational and the other operational and a matter of Allied air policy.

At the time Hap Arnold informed Spaatz he was going to head USSTAF, Spaatz's reaction was that he would like to stay right where he was and manage the show as he was doing. He did not favor OVERLORD any more than Winston Churchill, and he agreed with the British plan of going through the Balkans, believing it was the shortest way to Berlin. Further, he believed that strategic air power out of Italy—with its much better weather—could, if built up properly, pave the way better than operations out of the U.K. Now, in taking over as Commanding General of USSTAF, Spaatz had made clear his own organizational conditions. One was dealing directly with Eaker, which was no reflection on Major General Nathan F. Twining, the new Commanding General of the Fifteenth Air Force. That Nate Twining was eminently qualified for his command there was no question. His military career dated back to 1916 and Mexican border duty with the Infantry. His most recent assignment had been Commanding General of the Thirteenth Air Force, in the South Pacific. There, among other distinctions, he and fifteen others who had been on board his B-17 had been shot down and spent six days on a life raft in the Pacific before being rescued by a Navy PBY. Aside from good luck, Twining's career had been a distinguished one in the Pacific fighting, and Spaatz regarded him highly. But, for simplicity's sake and because he and Ira understood each other completely in all things, their relationship as old as their wings, he wished to deal directly with him and no one else. The fact that Eaker remained in England for two weeks after Spaatz's arrival to assist in the wrenching changeover was part and parcel of their close friendship.

When Barney Giles came over bearing messages of support and instruction from Arnold, they sat him down privately and told him what they were going to do to make operations between the Eighth and the Fifteenth Air Forces work. Giles accepted the conditions, including a new form of internal organization. It was Hugh Knerr's idea for streamlining a cumbersome staff system, made even more so by the functioning of two air forces far distant from one another. Knerr's plan was to put the administrative and operational functions of USSTAF on an equal footing, each commanded by a deputy answerable to Spaatz. Knerr quickly convinced Spaatz of the value of the plan, and Tooey adopted the system as his own, making Knerr Deputy for Administration and Fred Anderson Deputy for Operations. Anderson would control strategic operations, which included POINTBLANK missions for the Fifteenth as well as coordination with the RAF and the Ninth Air Force. Knerr would handle coordination of personnel and logistic requirements between the Eighth and the Ninth Air Forces. In that regard, it was his position that operations won battles but logistics won wars. It had always been Spaatz's belief that you couldn't delegate responsibility without delegating authority, but he knew perfectly well that if Knerr and Anderson were not loyal to him, were not good men, the system—which was later said to be "peculiar to his personality" —could not have worked. He was the type of officer who refused to spend his time at a desk poring over papers. He wanted time to think, and in the present situation he certainly needed it.

If working out the bugs in the internal structure of USSTAF posed some knotty problems, the overall command system of Allied air power as supposedly worked out at Cairo by the Combined Chiefs of Staff was an unqualified mess. Spaatz's word for it was "lousy." When Eisenhower returned from a brief secret trip to Washington directly after New Year's, he still was not sure whether as Supreme Commander he was to have command of the Allied Air Forces. Marshall told him had he been named to the post, it was his intention to insist on it, and if such a point of unification was not agreed on, he would take it to the press.

This detail was but the tip of the iceberg. The convoluted problem was one that Hap Arnold had referred to as a compromise. In North Africa a single unified air command for both tactical and strategic operations had been worked out, with Tedder as the head man and Spaatz as his deputy.

Before leaving for England, Spaatz tried to impress on Eisenhower and Tedder that the same system should be established in the U.K. He told them he would be perfectly willing to have Tedder again in command and he his deputy, heading the U. S. Strategic Air Forces as he had done with the Northwest Africa Air Force. When he arrived in England he made the same recommendation to Portal, who said he had heard nothing from the Combined Chiefs on the matter but that he would take it up in Washington, where he was headed.

The confusion arose from the appointment of Air Marshal Sir Trafford Leigh-Mallory, Chief of RAF Fighter Command, to head the Allied Expeditionary Air Force. Consisting of RAF units and Brereton's Ninth Air Force, they were to be used tactically in the softening up of enemy defenses prior to D day and then in support of the invasion forces. Leigh-Mallory assumed that he would also be giving orders to Spaatz and Bomber Harris in the employment of their strategic forces. However, on POINTBLANK, Spaatz and Harris were taking their orders from Portal, who acted as the agent of the Combined Chiefs of Staff. Hence there was no clear-cut line of authority between Leigh-Mallory's burgeoning headquarters, Spaatz's USSTAF, and RAF Bomber Command. Yet, at a still undetermined date, supposedly control of all the air components involved was to pass to the Commander of the Allied Expeditionary Air Force, who would direct them up to an also undetermined date. Of one point Eisenhower did make certain indeed. Leigh-Mallory would report to him, and thus, as Supreme Commander, the Air would be unified under Ike's headquarters. One wag described the system as "a hydra-headed bird with five wings, a brass ass and nowhere to fly but straight down."

Most of those having to cooperate on the various Allied staffs in this less-than-simple organizational mix knew each other, had worked together before, and were therefore familiar with each other's manner of approach. As far as Spaatz was concerned, the bumps that had come out of the compromises in Cairo could be worked out. Then he attended a meeting at Norfolk House on January 3 and came away less than enchanted. The subject was OVERLORD, and one of the principals present was Leigh-Mallory.

Afterward Spaatz observed, "Am not sure L-M has proper conception of air role. Apparently accepts possibility of not establishing Air supremacy until landing starts." Which, needless to say, to Tooey was, in the English vernacular, *just bloody nonsense.*

It was recognized at the end of the year that German aircraft production was expanding and that German fighter strength was growing in spite of the bombing done and the claims of planes shot down that, when added up, totaled the entire Luftwaffe force in the West. This was why Arnold's New Year's message to Spaatz and his command was an echo of what Eaker had been proclaiming for months: ". . . my personal message to you—this is a MUST—is to 'Destroy the Enemy Air Force wherever you find them, in the air, on the ground and in the factories.' " Otherwise, as Arnold declared, neither OVERLORD nor ANVIL (DRAGOON) would be possible. Everyone concerned seemed to know this but Air Chief Marshal Leigh-Mallory, who was doubtful it could be done before the landings were attempted. Spaatz, in turn, from then on was, to put it mildly, doubtful about Leigh-Mallory.

Someone had once said that Tooey Spaatz had the look of a rusty nail. If so, Leigh-Mallory could be described as having the aspect of a melon, smooth of skin and bland of eye, but he had a hard core. During the Battle of Britain, he had commanded 12 Group, and a bitter feud had developed between him and Air Vice Marshal Sir Keith Park, of 11 Group, responsible for defending the South of England. Leigh-Mallory having failed to send his forces to Park's aid during the desperate climax of the battle, Park never forgave him. Sides were chosen within the RAF and hard feelings remained. Irrespective of the past, Spaatz viewed Leigh-Mallory as stubborn, arrogant, unimaginative, and an officer who knew absolutely nothing about strategic bombardment and the purpose thereof. Bomber Harris no doubt used more pungent language. Aside from Hap Arnold's New Year's war whoop, the POINTBLANK directive from the Combined Chiefs was a command to eliminate the German Air Force, and this Tooey Spaatz fully intended to do.

In the following month, Jimmy Doolittle's Eighth and Nate Twining's Fifteenth air forces flew a conglomerate of thirty missions against a variety of targets, concentrating on German aircraft factories and component industries. As many as 875 heavy bombers were launched on one mission, but it, like many of those flown from England, was less than successful, plagued by impossible weather and fierce German fighter resistance. Again, in a single attack, as many as sixty B-17's were lost. But in this period some advances were made. B-24's began to be utilized along with the Mosquitoes as pathfinder aircraft. The long-awaited P-51's had first been used as long-range escort on December 13 in a raid on Kiel, and on January 24 it was agreed that from then on the Mustang would be the principal escort for the heavies. New blind-bombing equipment was put into use.

It was Jimmy Doolittle who introduced two new tactics, one of which was to cause a great deal of controversy. He was visiting Bill Kepner at his headquarters at Bushey Hall. On the wall was the motto of the 8th Fighter Command: *Our Mission Is to Bring the Bombers Back*. Doolittle studied the words for a bit and said, "That's not so. Your mission is to destroy the German Air Force." That's exactly what Monk Hunter had thought, and that's what Kepner had been arguing that he should be free to do. Sure that Doolittle meant it he said, "Thank God, we can now operate like fighters ought to!" They discussed the ways in which that should be done, and when Doolittle departed, he glanced at the motto and said, "Take that damned thing down."[1]

Bomber commanders did not take kindly to the change in tactics, feeling that the crews would now be abandoned by their "little friends" and their losses would skyrocket. This was not so. With numbers, the *Indianers,* as the German pilots called them, would be there, ranging all over the sky, ahead, above, and behind the bombers.

Doolittle's second innovation was sold to him by Colonel Budd Peaslee. Before launching a zillion bombers into a mess of weather over a particular target, Peaslee suggested why not send out a long-range P-51 to scout the weather and see first-hand whether the target could be bombed, and if it couldn't, search around to find one that could? When the bombers took off, the scout could give them an update. Doolittle told Peaslee to go ahead and organize what became the 1st Scouting Force. His most unpopular decision was to recommend that the number of bomber missions be increased from twenty-five to thirty. His reasoning was that with the great increase in fighter groups, thirty-three in all, including those in the Ninth, plus twenty-five heavy-bomber groups, the odds on the bomber crews surviving were much improved and that such a crew reaching twenty-five missions was at its professional peak and its capability was of great importance.

During their long association in Africa, Tooey Spaatz had formed a high regard for Dwight Eisenhower. In fact, during the difficult days involving Arnold's reorganization, which had put Spaatz in Marshall's doghouse, Tooey had stated in his diary that he considered Ike the finest man he knew. This high regard was mutual, and it included Arthur Tedder. The three had formed the habit of getting together frequently and privately to talk out problems and plans. Later, Spaatz was to remark that if any one of them had dropped dead from a heart attack there would have been no invasion. As it was, on the morning of February 15, Eisenhower came to call on Tooey at Park House, which doubled as dwelling and office. The major topic for discussion was Air Chief Marshal Leigh-Mallory. Spaatz expressed his feelings frankly. He had no confidence in the Air Chief Marshal's ability to handle his job, and he viewed with alarm any setup that placed the Strategic Air Forces under Leigh-Mallory's control. He was going to a meeting at Stanmore shortly, headquarters for the Allied Expeditionary Air Force, where they would be discussing Leigh-Mallory's plan for pre-D-day targeting.

Eisenhower was disturbed by Spaatz's obvious dislike of Leigh-Mallory, which had become fixed as a result of conferences held during the past month in which the British fighter commander had continued to stress that he did not believe air supremacy could be gained until the invasion was actually taking place. Actually, it was still Spaatz's private belief, which he shared with Eaker, Arnold, and a few others, that if he and Harris were free to use their bombers as they saw fit, there would be no need for landing forces on the Continent except to mop up. Although he did not say so, he remained an unenthusiastic supporter of OVERLORD.

His enthusiasm was in no way encouraged by the meeting that followed at Stanmore. There, Leigh-Mallory unveiled his softening-up plan, which was aimed at blotting out the enemy's transportation system from the beachhead to western Germany. Spaatz, whose axiom was *I never learned anything by talking,* felt it was time someone else did some learning. He told Leigh-Mallory his plan failed to take into account the purpose of POINTBLANK, whose first priority was to destroy the German Air Force. Bombing rail lines was not going to do that. When Spaatz asked when the AEAF Commander visualized taking operational control of the Strategic Air Forces, the answer was March 1, and Tooey said he could not concur. He was not going to limit his targets. He would bomb wherever it was necessary to make the German Air Force fight. Bomber Harris seconded the motion, whereupon Leigh-Mallory blandly argued that the landing of the ground troops on the beaches would make the Luftwaffe fight. What tone of voice Spaatz used in reply was not recorded, but he made it patently clear that was entirely too late! The job had to be done *before* the landing if the landing was to stand a chance of success. This had long been the Combined Chiefs of Staff's view. Totally unimpressed, Leigh-Mallory replied that was a matter for higher decision. Harris said the whole idea was based on a fallacy anyway: that rail communications could not be sufficiently interrupted by air attack to impede military movements in the first place.

The author of the Transportation Plan was Professor Solly Zuckerman, who had been Tedder's scientific adviser and was credited with planning the bombing of Pantelleria. He had developed this new plan as a result of a similar approach in Italy, bombing key rail centers. He now worked for Leigh-Mallory, who called on him to explain why the Transportation Plan was feasible. The professor did so and was promptly challenged by Harris and others. The argument went around and around, and Spaatz finally said that the entire subject needed more study and he would not commit his force to the plan as it now stood. He had already appointed his own committee to examine it carefully. Tedder, the quiet pipe smoker, then suggested a joint planning committee be formed with equal representation from the contesting sides. Spaatz agreed and named Colonels Pre Cabell and Robert Hughes, Assistant Director of Intelligence, as USSTAF representatives.

After the conference ended, Spaatz promptly informed Tedder and then Eisenhower that his forces would not be operating under Leigh-Mallory. And, for the time being, the issue remained unresolved, not only because of Leigh-Mallory and Zuckerman's Transportation Plan but also because Spaatz had a plan of his own.

The theme of the Committee of Operations Analysts had been don't use the shotgun technique, find the few critical targets in Germany's war machine that it can't operate without. Spaatz had come to believe that the synthetic oil system, which went to fuel tanks and trucks as well as aircraft, was such a target, and to eliminate it might well end the war. Within the Reich there were twenty-seven such installations of major importance, all of them now within range of either the Eighth or the Fifteenth Air Force. Spaatz's planners had developed what he considered to be a far more effective approach to crippling the Wehrmacht before D day, and it became known as the Oil Plan.

Meanwhile, continued division of command encouraged Spaatz to recommend again to Eisenhower that a single Air commander be appointed, but he learned from Ike that the political conditions prevailing, the delicacy of interrelations with the British, prevented the recommendation from being made. The impasse turned Spaatz's thoughts to the long-held belief in a Department of Defense to be established *"now,"* with coequal branches of Army-Navy-Air Force. Under the circumstances they were thoughts, however, that could not be openly discussed.

On the operational scene, in spite of the weather, he determined to send some sort of force, no matter how small, over Germany every day. This brought into question the devoutly held faith of precision as opposed to area bombing and the degree of morality therein. In his press conference following the October Schweinfurt raid, Hap Arnold had admitted that under certain conditions the Eighth Air Force did "pattern bombing" and Ira Eaker had put it a bit more bluntly to Arnold in referring to bombing through the overcast, saying that "we can dump our bombs in the heavily built-up industrial *areas* [my emphasis]." A February draft of a new directive prepared for the Combined Chiefs of Staff on POINTBLANK, the Combined Bomber Offensive, made direct reference to "Attack on target *areas* [my emphasis], as distinct from precision targets," by USSTAF, using "blind bombing devices." Spaatz went a step farther. In his position on the importance of sending out a small force daily, he told Anderson that the targeting should be aimed at hitting small towns in Germany where there were railheads or marshaling yards. Success of such attacks would depend on finding breaks in the clouds, and he felt that destroying these small towns would be just as important as hitting a railroad yard. Thus, to Tooey Spaatz, precision bombing was no longer a sacrosanct doctrine, although the Joint Chiefs of Staff refused to ever make mention of area bombing.

However, first and foremost in Spaatz's thinking was the elimination of the German Air Force. In a weekly "eyes only" message for Arnold in late January he said: "Basically, principal enemy we face is weather. Destruction of remaining fighter factories and ball bearing plants is entirely dependent on few days of visual bombing. Losses will be heavy but we must be prepared to face them.

"All other attacks will be made on basis of destroying enemy air force in air and on ground. . . ."

Arnold's admonitions to Spaatz to get his planes over Germany were far softer in tones and in numbers than they had been to Eaker, but in a late January message he pleaded, "Can't we some day and not too far distant, send out a big number—*and I mean a big number*—of bombers to hit something in the nature of an aircraft factory and lay it flat?"

Spaatz gave him the answer a month later, February 20–25, in what became known in the press as The Big Week. It was truly a combined operation and began on Saturday night, the nineteenth, when the RAF hit Berlin and Leipzig, where Messerschmitt parts were assembled. Sunday dawned with the usual mess of fog and an ice-coated overcast. Neither Doolittle nor Kepner was willing to take the responsibility to give the mission the green light. The force to be launched was made up of more than one thousand bombers and nine hundred fighters. Anderson brought the command decision to Spaatz, who, knowing the reported weather over Germany was good, considered the risks and simply said, "Let 'em go." And they went for the next five days—to Leipzig, Oschersleben, Gotha, Bernburg, Brunswick, Halberstadt, Tutow, Stuttgart, Regensburg, Schweinfurt again, and to Posen, in Poland. It wasn't until Tuesday that Eaker could send the Fifteenth on what was the first joint attack on Regensburg, his forces having been deflected earlier to aid in the desperate situation on the beachhead at Anzio. In coordination, Bomber Harris sent his Lancasters and Halifaxes to Stuttgart, Augsburg, and also to that so-called "panacea target," Schweinfurt. What it all added up to was thirteen major strikes on fifteen aircraft centers. Doolittle's bombers dropped more tons of bombs than the Eighth Air Force had dropped in its first year of operation. As Spaatz had foreknown, the enemy came up to fight, and the cost over the five days of operations was two hundred ten heavies and thirty-eight fighters against claimed totals of more than six hundred German interceptors.

And the results on the ground? *Time* magazine was to report that photo reconnaissance indicated: "30% of Germany's twin-engined fighter plane production had been knocked out; 60% of her single-engined production is gone. In addition, the raid destroyed 25% of the Reich's heavy bomber building capacity, and 60% of transportation production. Strategic bombing officials believe that if the victory is followed up, the Luftwaffe cannot make up its losses."

At first, the results of The Big Week, or Operation ARGUMENT as it was code-named, appeared catastrophic to the Luftwaffe high command. Then, incredibly, it was found that in spite of the apparent devastation, the damage to important machinery and assembly equipment was not nearly as complete as feared. This, added to Albert Speer's plan of dispersal of essential plant components already underway, also helped, as did a reorganization that took aircraft production away from the Reich Air Ministry and placed it in the Ministry of War Production. Some aircraft factories were back in production by early March, the BF Plant at Regensburg, first considered beyond repair, back to full production by June. That the concerted attacks had hurt the Luftwaffe badly there was no doubt. Field Marshal Erhard Milch, visiting Speer in the hospital on February 23, told him that he estimated that the bombing so far had reduced aircraft production by one third for at least a month. Even more serious was the loss of experienced fighter pilots. Although claims by bomber crews were always far off the mark, General der Jagdflieger Adolf Galland was to report that "Between January and April daytime fighters lost over 1,000 pilots." They included, he said, the best commanders. "Each incursion of the enemy is costing us some fifty aircrews. The time has come when our weapon is in sight of collapse."[2]

Just as German planners expected after the second bombing of Schweinfurt that the attack would be followed up by a third and a fourth strike, so they anticipated that the American bombers would be back to continue the destruction of what was left of the aircraft industry. With Schweinfurt, when the double attack finally came, during The Big Week, much of the ball-bearing production had been moved elsewhere; so, too, the latter strikes on aircraft factories, which, in spite of all, produced over twenty-five thousand fighters in 1944, the highest number of any year in the war.

* * *

Those in Germany who believed that their enemies had blundered in failing to continue the air attacks on aircraft industries were, of course, unaware of the internal Allied battle that centered around OVERLORD and the targeting that would precede the invasion, as well as who was going to command the Air.

Early in March, Eisenhower had lunched with Churchill and talked over the contentious matter. Sir Winston was no more enamored of the idea of Leigh-Mallory dictating bombing policy than was Spaatz, since the Air Chief Marshal had spent all his time in fighters. Ike informed him he had become thoroughly fed up with the infighting that was going on and with the British Air Staff's plan to retain elements of the RAF to use as it saw fit outside the requirements of OVERLORD. He had already told Tedder he was sick and tired of dealing with prima donnas, and if the quarreling didn't stop he would tell Churchill to get someone else to run the damn' war! What quickly followed was that Tedder became Ike's air commander, and Spaatz, Harris, and Leigh-Mallory would be under his direction. That was fine with Tooey. His major criticism of Sir Arthur was that while he enjoyed authority he was not so keen on responsibility, which in this case might work out. Eisenhower had assured Spaatz that he would be the adviser on strategic bombing, and conversely, Spaatz had made it clear that under no circumstances would he take orders from Leigh-Mallory. Further, although the Ninth Air Force was to come under the Allied Expeditionary Air Force command, Leigh-Mallory's staff would have no say in its training or operational methods.

As April approached—and time to prepare was fast running out—there was still no agreement on a bombing plan. In the appointment of Tedder, the directive to him had made note of the tremendous advantages accruing to OVERLORD "through current *Pointblank* operations," and therefore in any air plan "there must be complete integration of both *Pointblank* and *Overlord*." Toward this end, Spaatz's Oil Plan had been developed as an alternative to the Transportation Plan, and on Saturday, March 25, at the British Air Ministry the opposing supporters of the two points of view met to thrash it out. Spaatz had already discussed his proposal with Eisenhower and Tedder. He had pointed out to them "that the German military rail requirement into the assault area [would] be about 80 trains a day," which was but a fraction of the available capacity. Through the benefit of ULTRA he also presented an order from the Quartermaster General of the German High Command. It was dated December 13, 1943, and stressed the critical shortage of motor fuel. "At a decisive hour, we will not be able to move either our tanks or our fast units if there is no motor fuel," the Quartermaster General admitted. "The motor fuel situation is serious. In 1944 it may become still more serious. Restrictions have to be imposed in January. It is impossible to give more than there is."

Spaatz's plan was aimed at seeing there wasn't any to give at all. Its premise, of course, was the destruction of the German Air Force, and its method was to select targets the Luftwaffe would defend at all costs. If these targets were also essential to the German war effort, their destruction would have the obvious effect. "Of all systems examined, oil best meets these requirements. All our evidence shows the attack on the transportation potential will fulfill neither." The plan also pointed out that the weight of the attack on a large marshaling yard was about the same as that required to hit a synthetic oil plant. The number of targets had been reduced from the original twenty-seven, the plan concluding:

> Fourteen synthetic oil plants produce 80% of all the German synthetic petrol and oil, whereas any fourteen marshalling yards comprise only a fraction of the German rail potential, which can be readily dispensed with without seriously disrupting German military operations. In this connection, it is of value to note the complete disinterest of the Germans in

our current attacks on the marshalling yards in France, and his similar
disinterest during the STARKEY operations last year.

What met head on at the March 25 conference were the concepts of
strategic bombardment as opposed to tactical operations. And here there
was irony in it, for at first it appeared that Eisenhower, the ground commander, favored the Spaatz plan, but Tedder, the air man, came out
against it, saying that while such a series of attacks would no doubt cause
great harm, the time to do the job properly was too short and would not
contribute to the success of the invasion. On the other side, Portal was
not at all enthusiastic about the Transportation Plan. He did not believe
the French rail system could be so knocked out as to prevent supplies
from getting through. Further, there appeared to have been no consideration of just how many French civilians were going to get killed in the
bombings.

If what was envisioned occurred, civilian casualties would be unfortunately high, a point the Transportation advocates had somehow overlooked. Portal also came up with what was considered an acceptable remedy. Leaflets would be dropped, warning everyone within a mile of the
intended target that it was going to be bombed. In the end, it was Eisenhower who made the final decision and, predictably, he accepted the
Transportation Plan, because the results would be tangible and of immediate value to the landing forces in holding the bridgehead.

Spaatz's reaction was philosophic and not all that disturbed. POINT-
BLANK would continue. He would work through Tedder. Eisenhower
would listen to his ideas. Two days later, in his report to Arnold, he informed him that POINTBLANK targeting would continue to concentrate on
the Luftwaffe, its factories, and supporting installations, including ball-
bearing plants. On the defeat of his Oil Plan, he said he believed the "decision reached was justified, based on all factors involved, which are predominantly the absolute necessity to insure the initial success of
OVERLORD." He also added that he was now satisfied with the command
setup. "I feel the time has arrived now when the most essential thing is
the fullest coordination of the air effort in the support of OVERLORD."

But there was still a major block in transferring control of the Strategic
Air Forces to Eisenhower. Churchill and his War Cabinet were refusing
to accept the bombing of marshaling yards and repair centers in popu-
lated areas of the occupied countries because of anticipated huge civilian
casualties.* It wasn't until mid-April that the matter was resolved by the
presentation of lower casualty estimates, Portal's suggestion to warn the
population, and temporary acquiescence.

During this entire period leading up to D day, which had been ad-

* It was estimated that there would be forty thousand civilian casualties; the actual
figure was twelve thousand.

vanced from May to June, there had been a target priority on which the British were extremely anxious to have focused a continuing maximum effort. Under the code name CROSSBOW, these were the rocket and missile sites the Germans were rushing to completion in France and Belgium in order to attack England with their V-weapons. Spaatz was perfectly willing to include the small, dug-in, heavily cemented sites as pre-D-day targets along with the marshaling yards, but when Tedder told him, in mid-April, they were to take priority over the German Air Force, he balked, protesting to Eisenhower. His disgruntlement with the British had been growing apace, and his anger was focused as much on an Air Ministry press conference the week before, in which Air Vice Marshal Robert H. Peck, Portal's principal Public Information deputy, had blithely stated that German fighter production had increased 300 percent since November. This news did nothing to improve the morale of Jimmy Doolittle's bomber crews, who had accepted fiercely high losses, brutal missions, and battle fatigue in the belief that they were breaking the back of the Luftwaffe. Letters of apology from Sinclair, Portal, and Peck—who was truly chagrined—did nothing to remove the acceptance of the statement. When Spaatz visited a bomber base and talked the gaffe over with some of the group commanders, showing them a joint press release intended to correct the error, one of them handed it back, saying, "General, it will be hard to make the crews believe anything just now. They're dubious of anything they read."[3]

Whether the Air Ministry spokesman's inaccurate estimate, which made for stunned reading on both sides of the Atlantic, was the final blow that brought the explosion from Park House or simply the latest in Tooey Spaatz's black book of record is unknown, but on April 22, his headquarters came out with a blistering white paper on the record of U.S.-British air relations which literally tore RAF tactics, doctrine, strategy, and overall policy to shreds. It was an utterly damning indictment that fashioned the RAF as a millstone around the neck of U.S. air power in Europe. It concluded with the recommendation "that immediate consideration be given to a revision of Command Channels in the European Theater. Our primary concern is that of getting a unified American Air Command for all American forces operating in Europe. Concurrently it is believed that the best interest of all concerned will be best served by accomplishing the same for all forces, all Commands to be responsible to one Supreme Allied Commander who will designate the responsibilities of each." What Spaatz was trying to do was to get rid of what he considered the undue British-inspired influence of Portal, Tedder, and Leigh-Mallory. All, he felt, were deflecting him from his primary goal. He and Ira and Nate Twining had worked out an operation to hit Ploesti on a day of fair weather. Portal had advised against it, saying the Combined Chiefs of Staff recommended hitting Sofia, Bucharest, and Budapest. Tedder was still pushing for CROSSBOW to be number one on the target list, and Leigh-Mallory's Transportation Plan was killing a great many noncombatants. On this last, Ike shook his head and said there was no way around it, but he was in favor of Eaker's hitting Ploesti and agreed with pressure from Washington exerted by Arnold to give Spaatz a chance to carry out two attacks against synthetic oil plants. The Transportation Plan, as Tooey had predicted, had not brought the Luftwaffe up to fight.

On May 12, Doolittle dispatched eight hundred B-17's and B-24's in three forces against German oil installations. The weather was bad and a number of other targets were attacked. An estimated four hundred thirty German fighters rose to take on the bombers and their escorts. Forty-six bombers and ten U.S. fighters were lost. But because of the weather the mission did not have the effect Spaatz was seeking, although considerable damage was done. It was not until the end of the month, May 28 and 29, that he proved his point. On the twenty-eighth, close to nine hundred bombers struck eight synthetic oil plants and thirty targets of opportunity. The next day, nearly the same number of heavies hit the synthetic oil plant at Pölitz as well as airfields and assembly plants in five key locations. Again the Luftwaffe sent up its fighters, and again the losses were heavy on both sides but heaviest on the targets bombed.

Although at the time the results had to be estimated through photographs and intelligence gathering, in actuality the figures were dramatic proof of what Spaatz was attempting to impress upon the minds of his military and political peers. The Luftwaffe's supplies of aviation fuel plummeted from one hundred eighty thousand tons in April to only fifty thousand tons in June, and by August they would drop to only ten thousand tons.[4] As for German fighter losses in the epic air battle over Berlin on March 6, while the Eighth lost sixty-nine heavies, or 10 percent of the attacking force, the Luftwaffe lost eighty fighters, or nearly half the defending force. By the time Eisenhower gave Spaatz the go-ahead on his two missions in May against the oil targets, the Eighth and the Fifteenth air forces, with their escorts of P-51's and P-38's, had gained air supremacy, for, as Major General Walter Grabmann, commander of the Luftwaffe's 3rd Fighter Division, was to say of the time, "The total number of fighters we still had left represented, at best, less than half the number of escort fighters . . . used on a single raid."[5] By D day, total German fighter strength was less than three hundred first-line aircraft, and in further reducing the Reich's fuel supplies, Eaker had sent the Fifteenth against Ploesti on no less than twenty raids in six weeks.

In the month prior to the invasion, the Eighth and Ninth air forces and the RAF flew thirty-three thousand sorties and destroyed over one thousand German aircraft. In tearing apart the enemy's transportation system, they wiped out much of his locomotive and other rolling stock. Perhaps of most importance to the ground generals who would command the invasion forces—Field Marshal Bernard Montgomery and Lieutenant General Omar N. Bradley—was the destruction of the bridges across the Seine and the Loire rivers. As Spaatz was to report in a letter to Barney Giles after the fact: "The Air Forces had opened the door for the invasion by the constant hammering of the communication targets. This hammering . . . has been a continuous process, the tempo of which has risen to a peak during the month previous to D day. Perhaps the most important phase of these operations on and after D day was the destruction of the bridges across the Seine and Loire, the Ninth taking care of the Seine and the Eighth concentrating on the Loire. These attacks on the communications system harassed the enemy to the extent that the whole system was pretty well confused."†

On June 5, Jimmy Doolittle sent to Spaatz his schedule for bombing operations of German defenses behind the landing beaches. The Eighth Air Force would spend twenty-five minutes hitting targets facing the five areas where U.S. and British forces would land. The attacks would begin at 0600 and be completed by 0720. Doolittle pointed out that simultaneously there would be strikes on the flanks and within the French interior.

Before the day was far advanced on the fateful morning of June 6, the invasion forces succeeded in gaining a lodgment on the Normandy coast, a huge and perilous undertaking which, in the minds of many, had only a thin chance of success. In that first handhold to victory, the greatest victory in the minds of the airmen whose job it was to clear the skies of German aircraft was simply that there were no German fighters or bombers to contest the invasion. There were, of course, German ground forces, and ten days after the landing, while the Allied bridgehead was holding, it wasn't being expanded, and a method had to be found to force a breakout.

Following a meeting at Stanmore, Spaatz talked with Eisenhower, who spoke of the necessity for exercising full imagination in the employment of forces. Later Spaatz noted, "Developments indicate complete lack of imagination exists in minds of Army command, particularly Leigh-Mallory and Montgomery, who visualize best use of tremendous air potential lies in plowing up several square miles of terrain in front of the ground forces to obtain a few miles of advance. Our forces are now far superior to Germans opposing us, both in men and material. The only thing necessary to move forward is sufficient guts on the part of the ground commanders."

A month later, Montgomery's operation GOODWOOD began, with the largest air attack in support of ground troops in history. Nearly sixteen

---

† U. S. Army Engineers maintain the bombing of the bridges hampered rather than helped the Allied forces after the breakout of St.-Lô.

hundred heavies, supported by medium and light bombers, dropped seventy-seven hundred tons of bombs on German positions facing the British forces. Even so, the British-Canadian attempt to capture Caen failed. The bombing took place on July 18, and less than a week later there was a repeat on the American side of the line with some tragic consequences. Operation COBRA, devised by General Omar Bradley and his staff, was a plan to break through the German lines at St.-Lô, where bitter hedgerow fighting had stymied the First Army in its attempt to advance. Two solid weeks of rain had done nothing to help, and Bradley wanted air power to pave the way. His idea was to use the bombers in an attack that would pulverize an area in front of General Joe Collins' VII Corps seven miles wide and five thousand yards deep. Leigh-Mallory agreed to supply a force of nearly twenty-five hundred aircraft, fifteen hundred of which would be Eighth Air Force B-17's and B-24's. Spaatz and Doolittle did not like the idea worth a damn, and General Hoyt Vandenberg, Leigh-Mallory's Deputy Commander, did not like the method by which the British airman ordered the bombing attack, the planes to fly on a lateral instead of a perpendicular course to the American front, a single road dividing the two forces.

On the night of July 23, Brigadier General Orville Anderson, Eighth Air Force Operations Officer, recommended postponing the attack, scheduled to take place in the morning, because there was only a 50 percent chance of the weather being good enough to carry out the mission safely. The mission was not canceled, not, at least, until the three divisions were airborne and Leigh-Mallory had personally flown over the battle area and decided indeed the cloud cover was too thick. Two of the divisions got the message to abort, the other did not, and then, through a foul-up by a lead bombardier of one group, the entire group dropped its bombs on American forward positions. Sixteen G.I.'s were killed and nearly seventy wounded. The following day the entire force, of twenty-five hundred aircraft, struck again. The devastation in the target area was beyond description, but again some of the bombs had fallen among the leading echelons of U.S. troops. More than one hundred were killed and five hundred wounded. The most notable of the casualties was Lieutenant General Lesley J. McNair. He had nearly been killed the day before in the same manner. Even at the cost of error the job had been done, and Bradley and his commanders would ever after insist that the Eighth Air Force made possible the Army's breakout at St.-Lô and the rapid victories that followed.

Bedell Smith, however, took issue with Jimmy Doolittle, blaming him for the tragic accident which airmen had known would be unavoidable. "Goddammit, Beetle," Doolittle said angrily, "we shouldn't have even been there!" Because no matter how precise precision bombing had become, twenty-five hundred aircraft simply could not be that accurate, particularly when the target area was quickly smoke-covered from the bombing effect.

In studying Doolittle's bomb plot, Spaatz saw that about sixty heavy bombers had dropped short, and he noted, "It had previously been explained to Bradley that in a large-scale operation of this kind, placing a heavy concentration in a small area in the proximity of our front lines would inevitably result in some casualties. The casualties were higher than I had hoped, but not so great as anticipated under conditions prevailing." Holding a postmortem with Eisenhower, Spaatz tried to impress upon him that in the future "we must not send large formations of bombers over our troops to make the assault." Still, Eisenhower maintained it was perfectly feasible and made good military sense to use strategic bombers in support of the ground forces when the situation so demanded.

Spaatz's strategic air power was used in ways that were equally important if not exactly "strategic." On June 11, the first V-1 bombs began to rain down on London, and the efforts of CROSSBOW were stepped up, utilizing elements of the Eighth and Ninth air forces and the RAF in attempts to destroy the well-protected launching platforms in the Pas-de-Calais and other regions that ground forces had been unable to capture. Spaatz felt this was a deflection of his bombers that could best be handled by the British and Major General Pete Quesada's 9th Air Force Tactical units. At this time he wrote to Arnold, sending him two books showing the results of his efforts against the Axis oil system, which since D day had become his number one priority. He wanted one of them presented to the President. He said he was continuing his attacks against these targets and that he felt more strongly than ever in what he had started in January: "That if the Strategic Air Forces were directed against Germany's oil capacity such action would prove a decisive factor in bringing victory to the Allies."

Another diversion was sending B-17's to drop arms to the Maquis (Resistance forces in the South of France), but now, with the enormous preponderance of air power under his command, it was possible to mount the missions Eisenhower required for tactical support and at the same time send masses of bombers and fighters into Germany.

* * *

Just prior to D day, Ira Eaker went on his second combat mission of the war. He flew with the 97th Group, as he had done on August 17, 1942, in the first Eighth Air Force bombing raid of the war. This 1944 flight was also a first—the first shuttle to the U.S.S.R.

It was a plan to establish fields and facilities in the Ukraine so that long-range missions could be conducted without the return flight. Code name FRANTIC had been under preparation since the Tehran Conference.

On June 2, Twining bade farewell to Eaker and the one hundred-plus

B-17's making the flight. The 97th would bomb railroad yards at Debrecen, Hungary, and go on to land at Poltava. This they did, accompanied by two other heavy groups and a fighter escort. In the attack, only one Fort was lost to flak, and the others flew on to their assigned fields at Mirgorod and Piryatin.

When Eaker climbed out of *Yankee Doodle II* at Poltava, waiting to greet him was old friend Ambassador Averell Harriman, Harriman's daughter Kathleen, and a number of the U.S. and British press corps, not to mention a large gathering of Russian brass.

Spaatz and Arnold had had mixed feelings about FRANTIC. Fred Anderson, on the other hand, was all in favor, but Hugh Knerr, who had gone to the U.S.S.R. and been in on the logistical side of the preparations, believed the operation was more a political ploy than a military necessity and that the Russians were out to "rob us blind of everything they could get their hands on."

Eaker, however, was wined and dined in Moscow, where he informed Foreign Minister Molotov that the Russians were welcome to all intelligence information in Allied hands plus the record of U.S. battle experiences. He also said that Russian air officers would be welcome to return to Italy as observers.‡

In all, six FRANTIC missions were flown, and the first one carried out by the Eighth Air Force, on June 21, brought a staggering result, the Eighth suffering one of the heaviest losses of the war. Not in the air but on the ground. A German reconnaissance plane had tracked the force to Poltava after it attacked targets in Poland. That night the German bombers came. Russian antiaircraft was incapable of harming them. When the smoke cleared, forty-three of the 114 Forts were finished. So were fifteen Mustangs, and another twenty-six aircraft were damaged. Fortunately, there was only one American fatality.

As Eaker and Spaatz could both attest, there were other missions that were more successful, one of them Very Secret. The DRAGOON landings, in southern France on August 15, which Winston Churchill had opposed so vigorously and then showed up on the bridge of a destroyer to observe, was a walk-in for the troops of General Jake Devers' VI Corps. There were fewer than one hundred casualties on the three landing beaches at St.-Tropez, St.-Maxime, and St.-Raphaël. The Navy wished to take credit for the smoothness of the operation, although it was unnecessary for them to shell the landing sites. Joe Cannon's Twelfth Air Force believed it was responsible for the undisturbed air above the French resort towns. However, Eisenhower and Spaatz and a few others came to know that credit for the all-but-unopposed landings was not exactly due to the Navy, the Army, or the Air Forces.

‡ Two later did.

During the fighting in North Africa, an American intelligence officer was hidden in the attic of a brothel in Gafsa, Tunisia, by the madam of the house, a staunch supporter of the Allies. He was there two days before he was able to escape, with the madam's help. He didn't forget her, and when plans were going forward for DRAGOON and there was need for accurate information on enemy movements in the landing region, he went to his superior in G-2 with an idea. He knew the madam was now running a successful business in Tunis, and he suggested that she be enlisted in a more patriotic and possibly profitable venture. They would teach her how to operate a radio and send in code. They would baste her with a large supply of money and drop her into France, where she would set up business in Marseilles. The madam, as adventurous as she was naughty, cried *Vive la France! Allons! Allons!* On a stormy night she went, right out the bottom of a B-24, parachute billowing. Very soon thereafter, she and her new troop of girls were picking up valuable information on German troop movements and military intentions, and while not so sophisticated as ULTRA, her reports were not only of major importance to the planning of DRAGOON but ultimately saved thousands of G.I. lives as well.

After the landings were made, the officer who had trained the madam in espionage went to his commander, Lieutenant General Alexander M. Patch, and recommended that she be given the Legion of Merit. Patch thought it an excellent idea, but it would be necessary to get Eisenhower's approval. When they called on Ike, he was relaxing with Tooey, having a drink. Patch told them the story and Eisenhower got a great kick out of the tale and said that Spaatz should sign the order since it might not be politic if he did. Rasped Tooey, "I've signed some stupid orders in this war but this one makes it all worthwhile."*[6]

* * *

When Ira Eaker left England, on January 10, with the sad farewells of a great host of American and British friends echoing amid the sense of "heartburn," his first stop was Marrakesh. There he had been asked to call on a Colonel Holt. He did so and found that Holt was the cover name for Winston Churchill, who was ensconced in a spacious, flower-decked villa, recovering from a serious bout of pneumonia acquired during the hard debates at Cairo and Tehran.

Churchill said to Eaker, "I know of your disappointment, but . . ." and then went on to describe the size and importance of the Mediterranean Air Command that Ira was about to take on. He pointed out that Mediterranean Allied Air Forces consisted of not just two American but two British Air Forces and French air units as well. It was, in fact, a larger, more broadly based command than the one Eaker had given up, consist-

---

* The patriotic madam was decorated in a ceremony in which members of the French Resistance were cited for bravery in action.

ing of over one hundred ten thousand officers and men. For the moment this was true, and the Prime Minister's continued emphasis on its importance made Eaker realize for the first time that while he had lost his pride and joy he had indeed been given a new opportunity. What the Prime Minister did not say was that neither Eaker nor Jumbo Wilson, the Mediterranean Theater Commander, was to have any strategic responsibility. That would be dictated from Washington and London, and for the moment Marrakesh, for even as Churchill was expounding to Eaker on the breadth and depth of the task he was about to assume, he was planning the costly end run at Anzio. Later, the failure of the commanding general there would necessitate the use of the Fifteenth Air Force, deflecting, over Eaker's futile protest, its heavy bombers away from targets in Germany. But at the time Eaker departed Marrakesh for Algiers and Wilson's headquarters at the St. George Hotel, he was reassured. He and Jumbo would get on well, and there were other personnel shifts that were equally positive.

Barney Giles had brought the suggestion from Arnold's office that Eaker make Major General Ralph Royce his chief of staff. Eaker chose Idwal Edwards instead, their friendship and appreciation for each other having grown since Andrews' death. On the RAF side, his deputy was to be another old friend, Air Marshal Jack Slessor, whose Coastal Command had done so much in helping to win the desperate battle against the U-boats. Unlike Spaatz, however, Eaker brought only two members of his former staff with him: Harris Hull, his Intelligence Chief, and Jim Parton, his aide for all seasons.

Eaker established his headquarters at Caserta, a pastoral site north of Naples, and Wilson and Devers joined him there. It was an arrangement that suited them all. From that point on, he was in daily communication with Spaatz via the Redline. As planned, they held frequent meetings at which the centerpiece in the evening was a table with poker chips on it surrounded by a select few prepared to go down fighting to the last inside straight.

As for his relationship with Arnold, shortly after he had gotten established, Ira wrote to Tooey saying, "Again, all my thanks for your many kindnesses and further evidences of friendship in connection with this change of duty. I think you know there was never the slightest suspicion on my part that you had bounced me from my job. I well knew the name of the author of the idea and that any such thing was absolutely foreign to your nature, character, or way of doing business."[7]

Whatever Eaker thought about some individual on the Air Staff managing to knife him in the back and influence Arnold against him, it was Arnold who made it clear that it was he who was responsible for Ira's new command. In February, he wrote Eaker on the matter of the latest edition of their revised book *This Flying Game* saying he thought it a very attractive volume although it was still too early to get any feel for sales. He also broke the news that after talking it over with the editors they had decided to eliminate the authors' biographical sketches from the dust jacket, but alas, the foreword by Donald Douglas, written for the original version, was more of a plug for Arnold than for Eaker. "It is to be regretted that we did not have more time to get together on this after the manuscript was completed so as to iron out some of these difficulties," he said. "I have every hope that the book will go across big and you will not suffer because your biography was not included."

Then he got down to business on Eaker's new job and attempted to assuage Ira's pain by preaching to him and then letting him know where his gratitude should lie:

> It is an entirely different kind of job and requires different technique for the employment of your aircraft. It also requires a different kind of technique on your part in your relationship with the various commanders. I am of the opinion that it will do you a considerable amount of good. It will increase your experience and give you a reputation along other lines than that in which you were engaged in England. In other words, you should come out of this a bigger man by far than when you went into it.

> When I thought the matter over and discussed it with my superiors, I told them the troubles down there were going to be many, and the difficulties would test the ability of any Air Commander. I have seen nothing to change my opinion.

There were, of course, difficulties, mostly a problem of relationships similar to those Spaatz was facing in England, but whereas Tooey, on the surface, was abrupt and taciturn and did not suffer fools lightly, part of Eaker's nature was his ability to get along with all shades of officialdom. However, one difficulty he would no longer have to suffer was having Arnold ride close herd on his actions. In closing, Arnold had said to him, "I would like very much to have you write me from time to time as you have in the past—tell me your troubles, how you are getting along and wherein I can be of help to you."

Now, as the war progressed, they worked as a team, Spaatz through Doolittle, Eaker through Twining, the target ever Germany. Yet the war in Italy caused the same kind of deflections from strategic operations that Spaatz faced in France, none more wasteful and nonproductive than the bombing of the Benedictine Abbey of Monte Cassino. There, over Eaker's, Slessor's, and the objections of other airmen, five hundred tons of bombs converted the ancient shrine to rubble. Jumbo Wilson, Mark Clark, and other ground generals believed the abbey to be a German strong point blocking the Allied advance. Before the attack, Eaker flew Jake Devers, who was now Wilson's deputy, over the abbey in a Piper Cub, and they did spot a radio antenna, but the destruction that followed, first of the monastery and then of the town of Cassino, at its foot, did nothing whatever to speed the advance of the Allied forces up the peninsula. In fact, it slowed them, for as Eaker had warned, the shell holes caused by the bombs dropped on Cassino simply impeded the movement of men and armor.

Such "tactical operations" aside, Eaker directed the Fifteenth from its bases in the Foggia region in concert with Spaatz's overall strategic plan. But from whatever bases the bombers flew, it was a hard, grinding war of aerial attrition, and all too often the price was wickedly high.

At about the same time Eaker was moving to take command of the MAAF, Colonel Jake Smart was getting free of duty on the Air Staff, and he asked to be assigned to Eaker because the then Eighth Air Force Commander had promised him a combat group. In February he got his wish, with the Fifteenth Air Force taking over the veteran 97th. In the next three months he flew twenty-nine missions, and on May 9, Eaker called him in and said, "Jake, that's enough. I'm relieving you. I want you to move up to Wing." Eaker had already talked the matter over with Nate Twining, and he, in turn, with the Wing Commander, Colonel Lawrence. The following day, there was to be a very big mission against the Messerschmitt works at Wiener-Neustadt, and it was agreed that "as postgraduate job" Smart would lead the wing and the whole air force in the attack. In all, nearly four hundred bombers were allotted to make the strike, but over three hundred were forced to abort because of rotten weather. Smart pressed on with the rest. Nearing the target, they were met by a force of more than two hundred German fighters. Flak was particularly heavy and accurate, and the defenses were the toughest the Fifteenth had yet encountered. Thirty seconds before "bombs away," Smart's aircraft took a direct hit and exploded.

In his letter to Arnold, Eaker said of Smart: "No officer has come under my observation in this war who showed quite such promise. He had a vision and imagination well beyond the average. He was one of the little group I counted upon to carry the new Air Force after the war. His loss can only be classed as a definite tragedy for the whole Air Force." Eaker had also recommended to Twining that same day that Smart be awarded the Distinguished Service Cross posthumously "to help General Arnold and Mrs. Smart to bear the loss."

Miraculously, in this case, Jake Smart might be gone for a while but he was far from being gone for good. Blown clear of the exploding Fortress, he was struck by pieces of flak as he fell, and then again after his chute opened. Wounded in the back and legs, he came down in a soggy meadow, but when he tried to stand up, the wind caught his chute and he was dragged across a slimy expanse of water. In shock, half drowned, he knew his wounds would be infected, and he tried to get his first-aid kit open. It was too much, and his next thought was escape. To do that, he decided, he must rest first. He managed to get out of his chute harness and crawl under some brush in a ditch, where he either passed out or fell asleep. It was not until three hours later that he was awakened by some German soldiers from a nearby flak battery. The noncom in charge, seeing that the American was badly injured, opened Smart's first-aid kit and poured iodine on his wounds, brutally painful but necessary. Jake Smart would live to fly another day and come home to his wife and three children.[8]

Some months later, a similar letter was written, this one by Arnold to his West Point classmate Colonel Benjamin F. Castle. It concerned Brigadier General Frederick W. Castle, who had been one of Eaker's stalwart six in the founding of the Eighth Air Force. Castle, at thirty-six, was not the type to sit out the war flying a desk. He had asked Eaker to give him a combat assignment, and in June 1943 he took over the badly battered 94th Group at Bury St. Edmunds. The following April, he became Wing Commander and then replaced Curt LeMay as 3rd Division Commander (4th CBW).† In all, by December, like Jake Smart, he had flown twenty-nine missions and Arnold thought that was quite enough. Again paralleling Smart, Arnold recognized that "Freddie" was much more than a fly-boy and that his talents would be needed after the war.

The word came down to Harris Hull from Castle's West Point classmate Lauris Norstad, who told him, "We feel Castle is flying too much."

"What do you want me to do about it, sir?" asked Hull, up from Caserta with Eaker.

"You know him better than anyone else. Will you tell him to slow down?"

Knowing Fred better than anyone else, Hull knew how stubborn he was, and when he dropped in at Castle's headquarters, he suggested they go out for a drink. Later he got down to it, saying, "Fred, you're going to be a valuable asset to the Air Force after the war. Hap's worried you're going to get hurt. Why don't you give some thought to cutting down?"

Replied Fred, "You tell Hap to run his show, I'll run mine. I'll pick the missions I want to fly." The last one he picked was on Christmas Eve, and Arnold later described it to Castle's father.

"Freddie was on a mission to Eaeenhausen, Germany . . . The formation was flying at 23,000 feet in the vicinity of Liège, Belgium, when Freddie's plane lost an engine. He started to leave the formation and was immediately jumped by German fighters who were evidently hitting hard. Two other engines caught fire, and at 12,000 feet, the fuel tank in the right wing was hit and exploded. Freddie's plane went into a spin and eight chutes were seen to open, which, of course, meant that two of the occupants were still in the plane. . . ."

† LeMay, after his tour in Europe, went to the Pacific to command the Twentieth Air Force and conduct B-29 operations against Japan.

They were still in the plane when it hit the ground.‡

On the plus side of the life-and-death scale, Colonel Beirne Lay, Jr., was not in his B-24 when it spun in. Lay, like Castle, as one of Eaker's originals, was not content with an Eighth Air Force career that included being a publicist, historian, and aide to Hap Arnold when he came to visit. He had flown on five missions as a volunteer crew member—the fifth being the Regensburg shuttle—before returning to the States to take further training. In February 1944, he became Commanding Officer of the 487th Bomb Group, and on May 11, on a strike against marshaling yards near Châteaudun, flak knocked his Liberator out of the sky but not before his entire crew bailed out. Unlike Jake Smart, Lay was unhurt, avoided capture, and was picked up by the Resistance, which, as its intrepid members had done for hundreds of other downed airmen, spirited him to safety so that he could fight another day, which he did with the Fifteenth Air Force.

* * *

It was mid-September when Eisenhower relinquished his hold on USSTAF and Spaatz was free, except in an emergency situation, to return to what he considered his primary goal in the war. At the time, the defeat of the German armies in France, the liberation of Paris, the capture of thousands of enemy soldiers, had produced a sense of euphoria among the Allied leaders, and bets were being made on how soon the war in Europe would be over. Many thought, before the end of the year. In view of the seeming disintegration of the Wehrmacht forces following the breakout at St.-Lô, in July, and the closing of the Falaise pocket, in August, the belief was at least understandable. Control of the air made it seem more so.

But the German soldiers, once back behind the Siegfried Line, in their own fatherland, regained their resolve and dug in to fight. The fear of "unconditional surrender," coupled with the wording of the Morgenthau Plan, which was aimed at turning Germany into a pasture land, aided their determination. This was equally true of the worn and dwindling Luftwaffe.

In the nine months that Tooey Spaatz had commanded USSTAF, he had fought a bloody, unyielding strategy of attrition against the Luftwaffe. He was, in a real sense, the Ulysses S. Grant of the air war, and The Big Week was the beginning of his Wilderness Campaign. In a partnership with Eaker—which not Arnold but Spaatz had insisted on—he drove for the Luftwaffe's jugular, the attrition on both sides brutal.

He had the force, and he used it whatever the immediate cost, knowing that Arnold would replace the losses. Although he believed in precision bombing, he was willing to accept any kind of bombing so long as it damaged the enemy's capacity to fight back. He did not agree with Bomber

‡ Castle was posthumously awarded the Medal of Honor.

Harris' concept of laying waste to cities in the mistaken belief that such destruction would break German morale, but before the fighting ended, he acquiesced in permitting Doolittle's bombers to participate in the terror raids on Berlin and Dresden. War, after all, was madness to begin with, and the one sure way to stop the madness was to finish the war by whatever means were at hand, or so it was possible to reason.

Shortly after The Big Week, he had written to Arnold suggesting that it might be a good idea to form an investigating committee of knowledgeable civilians who, directly after the fighting ended, would go into Germany and make a study of just exactly how effective precision bombing had been. He had no thoughts whatever about the need to defend the strategy against academicians, such as John Kenneth Galbraith, who would come later to pronounce from their lofty position of all-knowing that the effort had largely failed in its purpose. He already knew better. So did the Germans.* His reason for the suggestion was that such an examination would be helpful in fighting the Pacific war and would reveal how effective the ordnance had been and what changes should be made in the tactics being used.†

Perhaps the one error of approach Spaatz shared with Eaker and both shared, to a lesser degree, with Arnold was a sense of optimism that if given the crews and equipment needed they could end the war sooner than anyone anticipated. Following second Schweinfurt, Arnold was willing to tell the press that yes, it might still be possible to defeat the Germans from the air without need of an invasion. And just prior to the invasion, Spaatz felt it wasn't really necessary, that air power alone could do the job. And, as noted, Eaker's ever-optimistic letters to Arnold probably helped to sour him, particularly after Lovett's inspection trip in June 1943. Frank Andrews, although more modified in his outlook, particularly during the last three months of his life, was possessed of the same can-do and can-do-sooner-than-later approach. The fact is that optimism was endemic in all of them, a characteristic that was ingrained in the very nature of their lives. They had begun with flight. They had fought for the cause of flight in peace. Now they were fighting to show what it could do in war, and their faith in its power to bring victory was unshakable. What the critics could not understand, would never understand, was that the use of strategic air power was brand-new, and the few, like Spaatz and Eaker, who were employing it, were pioneers in a conflict whose cruel proving ground was the sky. And because they themselves were men of the sky, their optimism never faltered, and often their predictions were far in advance of the goals they sought. But had they been commanders of lesser resolve and faith in their trade, the war in Europe might have told a

---

* See Albert Speer, *Inside the Third Reich* (New York: Macmillan, 1970).
† Spaatz's suggestion was the origin of the Strategic Bombing Survey.

different story. That it almost did, offered an ironic and fateful comparison between themselves and their adversaries. None of them knew it at the time, but they had a pair of secret weapons in the guise of the Reich Air Ministry and Adolf Hitler.

German aeronautical ingenuity was such that by July 1942 Luftwaffe pilots were test-flying the first jet fighter, the Me 262. Its performance capabilities were far superior to any piston-driven aircraft and would offer an unparalleled advantage. The following month, on August 17, the very day the Eighth Air Force flew its first heavy bombardment mission, the jet fighter cracked up on a test flight. The accident not only retarded development, it convinced unenlightened Air Ministry officials this was not the time to approve production of the aircraft. For a comparative decision of equally momentous importance, there was the crash of the Boeing B-17 on its preemptive test flight in October 1935. Like Goering's Air Ministry, the War Department, as a result, was against going into production on the Fortress, but Major General Frank Andrews, Commanding General of GHQ Air Force, prevailed then, and thirteen of the planes were produced. The Germans had no Frank Andrews of their own and the end result was that on the day Eaker's B-17's made their debut, the Luftwaffe's jet fighter was shunted aside. Not until December was the Me 262 considered for production, and then not until sometime in 1944, at the rate of twenty planes a month. It wasn't until Luftwaffe fighter commander Adolf Galland flew the jet fighter, in May 1943, and became immediately aware of the potential, that the Air Ministry was forced into recognizing what lay within its grasp. Galland told both Goering and Milch that this was the plane that could save the day for Germany. In November, the Me 262 was demonstrated for Hitler, and his first question to Willi Messerschmitt was, "Can this aircraft carry bombs?" Messerschmitt had to reply in the affirmative, and Hitler, who wanted to think only in terms of attack, cried, "So there is our blitz-bomber!"[9]

And there vanished the Luftwaffe's last, best hope. It was eight months later, in July 1944, that an American fighter pilot reported the first sighting of an enemy jet, but it was not until February 1945 that the Me 262 apppeared in combat in squadron strength and, although few in number, began knocking Allied bombers and fighters down like duckpins. Luckily, they were too few and too late to do any real damage. Thus the most important aeronautical advance of the war, actually developed before it and then ignored during much of it, banned by Hitler, was finally thrown into the struggle at the eleventh hour.[10] Fortunately for Allied air power, its effect on the outcome of the war was negligible.

* * *

On a mild morning in mid-April 1945 a quartet of U.S. airmen sat around a table taking their ease over coffee at a villa near Cannes,

France. The background was one of palm and olive trees, oranges growing, wisteria flowering, overhead the sky blue, and the water blue and
flashing in the sun. In the distance there was the sound of artillery, inter-
mittent, perfunctory. Like the fragrance of things growing, the spring of
peace was in the air.

Host at the table was Hap Arnold, three months away from a nearly
fatal heart attack. He was looking perky and rested, whereas just a week
before Marshall had cabled him: "I read of your presence and statements
with various commands. Where is the Bermuda rest, the lazy days at
Cannes, the period of retirement at Capri? You are riding for a fall, doctor or no doctor."

Maybe so, but on his convalescent tour of Air Forces commands, he
was spending a few lazy days at Cannes—even if his thoughts would not
rest. Around the table with him were Tooey Spaatz, Jimmy Doolittle, and
Hugh Knerr. The news had come the previous evening that Roosevelt had
died. "The King is dead, long live the King," was Spaatz's comment. Now
in the early sunlight they were contemplating the future and making plans
for it. In their thinking, Roosevelt had never really been an air supporter;
the Navy was his pride and joy. President Harry Truman, however, was
an unknown entity, and they wished to move swiftly to gain his support.
There was no question any longer on when the move should be made to
create a separate, independent Air Force: just as soon as they could
prepare their strength to go for it. But in preparation, Spaatz was to say,
"The first move we must make now is to negotiate the installation of a senior military aide to the President." And who would that be? The agreed
choice was Pete Quesada. Pete had the personality, rank, and prestige to
do the job. Both Omar Bradley and Eisenhower doted on him. Hell, he'd
even flown Ike over enemy lines, halfway to Paris. Most likely the War
Department would not approve the idea of Quesada, but they must organize and fight. The President must have day-to-day contact with an airman from here on in.

The next point was that with the war about to shift fully to the Pacific,
it was essential that the Air Staff be strengthened, toughened up. It was
not necessary to say so, but Hap's illness could not have come at a worse
time. Even before he was stricken, his health was such that Barney Giles
and Larry Kuter had been practically running the office. It was not Arnold who was conferring with Marshall on war plans but Giles, and although Giles was sharp and competent, he couldn't sit down with
Marshall the way Hap could, and it made a difference.

Arnold had wanted Giles to go to the February Yalta Conference in his
place, and Marshall had said no. He wanted Giles in Washington, and so
Kuter had gone instead. Following Yalta, Marshall had met with Spaatz
and Eaker and talked over Arnold's illness. The result was that Eaker
gave up his leadership of the Mediterranean Allied Air Forces and re-

turned to the Pentagon on March 28 to take over as Deputy Commander, Army Air Forces. One reason for his return was that Giles was going to the Pacific to head up all the air forces there for the final attack on Japan. Another was that, at Eaker's request, Kuter was going with him. Timing was bad, because Ira was presently on a three-week tour of all the air forces in order to have a first-hand look at what he would need to know, and when he returned to Washington, Giles and Kuter would be leaving. The sudden death of Roosevelt, Arnold's incapacitation, weakness on the Air Staff, and a vacuum created by the absence and shifting of its top leadership were of major concern to those at the breakfast table.

In spite of Marshall's admonition, Spaatz told Arnold his place was back in Washington immediately. There he must be surrounded by enough strong-minded men who knew their business so that the Air Staff would be solid in all areas. Some of the strong-minded they discussed were Fred Anderson, Pre Cabell, and Hoyt Vandenberg.

As Spaatz was to write Giles following the two-hour breakfast, "You and Kenney must fight the Pacific war. The best talent must be fed as rapidly as possible into your theaters and into Washington without jeopardizing the rapid conclusion of the European war."

Over the coffee cups there were two central points behind the plotting and planning. One was to fly free, to finally gain independence as an equal service with the Army and the Navy, and the other was to try to prevent the kind of repeat that had happened at the end of World War I, the dissolution of air power. In 1918 air power was too new and untried to be understood by most. There was no excuse for doubting air power's primacy now. Of the four at the table, only Arnold knew of the Manhattan Project, but even he had no idea of what an atomic bomb could do. Spaatz did not believe the war with Japan would be ended until November 1946; he'd bet twenty dollars on it, but however long they thought it would take to bring final victory, none of them believed the conflict could be over and done in four months and that the doing would revolutionize warfare.

In the long, hard fight for independence, no civilian official had been keener or more supportive of the idea than Under Secretary of War for Air Robert Lovett. In his letters to Spaatz, he had promised that, once the war was done, he would devote all his energies to making the dream a reality. They knew he meant it, and talked about keeping him informed on all their moves. He was to tell Tooey that "Hap's absence from the top councils at this particular time is a serious blow."

One positive development was that the Army's position had changed, at least Eisenhower's. He and Tooey had frequently discussed the need for a department of defense and three coequal branches. No one would ever be able to measure the importance of the relationship between Ike and Tooey to the progress and success of the war against Germany in North

Africa and Europe, but Eisenhower was to tell Marshall that Tooey
Spaatz was the best operational airman in the world.

The Navy was still seen as the big threat to independence. It had power
and might in the halls of Congress and within the government. The fear at
the breakfast table was that the Navy would now try to control everything
in the Pacific. But Nimitz wasn't going to get control of the Twentieth Air
Force and its B-29's, hitting Japan. The Twentieth's strategic operations
were outside Nimitz's theater, and MacArthur's as well. Arnold was going
to keep it in his pocket. Barney Giles would do the administrating, Curt
LeMay the bombing.

A month previously, Spaatz had received his fourth star. Privately, he
was anxious to return home and retire, but he knew it wasn't over yet,
that it couldn't be over until there was a U. S. Air Force. As Ira was to
write him from Washington, "I think it is a tragedy that we have to come
home from a war, three and a half years of hard work, to start the
toughest struggle of our lives, but we can either do that or see the whole
thing fall apart."

Eaker was suffering the blues, and Spaatz told him to cheer up, it
wasn't as bad as he thought. It was too bad, of course, that he wasn't at
the table with them, where they could relax even while they were organizing for the big push. None of them would deny they were worn around
the edges, not as badly wounded as Hap, but they'd all been through it.
They agreed strategic bombardment would end now. The RAF had just
blasted Berchtesgaden in a kind of final blow. As for the target's strategic
worth, Spaatz showed them a cable from his Intelligence Chief, George
McDonald. The message was a statement from Hans Fay, a German test
pilot who had landed his twin-engine Me 262 jet at an American field.
Fay was quoted as saying, "The American Air Force has shortened the
war by years as well as decided its outcome. . . . Only bomber attacks
during daytime have crippled and destroyed our industry. . . . Bombing
attacks on cities did not exert a profound influence on German morale.
This was true even of the devastating bomb carpets." Later, after Spaatz
had visited Germany, he was to say that no country had been laid waste
so completely since Carthage.

And what of the cost in the lives of the young men whose battleground
was the sky? It was unknown then, but almost eerily, the numbers were
practically the same for all: 79,265 Americans, 79,281 British, 80,588
Germans.[11]

And so, at war's end in Europe, the four at the table, like their Old
Guard comrades scattered in positions of command around the globe,
their ranks thinned, would have rather reflected on days of peace and rest
ahead instead of planning a conflict that would outlast the war. But they
were the few, quite unlike any other few. Arnold and Spaatz, Doolittle
and Knerr, and some who were not there with them: Eaker and Giles,

Hal George, Monk Hunter, George Kenney, and all the others. The thinkers, the darers, the doers. As young men they had had a dream, but unlike most dreamers, they had never lost it, and it was still with them although they were no longer young.

As young men, they had looked to the sky and in flimsy kites dared the imperious blue. Such men never grow old in spirit: They leave a memory, a heritage that endures.

At a table in Cannes in April 1945, Hap Arnold and a few of his captains made plans for the future.

Author's Acknowledgment

Most of the personal interviews for *Forged in Fire* were conducted during my research for *A Few Great Captains,* the two books being contiguous. During both efforts I had the indefatigable and essential aid of Lieutenant General Ira C. Eaker, who for thirty years contributed his all to the development of military aviation. In war as in peace, he was one of the few great captains of U.S. air power, and his responses to my unending inquiries were of fundamental importance to the writing of both volumes.

To cite General Eaker is to bring to mind his remarkable contemporary and fellow airman Lieutenant General James H. Doolittle. No name ever did less to describe its bearer, for Jimmy Doolittle's aerial career offers the stuff from which legends are made. Interviewing him was a memorable experience, his enthusiasm and energy and wit helping to fill in the perilous days of yesteryear, when he went from Tokyo raider to bomber commander.

The fighting of the air war over Europe was in the hands of young commanders whose names became famous during the conflict and afterward. In my interviews with Generals Curtis E. LeMay, Laurence S. Kuter, Haywood S. Hansell, Frank O'D. Hunter, Elwood R. Quesada, Earle E. Partridge, Harris Hull, Edward S. Curtis, Thomas C. Darcy, Jacob E. Smart, and Theodore R. Milton, I was given invaluable insight into the conditions and decisions each faced in handling combat operations in their respective roles on the ground and in the air. All were unstinting in their efforts to answer my questions and to acquaint me fully with the demands made upon them. Much helpful information and detail were also supplied by James Parton, who served for most of the war as General Eaker's aide.

On the technical side, I not only had the benefit of General Doolittle's input but that of Generals Mark E. Bradley (through correspondence) and Benjamin A. Kelsey. Both were unsung heroes during World War II in the development of the long-range fighter, particularly the P-51, the Mustang.

On the personal side of the lives of Generals Andrews, Arnold, Eaker, and Spaatz, I had the warm cooperation of family members—sons and daughters and wives—Allen Andrews, Jean Andrews Peterson, Colonel Hiette S. Williams, Jr., Colonel William Bruce Arnold, and two very gracious ladies: Ruth Eaker and Ruth Spaatz.

Two combat airmen and old friends who contributed to my knowledge were Charles Wilson Smith and Russell Bradshaw—Smith a former B-17 pilot with the Eighth Air Force, and Bradshaw a mission-flying intelligence officer with the Fifteenth Air Force. Two nonairmen who supplied me with additional information were Burton A. Gale and Robert Bruskin —Gale an antiaircraft gunner at Pearl Harbor on December 7, 1941, and Bruskin a combat intelligence officer who served in Panama, North Africa, and the European Theater. Finally, my appreciation to General Truman H. Landon for describing the preparations for the departure of his squadron of B-17's from the West Coast on December 6, 1941, their destination Pearl Harbor.

My special thanks also to those who steered my efforts in the right direction and gave valued advice in doing so: Major General John W. Huston and his staff at the Office of Air Force History and, at the Air Force Academy, Colonel Alfred F. Hurley, Lieutenant Colonels John F. Shiner and David MacIsaac, and Academy Archivist Duane Reed. The staff at the Manuscript Division of the Library of Congress were ever helpful.

Editorially, my gratitude and thanks to John Frisbee for his fine editing and organizational suggestions. Again, as with *A Few Great Captains,* I had the benefit of Air Force Historian Thomas A. Sturm's eagle eye in the search for accuracy and clarity, this time joined by Dr. John Greenwood, whose suggestions and insight were of special importance.

As for my ever-faithful typists, Jeri Olsen and Alison Mabry, they deserve oak leaf clusters added to medals for intelligence, perseverance, and good humor. They, with the understanding and support of my wife, Susan, made it all possible.

Notes

ONE

1. The Washington *Daily News,* Mar. 6, 1940.

2. The Walsh-Healey Government Contracts Act, of 1936, sought to establish fair labor standards among contractors accepting government work.

3. For an account of the Woodring-Johnson feud and its effect on the Army Air Corps, see DeWitt S. Copp, *A Few Great Captains* (Garden City, N.Y.: Doubleday, 1980), pp. 402–5. President Roosevelt was fully cognizant of the antics of the two officials, which Secretary of the Interior Harold L. Ickes referred to as "the holy show."

4. Copp, op. cit., pp. 48–51.

5. The earlier account of Arnold's collision with Roosevelt was cited by him in his autobiography, *Global Mission* (New York: Harper & Brothers, 1948), although there is no mention in the book of the second encounter, a year later. However, documentation from Arnold's papers, particularly his daily office diary, supports the details of the second episode, as does Secretary Morgenthau's diary.

6. Arnold wrote a "Memorandum of Record" of the entire episode, covering the dates May 16–18, 1940.

7. There are a number of versions of the story of how the Air Corps and Boeing nearly came to a parting of the ways over the cost of the B-17. Much of the problem had to do with personalities: The hot temper of Maj. Gen. George Brett, who threw James Murray, of Boeing, out of his office, and the unpredictability of Assistant Secretary Louis Johnson, who also sent Murray marching, did nothing to solve the issue. All agree it was Spaatz who found the solution.

8. Gen. Claire Chennault, a first lieutenant in 1929, demonstrated the use of paratroops in maneuvers at Brooks Field, Texas. Using a formation of Douglas DH-4's with one paratrooper per plane and a Fokker Trimotor to carry equip-

ment, Chennault's volunteer platoon, which he had trained, bailed out on signal and were prepared to fight a minute after reaching the ground. Army Chief of Staff Maj. Gen. Charles P. Summerall watched the operation long enough to see the parachutes blossom, then turned his back and walked away, commenting, "Some more of this damned aviation nonsense." See Claire L. Chennault, *Way of a Fighter* (New York: Putnam, 1949), pp. 16–17.

9. Max Hastings, *Bomber Command* (New York: Dial, 1979), pp. 9–29. The Luftwaffe was to claim that the Wellingtons flew over Wilhelmshaven but dropped no bombs, that one of the captured RAF pilots maintained they were only on a navigational flight. The German Air Ministry accepted the figure of twenty-seven Wellingtons shot down, although the RAF insisted it had sent out only twenty-two aircraft. See Cajus Bekker, *The Luftwaffe War Diaries* (Garden City, N.Y.: Doubleday, 1968), pp. 76–79.

10. Forrest C. Pogue, *George C. Marshall.* Vol. 2, *Ordeal and Hope 1939–1942* (New York: Viking, 1966), p. 50.

TWO

1. The background information concerning Capt. Robert M. Losey was supplied by Mr. John F. Fuller, Air Weather Service Historian, through the aid of Maj. Richard H. Miller, USAF (Ret.).

2. Providentially for Great Britain, the German Air Force was neither as strong nor as well prepared for a cross-Channel strike. Goering and his subordinates had made no plans for such an attack. They were involved in the final push to defeat France. Their losses had been heavy, their pilots and air crews worn down, their equipment not designed for long-range strategic operations. Beyond that, Hitler was anxious to negotiate a peace with England.

3. Telephone interview and correspondence with Maj. Gen. Benjamin A. Kelsey, USAF (Ret.), May–July 1980.

4. James Leutze, ed., *The London Journal of General Raymond E. Lee 1940–1941* (Boston: Little, Brown, 1971), p. 5.

5. Ibid., pp. 5–6.

6. Interview with Maj. Gen. Frank O'D. Hunter, USAF (Ret.), Jan. 7, 1978.

7. Churchill and Kennedy had very little regard for each other. Churchill saw the Ambassador as a threat to Anglo-U.S. cooperation, and Kennedy saw the Prime Minister as "a self-righteous imperialist striving to disguise a war for empire in the garb of a moral crusade." Michael R. Beschloss, *Kennedy and Roosevelt* (New York: Norton, 1980), pp. 205–6.

8. Leutze, op. cit., pp. 18–20.

9. Stephenson didn't add, but it was nakedly apparent, that this "objective" individual must be objectively pro-British. William Stevenson, *A Man Called Intrepid: The Secret War* (New York: Harcourt, 1976), p. 108.

10. Leutze, op. cit., p. 19.

11. Ibid., pp. 27–28.

12. Stevenson, op. cit., pp. 114–26.

13. Beschloss, op. cit., pp. 206–7; Ladislas Farago, *The Game of the Foxes* (New York: David McKay, 1971), pp. 338, 341–45.

14. John Toland, *Adolf Hitler* (Garden City, N.Y.: Doubleday, 1976), pp. 723–24.

15. Spaatz's thinking on these essential questions as well as an account of his activities during his stay in Great Britain are found in the diary he kept throughout the period in question.

THREE

1. Keith D. McFarland, *Harry H. Woodring* (Lawrence, Kans.: University Press of Kansas, 1975), pp. 228–30.

2. Stimson Diary, June 19, 1940.

3. Bernard M. Baruch, *The Public Years* (New York: Holt, 1960), p. 260.

4. The members of the NDAC, aside from Knudsen, were Sidney Hillman, Labor; Edward R. Stettinius, Industrial Materials; Leon Henderson, Price Stabilization; Ralph Budd, Transportation; Chester C. Davis, Farm Products; Dr. Harriet Elliot, Consumer Protection. Donald M. Nelson would later be made Coordinator of National Defense Purchases. The formation of the Commission was the beginning of manpower mobilization in preparation for war. It was termed a government within the government and was not appreciated by Cabinet members, who saw their power being usurped, nor by members of Congress, who viewed the creation of the Commission as another move by Roosevelt to expand his control of all aspects of the national economy and defense. According to Robert Sherwood (*Roosevelt and Hopkins*), the President created the NDAC because he was convinced that the regular departments of government were not organized or geared to meet the demands of war. Pp. 158–60.

5. Henry H. Arnold, *Global Mission* (New York: Harper, 1948), p. 196.

6. Winston S. Churchill, *Their Finest Hour* (Boston: Houghton, 1949), p. 404.

7. Admiral Georges Robert later had a nervous breakdown and was reported to have gone insane.

8. The Martinique question concerned both the White House and Whitehall. The United States, from a diplomatic point of view, was able, in late 1941, to station a consular officer and a naval observer at Fort-de-France. Conversely, the War Department had made tentative plans to prepare an amphibious force for invasion of the island. Whether most of the estimated one hundred twenty to one hundred fifty P-36's aboard the aircraft carrier *Béarn* were uncrated and assembled is not known. That they were on board was due to Henry Morgenthau, who had made it possible for the planes to reach Canada to be loaded on the aircraft carrier, with the intent of aiding the French. British interest in the island centered on seizing the gold stored at Fort Desaix. German agents operating in the area were also anxious to lay their hands on the gold. After U.S. entry into the war, Martinique was immobilized as a U-boat refueling point.

9. Roberta Wohlstetter, *Pearl Harbor: Warning and Decision* (Stanford, Calif.: Stanford University Press, 1962), p. 88.

10. Copp, op. cit., pp. 55–56.

11. Stimson Diary, Sept. 27, 1940.

12. According to William Stevenson, in May 1941, U.S. naval officer Ensign Leonard Smith, flying a PBY out of a British base, was responsible for locating the German battleship *Bismarck,* which resulted in the *Bismarck's* sinking by units of the British Fleet. See *A Man Called Intrepid: The Secret War,* pp. 235–45.

13. The FBI learned as early as 1938 that German agents had managed to lay hands on vital blueprints of the Norden bombsight, referred to in 1940 as "this country's most jealously guarded air defense weapon." Roosevelt, on his own and against the wishes of the War Department, ordered that both the Norden and the Sperry bombsights be turned over to the British during the Battle of Britain. In a reciprocal move, the British dispatched Sir Henry Tizard, one of their most eminent scientists, to the United States loaded with Britain's most advanced technical secrets. Sir Henry was not only willing to trade secrets but also to safeguard them and interest the Administration in their production should England fall to Hitler. It appears, however, that at the time in question, neither Stimson, Marshall, nor Arnold was aware of Roosevelt's decision on the Norden bombsight.

14. Stimson Diary, Sept. 13, 1940.

15. John Morton Blum, *From the Morgenthau Diaries, Years of Urgency 1938–1941* (Boston: Houghton, 1965), p. 184.

16. Ibid., p. 185.

17. Stimson Diary, Sept. 20, 1940.

18. Leutze, op. cit., p. 62.

19. Stimson Diary, Oct. 10, 1940.

20. Davison crashed in New York Harbor, injuring his legs permanently. He had to wear specially made shoes, walked with a cane, and limped badly, but the injury did not affect his interest in aviation and politics.

21. Charles A. Lindbergh, *The Wartime Journals of Charles A. Lindbergh* (New York: Harcourt, 1970), pp. 257–58.

22. Two weeks after Pearl Harbor, on Dec. 20, 1944, Lindbergh wrote a letter to Hap Arnold, saying: "This is a personal note to tell you that if I can, at any time, be of assistance to you and to the Air Corps, there is nothing I would rather do. I fully realize the complications created by the political stand I have taken and by past incidents connected with that stand. However, I want you to know that if the opportunity should arise during the crises, I am ready and anxious to be of service. Meanwhile, I wish you the greatest success. May God strengthen you for the ordeal ahead." Three days later, Arnold replied: "Many thanks for your letter. . . . The response of the American people to the needs of our country in the defense of democracy has been a source of inspiration to all of us in the military service. I assure you that your offer of assistance in this critical period through which our nation is passing is greatly appreciated. With the season's greetings and all good wishes to you and yours, I am. . . ."

23. Stimson Diary, Oct. 25, 1940.

FOUR

1. The description of the meeting and what was said at it were related to the author by Col. H. S. Williams, USAF (Ret.). The quotes are recounted from Colonel Williams' memory.

2. When the Panama Canal opened for business, in 1914, its protection was the responsibility of Army ground and Navy sea forces. By 1917 the War Department recognized that the airplane could provide an adjunct to its ground units, particularly Army hydroplanes. In February of that year, Maj. Henry H. Arnold was dispatched to the Canal to first locate and then acquire a base for the 7th Aero Squadron. Even though Arnold's mission did not succeed—America's entry into the war catching him en route to Washington—in July 1918, an air base was established near the Atlantic entrance to the Canal. It was named France Field.

The field's location left a lot to be desired. Daily rain showers for nine months of the year made for very muddy going. A twenty-seven-hundred-foot coral runway that couldn't be extended didn't encourage going anywhere in bombers or heavily loaded aircraft. With the Navy operating from its Coco Solo air base—actually, an extension of France Field—the traffic pattern and the sky around it with its daily mass of clouds made for dangerous flying. The result was that in 1931 the Air Corps began to work on Albrook Field, on the Pacific side of the Isthmus. Here there was only half as much rainfall and the climate was far less humid. Albrook became the center of Air Corps operations, and the 19th Wing was headquartered at nearby Quarry Heights, where the Panama Canal Department was also headquartered.

3. Farago, op. cit., p. 53. Goering was undoubtedly referring to the Culebra Cut.

4. No record was ever found in the official files of the Third Reich indicating Hitler had a plan to attack the western hemisphere when he finished with the Soviet Union. Arguments on whether Roosevelt was being duped by the British into believing there was a threat continue. Evidence shows that he certainly believed the threat was there, as did Stimson, Knox, Marshall, and Stark, not to mention Arnold, Andrews, Spaatz, and a great many others, particularly those engaged in intelligence. See also William Stevenson, *A Man Called Intrepid: The Secret War,* pp. 297–98.

5. Ships transiting the Canal passed through two major lock systems, which raised vessels eighty-five feet above sea level at the continental divide before lowering them at the other end of the Isthmus. A ship entering from the Pacific was raised fifty-four feet by the Miraflores Locks in a two-step operation, and then sailed through Miraflores Lake, where it entered the Pedro Miguel Lock, whose one-step chamber raised it an additional thirty-one feet. The ship then traversed the narrow Gaillard Cut, given to sudden landslides that could close the Cut. But the most sensitive and most vulnerable point was Gatun Lake, where the ship began its downhill journey. The Lake was held in by a huge dam, and it was the key to the Canal's success. It allowed the locks to fill with water. If the dam were to be destroyed by sabotage or a bombing raid, the Canal would be inoperative, and an additional eight thousand miles of cruising would be necessary for ships wishing to travel from one ocean to the other.

6. Farago, op. cit., Ch. 5, pp. 51–54.

7. Robert E. Sherwood, *Roosevelt and Hopkins* (New York: Harper, 1948), pp. 198–99.

8. In a letter to Hugh Knerr dated Dec. 19, 1940, Andrews, having discussed global strategy with Col. William Donovan, remarked: "I will admit that the conception of a continent being required to fight against another continent had not occurred to me but with air power in the picture there is a good deal in the thought. I will have to mull it over a little more. It certainly would change the South American picture and give greater importance than ever to the Caribbean."

9. In 1937, Andrews, working through Congressman Mark Wilcox, tried to get a bill passed that would create the United States Air Corps. One key provision of the bill was for the Air Corps to provide aerial defense of the United States and its possessions. At the time, Arnold was Assistant Chief of the Air Corps, and he did not support the bill. See *A Few Great Captains*, pp. 374–88.

10. Such disparate figures as University of Chicago President Robert M. Hutchins and Sen. Burton K. Wheeler, archisolationist, were in essential agreement as to what passage of the bill would mean. Said Hutchins, "The American people are about to commit suicide." Wheeler proclaimed that Lend-Lease would mean "ploughing under every fourth American boy." Roosevelt replied that this was "the most untruthful, the most dastardly, unpatriotic thing that has been said in public life in my generation."

11. Thomas A. Sturm, "American Air Defense: The Decision to Proceed," *Aerospace Historian*, Vol. 19, No. 4, Dec. 1972.

FIVE

1. Stimson Diary, Apr. 15, 1941. In honoring a commitment made to the Greek Government, Churchill, against the wishes of his military commanders in Egypt and Libya, had over 70,000 well-equipped and combat-hardened desert troops transferred to Greece in March 1941. Since October 1940, Greek forces had been engaged against an Italian invasion force, but they feared an attack by Germany. When it came, in April, fifteen divisions and superior air power brought about a miniature Dunkirk in which the Royal Navy, while suffering severe losses from aerial attack, brought off some fifty thousand troops—British, Greek, Palestinian, and Yugoslav. Winston S. Churchill, *The Grand Alliance* (Boston: Houghton, 1950), pp. 220–33.

2. Arnold, op. cit., pp. 261–62.

3.   *MEMORANDUM FOR THE PRESIDENT*
                         STRICTLY CONFIDENTIAL

1. 10 destroyers a month beginning April 1st. Destroyers to be reconditioned in the United States—reconditioning to begin immediately.

2. The urgent need of more merchant shipping at once. British cannot wait until new ships are built.

3. 50 PBY planes in addition to the PBY which the British are receiving on their own account; fully equipped with radio, depth charges, bombs, guns and ammunition. Adequate operating spare supplies. Urgent need for crews.

4. There are 29 engineless Lockheed planes in England. They need 58 Wright 1820 engines at once.

5. There are 100 Curtiss Tomahawks without propellors in England. 764 fifty-caliber and 100 thirty-caliber machine guns required to complete armament. Curtiss Tomahawks already in England.

6. Consideration to be given immediately to the replacement of fifty-caliber guns manufactured by Colt which are unsatisfactory with the same gun which has already been manufactured by our own arsenals.

7. 20 million rounds of fifty-caliber ammunition and as many extra fifty-caliber gun barrels as are available urgently needed.

8. The maximum number of B-17, B's C's or D's in addition to the 20 already agreed upon to be sent to England immediately. Planes should be sent complete ready for immediate operation, including spare parts, bombs and ammunition. Crews urgently needed.

9. Transfer to the British 200 North American Harvards or Vultee Valiants trainers in excess of all present deliveries.

10. At least 5 additional civilian flying training schools completely equipped.

11. Work out plan to ferry bombers to England. This would release nearly 800 British R.A.F. personnel.

12. 250,000 Enfield rifles and 50,000,000 rounds of ammunition have been sent.

13. Give priority to tools for the manufacture of Point 303 rifles for the British. Same applies to Point 303 ammunition.

14. Send 80 trained observers—half from the factories and half from the Army and Navy—to acquaint Britain with the use of our planes.

HARRY HOPKINS

SECRET

4. Arnold, op. cit., p. 235.

5. Stimson Diary, May 6, 1941.

6. As noted, Lovett had joined Stimson's staff as a special assistant on air matters. It took several months of legal and legislative modification not only to institute a better and more workable command organization with the Secretary of War's office but also to reinstitute the office of Assistant Secretary of War for Air, held formerly by F. Trubee Davison and abolished by Roosevelt in 1933 through Gen. Douglas MacArthur's influence. Robert A. Lovett was named the new Air Secretary in January 1941.

7. Stimson Diary, Feb. 10, 1941.

8. Guido R. Perera, *Memoirs*, "Washington and War Years," unpublished ms.

9. Knerr was referring to the part he played in drafting the Wilcox bill for a separate air corps.

10. Stimson Diary, June 12, 1941.

11. Andrews was referring to Arnold's less-than-all-out support when Andrews was trying to sell the General Staff in 1937–38 on the procurement of B-17's. Arnold, as Assistant Chief of the Air Corps, was in charge of procurement.

SIX

1. Churchill, op. cit., p. 369.
2. On Apr. 11, 1941, the U.S. destroyer *Niblack* attempted to destroy a German submarine by dropping depth charges. Evidently its sonar contacts were misleading, for no U-boat in the vicinity reported the attack. See Thomas A. Bailey and Paul B. Ryan, *Hitler vs. Roosevelt: The Undeclared Naval War* (New York: Macmillan, 1979), pp. 127–31.
3. Leutze, ed., op. cit., p. 309; Sherwood, op. cit., pp. 290–91; Bailey and Ryan, op. cit., pp. 155–57.
4. Arnold, op. cit., p. 209.
5. Leutze, op. cit., p. 333.
6. Ibid., p. 374.
7. Stimson Diary, Apr. 11, 1941.
8. Pogue, op. cit., pp. 156–57.
9. Here again, General Chaney's evaluation had a modifying effect. He and his staff prepared an in-depth study of the German bombing effort of 1940 in which he showed that the German failure to destroy British industry and public morale was the fault of Luftwaffe tactics and equipment, not proof that the theory was incorrect.
10. Haywood S. Hansell, *The Air Plan That Defeated Hitler* (Atlanta, Ga.: Higgins-MacArthur/Longino & Porter, 1972), pp. 61–70; interview with General Hansell.
11. Ibid., pp. 89–90.
12. Ibid., pp. 93–94.
13. Ibid., p. 96.

SEVEN

1. Thomas A. Bailey and Paul B. Ryan, op. cit., pp. 197–98.
2. The fall of the Konoye government took the White House and official Washington by surprise. Roosevelt canceled his regular Cabinet meeting and huddled with his chief advisers, civilian and military. The result was that Admiral Stark sent a most secret dispatch to his three fleet commanders, warning that Japan might attack the U.S.S.R. or the United States and Great Britain. This message was passed from Admiral Kimmel at Pearl Harbor to General Short on Oct. 16, 1941.
3. Friction between General MacArthur and Asiatic Fleet Commander Adm. Thomas C. Hart did not help matters in the Philippines. Hart's mission in case of war was to withdraw southward from the Islands until the Pacific Fleet could move westward and the two could coordinate their strength. The Admiral, impressed with the proposed increase in air strength, recommended to the Navy Department that he be permitted to remain and fight it out. This suggestion was rejected in Washington. Hart's Patrol Wing 10—"Patwing 10"—had a strength of 32 PBY's. The disagreement between MacArthur and Hart over reconnaissance duties was resolved in late November, when Patwing 10 took over patrols southward of Luzon and westward to the coast of In-

dochina, while MacArthur's B-17's, under the command of Maj. Gen. Lewis Brereton, were assigned to patrol the coastal waters around Luzon northward toward Formosa.

4. In Washington, an internal battle raged between J. Edgar Hoover, Director of the FBI; British Intelligence; Army G-2; and Navy ONI as to who would have control of counterespionage in Latin America. Mostly the battle was over Hoover's determination to have control, and although the FBI's mandate did not include foreign intelligence operations, Hoover won out. Nevertheless, Andrews utilized his own people and was a close confidant of Col. "Wild Bill" Donovan, who, in turn, was linked to British Intelligence.

5. Correspondence with Gen. Mark E. Bradley, USAF (Ret.).

EIGHT

1. Leutze, op. cit., pp. 338–39.

2. Stimson Diary, Nov. 27, 1941.

3. Pogue, *Ordeal and Hope, 1939–1942*, pp. 193–97.

4. Stimson Diary, Nov. 27, 1941.

5. Wohlstetter, op. cit., pp. 258–59.

6. Ibid., pp. 66ff.

7. L. H. Brereton, *The Brereton Diaries, 3 October 1941–8 May 1945* (New York: Morrow, 1946), p. 31.

8. William Manchester, *American Caesar: Douglas MacArthur, 1880–1964* (Boston: Little, Brown, 1978), p. 201.

9. Brereton, op. cit., p. 10.

10. Wohlstetter, op. cit., pp. 24–25.

11. Ibid., p. 25.

12. Interview with Maj. Gen. Thomas C. Darcy, Jan. 30, 1980.

13. Interview with former Cpl. Burton A. Gale, of the 55th Coast Artillery Co., U. S. Army.

NINE

1. Manchester, op. cit., p. 332.

2. It was Col. Charles A. Lindbergh as a civilian technical representative who, with MacArthur's blessing, showed Kenney's fighter pilots, flying P-38's, how to greatly increase their combat range without additional fuel. Directly after Pearl Harbor, Lindbergh had written to Arnold offering his services. Word of this got out and a campaign of hate mail followed, evidently orchestrated by an organized few. One who was strongly opposed to Lindbergh's being given an active Army commission was Congressman John B. Snyder, Democrat of Pennsylvania, who told Roosevelt that Army pilots would shoot Lindy down. FDR needed no encouragement from Snyder; he was set against Lindbergh's serving in any military capacity. As a civilian, Lindbergh flew in combat in the Southwest Pacific and was credited with downing two Japanese Zeros.

3. The targets Doolittle's raiders hit were ninety buildings of the First Demolition Ministry, in Tokyo; the Japanese Diesel Mfg. Co.; Factory No. 1 of the Japanese Steel Corp.; a warehouse of Yokohama Mfg.; Mitsubishi Heavy In-

dustrial Corp.; the Nagoya Aircraft Factory; the naval ammunition dump; and the army arsenal.

4. Hastings, op. cit., p. 127.

5. Ibid., p. 132; R. V. Jones, *The Wizard War* (New York: Coward, 1978), p. 210.

6. Hastings, op. cit., pp. 132, 133.

7. Ibid., pp. 134, 138.

8. Letter from Andrews to his old friend Maj. Gen. Henry Conger Pratt, Commander Trinidad Base Command, 1/28/42. "If we are ever to have unity of command, and we have got to have it eventually in every theater, the directive for that unity of command has got to come from the top, starting from Washington. Regardless of this . . . both [Gen.] Short and [Adm.] Kimmel were guilty of unbelievable lack of judgment in their estimate of the situation and the measures they took. . . ."

9. Leutze, op. cit., p. 468.

10. Ibid., p. 469.

TEN

1. Howard T. Wright, "Changing Insignias," *Aerospace Historian*, Vol. 27, No. 2, June 1980, pp. 113–15.

2. Hastings, op. cit., p. 149.

3. Women pilots were first used by the Air Transport Command in Sept. 1942. A training program was begun in Sweetwater, Texas, for women pilots, and before war's end more than fifteen hundred women pilots were on active duty with the AAF. The acronym WASP was derived from Women's Air Force Service Pilots. See *Global Mission*, p. 358.

4. Later Eisenhower apparently forgot that he had upheld Chaney's organizational plan over Arnold's. Dwight D. Eisenhower, *Crusade in Europe* (Garden City, N.Y.: Doubleday, 1948), pp. 49–50.

5. Hastings, op. cit., p. 121.

6. Sherwood, op. cit., p. 529.

ELEVEN

1. *Marshall Memo for the President:* "The Pacific Theater versus Bolero," 5/4/42.

2. Eisenhower, op. cit., pp. 49–50.

3. Arnold, op. cit., p. 308.

4. Ibid., p. 318.

5. Arnold made no mention of such a plan in his autobiography, *Global Mission*. Nor is there anything that clarifies the decision in his official papers. There is just the quoted mention in his letter to Winston Churchill dated June 10, 1942.

6. Laurence S. Kuter, "The General Vs. The Establishment—Gen. H. H. Arnold and the Air Staff," *Aerospace Historian*, Vol. 21, No. 4, Dec. 1974, p. 187.

7. Churchill's "unexpected" visit was a result of word from Mountbatten and Sir John Dill, the British Chief of the Joint Staff Mission, to the Prime Minister that they believed Roosevelt was anxious to drop plans for SLEDGEHAMMER.

Churchill had never been for the plan (believing the Channel would run red with Allied blood, mostly British). Neither had his Army Chief of Staff, Field Marshal Sir Alan Brooke, who came with him. Churchill's aim was to sell Roosevelt on either JUPITER, an invasion of northern Norway, or GYMNAST, an invasion of North Africa, or both. Brooke, like Marshall, was not in favor of the latter and, with Churchill, was opposed to SLEDGEHAMMER. Since Roosevelt had permitted Harry Hopkins to announce the promise of a second front in 1942, Sir Winston was only too willing to aid in getting FDR off the hook by pressing for a change in plans. Previously he had stressed we "never must let Gymnast pass from our minds," and now, to Marshall's and Stimson's anguish, he sought to sell the switch. He was at the White House on Sunday morning, June 21, with Brooke when Roosevelt handed him a pink slip of paper that said the British bastion at Tobruk had fallen. It was a crushing blow, as stunning as the loss of Singapore, and turning the color of the paper, Churchill made a plea for immediate emergency aid. This was what Duncan had been referring to in his letter to Spaatz. Marshall promptly offered support of tanks and guns and an armored division under General George Patton. But Churchill, desperate as the situation was, with Rommel's Afrika Korps less than eighty miles from Alexandria, wanted more than emergency aid; he wanted a commitment to GYMNAST. Roosevelt, who had been opposed to the North African venture, now began to swing around and joined the Prime Minister, overriding everything Marshall and Brooke had to say on the matter. What was going to be diverted to Egypt to supply the very hard-pressed British forces would naturally be taken from forces and equipment previously allocated to BOLERO. This, to Marshall, meant a certain end to SLEDGEHAMMER and very possibly to ROUNDUP. Roosevelt's weather-vaning, his ambiguity in insisting that he wished second-front plans to continue while at the same time agreeing with Sir Winston, began to wear on Marshall. Late in the evening on the fourth day of the discussions he was alone with the President, and when Roosevelt said he was in favor of sending a large expeditionary force to Egypt to control the vast desert area between Alexandria and Tehran, Iran, the Chief of Staff came very close to losing his temper. He didn't trust himself to reply. Instead, he turned and left the room.

8. Copp, op. cit., pp. 305–7; interview with Maj. Gen. Darcy, Oct. 7, 1977–Jan. 30, 1980.

TWELVE

1. Albert C. Wedemeyer, *Wedemeyer Reports* (New York: Holt, 1958), p. 160; interview with General Wedemeyer, Mar. 17, 1977.

2. Sherwood, op. cit., p. 600.

3. Arthur Bryant, *The Turn of the Tide* (Garden City, N.Y.: Doubleday, 1957), p. 341.

4. Ibid.

5. Pogue, *Ordeal and Hope, 1939–1942*, p. 340.

6. Bryant, op. cit., p. 346.

7. Eisenhower, op. cit., p. 72

8. Eaker's reasons to Arnold: "1. We can hit point targets in day bombing. A smaller force can therefore destroy vital objectives. 2. The British bomb by

night and the German defenses sleep by day; when we are at them in the day time, they will be alerted 24 hours a day and get no rest. 3. The operational losses will be greatly reduced; it is much better to combat the normal weather in this theater in daylight than at night. 4. Navigation will be greatly improved; crews with much less training and experience can do an acceptable job. 5. Our aircraft super-charged and unflame-dampened are not well suited for night bombardment. 6. Tight formations can be flown and pursuit protection can accompany."

9. Although Bedell Smith was in favor of strategic bombardment, he did not believe that the war could be won by its use alone or that it should have precedence over other forms of attack. Hansell, op. cit., p. 263.

10. Harry C. Butcher, *My Three Years with Eisenhower* (New York: Simon & Schuster, 1946), p. 62.

11. RAF losses were 71 pilots and 10 air crew killed or missing, 106 aircraft downed, of which 88 were fighters. German losses were 78 fighters and an unknown number killed. See John P. Campbell, "Air Operations and the Dieppe Raid," *Aerospace Historian,* Vol. 23, No. 1, Mar. 1976, pp. 10–20.

12. Hansell, op. cit., pp. 100–12; interview with General Hansell, Jan. 7, 1977.

13. Eisenhower, op. cit., p. 77.

14. Ibid.

15. General Doolittle points out that others should share the credit for the development of 100-octane gasoline. Eddie E. Aldrin, father of astronaut Edwin E. Aldrin, Jr., was Aviation Manager for Standard Oil, and he, too, was at work on the process, as was Billy Parker, Aviation Manager for Phillips Petroleum. Interview with Lt. Gen. James H. Doolittle, Aug. 26, 1980.

THIRTEEN

1. On Dec. 8, 1941, the Eagle Squadrons volunteered to transfer to the U. S. Army Air Forces.

2. Vern Haugland, *The Eagle Squadrons* (New York: Ziff-Davis, 1979), p. 164.

3. Through their own sloppy attitude toward briefing and a built-in sense of confidence, the loss was a combination of carelessness, bad weather forecasting, and bad luck. The weather officer predicted a 35-knot headwind at twenty-eight thousand feet. Instead, there was a 100-knot tailwind. The 135-knot error resulted in twelve Eagle pilots lost and twelve brand-new Spitfire IX's destroyed. Haugland, op. cit., pp. 168–72.

4. Curtis E. LeMay and MacKinlay Kantor, *Mission with LeMay* (Garden City, N.Y.: Doubleday, 1964), p. 225; interview with author.

5. USAAF, *Target Germany* (New York: Simon & Schuster, 1943), pp. 47–48.

6. Hansell, op. cit., pp. 114–18; interview with author.

7. Haugland, op. cit., pp. 160–63.

8. Out of this incident, Beirne Lay, with Sy Bartlett, was to fashion the Hollywood classic *12 O'Clock High.*

9. General Miller's career came to a tragic end in April 1944. At a small dinner at Claridge's on the evening of April 18, Miller, who had drunk too

much, inadvertently talked openly of the top-secret date for the launching of OVERLORD. One of the dinner guests was Maj. Gen. Edwin L. Sibert, Chief of Army Intelligence in the ETO. The breach was reported to Eisenhower, who sent Miller home on the next boat, reduced in rank to lieutenant colonel. Miller protested his innocence, but friend though he was, Eisenhower had no choice but to act summarily.

10. Roger A. Freeman, *The Mighty Eighth* (Garden City, N.Y.: Doubleday, 1970), pp. 33–36.

11. Hastings, op. cit., pp. 218–19.

FOURTEEN

1. Sir John Slessor, *The Central Blue* (London: Cassell, 1956), pp. 438–39.

2. Sir Winston Churchill, *The Hinge of Fate* (Boston: Houghton, 1950), pp. 678–79.

3. Ibid., p. 679.

4. The recounting of what took place at Casablanca with regard to the parts played by Generals Arnold, Andrews, Eaker, and Spaatz is drawn from a number of sources. The principal documentation was a daily diary kept by Arnold, giving date, time, and brief indication of what was going on and who was present, as well as Eaker's daily diary kept by Parton. Andrews' memo to Marshall dated Jan. 20, 1943, indicated his role in the proceedings, as did a running account written by his aide, Lt. Col. Frederick Chapman. Col. Everett Cook wrote a recap of Spaatz's attendance as Spaatz related it to his staff upon his return to Algiers. There were also letters written directly after the conference, commenting on it, from Arnold to Eaker and Spaatz, and also from Eaker to Arnold and Spaatz. The author had the opportunity to interview General Eaker and James Parton on the proceedings and General Eaker's meeting with Churchill. The author also interviewed Generals Wedemeyer and Jacob E. Smart. Numerous books detailing the conference were also utilized. The author had the aid of Maj. Gen. John W. Huston, Chief of Air Force History, in the search for accuracy.

5. Elliott Roosevelt and James Brough, *A Rendezvous with Destiny: The Roosevelts at the White House* (New York: Putnam, 1975), p. 333.

6. Wedemeyer, op. cit., pp. 185–87; interview with the author.

7. Anthony Cave Brown, *Bodyguard of Lies* (New York: Harper, 1976), p. 276.

8. Hanson Baldwin, *Great Mistakes of the War* (London: Redman, 1950), pp. 13–15.

9. Churchill, *Hinge of Fate*, p. 687.

10. C. L. Sulzberger in his diary *A Long Row of Candles* (New York: Macmillan, 1969) makes this point in three different accounts, and in one attributes the source of his information to Ambassador Averell Harriman.

11. Slessor, op. cit., pp. 447–48.

FIFTEEN

1. Bernard Boylan, "Development of the Long Range Fighter/Escort," Historical Division Research Studies Institute, Air University, Sept. 1955, pp. 69–70.

2. Perera, op. cit.
Perera.

3. Letter from Elihu Root, Jr., to Perera, May 16, 1946.

4. Hansell, op. cit., Ch. 7, pp. 144–69.

5. Albert Speer, *Inside the Third Reich* (New York: Macmillan, 1970), pp. 333–34.

6. MEMORANDUM FOR GENERAL ARNOLD:

Subject: Bombing out of United Kingdom

What is your reaction to the proposal put forward by General Eaker yesterday?

Should we accept without qualification the full estimates?

I am interested in the completeness with which we should accept their bad-weather bombing prediction and technique; by this I mean do we immediately place full reliance upon this in making allocations?

The tentative operational estimates given by Wedemeyer yesterday would indicate that a major ROUNDUP is not possible until late in 1944. If this is so is the major bombing strength mandatory for the fourth period of their plan?

I am interested in what additional bombers we can start to Kenney or Burma commencing the end of August.

I am interested in what possible combinations might be made between the United Kingdom and Sicily or in other areas to insure uninterrupted air operations against Axis-controlled Europe.

There is no doubt in my mind as to the over-all importance of heavy bomber operations out of the United Kingdom, the more so as the likelihood of cross-channel ground operations appears less probable in 1943. Naturally the British favor heavy concentration in the United Kingdom. Also it is normal for General Andrews and General Eaker to propose the most complete operation they visualize as possible of arrangement, especially in view of the outstanding accomplishments to date.

In making the allocations we must balance all these factors against the other theaters. We have given Eisenhower practically everything he has asked for within the capabilities of ocean shipping. We are now to consider to what extent, as regards Air, we do the same for Andrews. Our problem is complicated by the fact that we have been unable to carry out our general conception as to the concentration of force in the United Kingdom. Furthermore, we are confronted at the present time with a most serious issue as to the decision regarding post-HUSKY operations in relation to the Mediterranean. If a vacuum, as it were, is created in that theater, it will probably mean a serious prolongation of the war, and would preclude the timely concentration of ground forces in the U.K. to exploit favorable conditions for invasion.

Under such circumstances to what extent should we go in allotting planes for an "all out" bombing program from the U.K. in contrast to what would amount, on a percentage basis, to a very small increase of our air strength for the Far East-Pacific area?

C/S G. Marshall

7. This account was given to the author by Lt. Gen. Ira C. Eaker, USAF (Ret.). The order in question has never been found. Apparently, it disappeared with General Andrews' files. Major Trotman, who was their custodian, was also killed in the crash.

8. This was determined by the accident investigators at the time and by questioning Staff Sergeant Eisel.

9. Dear Johnny,

It wasn't until yesterday that the tragic news of the General's accident reached me. Even at that, the news came from a British Officer who stated that he had picked up a radio report to the effect that there were fourteen in all, including Charlie Barth, on board the plane. I would like to hope otherwise, but I'm afraid we must assume that Major Trotman was along too.

I know what a shock the General's death must be to you. I too take his passing as a great personal loss. But actually, the General's death has such a far-reaching influence that the personal aspects should dwindle to relative insignificance when compared with the loss to the nation as a whole, and the specific loss to our Air Force of the future. There is no American alive today who has a clearer concept of things to come. There is no one to whom the average Air Force officer can look for that ultimate leadership which the General embodied, and which we all hoped and prayed would take over when political pettiness and personal ambitions had run their course.

You may, and I know I will, hear from some of our people that the General had it coming to him; that he had defied the laws of flying too long and his luck finally ran out; that higher authority should have forbidden him to pilot his own plane, especially under the adverse weather conditions which he took in stride. They are wrong, Johnny, entirely wrong—and they are only taking such means to apologize for their own deficiencies and weaknesses. The General's attitude toward flying was only another concrete manifestation of his basic character. As a pilot, he was in a class with the best. He was in a class with the experts who have devoted their entire lives to nothing but flying and never had to treat their pilotage as something incidental to carrying on the many other and more important phases of military leadership. With the exception of Sonny Williams, I don't believe that anyone has been in a better position than I was to pass judgment on such matters. He was an excellent pilot, and I only hope that I'll be half as good if I am fortunate enough to stay at the game as long as he did.

When these people tell you he shouldn't have been flying and all that sort of tripe, just ask them how well they knew the General professionally. Ask them how much they have ever flown in the cockpit with him. Ask them if they have stopped to realize that his flying was merely an expression of everything he felt and believed. He was more than a talker, he did things. I am convinced that our service has never made the progress it should simply because we were always lacking in a sufficient number of men of the General's foresight and leadership qualities.

Except for us who felt we really knew him, the full appreciation of the General's life and vision will not be realized immediately by the country as a whole. But, as time passes, his stature will increase in the eyes of many who are groping for a symbol to help give our Air Force its proper place in the sun. With this in mind, I feel that you should guard carefully his letters and papers which Totman [*sic*] so meticulously filed. Someday, those papers are going to play an important part in bringing about the organization for which the General fought so sincerely. Someday, those papers will also be the basis for a documentary representation of one of the most important chapters in the fight for the recognition of Air Power in the United States.

Just a few nights ago, while having dinner with Air Marshal Dawson of the British Air Force, it is rather ironical that the General's name came up for discussion when neither of us knew that the accident had already happened. I think that the remark I made to the Air Marshal at that time concerning the General is doubly applicable now and is the best summary I could possibly make: He is the most unselfish person I have ever known.

Please extend my sympathies to Josie and Allen and Jeannie. I too feel that I have lost "one of the family."

Sincerely,
THOMAS C. DARCY
Colonel, Air Corps.

The sad fact is that today the Air Force has all but forgotten General Andrews. The onrush of the war and the death of so many others was contributory. Hap Arnold saw to it that Andrews Field, outside of Washington, D.C., was dedicated to him, but even at this date General Andrews has not been enshrined in the Airmen's Hall of Fame, at Wright-Patterson Field. It is an incredible oversight.

10. The question as to whether General Andrews was in fact coming back to Washington for a secret meeting with Marshall remains unanswered. Col. Hiette S. Williams, Jr., Andrews' son-in-law, came to Washington at the time to aid in the details of the memorial service. In so doing, he dealt directly with both Generals Marshall and Arnold, and from what was said he was left with the definite impression that, indeed, General Andrews was on his way to the United States at the time of the crash. Williams also heard talk of a fourth star being awarded, to give Andrews sufficient rank to deal as an equal with the British leadership. Conversely, Andrews wrote to his daughter Jean on May 1, telling her he was leaving the U.K. in a few days. Bishop Adna S. Leonard's itinerary did not include returning to the United States at the time, and it could be that if Andrews was heading for Washington, his plane was to pick Bishop Leonard up on the way back to England. Unfortunately, the last ten days of Andrews' daily diary, kept by Fred Chapman, are missing. The answer to the mystery may be in them.

SIXTEEN

1. Butcher, op. cit., p. 297.

2. Freeman, op. cit., p. 56.

3. Ibid., p. 51n.

4. Post was one of a dozen newsmen who got permission to go on the Kiel raid; Walter Cronkite was another. Only Post was willing to fly in a B-24, as

opposed to a B-17, and only Post failed to return. (Edward Jablonski, *Flying Fortress* [Garden City, N.Y.: Doubleday, 1965], p. 116.)

5. James Dugan and Carroll Stewart, "Ploesti: German Defenses and Allied Intelligence," *The Airpower Historian,* Vol. IX, No. 1, Jan. 1962, pp. 1–20; interview with Col. J. E. Smart, Nov. 29, 1977.

6. Ibid., p. 16; Bekker, op. cit., p. 318; Butcher, op. cit., pp. 160–61.

7. Bekker, op. cit., p. 19.

8. USAAF, op. cit., pp. 100–1.

9. Albert Speer, *Spandau: The Secret Diaries of Albert Speer* (New York: Macmillan, 1974), p. 239.

10. Ed Rees, "A Tribute to Dutch Kindelberger," *The Airpower Historian,* Vol. IX, No. 4, Oct. 1962, pp. 197–206; Air Force Office of History oral interview with Lt. Gen. Barney Giles.

11. Correspondence with Gen. Mark E. Bradley, 1980; Mark E. Bradley, "The P-51 over Berlin," *Aerospace Historian,* Vol. 22, No. 3, Sept. 1974; ibid., Giles interview; transcript of telephone conversation between General Echols and Colonel Bradley, July 10, 1943.

SEVENTEEN

1. Brown, op. cit., pp. 406–11.

2. Jablonski, op. cit., pp. 182–83.

3. Brown, op. cit., pp. 352–53.

4. Arnold, op. cit., p. 408.

5. Excerpt from letter by Eaker to Arnold, Sept. 11, 1943: "In accordance with your direction, I have assembled all of the commanders and have gone over with them completely our maintenance position and have issued a definite directive that the Air Service Command is to have technical control and supervision over maintenance down to the airplane. I have also cautioned that every airplane which cannot be made ready for the next mission coming up must be transferred and tagged to the Air Service Command and the Air Service Command be made responsible for its maintenance. . . . I will report to you in about thirty days how this is working out.

"I personally appreciate very much the suggestions you made while here and your comment on our organization. I know that it was entirely constructive and every possible effort is going to be made by me to carry out your ideas."

6. Interview with Brig. Gen. Theodore R. Milton, Oct. 7, 1977.

7. The argument over the importance of Schweinfurt as a strategic target continues. Special insight into the question was supplied by Col. Stone Christopher, USAF (Ret.), in a Nov. 1980 letter to *Air Force* magazine of the same date, when he wrote: ". . . After the questionable success of the 1943 October raid, it was decided the United States would buy SKF's (Sweden's) 1944 bearing production to prevent the bearings from being shipped to Germany. . . . On New Year's Eve 1944, John Von der Lieth, U. S. Vice-Consul in Gothenburg, presented Mr. Hamberger, president of SKF, a U. S. Treasury check for $8 million. John . . . used farms in Western Sweden to bury bearings not shipped to the UK. In the spring of 1944, shipments to the UK were

increased, using Bernt Balchen's airline, which had just begun its operations (under the code name SONIE). The Swedes permitted us to strip the B-24's (and B-17's) that had landed in southern Sweden, load them with bearings, and fly them to the UK by interned U.S. crews.

"Shortly after the liberation of Paris [August 1944] I was instructed to visit the manager of SKF factories in France, a Mr. Gustafson. . . .

"Mr. Gustafson informed me that he and five European SKF managers had been ordered by the Germans to Schweinfurt to assess the damage [from the October 14 raid]. We found that your bombs had only blown off the roofs of the factories and started some small fires. As soon as the raid was over the Germans greased and wrapped the milling machines in tarpaulins to prevent rust damage. You should have used deep-penetration bombs to tilt the machines. . . . A slight tilt makes them useless. The Germans replaced the roofs and in a couple of months they were back in full production. . . ."

8. Ronald H. Bailey, *The Air War in Europe* (New York: Time-Life Books, 1979), p. 135.

9. Air Marshal Portal said: "The Schweinfurt raid may well go down in history as one of the decisive air actions of the war, and it may prove to have saved countless lives by depriving the enemy of a great part of his means of resistance." (*The Mighty Eighth,* pp. 78–79)

EIGHTEEN

1. Interview with General Doolittle, Aug. 26, 1980.

2. Bekker, op. cit., p. 351.

3. David Irving, *The War Between the Generals* (New York: Congdon & Lattes, 1981), p. 125.

4. Hastings, op. cit., p. 319.

5. Bekker, op. cit., p. 353.

6. The former officer in question related the account to the author but asked that his name not be used. In the patriotic madam's club in Marseilles, one entire wall of the vast living room was covered by a huge photographic blowup of the madam receiving her award.

7. General Eaker never said who he believed was responsible for the change in his command. Although it was known that General Arnold could be influenced by those close to him, all evidence, as far as the author is concerned, indicates that the decision was a natural progression of Arnold's thinking and plans. This is not to say there were not those who agreed, supported the idea, and helped to push it. The most likely is General Kuter.

8. Colonel Smart, badly wounded, had the good fortune to be put in a hospital by an Austrian doctor, who tended him, spoke English, and was anti-Hitler and the war. When the Colonel had recovered somewhat he was interrogated by an Abwehr (Intelligence) officer, who amazed Smart with a photograph, taken at the Casablanca Conference, in which Smart was included. The officer was anxious to know what had happened at the Tehran Conference, with particular regard to the policy of unconditional surrender. It was obvious to Smart that his captors knew the war was lost and were looking individually for any means to protect their families, especially from the Russians. The Abwehr

officer warned him that he was in danger of being executed by the Gestapo, who would be interrogating him determined to learn when and where the anticipated invasion would take place. He advised Smart not to tell them if he did know but to be very correct in his manner. As a result of his former position on Arnold's Advisory Council and his expertise as a planner, Smart not only knew the approximate date of the invasion but, of even more perilous importance, where the invasion forces would land. When he was asked the question by Gestapo interrogators, he replied blandly, "It is obvious it will take place somewhere between the Bay of Biscay and Kiel." They did not press the point, getting drunk instead. Later the Abwehr agent attempted to use Smart as a go-between in making peace overtures to the Allies behind the back of the SS and the Gestapo. (Interview with Col. J. E. Smart, Nov. 29, 1977)

9. Bekker, op. cit., pp. 324–25, 328–29.

10. Ibid., p. 330.

11. Ibid., p. 380; *The Air War in Europe*, p. 191.

Bibliography

BOOKS

Alexander, Field Marshal Earl. *The Alexander Memoirs 1940–1945*. New York: McGraw-Hill, 1961.

Arnold, Henry H. *Global Mission*. New York: Harper, 1948.

Bailey, Ronald H. *The Air War in Europe*. New York: Time-Life Books, 1979.

Bailey, Thomas A.; and Ryan, Paul B. *Hitler vs. Roosevelt*. New York: Macmillan, 1979.

Baldwin, Hanson W. *Great Mistakes of the War*. London: Redman, 1950.

Baruch, Bernard. *The Public Years*. New York: Holt, 1960.

Bekker, Cajus. *The Luftwaffe War Diaries*. Garden City, N.Y.: Doubleday, 1968.

Beschloss, Michael R. *Kennedy and Roosevelt*. New York: Norton, 1980.

Blum, John Morton. *From the Morgenthau Diaries, Years of Urgency 1938–1941*. Boston: Houghton, 1965.

Bradley, Omar. *A Soldier's Story*. New York: Holt, 1951.

Brereton, Lewis H. *The Brereton Diaries*. New York: Morrow, 1946.

Brickhill, Paul. *Reach for the Sky*. New York: Norton, 1954.

Brown, Anthony Cave. *Bodyguard of Lies*. New York: Harper, 1976.

Bryant, Arthur. *The Turn of the Tide*. Garden City, N.Y.: Doubleday, 1957.

Butcher, Harry. *My Three Years with Eisenhower*. New York: Simon & Schuster, 1946.

Chennault, Claire L. *Way of a Fighter*. New York: Putnam, 1949.

Churchill, Sir Winston S. *Their Finest Hour*. Boston: Houghton, 1949.

———. *The Hinge of Fate*. Boston: Houghton, 1950.

———. *The Grand Alliance*. Boston: Houghton, 1950.

———. *Closing the Ring*. Boston: Houghton, 1951.

Coffey, Thomas M. *Decision over Schweinfurt*. New York: David McKay, 1977.

Collier, Richard. *Nineteen Forty: The Avalanche*. New York: Dial, 1979.

Copp, DeWitt S. *A Few Great Captains*. Garden City, N.Y.: Doubleday, 1980.

Craven, W. F.; and Cate, J. L. *The Army Air Forces in World War II.* Vol. I, *Plans and Early Operations;* Vol. VI, *Men and Planes.* Chicago: University of Chicago Press, 1948.

Deighton, Len. *Fighter: The True Story of the Battle of Britain.* New York: Knopf, 1978.

Devine, David. *The Nine Days of Dunkirk.* New York: Norton, 1959.

Eisenhower, Dwight D. *Crusade in Europe.* Garden City, N.Y.: Doubleday, 1948.

Farago, Ladislas. *The Game of the Foxes.* New York: David McKay, 1971.

Fleming, Peter. *Operation Sea Lion.* New York: Simon & Schuster, 1949.

Ford, Corey. *Donovan of O.S.S.* Boston: Little, Brown, 1970.

Forrester, Larry. *Fly for Your Life.* Garden City, N.Y.: Doubleday, 1956.

Freeman, Roger A. *The Mighty Eighth.* Garden City, N.Y.: Doubleday, 1970.

Goddard, George W.; and Copp, DeWitt S. *Overview.* Garden City, N.Y.: Doubleday, 1969.

Goldberg, Alfred. *A History of the United States Air Force 1907–1957.* New York: Van Nostrand, 1967.

Hansell, Haywood S. *The Air Plan That Defeated Hitler.* Atlanta, Ga.: Higgins-MacArthur/Longino & Porter, 1972.

Hastings, Max. *Bomber Command.* New York: Dial, 1979.

Haugland, Vern. *The Eagle Squadrons.* New York: Ziff-Davis, 1979.

Hinton, Harold B. *Air Victory: The Men and the Machines.* New York: Harper, 1948.

Irving, David. *The War Between the Generals.* New York: Congdon & Lattes, 1981.

Jablonski, Edward. *Flying Fortress.* Garden City, N.Y.: Doubleday, 1965.

———. *Double Strike.* Garden City, N.Y.: Doubleday, 1974.

———; and Thomas Lowell. *Doolittle.* Garden City, N.Y.: Doubleday, 1976.

James, D. Clayton. *The Years of MacArthur.* Boston: Houghton, 1970.

Jones, R. V. *The Wizard War: British Scientific Intelligence 1939–1945.* New York: Coward, 1978.

Keegan, John, ed. *Who Was Who in World War II.* New York: Crowell, 1978.

Killen, John. *A History of the Luftwaffe.* Garden City, N.Y.: Doubleday, 1968.

LaFeber, Walter. *The Panama Canal.* Oxford, England: Oxford University Press, 1978.

Lawson, Ted (ed. Considine, Robert). *Thirty Seconds over Tokyo.* New York: Random House, 1943.

LeMay, Curtis E.; and Kantor, MacKinlay. *Mission with LeMay.* Garden City, N.Y.: Doubleday, 1964.

Leutze, James, ed. *The London Journal of General Raymond E. Lee 1940–1941.* Boston: Little, Brown, 1971.

Lindbergh, Charles A. *The Wartime Journals of Charles A. Lindbergh.* New York: Harcourt, 1970.

MacArthur, Douglas. *Reminiscences.* New York: McGraw-Hill, 1964.

McFarland, Keith D. *Harry H. Woodring: A Political Biography of FDR's Controversial Secretary of War.* Lawrence, Kans.: University Press of Kansas, 1975.

Manchester, William. *American Caesar: Douglas MacArthur, 1880–1964.* New York: Dell, 1978.

Momyer, William W. *Air Power in Three Wars.* Washington, D.C.: Department of the Air Force, 1978.

Morison, Samuel Eliot. *The Two Ocean War.* Boston: Little, Brown, 1963.

Mosley, Leonard. *The Reich Marshal: A Biography of Hermann Goering.* Garden City, N.Y.: Doubleday, 1974.

Parkinson, Roger. *Summer 1940.* New York: David McKay, 1977.

Pogue, Forrest C. *George C. Marshall.* Vol. 2, *Ordeal and Hope 1939–1942.* New York: Viking Press, 1966.

———. *George C. Marshall* Vol. 3, *Organizer of Victory 1943–1945.* New York: Viking Press, 1973.

Price, Alfred. *Luftwaffe Handbook, 1939–1945.* New York: Scribner, 1977.

Roosevelt, Elliott; and Brough, James. *A Rendezvous with Destiny: The Roosevelts at the White House.* New York: Putnam, 1975.

Sherwood, Robert E. *Roosevelt and Hopkins.* New York: Harper, 1948.

Slessor, Sir John. *The Central Blue.* London: Cassell, 1956.

Speer, Albert. *Inside the Third Reich.* New York: Macmillan, 1970.

———. *Spandau: The Secret Diaries.* New York: Macmillan, 1974.

Stevenson, William. *A Man Called Intrepid.* New York: Harcourt, 1976.

Sulzberger, C. L. *A Long Row of Candles: Memoirs and Diaries 1934–1954.* New York: Macmillan, 1969.

Toland, John. *Adolf Hitler.* Garden City, N.Y.: Doubleday, 1976.

Toliver, Raymond F.; and Constable, Trevor J. *Horrido.* New York: Macmillan, 1968.

Townsend, Peter. *Duel of Eagles.* New York: Simon & Schuster, 1971.

USAAF. *Target Germany.* New York: Simon & Schuster, 1943.

Wedemeyer, Alfred C. *Wedemeyer Reports.* New York: Holt, 1958.

Whalen, Richard J. *The Founding Father: The Story of Joseph P. Kennedy.* New York: New American Library, 1964.

Wilson, Sir Charles. *Churchill—Taken from the Diaries of Lord Moran.* Boston: Houghton, 1966.

Winterbotham, F. W. *The Ultra Secret.* New York: Dell, 1974.

Wohlstetter, Roberta. *Pearl Harbor: Warning and Decision.* Stanford, Calif.: Stanford University Press, 1962.

SPECIAL PUBLICATIONS AND ARTICLES

The Army Air Forces in World War II Combat Chronology 1941–1945. Compiled by Kit C. Carter and Robert Mueller. Albert F. Simpson Historical Research Center, Office of Air Force History, 1973.

The U. S. Army in World War II. *The Western Hemisphere—The Framework of Hemisphere Defense.* Stetson Conn and Byron Fairchild. Office of the Chief of Military History, Department of the Army, Washington, D.C., 1960.

The U. S. Army in World War II. *The Western Hemisphere—Guarding the United States and Its Outposts.* Stetson Conn, Rose C. Engelman, and Byron Fairchild. Office of the Chief of Military History, Department of the Army, Washington, D.C., 1964.

Andrews, John C. "The Forty, the Spit and the Jug," *Aerospace Historian*, Vol. 26, No. 4, Dec. 1979.

Bouche, Georges G. "Grandpappy: The XB-15," *Aerospace Historian*, Vol. 26, No. 3, Sept. 1979.

Boyle, James N. "The XXI Bomber Command," *Aerospace Historian*, Vol. 11, No. 2, Apr. 1964.

Bradley, Mark E. "The P-51 over Berlin," *Aerospace Historian*, Vol. 22, No. 3, Sept. 1974.

————. "The XP-40," *Aerospace Historian*, Vol. 25, No. 3, Sept. 1978.

Bradshaw, Russell. "To Russia One Way," *Aerospace Historian*, Vol. 25, No. 4, Dec. 1978.

Campbell, John P. "Air Operations and the Dieppe Raid," *Aerospace Historian*, Vol. 23, No. 1, Mar. 1976.

Clodfetter, Mark A. "Culmination Dresden 1945," *Aerospace Historian*, Vol. 26, No. 3, Sept. 1979.

DeWeed, Harvey A. "Churchill, Coventry and Ultra," *Aerospace Historian*, Vol. 27, No. 4, Dec. 1980.

Dugan, James; and Stewart, Carroll. "Ploesti: German Defenses and Allied Intelligence," *The Airpower Historian*, Vol. IX, No. 1, Jan. 1962.

Eaker, Ira C. "Some Observations on Leadership," *The Airpower Historian*, Vol. VIII, No. 3, 1961.

————. "The Lindbergh I Knew," *Aerospace Historian*, Vol. 24, No. 4, Dec. 1977.

————. "Soviet Leaders and People," *Aerospace Historian*, Vol. 25, No. 2, June 1978.

————. "The Flying Fortress and the Liberator," *Aerospace Historian*, Vol. 26, No. 2, June 1979.

Eastman, James N., Jr. "The Development of Big Bombers," *Aerospace Historian*, Vol. 25, No. 4, Dec. 1978.

George, Harold L. "The Most Outstanding Leader—An Aerospace Profile of Maj. Gen. Robert Olds," *Aerospace Historian*, Vol. 15, No. 2, June 1976.

Glasebrook, Rick. "Flying the North American O-47 and the Curtiss Wright O-52," *Aerospace Historian*, Vol. 24, No. 1, Mar. 1978.

Hansell, Haywood S. "General Laurence S. Kuter 1905–1979," *Aerospace Historian*, Vol. 27, No. 2, June 1980.

Hicks, Dr. Edmund. "Soviet Sojourn: The First Shuttle Bombing Mission to Russia," *The Airpower Historian*, Vol. XI, No. 1, Jan. 1964.

Holley, I. Bruce, Jr. "Air Force General Laurence Sherman Kuter," *Aerospace Historian*, Vol. 27, No. 2, June 1980.

Holloway, Bruce K. "The P-40," *Aerospace Historian*, Vol. 25, No. 3, Sept. 1978.

Kuter, Laurence S. "The General Vs. The Establishment—Gen. H. H. Arnold and the Air Staff," *Aerospace Historian*, Vol. 21, No. 4, Dec. 1974.

LeMay, Curtis E. "Strategic Air Power: Destroying the Enemy's Resources— The Command Realities," *Aerospace Historian*, Vol. 27, No. 1, Mar. 1980.

Maurer, Dr. Maurer. "The 6th Aero Squadron 1919–1947," *The Airpower Historian*, Vol. VII, No. 3, July 1960.

Parish, Noel L. "Hap Arnold and the Historians," *Aerospace Historian*, Vol. 20, No. 3, Sept. 1973.

————. "Reflections on the Tuskegee Experiment" (interview by Hasdorff, James C.), *Aerospace Historian*, Vol. 24, No. 3, Sept. 1977.

Paszek, Lawrence J. "Separate But Equal? The Story of the 99th Fighter Squadron," *Aerospace Historian*, Vol. 24, No. 3, Sept. 1977.

Peaslee, Budd J. "Blood in the Sky," *Aerospace Historian*, Vol. 16, No. 2, Jan. 1969.

Potts, Thomas. "L'Operazion Cinzano," *Aerospace Historian*, Vol. 28, No. 1, Mar. 1981.

Rees, Ed. "A Tribute to Dutch Kindelberger: The Mustang a Great War Horse," *The Airpower Historian*, Vol. IX, No. 4, Oct. 1962.

Scamehorn, Dr. Howard. "American Air Transport and Air Power Doctrine in W.W. II," *The Airpower Historian*, Vol. VIII, No. 3, July 1961.

Sturm, Thomas A. "American Air Defense: The Decision to Proceed," *Aerospace Historian*, Vol. 19, No. 4, Dec. 1972, pp. 188–94.

Whalen, Norman N. "Ploesti: Group Navigator's View," *Aerospace Historian*, Vol. 23, No. 1, Mar. 1976.

Wright, Howard T. "Changing Insignias," *Aerospace Historian*, Vol. 27, No. 2, June 1980.

Historical studies at the Office of Air Force History, Bolling AFB, Washington, D.C., from the Albert F. Simpson Historical Research Center, Maxwell AFB, Alabama:

"Organization of the Army Air Arm, 1939–1945," Money and Williamson, 1956;

"Development of Air Doctrine in the Army Arm, 1917–1941," Greer, 1953;

"The Development of the Heavy Bomber, 1918–1944," Dubuque and Gleckner, 1951;

"Development of the Long Range Fighter/Escort," Boylan, 1955;

"Air Defense of the Panama Canal, 1 January 1939–31 December 1942," K. Williams, 1946;

"The Question of Autonomy for the United States Air Arm, 1907–1945," Air University, 1951.

DOCUMENTARY SOURCES

The documentary sources for *Forged in Fire* were drawn essentially from the same collections as those of *A Few Great Captains*. The two volumes form a continuous historical account, focusing on four principal Army air officers: Generals Henry H. Arnold, Frank M. Andrews, Carl A. Spaatz, and Ira C. Eaker. The official, unofficial, and personal papers of the four in the Manuscript Division of the Library of Congress, in Washington, D.C., formed the basis for the work. Selected research was also done at the Manuscript Division into the papers of John C. O'Laughlin.

Also at the Library, applicable congressional hearings and news and magazine stories were reviewed. Key news sources were the New York *Times,* the New York *Herald Tribune,* the New York *Daily Mirror,* the Washington

Times-Herald, the Washington *Post,* and the Washington *Star.* The major magazine of reference was *Time.*

Other primary sources of documentation were the Office of Air Force History and the National Archives, in Washington, D.C., and the Air Force Academy, Colorado Springs, Colorado. Documentation examined at the Office of Air Force History was supplied in major part from the Albert F. Simpson Research Center, Maxwell Field, Alabama, the period covered being 1940–45. Included as well were oral interviews from the American Heritage and Air Force collections. The papers of Major General Hugh J. Knerr were of special interest.

At the Air Force Academy's Special Collection Branch, the papers of Generals Frank M. Andrews, Laurence S. Kuter, Haywood S. Hansell, and Follett Bradley were examined, as was the Arnold Columbia University Oral Collection.

At the National Archives, research centered on the general correspondence files in the Military Records Section of the Division of the Army Air Forces, covering the people and the period in question.

Outside of official repositories and historical collections, letters, personal papers, and private transcripts of interviews were obtained. Particular thanks goes to Brigadier General George W. Goddard, USAF (Ret.), for supplying the author with information from his own files, which included personal interviews with Generals Carl A. Spaatz, Hugh J. Knerr, George C. Kenney, and Howard Davidson, as well as Elliott Roosevelt and Alexander de Seversky. In addition, personal letters from General Frank Andrews to members of his family were made available by his son and daughter, as was Mrs. Andrews' diary, covering the years 1935–45.

Index

ABOUT THE AUTHOR

DeWitt S. Copp was an Army Air Force pilot during World War II and has written numerous books and filmscripts on military and civilian aviation. A former history teacher and global newsman, Mr. Copp has served as a correspondent in Europe and the Far East. In his research for this book, he has used many previously untapped sources, including personal diaries, newly declassified documents, and interviews with many of the characters in the book. Mr. Copp and his wife, Susan, presently make their home in Manchester Center, Vermont.